Oracle Press™

Oracle Application Server Portal Handbook

About the Author

Chris Ostrowski is a Technical Management Consultant with TUSC. He has 15 years' Oracle experience and 10 years' experience as an Oracle DBA. Chris specializes in all aspects of the Oracle Application Server including Oracle WebCenter and BPEL/SOA solutions. Chris is also an instructor and class content owner for TUSC. Over the past seven years, he has presented at PPOUG, RMOUG Training Days, COAUG, IOUG, ODTUG, and Oracle's OpenWorld. He is the co-author of Oracle Press's *Oracle Application Server 10*g *Web Development* with TUSC founder Brad Brown, and is an Oracle Fusion Middleware Regional Director.

About the Technical Editors

Bill Lankenau has 12 years of IT experience including 7 years at Oracle where he has served in senior product management and consulting positions specializing in thin client architecture, Web technology, and portal products and solutions. He has been a featured speaker on these topics at several industry conferences including Oracle iDevelop, Oracle International Users Group, and Oracle OpenWorld. Prior to joining Oracle, Bill served as a managing consultant with Unisys Corporation. Currently, Bill is a Product Manager for Oracle Fusion Middleware.

Jay Daugherty is a 20-year veteran of the software industry, with 17 years' experience at Oracle. For the past 8 years he has been responsible for Product Management for Oracle Portal, working with the product from its initial concepts through the current production release. Prior to his work on Portal, he was a technical consultant and manager on projects ranging from pharmaceuticals and higher education to digital video on demand systems.

Philipp Weckerle joined Oracle originally in 1999 as support analyst for tools in Austria and transferred to Oracle Headquarters as Product Manager for Oracle Reports in 2001, where he took over the team lead role in 2003. His responsibilities expanded to Oracle Portal and Content Integration in 2004, and he is now leading both the Product Management efforts on Oracle Reports as well as Content Integration, located in the Oracle Austria office in Vienna.

Peter Moskovits is a principal product manager in the Portal and WebCenter Suite product group at Oracle Corporation. Peter is responsible for the Oracle WebCenter Framework, as well as portal development tools and technologies. He joined Oracle in Europe in 1998. During his years at Oracle, Peter has gained significant experience in Java EE Web development on the Oracle platform. Peter holds a Master of Science degree in computer science.

Michael (Mick) Andrew has worked for Oracle Corporation since January 1990 after completing a Bachelor of Applied Science in Computer Science at RMIT (Royal Melbourne Institute of Technology) in Melbourne. Mick worked initially with Oracle Australia before joining Product Development in 1999 as part of the Hosted Tools Division focusing on Oracle WebDB, OracleAS Reports, OracleAS Forms, Oracle Designer, and Oracle Software Configuration Manager. More recently Mick has been focused on Oracle Portal as part of Oracle Server Technologies Development. Prior to joining the Product Development group, Mick worked mainly as a sales consultant/representative in Sydney and Melbourne, focusing primarily on the Oracle Development Toolset.

Vince Casarez has held many key positions at Oracle over the past 12 years. Currently, he is Vice President of Product Management for WebCenter, Portal, and Reports. He also has responsibility for managing the WebCenter development team handling the Web 2.0 services. Prior to this, he focused on hosted portal development and operations, which included Oracle Portal Online for external customers, Portal Center for building a portal community, and My Oracle for the employee intranet. Previously, he was Vice President of Tools Marketing handling all tools products including development tools and business intelligence tools. Prior to running Tools Marketing, Vince was Director of Product Management for Oracle's JDeveloper.

Karthika Siva was product manager for Oracle Application Server for six years. In November 2006, she resigned from Oracle to spend more time with her two young sons. Karthika first joined Oracle in 1997 in the consulting organization where she helped to spearhead eCommerce and portal solutions. She then joined the product group and partnered with leading companies to build portal solutions. From that role, she went on to champion Oracle's portal application for mid-market companies. It was in that role that she helped to define Oracle Instant Portal, an out-of-the-box portal solution ideal for smaller companies and organizations. Prior to resigning, Karthika worked to bring collaborative services to Oracle WebCenter Suite.

Oracle Press™

Oracle Application Server Portal Handbook

Christopher Ostrowski

New York Chicago San Francisco
Lisbon London Madrid Mexico City Milan
New Delhi San Juan Seoul Singapore Sydney Toronto

The McGraw·Hill Companies

Cataloging-in-Publication Data is on file with the Library of Congress.

McGraw-Hill books are available at special quantity discounts to use as premiums and sales promotions, or for use in corporate training programs. For more information, please write to the Director of Special Sales, Professional Publishing, McGraw-Hill, Two Penn Plaza, New York, NY 10121-2298. Or contact your local bookstore.

Oracle Application Server Portal Handbook

1234567890 DOH DOH 01987

ISBN-13: 978-0-07-226460-9
ISBN-10: 0-07-226460-8

Sponsoring Editor
Lisa McClain

Editorial Supervisor
Jody McKenzie

Project Editor
Carolyn Welch

Acquisitions Coordinator
Mandy Canales

Technical Editors
Bill Lankenau, Jay Daugherty, Philipp Weckerle, Peter Moskovits, Michael Andrew, Vince Casarez, Karthika Siva

Copy Editor
Bob Campbell

Proofreader
Carolyn Welch

Indexer
Claire Splan

Production Supervisor
Jean Bodeaux

Composition
EuroDesign - Peter F. Hancik

Illustration
Lyssa Wald

Series Design
Peter F. Hancik, Lyssa Wald

Art Director, Cover
Jeff Weeks

Cover Design
Pattie Lee

To my wife Karen.
They say everyone has a perfect match.
With 7 billion people on the planet, I can't believe
I found mine in you.

Contents

PART II
Page Design and Content Management

PART IV
Administration

Acknowledgments

would like to personally thank everyone at TUSC. Having worked with hundreds of clients has made me truly appreciate what a world-class organization TUSC is and continues to be. I am forever indebted to the founders of TUSC—Brad Brown, Rich Niemiec, and Joe Trezzo—for assembling an incredible group of individuals and letting me be a part of it. So many other people who worked with me on this book were incredibly gracious and selfless, and I'm afraid my words will not fully express how profoundly grateful I am for having had the opportunity to work with all of you but here goes.

Karen Ostrowski, my wife, has made incredible sacrifices to give me the opportunity to write this book. There is no way I would have been able to complete it without her support and encouragement. I can't imagine a life without you. I love you with all of my heart.

Brad Brown, thank you so much for giving me the opportunity to do this and for creating a company where everyone is encouraged to grow not only as employees but also as human beings. Your unselfish words of encouragement kept me going through many a dark hour. I am so grateful for having the opportunity to work along side you, and I admire you for living the "Traits of the Uncommon Leader" every day.

Lisa McClain and Mandy Canales make up the Osborne/McGraw-Hill editorial team I worked with as this book was being written. I am grateful for having the opportunity to work with you.

At the beginning of this project, Bill Lankenau (Senior Manager of Oracle Portal Product Management) and Pascal Gilbert (Director of Oracle Portal Porduct Management) graciously altered their travel plans to sit down and talk with me about Oracle Portal. Their input was invaluable when putting this book together. In addition, I want to thank Jay Daugherty, Philipp Weckerle, Barry Hiern, Mick Andrew, Vince Casarez, and Karthika Siva—technical editors extraordinaire! I am greatly indebted for all of their tireless, unselfish work.

Introduction

asn't the Web supposed to make everything easier? Oh sure, the maturation of companies doing business on the Web has made things more reliable and more secure, but easier? If you've been using the Web for a while (5+ years), you've noticed the evolution from static web pages to dynamic content. AJAX and other technologies provide an even greater level of interactivity giving end-users a richer Web experience. Google has pioneered the simple-interface approach. There are web sites devoted to every conceivable human activity and subject imaginable. (Don't believe me? Point your browser to http://www.kli.org/tlh/newwords.html.)

Yes, all of these things make us more productive, more interested in the world around us, more connected to people and places we might never have a chance of knowing about. But is it easier? You should be able to do everything by yourself by now: fix your car, pick up girls (or guys), start your own company. Yet there is still a deep thirst for knowledge. Part of this has to do with customer expectations, and by customer, I mean anyone who visits your site. Customers demand more and more information. There is an almost insatiable desire for knowledge. At what point does the sheer volume of information make it impossible to present information to a user in a meaningful way? At what point do the scales tip and users become less interested in what information is presented to them and more interested in how it is presented to them?

I believe we've reached that point. Don't get me wrong; users are still interested in the content of what they're looking for, but more and more people, overwhelmed by the quantity of information available, are either turning to sites or products that summarize and organize content, using the first thing Google returns to them, or giving up altogether. Even inside a company or organization (where the choices of where to gather information are much more limited), users (employees) will choose what they are comfortable with, whether it's an Oracle Portal system, a set of binders, or just walking over to a colleague's desk to ask about the information they need. As a developer, your challenge is not only to present the data your customers want but present it in a meaningful way. In short, modern web development should be just as concerned with how information is presented as with what is presented.

I know that's a radical concept and many will (vehemently) disagree with me, but my experience has taught me over and over again this simple fact: Even if the information is there, *and users know it's there,* if it isn't easy to get to, people just won't do it.

I'm painting with a very broad brush here. Motivated people will dig until they get the answers they want, but how many people are truly motivated? How many people use Google to search for something, then continue to the third or fourth page of results to find what they're looking for? How many go past the first page? How many even go past the first result?

Google tracks these things and the answers are surprisingly small (some would say infinitesimal). That's why companies are willing to pay so much to get their links *at the top* of a Google page. It's why entire books have been written about how to optimize your web sites so that they show up at the top of a Google search. It's why there are consulting firms that specialize in this very activity for organizations. Hopefully, I've convinced you that making the effort to organize and present your data in a meaningful way is just as important as the actual data itself. How do you go about designing a system like that? There are numerous options available to you.

You could write a proprietary client-server type system in a language like C#. Systems like this are hard to update (as every client would need to be updated when a new feature was added). Also, you'd be limited by the operating system, unless you developed in a cross-platform development tool like Java. With users demanding up-to-the second updates in functionality, this solution would only work for a very small number of users.

You could develop a Web-enabled system using Java and J2EE technologies (or C# and .NET technologies). This would solve the problem of updating your system (any time a new enhancement is rolled out, it only needs to be deployed to the Application Server), but it introduces new issues: a tremendous amount of code needs to be written to handle things like security, persistence (the ability of data to outlive the process that created it), object-relational mapping (the mapping of Java objects to relational database tables), and graphical design elements. There is also the challenge of storing things that don't traditionally fit into a database like Microsoft Word documents or Adobe PDF documents, commonly referred to as content. A lot of programming would be needed to store and secure these types of objects.

Graphical design elements cannot be understated. Although modern Java development has embraced the concept of separating the business logic code from the code used to display elements to the end user, it still requires the effort of multiple programming skill sets to pull this off. Making a change to a system like this might require a full round of testing (unit, system, integration) before it could be deployed.

OracleAS Portal provides an environment that makes everything developers are trying to do easy. It has a simple structure to set up and maintain security, a page design system that supports templates for easy page design and visual consistency, wizards for creating simple database-centric portlets and integration with advanced development tools like Oracle JDeveloper for advanced business requirements, a rich set of functions for content and content management, and a graphical system for administrators. OracleAS Portal is a mature environment that makes Web development easy, and, at the risk of sounding like an OracleAS Portal fanatic, fun!

Components Needed

To run the examples in this book you will need the following:

- Access to an installation of Oracle Application Server 10*g*, with either the Portal and Wireless or Business Intelligence and Forms installation options installed.
- A Java-enabled Web browser. (The screen shots in this book are taken from Microsoft's Internet Explorer 6. I've tested most of the screen shots with Internet Explorer 7 and Mozilla's Firefox 1.5.0.7 with no issues.)
- Oracle JDeveloper 10.1.2. If you are running an Intel-based machine (Windows or Linux) you will need a PC with at least a 1.5GHz processor, 512MB of RAM, and 15GB of disk space. If you are running on a Unix-based machine, the guidelines above should meet all of your needs, but check your installation guide for specifics.

Audience

This book is intended for those developers who wish to implement OracleAS Portal and OracleAS Portal components in their organization, and develop Web-based applications that use Oracle development technologies. Exercises are included at the end of most chapters that encourage readers to expand their OracleAS Portal knowledge. This book focuses on all major aspects of OracleAS Portal: page design, development, security, content management, and administration.

How This Book Is Organized

This book is divided into six parts, twelve chapters, and three appendixes.

Part I—Introduction

Part I lays the groundwork for everything discussed in the book. It is important to understand the fundamentals of OracleAS Portal terminology because many of the terms are unique to portals and OracleAS Portal.

- **Chapter 1** This chapter provides an overview of what OracleAS Portal is capable of. Out of the box, OracleAS Portal provides a tremendous amount of functionality. This chapter discusses fundamental OracleAS Portal concepts.
- **Chapter 2** Chapter 2 discusses the different types of skill sets needed within an organization to utilize OracleAS Portal effectively.

Part II—Page Design and Content Management

This part discusses the page design and content management features of OracleAS Portal.

- **Chapter 3** One of the fundamental activities of using OracleAS Portal is the design of pages. Pages are how end users interact with your portal. The basics of page design are discussed in this chapter.

- **Chapter 4** In response to feedback from existing OracleAS Portal users, Oracle has provided some exciting new page design features in its latest version of OracleAS Portal (version 10.1.4). Some of the features discussed in this chapter include HTML Page Skins and HTML Content Layouts.
- **Chapter 5** Managing content is essential to any portal system. This chapter discusses the content management features of OracleAS Portal.
- **Chapter 6** OmniPortlet is a seeded portlet builder that allows developers to design portlets quickly and easily. Web clipping enables you to "grab" (clip) an existing web page and incorporate it into your OracleAS Portal page. This chapter shows how to use these tools.

Part III—Development

One of the two main activities in OracleAS Portal, along with content management, is the development of portlets: small pieces of code that perform a specific function that are placed on OracleAS Portal web pages. This section discusses how to use nondeclarative tools like Oracle JDeveloper to design and deploy OracleAS Portal portlets.

- **Chapter 7** Oracle provides an add-in for its Oracle JDeveloper product that allows developers to develop Java-based portlets quickly and easily.
- **Chapter 8** Advanced development topics like Service Oriented Architecture (SOA) and Business Process Execution Language (BPEL) are popular today. This chapter looks at these technologies and examines why they are relevant to OracleAS Portal.

Part IV—Administration

OracleAS Portal has numerous administration duties associated with it. This section looks at the main administration duties that need to be performed on a regular basis.

- **Chapter 9** This chapter shows where to find the administration and performance tuning page for OracleAS Portal.
- **Chapter 10** A portal is useless without users. This chapter shows how to define users for your system and how OracleAS Portal's security model works.

Part V—Miscellaneous

- **Chapter 11** This chapter talks about ways to take Oracle Forms, Oracle Reports, and Oracle Discoverer workbooks and worksheets and integrate them with OracleAS Portal pages. By doing this, we can integrate these components with OracleAS Portal's security features and visual templates, allowing you to maintain a consistent look across your portal.
- **Chapter 12** Oracle has created Oracle Instant Portal, addressing the need for simple content-based portals. Although limited in its features, Oracle Instant Portal provides

a quick way for designers to create content-based portals. This chapter provides an overview of this feature.

Part VI—Appendixes

Part VI contains three appendixes: Appendix A: Future Direction of OracleAS Portal; Appendix B: OracleAS Portal Resources; and Appendix C: Exercise Commentary.

Getting the Most out of This Book

In my previous book, *Oracle Application Server 10g Web Development*, co-written with Brad Brown, I finished the Introduction with the line "Experiment, play around, but most importantly, have fun!"

For the life of me, I can't think of a better way to end the Introduction to this book. OracleAS Portal is unique because the pages you work with are themselves OracleAS Portal Pages, so you're already in the OracleAS Portal environment. I know of no other Web-development tool that gives as much instant feedback as OracleAS Portal. When you define a page, or apply a template to a page, right after you hit the OK button, it gets displayed. As soon as you place a portlet on a page, you see the page with the portlet displayed immediately. This kind of instant feedback is great for developers starting with OracleAS Portal. Experiment and keep trying out new things; it's very hard to do something truly destructive in OracleAS Portal. In a short while, you'll be able to create simple portlets and pages in minutes—give them to your end users and get feedback. They'll be amazed at how quickly you can turn around a change request. After a while, when you start taking all of this for granted, you won't be able to go back to a traditional Web-development environment.

Oh yeah, I almost forgot: Experiment, play around, but most importantly, have fun!

Chris Ostrowski
June 2007
oski.oracle@gmail.com

PART I

Introduction

CHAPTER 1

Out-of-the-Box Oracle Application Server Portal Technologies

racle defines Oracle Application Server Portal as "a rich, declarative environment for creating a portal Web interface, publishing and managing information, accessing dynamic data, and customizing the portal experience, with an extensible framework for J2EE-based application access." While that one-sentence summarization is quite a mouthful, it does not do OracleAS Portal justice. OracleAS Portal is an incredibly powerful environment that enables developers to create and test sophisticated applications, all while writing and maintaining a very small amount of code, if they desire. Like any truly powerful development environment, OracleAS Portal can be used in a multitude of ways. For example, beginning developers can use OracleAS Portal's wizards to generate applications consisting of forms, reports, and graphs and deploy those Oracle Application Server components quickly, easily, and with a minimum of code. Advanced developers can enhance the generated components through the use of the OracleAS Portal Application Programming Interface (API) or even bypass the wizards altogether and use Java and/or PL/SQL to create OracleAS Portal portlets. The portal you create can pull data from a single database, from multiple databases (including non-Oracle databases), and even from other sites on the Web. OracleAS Portal can be used to create portlets that interact with other sites on the Web and use their content in your portal. This chapter will briefly discuss all of the major components of OracleAS Portal. Subsequent chapters will go into the major topic areas in greater detail. This chapter also outlines how to create portlets with the wizards built into OracleAS Portal. The development chapters that form most of this book, however, will focus on using OmniPortlet, Oracle JDeveloper, and the OracleAS Portal Development Kit (PDK) to create advanced portlets.

OracleAS Portal leverages open standards, enabling developers to build Java 2 Platform, Enterprise Edition/eXtensible Markup Language (J2EE/XML) components that can be exposed within the framework as pure HTML. With the introduction of Web Services for Remote Portals (WSRP) and Java Specification Request (JSR) 168, OracleAS Portal support includes the capability to build interoperable applications that can be deployed across multiple vendor platforms. Furthermore, since OracleAS Portal is a component of the Oracle Application Server, it can integrate with other components such as Oracle Application Server Discoverer and Oracle Application Server Reports to expose rich Business Intelligence Reports. Chapter 11 discusses integrating Oracle's other development tools (Oracle Forms, Oracle Reports, and Oracle Discoverer) into OracleAS Portal. As part of the Oracle Application Server, OracleAS Portal can also be deployed in a number of different architectures to support scalability and high-availability scenarios. Chapter 9 will discuss some of the options available to OracleAS Portal administrators.

Logging in to OracleAS Portal for the First Time

When Oracle Application Server 10*g* is installed with either the Portal and Wireless or Business Intelligence and Forms option, OracleAS Portal is installed also. Before we can access the OracleAS Portal environment, the necessary components must be up and running. Use the opmnctl tool (in the $ORACLE_HOME/opmn/bin directory) to see if the OracleAS Portal Oracle Application Server Containers for J2EE (OC4J) container is running:

```
O:\MT_HOME\opmn\bin>opmnctl status

Processes in Instance: MT_HOME.oski-2k3
-------------------+--------------------+---------+---------
ias-component      | process-type       |     pid | status
-------------------+--------------------+---------+---------
DSA                | DSA                |     N/A | Down
LogLoader          | logloaderd         |     N/A | Down
dcm-daemon         | dcm-daemon         |    3584 | Alive
OC4J               | home               |    5940 | Alive
OC4J               | OC4J_Portal        |    2256 | Alive
OC4J               | OC4J_BI_Forms      |    3664 | Alive
WebCache           | WebCache           |    2756 | Alive
WebCache           | WebCacheAdmin      |    2616 | Alive
HTTP_Server        | HTTP_Server        |    2820 | Alive
Discoverer         | ServicesStatus     |    2884 | Alive
Discoverer         | PreferenceServer   |    2904 | Alive
wireless           | performance_server |       0 | NONE
wireless           | messaging_server   |       0 | NONE
wireless           | OC4J_Wireless      |    4116 | Alive
```

If you are running on a server that has both the infrastructure and the middle tier on the same machine, make sure you run this command from the ORACLE_HOME location of the middle tier. If the OC4J_Portal component is not running for any reason, you can start it by executing the following command:

```
opmnctl startproc ias-component=OC4J
```

OracleAS Portal also depends on the security functions built into Oracle Application Server 10*g*. All of the security features of Oracle Application Server 10*g* are contained in the infrastructure. The infrastructure is another instance of the Oracle Application Server installation that can either reside on the same server as the mid-tier (where Portal lives) or on another server. To check to make sure that the security piece is up and running, cd to the ORACLE_HOME of your infrastructure, then to the opmn\bin directory. Execute the following command:

```
O:\IS_HOME\opmn\bin>opmnctl status
Processes in Instance: IS_HOME.oski-2k3
-------------------+--------------------+---------+---------
ias-component      | process-type       |     pid | status
-------------------+--------------------+---------+---------
DSA                | DSA                |     N/A | Down
LogLoader          | logloaderd         |     N/A | Down
dcm-daemon         | dcm-daemon         |    5644 | Alive
OC4J               | OC4J_SECURITY      |    4056 | Alive
HTTP_Server        | HTTP_Server        |    1104 | Alive
OID                | OID                |    2596 | Alive
```

If the OC4J_SECURITY component is not running for any reason, start it with the following command:

```
opmnctl startproc ias-component=OC4J
```

To access OracleAS Portal for the first time, enter the URL in your web browser from the following template:

```
http://<server>:<port>/pls/portal
```

The machine I used for the examples in this book is called oski-2k3, and the middle tier was installed on port 80 (since 80 is the default for http, you do not have to specify it in your URL), so to access OracleAS Portal on this server:

```
http://oski-2k3/pls/portal
```

During installation, Oracle will attempt to use port 7777 for your Oracle Application Server 10*g* infrastructure instance. If, for whatever reason, port 7777 is not available, Oracle will try 7778, then 7779, and so on. If you chose to install both the infrastructure and middle tier on the same machine, then, most likely, the infrastructure will use 7777 and the middle tier will use 80. OracleAS Portal "lives" in the middle tier, so use the middle-tier port number to access it. It is important to note that while Oracle Application Server's Portal Page Engine (PPE) lives in the middle tier, it is dependent on both the middle tier and the infrastructure for both metadata and identity management.

If all of the necessary components are up and running, you should see a page similar to the one shown in Figure 1-1.

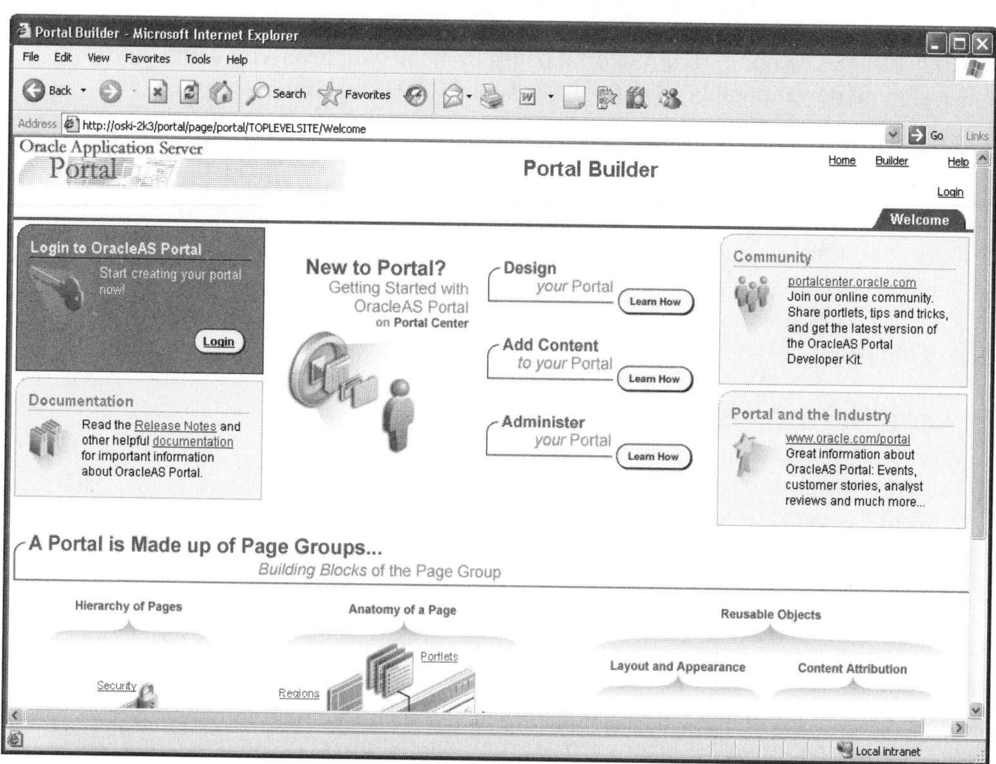

FIGURE 1-1 *The initial OracleAS Portal page*

Getting Around in OracleAS Portal

As with virtually every OracleAS Portal page developers or administrators will work with, a lot of information is displayed. The page in Figure 1-1 serves as both a welcome to the OracleAS Portal environment and an example of a typical OracleAS Portal page. Pages like this one that end users will display initially are commonly referred to as *landing pages.* This page contains a lot of OracleAS Portal–specific information that end users will not have any interest in, so it is not appropriate to have this page serve as your landing page. Chapter 12 describes how to change what the end users see as their landing page.

As you work with OracleAS Portal, you will become comfortable with the basic layout of an OracleAS Portal page (although, as a developer, you have great flexibility to make your OracleAS Portal pages look like whatever you want), and this welcome page contains all of the basic OracleAS Portal page elements.

Along the top of the page (above the first horizontal line) there is a page region called the *banner.* Although your portal pages do not have to contain a banner, it is included in all OracleAS Portal templates when it comes time to build and deploy your OracleAS Portal pages. You will find an image on the left, a title (Portal Builder), and links on the right. Below the links on the right is a tab that says Welcome. Tabs are similar to banners in that they are not required but are included as standard page elements in OracleAS Portal. Below the Welcome tab is the main part of the page.

NOTE
For those of you unfamiliar with graphical elements, tabs are standard page elements that look like the tabs that separate folders in your filing cabinet. Tabs can be used to provide easy navigation between a group of OracleAS Portal pages.

A key concept to understand when working with OracleAS Portal and the various OracleAS Portal elements is the one-to-many relationship. Oracle used this concept many times when constructing the OracleAS Portal environment. A one-to-many relationship describes one where there is one parent record and one or more child records. Child records cannot exist without a parent record, but a parent record may exist without any child records. As an example, say one of us walks into our local bookstore and purchases some books. The invoice might look like this:

```
Order # 12345
Customer: 67890    Ostrowski, Chris
                   215 Union Blvd
                   Lakewood, CO 80228
Quantity      Title
1             Oracle Application Server 10g Web Development, Ostrowski/Brown,
              Oracle Press
1             Oracle9i Performance Tuning Tips & Techniques, Niemiec, Oracle Press
1             Oracle PL/SQL Tips and Techniques, Trezzo, Oracle Press
Total:        179.97
Tax:           10.80
Total:        190.77
Payment Method: Mastercard xxxx-xxxx-xxxx-1234 Exp: 01/05
```

If the database used to store this information is normalized, there would be a database record that stores information about the order (Order id = 12345) and a line-items table that stores the line items that constitute this order (the three books). In this case, the order record is the parent and the line items are the children. The parent (the order) consists of one or more children (the line items). Line items cannot exist independent of an order. It is also possible to split the payment due on the order. Perhaps Chris has a gift certificate for $100. The payment to satisfy this order might constitute the $100 gift certificate and $90.77 charged to his credit card. Anticipating this possibility, the database is also designed with a one-to-many relationship between the orders and payments tables.

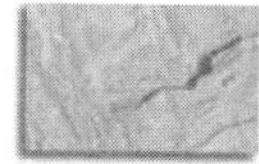

TIP

"Normalized" and "normalization" are fancy words for structuring your database so that there is as little redundancy as possible. The objective is to increase capacity by eliminating wasted storage.

For DBA-minded types out there, another example of the one-to-many relationship is the one between tablespaces and datafiles in an Oracle database. A tablespace (the parent) consists of one or more datafiles (children). A datafile cannot exist independent of a tablespace.

In OracleAS Portal, developers will visit this one-to-many relationship many times, and here is the first example of it. Every OracleAS Portal page, including the Welcome page in Figure 1-1, is made up of regions. A *region* is nothing more than a section of a page. Many aspects of content display are defined at the region level, such as the width of the region or whether to display borders around the portlets in a portlet region. Regions can also include one or more tabs. A region can be defined to hold portlets, items, subpage links, and tabs, or it can exist as undefined (undefined regions become defined when an OracleAS Portal object first gets placed on them). You cannot add portlets to an item region, nor can you add items to a portlet region. You cannot add anything to a subpage links region; these regions automatically populate with links to subpages of the current page. You cannot add anything other than a tab to a tab region; although you can configure the tab to include, for example, rollover images. There is a one-to-many relationship between pages and regions. In regions defined as portlet regions, there is also a many-to-many relationship between regions and portlets. These relationships are shown in Figure 1-2.

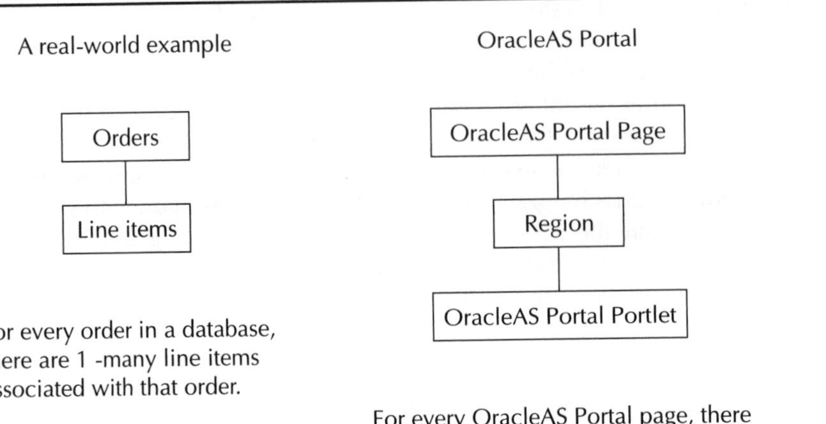
A real-world example
Orders
Line items
For every order in a database, there are 1 -many line items associated with that order.
OracleAS Portal
OracleAS Portal Page
Region
OracleAS Portal Portlet
For every OracleAS Portal page, there are 1 -many regions associated with that page. For each region, there are 1 -many OracleAS portlets associated with that region.

FIGURE 1-2 *One-to-many relationship between pages, regions, and portlets*

TIP
Another way to think about regions is to picture each OracleAS Portal page as divided into a section of "Web real estate." Each region exposes an OracleAS Portal object such as a portlet or an item and can be seen as a "container." Every OracleAS Portal page consists of one or more regions.

The many-to-many relationship is slightly different from the one-to-many relationship discussed earlier. In this example, one region may have many portlets placed on it, but a portlet may be placed on one or many different regions on different pages. Item regions have the same one-to-many relationship: an item region may contain many items.

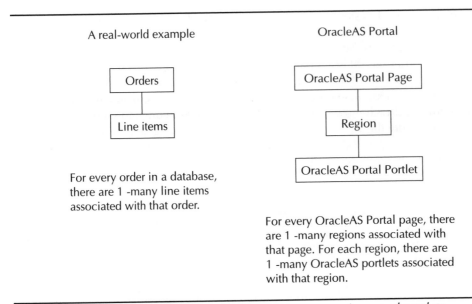

One of the many benefits of developing in OracleAS Portal is the ability to display pages with certain elements shown and others hidden, depending on the privileges of the user signing in to your portal. These changes are handled by OracleAS Portal automatically and require no additional programming from the developer. As an example, let's log in to OracleAS Portal as if we were going to begin our OracleAS Portal development work. You can log in either by clicking the

Definition of Items

What, exactly, are "items"? To fully understand items, we must take a step back and look at the definition of a portal. In the most general sense, a portal is a highly trafficked Web site with a wide range of content, services, and vendor links. It acts as a middleman by selecting the content sources and assembling them in a simple-to-navigate, customizable interface for presentation to the end user. Given this definition, many pieces that constitute a typical portal don't fit into traditional programming constructs like forms or reports. A good example might be a company's internal portal site that delivers private company information to its employees. Some of these portal elements may be things like Microsoft Word documents or Adobe Portable Document Format (PDF) files that outline company policies. The designers of OracleAS Portal were smart enough to know that some (if not most) information included in a typical portal would be nonstructured data like the aforementioned Word documents or PDF files. Chapter 5 discusses items in the context of Content Management.

small Login link on the top right of the page, or by clicking the Login link under the Login To OracleAS Portal portlet on the top left of the page. By default, a couple of OracleAS Portal logins are created for you automatically when you install OracleAS Portal. On the login screen, log in with the username of "portal" (without the quotes). The password will be the same as the password given when you or your administrator installed the Oracle Application Server 10*g* Application Server middle tier.

CAUTION

The portal user in OracleAS Portal is similar to the sys user in the database. It has every privilege within OracleAS Portal and should be used very sparingly. Just as when working as the sys user in the database, you should never create OracleAS Portal objects as the "portal" user. The portal user should be used for system administration purposes only.

After a successful login, you will see a page similar to Figure 1-3.

The page looks similar to Figure 1-1, and in fact, the URL is exactly the same. But if you look closely, you'll notice that there are many new elements on the page. On the top right of the page there are also many more links. Previously, only Home,

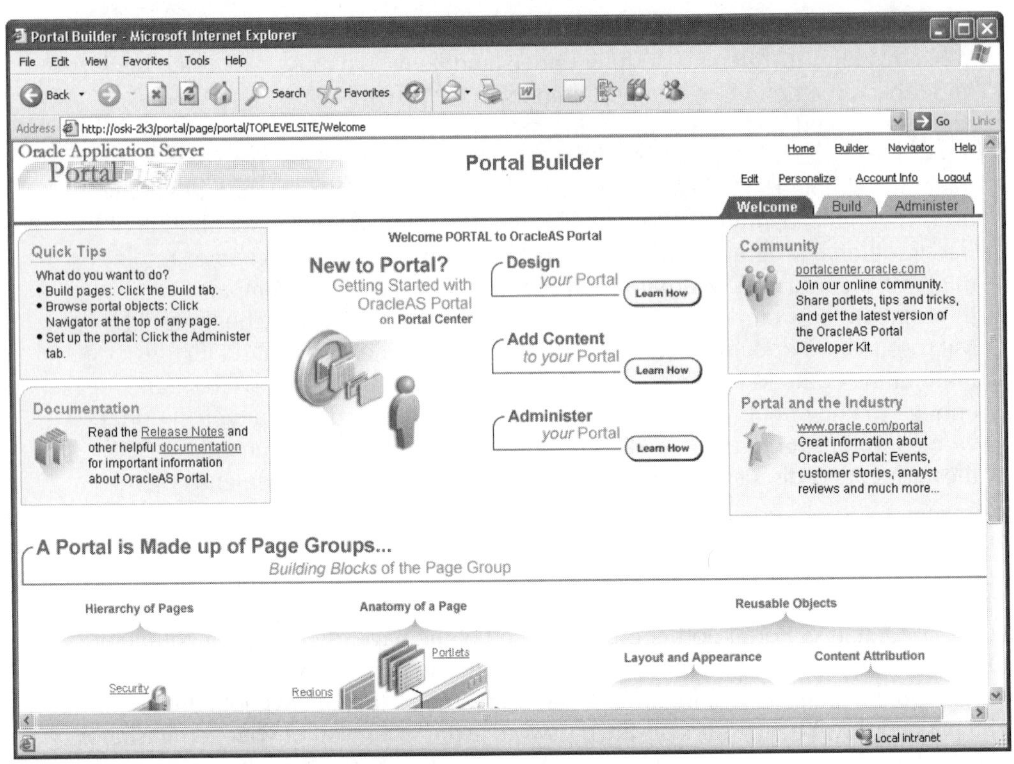

FIGURE 1-3 *The OracleAS Portal welcome page after a successful login*

Builder, Help, and Logon were displayed. Now, Navigator, Edit, Customize, and Account Info are displayed and the Login link has been replaced with the Logout link. We also have three tabs along the top right: Welcome, Build, and Administer. Finally, the login portlet on the top left of the page has been replaced with a Quick Tips portlet. This is an example of how your OracleAS Portal pages can be designed to behave differently, depending on who is looking at them, with no additional programming whatsoever. When we first viewed the Welcome page, we had not authenticated ourselves to OracleAS Portal (authenticated is a fancy word for logging in). After we logged in, we became part of an Oracle Application Server group called the Authenticated Users group. As a member of that group, we saw a different version of the page. Our user login, portal, also gave us privileges to see other aspects of the page.

A Quick Tour of OracleAS Portal Pages

Because there are so many pages and tabs available to developers after they log in to OracleAS Portal, it is easy to become quickly overwhelmed. This section will walk through the basic OracleAS Portal pages and give a brief explanation of each so that later on, we can easily navigate among them as we visit them in detail.

Like most Oracle development tools, OracleAS Portal provides developers with many ways of performing the basic tasks of development and administration. None of these methods is the "right" way of doing things; they are simply different techniques for accomplishing your development goals that give developers the ability to choose which methods are suitable for them. Some of the methods require more steps than other methods, so after exploring the different methods, we will (generally) use those techniques requiring the fewest number of steps.

The Build Tab

As the portal user, you have all privileges in OracleAS Portal. As we have already discussed, OracleAS Portal pages display different elements according to the privileges granted to the user logging in, so many of these pages will look subtlety different if you should log in as a different user. Clicking the Build tab in the top right will display a page similar to the one in Figure 1-4.

On this page there are four portlets:

- **Recent Objects portlet** This portlet allows developers and content administrators to quickly jump to one of the last five OracleAS Portal objects they've edited.
- **Developer News portlet** This portlet provides a link to Oracle's Portal Development site (http://portalcenter.oracle.com/).
- **Page Groups portlet** This portlet allows developers to work with Page Groups, along with the banner page element discussed earlier. Page Groups are at the top of the hierarchy in Figure 1-2. Pages are children of Page Groups and cannot, therefore, exist without them. Every Page Group has a default root page, and any attribute defined for a Page Group automatically cascades down to its Pages (although many attributes can be overridden at the Page level).
- **Instant Portal portlet** Instant Portals are discussed in detail in Chapter 12.

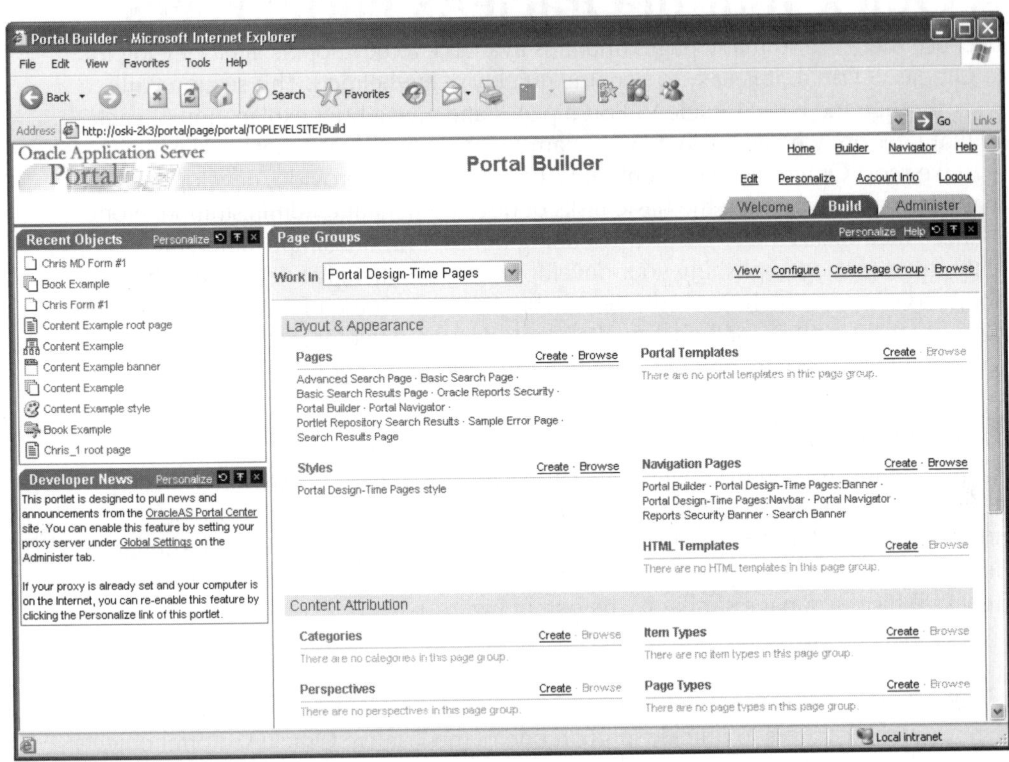

FIGURE 1-4 *The Build tab displayed in OracleAS Portal*

The two portlets on the left-hand side of the page—Recent Objects and Developer News—give an example of OracleAS Portal's security mechanisms. Both have a Personalize link in their title bars. These Personalize links allow end users to change certain characteristics of the portlet. Depending on the privileges granted to a particular user, the Personalize links will appear or be hidden. Any changes made to the portlet will be made for that user only. For example, if the portal user chooses to personalize the Recent Objects portlet to limit the list to only the three most recent objects (Figure 1-5), another user logging in will still see the five most recent objects in that portlet.

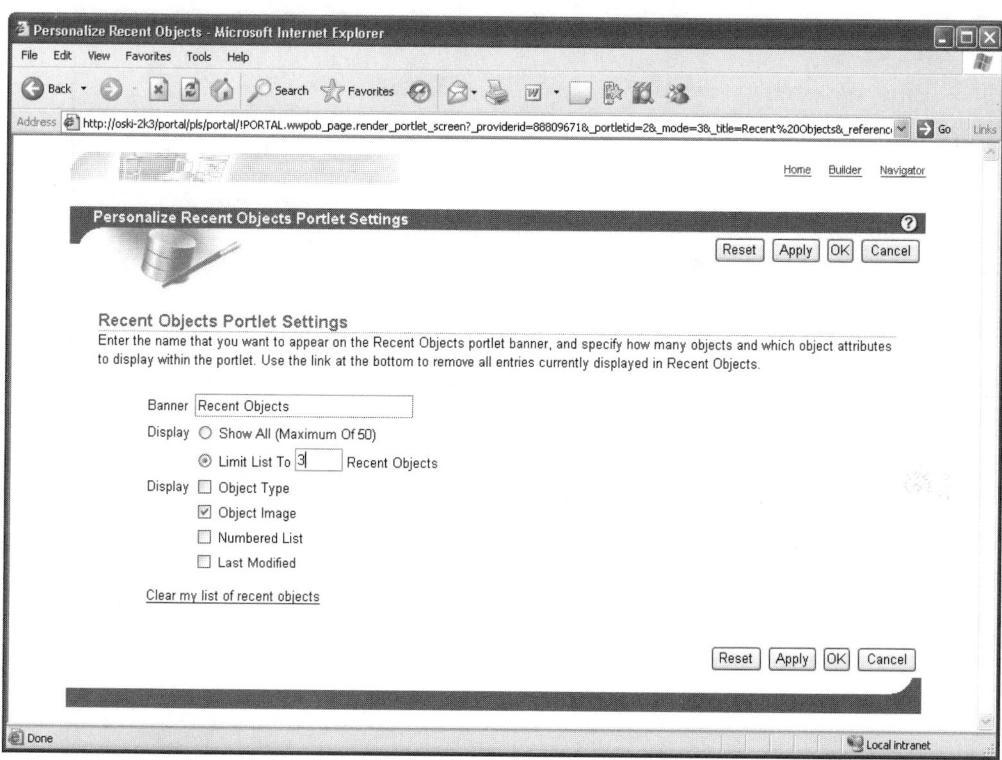

FIGURE 1-5 *The Personalize Recent Objects portlet screen*

The Administer Tab

The third tab in Figure 1-4, Administer, is where OracleAS Portal administrators will spend most of their time. It has three subtabs along the left-hand side: Portal, Portlets, and Database. The Portal subtab (see Figure 1-6) has portlets that allow administrators to change the basic functionality of the OracleAS Portal as a whole. The Portlets subtab (see Figure 1-7) has portlets that allow administrators to display the Portlet Repository and define remote providers.

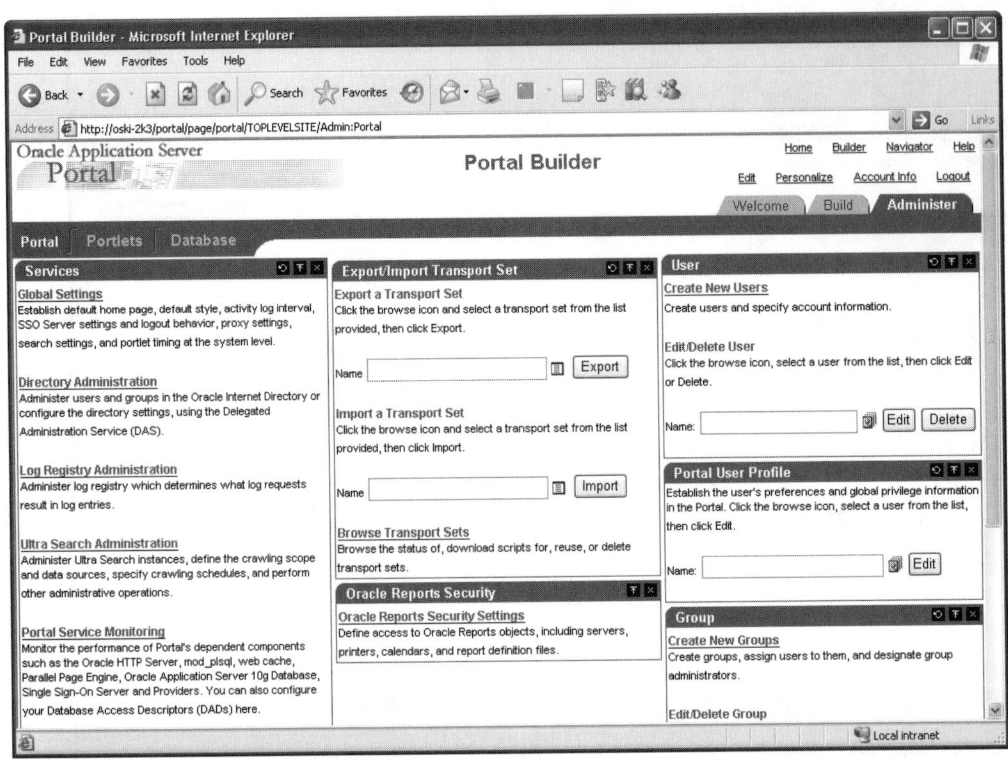

FIGURE 1-6 *The Portal subtab in the Administer tab*

Providers

In yet another example of the one-to-many relationship found throughout the OracleAS Portal product, a provider can be thought of as a way of grouping portlets together. Any attribute assigned to the provider will cascade down to the portlets in that provider (unless it's overridden by the portlet). In addition, providers are also members of provider groups, which can also define attributes. The provider is the parent and the OracleAS Portal components (forms, reports, graphs, etc.) that can eventually become portlets are the children.

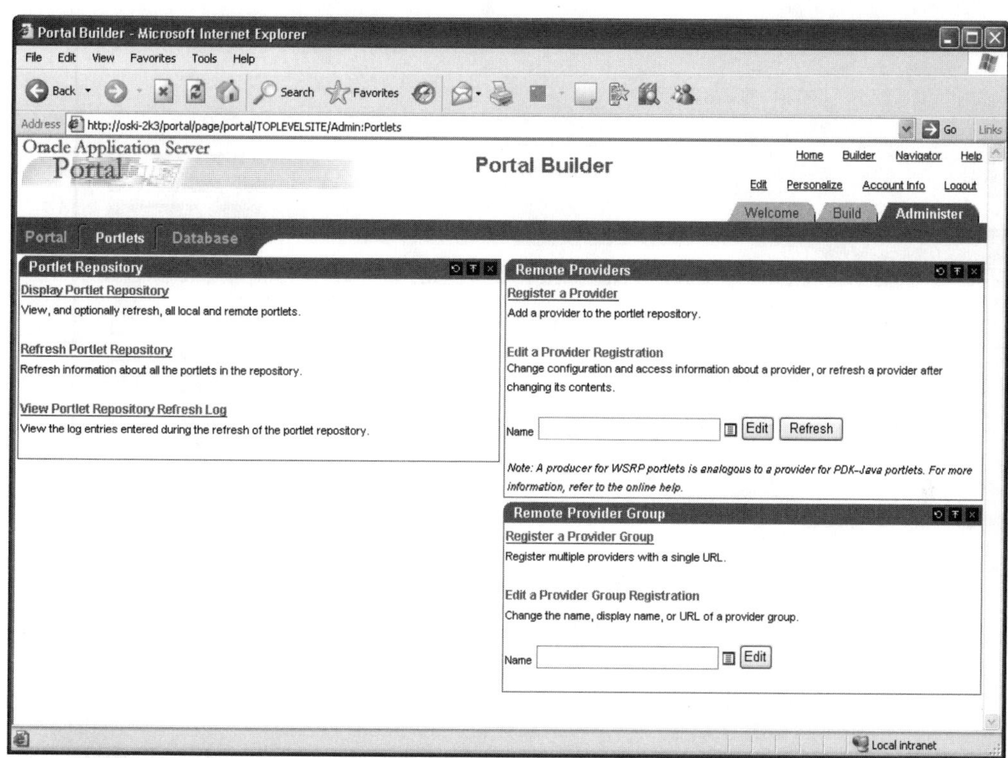

FIGURE 1-7 *The Portlets subtab in the Administer tab*

The last subtab, Database (see Figure 1-8), allows administrators to create and modify both database objects and rows within a table. This functionality is limited to the infrastructure database.

Here is another example of OracleAS Portal's security mechanism: Out of the box, OracleAS Portal defines Groups that have various privileges within OracleAS Portal (the portal user, of course, has all privileges). Becoming a member of any OracleAS Portal group automatically grants all privileges to that user. Three of the basic groups defined during the install of OracleAS Portal are

- PORTAL_ADMINISTRATORS
- PORTAL_DEVELOPERS
- PORTLET_PUBLISHERS

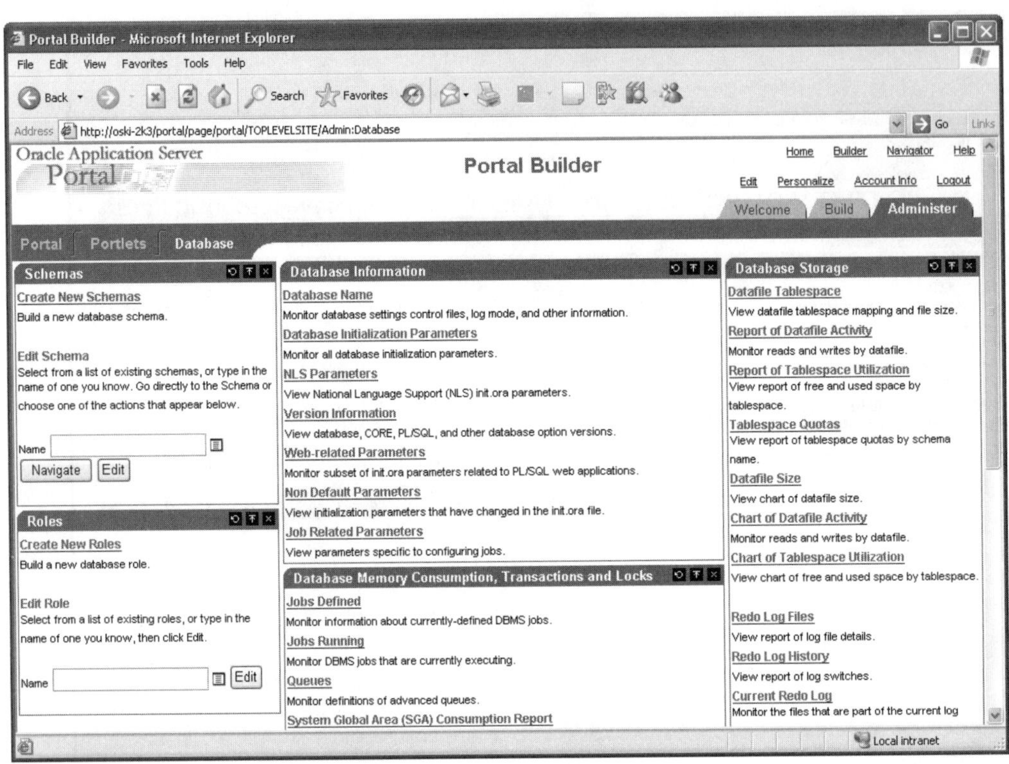

FIGURE 1-8 *The Database subtab in the Administer tab*

The OracleAS Portal elements on each of the tabs displayed along the top of the page will differ depending on what groups the OracleAS Portal user is assigned to. As an example, if a user is only a member of the PORTAL_DEVELOPERS group, nothing will be displayed in the Database subtab of the Administer tab. In general, these default groups were set up with the following privileges and for the following reasons:

- **PORTAL_DEVELOPERS** Users in this group can create portlets but cannot place them on a page. In general, users in this group are usually more concerned with the functionality of the various portlets that will make up an OracleAS Portal site and less concerned with the look and feel of a site.

- **PORTLET_PUBLISHERS** Users in this group can take developed portlets and place them on a page as well as construct pages and page templates, but they cannot create new portlets. In general, users in this group are generally more concerned with the aesthetics of a portal site and less concerned with the code that makes up the various portlets to be placed on a site.
- **PORTLET_ADMINISTRATORS** Users in this group have responsibilities across all facets of the site, including creation and deletion of users and groups, design and code modifications, and overall OracleAS Portal functionality. In general, users in this group have control over all aspects of the OracleAS Portal site.

You are not limited to these groups; you can create other groups that have distinct privileges and assign users to these groups. In some organizations, there may be a group of portlet users that is in charge of both designing portlets and placing them on pages. In this case, a new group with the privileges of both PORTAL_DEVELOPERS and PORTLET_PUBLISHERS can be created and users can be assigned to that (or users can just be assigned to both groups). If you have a small number of administrators and developers at your OracleAS Portal site, you may not even need groups at all, as you can assign these privileges directly to OracleAS Portal users.

OracleAS Portal Navigator

Up to this point, we have seen OracleAS Portal pages where developers can create users and groups, page groups, register providers, and change OracleAS Portal settings and database objects, among other things. What we haven't seen is the ability to design pages that end users will typically view and interact with or to create Oracle Application Server portlets such as forms and reports. To do those things, we'll need to explore another major piece of OracleAS Portal: the OracleAS Portal Navigator. Page developers can create/edit page groups, pages, styles, and templates, among other object types, directly from the build page. Oracle introduced this feature to make it easier for people to manage objects without relying on the OracleAS Portal Navigator so much.

The OracleAS Portal Navigator (see Figure 1-9) is where developers who will be using the wizards built into OracleAS Portal will spend most of their time. Its three tabs, Page Groups, Providers, and Database Objects allow developers to create, modify, and delete all of the OracleAS Portal objects that make up a portal. Again, only certain tabs and certain options within those tabs will be available to you as

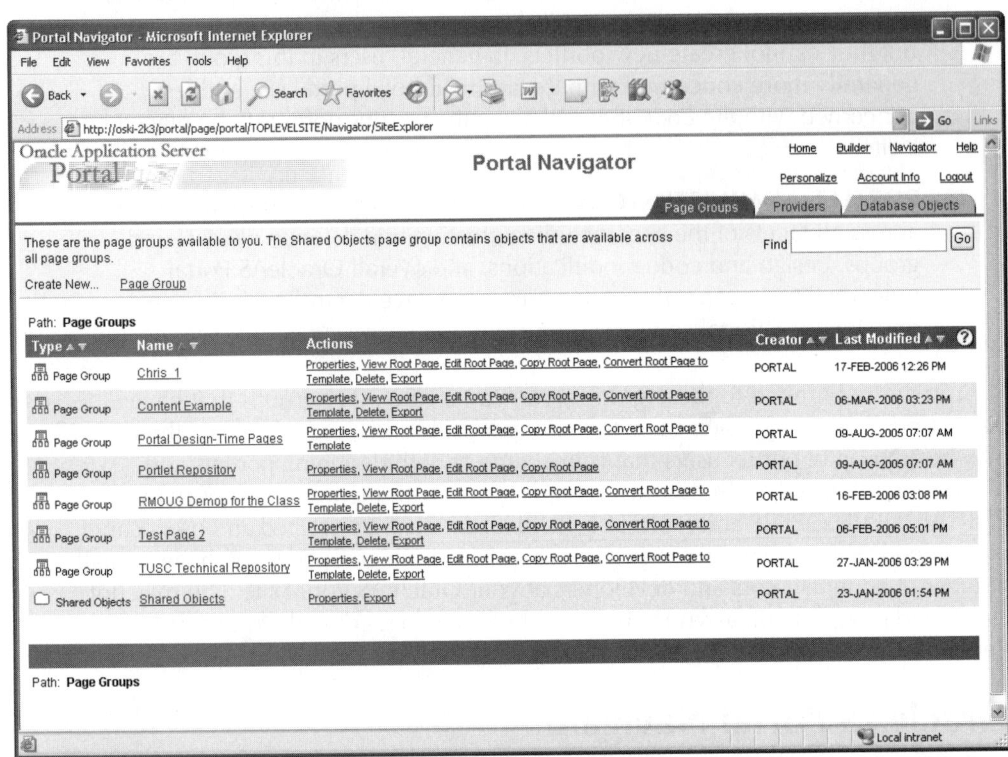

FIGURE 1-9 *The Page Groups tab of the Portal Navigator*

the OracleAS Portal developer, depending on your privileges. You can exit the Navigator at any time by clicking the Builder link on the top right of the page.

The Page Groups Tab

The Page Groups tab allows the creation of all page elements. On this tab, developers can perform the following actions:

- **Create a new Page Group** This action, which also automatically creates the root page of that group, is used to define a group that will incorporate pages that make up your portal or a section of your portal. As an example, an organization may have a set of OracleAS Portal pages with a certain look for a corporate office, another set for external suppliers, and other sets of pages for various satellite locations. Any attributes applied at the Page Group level cascade down to all subpages (unless they're overridden at the subpage level).

- **Edit properties of the Page Group** This action allows developers to define attributes of the Page Group such as the total amount of disk space used for items placed on pages within this page group, whether privileged users can alter the pages within the Page Group, what types of pages can exist within the Page Group, how items are to be displayed and versioned, if language translations are to be made available, and which users can perform which actions against pages in the page group.
- **Create new subpages** Every page group has a root page; other pages can be created as subpages to the root page. A breadcrumb menu, showing where the user is in the hierarchy of pages, is generated automatically.
- **Edit the root page or any of the subpages** This is where users typically assigned to the PORTLET_PUBLISHERS group will design pages and place portlets and items on them.
- **Create, modify, and apply Templates** These are used for enforcing a particular layout, style, set of privileges, and content for multiple pages.
- **Create and modify Categories** The purpose of a category is to enable users to quickly display a listing of a particular type of content. Categories answer the question, "What is this item or page?" and are used to classify content. For every item or page that you create, you can assign it to one category.
- **Create and modify Navigation Pages** A navigation page is a special type of page that can be included on other pages to provide a consistent set of navigational elements. A typical navigation page might contain a logo, the page title, a login link, and a link to the home page. Navigation pages differ from other pages in that they are excluded from searches and bulk actions performed on pages in the page group. Additionally, they have their own node in the Navigator (Navigation Pages). Although you can add any item or portlet to a navigation page, and even divide your navigation page into several regions, you should bear in mind that the idea is to add navigation pages to other pages.
- **Create and modify Perspectives** The purpose of perspectives is to enable users to quickly display a listing of content that is pertinent to them. Perspectives often answer the question, "Who will be interested in this item or page?" and are used to further classify content by a cross-category grouping. When an item is added to a page in the page group, it can be

Attribute	Description
Display Name Link	The display name of the item or portlet as a link pointing to the item or portlet content.
Display Name And Image Link	The display name and image of the item or portlet as links pointing to the item or portlet content. If the item has both a display name and an image, these will appear next to each other. If the item does not have an associated image, only the display name will appear.
Document Size	The size of the uploaded file.
Expire Date	The date (in the format, DD-MON-YYYY HH12: MI PM) when the item is due to expire.
Gist	The Gist icon next to items. Users can click this icon to display an overview of the item created by Oracle Text.
Help URL	The help icon next to the portlet item. Users can click this icon to display help for the portlet.
Image	The image associated with the item. If the item does not have an associated image, nothing is displayed.
Image Link	The image associated with the item as a link pointing to the item content. If the item does not have an associated image, nothing is displayed.
Image Or Display Name Link	The image associated with the item as a link pointing to the item content. If the item does not have an associated image, the display name is displayed instead.
Image URL	The image icon next to the portlet item. Users can click this icon to display a preview of the portlet.
Item Content	The content of the item.
Keywords	The keywords associated with the item or portlet.
Last Updated By	The user name of the user who last updated the item or portlet.
Mime Type Image	The image associated with the MIME type of the uploaded file.

Attribute	Description
New Item Indicator	The New icon next to a new item or portlet. Users can click this icon to display a list of all new content in the page group.
Perspectives	The names of the perspectives associated with the item or portlet.
Portlet Content	The portlet itself if the Item Displayed Directly In Page Area display option is selected.
Portlet ID	The ID of the portlet.
Portlet Name	The name of the portlet.
Property Sheet	The Property Sheet icon next to items and portlets. Users can click this icon to view the properties of an item or portlet.
Provider ID	The ID of the provider.
Provider Name	The name of the provider.
Publish Date	The date when the item is published on the page (i.e., when the item is visible to users in View mode).
Subscribe	The Subscribe or Unsubscribe icon next to items. Users can click this icon to subscribe to an item and be notified, via the Notifications portlet, when it is updated.
Themes	The Themes icon next to items. Users can click this icon to display the nouns and verbs appearing most often within an item.
Translations	A list of the languages in which the item or portlet is available.
Updated Item Indicator	The Recently Updated icon next to a recently updated item or portlet. Users can click this icon to display a list of all recently updated content in the page group.
Versions	The Versions icon next to items that have multiple versions. Users can click this icon to view other versions of the item.
View As HTML	The View As HTML icon next to items. Users can click this icon to view an HTML version of an item.

Attribute	Description
View As HTML With Highlight	The View As HTML With Highlight icon next to items. Users can click this icon to view an HTML version of an item with search terms highlighted.

- **Create and modify Page Types** Page types define the contents of a page and the information that is stored about a page. The information stored about a page is determined by the attributes of the page type. There are five base page types included with OracleAS Portal:
  - **Standard** Displays items and portlets
  - **URL** Displays the contents of a particular URL
  - **Mobile** Displays item and portlets in a hierarchical tree structure for viewing on a mobile device
  - **PL/SQL** Displays the results of executing PL/SQL code
  - **JSP** Displays the results of executing a Java Server Page (JSP)

Custom Page Types

In addition to these basic page types, developers and page designers can also create custom page types. Items are one of the basic components of a portal page. Items in OracleAS Portal are based on item types. Item types define the contents of an item and the information that is stored about an item. The information stored about an item is determined by the attributes of the item type. There are two kinds of item types: base item types and navigation item types.

Base Item Types Base items can be broken down further into these subtypes:

- **Content item types** These allow users to add content (for example, images, documents, or text) to a page. Base content item types are not available for users to add to pages. OracleAS Portal provides extended item types (listed next) that are based on the base content items. Oracle offers the following base content item types:
- **Base File** Uploads a file and stores it in the page group
- **Base Image Map** Uploads an image and allows the contributor to identify areas within the image that users can click to go to different URLs
- **Base Image** Uploads an image and stores it in the page group
- **Base PL/SQL** Executes PL/SQL code and displays the results

- **Base Page Link** Links to another page in the page group
- **Base Text** Displays text (up to 32KB)
- **Base URL** Links to another Web page, Web site, or document

Navigation Item Types These allow users to add navigational elements (for example, a login/logout link, basic search box, or list of objects) to a page. The following are the base navigation item types provided by Oracle:

- **Portal Smart Link** Adds a smart link (and associated image) to the page. A smart link is a link that users can click to access areas of the OracleAS Portal quickly, such as Account Information, Advanced Search, Contact Information, Help, and Home.
- **Login/Logout Link** Adds links and/or icons to the page that users can click to log in to or log out of the portal.
- **Basic Search Box** Adds a basic search box (and associated image) to the page in which users can enter search criteria. Users can specify whether users of the search box can search all page groups or only the page group specified.
- **List of Objects** Adds a list of objects (pages, categories, and perspectives) that users specify to the page. Users can choose to display this list as a drop-down list or as links (with or without associated images).
- **Portal Smart Text** Adds smart text, such as the current date, current user, or current page, to the page.
- **Object Map Link** Adds a map of objects available in the portal.
- **Page Path** Adds the page path to the page. Users can choose the number of levels for the path, and the character that separates the path levels.
- **Page Function** Adds a page function to the page. If there are no page functions associated with the current page, this item type is not displayed.

Extended Item Types These types are available to users to add to pages:

- File and Simple File
- Simple Image
- Image and Simple Image Map
- PL/SQL and Simple PL/SQL

- Page Link and Simple Page Link
- Text and Simple Text
- URL and Simple URL
- Zip File

Chapters 3 and 4 discuss OracleAS Portal page design in detail. Chapter 5 discusses content management and the various functions associated with types, items, and item attributes.

The Providers Tab

As we mentioned earlier, a provider can be thought of as a way of grouping portlets together. On the Providers tab of the Navigator in Figure 1-10, you can see that there are three categories of providers available: Locally Built Providers, Registered Providers, and Provider Groups.

Locally Built Providers This is where developers will define providers when they are ready to build OracleAS Portal objects such as OracleAS Portal forms, reports, and graphs. This chapter focuses on using the OracleAS Portal wizards and therefore deals mainly with Locally Built Providers.

Registered Providers This is where providers built outside of the OracleAS Portal are. Registered providers can include the following:

- **Database providers** A database provider is one that is written as a PL/SQL package. Use database providers for creating PL/SQL portlets that reside in the database. PL/SQL portlets are implemented as stored procedures and executed in the database. They can be written in PL/SQL or Java Stored Procedures wrapped in PL/SQL. Use PL/SQL portlets whenever your portlets require significant database interaction or when the development team has Oracle experience.
- **Web providers** A Web provider is one that is written as a Web application. It is installed and hosted on a Web server and is remote from the portal. A portlet exposed as a Web provider can be developed in any Web language. The portal communicates to the Web provider using the HTTP protocol. There are several benefits when developing portlets and exposing them as Web providers:
    - Leverage existing Web application code to create portlets
    - Manage outside of OracleAS Portal

- Provide hosted servers for OracleAS Portal users
- Create portlets using any existing Web language

NOTE
This chapter deals mainly with locally built providers. Chapters 7 and 8, however, discuss Web providers.

Provider Groups A provider group is a mechanism for organizing and simplifying the registration of providers. Provider groups often define a group of providers that share a common feature, such as belonging to the same organization, or providing similar content or functions.

Part III of this book discusses providers in more detail.

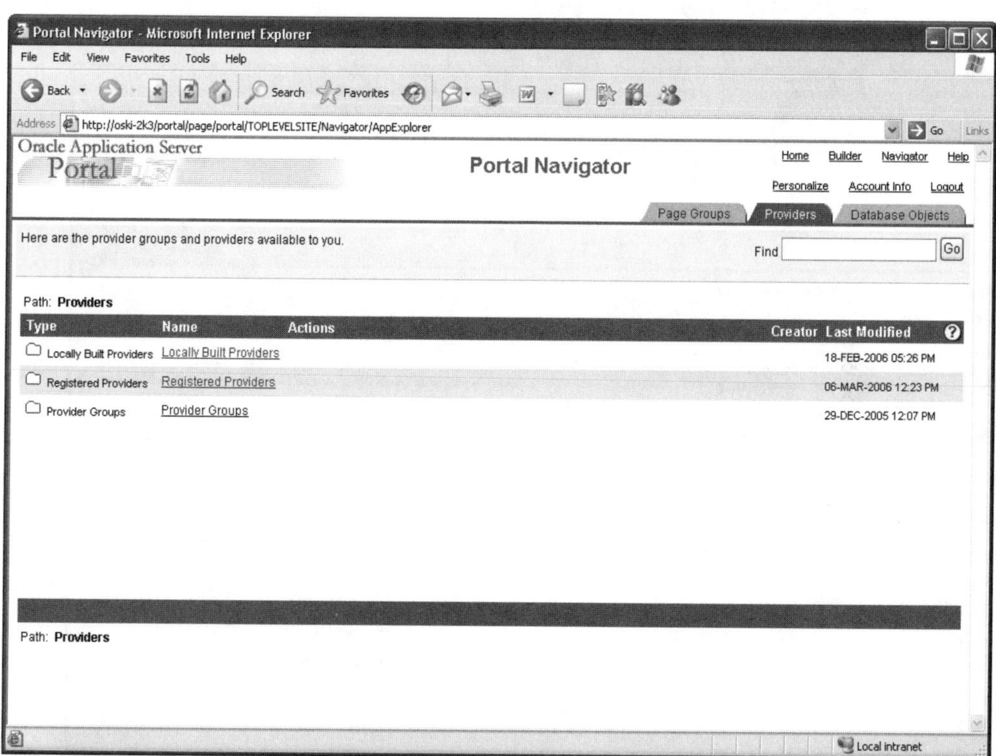

FIGURE 1-10 *The Providers tab of the OracleAS Portal Navigator*

The Database Objects Tab

The Database Objects tab allows OracleAS Portal users with the necessary privileges to manipulate database objects in the infrastructure database (see Figure 1-11). Some of the actions that can be performed include

- Creating new schemas
- Creating and modifying these database objects: tables, views, procedures, functions, packages, sequences, synonyms, indexes, triggers, database links, Java objects, and scripts
- Querying rows in tables and views
- Modifying columns and column attributes
- Modifying rows in tables and views
- Viewing able constraints and column attributes

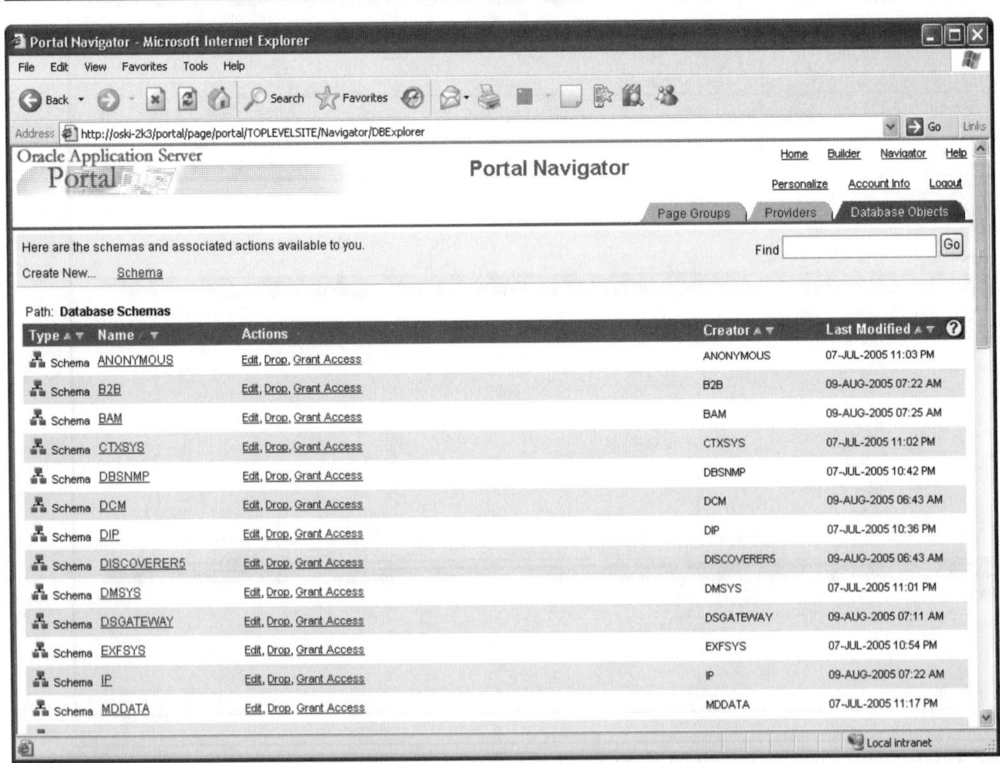

FIGURE 1-11 *The Database Objects tab of the OracleAS Portal Navigator*

The Help System

Last, but certainly not least, is the OracleAS Portal Help system (see Figure 1-12). Oracle has greatly improved the help system included with OracleAS Portal, including context-sensitive help for most (but not all) screens in OracleAS Portal version 10.1.4. The Search tab on the help pages is invaluable, as it allows developers to search through all of the OracleAS Portal documentation in one place.

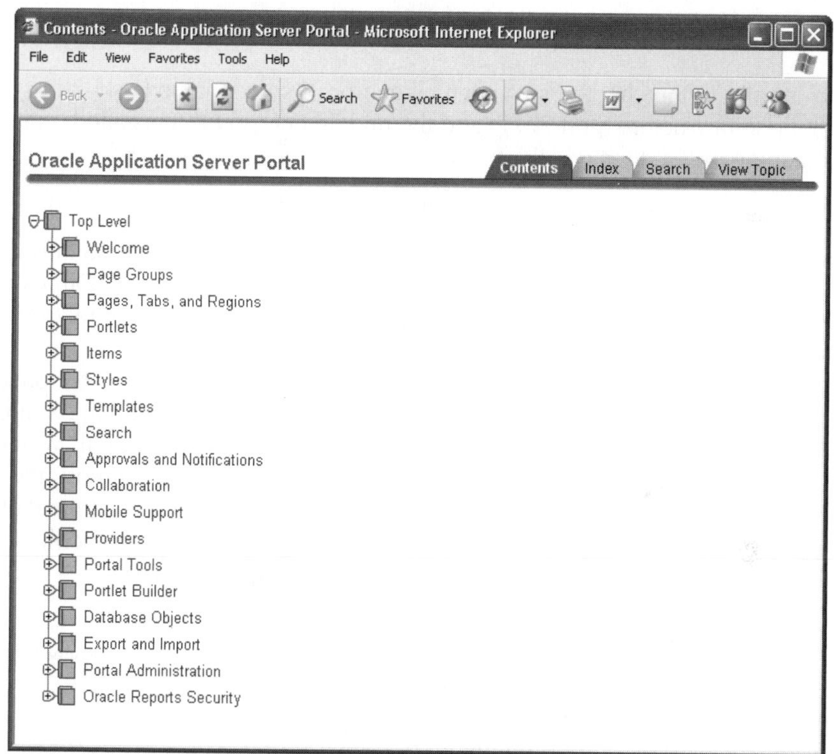

FIGURE 1-12 *The OracleAS Portal help system*

Creating an OracleAS Portal User

The first order of business we should take care of is the creation of a user to develop OracleAS Portal objects. The creation of initial users is one of the main reasons you would ever log in to your portal as the portal user. Assuming you are still logged in as the portal user, click the Administer tab on the top right of the Welcome page. Make sure the Portal subtab is selected on the top left of the page and click the Create New Users link on the top right of the page. After you select that link, your browser will be directed to a long URL that starts something like this:

```
http://<infrastructure server>:<infrastructure
port>/oiddas/ui/oracle/ldap/das/user/AppCreateUserInfoAdmin ...
```

The examples in the chapter have been taken from a server named oski-2k3 with both the infrastructure (port 7777) and the middle tier (port 80) installed on it. On this machine the re-directed URL begins like this:

```
http://oski-2k3:7777/oiddas/ui/oracle/ldap/das/user/AppCreateUserInfoAdmin ...
```

It is important to note this for the following reason: when creating OracleAS Portal users, we are creating users in Oracle's implementation of the Lightweight Directory Access Protocol (LDAP) standard, Oracle Internet Directory. Creating an OracleAS Portal user does not create a user in the Infrastructure database.

LDAP (Lightweight Directory Access Protocol) is a set of protocols for accessing information directories. LDAP is based on the standards contained within the X.500 standard but is significantly simpler. And unlike X.500, LDAP supports TCP/IP, which is necessary for any type of Internet access. LDAP makes it possible for almost any application running on virtually any computer platform to obtain directory information, such as e-mail addresses and public keys. Because LDAP is an open protocol, applications need not worry about the type of server hosting the directory.

TIP
You can also create and edit Oracle Internet Directory users at any time by going to http://<infrastructure server>:<infrastructure port>/oiddas. The root user for Oracle Internet Directory is orcladmin, and the password will be the same one assigned to the infrastructure instance during installation of the infrastructure.

We will now create users to handle the various tasks associated with development and administration of our portal. After selecting the Create New Users link, you should see a page similar to the one in Figure 1-13. On this page, you will create a new user and assign privileges that will allow that user to create OracleAS Portal components. Fill in the required fields for a user you will use for OracleAS Portal development and click the Roles Assignment link (see Figure 1-14).

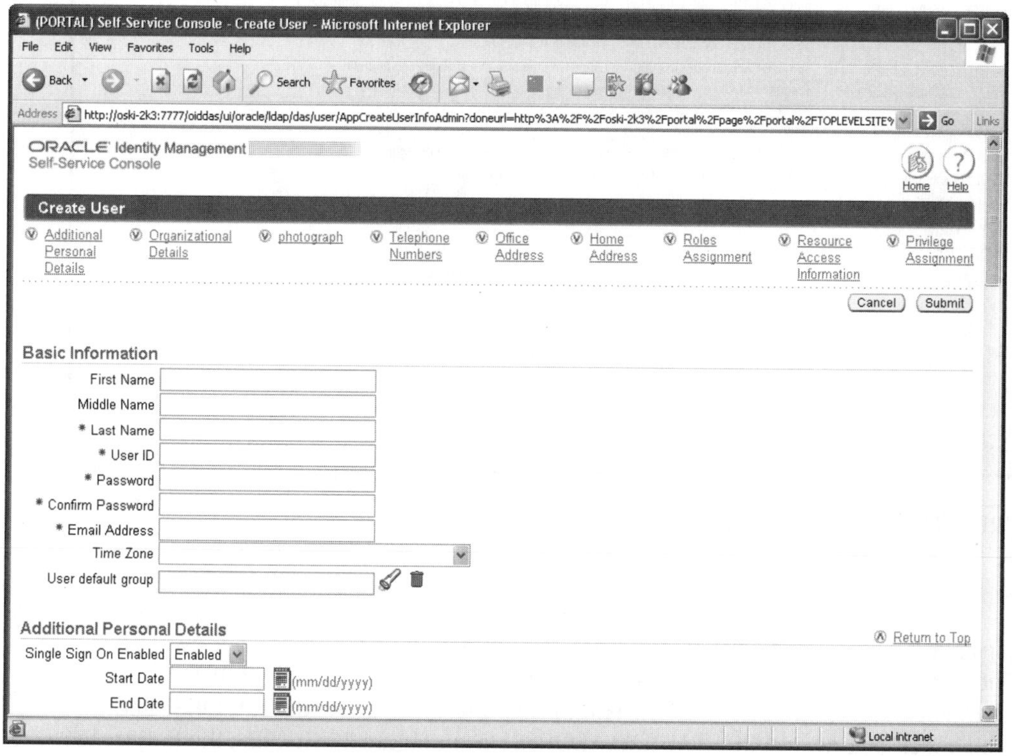

FIGURE 1-13 *The Create User page of the Oracle Internet Directory*

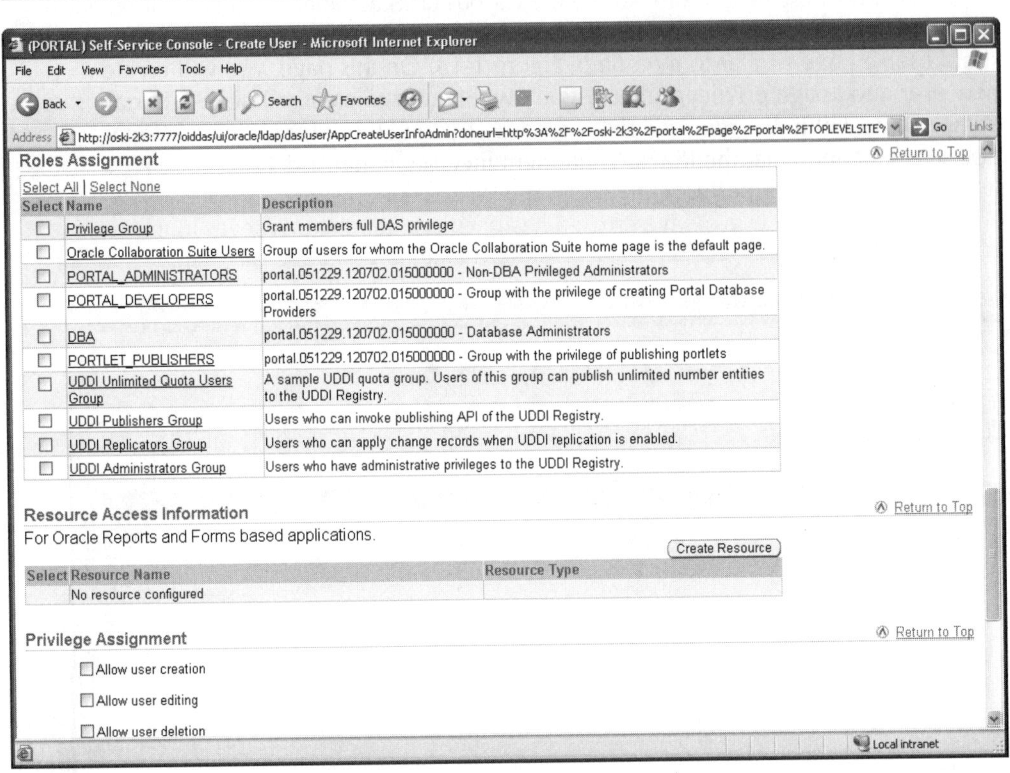

FIGURE 1-14 *The Roles Assignment section of the Create User page*

Figure 1-14 lists the default roles that are provided when OracleAS Portal is installed. You are not limited to these default roles; you can create your own. For now, pay attention to the roles listed earlier in this chapter, namely PORTAL_DEVELOPERS, PORTLET_PUBLISHERS, and PORTLET_ADMINISTRATORS. Click the check box next to PORTAL_DEVELOPERS as in Figure 1-14. Click the Return To Top link and then click the Submit link to create the new user. In another browser, log in to OracleAS Portal with this new user's name and password.

Clicking the Administration tab and then the Database tab will not reveal any portlets, since this user does not have administration privileges. This user does, however, have the ability to create OracleAS Portal components. Click the Navigator link on the top right of the page to be taken to the OracleAS Portal Navigator. Since all OracleAS Portal components must be associated with a provider, select the Providers tab, and then select the Locally Built Providers link on that page. The Locally Built Providers page is displayed (see Figure 1-15), but it contains no links to create a new provider. This is one of the security features that frustrate many new OracleAS Portal developers. Instead of presenting a link or option that brings you to a page or screen explaining the fact that the OracleAS Portal user does not have sufficient privileges to perform an action, the link or option simply is not displayed on the screen. The user we have created has been granted the privileges in the PORTAL_DEVELOPERS group, which gives us the ability to create OracleAS Portal components, but not Oracle Application Server Providers. Why?

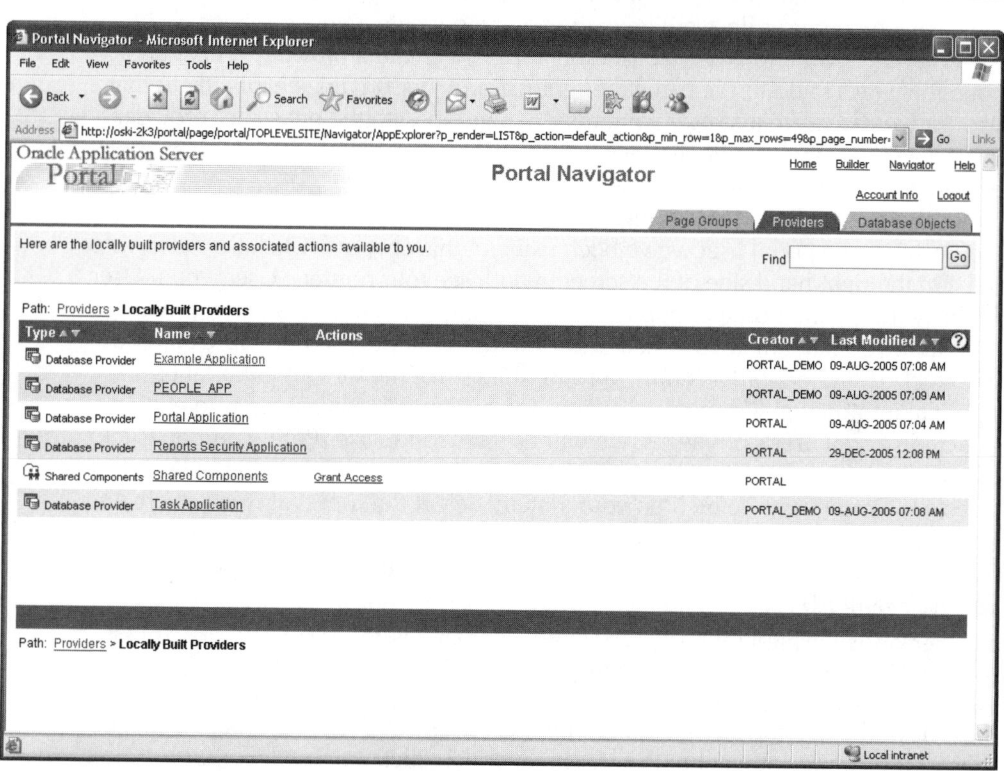

FIGURE 1-15 *The Locally Built Providers page*

The OracleAS Portal wizards that are used to generate forms, reports, and graphs (among other OracleAS Portal components) are really sophisticated code generators. While you have the ability to embed JavaScript code with your OracleAS Portal Forms and Reports, the majority of code that is generated by the OracleAS Portal wizards will be PL/SQL code. This PL/SQL code needs to be stored somewhere: it is stored in the infrastructure database. When an OracleAS Portal Provider is created, one of the first things we will need to specify is a database schema that this provider is associated with. This database schema is the one that will be used to hold the generated PL/SQL code that makes up the various OracleAS Portal objects that we generate from the wizards. In order to create an Oracle Application Server Provider, we must have access to the database (the database installed in the Oracle Application Server infrastructure) to specify which schema we want to use. In most cases, you would not want to give that privilege to an OracleAS Portal developer, which is why our user does not have the ability to create a new provider.

What if we want to give that user the ability to create a provider? There are a couple of ways to do it. We can either grant a provider privilege explicitly to that user, or we can make that user a member of a group with the necessary provider privilege so that the user implicitly gets the necessary privilege. Let's look at explicitly granting the privilege first.

Log in to Oracle Portal Provider Portal as a user with administration privileges (you can use the portal user we've been using in this chapter). Click the Administer tab. On the right-hand side of the screen, you'll see four portlets: User, Portal User Profile, Group, and Portal Group Profile. To change the OracleAS Portal privileges for a user, you may think you need to go into the User portlet, but you would be incorrect. The User portlet is only used for things like the OracleAS Portal user's personal information (username, password, group memberships, etc.). To edit an OracleAS Portal user's privileges, we will use the Portal User Profile portlet. Click the small icon between the Name: field and the Edit button to bring up a list of OracleAS Portal users defined on your system. Select the user that was just created and click Select to close the selection window. Click the Edit button to bring up the Edit Portal User Profile screen. Click the Privileges tab to display privileges for that user (see Figure 1-16).

It looks like this user does not have any privileges to do anything in our portal, but remember that the user inherits the privileges of any group that user is assigned to. In this case, no explicit privileges have been assigned to this user, but he has implicitly inherited the privileges from the PORTAL_DEVELOPERS group. Click the Builder link on the top right of the screen, and then click the small icon between the Name: field and the Edit button in the Portal Group Profile portlet at the bottom of the page. Select the PORTAL_DEVELOPERS group, click Edit, and select the Privileges page. As you can see in Figure 1-17, members of the PORTAL_DEVELOPERS group have the ability to create Oracle Application Server Providers.

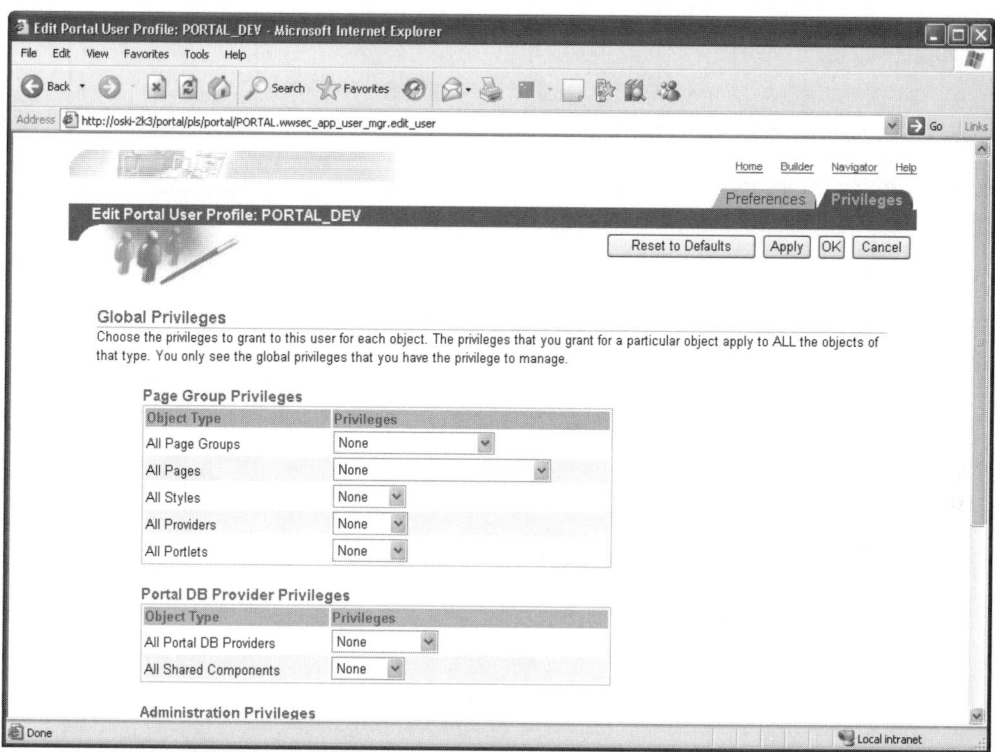

FIGURE 1-16 *The Privileges tab of the Edit Portal User Profile screen*

So what's going on here? We know that the user we have just created is a member of the PORTAL_DEVELOPERS group and that the PORTAL_DEVELOPERS group has the ability to create providers. Why doesn't the Create Provider link show up when we log in as that user? Remember, we said that providers must be associated with a database schema so that the PL/SQL packages that are generated from the various OracleAS Portal wizards can be stored. The OracleAS Portal user must have privileges on those schemas so that these packages can be created. We must grant an additional privilege to this OracleAS Portal user so that the user can create providers. On the Administration tab and on the Portal subtab, type the name of your OracleAS Portal user in the name field of the Portal User Profile portlet and click Edit. On the Privileges tab, select the drop-down box next to All Schemas. You'll see six options: Create, View Data, Insert Data, Modify Data, Manage, and None. The order in which they are listed is a little confusing: moving from the

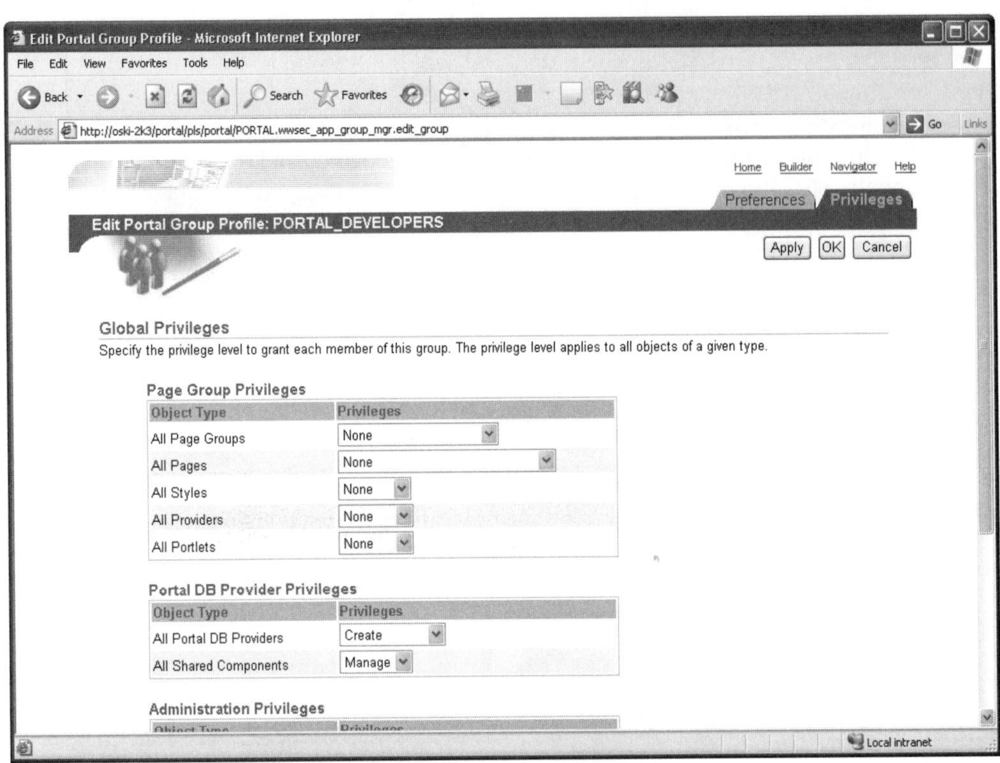

FIGURE 1-17 *The Privileges tab for the PORTAL_DEVELOPERS group*

bottom of the list (Create) up, the privileges encompass more and more capabilities, except for the top-most selection (None), which revokes all privileges. It would seem to make more sense to put None at the bottom of the list, but it is at the top for all drop-down boxes on this page.

The Create option gives the OracleAS Portal user the ability to create a new schema in the infrastructure database, but nothing else. View Data gives the OracleAS Portal user the ability to create a schema and query the data in that schema, but no privileges to add or insert data. Insert Data has all of the privileges of those below it, plus the ability to insert data into the schema. Granting our OracleAS Portal user any of the three privileges we've mentioned will not give the user the ability to create an OracleAS Portal Provider. Providers not only need the ability to view and insert data as various elements of the OracleAS Portal components are created, but also need the ability to modify data in that schema as OracleAS Portal components are changed and updated. We need a privilege higher than Insert Data before our OracleAS Portal user will have the ability to create providers. The last two options—Modify Data, which has all of the privileges below it plus the ability to actually modify data in the schemas, and Manage, which has the ability not only to perform Data Manipulation Language (DML) statements like insert, update, etc., but also to perform Data Definition Language (DDL) statements like "Create Index"—give the necessary privileges for our user to create Oracle Application Server Providers. For now, as an example, grant the user the Manage privilege and click OK. Log back in as the new OracleAS Portal user, click Navigator, then the Providers tab, and then the Locally Built Providers link. The page should look similar to before, except with the addition of the Create New... Database Provider link at the top of the page (see Figure 1-18).

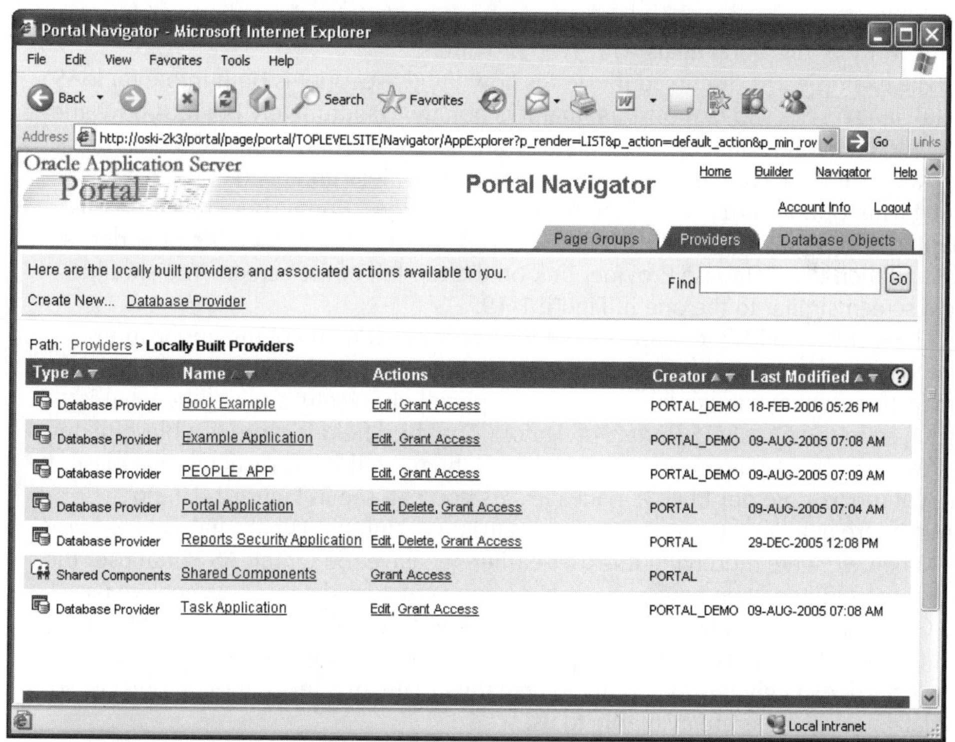

FIGURE 1-18 *The Locally Built Providers page of the Portal Navigator with the Create New Database Provider link available*

There are two types of providers—database providers and Web providers—in OracleAS Portal. *Database* providers are those packages written as PL/SQL packages. They're used for creating PL/SQL portlets that reside in the database and are implemented as stored procedures and executed in the database. They can be written in PL/SQL or Java Stored Procedures wrapped in PL/SQL. You use PL/SQL portlets whenever your portlets require significant database interaction or when the development team has Oracle experience. *Web* providers are those applications written as Web applications. They are installed and hosted on a Web server and are remote from the portal. A portlet exposed as a Web provider can be developed in any Web language. The portal communicates to the Web provider using the HTTP protocol. There are several benefits when developing portlets and exposing them as Web providers: You can leverage existing Web application code to create portlets, manage outside of OracleAS Portal, provide hosted servers for OracleAS Portal users, and create portlets using any existing Web language. Web providers use Simple Object Access Protocol (SOAP) to communicate with the Portal. Web providers, such as OC4J (along with the PDK), can also be installed locally on the Oracle Application Server. This chapter deals primarily with database providers, but the majority of this book deals with Web providers.

The example just discussed illustrates how tightly security is built into OracleAS Portal. It also serves to demonstrate that it is not always intuitively obvious how and where to make the changes necessary to grant access to your OracleAS Portal users.

Now that we have the ability to create providers, let's go ahead and create one to see what options are available to us. As the OracleAS Portal user created in this chapter, click the Navigator link on the top right of the screen, then the Providers tab, and then the Database Provider link on the top left of the screen. You should see a screen similar to the one in Figure 1-19.

The first two fields are self-explanatory: the internal name of the application (which cannot contain any spaces or special characters) and the display name of the application (which can contain spaces and special characters and will be what is displayed in the OracleAS Portal Navigator). The third field is more troublesome in this example. It requires us to specify which schema in the infrastructure database we will use to store our PL/SQL packages. As you can see in Figure 1-19, no schemas are available to us, preventing us from continuing. What's happening here?

When we were modifying this user earlier, we gave the OracleAS Portal user the ability to modify data in any schema in our infrastructure database. When we use the OracleAS Portal wizards to create forms, reports, graphs, etc., we will need the ability to create various database objects in the schema; granting Modify Data privileges doesn't give us the ability to actually create any new database objects, so no database schemas are available to us.

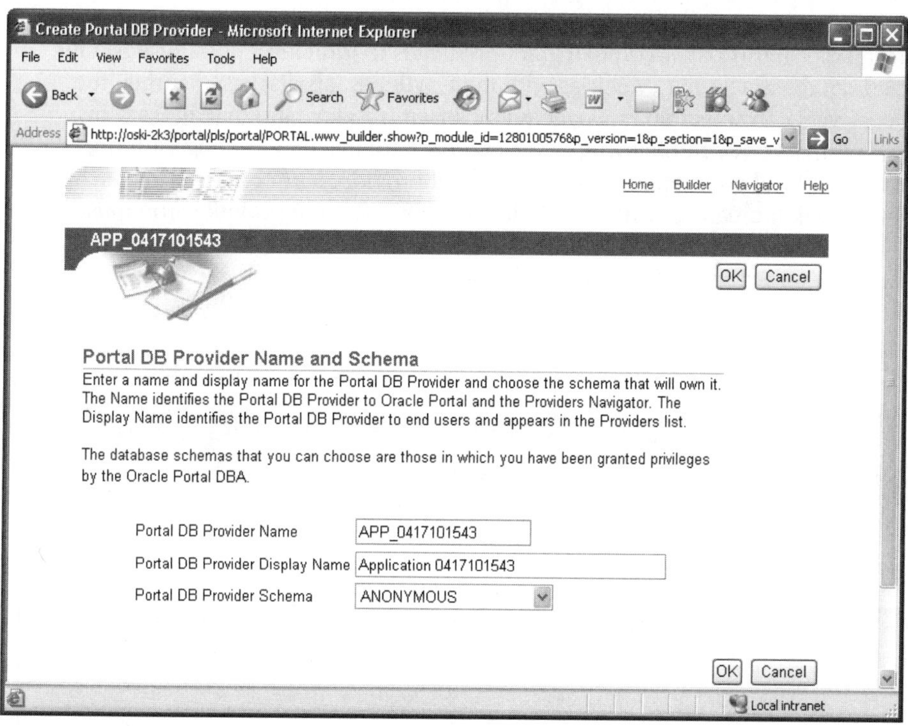

FIGURE 1-19 *The Create Portal Database Provider screen*

So the answer is simple, right? Go back and grant Execute privileges to our OracleAS Portal development user. That will give the OracleAS Portal developer the necessary privileges to create a provider, but that may not be such a great idea, either. By granting that privilege, an OracleAS Portal developer can do anything to any of the schemas in the infrastructure database. The potential for disaster, unintentional or on purpose, is great in this scenario. A better solution would be to define a schema to hold Oracle Application Server Portal–generated PL/SQL packages and grant privileges on that schema to the necessary OracleAS Portal developer(s).

You can use OracleAS Portal to create a schema in the database. Log in as a user with administration privileges (like the portal user) and select the Navigator link. Select the Database Objects link and then the Create New... Schema link. Fill in the necessary fields and make sure the Use This Schema For Portal Users check box is selected. Click Create. Back on the Navigator page, select the Grant Access link next to the schema you just created. You should see a page similar to the one in Figure 1-20. On this page, you can grant privileges to OracleAS Portal user on the selected database schema. Much as with the Privileges tab discussed earlier, the privileges you can select on this page (view, insert, modify, and manage) are in order from least powerful (view) to most powerful (manage). Granting view, insert, or modify will not grant enough privileges for the OracleAS Portal user to use this schema to begin creating OracleAS Portal components for a provider. You must grant the Manage privilege for your OracleAS Portal developer to use this schema. Click Add before clicking OK to close the page.

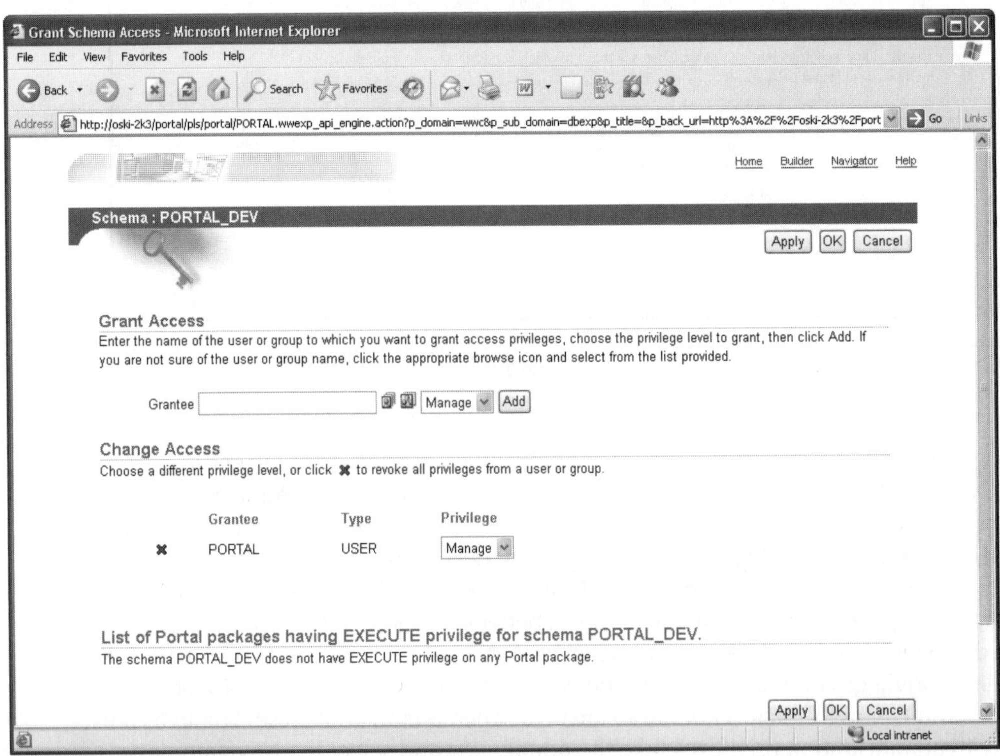

FIGURE 1-20 *The Grant Access page*

Logging back in to OracleAS Portal as the developer user, you can now create a new provider using the schema that has been granted the necessary privileges (see Figure 1-21).

The granting of Manage privileges on the portal_dev schema in the preceding example is all the OracleAS Portal developer user needs to create providers (along with, of course, the Create Provider privilege implicitly granted by being a member of the PORTAL_DEVELOPERS group). There is no need to grant the individual user the Manage privilege for all users that we performed earlier (just before Figure 1-18). To keep security tight in your database, it's best to go back and revoke that privilege.

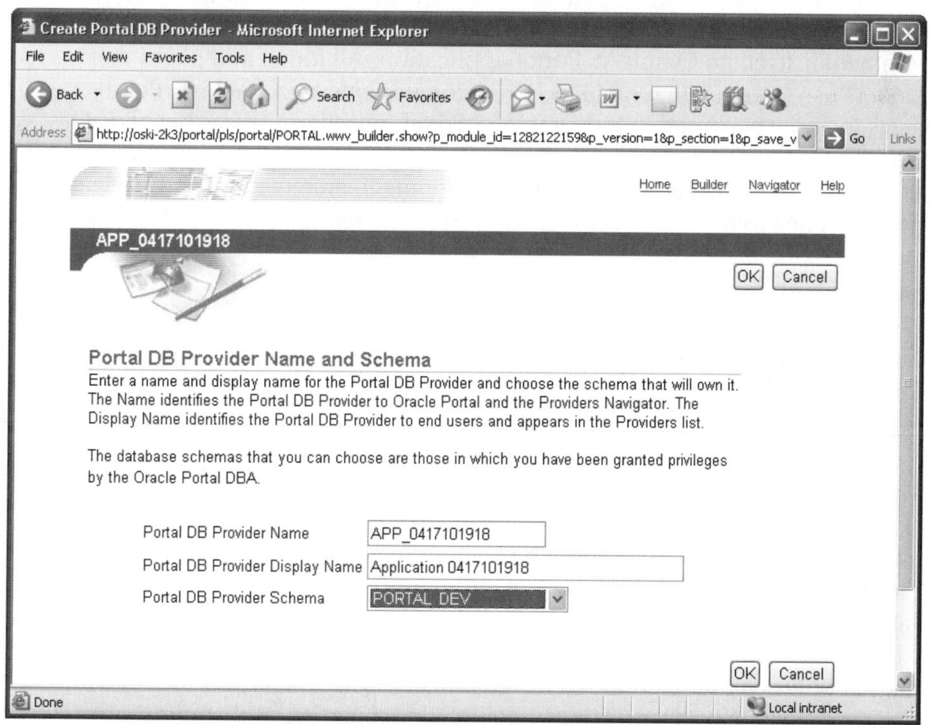

FIGURE 1-21 *The Create Provider page with the available "portal_dev" schema*

Portlets

What is a portlet? Oracle's definition is that they are "reusable building blocks for easily publishing information and applications." You can think of a portlet as a small application that performs a specific function. Portlets are then placed and arranged on a page so that the end user can interact with them. Portlets can be forms, reports, graphs, links to other Web sites, ad hoc query tools—the list goes on and on. All portlets come from a data source registered within OracleAS Portal, called a portlet provider. You can use OracleAS Portal's wizards to easily create reports, forms, charts, and other types of dynamic components or even publish pages, navigation pages, and other OracleAS Portal components as portlets. You can also build components with your own tools and integrate them through OracleAS Portal's APIs, available in the Portal Developer Kit (PDK).

One of the most difficult, yet ultimately beneficial, concepts for many beginning OracleAS Portal developers to grasp is the fact that the OracleAS Portal development environment is itself an OracleAS Portal application. All forms and pages that developers use to generate OracleAS Portal components are OracleAS Portal elements themselves, stored in the OracleAS Portal repository. This is beneficial to developers because they can work with a well-designed portal environment and understand the basics of OracleAS Portal development, architecture, and navigation before attempting to build and deploy their first portal pages.

NOTE
The wizards, even though they look just like OracleAS Portal pages, are technically not really OracleAS Portal objects. They are PL/SQL-coded solutions, and the source code is not published.

This chapter is designed to show the architecture of OracleAS Portal and to provide a road map so that developers and administrators can find their way around OracleAS Portal quickly. Even though OracleAS Portal is a true declarative development environment that requires little, if any, coding for a complete application, it is still beneficial to define and explore the structure of OracleAS Portal and how applications and portals are constructed. Given the fact that OracleAS Portal is a true Web-based development environment, you are probably anxious to jump in and start creating OracleAS Portal portlets and applications immediately; some of the material in this chapter may appear dry in that context, but mastering the basics of OracleAS Portal navigation will save you much time as your development efforts move forward.

Types of Portlets

OracleAS Portal supports numerous types of portlets:

- **Java** A portlet implemented using Java technologies. Part III of this book focuses on developing these types of portlets using Oracle JDeveloper.
- **PL/SQL** A portlet implemented using PL/SQL technologies. PL/SQL portlets can be developed from scratch but are most commonly developed using the OracleAS Portal wizards. This chapter discusses this technique, but the majority of this book focuses on developing portlets using Java technologies.
- **OmniPortlet** A Web provider that provides portlets that can display spreadsheet, XML, and Web Service data as tabular, chart, news, bullet, and form layouts. OmniPortlet is discussed in Chapter 6.
- **Web Clipping** A feature that enables page designers to collect Web content into a single centralized portal. It can be used to consolidate content from hundreds of different Web sites scattered throughout a large organization. Web Clipping is also discussed in Chapter 6.
- **Seeded portlets** Numerous portlets are available to developers when OracleAS Portal is installed. In Chapter 3, a section called "Seeded Portlets" discusses these portlets.

OracleAS Portal Content

OracleAS Portal contains sophisticated methods and programs to store, display, and manage content, giving administrators almost limitless ways to administer content on their portals. The Content Management SDK gives administrators and developers the ability to automate many of the tasks of content management. Content Management and the Content Management SDK are discussed in detail in Chapter 5.

TIP

For more information on the Content Management SDK, go to http://www.oracle.com/technology/products/ifs/index.html.

A good place to start our discussion of OracleAS Portal content would be the definition of content. As we have seen, OracleAS Portal allows developers to build components such as forms, reports, charts, calendars, etc. But what if you have information that you wish to display on your portal that does not fit into one of these component types; for example, a Microsoft Word document or an Adobe PDF file? The developers of OracleAS Portal were smart enough to design it so that both types of objects can be displayed on your Portal: portlets, which can query Oracle databases and display that data in a form, report, calendar, etc.; and items, which can display content such as word processor files, spreadsheets, or images. Within the context of OracleAS Portal, content can be defined as any piece of information that is to be displayed on a portal that does not fit into the traditional interface of an OracleAS Portal component such as a form or report. There are two basic types of items that can be placed on a page: Content Item Types and Built-in Navigation Types.

Content Item Types

The following is a list of Content Item Types you can place on your OracleAS Portal pages:

- **File** This option allows you to place a file on your portal and is the most common option selected when placing content on your portal. When a file is selected, it is converted to a binary large object and stored in the infrastructure database automatically. You also have the option of displaying a Simple File, which does not prompt you for advanced content attributes such as publish or expiration dates (advanced content attributes are discussed in Chapter 5).
- **Text** This option displays a WYSIWYG (What You See Is What You Get) editor that allows you to enter text for your content area. Just as with the File option, there is a Simple Text option.
- **URL** This option allows you to place a URL in your content area. Alternatively, the editor displayed in the preceding text option allows you to create links in your text area. As with the File and Text options, there is also a Simple URL option.
- **Page Links** This option allows you to place links in your content area to other OracleAS Portal pages. There is also a Simple Link option.
- **Images** This option allows you to place an image in your content area. There is also a Simple Image option.
- **Zip Files** This option allows you to upload a Zip (compressed) file to your content area. The only difference between this and a File is the existence of

a link titled Unzip next to the item when displayed. Clicking the Unzip link gives end users the ability to unzip and store whatever is in the Zip file on a page in the portal.

- **PL/SQL** This option allows you to store a PL/SQL code fragment as a content item in the content area. Clicking this link will execute the PL/SQL code.
- **Oracle Reports** This option allows developers to embed an Oracle Report (not to be confused with an OracleAS Portal Report) in a content area. Clicking the link will display the Oracle Report on the Web.

Built-in Navigation Types

The following is a list of Built-In Navigation Types you can place on your OracleAS Portal pages:

- **Portal Smart Links** This option allows you to place various links in the content area to perform actions such as edit user account information, edit the page, display a help menu, take the user to his or her personal page, refresh the page, etc.
- **Login/Logout Links** This option places a Logout link on the content area page.
- **Basic Search Box** Two types of searches are available to end users in OracleAS Portal: A basic search allows users to search through their portals without reducing the information returned by category or perspective. An advanced search gives end users the ability to use various methods of reducing information returned by their search as well as utilize advanced features such as Boolean operators. The Basic Search box places a Search field on the content area, allowing end users to perform a basic search through content on the portal.

NOTE

For now, understand that categories and perspectives are ways of organizing content in your portal. Categories organize the content according to what the content is. Perspectives organize the content according to who might be interested in it.

- **List Of Objects** This option allows you to return a set of OracleAS Portal content that meets certain criteria. You can return a drop-down list or a set of links that point to a page group, a perspective, or a category.
- **Portal Smart Text** This option can be used to display the current date, user, or page.
- **Object Map Link** This option can be used to create a link that will display a hierarchical map of pages and subpages when clicked by an end user.
- **Page Path** This option creates a breadcrumb menu on the page that allows end users to see where they are in the portal site and gives them the ability to navigate through levels quickly. Placing a Page Path navigation link on a root page has no effect; it is only useful on subpages.

TIP
Not all of these types are available for pages by default. Some of the items will have to be enabled for a page group. To add these types, select the Properties link next to Page Group on the top left of the page editor. Select the Configure tab, and then click the Edit link in the Content Type and Classification section of the page. Add the Item Types in the Item Types section of the page and click OK.

Declarative Development

The term *declarative development* refers to the process of using the OracleAS Portal wizards to build and deploy your portlets. While this method has been available to Portal developers since the inception of Oracle Portal (known in its first public iteration as "WebDB"), Oracle has focused less on enhancing the OracleAS Portal wizards and more on features and functionality related to Web-based providers (Java, etc.). In the 10.1.4 version of the OracleAS Portal Developer's Guide (http://download-east.oracle.com/docs/cd/B14099_19/portal.1014/b14135/toc.htm), the section on declarative development has been relegated to the appendix.

What does this mean for OracleAS Portal developers? Oracle will continue to support the OracleAS Portal wizards but will probably not add much functionality to them in the future. To explore the advanced features of OracleAS Portal development, the developer should concentrate on Web-based providers using a tool like Oracle JDeveloper. As such, this chapter briefly discusses the OracleAS Portal wizards, but all other development-based chapters in this book will focus on using Oracle JDeveloper to create Web Provider–based portlets.

The OracleAS Portal Wizards

The OracleAS Portal wizards allow developers to create, with a minimum amount of hand-written code, portlets that can be deployed to the OracleAS Portal easily and securely. While this functionality gives beginning developers an easy way to achieve quick success, any wizard-based development tool, by its very nature, will have its limitations. While the advanced page design features give developers and publishers great functionality over how their applications look and feel, end users are demanding more and more functionality from their Web-based applications every day. It is difficult to create a sophisticated application that will satisfy a majority of users in a production environment using the OracleAS Portal wizards alone.

Common Features of all Wizards

All of the wizards have a common look and feel (many of the wizards for the different OracleAS Portal components have the exact same wizard pages), allowing developers to create and modify portlets quickly and easily. All of the wizards use a standard notation of "Step X of Y" along the top of the screen to show developers how far they are along in the development process for that particular portal component. Beyond the first couple of screens, where the type of portlet is selected and named, it is possible to change almost any facet of the portlet, either during the initial run of the wizard or by modifying the portlet after it has been generated.

For every portlet created using the OracleAS Portal wizards, there is a Manage screen that allows developers to modify the portlet, set privileges for the portlet, and view the portlet before it gets placed on an OracleAS Portal page. The Manage page also allows developers to export the portlet (useful for moving a portlet from a development environment to a production environment). The Manage page also gives you the ability to view the code that the wizard has generated and see the call interface, which shows what parameters can be passed to call the portlet as well as examples of calling the portlet from a PL/SQL stored procedure or from a URL.

What Do the Wizards Generate?

Upon completion of the final step of an OracleAS Portal wizard, the OracleAS Portal engine generates PL/SQL code to reflect the choices the developer made on the various pages of the OracleAS Portal wizard. The resulting PL/SQL code is stored in the infrastructure database under the schema the developer selected on the first step of the wizard. Developers often wonder if they can use the OracleAS Portal wizards to generate most of the code needed for the portlet and then go in and customize the resulting code to their specifications. While this certainly is possible, it's highly unlikely that a developer could use this method for two reasons: 1) the generated code is extremely large—even a simple report or form will generate almost 1,000 lines of code and 2) any changes made to the generated code by the developer will be lost if the wizard is run again. If developers want more control over the portlet than the wizards can provide, those developers would be much more productive using a tool like Oracle JDeveloper to create their portlets.

Creating Your First OracleAS Portal Objects

Earlier in this chapter, in the section titled "Creating an OracleAS Portal User," we created a user with the ability to create providers. Let's go ahead and start creating some OracleAS Portal components as that user. Later in the chapter, we'll take some components and place them on an OracleAS Portal page.

If you are not logged in already, log in as the development user created earlier in this chapter. Select the Navigator link and click the Create New... Database Provider link. Give your Provider a name (no spaces or special characters) and a display name, and select a database schema to use for this application (see Figure 1-22). Click OK.

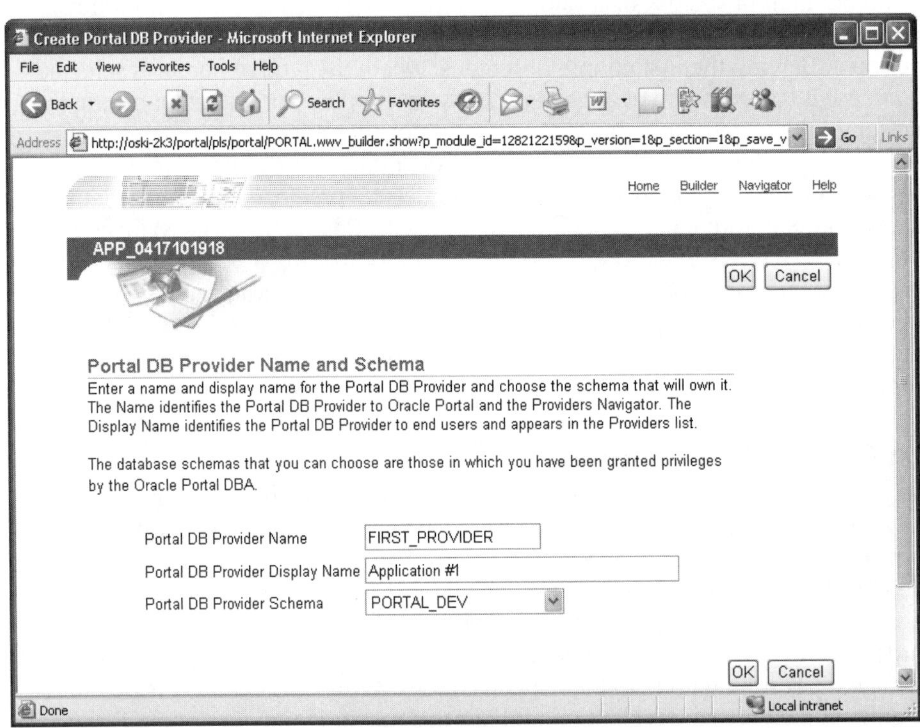

FIGURE 1-22 *The Create Portal DB Provider screen*

Back in the OracleAS Portal Navigator screen, click the link with your provider's name. You are taken to a navigator page where you can build the following OracleAS Portal objects:

- **Form** Forms display a customized form that can be used as an interface for updating tables, executing stored procedures, and generating other customized forms. You can build three types of forms:
- A form based on a table or view enables end users to insert, update, and delete data in a database table or view.
- A master-detail form displays a master row and multiple detail rows within a single HTML page. The form contains fields for updating values in two database tables or views.
- A form based on a procedure enables end users to insert, update, and delete data in a database-stored procedure.
- **Report** Report objects display data you select from the database table or view in a report. Your report can have a tabular, form, or custom layout.
- **Chart** Chart objects display data you select from a database table or view as a bar chart. You can also create Java-based image charts.
- **Data component** Data components display data in spreadsheet format.
- **Calendar** Calendar objects display data you select from a database table or view as a calendar.
- **Dynamic page** Dynamic pages display dynamically generated HTML content on a Web page.
- **Hierarchy** Hierarchies display data you select from a database table or view as a graphical hierarchy of items containing up to three levels.
- **Menu** Menu objects display an HTML-based menu containing hyperlinked options to other menus, OracleAS Portal database portlets, or URLs.
- **Frame driver** Frame drivers display a Web page with two frames. End-user queries in one frame control the contents of the other frame.
- **Link** Link objects display a clickable link that provides a hypertext jump between OracleAS Portal database portlets and other database portlets, database portlet customization forms, or any HTML page.

- **List of values (LOV)** LOVs enable end users to choose entry field values in a form or database portlet customization form. You can use LOVs when creating database portlets to preselect the possible values in an entry field. The end user clicks the mouse to select a value rather than type it. You can also build LOVs based on other LOVs. LOVs are assigned to fields on a Form or Report and are the only OracleAS Portal components not placed directly on a page.
- **URL** URL objects display the contents of a URL.
- **XML Component** XML components display an XML page.

OracleAS Portal Forms

One of the basic OracleAS Portal components is that of an OracleAS Portal Form (Figure 1-23). A form allows end users to interact directly with the database and can be designed to query, insert, update, or delete data, or most likely, to enable the end user to perform a combination of these activities. The OracleAS Portal wizard used to create an OracleAS Portal form, like all of the other wizards discussed in this chapter, can be used to create a component that can be run by itself over the Web and accessed via a Web browser. These components run outside of OracleAS Portal's security and page structure and can be used to create components that are not placed on OracleAS Portal pages. Running the OracleAS Portal components in this manner is commonly referred to as *full page* or *standalone* mode. As this is unusual, the focus of this chapter will be on the creation of OracleAS components that are designed to be used as portlets (i.e., those to be placed on an OracleAS Portal page).

NOTE
To see the steps involved in creating the different types of OracleAS Portal Forms and other objects, go to http://www.tusc.com/. I recommend that you go through all examples referenced in this book in order, as concepts introduced in the early lessons are referenced in the later ones.

OracleAS Portal Reports

The Reports component of OracleAS Portal gives developers the ability to create great-looking OracleAS Portal Reports. Developers can change the look of the report according to values queried (or calculated) from the database, and then they can grant power users the ability to modify the query used to drive the report and can even create links in their reports that allow users to click a report and be taken to another OracleAS Portal component.

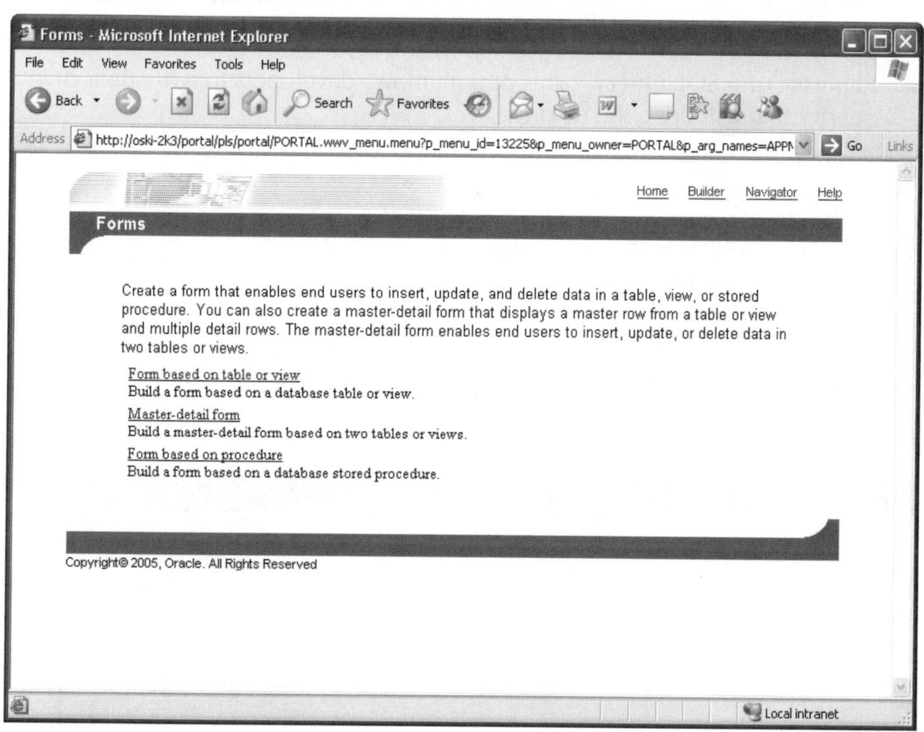

FIGURE 1-23 *The first page of the OracleAS Portal Form Wizard*

When you select the Create New... Report link in the Navigator, you are presented with a page similar to the one used to create our first OracleAS Portal Form (Figure 1-24).

Your choice of the three different types of OracleAS Portal Reports will depend on your reporting requirements:

- **Query By Example (QBE) Reports** Choosing this type of report will not only generate the report itself but will also generate a customization screen along with the OracleAS Portal Report. Power users can be granted privileges that allow them to modify what data is returned to the portlet and to insert/update/delete records in the reports' tables.
- **Reports From Query Wizard** This type of report is similar to a QBE report except for the fact that the customization page contains many fewer

options—the ability to insert/update/delete records is not available, nor is the ability to change the WHERE clause of the query driving the report.

- **Reports From SQL Query** This option allows developers to write their own queries that will drive the report.

NOTE
To see the steps involved in creating the different types of OracleAS Portal Reports, point your browser to http://www.tusc.com/. It is the author's recommendation that you go through all examples referenced in this book in order as concepts introduced in the early lessons are referenced in the later ones.

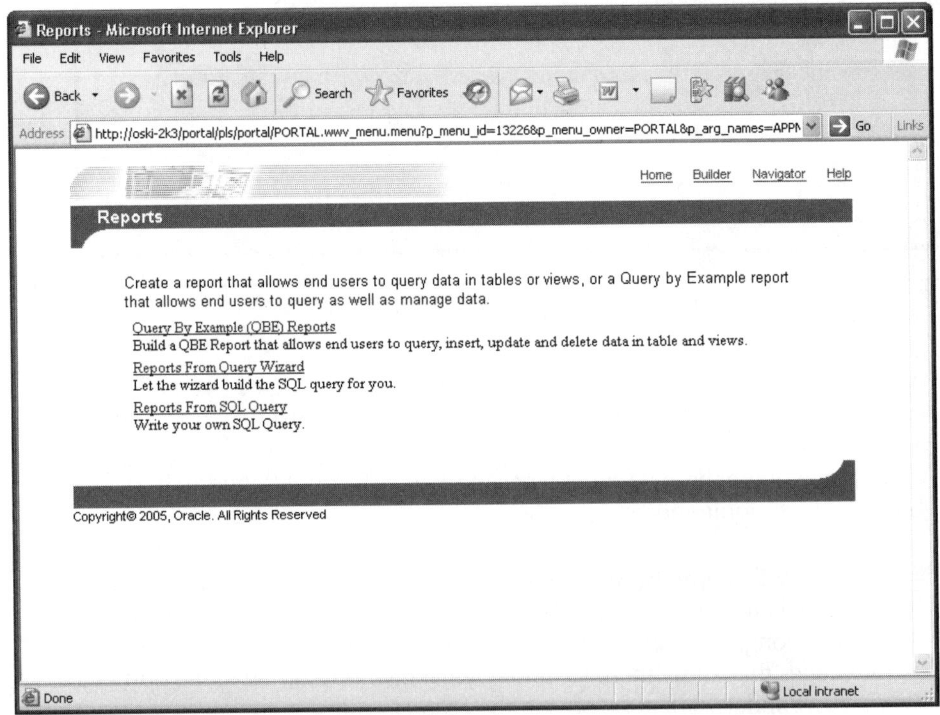

FIGURE 1-24 *The first page of the OracleAS Portal Report Wizard*

OracleAS Portal Charts

OracleAS Portal Charts give developers the ability to graphically display information as a portlet on their OracleAS Portal pages. Like OracleAS Portal Forms and Reports, OracleAS Portal Charts are developed using a series of wizard pages and can be created with various customization options that can then be granted to certain users. As you will see, OracleAS Portal gives developers great freedom in choosing the type of chart to display and what formatting options are to be used when displaying the chart.

To create a new OracleAS Portal Chart, bring up the Navigator by clicking the Navigator link on the top right of any OracleAS Portal page. Click the Providers tab if it is not already selected. Click the Locally Built Providers link, and then the name of the provider you have been using to build the examples so far. On the top left of the page, click the Create New... Chart link.

The first page gives you the option of creating a chart from the Query Wizard or a chart from a SQL Query. Building the chart using the Query Wizard allows you to quickly build and deploy a chart, but developers are restricted to a limited number of features. Building a chart from a SQL Query gives the developer greater flexibility but requires more work (particularly when constructing the driving SQL query). With either selection, you are presented with the now-familiar first page of the Chart Wizard (Figure 1-25) after choosing what type of chart to build.

NOTE
To see the steps involved in creating the different types of OracleAS Portal Charts, point your browser to http://www.tusc.com/.

OracleAS Portal Dynamic Pages

An OracleAS Portal Dynamic Page allows developers to control every aspect of their OracleAS Portal component. Unlike in the OracleAS Portal Reports and Forms wizards, there are no wizard pages here to specify column or page formatting, color of font specification, or portlet settings. While this OracleAS Portal component gives the developer the most flexibility when designing his or her portlet, the developer must handle all details of formatting, validation, and appearance.

OracleAS Portal List of Values

An OracleAS Portal List of Values is a unique component in the sense that, along with OracleAS Portal Links, it is not designed to be placed on a page; rather, the purpose of an LOV is to be used as an attribute to provide data to other OracleAS Portal components. An LOV is invaluable when used in data entry–type applications

OracleAS Portal Dynamic Page

The name Dynamic Page can be a little misleading. Most of the time, developers create these components to be used as portlets that are then placed on OracleAS Portal pages. Placing a Dynamic Page portlet on a page does not affect the characteristics of that page; it's still an OracleAS Portal page. If the Dynamic Page is displayed in standalone mode, then it truly is a dynamic page; otherwise, it is just a dynamic portlet that is placed on an OracleAS Portal page. To see the steps involved in creating the different types of OracleAS Portal Dynamic Pages, point your browser to http://www.tusc.com/.

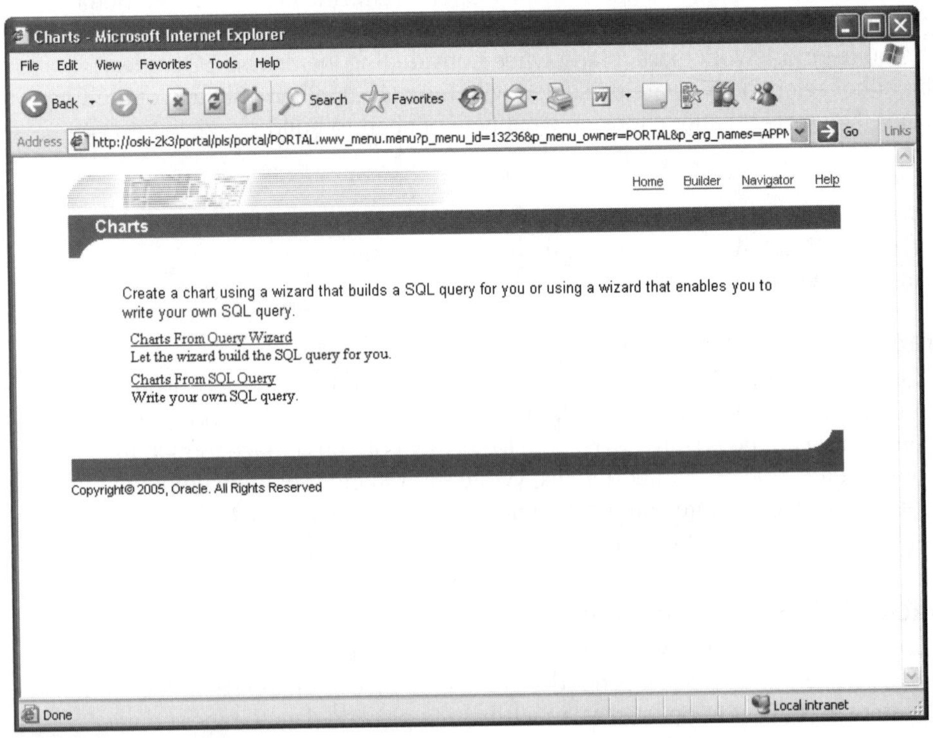

FIGURE 1-25 *The first page of the Chart Wizard*

for two reasons: 1) it eliminates incorrect data from being entered, and 2) it eliminates the need to memorize various codes needed to drive applications.

An LOV, after it is created, exists in OracleAS Portal but is not available to be placed on an OracleAS Portal page. Any new OracleAS component can use the LOV, and any existing OracleAS component can be modified to include the new LOV. LOVs can display values in different formats:

- **Combo box** This displays the data in a text box with a drop-down arrow on the text box's right side. When a user clicks the arrow, the box drops down to display all of the values of the LOV. Only a single value can be selected. Combo boxes are good for application screens that do not have a lot of free space on them.
- **Popup** This displays the data in a text box with a small notepad icon to its right. Clicking the icon opens another window, where the appropriate value can be selected. As in combo boxes, only a single value can be selected. We've seen popups for selecting tables or views when we created our example OracleAS Portal Forms and Reports earlier in this chapter.
- **Check box** This displays all of the data for the LOV with a small check box to the left of each entry. Check boxes are good when you want to display all values in the LOV and give the end user the ability to select multiple values.
- **Radio group** This displays all of the data for the LOV with a small circular button to the left of each entry. Only a single value can be selected. Radio groups are good for applications that need to display all LOV data to the user at one time and then allow one selection to be made.
- **Multiple select** This displays the first couple of data elements for the LOV in a text box. The user can scroll through the values and select multiple values by holding down the SHIFT key and single-clicking the appropriate values.

Figure 1-26 displays a simple LOV in different formats.
Figure 1-27 shows the two types of LOVs you can build (Dynamic and Static).

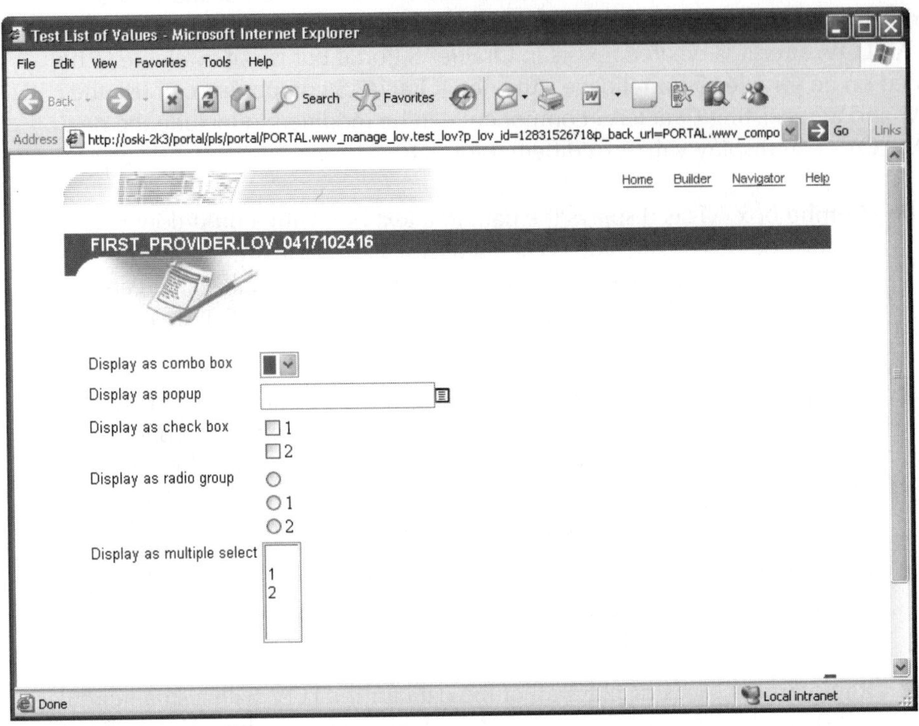

FIGURE 1-26 *The different formats in which an LOV can be displayed*

NOTE
To see the steps involved in creating the different types of OracleAS Portal LOVs, point your browser to http://www.tusc.com/.

OracleAS Portal XML Components

The first step of the XML Component Wizard (Figure 1-28) shows the ubiquitous naming page of the wizard. Step 2 of the wizard gives developers the opportunity to either enter a URL that points to an existing XML file or place the XML code on the page. As in the dynamic pages created earlier, OracleAS Portal allows developers to

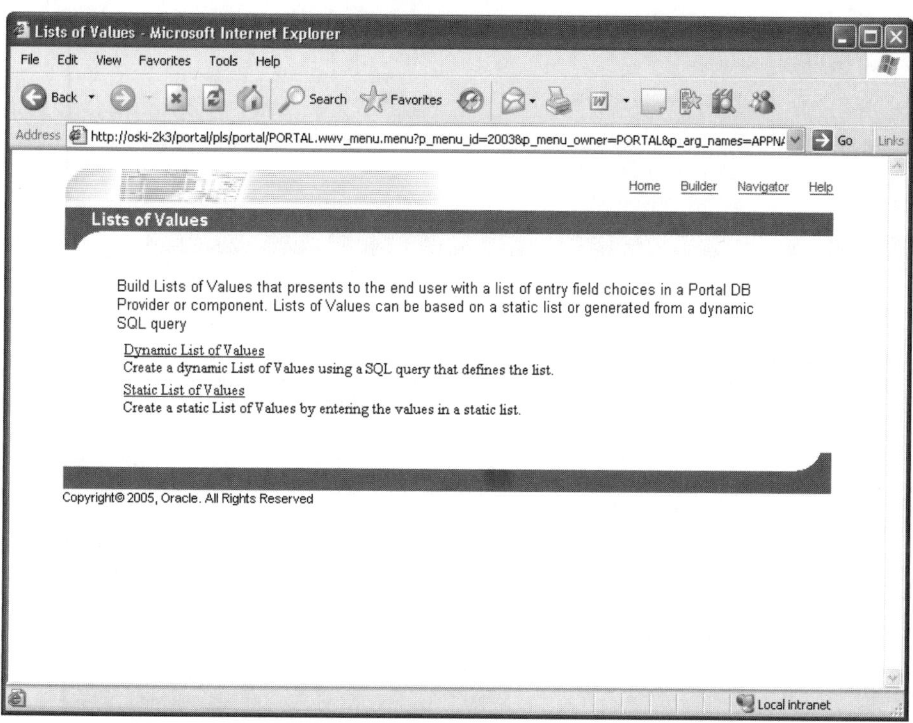

FIGURE 1-27 *The first page of the LOV wizard*

embed SQL or PL/SQL code within the XML text box by surrounding it with the <oracle> and </oracle> custom tags. You can also make use of bind variables to give your end users another layer of interaction with the portlet. Step 3 lists all of the code between the <oracle> and </oracle> tags so that you can check it and make any modifications to it.

NOTE
To see the steps involved in creating the different types of OracleAS Portal XML Components, point your browser to http://www.tusc.com/.

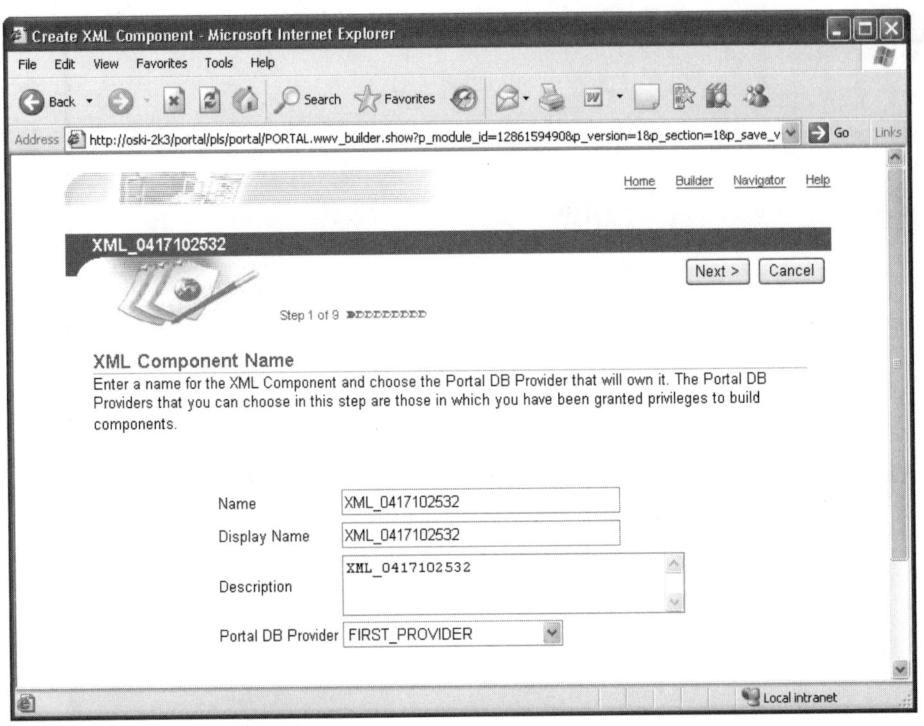

FIGURE 1-28 *The first page of the XML Component Wizard*

OracleAS Portal Calendars

A *calendar* is a graphical object that can be used to display links that reference specific records in your database. By default, the record must have a date field, or a field that can be converted into a date field by way of the TO_DATE SQL function if you intend to use it with an OracleAS Portal Calendar. The calendar then displays with the corresponding links in the calendar, where the end users can drill down for more information. The trickiest part of building a calendar for use in our portal will be constructing the appropriate query to return data that will drive the calendar. This query is similar to the query we constructed when building the OracleAS Portal Chart component earlier. The first step of the Calendar Wizard is shown in Figure 1-29.

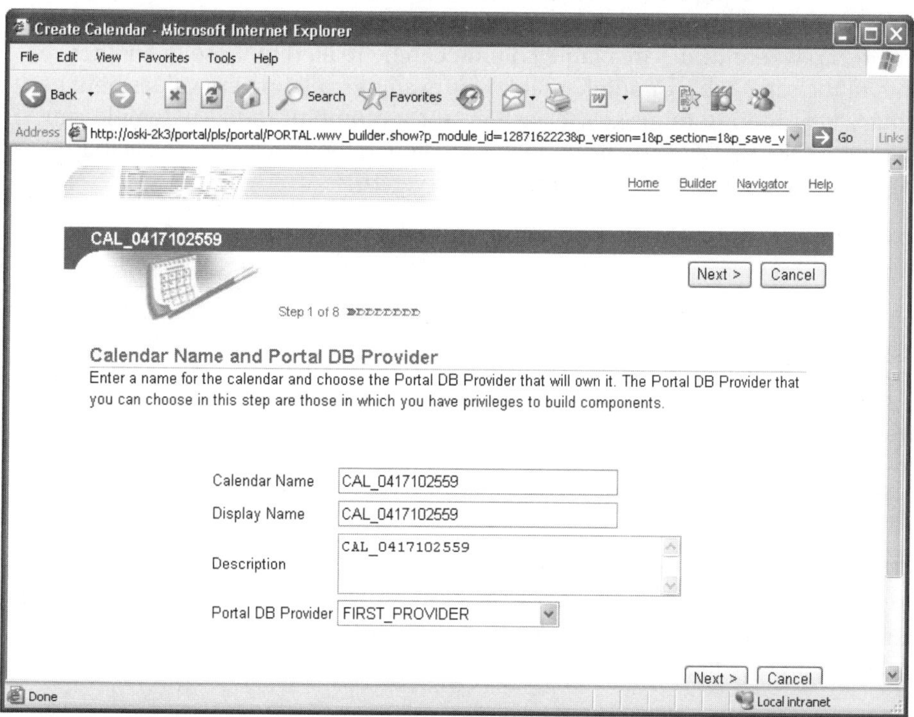

FIGURE 1-29 *The first step of the Calendar Wizard*

NOTE
To see all the steps involved in creating the different types of OracleAS Portal Calendars, point your browser to http://www.tusc.com/.

OracleAS Portal Hierarchies

A *hierarchy* is a graphical representation of elements in a list that has been queried from the database. Hierarchies are very useful for things such as employee charts or a list of parts that makes up a large component such as an automobile or a computer server. Hierarchies can also be created with links so that they become a way of allowing end users to interact and "drill down" for more information based on what is displayed in the hierarchy.

The part of creating an OracleAS Portal Hierarchy that can be complex is understanding the fact that the table you wish to base your hierarchy on must have a relationship where values in a table column can be related to those in another column in the same table or another table; for example, relating the values between a primary key and a foreign key. Consider, for a moment, the EMP (employee) table in the PORTAL_DEMO schema that is created in the infrastructure database during the installation of Oracle Application Server 10*g*:

```
SQL> desc portal_demo.emp;
 Name                                      Null?    Type
 ----------------------------------------- -------- ------------
 EMPNO                                     NOT NULL NUMBER(4)
 ENAME                                              VARCHAR2(10)
 JOB                                                VARCHAR2(9)
 MGR                                                NUMBER(4)
 HIREDATE                                           DATE
 SAL                                                NUMBER(7,2)
 COMM                                               NUMBER(7,2)
 DEPTNO                                             NUMBER(2)
```

This table contains a recursive relationship between the MGR and EMPNO fields that makes it a good candidate for a hierarchy. Step 1 of the Hierarchy Wizard asks us to specify the name of the hierarchy. Step 3 asks us to specify what table or view the hierarchy will be based on.

NOTE
To see the steps involved in creating the different types of OracleAS Portal Hierarchies, point your browser to http://www.tusc.com/.

OracleAS Portal Menus

An OracleAS Portal Menu is an HTML page that displays links to submenus, OracleAS Portal database portlets, or external URLs. The menu, its submenus, and any links to OracleAS Portal database portlets or URLs can be secured at the OracleAS Portal role level to prevent access by unauthorized users. OracleAS Portal Menus can display as many as five levels of a menu hierarchy, with each level indented on the menu to the right. Descriptive text can be added to links, and hyperlinks can be added. You can set an overall different look and feel for the menu and its submenus based on a template, or you can set a different look and feel on a submenu-by-submenu basis.

To create a new menu, click the Navigator icon on the top right of any OracleAS Portal page. Click the Providers tab if it isn't already selected. Click the Locally Built Providers link and then click the provider you have been using to work thorough the examples. Click the Create New... Menu link on the top left of the page. Menu creation via the wizard only has four steps (the first is shown in Figure 1-30), so it is one of the least complicated OracleAS Portal components we can create.

NOTE
To see the steps involved in creating the different types of OracleAS Portal Menus, point your browser to http://www.tusc.com/.

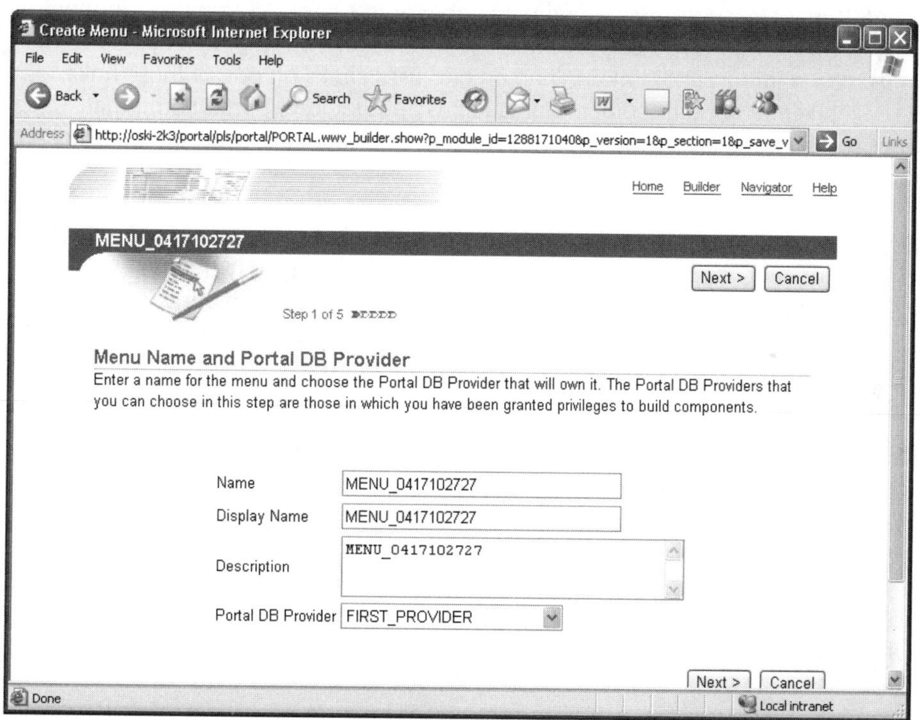

FIGURE 1-30 *The Menu Items and Submenus page of the Oracle AS Portal Menu Wizard*

OracleAS Portal URLs

An OracleAS Portal URL is, perhaps, the simplest component you can create in OracleAS Portal. A URL portlet that is placed on a page does not display the HTTP hyperlink; rather, it resolves whatever is in the URL and displays that page in the portlet. To create an Oracle Portal URL, navigate to your provider page. Click the Create New... URL link on the top left of the page.

NOTE
To see the steps involved in creating the different types of OracleAS Portal URLs, point your browser to http://www.tusc.com/.

OracleAS Portal Links

OracleAS Portal Links are a way of tying together your OracleAS Portal components. With links, for example, you can produce a report, as an example, that has one of its columns turned into a set of links. When an end user clicks on one of those links, that user is taken to another component (such as an OracleAS Portal Form) that provides more information about the selected record. There are two aspects of links that make them extremely powerful:

- **They can be used in multiple places.** Once a link is defined to a particular component, a component's customization form, or an HTML link, it can be placed on as many components as you like. This is very powerful, as it easily gives you a way to allow a high level of interaction among portlets on your OracleAS Portal and provides a standardized, consistent way of handling this interaction.
- **They allow parameters to be passed.** Links are "smart" enough to pass the appropriate value(s) to the target (destination) OracleAS Portal component. By doing so, the overhead of complex programming involving parameters is eliminated.

To create a new link, select the Create New... Link link on the Providers page in the OracleAS Portal Navigator to bring up the OracleAS Portal Link Wizard shown in Figure 1-31.

NOTE
To see the steps involved in creating the different types of OracleAS Portal Links, point your browser to http://www.tusc.com/.

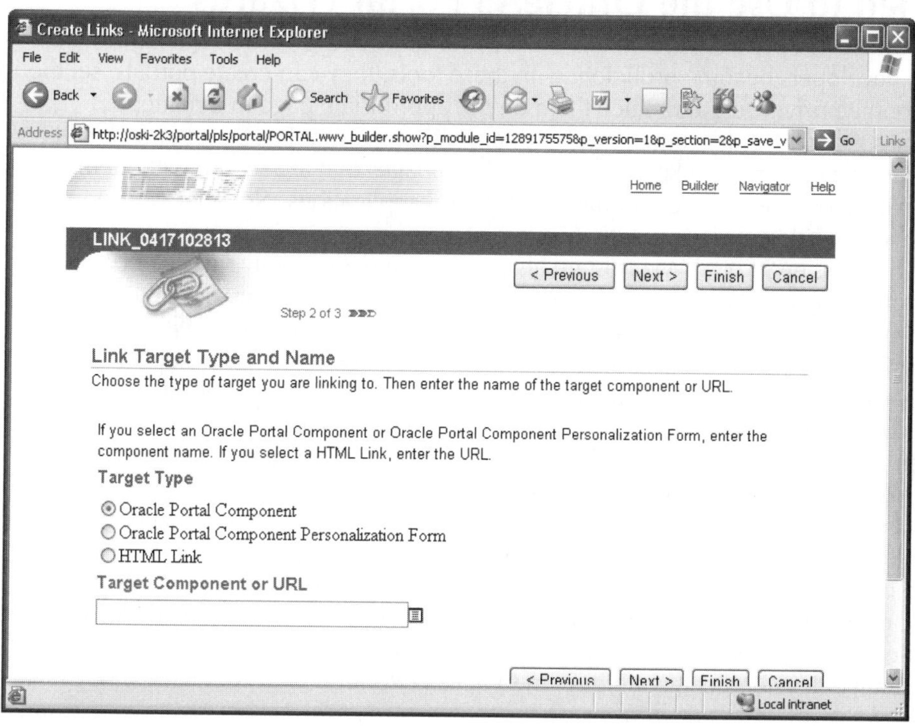

FIGURE 1-31 *The second page of the OracleAS Portal Link Wizard*

OracleAS Portal Data Components

An OracleAS Portal Data Component is the equivalent of embedding a spreadsheet into your OracleAS Portal pages. The wizard does not prompt you for any source information (such as a database table), since the spreadsheet is not populated upon being displayed on an OracleAS Portal Page. Depending on whether you select a report or a chart in Step 3 of the wizard, you will see an entirely different set of wizard pages for this component.

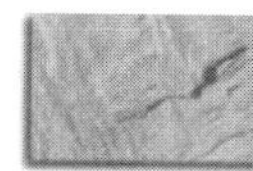

NOTE
To see the steps involved in creating the different types of OracleAS Portal Data Components, point your browser to http://www.tusc.com/.

When to Use the OracleAS Portal Wizards

The OracleAS Portal Wizards are great tools for developing portlets quickly. In fact, once developers become proficient with these tools, they can create portlets, set the appropriate privileges, and place them on the appropriate page in a matter of minutes. Beginning developers, with just a small amount of JavaScript and PL/SQL knowledge, can create relatively complex Web pages that are secure without the complex knowledge needed for most Web-based applications. No other development tool can provide developers with this type of productivity.

The OracleAS Portal Wizards are also appropriate for prototyping. In today's ever-changing environment, sophisticated users are expecting increasingly complex Web-based applications to perform their job duties. This, combined with ever-shrinking development times, makes the Web-based application developer's job increasingly more difficult. Using the OracleAS Portal Wizards to rapidly prototype Web-based, database-centric applications can greatly reduce the developer's time when it comes to delivering production-quality applications to end users when rigorous end-user requirements cannot be gathered.

Having said that, there are some significant limitations to declarative-based development with the OracleAS Portal Wizards. Any application that requires the developer to have a level of control beyond what is provided in the wizards is not a good candidate. Most developers will hit this limitation relatively quickly. Also, any application that is not strictly database-centric in nature is not a good candidate for declarative development techniques in OracleAS Portal.

OracleAS Portal Page Design

Up until this point, we have looked at creating various OracleAS Portal components. How do we take them and place them on a page to be viewable by our end users? The answer lies in the OracleAS Portal Design Page. To create a new page, enter the Navigator by clicking the Navigator link on the top right of any OracleAS Portal page. Up until this point, all of our OracleAS Portal examples have utilized the Providers tab on this page. To create a new page that can hold content, however, we will select the Page Groups tab (Figure 1-32).

Page Groups

All pages must be associated with a Page Group page. The Page Group tab on the Navigator allows us to create new page groups, where we can then create *sub-pages, templates, categories, navigation pages, perspectives, styles, attributes, page*

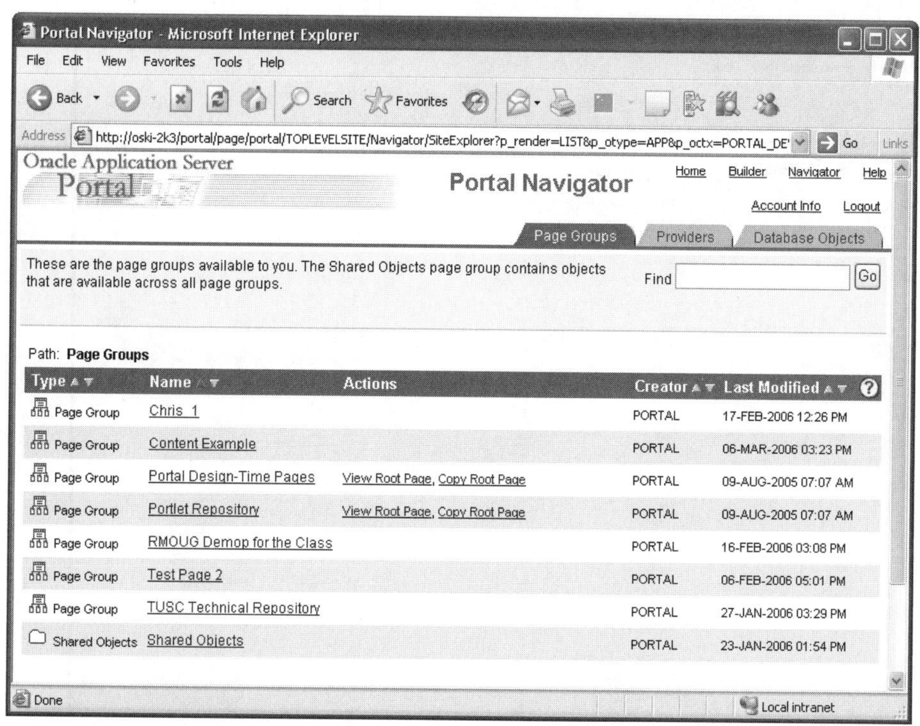

FIGURE 1-32 *The Page Groups tab displayed in the Navigator*

types, and *item types.* Each of these components will be discussed in depth in Chapters 3 and 4. For now, click the Create New... Page Group link on the top left of the screen. The Create Page Group Wizard is a simple one: It consists of one page that prompts for a name, display name, and language. Only English will appear in the Default Language drop-down box unless you have installed other language packs for OracleAS Portal. Every page group has at least one page associated with it called the root page, and this page is created automatically for you when the page group is created. After entering the necessary information, you are automatically taken to the Page Layout screen for the root page of the group you have just created (Figure 1-33).

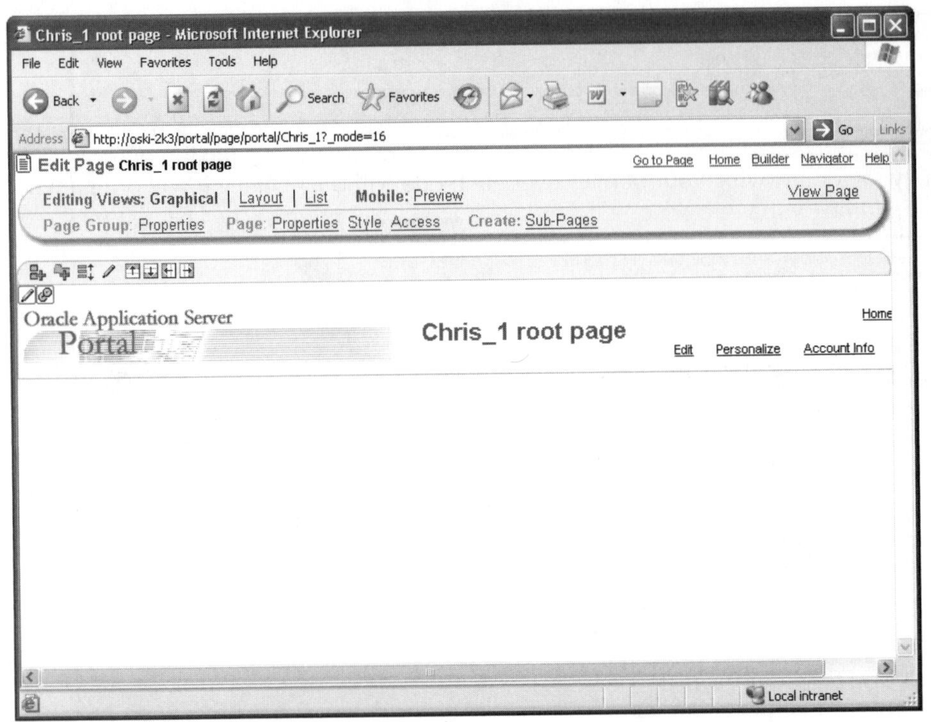

FIGURE 1-33 *The Edit Page screen of OracleAS Portal*

The Edit Page Window

You can edit a page in OracleAS Portal one of three ways, depending on the link selected on the top left of the screen:

- **Graphical** This will display a rough estimate of how the page will look as you add regions, content, and portlets to it.
- **Layout** This will display a layout page for adding regions, content, and portlets to a page (developers who have used earlier versions of Oracle Portal will be familiar with this page).
- **List** This provides a convenient way for developers to manage content on a page. It is not much use for managing portlets.

Click the Graphical link on the top left of the page. By default, there are two regions created for you on the page: a banner region along the top of the page and an empty region below that. The banner region is considered a navigation page, which is one of the subcomponents of a page group listed at the start of this section. After adding some portlets to our page, we will look at editing that part of the page. In the region below the banner, there is a set of nine icons along the top of the empty region. Moving your pointer over each one without clicking it will bring up a tooltip telling you what action clicking each icon will perform. The first (left-most) icon is the Add Item icon. Next to that is the Add Portlet icon.

Adding Portlets

A region, as you will soon discover, can contain items (content) or portlets but not both. If that's the case, why are both the Add Item and Add Portlet icons available for this region? The answer lies in the fact that, by default, the region is created as "undefined," meaning we can place either items or portlets in the region now. As soon as either an item or portlet is placed in the region, the region type becomes defined as that type. Place a portlet on the region by clicking the Add Portlet icon in the region below the banner.

The Add Portlets page (Figure 1-34) is displayed. From this page, we can select portlets that will be placed in the region we have selected. There are two ways to search for portlets that you would like to place in the region: If you know the name of your portlet (or a part of the name), type that in the search text box at the top of the screen and click Go. You can also search for portlets by looking through the categories provided to you by Oracle (portlets provided by Oracle are called "seeded" portlets):

- Portlet Builders
- Portal Community News
- Portal Content Tools
- Administration Portlets
- Published Portal Content
- Shared Portlets

Or as another option, you can search for portlets you have created by looking in the Portlet Staging Area category.

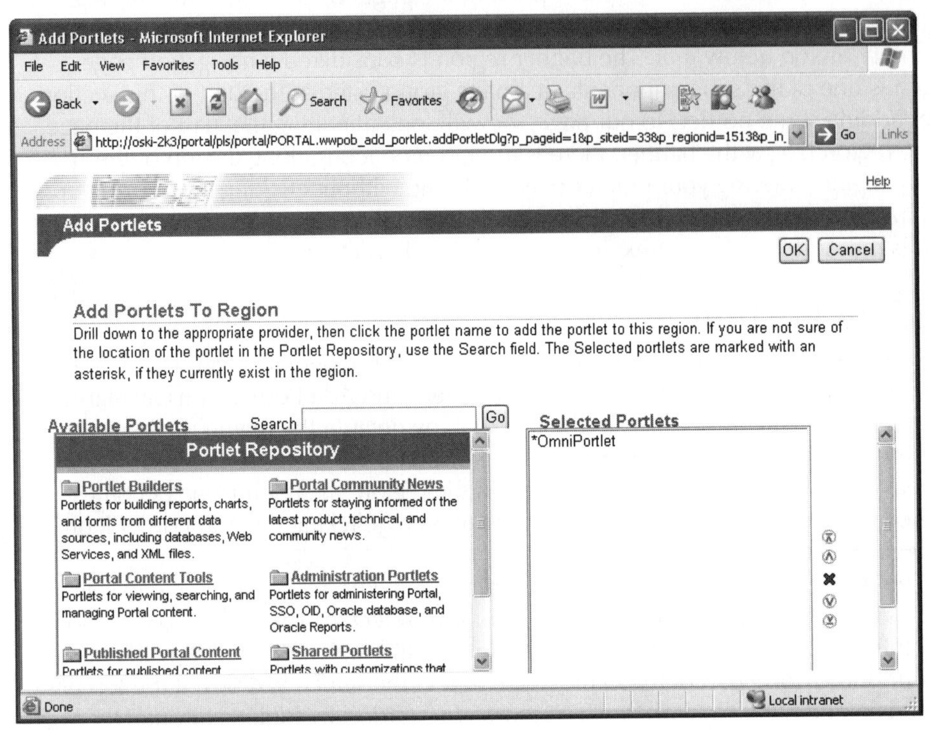

FIGURE 1-34 *The Add Portlets page*

Clicking the portlet will move it to the right-hand side of the screen. Go to the Portlet Staging Area and click the name of the provider you have been creating your portlets under. You will see a list of the portlets you have created up to this point. Single-click one of them and it will display on the right side of the page. Click OK to return to the Page Edit mode of your page with the portlet displayed graphically (Figure 1-35).

Click the View Page link on the top right of the screen to see how the page will be displayed when end users request it. Click the Back button of your browser to return to the Edit Page window. Click the pencil icon (fourth from the left) in the region where you have just added your portlet. This displays the Edit Region page (Figure 1-36).

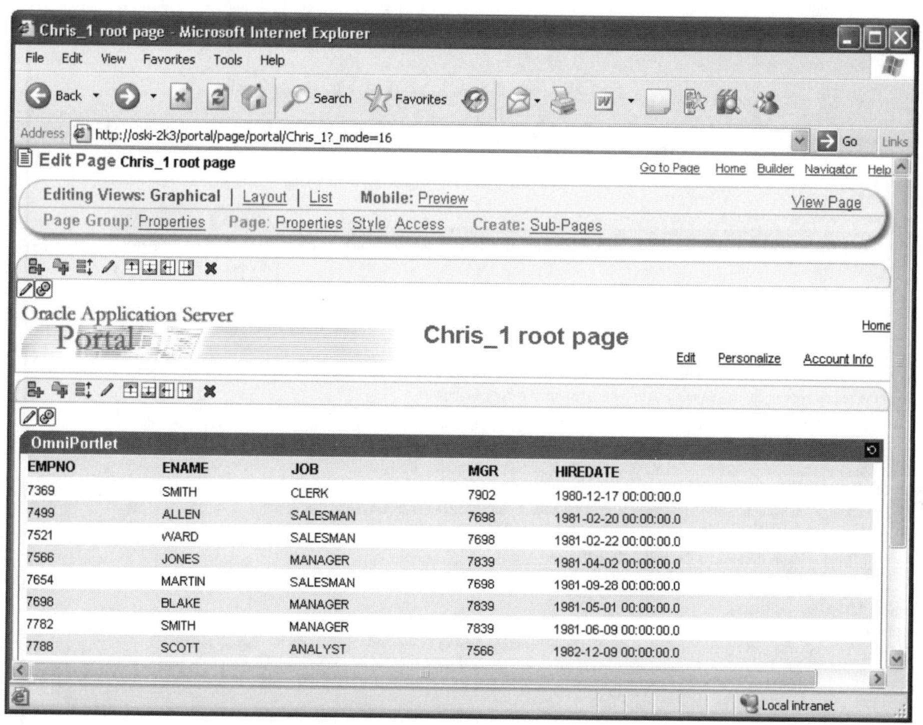

FIGURE 1-35 *The Edit Page screen with a portlet rendered*

Regions

Regions are sections of a page. They can contain either items or portlets, but not both. They can be sized so that they take up a certain number of pixels on a page or a certain percentage of the page. Each region has its own set of attributes that affect how it displays items or portlets contained within it. The Edit Region page allows you to set attributes for a region on the page. The Main tab allows you to define whether the region is titled and how much space on the page it will take up. When we add regions to our pages in the next step, the OracleAS Portal engine will automatically resize existing portlets so that they can fit on the page. The OracleAS Portal engine will evenly divide the page depending on where we add regions, so

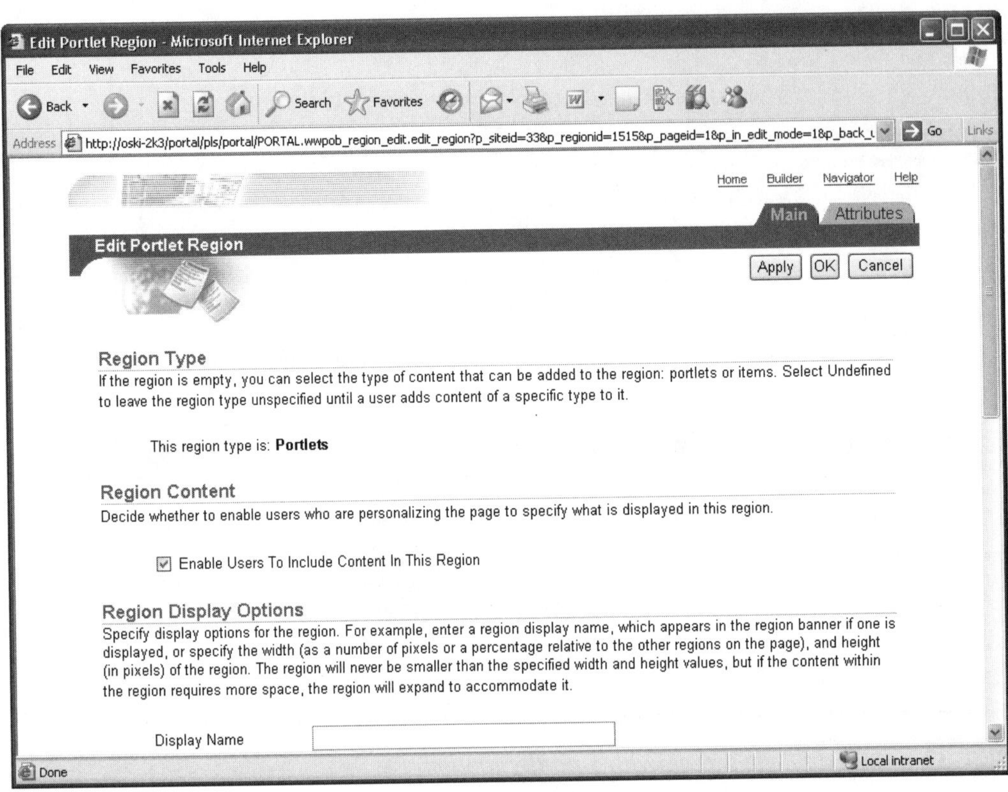

FIGURE 1-36 *The Edit Region page*

we can return to this page to change the region size if we do not want evenly sized regions. The Attributes tab allows you to define what will be displayed, along with which portlets or content that are in the region. When we look at adding items (content) in the next section, we will revisit this page. Click Close to return to the Page Edit page.

Next to the pencil icon for the region there are four icons. These icons are used to add regions to the page. A region will be added in the direction that the arrow is pointing in the four icons. For this example, click the icon with the arrow pointing to the right (the eighth icon from the left). As we mentioned before, the OracleAS Portal engine will automatically size the new and existing regions equally (Figure 1-37).

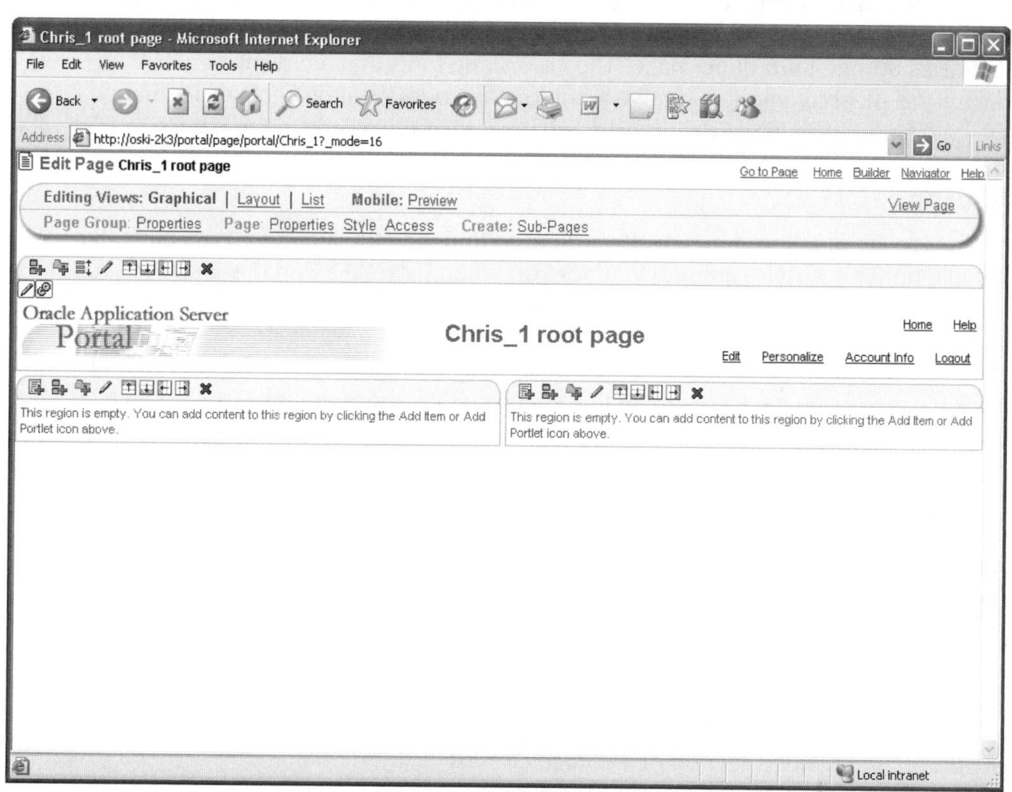

FIGURE 1-37 *The page with two equal-sized regions on it*

Changing the attributes for one of the regions will resize the others it affects automatically. To see an example of this, click the pencil icon for the leftmost region. Change the Width field on the Main tab to 66%. Click OK to redisplay the page. As you can see, the leftmost region now takes up 66% of the screen and the right-most region takes up 33% of the screen. To verify this, click the pencil icon on the rightmost region and note how it has automatically been resized to have a width of 33%.

TIP

Since the rightmost region is an undefined region, the page properties will not display. Click the radio button next to Items and click the Apply button.

We now have a page with two regions on it: a portlet region on the left-hand side that takes up two-thirds of our page and an item region on the right-hand side that takes up one-third of our page. The colors and fonts that are displayed by default are pleasant enough, but we want to make our Portal distinctive. To change the colors and fonts that are displayed, we need to apply a style to the page.

Styles

A *style* is a set of colors and fonts that are used to define the look of a Web page. By default, numerous styles are provided for you when OracleAS Portal is installed. You are not limited to the seeded styles; you can create your own styles and then apply them to pages if you'd like. To create a new style, click the Navigator link on the top right of any OracleAS Portal screen. Click the Page Groups tab and then the link of the page group you have created in this chapter. Click the Style link. You'll notice that there are no styles there. What about the seeded styles? To see those, you'll have to navigate up to the root of the Page Groups section by clicking the Page Groups link in the breadcrumb menu. From there, click the Shared Objects link, and then the Styles link. This will display all of the seeded styles available for you. If you choose to create a style here, it will be available to all pages across all page groups. If you choose to create a style under a specific page group, it will only be available for that page group.

NOTE
The preceding sentence is true for all objects in the Shared Objects section of the Page Groups tab: Templates, Categories, Navigation Pages, Perspectives, Styles, Attributes, Page Types, and Item Types.

Return to the page group by clicking the Page Groups link in the breadcrumb menu, and then clicking the link of the page group we have been working with. From here, click the Styles link and then the Create New... Style link to create a new style. After defining the name and display name, you are automatically taken to the Properties tab for the new style. Here, you can define virtually every aspect of how things will appear on your page. The first drop-down box on the top left of the screen under the header Style Element Type lists the four types of elements you can affect on the page: Items, Tabs, Portlets, and Common. Depending on what is selected there, the second drop-down box under the header Style Element

Properties will change to reflect the first selection. The elements under the color palette will also change depending on what is selected in the first two drop-down boxes. Table 1-1 lists what can be specified on this page.

Experiment by changing some of the properties to something distinctive (it's easiest to change something in the Common section such as Background Color) and saving the Style by clicking Close. Return to the root page of the page group by clicking the Page Group link in the breadcrumb menu and then clicking the Edit Root Page link next to the page group you've been working with. Click the Style link on the top of the page to be taken to the Style tab for the page. Select the style you've just created from the Choose Style drop-down box. Click OK to return to the graphical editing view for the page. Click the View Page link on the top right of the screen (Figure 1-38).

Style Element Type	**Style Element Properties**
Items	Group By Banner, Group By Text, Group By Link, Default Attribute, Sub Page Title Associated Functions, Author, Base Item Type, Category, Create Date, Creator, Date Updated, Description, Display Name, Display Name and Image Link, Display Name Link, Document Size, Expiration Period, Expire Date, Help URL, Image or Display Name Link, Item Content, Keywords, Last Updated By, Page, Page Group, Perspectives, Portlet ID, Portlet Name, Provider ID, Provider Name, Publish ID, Score
Tabs	Active Tab Color, Active Tab Text, Inactive Tab Color, Inactive Tab Text
Portlet	Portlet Header Color, Portlet Header Text, Portlet Header Link, Portlet Header Style, Portlet Subheader Color, Portlet Subheader Text, Portlet Subheader Link, Portlet Body Color, Portlet Heading1, Portlet Text1, Portlet Heading2, Portlet Text2, Portlet Heading3, Portlet Text3, Portlet Heading4, Portlet Text4
Common	Background, Region Banner, Region Banner Text

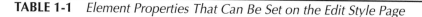

TABLE 1-1 *Element Properties That Can Be Set on the Edit Style Page*

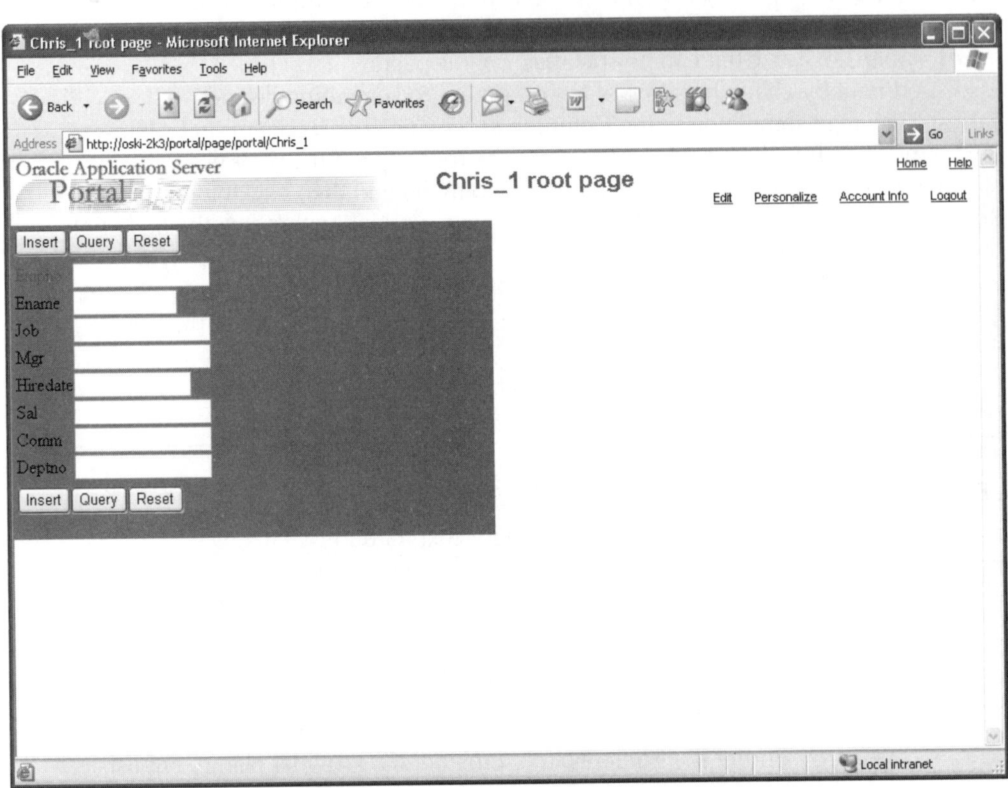

FIGURE 1-38 *A page with a style applied to it*

Templates

A *template* can be used to predefine the tabs and regions on a page. A template can be associated with a page when it is created, or it can be associated afterward. If a template is associated with a page after items and portlets have been placed on it, you will be asked which regions and tabs on the template move the items and portlets. It is much easier to associate a template to a blank page right after it has been created.

NOTE
Pages can also be "detached" from templates.

The latest version of OracleAS Portal (10.1.4) has two types of templates: Portal Templates and HTML Templates. Portal Templates are created with an OracleAS Portal Wizard. Portal Templates are used to enforce a particular layout, style, set of privileges, and content across multiple pages. As with a standard page, you can divide a Portal Template for pages into regions and tabs, apply a style, grant access privileges, and add items and portlets. Page Designers can also define parameters for the template and use them in conjunction with the portlets placed on the pages that are based on the template. HTML Templates can be created with either an OracleAS Portal wizard or a third-party HTML editor. You can extend an HTML Template using OracleAS Portal substitution tags or your own developed JavaScript. HTML Templates include two subtypes: HTML Page Skins and HTML Content Layouts.

HTML Page Skins can be used to define the appearance of the area surrounding page content. With HTML page skins, you define where the body area of the page is placed. The body area is where portal content displays, that is, the regions, tabs, items, and portlets. You can introduce portal elements into your page skin through the use of HTML page skin substitution tags. Use these to introduce such OracleAS Portal elements as page Edit or Personalize links, the name of the currently logged-in user, the current page's display name, and so on.

HTML Content Layouts can be used to define a formatting scheme for individual regions. Design HTML templates for either item or portlet regions. Page designers can use HTML to create tables, font designs, colors, and any other encoding or object type you could place in any other HTML template. You could even call a cascading style sheet (CSS) to apply a standard format. HTML Templates are discussed in detail in Chapter 4.

Create a new Portal Template by clicking the name of the page group we have been working with in this chapter, and then clicking on the Portal Templates link. Click the Create New... Portal Template link on the top left of the page. Give the template a meaningful name, display name, and description, and then click the "Make available for use in this page group" check box and click Next. If you would like to restrict the style to maintain a consistent look and feel, de-select the "Enable Pages to Use a Different Style" check box. When you click Finish, you will be taken to a page that looks similar to the Edit Page screen (Figure 1-39).

On this screen you can define regions and tabs, as well as place items and portlets, although the last two actions are rare. Experiment by adding some tabs and regions to this template. Changes are saved automatically as you add regions or tabs to the template. When you're finished, click the Navigator link in the top right of the screen. Click the name of the page group in the breadcrumb menu and then click the Pages link. Click the Create New... Page link on the top left of the screen. Leave Page Type as standard and enter meaningful information for the name, display

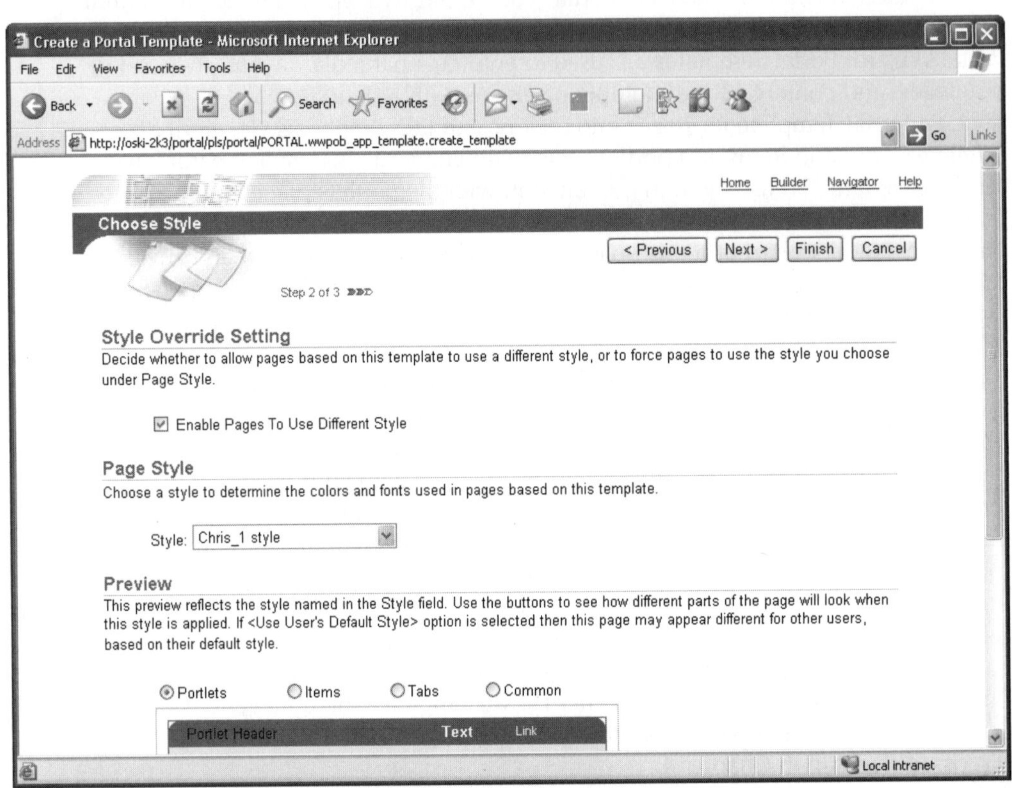

FIGURE 1-39 *The Edit Template Page screen*

name, and description fields. Click Next. On the second page of the wizard, select the template you created in the previous step. Automatically, the screen repaints to display what the new subpage will look like (Figure 1-40). Clicking Finish after this step will display the page in graphical edit mode. Note that the developer has no way to delete or add regions (they are "locked" by the template). It is also impossible to add portlets or items to the existing tabs, as they have not been defined as portlet or item regions in the template.

Navigation Pages

Navigation pages are a special type of subpage that are intended to be used as a navigation area for your portal pages. During creation of a navigation page, the

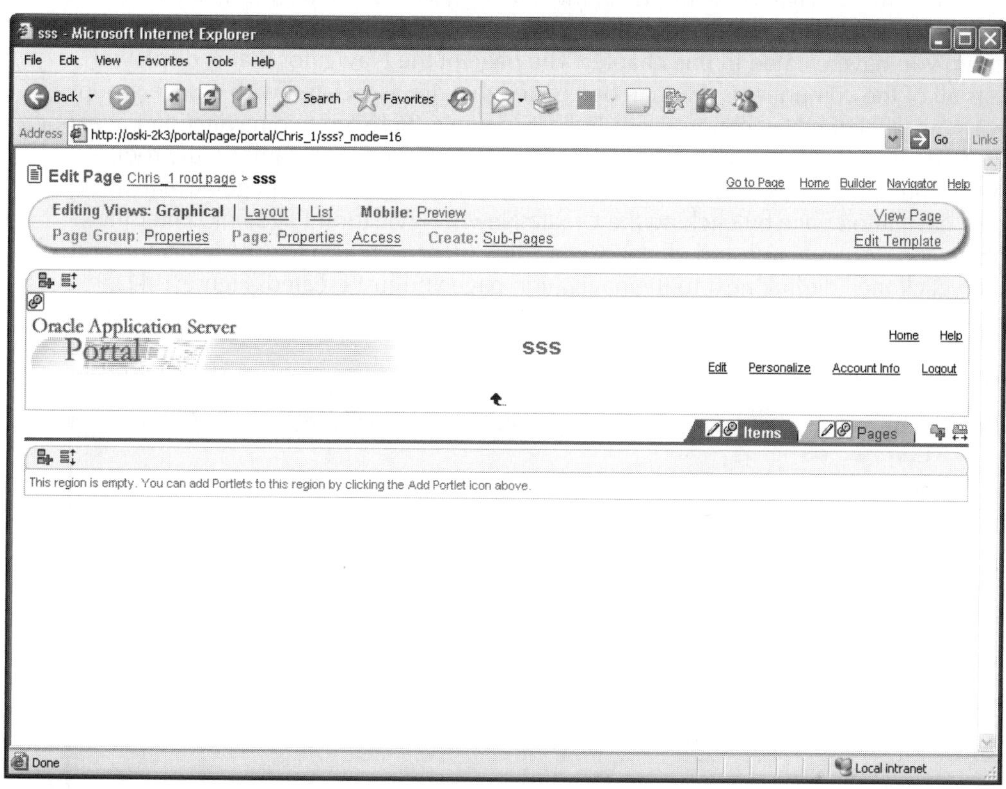

FIGURE 1-40 *The Create Page Wizard after a template has been selected*

steps and attributes of the navigation page are exactly the same as a subpage except for the following:

- Navigation pages can only be "standard" pages; subpages can be either "standard" or "URL"-type pages and can have their attributes modified.
- Navigation pages can be created from other navigation pages by selecting another page in the Copy From drop-down box.
- By default, navigation pages are published as portlets with the intent of placing them on a page.
- There is no banner region created automatically.

Let's add a navigation window on the left-hand side of the page. Click the Navigator link on the top right of the page, and then click the name of the page group you have created in this chapter. The page of the Navigator that is displayed lists all of the components that can be created that are associated with a page group. For now, click the Navigation Pages link. By default, there are two navigation pages created for each page group: a banner (which is displayed by default on the root page) and a navbar (which is not displayed by default on the root page). Create a new navigation page by clicking the Create New... Navigation Page link. Enter the name and display name and click Create. Click Close to return to the Navigator, and then click the Edit link next to the navigation page you just created (Figure 1-41).

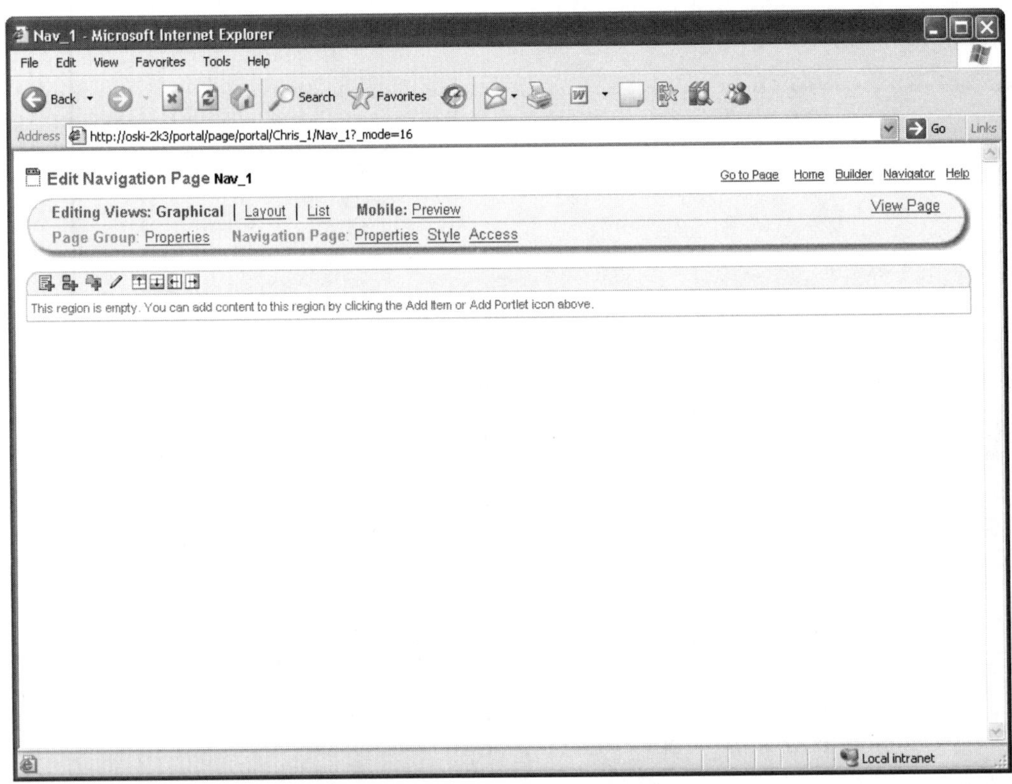

FIGURE 1-41 *The edit screen for the Navigation Page*

As you can see, this page looks very similar to the edit page screen except that no banner region is created automatically. You can place either items or portlets on the default region and you have full capabilities to create other regions and place tabs on them, but it is far more common to maintain one region and place items (usually links to other OracleAS Portal pages or components) in this region. Click the Add Item icon on the top left of the page, select Page Link from the Content Item Types drop-down box, and click Next. Click the notepad icon next to the Path text box and select an OracleAS Portal page from the list by clicking Return Object next to our selection. Returning to Step 2 of the Add Item Wizard, fill in the fields on this page with meaningful values, and click Finish.

After returning to the edit page screen, click the Navigator link on the top right of the screen. Click Page Groups in the breadcrumb menu of the navigator, then click the Edit Root Page link next to the page group we have been working with in this chapter. Add the navigation page by creating a new region on the left of the screen. Click the Add Portlet icon for that new region and search for the navigation page you just created. Place it in the region by single-clicking it. Click OK to return to the page.

Page Properties and Page Group Properties

Both *pages* and *page groups* have properties associated with them that affect how the page looks and behaves. A Page Group setting will affect all pages (root and subpages) associated with that page group. At the top of the Edit Page screen, there are two links: a Properties link next to Page Group: and a Properties link next to Page:. Click the Properties link next to Page Group: (Figure 1-42).

The properties for the page group include the following:

- **Main** This tab can be used to change the page group name, display name, or quotas for the size of items that can be placed on pages in the page group. It can also be used to allow or deny end users the privilege to use or modify page styles.
- **Configure** This tab can be used to allow or deny different page types and different types of content on the page(s) in the page group.
- **Items** This tab allows you to enable/disable item versioning, set characteristics for unpublished (unviewable) items, and purge expired items.
- **Translations** This tab allows you to manage different language packs that may have been installed.
- **Access** This tab allows you to set permissions on the pages in the page group.

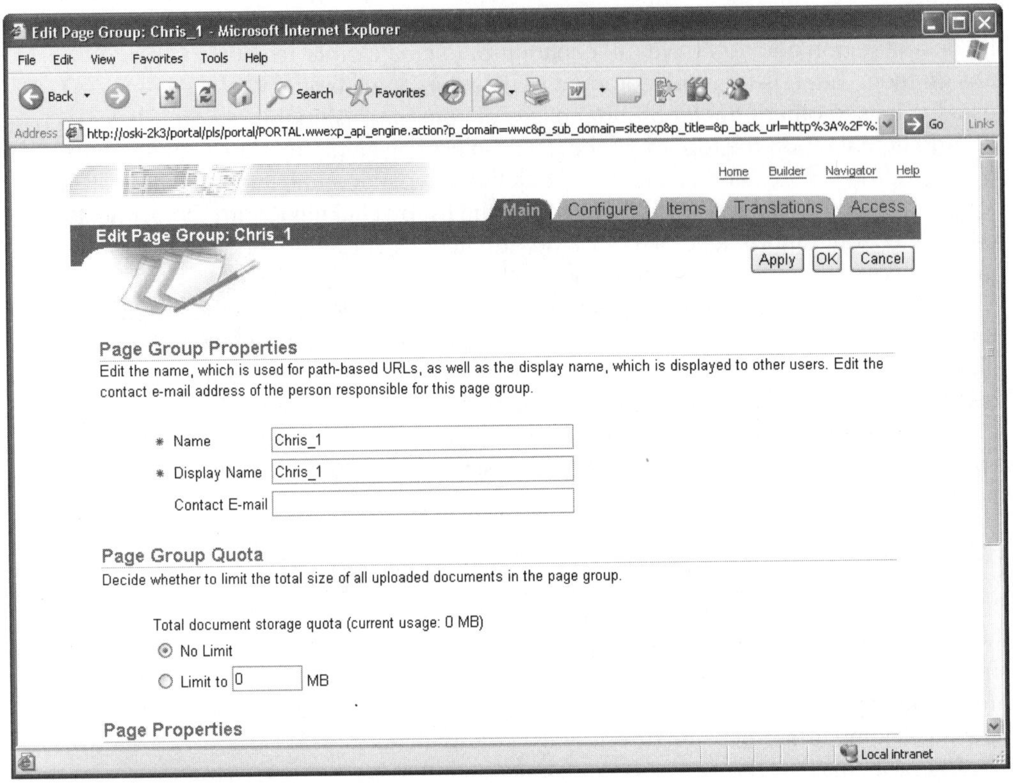

FIGURE 1-42 *The properties page for the page group*

Click OK to return to the edit page screen. Click the Properties link next to Page: to go to the properties page (Figure 1-43).

This page shows a slightly different set of properties. Along the top, there are now eight tabs:

- **Main** This tab allows you to change the name/display name of the page and control its caching behavior.
- **Template** This tab allows you to attach the page to or detach the page from a template.

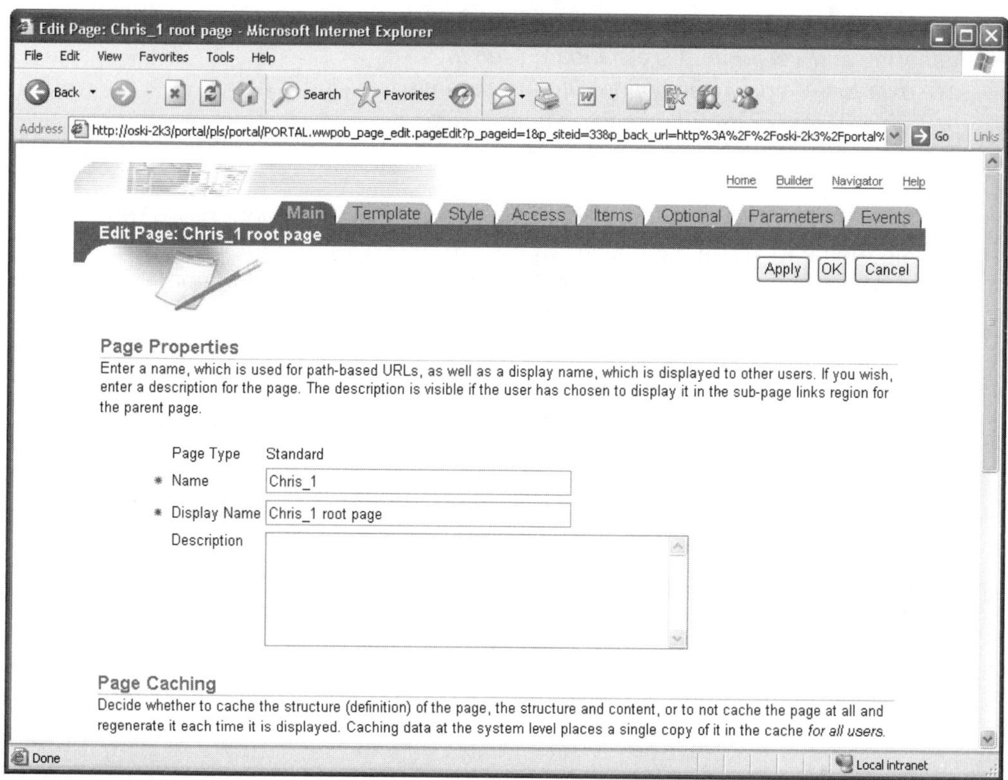

FIGURE 1-43 *The properties page for the page*

- **Style** This tab allows you to select a style for the page.
- **Access** This tab allows you to set access privileges for the page. You can use this tab to override settings made in the Access tab of the Page Group properties described in the preceding list.
- **Optional** This tab allows you to publish your page as a portlet (which can then be placed on other pages), set default WebDAV properties, enable/disable item versioning, specify page images, and enable/disable links to subpages.

NOTE
WebDAV (the term stands for WWW Distributed Authoring and Versioning) is a standard used to save data to a Web site (as opposed to just reading it). WebDAV is very useful when you have a large amount of content you wish to publish on your site.

- **Parameters** This tab allows you to define parameters for your page. You can then pass those parameters in calls to the page from the various packages in the Portal API. Parameters are most often passed to portlets on the page to synchronize portlet behavior. An example of this might be a stock symbol parameter that can be used to drive quote and news portlets relating to the stock symbol.

TIP
The Portal API is described in the Portal Development Kit (PDK), downloadable from http://portalcenter.oracle.com/.

- **Events** This tab allows you to define events for your page. Events can be used to trigger certain actions when various events happen on the page.
- **Regions** This tab allows you to define a default item and default portlet region for the page.

Exercises

At the end of each chapter, there will be a series of exercises that will explore the topics discussed in the chapter. It is recommended that you do these exercises in order. The first couple of exercises are relatively simple and should take a very short amount of time to perform. The later exercises, which introduce more complex topics, will obviously take longer.

While it is strongly encouraged that you work through the exercises, the author realizes that, depending on the reader's existing skill level, some exercise topics may be review material. If you wish to skip over some of the beginning exercises and focus on the later ones, you can download the pages and portlets for these beginning exercises from the author's Web site listed in the Introduction to this book.

- Exercise 1: Create a Page Group named "Executive Dashboard."
- Exercise 2: Create three pages: one that holds only content, named "Content Page," one that holds only portlets, named "Portlet Page," and one that holds both, named "Mixed Page."
- Exercise 3: Place a piece of content on your content page. If you don't have a common file like a Microsoft Word (.doc) document or an Adobe Portable Document File (.pdf) available, simply create a text file, put some random text in it, save it with a .txt extension, and place that .txt file on the page.
- Exercise 4: Place a portlet on your Portlet Page. If you haven't created any portlets yet, you can place one of the seeded portlets on the page; seeded portlets are discussed in Chapter 3.

Summary

OracleAS Portal is a feature-rich development environment that gives developers a multitude of tools and constructs that allow the creation and deployment of Web-based applications quickly and easily. This chapter has introduced the basic architecture of OracleAS Portal and the OracleAS Portal components that can be built using the wizards provided by Oracle, but we've just scratched the surface of what it is truly capable of. In subsequent chapters, details of OracleAS Portal development, security, and advanced topics will be discussed.

CHAPTER 2

OracleAS Portal Responsibilities within an Organization

ears ago, it was possible for a single, talented individual to be the "guru" of a department within an organization. This individual kept things running pretty smoothly; whether it was closing the month-end in accounting or managing the backup tape system, the guru was always there with a quick answer or a clever solution to whatever thorny problem came his or her way. Even when things did go wrong, the guru was on the job, and most people within the organization could rest easy knowing problems would be eventually resolved.

In most organizations, those days are long gone. As technology, government regulations, and an ever-increasingly competitive marketplace for products, services, and talent continue to put extreme pressure on IT departments to get more and more things done faster and with fewer resources, the members of those IT departments are being called on to perform tasks further and further from their original skill sets. For many, this is eagerly taken up as a challenge; for others, inertia and the fear of change makes even the simplest new skill an arduous task.

OracleAS Portal, currently in its fifth major revision, is a mature development environment that gives organizations the ability to get information to the people who need it quickly and easily. As Oracle has continually shown its support of open standards, OracleAS Portal incorporates many cutting-edge tools to give your end users the richest Web-based experience possible. The robust set of features OracleAS Portal provides also requires a robust set of skills to maximize the implementation of any OracleAS Portal solution.

Back when OracleAS Portal was known as WebDB, it was common for a single person to handle all of the responsibilities of a company's portal: managing content, developing portlets, designing pages, etc. Today, each of the major development activities associated with developing a portal with OracleAS Portal has such a rich set of features, it is far more common to divide the work among people with specific skills. While it certainly is possible for a single person to handle all of the tasks associated with developing a portal, the new features of OracleAS Portal require enough specialized skills that most organizations would benefit from having multiple people devoted to developing and enhancing the portal. This chapter discusses the major responsibilities organizations can put to use when designing, implementing, and maintaining their portals.

Skill Sets

As someone much smarter than me once said, "No Web site is ever 'finished'." Your portal is no exception. It is in this spirit that this chapter attempts to list out the types of skills your organization will need when undertaking the task of building a portal using OracleAS Portal.

NOTE

Please keep in mind that these are not rigid classifications and that it is very common for someone to have skills and responsibilities that "bleed across" these classifications. This chapter is an attempt to list the crucial skills that every organization should have access to before beginning a medium- to large-scale OracleAS Portal project.

Every IT department needs specific skills, whether those of Java or C# programmers to perform large-scale custom development or those of business architects to help manage implementation of software that drives an organization from top to bottom, like Oracle's E-Business Suite. In those two broad classifications, there are numerous references for managers and developers to turn to that help define the architecture of skills needed within the organization before beginning a project. OracleAS Portal demos extremely well, and most people, upon seeing the relative ease with which dynamic, Web-based solutions can be implemented with it, are excited to start using it as quickly as possible. There is, however, a significant dearth of information regarding the types of skills and development methodologies needed for those organizations interested in implementing robust OracleAS Portal solutions. The following job titles can be thought of as skills that an organization must have to (whether through internal employees or through consultants) fully take advantage of everything OracleAS Portal has to offer.

Developers

There are two general ways to work with OracleAS Portal, and most portal sites use a combination of both: by using portlets to display information usually queried from a database and by using the content management features in OracleAS Portal to make information available that doesn't easily fit into databases. What is the difference between the two? Portlets can be thought of as small programs that are placed on a page and retrieve information from a data source, like an Oracle database. Content management allows you to provide information that doesn't fit into a traditional data source to your users easily. Examples of content might include things like an Adobe Acrobat PDF, a sound file, or a video file. OracleAS Portal's content management features handle things like these that don't fit into a database easily. While it is possible to have an OracleAS Portal site solely made up of content, it is much more likely that your portal will consist of both content and the need to programmatically query information from a data source. In order to create these components, a developer will have to create them.

NOTE
In this context a data source can be a traditional data source (like an Oracle database) or something like an XML file.

What types of developer skills are needed to create OracleAS Portlets? The answer to that question depends on the types of portlets you wish to incorporate into your portal. Developing portlets falls into two basic categories: declarative development and programmatic development.

Declarative Development

As mentioned in Chapter 1, OracleAS Portal provides wizards that allow you to "declare" what you want your portlet to look like. These wizards ask you a series of questions and then generate PL/SQL code for your portlet based on the answers you provide. This type of development has many advantages:

- **Rapid development** There is no other way to create Web-based portlets as quickly as by using the OracleAS Portal wizards.
- **Lack of code development/maintenance** Using the wizards guarantees syntactically correct code and eliminates the need for any code maintenance.
- **No need for coding skills** Since the wizards generate all of the necessary code for you, there is no need for developers (in the traditional sense of the word) to write code to create a portlet. Of course, developers can enhance their portlets using this development method with JavaScript and/or PL/SQL, but this is not required.

With these advantages, why is it, as mentioned in Chapter 1, that declarative, wizard-based development is, in effect, almost never used in modern OracleAS Portal development? These are among the drawbacks to this method:

- **Limited functionality** The wizards attempt to incorporate as much functionality as they can, but all declarative development environments are limited by the types of questions they pose to the developer. Most end users expect a plethora of modern features in their Web-based applications. The OracleAS Portal wizards cannot incorporate all of these new features.
- **Fundamental purpose of the wizards** Originally, the wizards were designed to provide an easy way for developers to create Web pages that access databases quickly, and they do that job quite well. Most

users, however, demand more functionality than this—the ability to pull information for multiple data sources and even other Web sites, the integration of various applications from internal and external sources, the ability to have only one login to access these applications—and all of these requirements are far beyond what the OracleAS Portal wizards were designed to do.

- **Lack of new functionality** Oracle has realized that developers and end users want a rich Web experience from their portals. Accordingly, the OracleAS Portal development team is focusing its energy on providing enhancements to the programmatic development tools, discussed in the next section. While there have been some minor enhancements to the wizards, the last couple of versions of OracleAS Portal have seen the wizards basically unchanged. The programmatic tools, however, have seen significant enhancements over the last couple of OracleAS Portal versions.

There are three basic types of declarative development methods within OracleAS Portal:

- **OracleAS Portal wizards** These wizards allow developers to create the following types of portlets: Forms, Reports, Charts, Calendars, Dynamic Pages, XML Components, Hierarchies, Menus, URLs, Frame Drivers, Links, Lists of Values, and Data Components. The portlets that are generated by these wizards can be enhanced through the use of JavaScript, so while no programming knowledge is needed to create these types of portlets, understanding JavaScript will enable developers to add some basic functionality to the end-user experience that the standard wizards cannot. Also, there are places in each of these wizards to execute PL/SQL code and display text using HTML tags, so knowledge of these will help in the development and enhancement of these portlets.

NOTE
It's important to note that an OracleAS Portal Form is not the same as a form created with the Oracle Forms product that is part of Oracle's Developer Suite. The same holds true for Reports. In Chapter 11, the integration of Oracle Forms, Oracle Reports, and Oracle Discoverer, developed using the Oracle Developer Suite into OracleAS Portal, is discussed in detail.

- **OmniPortlet** This wizard, discussed in detail in Chapter 6, gives developers the ability to pull data from multiple sources (including non-Oracle databases) and return the data to end users in a number of different formats. OmniPortlet can be thought of as the next generation of the OracleAS Portal wizards. While Oracle has never explicitly said that OmniPortlet is intended to replace the OracleAS Portal wizards, it continues to be enhanced in each release of OracleAS Portal, unlike the OracleAS Portal wizards. You can think of OmniPortlet as Oracle's "method of choice" for those developers interested in moving forward with declarative development. Like the OracleAS Portal wizards, OmniPortlet does not require any knowledge of programming languages to use, but it does require an understanding of the data source to be used in the portlet. OmniPortlet supports the following data sources:
  - **Spreadsheet** Developers can specify a URL that points to a spreadsheet containing data to be displayed in the portlet.
  - **SQL** Developers can specify connection information and the SQL to be run against the data source. This is one of the significant things that separates OmniPortlet from the OracleAS Portal wizards: namely, the ability to query from any data source that has a JDBC driver installed on the server running OracleAS Portal. You could, for example, install a JDBC driver for Microsoft SQL Server or MySQL and have OmniPortlet query data from those databases. This functionality demonstrates the true spirit of OracleAS Portal (and portals in general) by having OracleAS Portal be the interface through which end users can get at all forms of data, whether they be Oracle or non-Oracle data sources.
  - **XML** Developers can specify an XML source, an XSL filter, and an XML schema to make XML data available.
  - **Web Service** Here, developers can specify a WSDL URL, the method of the Web service, and the XSL filter URL to make data returned from Web services available to OmniPortlet.
  - **Web Page** This method is very similar to Web Clipping (discussed next).
- **Web Clipping** This wizard, also discussed in Chapter 6, falls into the "in-between" category of OracleAS Portal development. Web Clipping allows you to "clip" Web pages (or, most impressively, parts of Web pages) and incorporate them into your OracleAS Portal pages. The clips are dynamic, so if the underlying Web page changes, your OracleAS Portal page changes also. Since assembling clipped pages does not require any programming, you could consider this to be part of a Web designer's responsibility and not one of a developer's, but in the strict delineation of responsibilities,

many organizations consider a Web designer's job to control things like the look and feel of a Web page, and the developer's job to perform the necessary activities to create what is placed on the page. Most of the time, that entails traditional development (like using the OracleAS Portal wizards or writing Java code), but it could include Web Clipping in this particular circumstance. Web Clipping is the easiest way to create OracleAS Portal pages, since all of the content that will make up your pages has already been developed. As such, Web Clipping does not require any knowledge of programming languages, although a basic knowledge of Web page design is essential for using Web Clipping effectively.

Typically, an organization will employ a few users to provide declaratively developed portlets to end users. These developers usually have a basic understanding of the underlying database structures along with enough programmatic skills to model basic business processes in the portlets. In many cases, these developers are not part of the traditional IT departments; they may be power users in specific departments who can help take the burden of the creation and maintenance of forms or reports off of IT's shoulders.

Programmatic Development

The OracleAS Portal wizards, OmniPortlet, and Web Clipping are all great techniques for developing OracleAS Portal portlets quickly, but for most portal sites, developers bump up against the limitations of these tools pretty quickly. In order to get greater control over their portlets, developers need to go outside of the OracleAS Portal environment and use other languages. There are two languages that can be used to develop portlets: PL/SQL and Java.

PL/SQL is what the OracleAS Portal wizards, discussed in the preceding section, generate. Many developers wonder if they can use the wizards to generate the portlet, and then go back and manually modify it. While this technique is certainly possible in principle, in reality, it is almost impossible to carry out in practice, as the wizard generates a significant amount of "overhead" code (code used to maintain various variables and states). While it is possible for a developer to use this code, the amount of time and effort needed to keep track of this makes it much more practical to create a PL/SQL portlet from scratch.

On Oracle's Web site, there is a page devoted to OracleAS Portal development. This site (http://www.oracle.com/technology/products/ias/portal/index.html, formerly located at http://portalcenter.oracle.com) contains downloads for developers called Portal Development Kits (PDKs). There are separate PDKs for PL/SQL and Java developers. The PDKs contain code samples, API references, and other tools to make your development easier. Using the PDK for PL/SQL requires developers to have intermediate to advanced PL/SQL skills in order to take advantage of the PL/SQL PDK effectively.

One of the tools in the PL/SQL PDK is called the PL/SQL Generator. This utility generates installable PL/SQL code for a database provider and its PL/SQL portlets based on the provider and portlet definitions that are stored in the source XML file. Providers are discussed in Chapter 7, but for now, think of a provider as a container that "holds" portlets. You can set attributes for the container, and the portlets placed in that container will inherit the attributes of the provider. A portlet cannot exist in your portal without being associated with a provider.

NOTE
While the PL/SQL PDK gives developers enhancements beyond the capabilities of the OracleAS Portal wizards, there are still significant limitations to choosing this development method when developing OracleAS Portal portlets. Accordingly, the development chapters in this book focus on the development language that gives developers the greatest amount of flexibility: Java.

The other PDK that Oracle provides is the PDK for Java. As its name implies, this PDK contains code samples, API references, and other tools for those developers interested in using Java to develop their portlets. Java and the PDK for Java give developers the most flexibility when developing portlets. While it is possible to use any Java environment to create portlets, Oracle provides an add-in for their Java Integrated Development Environment (IDE) called Oracle JDeveloper that greatly simplifies the creation of Java-based portlets. In addition to the portlet add-in, Oracle JDeveloper also contains a framework called Application Developer Framework (ADF) that makes the development of applications that access databases much easier. Chapters 7 and 8 discuss how to develop portlets in Java using Oracle JDeveloper and ADF.

What Is a Framework?

A *framework* is a fancy word for a set of rules and code for maintaining your development efforts. Wikipedia defines it as "a defined support structure in which another software project can be organized and developed. Typically, a framework may include support programs, code libraries, and a scripting language, amongst other software to help develop and glue together the different components of your project."

OracleAS Portal programmatic developers are part of the IT department in most organizations. This is true for two main reasons:

- Development of these portlets is code intensive, and advanced Java and/or PL/SQL skills are usually possessed only by those in the IT department.
- The scope of what can be accomplished with programmatic-based portlets (integration with advanced security functionality [discussed in Chapter 10] and integration with external [non-OracleAS Portal] systems, to name but two examples) is significant enough to warrant control by the IT department.

Typically, although not always, developers are more focused on the functionality of a particular piece of code and less with the details of how the information is presented to the user. Chapter 10 discusses OracleAS Portal users, groups, and security, but for now, know that Oracle provides two groups out of the box: PORTAL_DEVELOPERS and PORTLET_PUBLISHERS. Any user who is a member of the PORTAL_DEVELOPERS group has the ability to create portlets but not to place them on a page. Any user in the PORTLET_PUBLISHERS group has the ability to place a portlet on a page but not to create one. This (very general) classification is used to separate developers (who are usually more interested in functionality) from Web designers (who are usually more interested with aesthetics). Of course, you are not limited to these classifications—a user can be a member of both, or you can create your own groups, depending on your needs.

It's important to note that portlets encompass both functionality and a user interface. Developers do have to work closely with the Web designers to make sure they create portlets that fit the overall look of the portal.

If you have a background in Java development, you are probably familiar with the MVC (Model View Controller) paradigm. If you design your application to MVC standards, the code used to model the database structures (Model) is separated from the end-user interface (View), which is separated in turn from the business logic (Controller). This makes it easier to modify a part of the application at a later time. For instance, if the business rules change, only the controller part of the code needs to be changed. In relation to OracleAS Portal, developers using the declarative method already have the Model piece taken care of when they are prompted for which database tables they want to use. The controller part is generated by the answers they provide in the various wizard screens. The view part of the portlet is a combination of the developer's choices (what labels to display on the form/report, etc., along with any format masks applied to the data) and the Web designer's choices in regard to font, coloring, and templates. For programmatic developers, the Portal Wizard that works with Oracle JDeveloper will effectively generate the

View/Controller part of the code for you. It is the developer's responsibility to write the Model code that interfaces with your data source (if you so desire).

To be an effective programmatic developer in OracleAS Portal, a sophisticated set of skills is required. Obviously, you will need intermediate-to-advanced skills in either PL/SQL or Java, depending on which language you decide to pursue. For Java developers, the skill sets also include a thorough understanding of the Java 2 Enterprise Edition (J2EE) technology stack, HTML, Java servlets, XML, Java Server Pages (JSP), and the JSP Tag library.

Content Managers/Approvers

As mentioned earlier, there are two basic ways of using OracleAS Portal: portlets and content management. Content management is the process by which content (things that don't fit into a data source easily, like Microsoft Word documents or Adobe PDF documents) is added to the portal, made available to users, removed from the portal, etc. While adding and removing content may seem like a trivial task, modern content management systems provide sophisticated features that give content managers great control and automation of the various content management functions. Chapter 5 will discuss these features in detail.

A *content manager* is responsible for the content that is made available on the OracleAS Portal site. Responsibilities usually include checking to make sure the content is grammatically correct and spell-checked, that the content is available at

Where to Find More Information about Java and Oracle JDeveloper

While this book will give you the understanding and knowledge to create Java-based portlets, it is not intended as a reference to learn the Java language or the Oracle JDeveloper development tool. In Oracle Press's *Oracle JDeveloper 10g Handbook,* written by Dr. Avrom Roy-Faderman, Peter Koletzke, and Dr. Paul Dorsey (McGraw-Hill, 2004), the first line of the introduction states: "This is not the only book you will need to learn how to create Java-based Web applications." Considering the fact that this is a very dense 700+ page book, it is an indication of the complexity of the Java and the Oracle JDeveloper 10*g* products. I heartily recommend this book along with Brad Brown's excellent presentations and white papers on Oracle JDeveloper available on TUSC's Web site (http://www.tusc.com/) to help further your understanding of Java and, specifically, of using Oracle JDeveloper to create Java-based applications that access an Oracle database.

the appropriate times, and that the content can be viewed only by appropriate end users. In addition to these responsibilities, some organizations allow content managers to designate other users who can add or update content.

One of the most important features when dealing with content management is the concept of approvals. In OracleAS Portal, it is possible to establish a set of users who will need to approve a piece of content (referred to as an "item" in Oracle's documentation) before the content is available for users to see. For example, a human resources document intended for all employees may need to be approved by a member from the legal department, an HR manager, and a set of VPs before becoming available. The content manager will usually be responsible for setting up the approval process and be ultimately responsible for all content made available on the site.

Page Designers

OracleAS Portal provides a rich environment for creating pages. All of the tools for creating pages are contained within the OracleAS Portal product. Oracle provides templates (for maintaining consistency when laying out your pages), styles (for maintaining color and font consistency), and the ability to define what colors and fonts are available to a page or a set of pages. All of this is contained within the OracleAS Portal environment, so there is no need to go to any other tool to create a rich end-user experience.

While all of these features are great for those organizations getting started with OracleAS Portal, many departments have already invested time and money in more traditional Web development environments and don't wish to re-write existing HTML code and re-train their Web designers in a new tool. Up until now, there was no other choice if you wanted to take advantage of OracleAS Portal effectively.

In OracleAS Portal 10.1.4, all of that changes. Oracle introduced the concept of HTML and Content Templates, which give page designers the ability to use tools outside of Oracle to create their Web pages. By using this functionality, Web designers can use a tool like Dreamweaver to generate the HTML that will serve as the foundation of their Web pages, export the HTML into OracleAS Portal, and then place OracleAS Portal–specific tags in the code to represent content and/or portlets. Chapter 4 discusses these new features in detail.

Administrators

OracleAS Portal administrators have the responsibility to maintain security and privileges for the portal site. Since the development wizards and content management administration screens are themselves part of OracleAS Portal, the administrator's job includes the setting of privileges for internal users (those developing portlets, designing pages, and managing content) as well as end users using the portal to do their daily jobs.

Many people using OracleAS Portal are confused by Oracle's implementation of security in OracleAS Portal. While the database that is installed in the Oracle Application Server infrastructure holds all of the security information, there is a clear separation between database users and OracleAS Portal users. Creation of a user in OracleAS Portal does *not* create a user in the infrastructure database. Oracle uses a technology called LDAP to maintain OracleAS Portal users. Oracle's implementation of LDAP is done through a product called Oracle Internet Directory (OID). The LDAP standard specifies how to structure and access information about users, but it does not specify how the information is to be stored (vendors of the LDAP system are given the choice of how to store their data). What do you think Oracle chose to store the LDAP information? You guessed it—an Oracle database.

LDAP (the term stands for Lightweight Directory Access Protocol) is an open standard that has been used for many years and is highly secure and stable. Wikipedia.org defines it as ". . . an application protocol for querying and modifying directory services running over TCP/IP." An LDAP directory usually follows the X.500 model: it is a tree of entries, each of which consists of a set of named attributes with values. While some services use a more complicated "forest" model, the vast majority use a simple starting point for their database organization. Microsoft has a similar product, called Active Directory.

NOTE
You can think of the separation of database users and LDAP users this way: Database users get privileges to see data and run pieces of code in a database. LDAP users get privileges to Web resources, including the ability to view OracleAS Portal pages, run Oracle Forms or Reports on the Web, or access Web-based development environments like Oracle Discoverer Plus.

Assignment of privileges in OracleAS Portal is made simpler by the use of groups. Groups are very similar in concept to the roles in the database. Privileges in the database can be granted to a role, and then any user who is granted that role inherits those privileges. Similarly, groups in OracleAS Portal can be granted privileges like the ability to create pages or place a portlet on a page. Any user who becomes a member of that group automatically inherits the privileges of that group. As mentioned earlier, default groups are created for you automatically when OracleAS Portal is installed—for instance, PORTLET_PUBLISHERS (users who can place portlets on a page) and PORTAL_DEVELOPERS (users who can create new portlets)—but you are certainly not limited to those. Most administrators will create groups of end users (such as "HR" or "C-Level") that give end users various privileges to do their daily work with the portal.

It is also the portal administrator's responsibility to maintain system settings concerned with, for instance, allowing users to create their own portal pages, specifying file quotas to limit the amount of content uploaded to the portal, allowing users to register themselves (create their own accounts), applying patches, configuring Ultra Search parameters, and monitoring performance. In some instances, it will be the administrator's job to register new providers as developers create them. All of these advanced responsibilities are discussed in Chapters 9 and 10.

Exercises

The exercises in this chapter don't require any technical skills. Rather, they are intended to show some of the "soft" skills you may require when working on an OracleAS Portal project. While other languages have business modeling tools such as UML, those tools don't translate easily to OracleAS Portal development. In Chapter 8, Business Process Execution Language (BPEL) is discussed—while in its infancy, it provides a good first step to establishing a formal development methodology and business model process—but in most cases, OracleAS Portal portlets and content management pages are developed in an informal manner. For this reason, the examples in this chapter don't have a "right" answer.

In every install of OracleAS Portal, there is a user in the infrastructure database named PORTAL_DEMO. We will be using that user and the objects defined in that schema to perform the exercises.

- Exercise 1: Drawing on the tables in the PORTAL_DEMO schema, try to identify what information would be useful for a dashboard application. A dashboard application can be thought of as a user interface that organizes and presents information in a way that is easy to read. The name refers to the fact that it can sometimes look like the dashboard of a car. Again, there is no "right" or "wrong" answer to this question.

- Exercise 2: Since the PORTAL_DEMO schema is fairly limited, download the Ch02_scripts.sql file from the author's Web site (http://www.oski-oracle.info) and add the tables and data to your PORTAL_DEMO schema. Look at the tables and see what would be good candidates for inclusion in a dashboard application.

Summary

OracleAS Portal is a mature development and content management environment that requires numerous technical skills to implement effectively. While it is certainly possible for a single person to handle all of the technical requirements, it is much more common to divide the different types of responsibilities among multiple employees. This chapter attempts to outline the basic technical responsibilities needed to work with OracleAS Portal efficiently.

PART II

Page Design and Content Management

CHAPTER 3

OracleAS Portal Page Design

In the Java development world, there is a common framework for developing Java-based Web applications. This framework is called MVC, which stands for model-view-controller. The thought behind the MVC framework is this: by separating the major parts of an application, that is, the code that interacts with a data source (the *model* part) from the code that handles users interaction (the *view* part) from the code that contains the business logic of the application (the *controller* part), development, modification, and testing of the application is greatly simplified. While there are other development frameworks available, the MVC framework is one of the most popular ones today.

What does this have to do with OracleAS Portal page design? The MVC framework allows large projects to be divided among developers with differing skill sets, all the while using a common development tool (if they so choose). Developers who are familiar with the data source (like an Oracle database) can focus on the model parts of the application, a developer focused on the user interface can focus on the view parts, and developers implementing business rules can focus on the controller parts. Often, a single developer is responsible for all aspects of a Web-based application, but as systems, business rules, industry regulations, and end-user requirements get more complex, this is increasingly rare. For more on the importance of the MVC framework, see the sidebar "The MVC Framework."

In the same way, OracleAS Portal provides tools within its development environment to support declarative-based development, page design, and content management. By separating the page design from the development of portlets, OracleAS Portal implements its own version of the MVC paradigm: you develop portlets using the OracleAS Portal wizards to model the data source(s) and handle the business logic for the portlet, effectively taking care of the *M* and *C* parts of the MVC framework. The page design function of OracleAS Portal handles the *V* part.

It is important to note that there is no rigid delineation between the model-controller part of portlet development and the view part of OracleAS Portal page design. Portlet developers can, for example, use JavaScript or formatting conditions built into the OracleAS Portal wizards to change how portlets are presented to the end user, which affects the view part of the MVC framework. Page designers can also set up their pages to accept parameters that can then be used to affect what is displayed in a portlet, which affects the controller part of the MVC framework. In Chapters 7 and 8, you will see that when using Oracle JDeveloper to create Java-based portlets, the developer has full control over how the data is presented to the end user. The Portal add-in for Oracle JDeveloper will generate a user interface

The MVC Framework

You may be thinking, why is the model part of the MVC framework given such importance? If you are a PL/SQL developer, you know that modeling database structures in your code is as simple as declaring variables using the %TYPE or %ROWTYPE attributes. In object-oriented languages like Java, mapping objects to relational database elements is a lot more complicated. There is also the concept of persistence, defined as the process of having data outlive the object that created it. As Java objects are no longer needed, they are de-allocated from memory; in a complex application, how do you preserve the data you may have manipulated in one of your application's forms? These are very complex issues for a developer working on a relational database-driven Web application. There are persistence frameworks available to help developers handle the tasks associated with issues like these. Two common ones are Hibernate and Oracle's offering: Toplink. As part of Oracle's Java Integrated Development Environment, Oracle JDeveloper, a developer framework called Application Developer Framework (ADF) also handles much of this complexity for you. ADF is discussed in Chapters 7 and 8.

(usually a JSP page) that can then be modified by the developer. The latest version (as of May 2007) of the Oracle JDeveloper development tool (now referred to as Oracle WebCenter) has the portal development wizards built in.

As you will see in Chapter 4, you are no longer limited to using the OracleAS Portal tools to design and enhance your pages. You can do all of your page design from within the OracleAS Portal environment if you so choose, but there are some exciting new enhancements in OracleAS Portal 10.1.4 that allow you to design pages that give your end users an enhanced Web experience.

Pages and Page Groups

A page in OracleAS Portal is where developers and content managers place portlets and content for end users to work with. When you type in the URL to get to your portal, an OracleAS Portal page is displayed. After you log in and navigate to places where you can create portlets, add content, administer users, or create pages, you are viewing OracleAS Portal pages.

NOTE

Out of the box, OracleAS Portal contains prebuilt pages and portlets for you to use. These are called "seeded" pages and portlets. There are seeded portlets like a Login portlet and a Search portlet that you can place on any of the pages you create. It is less common to use one of the existing seeded pages in your portal, but you could if you wanted to. A far more common thing to do is to take the structure of an existing page by copying it and modifying it.

As with the OracleAS Portal wizards that are used in declarative development, OracleAS Portal page design is handled through OracleAS Portal. In Chapter 4, we will see how to use a non–OracleAS Portal page design tool such as Dreamweaver to design portal pages, but even in this scenario, we need to use the OracleAS Portal design pages to define the page first.

If you haven't done so already, log in to your portal. In order to create pages, you need certain privileges. Without those privileges, the options to create and modify pages will not be available to you.

This is a very important concept to note in all aspects of your interactions with OracleAS Portal: If you don't have the necessary privileges in OracleAS Portal to perform an action, the pages, portlets, and links associated with that action are simply not displayed. You won't see a message like "You do not have the necessary privilege to perform this action." This can be frustrating for new users of OracleAS Portal. In the case that the screen you are viewing in your portal does not match the screen shots in this book, most likely it is a permission issue. Talk to your portal administrator or see Chapter 10 for more information.

CAUTION

The portal user has all privileges in OracleAS Portal, so you could log in as that user, but do so with caution. Since the portal user has all privileges, you can do things that will make your portal unusable. For DBAs reading this, logging in to OracleAS Portal as the portal user is like logging in to a database as the sys user. It is also not a good idea to be the portal user when you start development, as complications can arise when it comes time to move parts of your portal from a development environment to a test or production environment. Moving portal pieces from and to different environments is discussed in Chapter 9.

If necessary, create a user in OracleAS Portal (or have your Portal administrator do it) and grant that user DBA privileges. After creating that user, log out, and then back in as the user you just created.

In Chapter 1, the concept of the one-to-many relationship was discussed. To quickly review, Oracle uses the one-to-many relationship in many places within OracleAS Portal. These relationships between OracleAS Portal elements provide the following benefits:

- It allows administrators to perform bulk operations on many elements (such as move, delete, or exports) at once.
- It gives administrators the ability to define attributes at the parent level that can cascade down to all child elements associated with that parent.
- It makes the administration of privileges and security much easier. A privilege can be assigned to a parent element and all child elements associated with that parent will automatically inherit those privileges. Individual children can also override those privileges to give administrators an even greater level of security.

The one-to-many relationship that is important here is the one between *page groups* and *pages.* In this relationship, the page group is the parent and the pages are the children. Before you can create a page, there must be an existing page group. When a page group is created, a special page is created for that page group automatically. This special page is called the *root page.* You can create, modify, and delete other pages for this page group, but you cannot delete the root page. For most of the exercises in this book, we will be using a page group called "Dashboard_1."

Page Groups and Pages

You can think of a page group as a way of organizing the pages in your portal. It is common to set up page groups either by application or by the groups within your organization who will be accessing the pages. For example, you may have a page group called HR for all of the pages that are related to Human Resources in your portal. You might also have a page group called Inventory that has all of the pages with portlets on them that are related to inventory and inventory management. By taking time to organize your portal pages up front, you can save yourself a lot of time later on when it comes time to set up your users and privileges.

There are two ways to get to the page design screen within OracleAS Portal. One method gives you the opportunity to create a new page group; the other does not. After logging in, click the Build tab on the top right of the page. In Figure 3-1, the main part of the screen is devoted to working with existing page groups. Here, you can use the drop-down box to select what page group you wish to work with, and you can create or modify pages, styles, templates, categories, perspectives, item types, page types, or attributes.

NOTE

All of the items under the heading Layout & Appearance are discussed later in this chapter. The items under Content Attribution are discussed in Chapter 5.

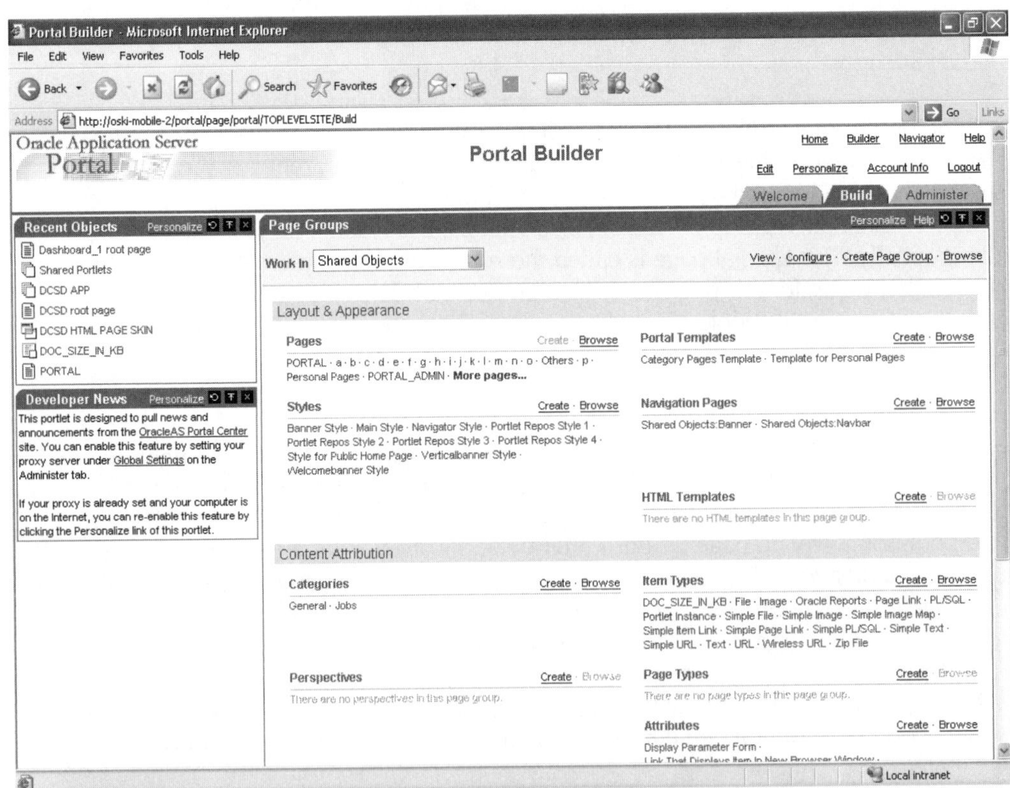

FIGURE 3-1 *The Portal Builder page*

If this is a new installation of OracleAS Portal, you will see three page groups in the Work In drop-down box: Portal Design-Time Pages, Portlet Repository, and Shared Objects. If this is not a new installation, you will see these page groups plus any more that you or your team have created. The Portal Design-Time Pages are the seeded pages that developers, content managers, and administrators use to build and administer your portal. The page you are currently looking at is one of the Portal Design-Time Pages. The Portlet Repository is a special group that allows you to see a page with a selected portlet on it. From here, you select a portlet and a page is temporarily created with that portlet on it. This is not a common use of OracleAS Portal; most likely, developers will create portlets, create pages, and then place the portlets on a page manually. The final seeded page group is called Shared Objects. When one of the categories in Figure 3-1 (styles, templates, types, etc.) is created in a page group, it is only available to pages within that page group. Anything created in the Shared Objects page group becomes accessible to all page groups.

TIP

The portlet repository page group is there to allow developers and page designers to organize the portlets in any way they choose. Changing the page hierarchy and/or moving portlets around will change the portlet selection window when adding portlets to pages. This allows developers and designers to tailor the portlet selection experience in any way they want. The fact that you can preview the portlet directly in from the repository page is an additional benefit.

Since we are unable to create page groups here, it is time to explore the second way of getting to our design pages (users with the right privileges can create a page group directly on the builder page). Click on the Navigator link in the top right of the portal page. In Figure 3-2, you'll see the Portal Navigator. From the Portal Navigator you can create Page Groups, Pages, all of the items associated with pages (Styles, Items, etc.), Providers (which, in the one-to-many relationships we've seen so far, are the parents to individual portlets), Portlets, and Provider Groups. You can also query, create, and modify database objects in the infrastructure database (provided that you have the necessary permissions, of course). Since the Portal Navigator is so flexible, most developers, page designers, and content managers do most of their work here, although you can certainly use the Portal Builder if you are more comfortable with that. You'll notice that there are no administration functions (create users/groups, etc.) here, so administrators will do most of their work in the Portal Builder.

Click on the Page Groups tab if it's not already selected. Here, you'll see a list that corresponds to the drop-down box in Figure 3-1. Click the Create New Page Group link in the top right. You are taken to a simple wizard that asks you for the name of your page group. As mentioned earlier, creation of a page group will also automatically create a root page associated with this page group. The Default Language drop-down box will contain only English unless you have installed other language packs. Type **Dashboard_1** in the Display Name field and click Create. You will see a screen similar to Figure 3-2.

What just happened? After you specified the name of the page group, the page group itself was created, the root page for the page group was created, and you were taken to the Edit page for the root page. Click the Navigator link in the top right—you will see a new page group called "Dashboard_1."

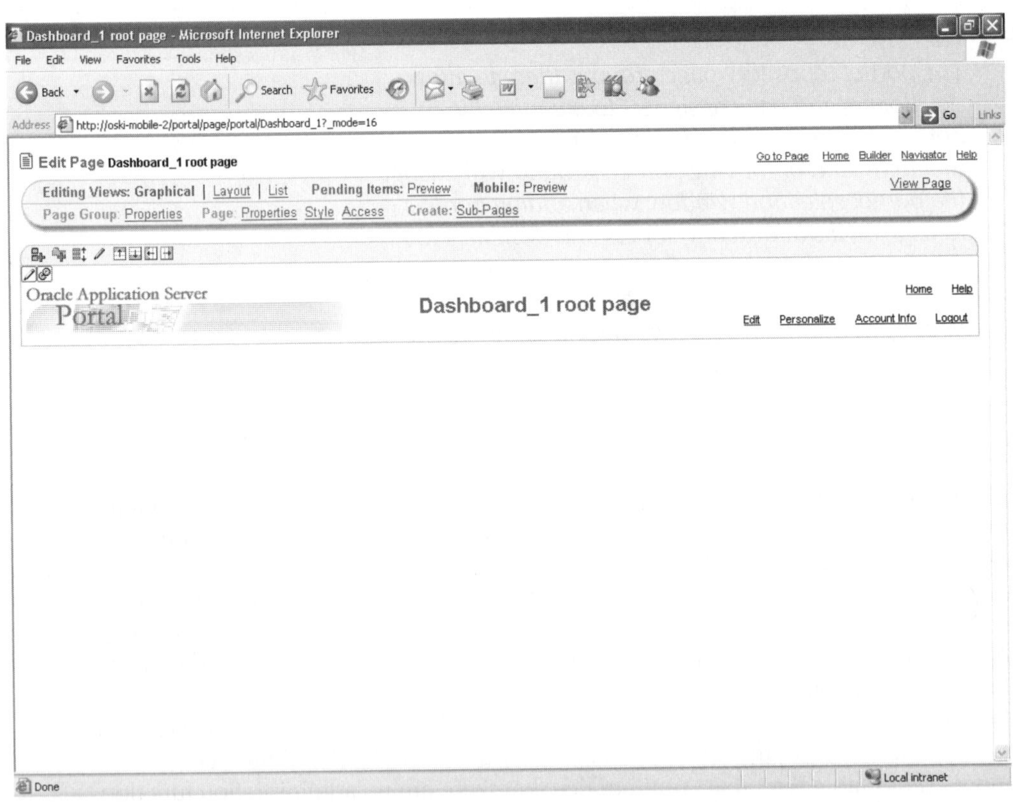

FIGURE 3-2 *The Edit page for the Dashboard_1 root page in Graphical mode*

NOTE

You may be wondering where all of these things are created. All of it is created and stored in the infrastructure database of your Oracle Application Server installation. The infrastructure database holds three basic pieces of information: 1) security information from the LDAP server installed with Oracle Application Server, 2) clustering information for the instances of the Oracle Application Server, and 3) Portal information—content, templates, page design, etc.

Clicking the Dashboard_1 link shows all of the OracleAS Portal objects that are associated with that page group:

- **Pages** This link lists all of the subpages associated with this page group. Click that link now. You'll notice that no pages are displayed. As an unusual quirk of OracleAS Portal, you cannot edit the root page from here. The only way to edit the root page is to go up one level (you can do this by clicking the Page Groups link in the top left of the page in the breadcrumb menu) and then click the Edit Root Page link in the center of the page next to the page group you are interested in.
- **Portal Template** This link allows you to create a template that can be used to create other pages quickly and easily. For example, you can create a portal template that has your company logo along the top of the page and a legal disclaimer at the bottom. You can then use that page template to create other pages without having to go through the effort of defining the logo and legal information over and over again.
- **HTML Templates** This is one of the most exciting new features of OracleAS Portal 10.1.4. By using HTML Templates, you can use a page design tool like Dreamweaver to create your pages and use them in OracleAS Portal with minimal modification. There are two types of HTML Templates: HTML Page Skins, which are used to add a "wrapper" of HTML around a page, and HTML Content Layouts, which are used to format a region. HTML Content Layouts are named a little misleadingly, as they can be used for regions that contain content and regions that contain portlets.

NOTE
Regions will be discussed shortly, but for now, understand that regions are parts of a page that can be defined to hold either content or portlets, but not both. To revisit the one-to-many relationship, regions are the children and pages are the parents.

- **Categories** As your portal grows, you may have large amounts of content. Categories are use to help classify content that users can search through. A particular piece of content (referred to, in Oracle's documentation, as an "item") can only belong to one category.
- **Navigation Pages** A navigation page is a special type of page that can be added to other pages to provide a consistent set of navigational elements. These pages differ from other pages in that they are excluded from searches and bulk actions performed on pages in the page group. Although you can add content or portlets to a navigation page, the idea is to add navigation pages to other pages.
- **Perspectives** Perspectives are very similar to categories in the sense that they help organize the content in your portal. The key difference between the two is that an item can belong to multiple perspectives. Oracle separates these two classifications by saying that categories help organize items according to their content, while perspectives organize items according to who might be interested in them. For instance, you may have a technical note for one of your software products. You can set up a perspective for the product and another one for the operating system it runs on. The technical document could then be associated with two perspectives: "Product *x* version 2.0" and "Red Hat Enterprise Server 4.*x*." End users can then use perspective filters in the Advanced Search portlet (a seeded portlet available for you to place on your pages) to narrow their search automatically to the perspectives they are interested in.
- **Styles** Styles define visual attributes of your pages and the things placed on them such as portlets, items, tabs, etc. Each one of the things you can place on a page has further attributes you can define for your style. As an example, for portlets, you can define the portlet header color; the color, font, font size, and font style of the text in the portlet header; the subheader colors and text attributes; etc. If the developer of the portlet has defined

things like these and the page designer has also defined a style for the page, the page style will override the developer's settings.

- **Attributes** An attribute is an element that takes a value and is associated with an object, such as an item, a region, a page. An example of such an element is Author, whose value is typically the name of the object creator. Typically, an attribute value is provided by a user, though there are some attributes that provide their own default values. For example, the Publish Date attribute has a default value of the current date and time. In most cases, users can revise an attribute's default value. There are two types of attributes, with all attributes falling into either one or both types: Content attributes are associated with item types and page types, and store information about an item or page, such as the associated category, description, or perspectives. These attributes are included in the add and edit screens where users can provide information about the item or page they are adding or editing. Page group administrators can create their own item types and page types and specify exactly what information they want users to supply by choosing which attributes to include. In addition, page group administrators can create their own attributes for containing extra information. Display attributes are associated with regions and display information about an item or portlet, such as the author, display name, and creation date. Page designers can choose which attributes to display in a region. Note that some content attributes, such as author and description, are also display attributes. Any custom attributes created by the page group administrator are also display attributes.
- **Page Types** Page types define the contents of a page and the information that is stored about a page. The information stored about a page is determined by the attributes of the page type. Base page types are the page types included with OracleAS Portal. Following are the five base page types:
- **Standard** Displays items and portlets.
- **URL** Displays the contents of a particular URL.
- **Mobile** Displays items and portlets in a hierarchical tree structure for viewing on a mobile device.
- **PL/SQL** Displays the results of executing PL/SQL code.
- **JSP** Displays the results of executing a JavaServer Page (JSP).

TIP

If you want to store more information than the default page types allow, you can create a custom page type. You base a custom page type on one of the base page types. The custom page type automatically inherits all of the base page type's attributes. After creation of a custom page type, developers can edit it to add attributes that are specific to your requirements.

- **Item Types** Item types define the content of an item and the information that is stored about an item. Items in OracleAS Portal are based on item types. Items are one of the basic components of a portal page. The information stored about an item is determined by the attributes associated with the item type.
- **Base Item Types** Base item types are the item types included with OracleAS Portal. There are two types of base item types. Content item types allow users to add content (for example, images, documents, or text) to a page. Navigation item types allow users to add navigational elements (for example, a login/logout link, basic search box, or a list of objects) to a page. Base content item types include
- **Base File** Uploads a file and stores it in the page group.
- **Base Image Map** Uploads an image and allows the contributor to identify areas within the image that users can click to go to different URLs.
- **Base Image** Uploads an image and stores it in the page group.
- **Base PL/SQL** Executes PL/SQL code and displays the results.
- **Base Page Link** Links to another page in the page group.
- **Base Text** Displays text (up to 32KB).
- **Base URL** Links to another Web page, Web site, or document.
- **Base Item Link** Links to another content item (file, text, URL, image, and the like) within a page group and displays the content of that item or a link to the content, depending on the source's display option.

- **Base Item Placeholder** Identifies where the content from items that use a Portal Template display in relation to the rest of the template content. Select default content for the Item Placeholder; choose from file items of type text/html or text/plain, text items, PL/SQL items, and URL items.

Base navigation item types include the following

- **Portal Smart Link** Adds a smart link (and associated image) to the page. A smart link is a link that users can click to access areas of the portal quickly, such as Account Information, Advanced Search, Contact Information, Help, and Home.
- **Login/Logout Link** Adds links and/or icons to the page that users can click to log in to or log out of the portal.
- **Basic Search Box** Adds a basic search box (and associated image) to the page in which users can enter search criteria. Users can specify whether users of the search box can search all page groups or only the page group specified.
- **List of Objects** Adds a list of objects (pages, categories, and perspectives) that users specify to the page. Users can choose to display this list as a drop-down list or as links (with or without associated images).
- **Portal Smart Text** Adds smart text, such as the current date, current user, or current page to the page.
- **Object Map Link** Adds a map of objects available in the portal.
- **Page Path** Adds the page path to the page. Users can choose the number of levels for the path, and the character that separates the path levels.
- **Page Function** Adds a page function to the page. If there are no page functions associated with the current page, this item type is not displayed.

The base content item types are not actually available for users to add to pages. Instead OracleAS Portal provides extended item types based on the base content items. These include

- File and Simple File
- Simple Image

- Image and Simple Image Map
- PL/SQL and Simple PL/SQL
- Page Link and Simple Page Link
- Text and Simple Text
- URL and Simple URL
- Zip File
- Simple Item Link
- Item Placeholder

If these extended item types do not provide enough flexibility, you can further extend most of them to meet your requirements, provided you have the appropriate privileges. To extend these item types, you must have at least the page group privileges Manage Classifications and View on the Shared Objects page group. You can add different attributes to the item types to store exactly the information that you want. Developers and designers can also add calls to PL/SQL and HTTP procedures and even pass attributes to the parameters of those procedures.

Edit the root page of the "Dashboard_1" page group by clicking the Page Groups link in the top-left corner, and then clicking the Edit Root Page link to the right of the Dashboard_1 link. Along the top left of the page, there are three links next to the Editing Views: label: Graphical, Layout, and List. Clicking each one of these links gives you a different way of editing your page. Each of these editing views has its advantages and drawbacks:

- **Graphical** As you place portlets and content on the page in this view, they will display along with some extra editing icons and links. The advantage of this view is that you can see a rough estimate of what your page will look like to end users while you are editing it. The drawback of this mode is that you cannot do bulk actions such as delete or move a bunch of portlets and content with one action. Also, for pages with many portlets and much content, the amount of information on the screen can become overwhelming.

- **Layout** Layout mode does not display the portlets or content, but rather a one-line title of said portlet or content (Figure 3-3). This view can be very useful for bulk operations such as moving or deleting content and portlets and can make the design of complicated pages easier.
- **List** List mode is great for content (Figure 3-4). You can move, delete, and expire content easily as well as get more detailed information on the content such as author or date added. List mode has no functionality to administer portlets.

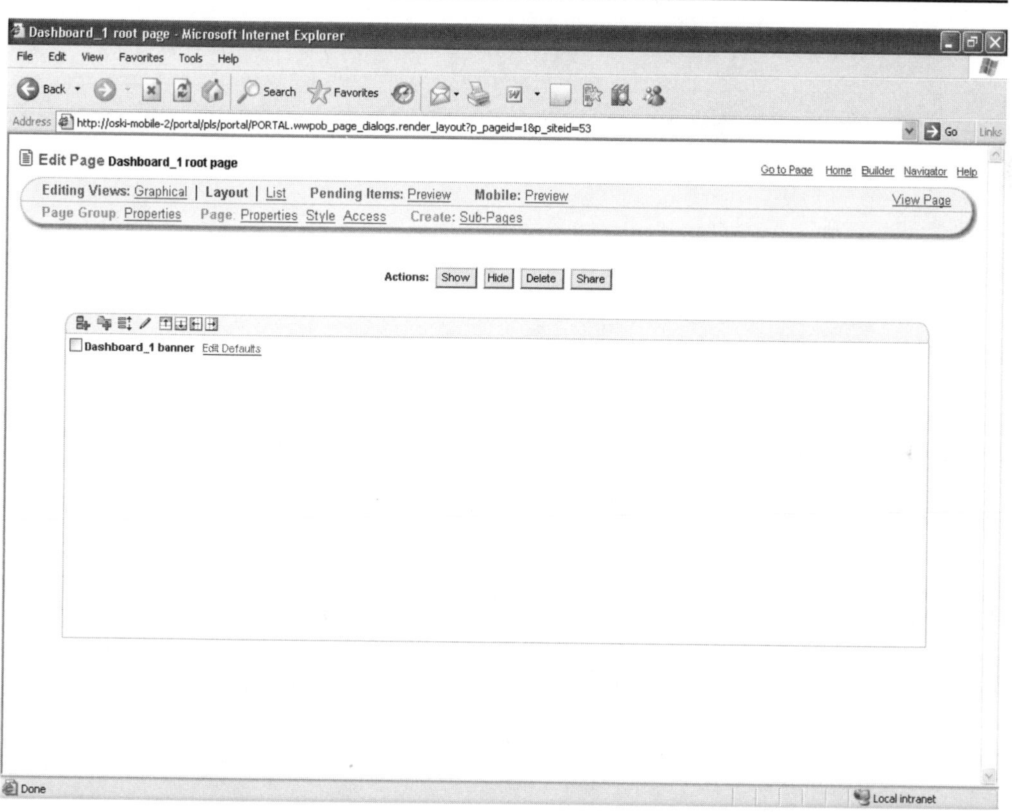

FIGURE 3-3 *The root page in Layout mode*

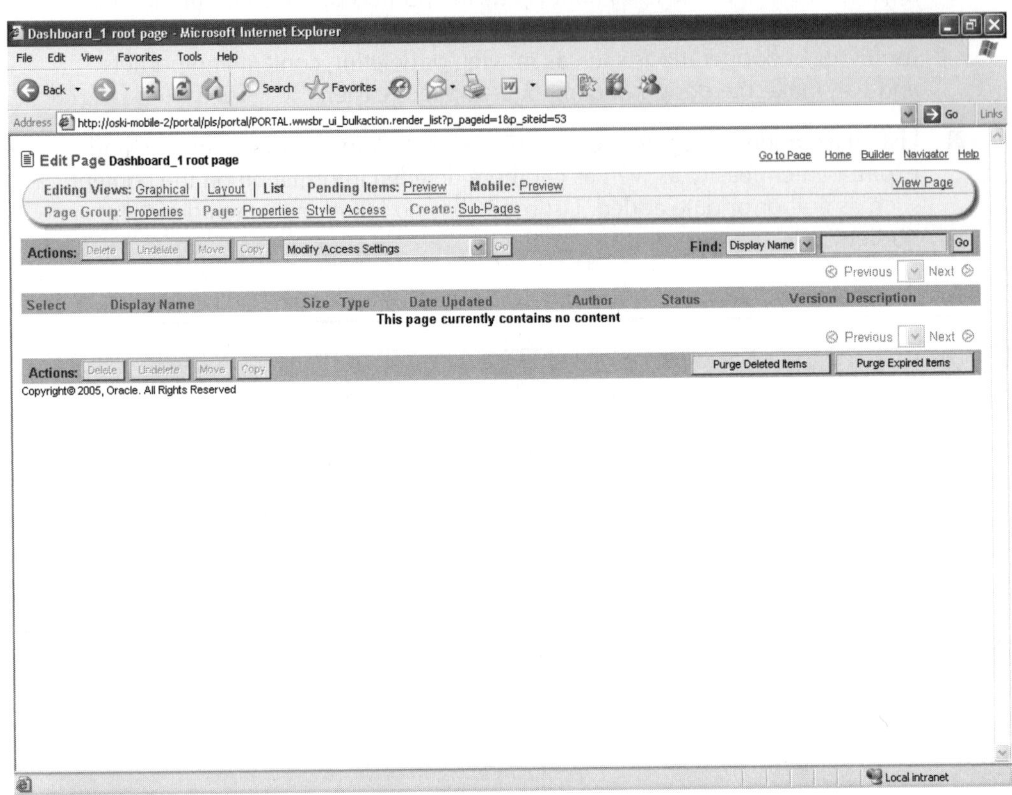

FIGURE 3-4 *The root page in List mode*

Page and Page Group Properties

Click the Graphical link on the top right of the page if you haven't already done so. Just below the Editing Views line on the top right is a line with five links: Page Group Properties, Page Properties, Style, Access, and Create Sub-Pages. The following sections describe the first two of these at length.

Page Group Properties

This link will take you to a tabbed screen where you can define various properties for the page (Figure 3-5). The tabs include

- **Main** This tab gives you the opportunity to change the name of the page, the display name (what displays in the Portal Navigator), the amount of content that can be added to the page group, whether users can change page styles, and whether tab persistence (whether OracleAS Portal "remembers" what tab was last selected when you re-visit a page) is active.

- **Configure** This tab gives page designers the ability to set various properties for the page group:
- **Page Defaults** Displays options for defining a default style (styles are discussed at the end of the chapter), defining a default navigation page, and defining a default template for all pages in the page group.
- **Types and Classification** Displays options for defining the types of pages permitted in the page group, the types of items that can be used when adding content to any of the pages in the page group, and the categories and perspectives that an item can be assigned to.
- **Edit Mode** Displays options for what edit modes are available, what the default edit mode for a page should be, and the number of items and attribute columns of those items that should be displayed in list mode.
- **View Mode** Displays the option of whether to define a default item that toggles between showing and not showing content on a page. See the sidebar "More about View Mode."
- **Parameters and Events** Displays the option to toggle between allowing and restricting parameters and events for all pages in the page group.
- **Content Management Event Framework** Enable this option to allow the integration of external processes into the portal.

More about View Mode

View mode allows developers or designers to treat the page group more like a file system if they want to use OracleAS Portal as a deployment platform for static HTML files. This is similar to the way static Web sites work in that if the OracleAS Portal Page Engine finds an index.html file in a folder, it uses that as the page to display if the URL only goes down "into" the folder. As a developer or designer, you can enable View mode and then use "index.html" as the default item—a URL to the page will show the contents of "index.html" rather than the page itself. This is a side effect of using the page as both a container (or folder) and a display vehicle.

- **Approvals and Notifications** Use this to enable or disable item approvals and item notifications in the page group. When approvals/notifications are enabled, a new tab called Approval displays in the Edit Page Group tab set, on which you can define the approval process and specify notification recipients for the page group.
- **JSP Access** This option specifies whether JSPs can access this page group.
- **URL Rewrite Rules** This option specifies the rewrite rules for the path-based URLs in this page group.
- **Items** This tab gives you the ability to specify item versioning, whether unpublished items are retained or displayed, how long the New icon will appear next to new content, whether to purge old content, and whether to enable the rich text editor when adding text items.
- **Translations** This tab is only meaningful if you have multiple languages installed. You can specify what languages you would like displayed and how the page translates to that language. Languages other than English are installed by using the Oracle Application Server installation program.
- **Access** This tab allows you to define who has access to a page and what type of access that user has. This is a confusing concept for many beginning OracleAS Portal developers and administrators. The access privileges at this level grant access only to the page, not necessarily to the content or portlets on the page. As an example, I can grant View privilege to user Kelsey on the page, but a portlet placed on that page may not have given user Kelsey the privilege to see it. When trying to view the page, user Kelsey sees a blank page. She has privileges on the page, but not on the portlet that is placed on the page. While the transparency of OracleAS Portal's security mechanism is a blessing to developers and administrators, it can be frustrating to new users accustomed to No access granted error messages. Security is discussed in Chapter 10.
- **Approval** This tab is only visible if Approval and Notifications has been selected in the Items tab. This tab allows administrators to set up a list of users (or groups of users) who need to review and approve a piece of content before it becomes available on the OracleAS Portal page. Approvals are discussed in Chapter 5.

Page Properties

These properties, which have many similarities to the Page Group properties, apply only to a specific page (Figure 3-6). Where Page properties duplicate Page Group

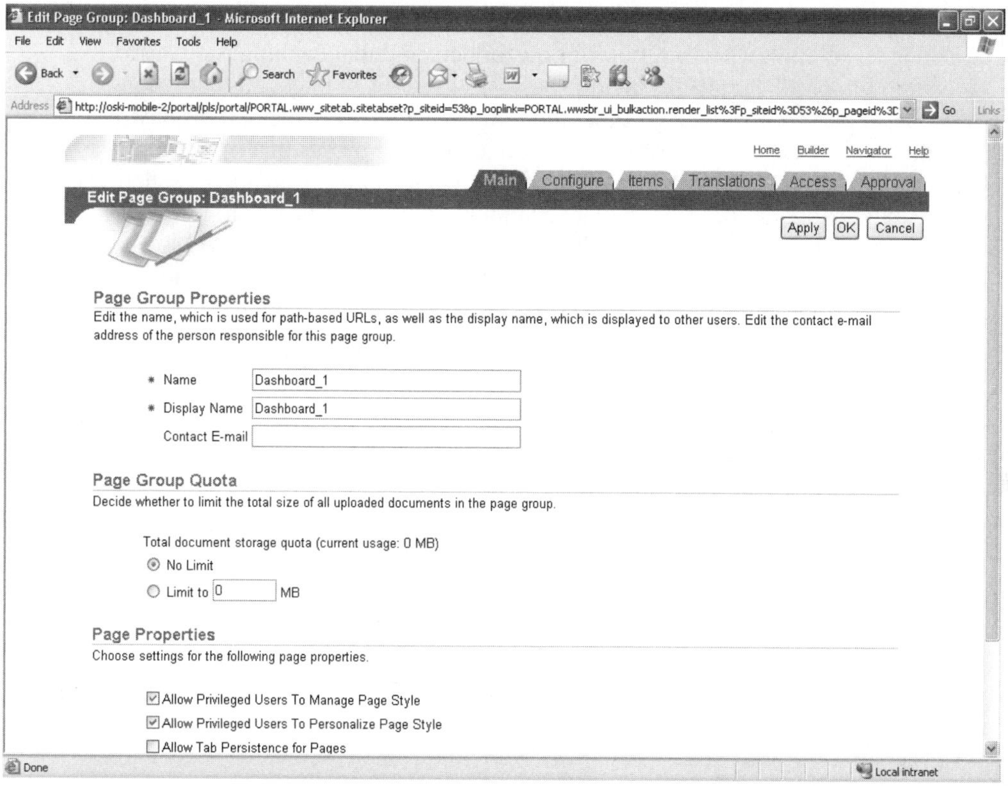

FIGURE 3-5 *The Page Group Properties page*

properties, properties set at the Page level will override those set at the Page Group level.

- **Main** This tab displays options that can be used to change the page name, change the caching rules, or set a time-out for page assembly. For more information about caching, see the "What Is Caching?" sidebar.
- **Template** This tab provides the option to use a template for the page. This is an example of the potential for Page properties to override Page Group properties. If a template is specified at the Page Group level and is not specified here, this page will inherit the template from the Page Group. If a template is specified at the Page Group level and a different one is specified here, the one specified here will override the Page Group template setting.

What Is Caching?

Caching is a complex subject, but for now, understand that caching is a way to speed up OracleAS Portal by "saving" previous versions of pages so that when they are requested after the first time, the OracleAS Portal engine can display the "saved" version without having to reconstruct all of the pieces that make up the portal page. There is also a component of the Oracle Application Server called, surprisingly enough, Web Cache that separately helps this process. To further complicate matters, most browsers (like Microsoft's Internet Explorer and Mozilla's Firefox) have caching mechanisms built into them also. Caching, performance tuning, and monitoring of OracleAS Portal are discussed in Chapter 9.

- **Style** This tab provides the same functionality as the Template tab, except in relation to styles.
- **Access** Like the Template and Style tabs, this tab allows you to define access privileges for the page. Again, it can be used to inherit or override settings from the Page Group.
- **Items** This tab allows you to set item versioning options, the ability to define a default template for items, and whether to define a default region on the page to hold items and WebDAV options.

NOTE
WebDAV stands for Web-Based Distributed Authoring and Versioning. It is a set of extensions to the Hypertext Transfer Protocol (HTTP) that allows users to collaboratively edit and manage files on remote Web servers. By adhering to this standard, OracleAS Portal allows any program that is "WebDAV-aware" to communicate with OracleAS Portal. Oracle provides a WebDAV tool called Oracle Drive that makes the transfer of files to OracleAS Portal repositories simple. Oracle Drive is discussed in Chapter 5.

- **Optional** The attributes defined on this page allow you to define the entire page as a portlet (which can then be placed on other pages) and to set keywords, categories, and perspectives (which can help users search through large portal sites). You can also define an image to represent the page that is used in certain portlets, listing all of the objects in a portal and whether to display subpages of a page.

- **Parameters** Page parameters are used to pass values to a page. Parameters can be used to change information displayed in accordance with where the page is called from or who is viewing the page.
- **Events** An event is a user action defined by a portlet developer. User actions include clicking a link, a button, or some other control on a Web page. A page designer can specify that an event forces the reloading of the current page or the loading of another page, optionally passing parameters to the newly loaded page. A portlet's events are specified in the provider.xml file (see the sidebar "The provider.xml File").

The Remaining Links

The remaining three of the five links mentioned on the Dashboard_1 root page design screen are as follows:

- **Page: Style** Takes you to the Style tab on the Page Properties page.
- **Page: Access** Takes you to the Access tab on the Page Properties page.
- **Create: Sub-Pages** Takes you to a wizard where you can create a sub-page (a page that inherits its attributes from the root page and Page Group).

The provider.xml File

Chapter 1 described Oracle's one-to-many philosophy when designing OracleAS Portal. In the context of portlets, every portlet must be associated with a provider. In this scenario, the provider is the parent (the "one" in the one-to-many relationship) and the portlets are the children. When you are ready to create a declarative portlet using the OracleAS Portal wizards, the process of creating the provider handles the creation of all of the necessary configuration files (of which the provider.xml file described here is one) behind the scenes. The provider.xml file is used to define how the provider will function. When creating Java-based portlets, you must explicitly declare the provider.xml file before deploying your application (deploying is a fancy word for moving all of the files that make up your application to the proper directories of the application server). In Chapter 7, the structure of developing Java-based portlets will be discussed and we will see how the Portal Add-in Wizard for Oracle JDeveloper handles many of the implementation details for you.

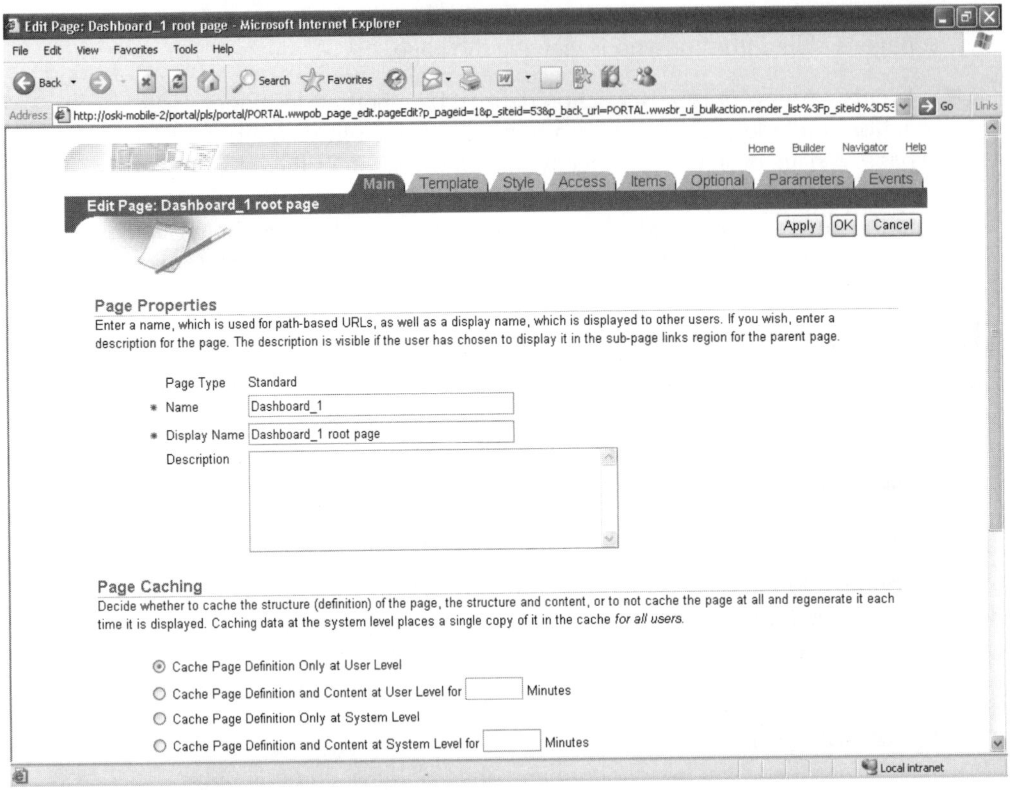

FIGURE 3-6 *The Page Properties page*

Page Design

After all of the attributes for your Page Groups and Pages have been set, it's time to start designing your OracleAS Portal page. Earlier in Figure 3-2, a new root page is displayed. There are standard elements available when editing a page in graphical mode to assist your development. Along the top of the page, there is a header that starts with "Edit Page Dashboard_1 root page." Below that, there is a rounded horizontal box with Editing Views in the top left, which contains links discussed in the preceding section of this chapter (Figure 3-7). These elements are not part of your final page. They are only visible when editing the page. To see what the page will look like to end users, click the View Page link in the top right of the page at any time. Clicking that link will show you a blank page (since we haven't added anything to it yet).

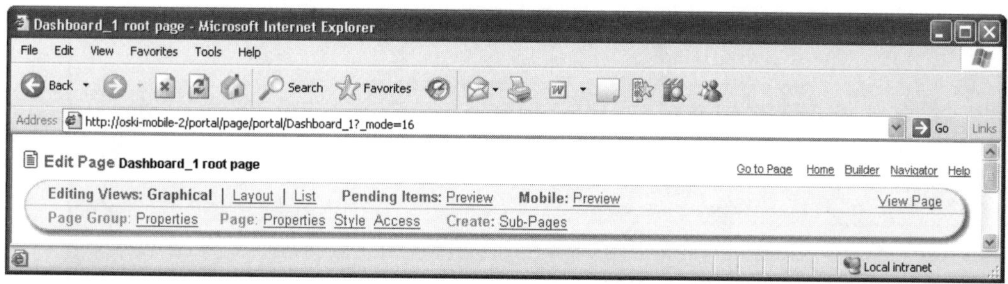

FIGURE 3-7 *Toolbar elements visible when editing an OracleAS Portal page in Graphical mode*

Below the horizontal box is a section of the page with eleven small icons on the top left, a graphic that says "Oracle Application Server Portal," a title in the middle that says "Dashboard_1 root page," and six links on the right-hand side (Figure 3-8). What is this and where did it come from?

It was mentioned earlier that a page cannot exist without a page group. It was also stated that all page groups must have at least one page associated with them, the root page. So when the page group is created, one default page is created automatically. In addition to this, another page element is created: a default navigation page. The default navigation page is given the name of <Page Group Name> banner, so in this case, if we go to the Portal Navigator and click the Dashboard_1 link, and then Navigation Pages, we'll see an entry entitled "Dashboard_1 banner." Navigation pages aren't *really* pages, per se—their intention is to be placed *on* a page. Clicking the Edit link in the middle of the page will display a graphical editing page for the navigation page that is similar to the root page we have been working with (Figure 3-9).

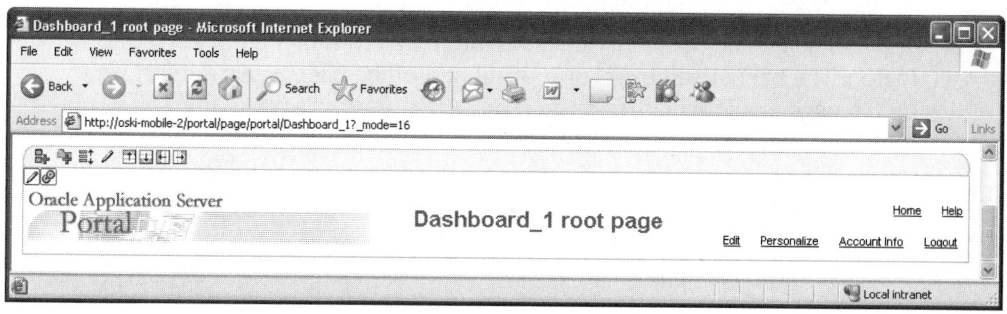

FIGURE 3-8 *The Dashboard_1 banner*

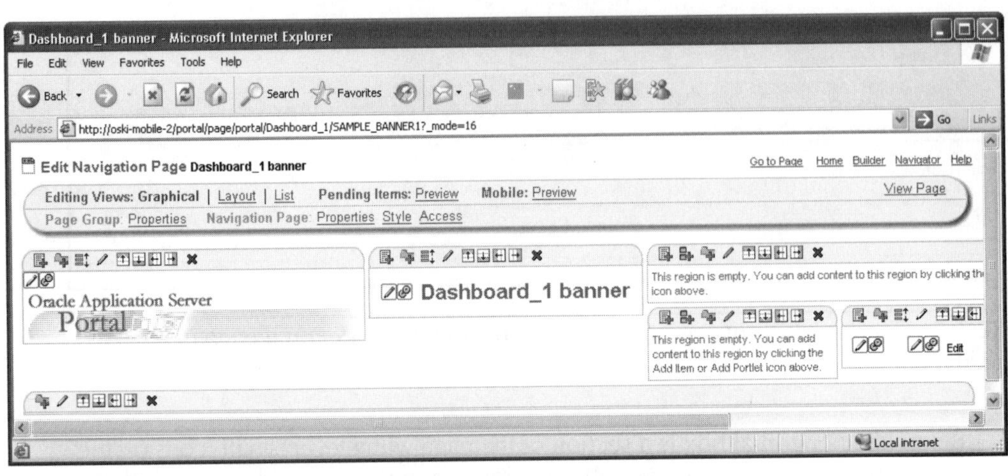

FIGURE 3-9 *The graphical editing page for the banner*

After viewing this navigation page, return to editing the root page for Dashboard_1. If you don't want to use the banner, there are several ways to dispense with it:

- You can select Page Group Properties, then the Configure tab, then the Edit link under page defaults and change "Default Navigation page" to None. This will stop the banner from being placed on all new pages created in that page group.
- You can, on that same properties page, use the radio button to select either an HTML Page Skin template or Portal Template in the Default Template section of that page. This will base all new pages for that page group on the template selected. Portal and HTML templates are discussed in Chapter 4.
- You can delete the banner by clicking the small red *X* in the top left of the region. The banner still exists and is still part of the page group—it just isn't on the page any longer.

CAUTION
If you delete the banner, you won't be able to edit the page directly any more. You can only edit it via the OracleAS Portal Navigator.

If you like the banner but want to change it (let's say, by replacing the Oracle Application Server Portal picture with your company logo), you can edit the navigation page. Any edits you make there will automatically be reflected on all of the pages to which that Navigation page has been added.

Under the banner section, there is another horizontal section with only nine icons in its top left and text that says, "This region is empty. You can add content to this region by clicking the Add Item or Add Portlet icon above." Now is a good time to discuss regions.

Region Properties

Regions are a way to divide your page into different sections. A region can divide the page horizontally or vertically, but not diagonally. You can have multiple regions on a page, and each of those regions can be defined to contain either portlets or content, but not both. Regions, like pages and page groups, have their own properties. By default, all new pages contain two regions: a region containing the banner (a navigation page, discussed in the previous section) and an empty, undefined region below it, unless you have specified an HTML Template or Portal Template in the Page Group properties.

The four icons to the left of the red *X* in the top left of the region (shown in the following illustration) give page designers the ability to create new regions on the page.

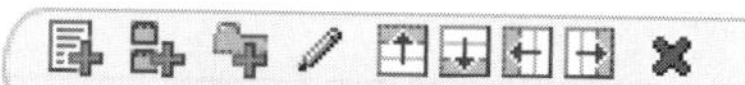

Clicking the icon just to the left of the *X* will create a new region to the right of the existing region. The OracleAS Portal Page engine will evenly divide the page so that the existing region will now occupy 50 percent of the page and the new region will occupy 50 percent of the page. Clicking the same icon (the one with the arrow pointing to the right) in either region will create a third region. All regions now occupy 33 percent of the page (Figure 3-10).

In the left-most region, click the icon with the arrow pointing down. A new region is created below with the same screen dimensions as the region above it. In effect, by dividing the first region three times, three columns were created on the page. To see the effect of this, click the icon with the arrow pointing to the right of the region in the second row. A new region is created to the right, but instead of taking up 50 percent of the entire screen, it takes up 50 percent of the column that takes up 33 percent of the entire screen (Figure 3-11).

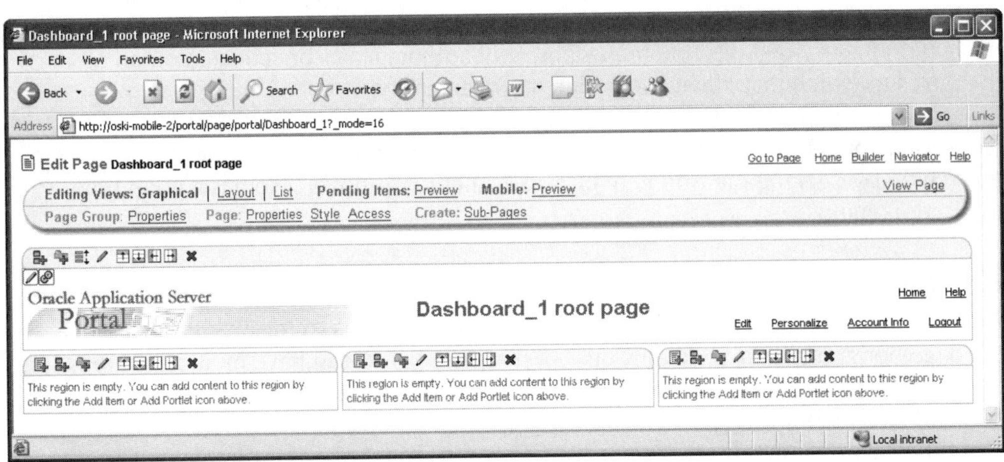

FIGURE 3-10 *The result of creating two new regions to the right of the existing region*

Remove all but one of the regions by clicking the red *X* in all of the other regions. Note how the regions automatically resize themselves as the others are deleted.

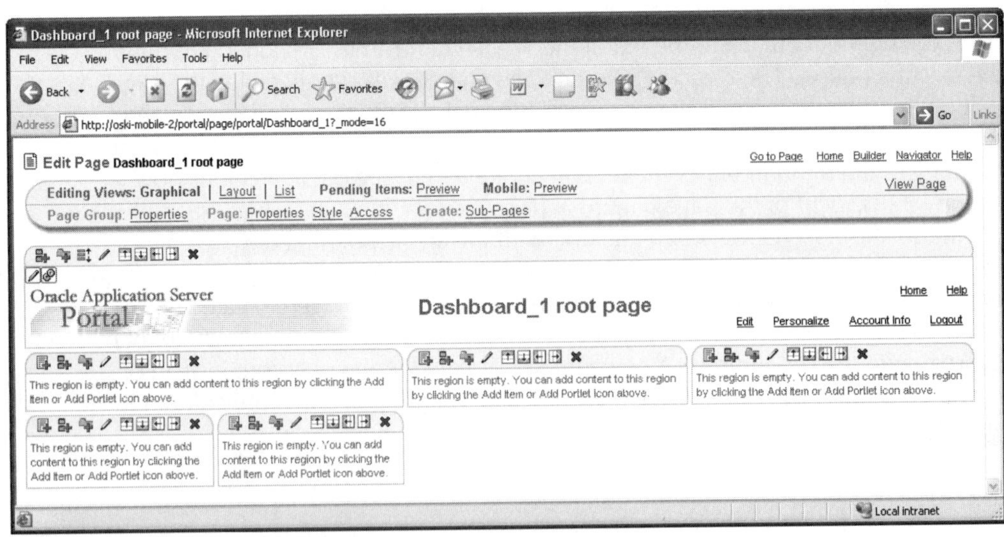

FIGURE 3-11 *Dividing regions*

We now know what the five right-most icons for each region do. Starting from the left, the icons provide the following functionality, as shown here:

- For an empty, undefined region, the icon that looks like a sheet of paper with a plus sign in front of it and the icon that looks like two small boxes with a plus sign in front of it will be visible. The first icon allows you to add an item (content); the second allows you to add a portlet. Once an item or portlet is added to a region, the region type changes to reflect the addition. Once the region is defined as a type, only the appropriate icon shows up in the graphical editing screen for the page.
- The icon that looks like a folder with a plus sign allows you to add a tab to the region. Tabs can be used to further subdivide a region. Like regions, each tab can hold items or portlets but not both, so it is possible to create a region with one tab for content and another for portlets. Tabs can hold other tabs and other regions and also have their own properties.

NOTE
One of the great challenges of working with OracleAS Portal is finding where the necessary changes need to be made in order to get your portal to do the things you want it to do. Just in terms of properties, we've seen how there are Page Group Properties, Page Properties, and Region Properties. As you work more with OracleAS Portal, finding the correct place to make modifications will become second nature.

- The icon that looks like a pencil allows designers to view and edit the properties for the region. Just like Pages and Page Groups, Regions have their own set of properties. A region has many fewer properties than a Page or Page Group, however.

Region Types

When a new region is created, it is created as an Undefined type. As mentioned earlier, a region can contain portlets or items, but not both. As soon as either an item or a portlet is placed in a region, it becomes a region of that type. You can also define a region to be of a certain type before placing anything in it by clicking the pencil icon in the region to edit its properties and manually specifying what type of region you would like it to be.

There is also a fourth type of region: a subpage links region. This is a special type of region designed to hold links to the subpages of a page. If a region is defined as this type, it will automatically be populated with links to all subpages from the page you are working on (as a designer) or viewing (as an end user).

Once a region has been defined as a particular type, designers no longer have the ability to place a different type of OracleAS Portal element in that region. To see how this works, click the Add Item icon in one of the regions on your page. Select Content Item Types and File on the first page of the Add Item Wizard. Click Next. On the Item Attributes page, click the Browse button next to the File Name box and select a file from your hard drive. Since this is just a demonstration, pick a small text file; if you don't have one available, use an editor like Notepad to create a small text file. Leave all of the other prompts the way they are and click Finish. OracleAS Portal will now copy this file from your hard drive and transfer it up to the OracleAS Portal repository. It also returns you to the page you were working on (Figure 3-12) showing a link for the text file you've added. The important thing to note here is how the region is now defined as an Item region and the icon for adding portlets is no longer available for that region.

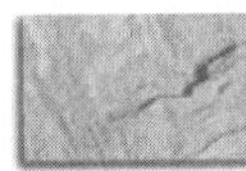

TIP
Don't worry if the screens to add items seemed complicated. Adding content is discussed in detail in Chapter 5.

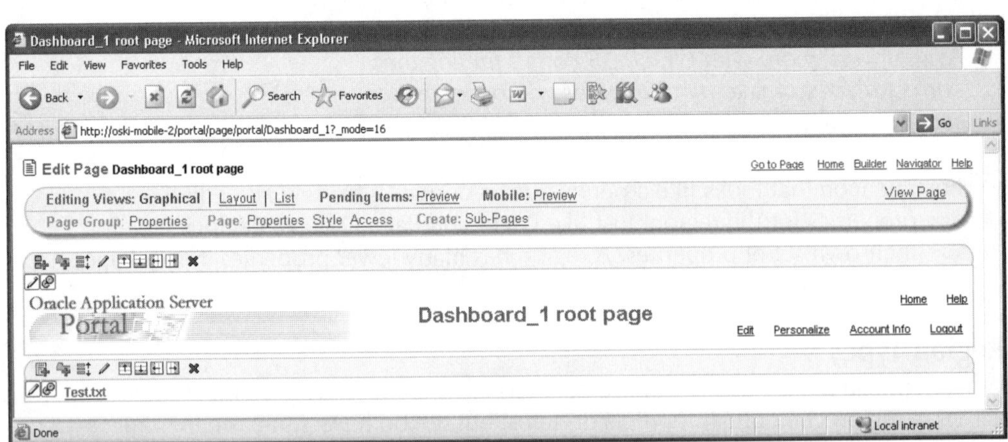

FIGURE 3-12 *The Page Design screen with an Item added to a region*

Adding Portlets to Your Pages

Portlets are reusable pieces of code that can be placed on a page. Out of the box, OracleAS Portal contains portlets that developers and designers can use. These portlets, called seeded portlets, can be used just like any portlets that developers at your site create. To add a portlet, find a region that is defined as either a portlet or an undefined region. If you don't have a region like that on your page, create a new region by clicking one of the four icons that create a new region on your page. After clicking the Add Portlet icon, you will see a page similar to Figure 3-13.

This page allows you to select a portlet from the Portlet Repository to add to your page. The Portlet Repository is where portlets are stored and organized. Out of

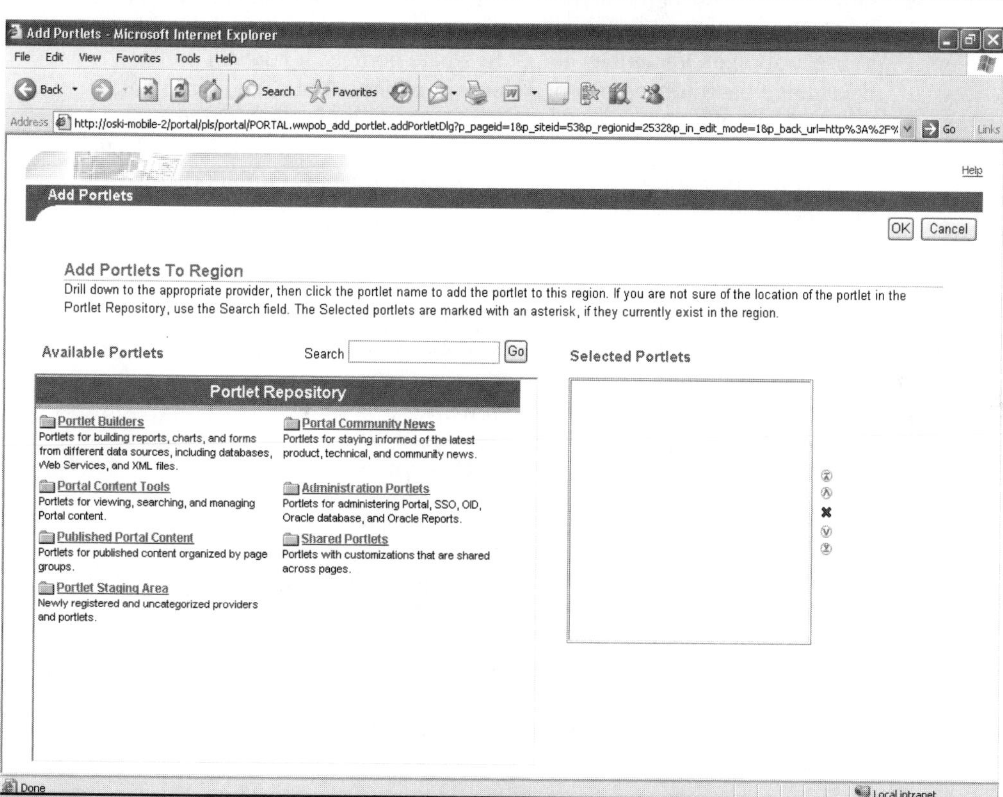

FIGURE 3-13 *The Add Portlets To Region page*

the box, OracleAS Portal provides numerous seeded portlets organized into six categories:

- **Portlet Builders** All of the screens we have been viewing (the Edit Page screen, the Add Portlet screen, the Add Item screen, etc.) are themselves OracleAS Portal pages. All of the portlets on these pages are stored here in the Portlet Builders category. Normally, a portal developer would not place a Create Portal Form or a Create Portal Report portlet on an end-user page (although you *could,* if you really wanted to), so this category may seem as if it would not be used much. There are, however, some very important seeded portlets in this category of interest to OracleAS Portal developers and page designers:
    - **OmniPortlet** As mentioned in Chapter 1, Oracle is moving away from the declarative-based OracleAS Portal wizards and encouraging developers to use tools like Oracle JDeveloper to create portlets. If you still prefer declarative-based development, Oracle provides a tool called OmniPortlet that gives developers access to some advanced OracleAS Portal features while still providing a declarative development environment. It is by selecting this link that developers get access to this functionality. OmniPortlet is discussed in detail in Chapter 6.

NOTE
Although I keep hammering away at the fact that Oracle is moving away from declarative-based development, it is important to note that the declarative wizards are still fully functional with OracleAS Portal release 10.x. This book does not discuss those wizards beyond what was covered in Chapter 1, however.

-
    - **Web Clipping** This portlet allows developers and designers to clip (copy) a Web page (or, what is more important, *part* of a Web page) and place it on the OracleAS Portal page they are designing. The clipped page can be an internal OracleAS Portal page, an internal non-OracleAS Portal page, or an external Web page. The Web Clipping portlet is a great way to assemble an OracleAS Portal page from existing sources without any programming skill needed.
    - **Survey Builder** This folder contains four seeded portlets for creating and reporting on surveys you can build into your portal. Many Web sites contain either a human-interest-type question or a question related to the relevance

of the site end users are viewing. These portlets allow you to develop a survey and run reports against those surveys.

- **Portal Community News** The portlets in this category pull information from Oracle's Portal site, http://portalcenter.oracle.com/. When you place these portlets on a page, various pieces of news and announcements are queried from Oracle's Web pages and displayed on your page.
- **Portal Content Tools** The portlets in this category perform various features related to content and content management. Some of the most useful are:
  - **The Search portlets (Advanced Search, Basic Search, Custom Search, and Saved Searches)** You can use these portlets to give your end users the ability to search though content that has been added to your site. The search capabilities of OracleAS Portal become invaluable as content is added to your site. Searching content will be discussed in detail in Chapter 5, but for now, know that the search capabilities of these portlets include the ability to search within Microsoft Word documents, Excel spreadsheets, PowerPoint presentations, and Adobe PDF Documents, among other types. There are also classifications (categories and perspectives) that give content managers further abilities to segment content and allow users to narrow their searches.
  - **Approvals (My Approval Status, My Notifications, and Pending Approvals Monitor)** These portlets play an important role in the approval of content to be displayed on a page. The page administrator can set up an approval chain which requires approval from users (or groups of users) within OracleAS Portal before a piece of content can be displayed to end users. These portlets give page designers a way of quickly constructing a page so that the users know when and if they have been assigned a piece of content to review and if an item has or has not been reviewed by those necessary for approval.
- **Administration Portlets** These portlets are used to perform administration on various parts of your portal. All of these portlets are already contained on pages that only users who are members of the portal_administrators group are allowed to view. It is unlikely that a developer or page designer would place any of these portlets on a page except where noted here. Administration portlets are divided into four subcategories:
  - **SSO/OID** This group contains the security portlets for OracleAS Portal. Under most circumstances, none of these would need to be placed on a page, other than the Login portlet, which might be placed on the first page end users would see (commonly referred to as the "landing page"). You don't have to use the seeded login portlet if you don't want to—it is fairly

common for developers to write their own. SSO (Single Sign-On) provides a mechanism for users to only have to sign in once and access data across heterogeneous systems. OID (Oracle Internet Directory) is Oracle's name for their implementation of the Lightweight Directory Access Protocol (LDAP) built into Oracle Application Server. OID and LDAP are discussed in Chapter 10.

- **Portal** This group contains portlets related to internal OracleAS Portal activities such as listing database providers or clearing the Portal page engine cache.
- **Database** This group contains portlets that interact with the infrastructure database that is installed automatically with Oracle Application Server 10*g*. There are portlets to create and change schemas, list database information, and show database storage statistics. Depending on the privileges of the OracleAS Portal user, it may be advantageous to allow direct interaction with the infrastructure database, but this functionality comes with a stern warning: by giving users the ability to modify data in the infrastructure database, you risk the possibility of data being modified that makes your OracleAS Portal (or worse, your entire application server) unusable.
- **Oracle Reports Security** This group contains portlets that allow you to set up rules for how Oracle Reports can be run within your portal. Note that this does *not* relate to the OracleAS Portal Reports Wizard briefly discussed in Chapter 1. Rather, these portlets relate to the integration of reports developed with the Oracle Reports product that is part of the Oracle Developer Suite. Integration with common Oracle development tools such as Oracle Forms, Oracle Reports, and Oracle Discoverer is discussed in Chapter 11.

- **Published Portal Content** One of the most interesting things you can do within OracleAS Portal is to check the Publish As Portlet check box in the Optional tab under the properties for a page. Checking this box allows you to treat the entire page as a portlet that can now be placed (as a portlet) onto another page. Any pages that have the Publish As Portlet check box checked will show up in this group. Navigation pages (like the banner at the top of the page that is created by default) have the Publish As Portlet check box selected by default, so they also show up in this category.
- **Shared Portlets** If appropriate, OracleAS Portal Portlets can be customized by users to their individual needs. Developers can allow or deny certain aspects of the portlet to be modified. Administrators can then allow or deny users or groups of users the ability to see and modify those customizations. The customizations are stored in the security mechanism for OracleAS

Portal, so when a user makes a customization and then logs in to OracleAS Portal from a different computer, the customizations are preserved. An example of a customization would be the ability to change the WHERE clause on a report. Users may want to customize a report to only show information for their department. These customizations can also be saved as shared portlets for other users. Any customized portlet that is saved will show up in this group.

The seventh category, Portlet Staging Area, is where portlets that you create will be stored. The portlets there are grouped by provider. If you don't know which provider the portlet you wish to add to a page is stored under, or you just don't feel like searching through the repository for the portlet you're looking for, you can always use the search box at the top of the screen.

NOTE
Providers, discussed briefly in Chapter 1 and in more detail in Chapter 7, are a way of grouping portlets together. Like all of the one-to-many relationships in OracleAS Portal (the provider being the "one" and the portlets being the "many"), any attribute defined at the provider level cascades down to the individual portlets, unless explicitly overridden at the portlet level. This mechanism makes the setting of privileges much easier.

When you click the portlet you wish to add, it appears on the left side of the screen. You have basic control as to where the portlet is placed in the region by using the up and down arrows on the right side of the Selected Portlets box, but that's about it—the OracleAS Portal page engine will do the work of arranging your portlets in the region. The red *X* on the right of the Selected Portlets box removes a portlet from the page. Select two or three of the seeded portlets and click OK.

TIP
It's important to remember that although the red X on the Add Portlets To Region page removes the portlet from the page, it is still there in the Portlet Repository.

You are returned to the Page Edit screen. In Figure 3-14, I have added the Login and Advanced Search portlets to my region. Since I'm already logged in, the Login

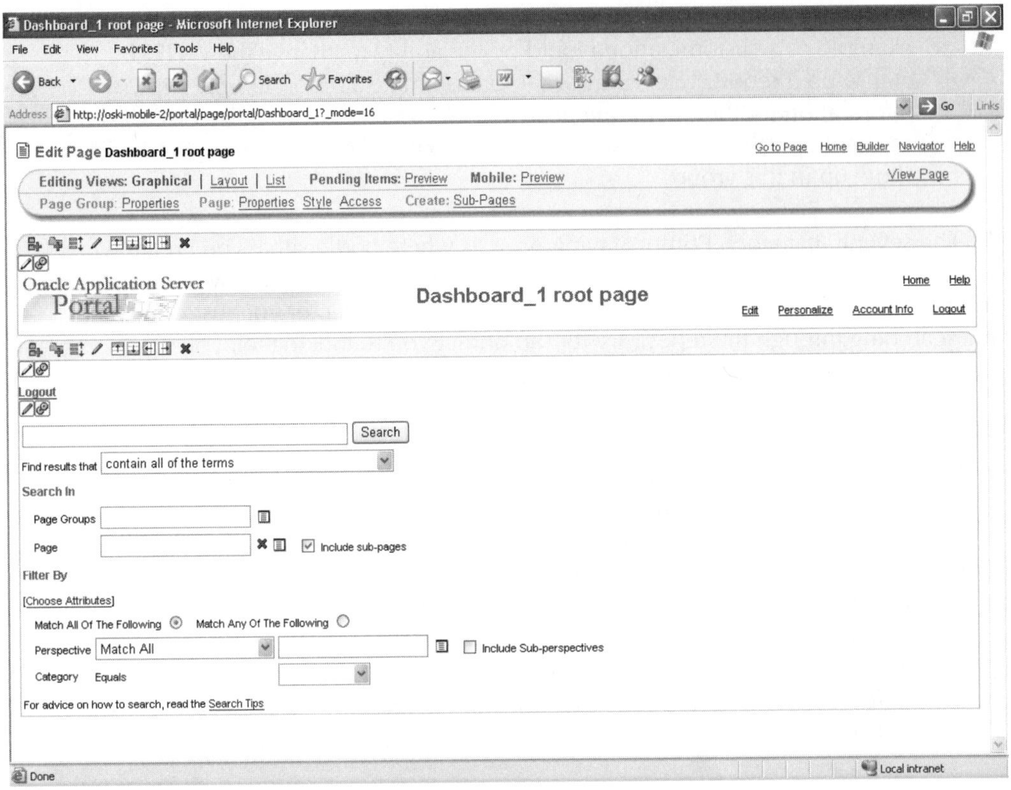

FIGURE 3-14 *An OracleAS Portal page with the Login and Search portlets on it*

portlet displays only a Logout link. If I were to make this page available to the "Public" user (i.e., a user that has not logged in to OracleAS Portal) and displayed this page before logging in, a prompt for username and password would be displayed.

Clicking the Layout link at the top left of the page brings us to the Layout display of the page (Figure 3-15). While there is certainly less information and no indication of how the final page will be displayed to end users, this page is useful when the page you are designing becomes so complicated that it becomes impossible to make sense out of it anymore. This view is also useful if the need should arise to move a portlet (or set of portlets) from one region to another. As you can see from the icons above each region, the functionality of adding and removing portlets and regions is the same here as it was when editing the page in graphical mode.

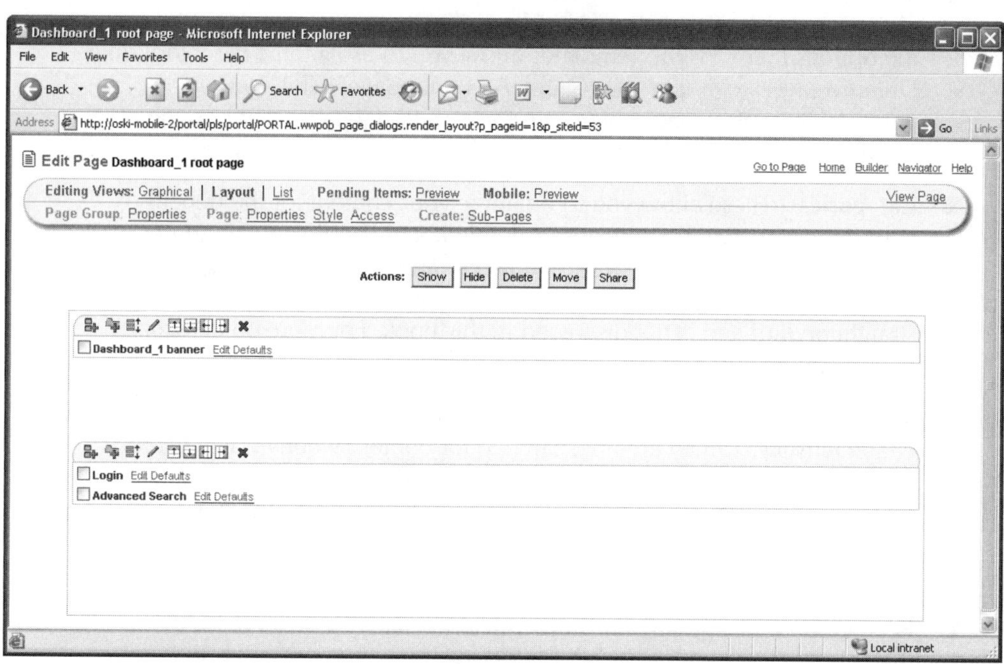

FIGURE 3-15 *The Layout version of the same page*

Other Page Elements

If you click the Navigator button in the top right of any page, then the Page Groups tab, and then the page group name (for the examples in this book, we've been using the "Dashboard_1" page group), you will be taken to a page that allows you to define other page elements that are associated with your page group:

- **Pages** This allows you to create subpages off the root page (discussed in Chapter 4).
- **Portal Templates** A template allows you to define the look and feel of a page. Subsequent pages can be created on the basis of this template, saving the page designer a great deal of work. Another powerful feature is that the application of templates to a page is dynamic, so that if a change is made to the template, all pages based on that template are immediately updated. Portal Templates are discussed in Chapter 4.

- **HTML Templates** The Portal Templates described in the preceding item give page designers a great deal of flexibility, but you are still limited to the options there. HTML Templates allow you to use a third-party tool (like Dreamweaver) to create your OracleAS Portal pages. This method also gives you granular control of your OracleAS Portal page, down to the pixel. HTML Templates are also discussed in Chapter 4.
- **Categories** These allow you to organize your content for the benefit of your end users. Once a category is defined, a piece of content (an item) can be assigned to it. This way, end users can limit their search. An item can belong to only one category. The creation of a category is pretty straightforward and is not discussed in this book. For more on category definitions, see the sidebar "Defining Categories."
- **Navigation Pages** These are just like subpages but have two distinct characteristics: 1) they are not searched for content when Oracle is told to index all content; 2) they have the Publish Page As Portlet box checked by default (meaning they show up in the Publish Portal Content category shown on Figure 3-13). As mentioned earlier, navigation pages are not *really* pages but rather elements designed to be placed on an existing page.
- **Perspectives** These are almost identical to categories except for the fact that an item can belong to multiple perspectives. As with categories, the creation of perspectives is trivial and not discussed in this book.

Defining Categories

While the creation of a category is simple, the definition of one is not. Many organizations struggle with this task when defining their portal. Great care must be taken so that categories and perspectives are created that are both functional and intuitive. Changing categories and perspectives after they have been defined and have had items associated with them is not an easy task. Likewise, adding a category or perspective and then updating all of the content in your portal can be arduous. Also, if categories and perspectives are not intuitive to your end users, their functionality will be severely crippled. It is imperative to do a thorough taxonomy definition before proceeding with the addition of content.

Styles, Attributes, Page Types, and Item Types

There are four other types of objects you can add to your page groups. Each of them provides the developer or page designer with additional ways of controlling how pages and the content on those pages are organized.

Styles

Many page designers confuse style and templates. A template can be used to define the structure of a page (how many regions, where they are placed, if a graphic is to be placed on the page, etc.), while a style is a set of attributes that can be applied to the elements on a page. The page elements are broken down into four basic categories:

- **Portlets** These affect how the portlets are displayed. Some of the portlet elements that can be modified include
  - **Portlet Header Color** The color of the horizontal bar on the top of the portlet
  - **Portlet Header Text** The color and font of the text that is in the portlet header
  - **Portlet Body Color** The background color of the portlet
- **Items** These affect how content is displayed. Some of the item elements that can be modified include
  - **Display Name** The font and color of the content name
  - **Group By Banner** The color, height, and alignment of text
- **Tabs** How active and inactive tabs are displayed
- **Common** How backgrounds and region banners are displayed

After a new style is defined (there is always a default style defined, named the <Page Group Name> style), it can be applied to a page by editing the page in Graphical mode, clicking the Style link on the top right of the page, and selecting the style to be used for the page. Page designers can also change the style for all pages in a page group by clicking the Properties link next to the Page Group heading in the top left of the page, selecting the Configure tab, selecting the Edit link in the Page Defaults section of the page, and changing the Default Style to the newly created style. You can experiment by creating a new style and applying it to the page without any fear of harming your page. You can always reassign your page back to the original style without altering any of the regions, portlets, or content on the page. The creation of a new style is as simple as clicking the Style link under the Page Group, giving it a name, and setting the various properties for that style.

NOTE

If you create a style under a page group, that style will be available only for pages in that page group. If you want to create a style that can be shared among page groups, return to the root of the page groups by clicking the Page Groups link in the top left of the screen. From there, you will see a link called Shared Objects. When you select that link, you will see links identical to those when you click one of the Page Group links. Anything created here is available to all page groups.

Attributes

Developers can add attributes to their pages to enhance the various attributes already provided by OracleAS Portal. Predefined content attributes are associated with item types and page types, and store information about an item or page, such as the associated category, description, or perspectives. These attributes are included in the Add and Edit screens, where users can provide information about the item or page they are adding or editing. There is also another category of attributes called *display* attributes. Display attributes are associated with regions and display information about an item or portlet, such as the author, display name, and creation date. Page designers can choose which attributes to display in a region. Note that some content attributes, such as author and description, are also display attributes. Any custom attributes created by the page group administrator are also display attributes. Adding and using attributes is discussed in Chapter 5.

Page Types

OracleAS Portal comes with predefined page types. You can see a list of these by going to the properties of a page group (by clicking the Properties link in the top left of the graphical editing page of any page or by going to the Portal Navigator and clicking the Properties link next to the Page Group in question), clicking the Configure tab, and then clicking the Edit link in the Types And Classification section of the page (Figure 3-16).

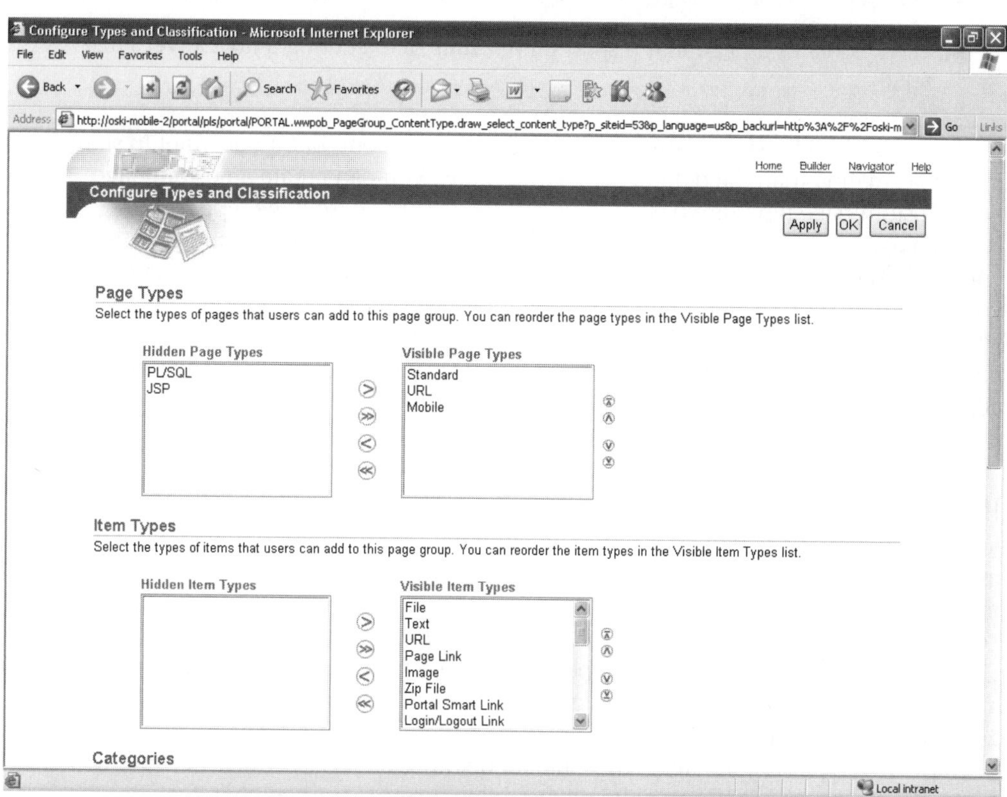

FIGURE 3-16 *The Configure Types And Classification screen*

Here you see a list of the five predefined page types for OracleAS Portal:

- **Standard** Creates a page that displays portlets and items. This is, by far, the most common page created in OracleAS Portal.
- **Mobile** Creates a page that displays portlets and items. Mobile pages provide a way to design pages specifically for display in mobile devices, such as cell phones. Standard pages can also be displayed in mobile devices; however, the standard page design environment is more suited to creating pages for larger display devices, such as PC monitors.
- **URL** Creates a page that displays the contents of a particular URL.

- **PL/SQL** Creates a page that displays the results of executing PL/SQL code.
- **JSP** Creates a page that displays the results of executing a JavaServer Page (JSP).

For most sites, these predefined page types are sufficient, but if you want to store more information than the default page types allow, you can create a custom page type. Custom page types are based on one of the existing base page types. The custom page type automatically inherits all of the base page type's attributes. After you create a custom page type, you can edit it to add attributes that are specific to your requirements. It is important to note that you must create an attribute before you can add it to a custom page type. In addition to adding attributes to custom page types, you can also add calls to PL/SQL or HTTP procedures. You can pass attributes as parameters to the procedures if required, but you cannot add attributes or procedure calls to base page types.

Item Types

Just as it includes page types, OracleAS Portal comes with standard item types. For most sites, these item types are sufficient, but OracleAS Portal provides the mechanism for you to add your own item types if needed. Item types define the content of an item and the information that is stored about an item. Items in OracleAS Portal are based on item types. Items are one of the basic components of a portal page. The information stored about an item is determined by the attributes associated with the item type.

Base item types are the item types included with OracleAS Portal. There are two types of base item types. Content item types allow users to add content (for example, images, documents, or text) to a page. Navigation item types allow users to add navigational elements (for example, a login/logout link, a basic search box, or a list of objects) to a page. The base content item types are not actually available for users to add to pages. Instead, OracleAS Portal provides extended item types based on the base content items.

If the extended item types do not provide enough flexibility, you can further extend most of them to meet your requirements, provided you have the appropriate privileges. To extend these item types, you must have at least the page group privileges Manage Classifications and View on the Shared Objects page group. You can add different attributes to the item types to store exactly the information that you want. You can also add calls to PL/SQL and HTTP procedures and even pass attributes to the parameters of those procedures. You can only base custom item types on one of the base content item types. You cannot base custom item types on any of the base navigation item types.

Exercises

Most of the time, when OracleAS Portal Pages are created, page designers will want to create them from an existing template to ensure consistency. One of the really nice features of OracleAS Portal is the ability to convert a page into a template. The exercises in this chapter will focus on creating a page for our dashboard application. We will then convert that page into a template that can be used to create other pages.

- Exercise 1: Edit the root page so that is has a basic look and feel for all of our subsequent pages. Take a good look at the page and see how it compares to other Web pages you have worked with, either internally in your company or on the Internet. You will spot a couple of obvious things to change:
  - **The banner** The default banner has an image the says Oracle Application Server Portal. You'll want to "brand" your site with your own logo. OracleAS Portal can accept images in the JPEG, GIF, or PNG format, and you can reference these images from either your local hard drive or a Web location. If you have an image you'd like to use already, modify the banner to use that. If you don't have an image, you can download an image from the author's site to your hard drive. The banner also has a title in the middle with the text "Dashboard_1 Banner." Change that to something meaningful, or remove it altogether.
  - **The style** The style of the page is rather plain. Change the style of the page group (or better yet, create a new style) and apply it to the page group. Make it so that it is pleasing to the eye yet captures the end user's attention.
  - **The regions** Most sites have a distinctive look and feel throughout all of their pages. As an example, go to Oracle's technology Web site (http://www.oracle.com/technology/index.html). Almost all of the pages on this site have the same basic look and feel—a region on the left with headings like Products, Technologies, and Community; horizontal choices along the top like Downloads and Documentation; and the main part of the page that displays content (Figure 3-17). Not all of the pages have this layout, but by creating a template similar to this, new pages can be added quickly. Create regions in your template that use 25 percent of the screen on the left, 25 percent of the screen on the right, and 50 percent of the screen in the middle.
- Exercise 2: Convert the page to a template by returning to the Portal Navigator and clicking the Convert Root Page to Template link. Save the template as **Dashboard_Page_Template**.

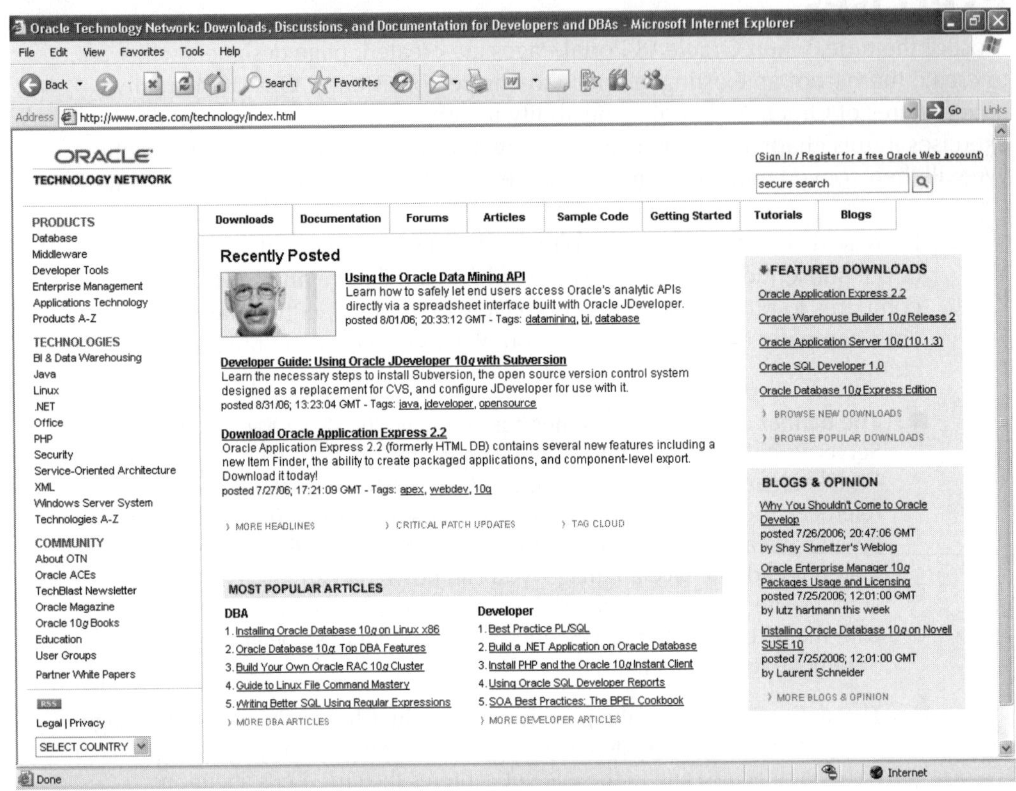

FIGURE 3-17 *The Oracle Technology Network page*

- Exercise 3: Create a new page based on the Dashboard_Page_Template template.

Summary

The page design features of OracleAS Portal enable page designers to create a rich end-user experience quickly and easily. The template features (discussed more thoroughly in Chapter 4) take the hassle out of maintaining visual consistency throughout the site by giving page designers a simple way of generating and using templates. In the next chapter, advanced page design features are discussed, including using page parameters and events and—perhaps the most exciting new feature of OracleAS Portal 10.1.4—HTML Templates.

CHAPTER 4

Advanced Portal Page Design

he OracleAS Portal page design features discussed up until this point provide page designers with all of the tools needed to build production-quality Web sites. Some of the benefits of the OracleAS Portal standard page design features include

- **Page groups** Page groups allow designers to group pages for easy site maintenance and privilege assignment. Grouping pages in this manner also eases administration tasks, such as exporting your pages from a development or testing environment to a production environment. Administration tasks are discussed in Chapter 9.
- **Templates** Templates provide a simple way of maintaining visual consistency across pages and allow page designers to add new pages to their portal site quickly and securely.
- **Page design environment** The fact that OracleAS Portal pages are created, edited, and previewed from within a Web browser greatly simplifies the design process, eliminating the need to use third-party tools to design the pages, copy those files to a server, check the result, and repeat the process again when errors are made or modifications are needed. OracleAS Portal also makes the copying of pages trivial, giving page designers a simple way of maintaining version control, with all copies (versions) of your pages stored in a single location.

These features allow page designers to be productive quickly, but there are some fundamental limitations with this approach:

- It forces page designers to adapt to the OracleAS Portal environment. In most cases, organizations have already spent a great deal of effort using other tools to design their Web pages. Forcing Web designers to learn another tool can be daunting for IT departments that are already stretched thin.
- It limits page design to the tools provided within OracleAS Portal. There are many exciting technologies for creating Web pages that provide a higher level of interactivity than the page design tools within OracleAS Portal can provide.

In Chapter 3, we discussed the basics of page design in OracleAS Portal. Some of the basic features discussed include pages and page groups, regions, categories and perspectives, navigation pages, styles, attributes, and page types. If OracleAS Portal contained only those features, page designers would have a sophisticated set

Oracle Infrastructure Database

If you're wondering where everything related to OracleAS Portal is stored, a special database is automatically created when the Oracle Application Server is installed. This database, referred to as the infrastructure database, serves three basic purposes: 1) it stores security information about users and groups (when you create a new Portal user, that user's information is stored in the infrastructure database; it also stores all of the privileges you grant to users and groups in regard to page and portlet privileges), 2) it maintains information about how the different pieces of the Application Server are clustered together, and 3) it stores all Portal information: Page definitions, PL/SQL portlets, Portal site settings, and Portal content are all stored in tables within the infrastructure database. As this database has a very specific purpose, Oracle strongly recommends that you *not* keep any of your organization's data (referred to, in Oracle's documentation, as "consumer" data) in the infrastructure database. It's also important to note that content stored within OracleAS Portal (like Microsoft Word documents, Excel spreadsheets, or .pdf files, to name but a few types) is converted into something the Oracle infrastructure database can understand (for technical types, the content is stored as a binary large object, or a "BLOB") and stored as a row inside of the database. This is important from a security standpoint: the content is not stored in the file system, so if your server is compromised, a hacker will have a much harder time getting access to your organization's sensitive information. Content is discussed in Chapter 5.

of graphical design elements to give their end users a rich Web experience when interacting with their portal. Oracle recognized that the limitations just listed needed to be addressed, however. One of the most exciting feature areas of OracleAS Portal 10.1.4 is the inclusion of advanced page design features that give page designers even greater flexibility and allow them to use all of the advanced design tools at their disposal. In this chapter, we will look at some of the advanced page design features that are available to OracleAS Portal page designers.

The main advanced page design feature available to page designers in OracleAS Portal 10.1.4 is called HTML Templates. These templates allow you to use a tool outside of OracleAS Portal (like Adobe's Dreamweaver or Microsoft's FrontPage) to construct the templates that will drive your site. HTML Templates also give page designers greater flexibility to customize their OracleAS Portal pages and provide features that Portal templates do not. HTML Templates are one of the most talked about features in OracleAS Portal 10.1.4.

NOTE
There are also two more advanced features, called Page Parameters and Page Events. These, however, are best understood in the context of creating and using a certain type of OracleAS Portal portlet called an OmniPortlet. As such, Page Parameters and Page Events are discussed in the OmniPortlet chapter, Chapter 6.

HTML Templates

For many organizations, a large amount of work has already been done to brand their Web site. In this context, branding refers to the effort expended designing the organization's site with a distinctive look and feel so as to distinguish it from other Web sites. For example, if you visit any of Oracle's Web pages, you will notice that all of their pages have a very consistent look to them—the fonts, basic navigation page elements, areas of categorization, and content areas all look the same on the various pages. While this may sound like a trivial fact, the definition of these page elements is crucial for providing an environment that end users will find easy to use and productive. Without the existence of templates in OracleAS Portal, the task of maintaining visual consistency throughout all of your pages would be an arduous one. In Chapter 3, we discussed OracleAS Portal templates and saw how they can be used to define the basic structure of a page. This functionality gives page designers a starting point when it comes to constructing new pages.

One of the most exciting features of OracleAS Portal 10.1.4 is the ability to construct pages using a tool outside of OracleAS Portal. As mentioned previously, many organizations have already done the work to brand their site and do not wish to convert all of that work into OracleAS Portal templates. By using the HTML template functionality in OracleAS Portal, page designers can take their existing work, and with a few adjustments, incorporate it into OracleAS Portal seamlessly. There are two types of HTML templates:

- **HTML Page Skins** An HTML Page Skin gives designers the ability to create a template that controls the area around the body of a page. The body contains OracleAS Portal content, such as items, portlets, regions, and tabs. The skin can contain anything any Web page can handle, including images, links, JavaScript, etc.
- **HTML Content Layouts** HTML Content Layouts can be used to format regions. Its name is a little misleading—HTML Content Layouts can be applied to all regions (content regions and portlet regions), not just content regions.

TIP

While it is not essential to be fluent in JavaScript and HTML to use HTML Page Skins and Content Layouts, you will have greater flexibility if you are familiar with these languages. The examples in this chapter make use of JavaScript to show the features and benefits of HTML Page Skins and Content Layouts.

One of the really nice features of HTML Templates is the fact that they are applied dynamically to your OracleAS Portal pages. There are two main benefits of this:

- If you've already created pages in OracleAS Portal, you don't have to go back and re-create all of them to take advantage of HTML Templates.
- If and when the time comes to change the branding of your site, it only has to be done in one place: the HTML templates that make up your site. Once the template has been changed, any page assigned to that template will automatically display with the new attributes of that template.

You may be wondering how OracleAS Portal knows how to display its page contents using a template generated by an external tool such as Dreamweaver. After all, an external HTML editor doesn't know anything about how OracleAS Portal displays items and portlets. The answer to this lies in what Oracle refers to as "tags as substitution variables." These tags allow page designers to specify where the content coming from OracleAS Portal is to be placed on the portal page that was generated with the third-party tool. In order to make use of HTML Templates, a page designer will need to perform the following steps:

1. Generate the page layout in the third-party tool.
2. Copy the generated HTML into OracleAS Portal.
3. Add the OracleAS Portal–specific tags to the template.
4. Modify any references (to files stored on the server) to be displayed or referenced on the page.

NOTE

Portal-specific tags can be added in the third-party tool if the designer prefers.

There are two sets of tags: tags for pages (which are used in conjunction with HTML Page Skins) and tags for Items and Portlets (which are used in conjunction with HTML Content Layouts). The tags and their descriptions are discussed in the following sections.

HTML Page Skins

An HTML Page Skin is a template that defines the appearance of the area surrounding page content. In this context, the word "content" refers to anything on the page, including both portal content (items) and portlets. You can use the wizards within OracleAS Portal to create your HTML Page Skin by typing in all of the code manually, but it is far more common to use a third-party tool to create the template and then copy the HTML code generated by the third-party tool into the OracleAS Portal HTML Template. For the examples in this chapter, we will use Dreamweaver, a tool from Adobe, to create our HTML Page Skins, but you can use any HTML design tool.

An HTML Template, whether it is an HTML Page Skin or an HTML Content Layout, is part of a page group. To create a new HTML Template, go to the OracleAS Portal Navigator, click the Page Groups tab, and click the page group you wish to work with. Click the HTML Templates link. Click the Create New HTML Template link on the top left of the page. You will see a page similar to Figure 4-1.

NOTE
In the previous chapters of this book, we have been working with a page group titled Dashboard_1. The examples and screen shots in the chapter will assume you are also working within this page group.

This is the page OracleAS Portal page designers use to create their HTML Templates. In the top left of the page is a drop-down box with the two choices of HTML Templates: HTML Page Skin or HTML Content Layout. Changing the Template Type also changes the default Template Definition in the middle of the page. The default Template Definition for HTML Page Skins looks like this (line numbers have been added for reference):

```
<HTML dir=#DIRECTION#>
<HEAD>
<TITLE>#TITLE#</TITLE>
#PAGE.STYLE#
#PAGE.BASE#
</HEAD>
<BODY leftMargin="0" rightMargin="0" topMargin="0" margin-
height="0"
marginwidth="0" >
#BODY#
</BODY>
</HTML>
```

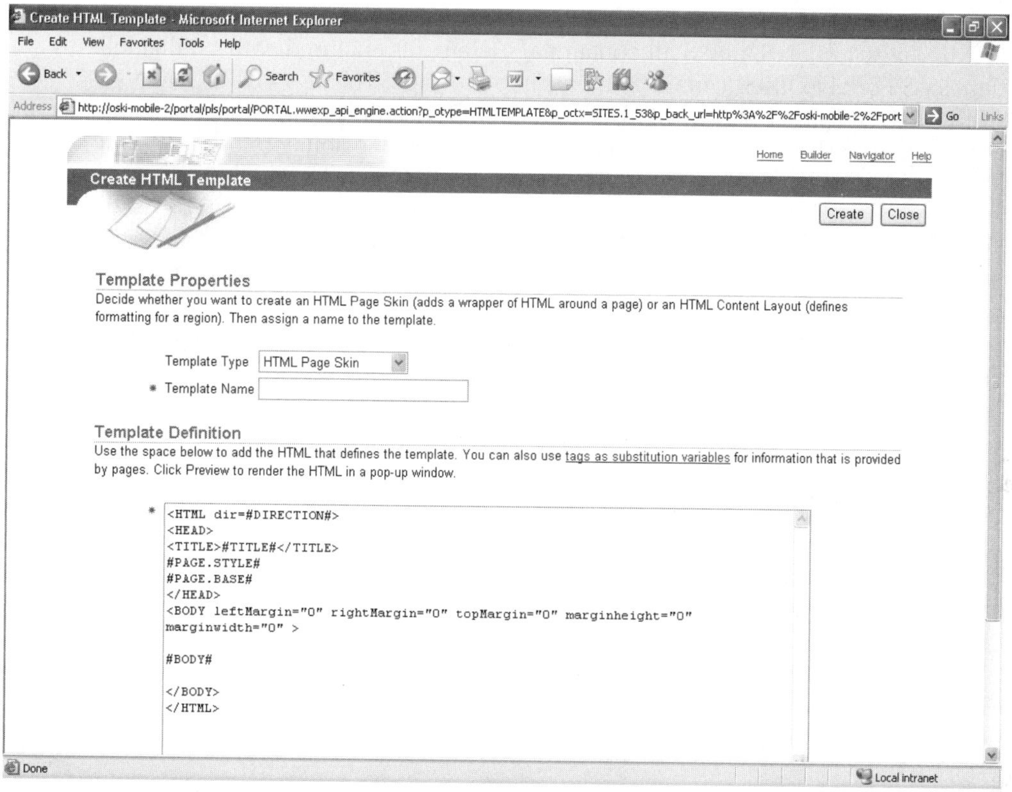

FIGURE 4-1 *The Create HTML Template page*

This code is HTML with a couple of OracleAS Portal–specific tags thrown in. HTML stands for Hypertext Markup Language, which is the language that defines how pages are displayed in your browser.

NOTE

HTML is beyond the scope of this book. There are several excellent books available if you want to learn HTML, including HTML: A Beginners Guide by Wendy Willard (McGraw-Hill, 2003) and HTML and XHTML: The Complete Reference by Thomas Powell (McGraw-Hill, 2003).

If you know HTML, most of the preceding code should make sense to you. There are, however, some OracleAS Portal–specific elements that are not part of HTML. Lines 1, 3, 4, 5, and 8 all contain tags (elements enclosed with #s) that tell OracleAS Portal to insert certain elements into the page. The tags #DIRECTION#, #TITLE#, #PAGE.STYLE#, #PAGE.BASE#, and #BODY# all have specific meanings, and it is these substitution tags that give page designers the ability to use an HTML file generated with a third-party tool to integrate with OracleAS Portal.

As mentioned earlier, there are two types of substitution tags that can be used. For either HTML Page Skins or HTML Content Layouts, you can click the Tags As Substitution Variables link in the center of the page to see a list. Clicking that link opens a pop-up window that lists all of the tags (Figure 4-2). It does not, however, provide an explanation of what the tags are used for. Table 4-1 lists the HTML Page Skin tags.

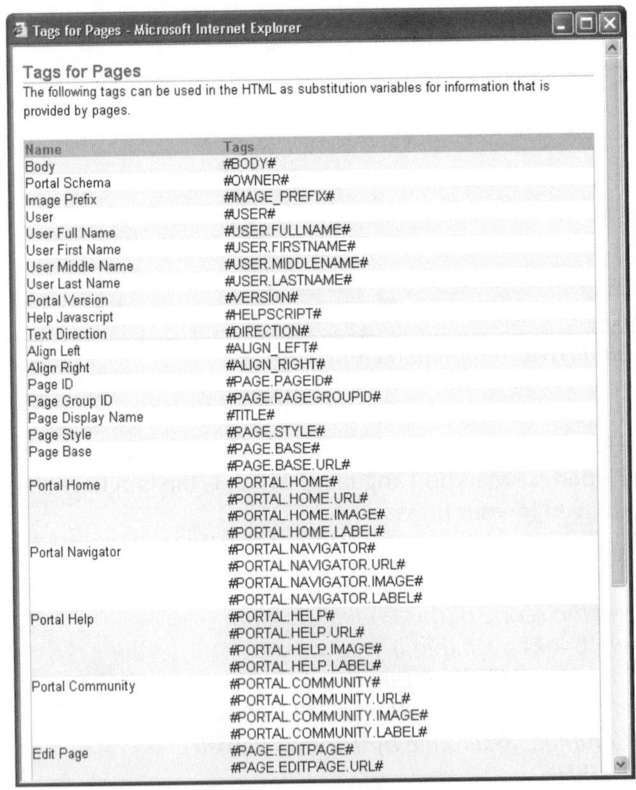
Tags for Pages - Microsoft Internet Explorer

Tags for Pages

The following tags can be used in the HTML as substitution variables for information that is provided by pages.

Name	Tags
Body	#BODY#
Portal Schema	#OWNER#
Image Prefix	#IMAGE_PREFIX#
User	#USER#
User Full Name	#USER.FULLNAME#
User First Name	#USER.FIRSTNAME#
User Middle Name	#USER.MIDDLENAME#
User Last Name	#USER.LASTNAME#
Portal Version	#VERSION#
Help Javascript	#HELPSCRIPT#
Text Direction	#DIRECTION#
Align Left	#ALIGN_LEFT#
Align Right	#ALIGN_RIGHT#
Page ID	#PAGE.PAGEID#
Page Group ID	#PAGE.PAGEGROUPID#
Page Display Name	#TITLE#
Page Style	#PAGE.STYLE#
Page Base	#PAGE.BASE# #PAGE.BASE.URL#
Portal Home	#PORTAL.HOME# #PORTAL.HOME.URL# #PORTAL.HOME.IMAGE# #PORTAL.HOME.LABEL#
Portal Navigator	#PORTAL.NAVIGATOR# #PORTAL.NAVIGATOR.URL# #PORTAL.NAVIGATOR.IMAGE# #PORTAL.NAVIGATOR.LABEL#
Portal Help	#PORTAL.HELP# #PORTAL.HELP.URL# #PORTAL.HELP.IMAGE# #PORTAL.HELP.LABEL#
Portal Community	#PORTAL.COMMUNITY# #PORTAL.COMMUNITY.URL# #PORTAL.COMMUNITY.IMAGE# #PORTAL.COMMUNITY.LABEL#
Edit Page	#PAGE.EDITPAGE# #PAGE.EDITPAGE.URL#

FIGURE 4-2 *A list of HTML page skin substitution tags*

Substitution Tag	Value Set By
#BODY#	The database portlet itself or the page's portlets
#OWNER#	The Portal schema
#IMAGE_PREFIX#	The OracleAS Portal images directory as specified in the plsql.conf configuration file
#USER#	The user name of the user who is currently logged on
#USER.FULLNAME#	The full name of the user who is currently logged on
#VERSION#	The version of this installation of OracleAS Portal
#HELPSCRIPT#	The JavaScript function used to open a window to display the OracleAS Portal online help
#DIRECTION#	The direction of character layout (left-to-right or right-to-left)
#ALIGN_LEFT#	Align text to the left
#ALIGN_RIGHT#	Align text to the right
#TITLE#	The page's display name
#PAGE.STYLE#	Fetches all relevant style settings and embeds them in the HTML
#PAGE.BASE#	The HTML base element for the base URL of the document
#PAGE.BASE.URL#	The base URL
#PORTAL.HOME#	The HTML image hyperlink to the portal home page
#PORTAL.HOME.URL#	The URL of the portal home page
#PORTAL.HOME.IMAGE#	The image used for the portal home page link
#PORTAL.HOME.LABEL#	The text used for the portal home page link
#PORTAL.NAVIGATOR#	The HTML image hyperlink to the Navigator
#PORTAL.NAVIGATOR.URL#	The URL of the Navigator
#PORTAL.NAVIGATOR.IMAGE#	The image used for the Navigator link
#PORTAL.NAVIGATOR.LABEL#	The text used for the Navigator link
#PORTAL.HELP#	The HTML image hyperlink to the OracleAS Portal online help

Table 4-1 *HTML Page Skin Tags*

Substitution Tag	Value Set By
#PORTAL.HELP.URL#	The URL of the OracleAS Portal online help
#PORTAL.HELP.IMAGE#	The image used for the OracleAS Portal online help link
#PORTAL.HELP.LABEL#	The text used for the OracleAS Portal online help link
#PORTAL.COMMUNITY#	The name of the Portal Community Web site
#PORTAL.COMMUNITY.URL#	The URL of the Portal Community Web site
#PORTAL.COMMUNITY.IMAGE#	The image of the Portal Community Web site
#PORTAL.COMMUNITY.LABEL#	The label of the Portal Community Web site
#PAGE.EDITPAGE#	This is the combined text and link to the page editor. By default it is "Edit" displayed as a link.
#PAGE.EDITPAGE.URL#	This returns the URL to the page editor for this page.
#PAGE.EDITPAGE.LABEL#	This returns the text defined as the label for the link to the page editor (by default "Edit") without the hyperlink behind it.
#PAGE.CUSTOMIZEPAGE#	The HTML text hyperlink to the customize page dialog
#PAGE.CUSTOMIZEPAGE.URL#	The URL that renders the personalize page view
#PAGE.CUSTOMIZEPAGE.LABEL#	The text used for the personalize page link
#PAGE.REFRESH#	The HTML text hyperlink used to refresh the page
#PAGE.REFRESH.URL#	The refresh URL
#PAGE.REFRESH.LABEL#	The text used for the refresh link
#PORTAL.LOGOUT#	The HTML text hyperlink to the logout URL
#PORTAL.LOGOUT.URL#	The logout URL
#PORTAL.LOGOUT.LABEL#	The text used for the logout link
#PORTAL.ACCOUNTINFO#	The HTML text hyperlink to the account information dialog
#PORTAL.ACCOUNTINFO.URL#	The URL of the account information dialog
#PORTAL.ACCOUNTINFO.LABEL#	The text used for the account information link

Table 4-1 *HTML Page Skin Tags* (continued)

Returning to the default template definition listing earlier in this chapter, line 1 references a tag called #DIRECTION#. This tag defines the direction of the characters used on the page. Line 3 uses the #TITLE# tag to retrieve the title of the page from the OracleAS Portal engine. Line 4 fetches all of the style settings for the page by way of the #PAGE.STYLE# tag. Line 5 establishes the base URL of the document by way of the #PAGE.BASE# tag. Line 8 is the key line in this template definition—the #BODY# tag is where OracleAS Portal will place the main part of the page. The body of the page, in this context, refers to all of the regions you have defined for the page.

The default temple is not terribly exciting. In fact, if you were to save it as is, you would not see any change when it was applied to any of your pages, as the code in the default template definition listing is what OracleAS Portal uses when it creates new pages. To see the effect of changing this template, modify line 7 of the listing to look like this, to give the template a blue background:

```
<BODY leftMargin="0" rightMargin="0" topMargin="0" marginheight="0" marginwidth="0"
bgcolor="#6600FF">
```

To see what it looks like, name the template **DEFAULT_TEMPLATE** and click the Create button on the top right of the screen. After the template is saved, click the Close button in the top right of the screen. Now that the template is created, a page must be assigned to it for the settings to take effect. Click the Page Groups link in the top left of the OracleAS Portal Navigator, then click the Edit Root Page link next to the Dashboard_1 page group. Click the Page Properties link on the top left of the page (be careful *not* to click the Page Group Properties link). Click the Template tab (Figure 4-3).

On this page, you have the ability to specify what template you would like to use for the page. If no HTML Page Skins have been created, the middle selection on this page will contain a drop-down box that is empty. Click the radio button next to Use HTML Page Skin and make sure DEFAULT_TEMPLATE is selected. Click the Preview button to the right. You will see a pop-up window similar to Figure 4-4.

Close the pop-up window and click OK. You are returned to the Edit mode of the page with the HTML Page Skin applied (Figure 4-5).

FIGURE 4-3 *The Template tab of the Page Properties screen*

CAUTION

This is a pretty unpleasant color scheme. Your end users would probably complain pretty loudly if they were forced to work on a screen like this all day. It is important to understand how important things like colors, fonts, page design, and application flow play in the success or failure of your Web development efforts. The advanced page design tools outlined in this chapter give you great flexibility, but with that flexibility comes the responsibility to be sensitive to your end users' needs. Change the page back to its original color scheme by entering the Page Properties screen, selecting the Template tab, and selecting the Do Not Use A Template radio button for now.

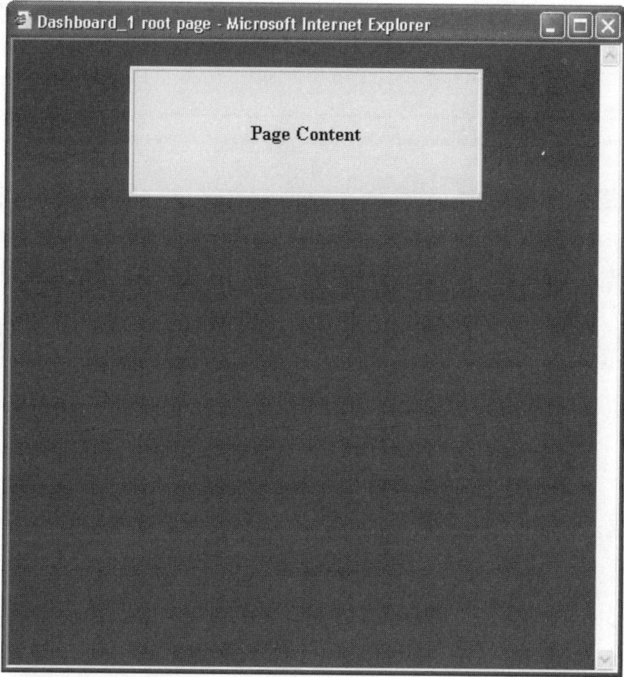

FIGURE 4-4 *The Preview pop-up window for HTML Page Skins*

You certainly could create HTML templates this way, but this functionality was really created for page designers using advanced third-party HTML tools to design and maintain their Web sites. Since many organizations implementing OracleAS Portal have already done a lot of design work to make their sites unique, taking that design work and implementing it in OracleAS Portal should be a simple task. In the next couple of pages, we're going to reverse-engineer an existing site, create the necessary HTML Templates, and apply those to our Dashboard_1 page, so that our OracleAS Portal pages match the look and feel of an existing set of pages that were designed outside of OracleAS Portal.

I maintain a personal Web site (http://www.oski-oracle.info/), where I make various papers I've written and presented and source code from my books available for download. None of the pages on this site were developed with any OracleAS Portal tools. Let's pretend that my page is a corporate site and, as an OracleAS Portal page designer, you have been given the mandate that all portal pages you create have the same look and feel as the pages on the http://www.oski-oracle.info/ site. How would you go about doing it? You could write all of the code by hand

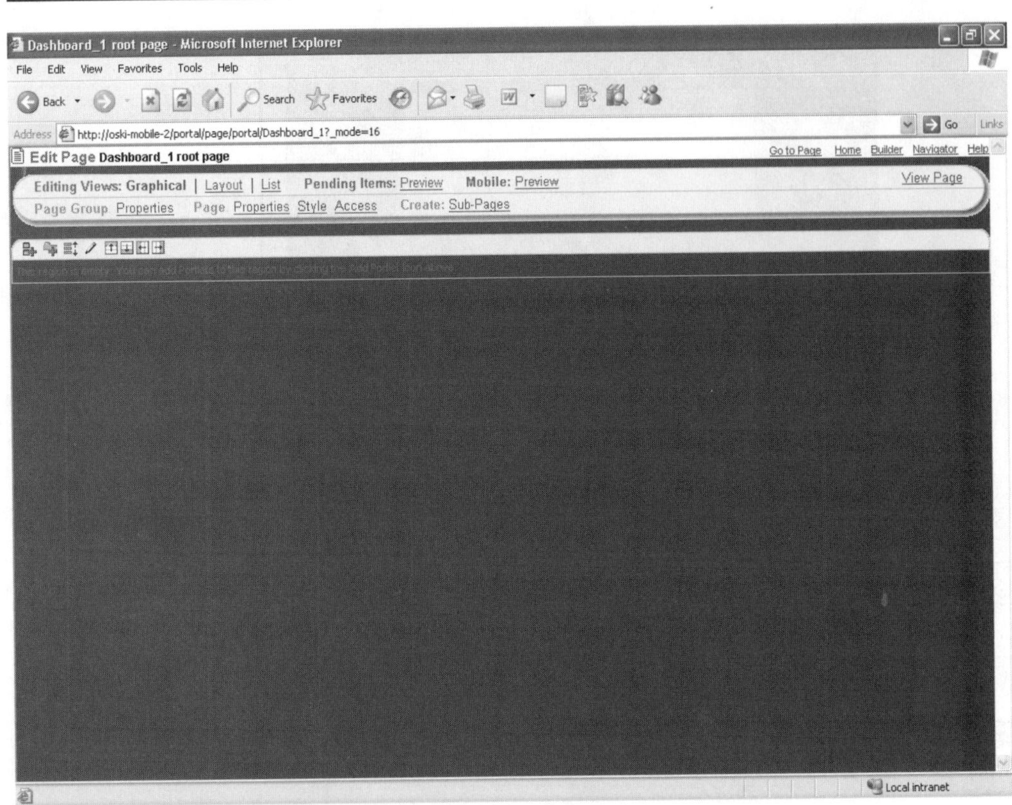

FIGURE 4-5 *The Dashboard_1 root page with the DEFAULT_TEMPLATE applied*

and, through trial and error, create a template that matches what's on that page. It's much more efficient, however, to use a professional HTML editing tool.

NOTE
For this chapter, I'm going to use a tool called Dreamweaver. You are certainly not limited to this tool, however. All HTML layout programs generate HTML code, and this is what we're really interested in. We're going to use this tool to lay out the page, generate the HTML code for the page, copy and paste that code into OracleAS Portal's HTML Page Screen Template Definition, and add the necessary tags so that OracleAS Portal knows how to display the portal content or portlets. You can use any tool to generate the HTML code.

The main page on my Web site consists of three images along the top of the screen: the oski-oracle image on the top left, the horizontal bars above and below the Roman columns, and the image of the Roman columns (Figure 4-6). My Web site uses a trick to place the image of the Roman columns on top of the image of the horizontal bars, so our template is not going to use the two horizontal bars. Right-click each of the two images (the oski-oracle image and the Roman columns image) and save them to your hard disk by selecting Save Background As for each. Save the oski-oracle image as **oski-oracle.bmp** and save the Roman column image as **roman_cols.gif**. Most HTML editors like Dreamweaver can't work with files with .bmp extensions, so open up the oski-oracle.bmp image with Paint (Start | Programs | Accessories | Paint) and then save it as a JPEG file: **oski-oracle.jpg**.

You should now have two files on your hard drive: oski-oracle.jpg and roman_cols.gif. We can now use a third-party editor like Dreamweaver to construct our

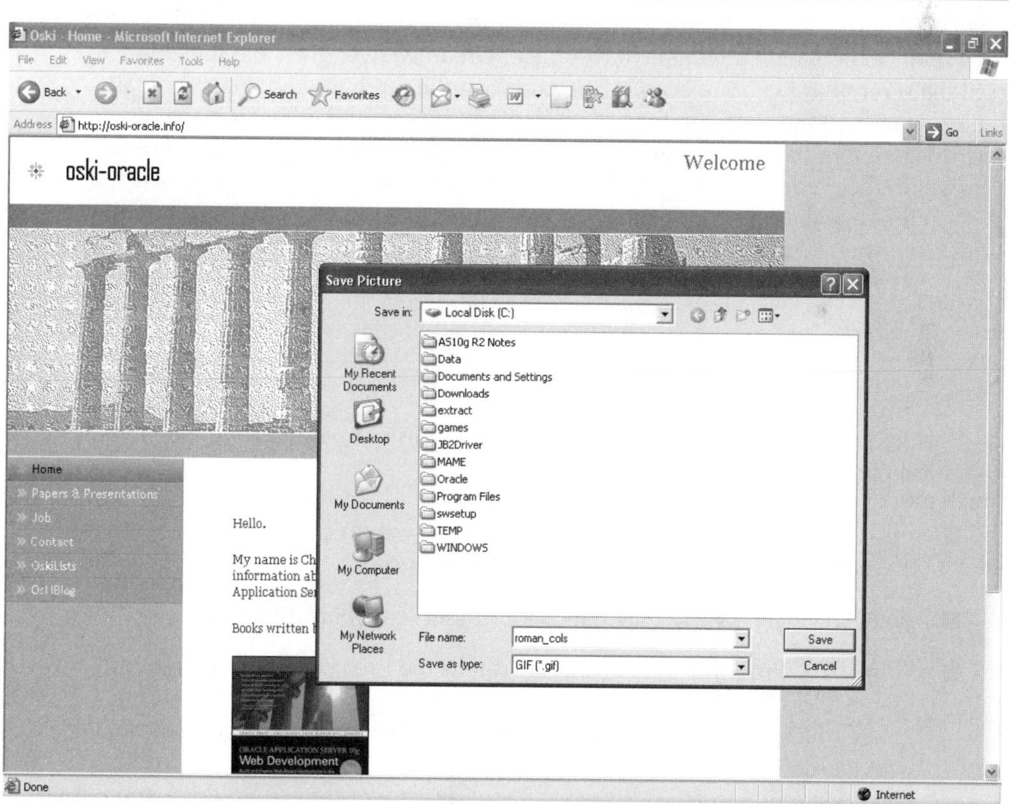

FIGURE 4-6 *Saving the images from the oski-oracle.info page*

File Formats

Files with a .bmp extension are called bitmapped image files. Bitmap files are much larger than other file formats that contain images. The de facto standards for image files on Web pages are: JPEG, which stands for Joint Photographic Experts Group, and GIF, which stands for Graphic Interchange Format. Image files in JPEG format have a .jpg or .jpeg extension, and image files in GIF format have a .gif extension. Both of these formats produce files that are much smaller than .bmp files. This makes them particularly useful for transmission over the Internet. If you have your own JPEG or GIF files that you'd like to use, feel free to do that for the examples in this chapter. Just make sure that they aren't too large, or the formatting in OracleAS Portal will make your page seem disproportionate.

page. In Figure 4-7, I have used Dreamweaver to place the images that will make up my HTML Template on a Dreamweaver page. Dreamweaver gives me the ability to split the screen, so I can see both HTML code (on the top half) and the graphical representation of the page (on the bottom half) at the same time. I can make changes to either half of the page, and the other half will change to reflect those changes immediately.

You'll notice that the code generated references the .jpg and .gif files that are stored (for now) locally on my hard drive:

```
<p><img
src="file:///C|/Program%20Files/Macromedia/Dreamweaver%20UltraDev%
204/Tutorial/UltraDev%20ASP%20tutorial/Compass%20Intranet/oski-
oracle.JPG" width="360" height="66">
```

This line of HTML code may look scary, but it's easier to understand when you break it down:

- **<p>** This is a tag in HTML that tells the browser to create a new paragraph. It creates a line break and a space between lines.
- **<img src=** This HTML tag tells the browser to display an image.
- **"file:///C|/Program%20Files...** This tells the browser where to find the image to display. Right now, it's looking at my local hard disk to find this image (the %20's correspond to spaces in the path of the image). This image is in the C:\Program Files\Macromedia\Dreamweaver UltraDev 4\Tutorial\UltraDev ASP tutorial\Compass Intranet directory on my hard drive and is called oski-oracle.JPG. We will have to update this to reflect the location where we're going to place the images on the server.

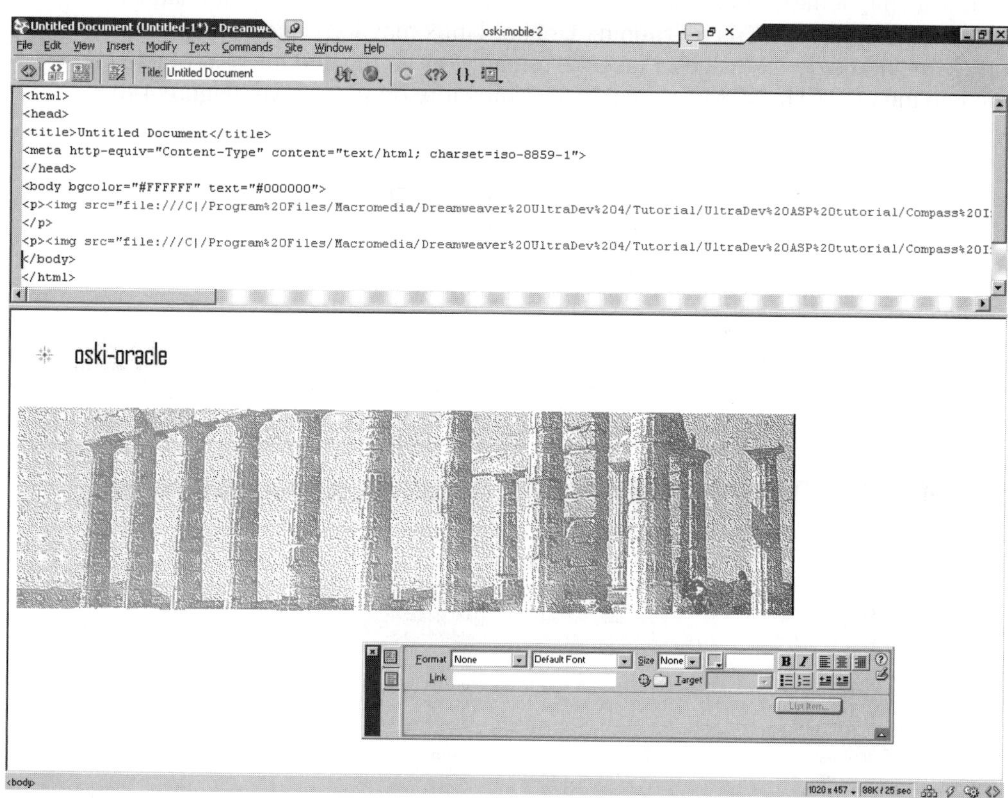

FIGURE 4-7 *A Dreamweaver page with images from oski-oracle.info placed on it*

- **width="360" height="66">** These are characteristics of the image to be displayed. If I were to shrink or expand the size of the image in Dreamweaver, these numbers would be updated automatically.

We now need to figure out where to place our images on our server. The server, in this case, is where OracleAS Portal is running. The code that references the directory where the images are stored in our HTML Template will need to reflect the operating system that is running on the server. All directories are specified in reference to the ORACLE_HOME\portal directory, where ORACLE_HOME is the location of your middle-tier installation on your server. By default there is a directory created underneath the ORACLE_HOME\portal directory called images. If, for example, the server is running Microsoft Windows, and the middle-tier was installed in the c:\oracle\mt_home directory, a c:\oracle\mt_home\portal directory and a c:\oracle\mt_home\portal\images directory will be created for you automatically. A similar directory on a server running Unix or Linux may look like this: /u01/oracle/mt_home/portal/images. Place the roman_cols.gif file and the oski-oracle.jpg file into the ORACLE_HOME\portal\images directory on your server (Figure 4-8).

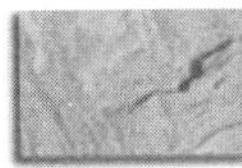

TIP

All of the examples in this book were performed on a server running Microsoft Windows 2003 Server, so all directories will reflect that environment. If you are working through the examples on a Linux or Unix server, make sure to adjust your directory names appropriately.

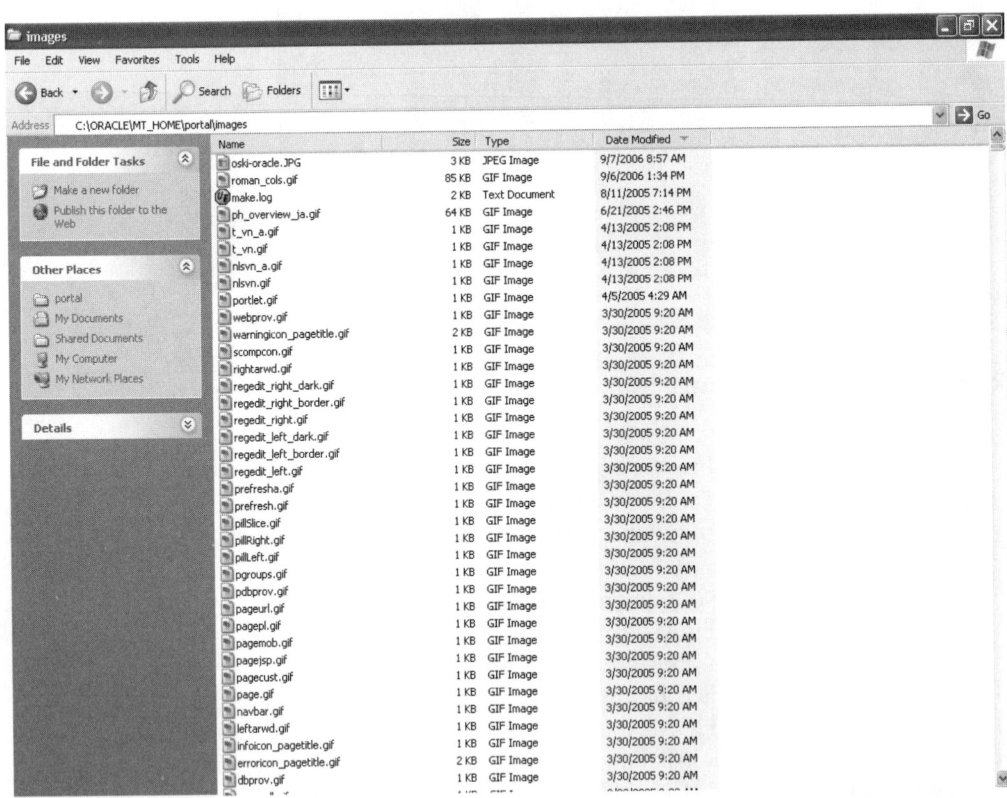

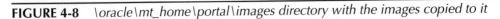

FIGURE 4-8 *\oracle\mt_home\portal\images directory with the images copied to it*

We can now copy and paste that code into our OracleAS Portal HTML Template (Figure 4-9).

```
<html>
<head>
<title>Untitled Document</title>
<meta http-equiv="Content-Type" content="text/html; charset=iso-8859-1">
</head>
<body bgcolor="#FFFFFF" text="#000000">
<p><img
src="file:///C|/Program%20Files/Macromedia/Dreamweaver%20UltraDev%204/Tutorial/Ultr
aDev%20ASP%20tutorial/Compass%20Intranet/oski-oracle.JPG" width="360" height="66">
</p>
<p><img
src="file:///C|/Program%20Files/Macromedia/Dreamweaver%20UltraDev%204/Tutorial/Ultr
aDev%20ASP%20tutorial/Compass%20Intranet/roman_cols.gif" width="792"
height="200"></p>
</body>
</html>
```

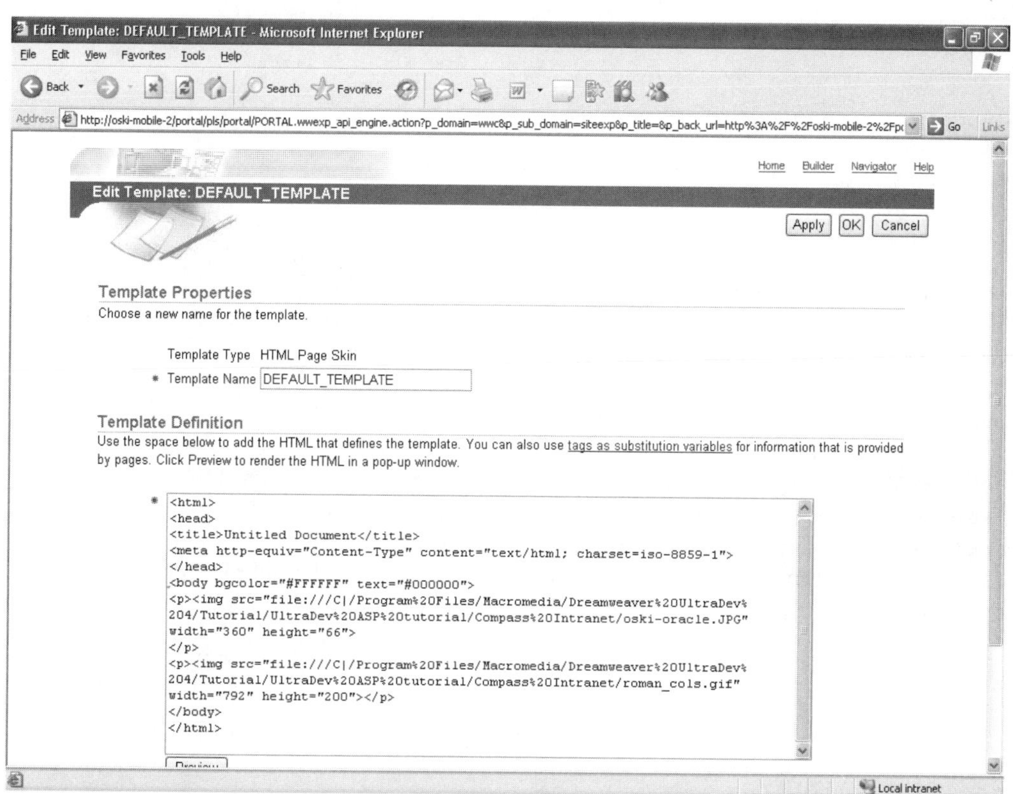

FIGURE 4-9 *The HTML Template page with the Dreamweaver code pasted in*

We have to make some changes to this code before it becomes a usable OracleAS Portal HTML Page Skin. First, replace whatever your HTML editing program generated between the <title> and </title> tags with the OracleAS Portal Substitution tag #TITLE#. This will place the title of the page from OracleAS Portal into the title of the HTML page when it's displayed. Next, place the #PAGE.STYLE# and #PAGE.BASE# tags after the <title> line so that OracleAS Portal can apply any styles defined in OracleAS Portal to the page. Next, change the two <img src= tags to point to the directory you created on your server to store your portal images. Finally, add the #BODY# tag, so OracleAS Portal knows where to place the body of your portal page. The final code should look something like this:

```
<html>
<head>
<title>#TITLE#</title>
#PAGE.STYLE#
#PAGE.BASE#
<meta http-equiv="Content-Type" content="text/html; charset=iso-8859-1">
</head>
<body bgcolor="#FFFFFF" text="#000000">
<p><img src="\images\oski-oracle.JPG" width="360" height="66">
</p>
<p><img src="\images\roman_cols.gif" width="792" height="200"></p>
#BODY#
</body>
</html>
```

Click the preview button to see if the code is correct. You will see a pop-up window similar to Figure 4-10.

Click OK to save the template. To apply this template to your work, return to the OracleAS Portal Navigator by clicking the Page Groups link on the top left of the page. Click the Edit Root Page link in the middle of the page of the Dashboard_1 page group. Click the Properties link on the top right of the page next to "Page:" (make sure not to click the Properties link next to "Page Group:"). Click the Template tab and select the radio button next to "Use HTML Page Skin." Make sure DEFAULT_TEMPLATE is selected in the drop-down box. Clicking Preview will bring up the same pop-up window as Figure 4-10. Click OK. You are returned to the page in Graphical editing mode (Figure 4-11). You can click the View Page link on the top right of the page to see what the page will look like to end users.

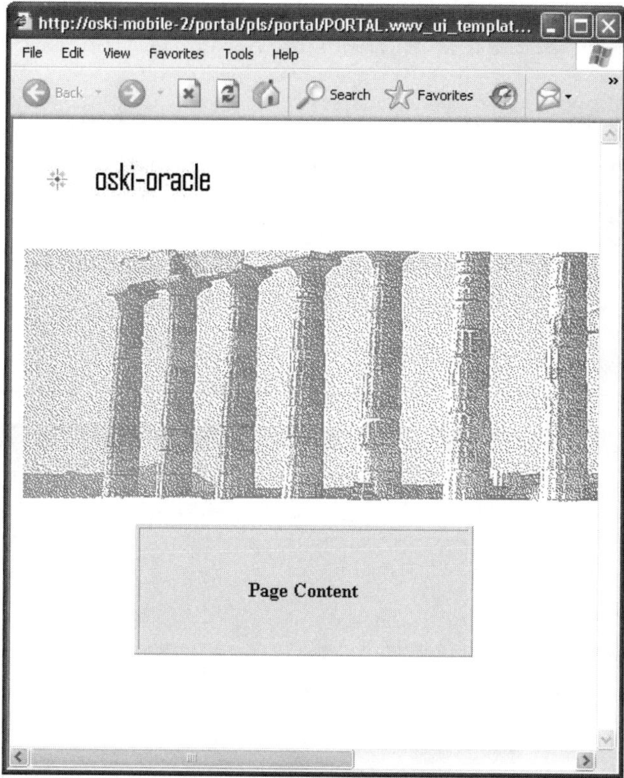

FIGURE 4-10 *The preview of your HTML Template*

You can make things more interesting by adding more of the tags shown earlier in Table 4-1. Consider this next listing (line numbers have been added for reference):

```
<html>
<head>
<title>#TITLE#</title>
#PAGE.STYLE#
#PAGE.BASE#
```

```
<meta http-equiv="Content-Type" content="text/html; charset=iso-8859-1">
</head>
<body bgcolor="#FFFFFF" text="#000000">
<p><img src="c:\oracle\portal_images\oski-oracle.JPG" width="360"
height="66">
</p>
<p><img src="c:\oracle\portal_images\roman_cols.gif" width="792"
eight="200"></p>
<p align="right"><font class="titleorimageid1siteid53">Welcome,
#USER#</font></p>
<p align="right"><a href="#PORTAL.HOME.URL"#><font
lass="titleorimageid1siteid53">Home</font></a></p>
<p align="right">#PORTAL.LOGOUT#</p>
#BODY#
</body>
</html>
```

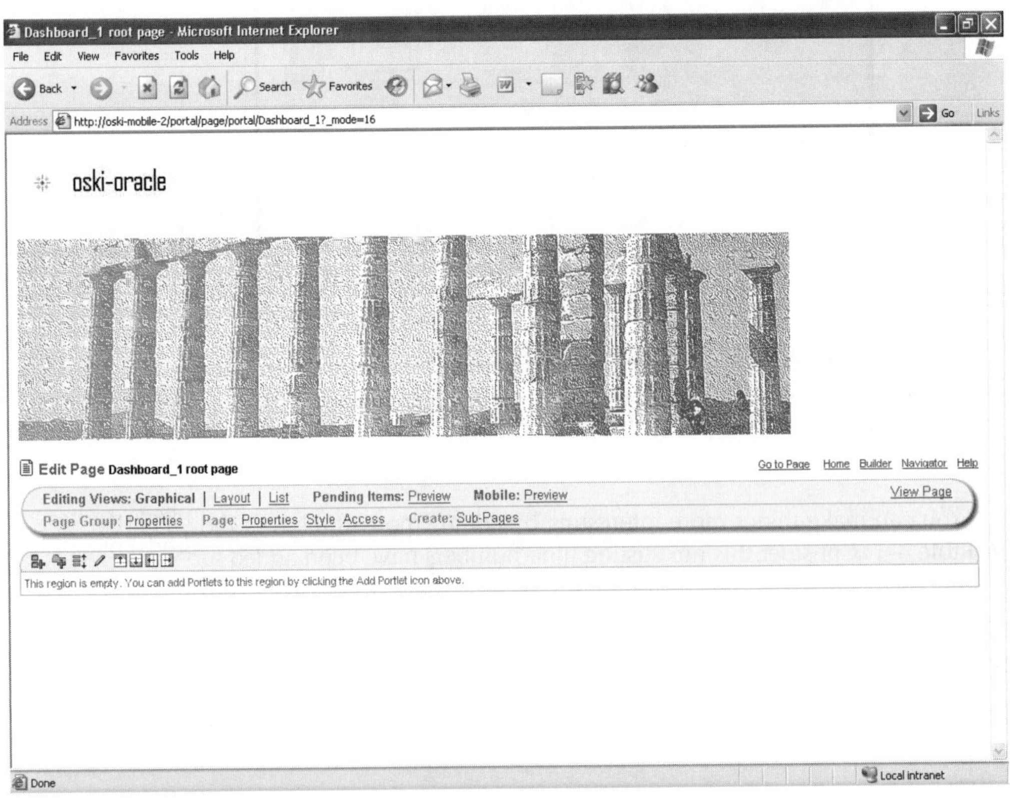

FIGURE 4-11 *The Dashboard_1 root page with the DEFAULT_TEMPLATE HTML Page Skin applied to it*

Line 12 contains a reference to #USER#, which will substitute the name of the user who is currently logged in. The <p align="right"> tag creates a new paragraph and aligns the text on the right side of the page. The <font class="titleorimageid1site id53"> tag makes the text consistent with the Logout link specified in line 14.

In Line 13, we construct a link that will be used to allow end users to click a link that will return them to their home page at any time. By placing this link in our template, we assure that users will never get "stuck" in our portal. If, for whatever reason, an end user gets "lost," that user can always click that link to return to the home page. Line 14 contains a link allowing the user to log out.

CAUTION

An important thing to remember: HTML does not display an error if you code something incorrectly—it just ignores whatever it doesn't recognize and moves on to the next tag. This can be a double-edged sword for beginning HTML developers; it allows you to experiment freely and try out new things without breaking an existing design, but it makes debugging HTML that much more challenging when your page doesn't display properly. Most advanced HTML editors like Dreamweaver will catch potential errors and alert you, but the Template Definition text box of the Edit Template page in OracleAS Portal has no such functionality.

Note how the changes made in the DEFAULT_TEMPLATE template are applied automatically to the Dashboard_1 root page immediately, as shown in Figure 4-12. This is true of any page that uses the DEFAULT_TEMPLATE template. So, imagine that your company decides to change from the Roman columns theme on its Web pages. Without templates, you might have to update dozens (or even hundreds) of pages. With HTML Templates, you only have to change one thing: the reference to the image file in the definition of the HTML Page Skin.

HTML Content Layouts

As mentioned earlier, HTML Content Layouts are a little misleadingly named. They apply to regions within pages, and judging by their name, you might think that they can only be applied to regions that are made up of items (content). This is not true, however—HTML Content Layouts can be applied to both regions that contain items and regions that contain portlets.

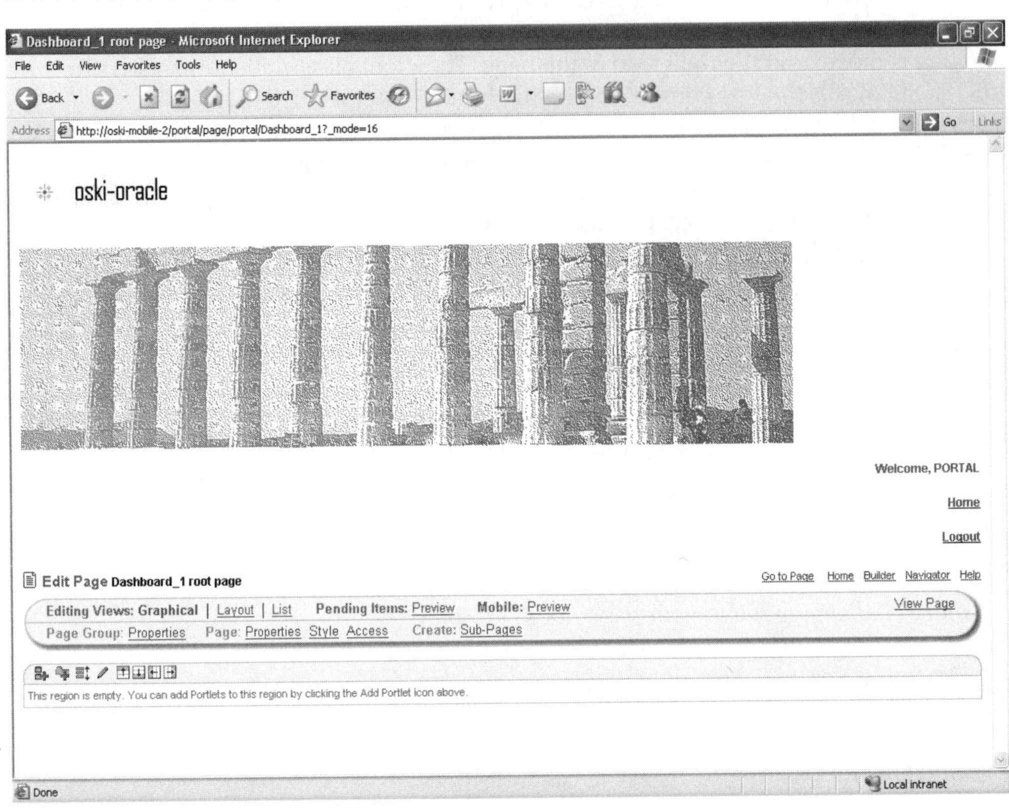

FIGURE 4-12 *The Dashboard_1 root page with added functionality in the DEFAULT_TEMPLATE displayed*

As with HTML Page Skins, there is a set of tags that can be used when developing HTML Content Layouts. The following table lists all of the tags that are available for HTML Content Layouts. The second column lists the type (scope) of the tag—any tag with a value of "common" can be applied to regions with either items or portlets. As you can see, most of the tags apply to items; there are only three tags (at the end of the table) that are specific to portlets. In addition to the tags listed, it is common for page designers to use JavaScript to enhance the functionality of HTML Content Layouts.

<table>
<tr><th>Substitution Tag</th><th>Type</th><th>Value Set By...</th></tr>
<tr><td>#ITEM.ID#</td><td>Common</td><td>The ID of an item that is rendered through the HTML Content Layout template. When items have multiple versions, this tag refers to a specific item version. Compare it with #item.masterid#, which is the ID of the item without regard to version. The #item.id# is different for each version. The #item.masterid# is the same for all versions of the item.</td></tr>
<tr><td>#ITEM.MASTERID#</td><td>Common</td><td>The master ID of an item that is rendered through the HTML Content Layout template. Compare this with #item.id#, which is the ID of a specific version of an item. See #item.id# for more information. This tag can be used with the #item.pagegroupid# tag in a query against the public view of a page. In the following example, assume that the privilege to view WWSBR_ALL_ITEMS is granted to the user or to PUBLIC:

```
<oracle>
begin
   htp.p('Item MasterID=#item.masterid#'); htp.br;
   htp.p('PageGroup=#item.pagegroupid#'); htp.br;
   for c1 in (
      select id, display_name, language
      from #owner#.WWSBR_ALL_ITEMS
      where masterid = #item.masterid#
      and caid = #item.pagegroupid#
      )
      loop
          htp.p('Item ID = '||c1.id||
          ' title = ' ||c1.display_name||
          ' language = '||c1.language);
          htp.br;
      end loop;
end;
</oracle>
```

</td></tr>
<tr><td>#ITEM.PAGEGROUPID#</td><td>Common</td><td>The ID of the page group that contains the item being rendered through the HTML Content Layout template. See the example in #item.masterid#.</td></tr>
</table>

Substitution Tag	Type	Value Set By...

#ITEM.TYPE#	Common	The type of the object, such as *File*. Possible values can be queried from the NAME column in WWSBR_ITEM_TYPES. Consider using this tag inside <oracle></oracle> tags to create a conditional entry. For example:
		`<oracle>`
		`if #ITEM.TYPE# in ('baseportletinstance',`
		`'portlet_instance') then`
		`htp.p('#ITEM.PORTLETCONTENT#');`
		`else`
		`htp.p('#ITEM.DESCRIPTION#');`
		`htp.p('#ITEM.CONTENT#');`
		`end if;`
		
		`</oracle>`

#ITEM.STATUS#	Common	The status of the object Values include:
		•Active
		•Expired
		•Deleted
		•Hidden
		•Draft
		•Pending
		•Rejected
		A single tag can return multiple values (separated by a space), for example:
		`Expired Hidden Deleted`
		`Expired Hidden`
		Consider using this tag inside `<oracle></oracle>` tags, for example, in `if` statements. See the text that follows this table for a usage sample of the <oracle></oracle> tags.

#ITEM.STATUSINHTML#	Common	The item status value in the language specified for the client browser. The value is returned formatted as highlighted bold. It is rendered only when the page is in Edit mode.

Substitution Tag	Type	Value Set By...
#ITEM.STATUSLINK#	Common	A fully formed hyperlink leading to the proper action for pending or draft items. This link displays only when the object's status is *Pending* or *Draft*. •Clicking a *Draft* link takes users to an action page where they can either delete the object or submit it for approval. •Clicking a *Pending* link takes users to the Approval Notification Details page. This page contains a link to the item, a summary of attribute values (both displayed and not displayed), a text box for the approver's comments, and the object's approval history.

#ITEM.DISPLAYOPTION#	Common	The object's display option:
		•**direct**—directly on the page
		•**link**—as a link on the page, link opens in current browser window
		•**linktonewwindow**—as a link on the page, link opens in new browser window
		You can use <oracle></oracle> tags to set up a condition that displays the object as specified in the object's attributes—in the current browser window or a new browser window—should this vary from object to object.
		For example:
		`<oracle>`
		`begin`
		`if '#item.displayoption#' = 'link' then`
		`htp.p('<a href="#item.url#">View item in current window</a>');`
		`elsif '#item.displayoption#' = 'linktonewwindow' then`
		`htp.p('<a href="#item.url#" target="_blank">View item in new window</a>');`
		`else`
		`htp.p('Display item directly in page');`
		`htp.br;`
		`htp.p('#item.content#');`
		`end if;`
		`end;`
		`</oracle>`

Substitution Tag	Type	Value Set By...
#ITEM.URL#	Common	The object's path-based URL. Use this tag in an HTML href tag. For example: <a href="#item.url#">#item.title.value#</a> Or <a href="#item.url#"><img src="#item.image.value#" alt="#item.title.value#"></a>
#ITEM.DURABLEURL#	Common	The object's durable (or globally unique ID–based) URL. Use this tag in an HTML href tag. For example: <a href="#item.durableurl#">#item.content.label#</a>
#ITEM.EDITURL#	Common	The URL to an edit view of the object. This tag renders only for users with the appropriate privilege. Use it in an HTML href tag. For example: <a href="#item.editurl#">Edit</a>
#ITEM.EDITLINK#	Common	The fully formed hyperlink to an edit view of the object. Only users with edit privileges on the item will see this link. Users who click this link are taken to the object's properties page. This tag renders the HTML to form the link as well as the link label, *Edit*. No additional encoding, such as an href tag, is required.
#ITEM.DELETEURL#	Common	The URL to a delete view of the object. This tag renders only for users with the appropriate privilege. Use it in an HTML href tag. For example: <a href="#item.deleteurl#">Delete</a>
#ITEM.DELETELINK#	Common	The fully formed hyperlink to a delete view of the object. Only users with delete privileges on the item see this link. Users who click this link are taken to a decision page where they choose either **Yes** or **No** to continue with deleting the relevant object. This tag renders the HTML to form the link as well as the link label, *Delete*. No additional encoding, such as an href tag, is required.
#ITEM.PAGENAME#	Common	The name of the object's host page.
#ITEM.PAGEURL#	Common	The path-based URL of the object's host page. Use this tag in an HTML href tag. For example: <a href="#item.pageurl#">#item.pagename#</a>

Substitution Tag	**Type**	**Value Set By…**
#ITEM.PAGEDURABLEURL#	Common	The durable (or globally unique ID-based) URL of the object's host page. Use this tag in an HTML href tag. For example: <a href="#item.pagedurableurl#”> #item.pagename#</a>
#ITEM.TITLE#	Common	The object's title or Display Name wrapped in its associated style. This tag is equivalent to: <font class="#item.title.style#”> #item.title.value# </font>
#ITEM.TITLE.LABEL#	Common	*Display Name*
#ITEM.TITLE.VALUE#	Common	The Display Name of the object
#ITEM.TITLE.STYLE#	Common	The style applied to the Display Name of the object. Use this tag inside a <font class=" "> tag. For example: <font class="#item.title.style#”>#item.title.label#: #item.title.value#</font>
#ITEM.DESCRIPTION#	Common	The Description of the object wrapped in its associated style. This tag is equivalent to: <font class="#item.description.style#”> #item.description.value# </font>
#ITEM.DESCRIPTION.LABEL#	Common	*Description*
#ITEM.DESCRIPTION.VALUE#	Common	The Description of the object
#ITEM.DESCRIPTION.STYLE#	Common	The style applied to the Description. Use this tag inside a <font class=" "> tag. For example: <font class="#item.description.style#”> #item.description.label#: #item.description.value#</font>
#ITEM.AUTHOR#	Common	The object's Author wrapped in its associated style. This tag is equivalent to: <font class="#item.author.style#”> #item.author.value# </font>
#ITEM.AUTHOR.LABEL#	Common	*Author*
#ITEM.AUTHOR.VALUE#	Common	The object's Author

Substitution Tag	**Type**	**Value Set By...**
#ITEM.AUTHOR.STYLE#	Common	The style applied to the name of the object's Author. Use this tag inside a <font class=" "> tag. For example: <font class="#item.author.style#"> #item.author.label#: #item.author.value#</font>
#ITEM.IMAGE#	Common	The object's representative image with ALT text, aligned as specified in the portal. This is the image selected by a user to represent the object, rather than an item of the *Image* type. This tag is equivalent to, for example: <img src="#item.image.value#" border="0" alt="#item.title.value#" align="*value defined on the item*">
#ITEM.IMAGE.LABEL#	Common	*Image*
#ITEM.IMAGE.VALUE#	Common	The URL leading to the uploaded image (a location within the portal). This is the image selected by a user to represent the object, rather than an item of the *Image* type. Use this tag in an HTML <img src> tag. For example: <a href="#item.url#"><img src="#item.image.value#" alt="#item.title.value#"></a> When used within an <img src> tag, the image is rendered in place. Otherwise, this tag renders a URL.
#ITEM.KEYWORDS#	Common	The object's assigned keywords and the Keywords label wrapped in their associated style. This tag is equivalent to: <font class="#item.keywords.style#"> #item.keywords.label#: #item.keywords.value# </font>
#ITEM.KEYWORDS.LABEL#	Common	*Keywords*
#ITEM.KEYWORDS.VALUE#	Common	The object's assigned keywords
#ITEM.KEYWORDS.STYLE#	Common	The style applied to the object's keywords. Use this tag inside a <font class=" "> tag. For example: <font class="#item.keywords.style#"> #item.keywords.label#: #item.keywords.value# </font>
#ITEM.CREATOR#	Common	The user name of the object's creator, labeled and wrapped in its associated style. This tag is equivalent to: <font class="#item.creator.style#"> #item.creator.label#: #item.creator.value# </font>

Substitution Tag	Type	Value Set By...
#ITEM.CREATOR.LABEL#	Common	*Creator*
#ITEM.CREATOR.VALUE#	Common	The user name of the object creator.

#ITEM.CREATOR.STYLE#	Common	The style applied to the object creator's user name. Use this tag inside a <font class=" "> tag. For example:
		
		`<font class="#item.creator.style#">`
		`#item.creator.label#: #item.creator.value#`
		`</font>`

#ITEM.CREATEDATE#	Common	The object's create date, labeled and wrapped in its associated style. This tag is equivalent to:
		
		`<font class="#item.createdate.style#">`
		`#item.createdate.label#: #item.createdate.value#`
		`</font>`

#ITEM.CREATEDATE.LABEL#	Common	*Create Date*
#ITEM.CREATEDATE.VALUE#	Common	The string value equal to the date the object was created (that is, the date it was uploaded to the portal). This tag uses the format: `DD-MON-YYYY`, that is, `06-MAY-2004`

#ITEM.CREATEDATE.STYLE#	Common	The style applied to the object's create date. Use this tag inside a <font class=" "> tag. For example:
		
		`<font class="#item.createdate.style#">`
		`#item.createdate.label#: #item.createdate.value#`
		`</font>`

#ITEM.TRANSLATIONS#	Common	The fully formed hyperlink to a translation. If no translation is present, the link does not display.

#ITEM.TRANSLATIONS.LABEL#	Common	Use this tag in conjunction with the VALUE tag to render a fully formed link to a list of translations of the current item. For example:
		
		`<a href="#item.translations.value#>`
		`#item.translations.label#</a>`

Substitution Tag	Type	Value Set By...
#ITEM.TRANSLATIONS.VALUE#	Common	The URL leading to the object's translation (a location within the portal) if such a translation exists. Use this tag in an HTML href tag. For example: <a href="#item.translations.value#"> #item.translations.label#</a> In contrast to the #ITEM.TRANSLATIONS# tag, consider placing the VALUE tag in a PL/SQL conditional statement to control whether it will render. Otherwise, there is a possibility that the link will render even if no translation is present; in which case, users will receive an HTML error message when they click the link.
#ITEM.TRANSLATIONS.IMAGE#	Common	You can use this tag in conjunction with the #item.translations.value# and #item.translations.label# tags to link the translations icon to a URL that dynamically assembles a page that lists links to all translations of this object in the portal. For example: <a href="#item.translations.value#"> <img src="#item.translations.image#" alt="#item.translations.label#"> </a> This tag must be placed in an <img src> tag to render properly: <img src="#item.translations.image#">
#ITEM.NEWFLAG#	Common	The fully formed hyperlink to a page listing all new objects. If the object does not fall within the time limit specified for new objects, the link does not display. For example, if the page group is configured to flag objects as new for three days after they are uploaded, and the current object was uploaded seven days ago, the object is no longer considered new, and the link no longer displays next to the object.
#ITEM.NEWFLAG.LABEL#	Common	*New Items*

Substitution Tag	Type	Value Set By...

#ITEM.NEWFLAG.VALUE#	Common	The URL that renders a page that lists hyperlinks to all objects labeled *New Items*. What qualifies as new is configured at the page group level on the page group properties Items tab. Use this tag in an HTML href tag. For example:
		
		`<a href="#item.newflag.value#">`
		`#item.newflag.label#</a>`
		
		In contrast to the #ITEM.NEWFLAG# this tag, consider placing the VALUE tag in a PL/SQL conditional statement to control whether it will render. Otherwise, there is a possibility that the link will render even if no objects fall within the New Flag time limit; in which case, users will receive an HTML error message when they click the link.

#ITEM.NEWFLAG.IMAGE#	Common	You can use this tag in conjunction with the #item.newflag.value# and #item.newflag.label# tags to link the new objects icon to a URL that dynamically assembles a page that lists links to all new objects in the portal to which the user has access privileges. For example:
		
		`<a href="#item.newflag.value#">`
		`<img src="#item.newflag.image#" alt="#item.newflag.label#">`
		`</a>`
		
		This tag must be placed in an <img src> tag to render properly:
		
		`<img src="#item.newflag.image#">`

#ITEM.PERSPECTIVES#	Common	All perspectives applied to the object, listed as HTML links, which, when clicked, return a search result of all objects sharing the same perspective. This tag renders the same information as the tag #ITEM.PERSPECTIVES.VALUE#.
#ITEM.PERSPECTIVES.LABEL#	Common	*Perspectives*
#ITEM.PERSPECTIVES.VALUE#	Common	All perspectives applied to the object, listed as HTML links, which, when clicked, return a search result of all objects sharing the same perspective.
#ITEM.PERSPECTIVES[*n*]#	Common	The fully formed hyperlink to a page that lists links to all objects that are classified under the specified perspective. If the relevant perspective has not been applied to the object, the link does not display.

Substitution Tag	Type	Value Set By...

#ITEM.PERSPECTIVES[*n*].LABEL	Common	The display name of the *n*th perspective. Use this tag in conjunction with the #ITEM.PERSPECTIVES[n].VALUE# tag to render the targeted perspective. For example:
		`<a href="#item.perspectives2.value#">`
		`#item.perspectives2.label#</a>`
		This construction will list the second perspective in the list of perspectives associated with the object. The perspective will display as a link, which, when clicked, will return a search result of all objects sharing the same perspective.

#ITEM.PERSPECTIVES[*n*].VALUE#	Common	The URL that renders the value of the *n*th perspective in the list of perspectives applied to the object. Use this tag in an HTML href tag. For example:
		`<a href="#item.perspectives2.value#">`
		`#item.perspectives2.label#</a>`
		In contrast to the #ITEM.PERSPECTIVES[n]# tag, consider placing the VALUE tag in a PL/SQL conditional statement to control whether it will render. Otherwise, there is a possibility that the link will render even if no *n*th perspective is present. In such a case, users receive an HTML error message when they click the link.

#ITEM.PERSPECTIVES[*n*].STYLE#	Common	The style applied to the object's perspective attribute. Use this tag inside a <font class=" "> tag. For example:
		`<a href="#item.perspectives4.value#">`
		`<font class="#item.perspectives4.style#">`
		`#item.perspectives4.label#`
		`</font></a>`

Substitution Tag	Type	Value Set By...

#ITEM.PERSPECTIVES[*n*].IMAGE#	Common	The icon image that is associated with a perspective. The value [*n*] refers to the perspective's position on the list of perspectives that are selected for the object. If the object has only one perspective, the value is 1. This tag must be placed in an <img src> tag to render properly:
		
		<img src="#item.perspectives3.image#">
		
		You can use this tag in conjunction with the #item.perspectives[*n*].value# and #item.perspectives[*n*].label# tags to set up a linked image. Users click the image to go to a page that lists links to all objects classified by the specified perspective. For example:
		
		<a href="#item.perspectives4.value#">
		<img src="#item.perspectives4.image#"
		alt="#item.persepctives4.label#">
		</a>
		
		If every perspective in a page group does not have a related perspective icon, you can set up a conditional statement using <oracle></oracle> tags and PL/SQL that renders the icon when it is present and prevents attempts at rendering when it is not present. For example:
		
		<oracle>
		if length('#item.perspectives1.image#') > 0 then
		   htp.p('<a href="#item.perspectives1.value#">
		   <img src="#item.perspectives1.image#"></a>');
		else
		   htp.p('<a href="#item.perspectives1.value#">
		   #item.perspectives1.label#</a>');
		end if;
		</oracle>

#ITEM.PROPERTYSHEET#	Common	The fully formed hyperlink to the object's property sheet.
#ITEM.PROPERTYSHEET.LABEL#	Common	*Property Sheet*
#ITEM.PROPERTYSHEET.VALUE#	Common	The URL that renders the object's property sheet. Use this tag in an HTML href tag. For example: <a href="#item.propertysheet.value#"> #item.propertysheet.label#</a>

Substitution Tag	Type	Value Set By...
#ITEM.PROPERTYSHEET.IMAGE#	Common	The icon that this tag renders depends on the type of object the property sheet describes. This tag must be placed in an <img src> tag to render properly: <img src="#item.propertysheet.image#"> You can use this tag in conjunction with the #item.propertysheet.value# and #item.propertysheet.label# tags to link to the object's property sheet. For example: <a href="#item.propertysheet.value#"> <img src="#item.propertysheet.image#" alt="#item.propertysheet.label#"> </a>
#ITEM.UPDATEDFLAG#	Common	The fully formed hyperlink to a page that lists links to all recently updated objects. If no objects have been updated recently, the link does not display.
#ITEM.UPDATEDFLAG.LABEL#	Common	*Recently Updated Items*
#ITEM.UPDATEDFLAG.VALUE#	Common	The URL that renders a page that contains a linked list of all newly updated objects. What qualifies as a newly updated object is configured at the page group level on the page group properties Items tab. Use this tag in an HTML href tag. For example: <a href="#item.updatedflag.value#"> #item.updatedflag.label#</a> In contrast to the #ITEM.UPDATEDFLAG# tag, consider placing the VALUE tag in a PL/SQL conditional statement to control whether it will render. Otherwise, there is a possibility that the link will render even if no object has been updated within the specified period; in which case, users will receive an HTML error message when they click the link.
#ITEM.UPDATEDFLAG.IMAGE#	Common	You can use this tag in conjunction with the #item.updatedflag.value# and #item.updatedflag.label# tags to link the updated icon to a URL that dynamically assembles a page that lists links to all updated objects in the portal to which the user has access privileges. For example: <a href="#item.updatedflag.value#"> <img src="#item.updatedflag.image#" alt="#item.updatedflag.label#"> </a> Used alone, this tag must be placed in an <img src> tag to render properly: <img src="#item.updatedflag.image#">

Substitution Tag	Type	Value Set By...
#ITEM.ITEMFUNCTION#	Common	A URL that renders a page listing hyperlinks to all functions associated with the object. This tag renders the same information as the tag #ITEM.ITEMFUNCTION.VALUE#.
#ITEM.ITEMFUNCTION.LABEL#	Common	*Associated Functions*
#ITEM.ITEMFUNCTION.VALUE#	Common	A URL that renders a page listing hyperlinks to all functions associated with the object.
#ITEM.ITEMFUNCTION[*n*]#	Common	A fully formed link to the *n*th function associated with the object. If the object does not have an *n*th associated function, the link does not display.
#ITEM.ITEMFUNCTION[n].LABEL#	Common	The display name of the *n*th function.
#ITEM.ITEMFUNCTION[n].VALUE#	Common	In the presence of multiple associated functions, the URL to the function in the *n*th position on the list of functions associated with the object. Use this tag in an HTML href tag. For example: <a href="#item.itemfunction3.value#"> #item.itemfunction3.label#</a> This will result in a linked label of the third function associated with the object. Users click the label to perform the related function. In contrast to the #ITEM.ITEMFUNCTION[*n*]# tag, consider placing the VALUE tag in a PL/SQL conditional statement to control whether it will render. Otherwise, there is a possibility that the link will render even if an *n*th function has not been associated with the object; in which case, users will receive an HTML error message when they click the link.
#ITEM.ITEMFUNCTION[*n*].STYLE#	Common	The style associated with the object function. Use this tag inside a <font class=" "> tag. For example: <a href="#item.function[n].value#"> <font class="#item.function[n].style#"> #item.function[n].label# </font></a>
#ITEM.PUBLISHDATE#	Common	The string value of the object's publish date, labeled and wrapped in its associated style. This tag is equivalent to: <font class="#item.publishdate.style#"> #item.publishdate.label#: #item.publishdate.value# </font> Note: This tag uses the format: Publish Date: DD-MON-YYYY HH12:MI PM, that is, Publish Date: 06-MAY-2004 01:45 PM

Substitution Tag	Type	Value Set By...
#ITEM.PUBLISHDATE.LABEL#	Common	*Publish Date*
#ITEM.PUBLISHDATE.VALUE#	Common	The string value of the object's publish date. This tag uses the format: DD-MON-YYYY HH12:MI PM For example: 06-MAY-2004 01:45 PM
#ITEM.PUBLISHDATE.STYLE#	Common	The style applied to the object's publish date. Use this tag inside a <font class=" "> tag. For example: <font class="#item.publishdate.style#"> #item.publishdate.label#: #item.publishdate.value# </font>
#ITEM.CATEGORY#	Common	The fully formed hyperlink to a search results page that links to all objects classified under the relevant category. If a category has not been applied to the object, the link does not display.
#ITEM.CATEGORY.LABEL#	Common	The display name of the category assigned to the object.
#ITEM.CATEGORY.VALUE#	Common	The URL that renders search results for a search run against the category's display name. Use this tag in an HTML href tag. For example: <a href="#item.category.value#"> #item.category.label#</a> In contrast to the #ITEM.CATEGORY# tag, consider placing the VALUE tag in a PL/SQL conditional statement to control whether it will render. Otherwise, there is a possibility that the link will render even if no category has been applied to the object; in which case, users will receive an HTML error message when they click the link.
#ITEM.CATEGORY.STYLE#	Common	The style applied to the object's category. Use this tag inside a <font class=" "> tag. For example: <a href="#item.category.value#"> <font class="#item.category.style#"> #item.category.label# </font></a>

Substitution Tag	Type	Value Set By...

#ITEM.CATEGORY.IMAGE#	Common	The image associated with a category. This tag must be placed in an <img src> tag to render properly:
		
		<img src="#item.category.image#">
		
		You can use this tag in conjunction with the #item.category.value# and #item.category.label# tags to set up a linked image. Users click the image to go to a page that lists links to all objects classified by the specified category. For example:
		
		<a href="#item.category.value#">
		<img src="#item.category.image#"
		alt="#item.category.label#">
		</a>
		
		If every category in a page group does not have a related category icon, you can set up a conditional statement using <oracle></oracle> tags and PL/SQL to render the icon when it is present and prevent attempts at rendering when it is not present. For example:
		
		<oracle>
		if length('#item.category.image#') > 0 then
		   htp.p('<a href="#item.category.value#">
		   <img src="#item.category.image#"></a>');
		else
		   htp.p('<a href="#item.category.value#">
		   #item.category.label#</a>');
		end if;
		</oracle>

#ITEM.UPDATEDATE#	Common	The string value of the date of the object's latest update, labeled and wrapped in its associated style. This tag is equivalent to: <font class="#item.updatedate.style#"> #item.updatedate.label#: #item.updatedate.value# </font> Note: This tag uses the format: Date Updated: DD-MON-YYYY, that is, Date Updated: 06-MAY-2004
#ITEM.UPDATEDATE.LABEL#	Common	*Date Updated*
#ITEM.UPDATEDATE.VALUE#	Common	The string value of the date of the object's latest update. This tag uses the format: DD-MON-YYYY, for example, 06-MAY-2004

Substitution Tag	Type	Value Set By...
#ITEM.UPDATEDATE.STYLE#	Common	The style applied to the object's update value. Use this tag inside a <font class=" "> tag. For example: <font class="#item.updatedate.style#"> #item.updatedate.label#: #item.updatedate.value# </font>
#ITEM.UPDATOR#	Common	The username of the user who last updated the object, labeled and wrapped in the associated style. This tag is equivalent to: <font class="#item.updator.style#"> #item.updator.label#: #item.updator.value# </font>
#ITEM.UPDATOR.LABEL#	Common	*Last Updated By*
#ITEM.UPDATOR.VALUE#	Common	The user name of the user who updated the object.
#ITEM.UPDATOR.STYLE#	Common	The style applied to the object updator attribute. Use this tag inside a <font class=" "> tag. For example: <font class="#item.updator.style#"> #item.updator.label#: #item.updator.value# </font>
#ITEM.EXPIREDATE.LABEL#	Item	*Expire Date*
#ITEM.EXPIREDATE.VALUE#	Item	The string value of the date the item will expire. This tag uses the format: DD-MON-YYYY HH12:MI PM, for example, 06-MAY-2004 01:45 PM
#ITEM.EXPIREDATE.STYLE#	Item	The style applied to the item's expire date. Use this tag inside a <font class=" "> tag. For example: <font class="#item.expiredate.style#"> #item.expiredate.label#: #item.expiredate.value#</font>
#ITEM.VERSIONS#	Item	The fully formed hyperlink to a page listing all available versions of the item. Item versioning must be enabled for the page group for this hyperlink to display.
#ITEM.VERSIONS.LABEL#	Item	*Versions*

Substitution Tag	Type	Value Set By...

#ITEM.VERSIONS.VALUE#	Item	The URL that renders a page that lists hyperlinks to each of the item's versions (a location within the portal), indicates which is the current (displayed) version, shows when the item was last updated, and lists the user who last updated the item. Use this tag in an HTML href tag. For example:
		
		`<a href="#item.versions.value#">`
		`#item.versions.label#</a>`
		
		In contrast to the #ITEM.VERSIONS# tag, consider placing the VALUE tag in a PL/SQL conditional statement to control whether it will render. Otherwise, there is a possibility that the link will render even if versioning is not enabled for the page group; in which case, users will receive an HTML error message when they click the link.

#ITEM.VERSIONS.IMAGE#	Item	You can use this tag in conjunction with the #item.versions.value# and #item.versions.label# tags to link the versions icon to a URL that dynamically assembles a page that lists links to all versions of the given item. For example:
		
		`<a href="#item.versions.value#">`
		`<img src="#item.versions.image#"`
		`alt="#item.versions.label#">`
		`</a>`
		
		This tag must be placed in an <img src> tag to render properly:
		
		`<img src="#item.versions.image#">`

#ITEM.DOCUMENTSIZE#	Item	The size of the uploaded file or image item, labeled and wrapped in its associated style. This tag is equivalent to:
		
		`<font class="#item.documentsize.style#">`
		`#item.documentsize.lable#:`
		`#item.documentsize.value#`
		`</font>`

#ITEM.DOCUMENTSIZE.LABEL#	Item	*Document Size*
#ITEM.DOCUMENTSIZE.VALUE#	Item	The size of the uploaded file or image item.

#ITEM.DOCUMENTSIZE.STYLE#	Item	The style applied to the item's document size. Use this tag inside a <font class=" "> tag. For example:
		
		`<font class="#item.documentsize.style#">`
		`#item.documentsize.label#:`
		`#item.documentsize.value#`
		`</font>`

Substitution Tag	Type	Value Set By...
#ITEM.VIEWASHTML#	Item	The fully formed hyperlink to the item displayed as HTML. This lets you see binary files with textual content as a Web page. Such files include Microsoft Word documents or Excel spreadsheets. If the item cannot be displayed as HTML, the link does not display.
#ITEM.VIEWASHTML.LABEL#	Item	*View as HTML*
#ITEM.VIEWASHTML.VALUE#	Item	The URL that renders the file item content as HTML. This tag enables you to see binary files with textual content as a Web page. Such files include Microsoft Word documents or Excel spreadsheets. Use this tag in an HTML href tag. For example: <a href="#item.viewashtml.value#"> #item.viewashtml.label#</a> In contrast to the #ITEM.VIEWASHTML# tag, consider placing the VALUE tag in a PL/SQL conditional statement to control whether it will render. Otherwise, there is a possibility that the link will render even if the item cannot be viewed as HTML; in which case, users will receive an HTML error message when they click the link.
#ITEM.VIEWASHTML.IMAGE#	Item	This tag must be placed in an <img src> tag to render properly: <img src="#item.viewashtml.image#"> You can use this tag in conjunction with the #item.viewashtml.value# and #item.viewashtml.label# tags to link to an HTML view of the binary file (that is, the Microsoft Word file, the Excel spreadsheet, and the like). For example: <a href="#item.viewashtml.value#"> <img src="#item.viewashtml.image#" alt="#item.viewashtml.label#"> </a>
#ITEM.THEMES#	Item	The fully formed hyperlink to the linguistic themes of the item's content. If Oracle Text is not enabled, the link does not display.
#ITEM.THEMES.LABEL#	Item	*View Themes.* This attribute is used in conjunction with a portal search. It displays only if Oracle Text is enabled and only for File and Simple File items, or items of a type based on the Simple File item type.

Substitution Tag	Type	Value Set By...
#ITEM.THEMES.VALUE#	Item	The URL that renders the linguistic themes of the content. This attribute is used in conjunction with a portal search. It displays only if Oracle Text is enabled and only for File and Simple File items, or items of a type based on the Simple File item type. Use this tag in an HTML href tag. For example: <a href="#item.themes.value#"> #item.themes.label#</a> In contrast to the #ITEM.THEMES# tag, consider placing the VALUE tag in a PL/SQL conditional statement to control whether it will render. Otherwise, there is a possibility that the link will render even if Oracle Text is not turned on; in which case, users will receive an HTML error message when they click the link.
#ITEM.THEMES.IMAGE#	Item	This tag must be placed in an <img src> tag to render properly: <img src="#item.themes.image#"> You can use this tag in conjunction with the #item.themes.value# and #item.themes.label# tags to link to the item's linguistic themes. For example: <a href="#item.themes.value#"> <img src="#item.themes.image#" alt="#item.themes.label#"> </a> This attribute is used in conjunction with a portal search. It displays only if Oracle Text is enabled and only for File and Simple File items, or items of a type based on the Simple File item type.
#ITEM.GIST#	Item	The fully formed hyperlink to a paragraph summarizing the item's content (its gist). If Oracle Text is not enabled, the link does not display.
#ITEM.GIST.LABEL#	Item	*View Gist.* This attribute is used in conjunction with a portal search. It displays only if Oracle Text is enabled and only for File and Simple File items, or items of a type based on the Simple File item type.

Substitution Tag	Type	Value Set By...
#ITEM.GIST.VALUE#	Item	The URL that renders a paragraph that summarizes the document. This attribute is used in conjunction with a portal search. It displays only if Oracle Text is enabled and only for File and Simple File items, or items of a type based on the Simple File item type. Use this tag in an HTML href tag. For example: <a href="#item.gist.value#">#item.gist.label#</a> In contrast to the #ITEM.GIST# tag, consider placing the VALUE tag in a PL/SQL conditional statement to control whether it will render. Otherwise, there is a possibility that the link will render even if Oracle Text is not turned on; in which case, users will receive an HTML error message when they click the link.
#ITEM.GIST.IMAGE#	Item	This tag must be placed in an <img src> tag to render properly: <img src="#item.gist.image#"> You can use this tag in conjunction with the #item.gist.value# and #item.gist.label# tags to link to a summary paragraph about the item. For example: <a href="#item.gist.value#"> <img src="#item.gist.image#" alt="#item.gist.label#"> </a> This attribute is used in conjunction with a portal search. It displays only if Oracle Text is enabled and only for File and Simple File items, or items of a type based on the Simple File item type.
#ITEM.CONTENT#	Item	The item content. • If the item display option is set to display item content directly on the page, the item content is rendered on the page. • If the item display option is set to display as a link, an HTML link, using the item's title or Display Name, is rendered on the page. This tag is equivalent to #ITEM.CONTENT.VALUE#.
#ITEM.CONTENT.LABEL#	Item	*Item Content.* To render the object's display name, use #item.title.value#.

Substitution Tag	**Type**	**Value Set By...**
#ITEM.CONTENT.VALUE#	Item	The item content. This tag renders differently for different item types and for each display option, whether content is displayed on the page or as a link on the page: TEXT—**On page**: The text is rendered; **As link**: The item's path-based URL is rendered. PL/SQL—**On page**: The string value from the execution of the PL/SQL code is rendered; **As link**: The item's path-based URL is rendered. FILE—**On page**: The file content is rendered; **As link**: The item's path-based URL is rendered. URL—**On page**: The content from the URL is rendered; **As link**: The item's path-based URL is rendered. IMAGE—Always displays the image path. You can view the image directly on the page by placing this tag in an <img src=" "> tag. If other types of items will be included in a region that uses an HTML Content Layout template, you can use <oracle></oracle> tags to set up a condition that considers the item type and renders the item appropriately. The value displayed in the browser window depends not only on the object type being rendered, but also on the display option that was selected for the object in OracleAS Portal. When the link display option is selected, the resulting URL that displays in a region formatted with a Content Layout template is not linked. That is, users cannot click the URL to navigate to the object. To make the URL navigable when an object's display option is set to *link*, enclose the substitution tag in an HREF tag. This will render a link that users can click to render the object. When an HTML Content Layout template is applied, problems can arise when different objects in the same region have different display option attribute values. See the example following this table for a way to successfully construct a Content Layout template that displays both linked and directly displayed objects in the same region. The example also demonstrates a template that can be applied to both portlet and item regions.

#ITEM.CONTENT.STYLE#	Item	The style applied to the item's label. Use this tag inside a <font class=" "> tag. For example:
		
		`<a href="#item.content.value#">`
		`<font class="#item.content.style#">`
		`#item.content.label#`
		`</font></a>`

Substitution Tag	Type	Value Set By...
#ITEM.ITEMTYPEICON#	Item	The icon denoting the item's type with ALT text, aligned and sized as specified in the portal. This tag is equivalent to, for example: `<img src="#item.itemtypeicon.value#" alt="#item.itemtypeicon.label#" border="0" align="absbottom" width="16" height="16">` The conditions that determine which image is rendered include: • For items that have an associated file of a recognized MIME type, this tag renders an image that identifies the MIME type, for example: The recognized MIME types are: doc, exe, gif, html, htm, jpg, peg, pdf, ppt, rtf, txt, wav, xls, zip. • For other items, this tag renders the image entered for the item type's Image attribute. If no image was provided, the built-in base-type icon is used.
#ITEM.ITEMTYPEICON.LABEL#	Item	The type of item. The conditions that determine which text is rendered are as follows: • For items that have an associated file of a recognized MIME type, this tag renders the text that identifies the MIME type, for example, `Adobe Portable Document Format`. The recognized MIME types are: doc, exe, gif, html, htm, jpg, peg, pdf, ppt, rtf, txt, wav, xls, zip. • For other items, this tag renders the value entered for the item type's Display Name attribute. When the page group is rendered in a language other than its default language, the text is translated automatically when a translation is available in the language. For example: • Translations for recognized MIME types and built-in item types are available. • Translation for a custom item type is available when a translation is provided for the item type's Display Name attribute.

Substitution Tag	Type	Value Set By...

#ITEM.ITEMTYPEICON.VALUE#	Item	The URL of the image that represents the item type. The conditions that determine which image is rendered include:
		
		• For items that have an associated file of a recognized MIME type, this tag renders a URL of an image that identifies the MIME type.
		
		The recognized MIME types are: doc, exe, gif, html, htm, jpg, peg, pdf, ppt, rtf, txt, wav, xls, zip.
		
		• For other items, this tag renders the URL of the image entered for the item type's Image attribute. If no image was provided, the built-in base-type icon is used.
		
		You can use two ITEMTYPEICON tags together to render an icon of a standard size and its Alt text. For example:
		
		`<img src="#item.itemtypeicon.value#"`
		`alt="#item.itemtypeicon.label#" WIDTH="16"`
		`HEIGHT="16">`
		
		The `WIDTH` and `HEIGHT` values guarantee consistency in the rendered icon's size.

#ITEM.SUBSCRIBE#	Item	A fully formed subscription link. If approvals and notifications are not enabled, the link does not display. Use this tag only when approvals and notifications are enabled for the page group that owns the page where the item is placed.

#ITEM.SUBSCRIBE.LABEL#	Item	*Subscribe* or *Unsubscribe*. You can use this tag in conjunction with the #item.subscribe.value# tag to render a subscription or an unsubscribe link. For example:
		
		`<a href="#item.subscribe.value#">`
		`#item.subscribe.label#`
		`</a>`
		
		You can also wrap the value tag around your own label text. But keep in mind, all items placed in the same region use whatever static label you enter. Use this tag only when approvals and notifications are enabled for the page group that owns the page where the item is placed. The value that is rendered by this tag depends on the state of the item. If the item is not yet subscribed to, #item.subscribe.label# returns *Subscribe*. If the item is already subscribed to, #item.subscribe.label# returns *Unsubscribe*.

Substitution Tag	Type	Value Set By...

#ITEM.SUBSCRIBE.VALUE#	Item	The URL that enables users to subscribe to an item or the URL that enables users to unsubscribe from an item. Use this tag in an HTML href tag. For example:
		
		`<a href="#item.subscribe.value#">`
		`#item.subscribe.label#`
		`</a>`
		
		In contrast to the #ITEM.SUBSCRIBE# tag, consider placing the VALUE tag in a PL/SQL conditional statement to control whether it will render. Otherwise, there is a possibility that the link will render even if item subscriptions are not enabled; in which case, users receive an HTML error message when they click the link. Use this tag only when approvals and notifications are enabled for the page group that owns the page where the item is placed. The value that is rendered by this tag depends on the state of the item. If the item is not yet subscribed to, #item.subscribe.value# returns the URL that allows users to subscribe to the item. If the item is already subscribed to, #item.subscribe.value# returns the URL that allows users to unsubscribe from the item.

#ITEM.SUBSCRIBE.IMAGE#	Item	This tag must be placed in an <img src> tag to render properly:
		
		`<img src="#item.subscribe.image#">`
		
		You can use this tag in conjunction with the #item.subscribe.value# and #item.subscribe.label# tags to render the item's subscribe link. For example:
		
		`<a href="#item.subscribe.value#">`
		`<img src="#item.subscribe.image#"`
		`alt="#item.subscribe.label#">`
		`</a>`
		
		Once an item is subscribed to, OracleAS Portal automatically switches this image to the Unsubscribe icon. Use this tag only when approvals and notifications are enabled for the page group that owns the page where the item is placed.

#ITEM.VERSION_NUMBER#	Item	The numeric value that identifies a particular item version, labeled and wrapped in its associated style. This tag is equivalent to:
		
		`<font class="#item.version_number.style#">`
		`#item.version_number.label#:`
		`#item.version_number.value#`
		`</font>`

Substitution Tag	**Type**	
#ITEM.VERSION_NUMBER.LABEL#	Item	*Version Number*
#ITEM.VERSION_NUMBER.VALUE#	Item	The numeric value that identifies a particular version.

#ITEM.VERSION_NUMBER.STYLE#	Item	The style applied to an item's version number. Use this tag inside a <font class=" "> tag. For example:
		
		`<font class="#item.version_number.style#">`
		`#item.version_number.label#:`
		`#item.version_number.value#`
		`</font>`

#ITEM.[*attribute_name*].LABEL#	Item	The custom attribute's display name.
#ITEM.[*attribute_name*].VALUE#	Item	The stored value of the custom attribute.

#ITEM.[*attribute_name*].STYLE#	Item	The style applied to the custom attribute. Use this tag inside a <font class=" "> tag. For example:
		
		`<font class="#item.[attribute name].style#">`
		`#item.[attribute name].label#:`
		`#item.[attribute name].value#`
		`</font>`

#ITEM.PORTLETCONTENT#	Portlet	The portlet. This tag renders the same content as the #item.portletcontent.value# tag.
#ITEM.PORTLETCONTENT.LABEL#	Portlet	*Portlet Content.* Use the tag #item.title.value# to render the object's display name.
#ITEM.PORTLETCONTENT.VALUE#	Portlet	The portlet. For example, if the Favorites portlet is added to a region formatted with an HTML Content Layout containing this tag, this tag will render the Favorites portlet.

What you can do with HTML Content Layouts is really only limited by your imagination (and your knowledge of HTML and JavaScript), but there are two standard examples that represent the types of things you can do with HTML Content Layouts: creating expandable regions and scrollable regions.

Creating an Expandable Region

As wonderful as the Internet is for finding information, we've all seen pages that have just too much information on them. Viewing these pages can be overwhelming for end users as they try to make sense of all of the information presented. Another problem can happen when the amount of information on a page causes the page to expand beyond the vertical size of the end user's screen. It's probably not an issue if the page extends a little bit beyond the size of the screen, but adding too much content to a page can result in a Web page that forces the user to scroll repeatedly. In many cases, this can be uncomfortable for the end user, especially if the user is trying to link up multiple pieces of information on the page.

To address this issue, we can create an HTML Content Region that takes content and only displays the title of the content. When the user clicks the title, the region expands to show all of the content. This way, the end user can select topics he or she wishes to get more information on, rather than be bombarded with too much information.

To see how this works, let's create a new region and add some content to it. If you are not in the OracleAS Portal Navigator already, go there now by clicking the Navigator link on the top right of any OracleAS Portal page. Click the Edit Root Page link next to the Dashboard_1 page group. Click the Add Region Right icon (it has a small icon pointing to the right in the top bar of the existing region—you can hover your pointer over the icons to see what they are). In that new region, click the Add Item icon (again, hover your mouse over the icons to find the Add Item icon). In the first page of the Add Item Wizard, select Text in the top drop-down box. Click Next. You will see a screen similar to Figure 4-13.

Add some text (what you enter really doesn't matter – just make sure it has multiple lines) and enter a title in the Display Name field. Click Finish. Repeat this process for a second text item. After entering the two text items, your page should look something like Figure 4-14.

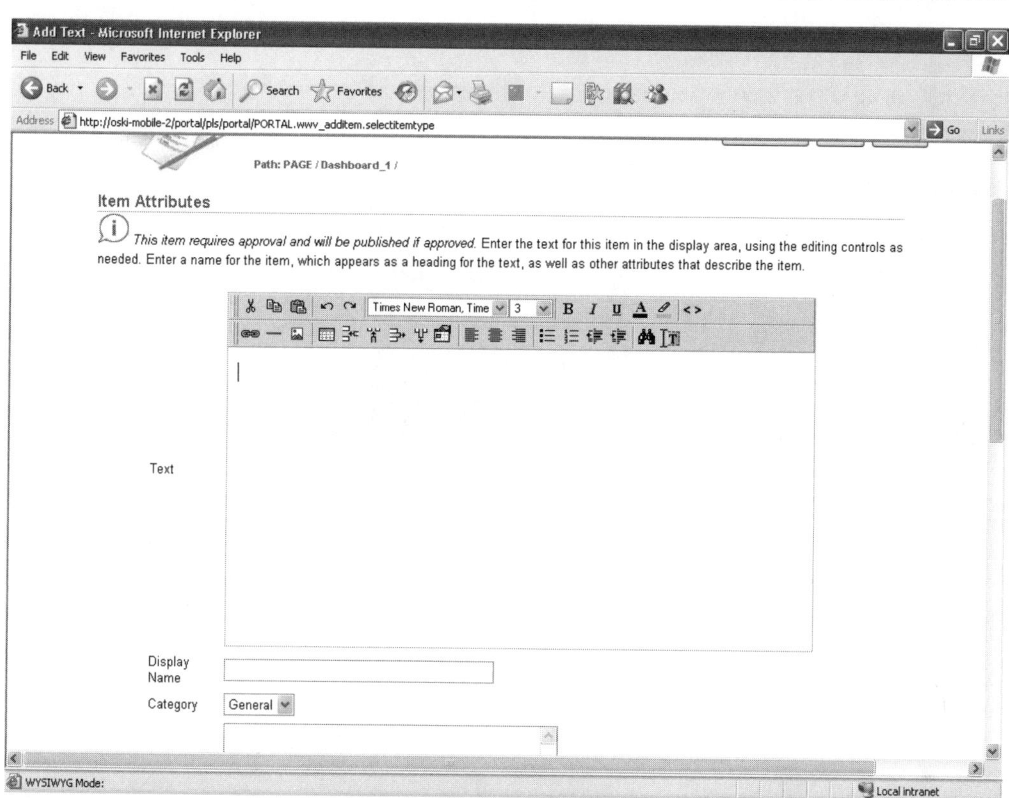

FIGURE 4-13 *The Item Attributes for the Add Item page*

This page is not extremely large, and an end user should be able to view that information relatively easily, but what if the content keeps getting updated and expanded? Create a new HTML Content Layout by selecting the Page Group in the OracleAS Portal Navigator, then HTML Templates, and then Create New HTML

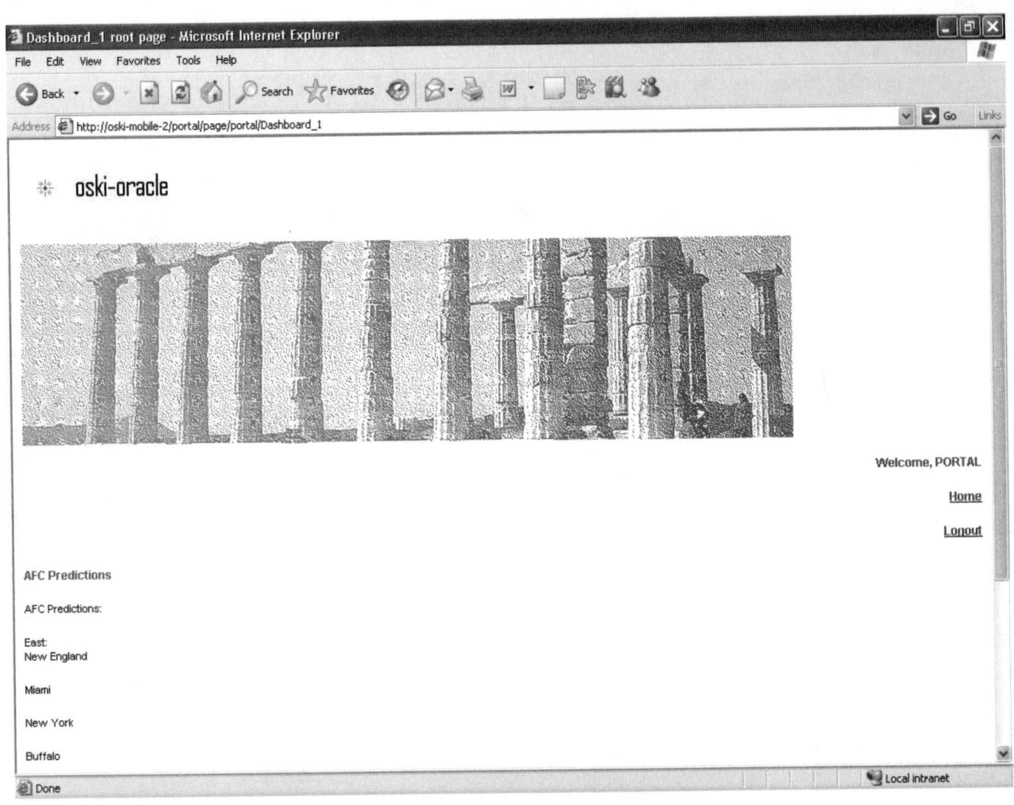

FIGURE 4-14 *The Dashboard_1 root page with two items added*

Template on the top left of the screen. Select HTML Content Layout from the drop-down box at the top of the page. Enter the following code (without the line numbers) in the Template Definition:

```
<SCRIPT language=JavaScript>
<!--
function expand(id) {
 if (document.getElementById)
   {
    if (document.getElementById(id).style.display == "none")
      {
```

```
8            document.getElementById(id).style.display = 'block';
9          } else
10           {
11            document.getElementById(id).style.display = 'none';
12          }
13      } else
14       {
15         if (document.layers)
16           {
17             if (document.id.display == "none")
18              {
19                document.id.display = 'block';
20             } else
21              {
22                document.id.display = 'none';
23             }
24         } else
25             {
26               if (document.all.id.style.visibility == "none")
27                {
28                  document.all.id.style.display = 'block';
29               } else
30                {
31                  document.all.id.style.display = 'none';
32               }
33             }
34         }
35      }
36      //-->
37      </SCRIPT>
38      <img src="/images/expand.gif" width="7" height="7"
    border="0"> <A onClick="expand('#ITEM.ID#');" ><span
    style="cursor: pointer; cursor: hand; font-size:70%;"
    >#ITEM.TITLE#</span></A>
39      <DIV id=#ITEM.ID# style="DISPLAY: none">#ITEM.CONTENT#</DIV>
```

This listing really starts on line 38. By default, only the title of the item is displayed (by way of the #ITEM.TITLE# tag). For every item in the region an action is defined (onClick). When the user clicks an item, the JavaScript procedure "expand" is called and the ID of the item (#ITEM.ID#) is passed as a parameter. The JavaScript procedure "expand" is declared in lines 1–37. That procedure checks to see what the current display mode is (if the item is expanded, then we want to collapse it; otherwise, it's already collapsed and we want to expand it) and changes the display mode to the appropriate setting. Save this content layout as **EXPANDABLE_ITEMS**.

TIP

If you look closely at line 38, you'll see a reference to an image called expand.gif in the /images directory. How did OracleAS Portal know where to find it? By default, OracleAS Portal starts searching from the ORACLE_HOME/portal directory (where ORACLE_HOME is the location of the mid-tier installation on your server) to find the specified files. In this example, I installed the Oracle Application Server middle tier in the c:\oracle\mt_home directory on my Microsoft Windows 2003 server. When I specified /images/expand.gif in line 38, the OracleAS Portal engine searched the c:\oracle\mt_home\portal\images directory and, upon finding the expand.gif file there, displayed it on the page.

Now that the HTML Content Layout has been created, we need to apply it to a region. Edit the root page for the Dashboard_1 page group and click the pencil icon in the new region you just added your two text items into. Click the Attributes tab and select the radio button next to Use HTML Content Layout. Make sure EXPANDABLE_ITEMS is selected in the drop-down box and click OK. Your page should now resemble Figure 4-15. Click the title of the text items repeatedly and notice how they expand and contract.

You could apply the EXPANDABLE_ITEMS to a region with portlets, but it wouldn't do much good. Why? The code in the "expand" JavaScript procedure only knows how to expand items—it won't be able to expand portlets, so you'll never see anything beyond the header of the portlet.

What Is AJAX?

There's been a lot of talk lately in the development community about a new way of programming called AJAX. AJAX stands for Asynchronous JavaScript and XML and is a term describing Web development techniques for creating Web applications using HTML and Cascading Style Sheets (CSS). The main benefit of designing pages using AJAX is the ability to update information on the page quickly. This is done by refreshing only the part of the page that needs updating. As you've seen, the use of HTML Content Layouts can provide much of this functionality without the technical knowledge needed to code AJAX implementations efficiently.

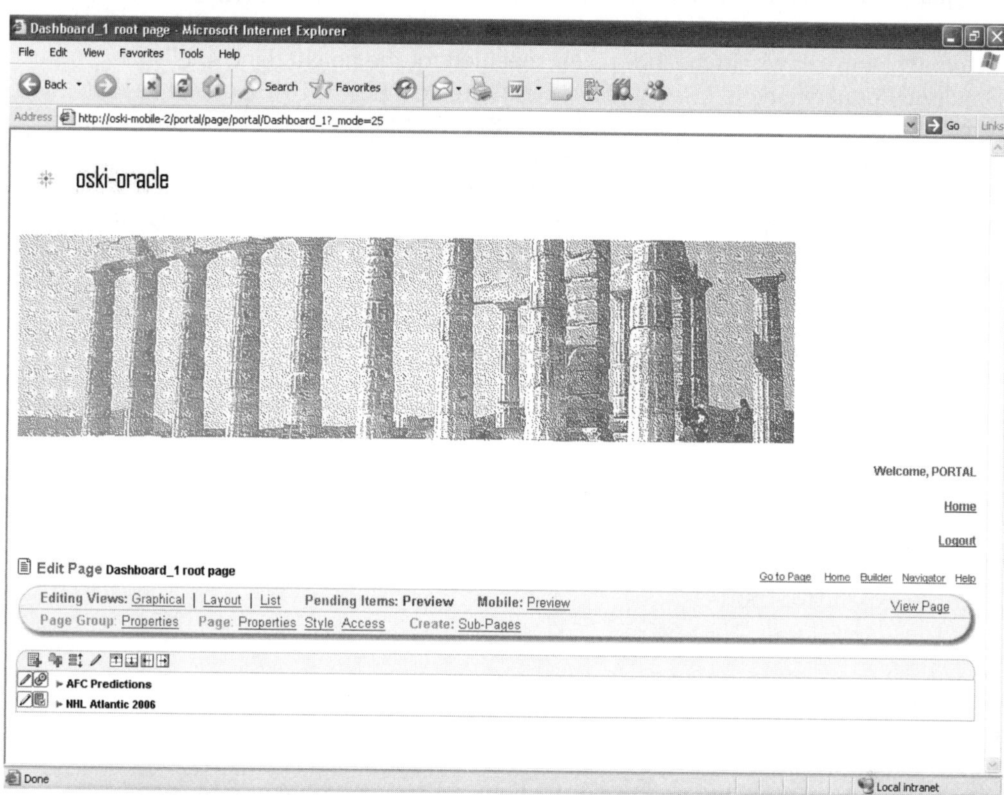

FIGURE 4-15 *The Dashboard_1 root page with an HTML Content Layout applied*

Creating a Scrollable Region

Another common use of HTML Content Layouts is the need to create regions that scroll: that is, the size of the region remains fixed, while a scrollbar on the right side of the region appears, allowing the end user to scroll through the information provided in the region. HTML makes it incredibly easy to implement this functionality. Consider the following listing (again, line numbers have been added for reference):

```
#ITEM.TITLE#
<br>
<div style='height: 100px; overflow:auto;'>
#ITEM.CONTENT#
</div>
```

Line 1 displays the title of the content. Line 3 specifies that the item is to take up 100 pixels within the region. The overflow:auto parameter creates a scroll bar when the content can't fit within the 100 pixels specified for the height. Line 4 tells the OracleAS Portal engine to display the content. Create a new HTML Content Layout with the preceding code and call it **SCROLLABLE_ITEMS**. Edit the Dashboard_1 root page and change the region that you defined to use the EXPANDABLE_ITEMS template. Re-display your page and note how the functionality is different. You can create a scrollable region for portlets by creating a new HTML Content Layout and substituting the appropriate tags:

```
1    #ITEM.TITLE.VALUE#
2    <br>
3    <div style='height: 100px; overflow:auto;'>
4    #ITEM.PORTLETCONTENT.VALUE#
5    </div>
```

Use the preceding listing to create an HTML Content Layout called SCROLLABLE_PORTLETS. Apply this HTML template to a portlet region on the Dashboard_1 root page. In the exercise at the end of this chapter, we are going to take the knowledge of tags and templates to create a new template that will allow us to create expandable portlets.

Exercises

One of my computer science professors in college posed the following question to us, his students:

"Do you think it's better to: a) Spend 5 hours solving a problem or b) Spend 4 ½ hours creating a tool to solve a problem and the other ½ hour using the tool to solve the problem? If you didn't answer b), just walk out right now."

A little harsh maybe, but there's wisdom in those words. Why re-invent the wheel over and over again when OracleAS Portal gives you the tools to design things once, and then use them over and over again? This cuts down on design time and makes the process of changing your OracleAS Portal page design a trivial one.

- Exercise 1: Use a third-party tool to create an HTML Page Skin. If you don't have any images available to you, you can grab images off of the Internet using the technique described in the chapter. You can create quite a hodgepodge of images from different sites, but note how the overall look and feel of the site changes as more and more images are added. Is the look of the site pleasing to the eye? Ask yourself how a non-technical end user would like your site. Think of ways to make your site unique and memorable while maintaining a pleasing experience for the end user.

CAUTION
Please do not use any images you get off of the Internet in your organization's intranet or Internet site(s) or on any commercial site. You will be violating the copyright of the sites you get the images from if you do this. This exercise is for instructional purposes only.

- Exercise 2: If you have access to an advanced editing program, create logos and images to brand your site. Tools like Paint Shop Pro and PhotoShop can be used to create professional-quality graphics easily and quickly. Take a look at some Web sites that get your attention and note what is done on those sites. Also, take a look at the different types of sites (technical sites like Oracle's or Microsoft's) and compare those to sites with different purposes, say an entertainment site like mtv.com. Note how the different type of expected user influences how the page is designed. Since we're focused on an executive dashboard, brainstorm about the types of things that might be on that type of page and how the layout can be designed to reflect that.
- Exercise 3: Create a new HTML Content Layout called EXPANDABLE_PORTLETS. Use the tags shown earlier in Table 4-1 to create a template that can expand portlets. Apply this content layout to a portlet region on your page.

Summary

For a long time, OracleAS Portal page designers were frustrated with the inability to integrate existing design work into OracleAS Portal easily. With OracleAS Portal 10.1.4, that limitation has been removed. Page designers can now use any tool that generates HTML code to lay out their pages and, through the use of HTML Page Skins, create a portal experience for end users that reflects all of the work already performed branding the sites within an organization. The advanced page design features of OracleAS Portal allow page designers to create a rich end-user experience quickly and easily. The HTML Template features take the hassle out of maintaining visual consistency throughout the site by giving page designers a simple way of using third-party tools to reuse existing design work within OracleAS Portal.

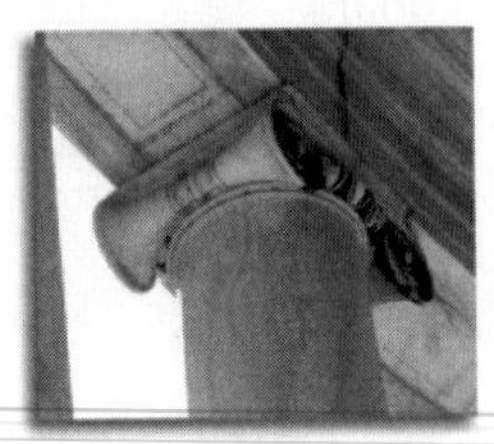

CHAPTER 5

Content Management

racleAS Portal is certainly not the only portal product on the market today. Microsoft sells a portal product called SharePoint, JBoss has a product called JBoss Portal, and IBM sells a product called WebSphere Portal. While all of these products have different philosophies and methods in relation to portlet development, page design, administration, and security, they all share one common feature: the ability to manage files that don't fit into a traditional database structure. These files can include virtually any piece of information that an organization might deem valuable and can be in virtually any format: text documents, Microsoft Word documents or Excel spreadsheets, Adobe PDF documents, etc. These files need to be organized, secured, and made available to the people who need them. The common term for these activities is *content management.*

A good place to start our discussion of OracleAS Portal content management features would be the definition of content management. Content management means acquiring, collecting, authoring, editing, tracking, accessing, and delivering both structured and unstructured digital information. A piece of digital information (a Word document, for example) is the "content" and is referred to, in Oracle's documentation, as an "item." While PL/SQL code can be written to convert, say, a Word document into something the Oracle database can understand and store, the term "content management" refers to a much larger scope. It refers to the overall management of these files, from an item's creation all the way through expiration (a content management term that refers to when an item is no longer needed or available) and possible deletion from the repository. OracleAS Portal has many features that allow content administrators to manage content easily.

OracleAS Portal Content Management Features

As we have seen in Chapter 1, OracleAS Portal allows developers to build components such as forms, reports, charts, and calendars. But how do you manage information that does not fit into one of these traditional component types? The developers of OracleAS Portal were smart enough to design it so that two fundamental types of objects can be displayed on your portal:

- **Portlets** These are small programs that query Oracle databases (or other data sources) and display that data in a form, report, calendar, etc.
- **Items** Items are pieces of unstructured content stored in the OracleAS Portal repository and displayed in a specific location on an OracleAS Portal page.

This chapter deals with items and the things content administrators can do with them within OracleAS Portal. While it is not mandatory to define a position with that title within your company, many organizations find it beneficial to do so. A *content administrator,* particularly for a large, public portal site, is usually tasked with making sure content is available, making sure the content is available at appropriate times, and making sure the content that is available is appropriate for potential end users. For smaller OracleAS Portal sites, it is common for a page designer or OracleAS Portal administrator to perform these duties, but as your portal site grows, this is one of the first administrative tasks that usually needs to be addressed by a dedicated resource.

NOTE
The OracleAS Portal wizards that are used to create portlets were referenced in Chapter 1, and using advanced tools to create portlets (like OmniPortlet and Oracle's JDeveloper) is discussed in Chapters 6, 7, and 8.

Items

Within the context of OracleAS Portal, *content* can be defined as any piece of information displayed on a portal that does not fit into the traditional interface of an OracleAS Portal component such as a form or report. Every item (a single piece of content) has numerous attributes, such as an author, category, perspective, or expiration date. These attributes allow content administrators to organize their content so that end users can easily find what they're looking for (which is, after all, the whole purpose of a portal). This type of organization also makes the administration of items within the OracleAS Portal repository much easier.

There are two basic types of items that can be placed on a page: *item types* and *built-in navigation types.* The following is a list of Item Types you can place on your OracleAS Portal pages:

- **File** This option allows content administrators to place a file on their portal and is the most common option selected when adding content. When a file is selected, it is converted to a binary large object, uploaded, and stored in the infrastructure database automatically. This fact is very important from a security standpoint. Many less-advanced portal products store content as files on the file system of the server and simply create a link on the portal page to the file. This increases the potential for a user with unauthorized access to view your organization's sensitive data. By storing the binary representation of the content as a row in the infrastructure database, it is an order of magnitude more difficult for a hacker to view non-authorized information. Content administrators also have the option of adding a Simple File, which does not prompt for advanced content attributes like publish date or expiration date. Advanced content attributes are discussed shortly.

- **Text** This option displays a WYSIWYG (What You See Is What You Get) editor in your Web browser that allows you to enter text for your content area. The editor has basic formatting options like bold, italics, font selection, bulleted lists, and tables, to name a few. Just as with the File option, there is a Simple Text option.
- **URL** This option allows you to place a URL in your content area. Alternatively, the editor displayed using the text option mentioned in the preceding bullet point allows content administrators to create links in their text areas. As with the File and Text options, there is also a Simple URL option.
- **Page Links** This option allows you to place links in your content area to other OracleAS Portal pages. Page Links differ from URLs in the fact that they are designed to redirect the end user to another OracleAS Portal page. URLs, on the other hand, can redirect the end user to anywhere on the Internet. There is also a Simple Link option.
- **Images** This option allows content administrators to place an image in their content area. There is also a Simple Image option.
- **Zip Files** This option allows content administrators to upload a Zip (compressed) file to their content areas. The only difference between this and a File is the existence of a link titled "Unzip" next to the item when displayed. Clicking the Unzip link gives end users the ability to unzip and store whatever is in the Zip file on a page in the portal.
- **PL/SQL** This option allows you to store a PL/SQL code fragment as an item in the content area. Clicking a PL/SQL link executes the PL/SQL code.
- **Oracle Reports** This option allows content administrators to embed an Oracle Report on a content area. Clicking the link displays the Oracle Report in a Web browser. Note that this refers to a report developed with the Oracle Reports product and does not refer to an OracleAS Portal Report developed using the wizards referenced in Chapter 1.

The following is a list of Built-In Navigation Types content administrators can place on their OracleAS Portal pages:

- **Portal Smart Links** This option allows content administrators to place various links in the content area to perform actions such as edit user account information, edit the page, display a help menu, take the user to their personal page, or refresh the page.

- **Login/Logout Links** This option places a Logout link on the content area page when the user is logged in. If the link is placed on a public page and the user has not logged in yet, it automatically changes to a Login link.
- **Basic Search Box** Two types of searches are available to end users in OracleAS Portal: a basic search that allows users to search through their portals without reducing the information returned by a category or perspective and an advanced search that gives end users the ability to use various methods of reducing information returned by their search as well as advanced features such as Boolean operators. The Basic Search Box places a Search field on the content area, allowing the end users to perform basic searches throughout all content on the portal.

NOTE
For now, understand that categories and perspectives are ways of organizing content in your portal. Categories organize the content according to what the content is. Perspectives organize the content according to who might be interested in it. Categories and perspectives are discussed later in this chapter.

- **List Of Objects** This option allows content administrators to return a set of OracleAS Portal content that fits certain criteria. You can return a drop-down list or a set of links that point to a page group, a perspective, or a category.
- **Portal Smart Text** This option can be used to display the current date, user, or page.
- **Object Map Link** This option can be used to create a link that will display a hierarchical map of pages and subpages when clicked by the end user.
- **Page Path** This option creates a breadcrumb menu on the page that allows end users to see where they are in the portal site and gives them the ability to navigate through levels quickly. Placing a Page Path navigation link on a root page has no effect; it is only useful on subpages.

Not all of these types are available for pages by default. Some of the items will have to be enabled for a page group. To enable these types, select the Properties link next to Page Group on the top left of the page editor. Select the Configure tab, and then click the Edit link in the Content Type and Classification section of the page. Add the Item Types in the Item Types section of the page and click OK.

For this example, let's create a region on the Dashboard_1 root page to hold content and place content in it. You will need some basic content from the hard drive of the computer you are doing these exercises on. The content for these examples is not important—a simple text file will do. Edit the root page of the Dashboard_1 page group by going to the OracleAS Portal Navigator and clicking the Edit Root Page link next to the Dashboard_1 page group on the Page Groups tab. On that page, click one of the create region icons (one of the four icons with an arrow in them in the top bar of an existing region) to create a new region. Click the

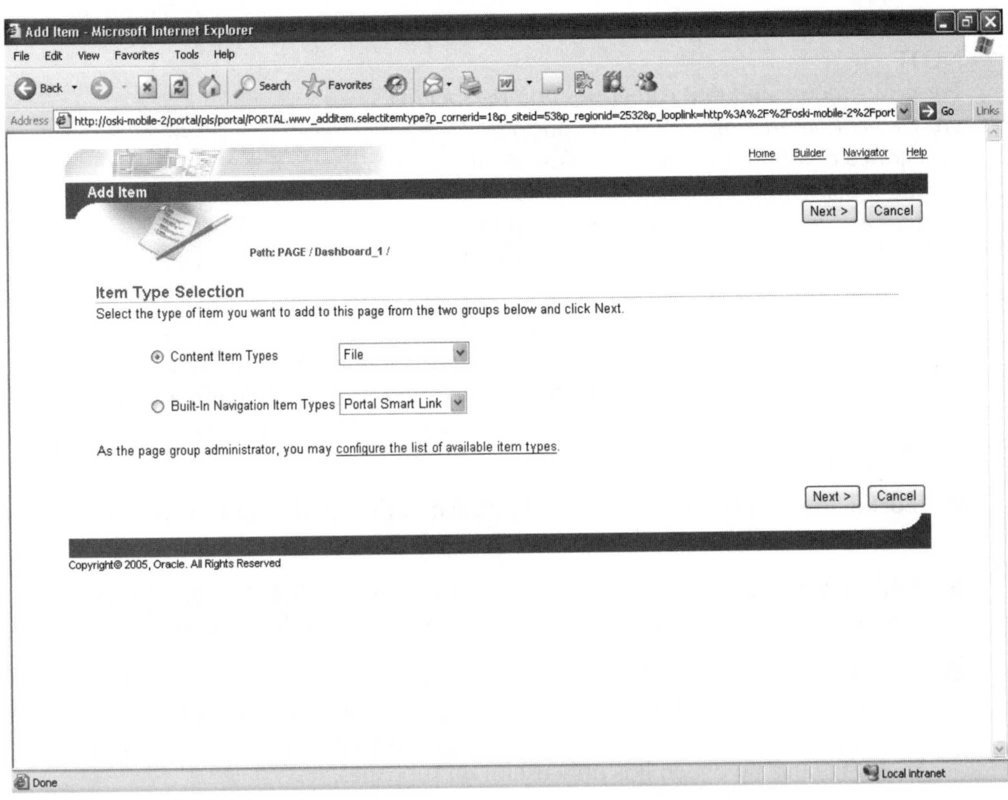

FIGURE 5-1 *The OracleAS Portal Add Item screen*

Add Item icon in the top bar of that new region. You will see the Add Item screen (Figure 5-1).

This wizard allows you to add content to your portal. As mentioned earlier, there are two basic types of content: item types and built-in navigation item types. Select the radio button next to Item Types, select File in the drop-down box to the right, and click Next. The following screen, the Item Attributes page (Figure 5-2), allows content administrators to set attributes for the content they want to add. If we had selected "Simple File" instead of "File" on the previous screen, this page would not display any of the attributes.

This page lists all of the attributes for a file item. You can think of attributes as adjectives that describe an item. An automobile, for instance, has the following

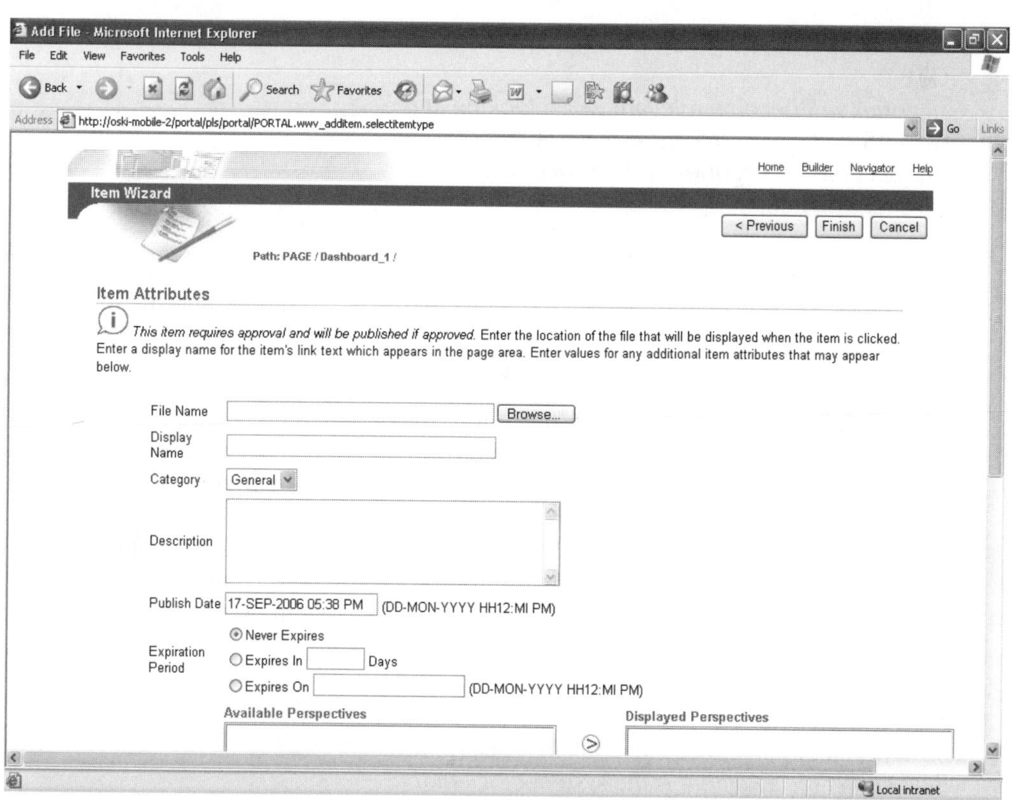

FIGURE 5-2 *The Item Attributes page*

attributes: Year, Make, Model, Color, Transmission, Number of Doors, Engine Type, Fuel Economy, etc. The following attributes are associated with File items:

- **File Name** The first field prompts for the location of the file to add to the content repository. After all of the fields on this page are entered, the OracleAS Portal engine converts the file specified here into a binary large object and stores it in the infrastructure database.
- **Display Name** This field represents what is displayed as a link on the page with the content region.
- **Category** This field represents what category the item will be associated to. An item can belong to only one category. By default, the only category available is "General." Later on, we will see how to go about creating new categories.

NOTE
Categories will become relevant when looking at the OracleAS Portal search features later in this chapter, in the sections "Categories and Perspectives" and "Advanced Search."

- **Description** This field serves two purposes: It allows content administrators to enter descriptive information about the item, and it provides information that the search capabilities of OracleAS Portal can use when building indexes that end users can use to search content.
- **Publish Date** This date, which defaults to the current date and time, gives content administrators the ability to control when a piece of content will become available to end users. If the default is taken, the content will be available immediately. If the time is set to the future, the content will not become available (displayed) until that time threshold is reached. Content administrators will see the content on the edit page screen regardless of this setting. End users, however, will not see it until the system time is greater than the time specified here.

NOTE
It is important to note that the clock that determines when content is available is the system clock of the server running your OracleAS Portal instance. This is very important when you are working on a server that is physically located in a different time zone.

- **Expiration Date** This field gives content administrators the ability to "expire" an item—that is, make it unviewable after a certain date and time. This is particularly useful for something like a monthly report, which can be made available on a site and set to expire on the final day of the month. In this scenario, an end user viewing the page on the last day of the month would see the item, but when viewing the same page after the start of the next month, would not. All of this is handled by the OracleAS Portal engine automatically, with no programming or administrative actions needed. To learn more about expired content, see the sidebar "Expired Content."
- **Perspectives** Perspectives are similar to categories in the sense that they organize content according to who might be interested in seeing it. The key difference between categories and perspectives is that fact that an item can belong to multiple perspectives simultaneously, whereas an item can only belong to one category.
- **Image** An image can be placed next to the link by specifying an image file or Web location in the Image field. The drop-down box next to the Image Alignment field allows content administrators to align the image in the content area.
- **Basic Search Keywords** This field allows content administrators to add keywords that will be indexed by the search engine. By default, the attributes of an item are indexed—its name, its description, and what is in the content—provided it is part of the list shown in Table 5-1.
- **Author** This field allows content administrators to enter an author for an item.
- **Enable Item Check-Out** This field allows content administrators to "lock" the item. In most organizations, there are numerous people who can add content. This can potentially be an issue if more than one person is updating

Expired Content

Expired content still exists within the Oracle infrastructure database. Content administrators must manually delete it, if they want the expired content to be permanently removed. You can delete expired content by clicking the Purge Expired Items button when editing the page in List mode. You can also use calls to built-in portal-specific PL/SQL packages to do this. Using PL/SQL to programmatically manipulate content is discussed in the section "Content Management APIs" later in this chapter.

a piece of content simultaneously. This issue can be overcome by clicking the check box next to this field. The content will not be able to be updated if someone has "checked" the item out. This will, in effect, lock the item, preventing anyone else from modifying it. While other users can still see the item, no one else will be able to modify it until it is checked back in.

- **Display Options** These radio buttons control whether the item is displayed in the same page of the browser (if it is a supported Multipurpose Internet Mail Extensions [MIME] mime type for your browser) when selected or if a new browser window opens up automatically.

Text and Markup	
Format	**Version**
ANSI (TXT)	All versions
ASCII (TXT)	All versions
HTML	2.0, 3.2, 4.0
IBM DCA/RFT (Revisable Form Text) (DC)	SC23-0758-1
Rich Text Format (RTF)	1 through 1.7
Unicode Text	3, 4
XHTML	1.0
Generic XML	1.0
Word Processing Formats	
Format	**Version**
Adobe Maker Interchange Format (MIF)	5, 5.5, 6, 7
Applix Words (AW)	3.11, 4.2, 4.3, 4.4, 4, 41, 4.2
DisplayWrite (IP)	4
Folio Flat File (FFF)	3.1
Fujitsu Oasys (OA2)	7
JustSystems Ichitaro (JTD)	8, 9, 10, 12

TABLE 5-1 *File Formats That Can Be Indexed and Searched by OracleAS Portal*

Word Processing Formats	
Format	**Version**
Lotus AMI Pro (SAM)	2, 3
Lotus Word Pro (LWP)	96, 97, Millennium Edition R9, 9.8 (supported on Windows 32-bit platform only)
Lotus Master (MWP)	96, 97, Millennium Edition R9, 9.8 (supported on Windows 32-bit platform only)
Lotus Master (MWP)	96, 97 (supported on Windows 32-bit platform only)
Microsoft Word for PC (DOC)	4, 5, 5.5, 6
Microsoft Word for Windows (DOC)	1 through 2003
Microsoft Word for Windows XML format	2003 (No formatting extracted)
Microsoft Word for Macintosh (DOC)	4, 5, 6, 98
Microsoft Works (WPS)	1 through 2000
Microsoft Windows Write (WRI)	1, 2, 3
OpenOffice (SXW)	1, 1.1
StarOffice (SXW)	6, 7
WordPad	Through 2003
WordPerfect for Windows (WO)	5, 5.1
WordPerfect for Windows (WPD)	6, 7, 8, 10, 2000, 2002, 11
WordPerfect for Macintosh	1.02, 2, 2.1, 2.2, 3, 3.1
WordPerfect for Linux	6
XyWrite (XY4)	4.12
Applix Spreadsheets (AS)	4.2, 4.3, 4.4
Spreadsheet Formats	
Format	**Version**
Corel Quattro Pro (QPW, WB3)	6, 7, 8, 10, 2000, 2002, 11
Lotus 1-2-3 (123)	96, 97, Millennium Edition R9, 9.8
Lotus 1-2-3 (WK4)	2, 3, 4, 5

TABLE 5-1 *File Formats That Can Be Indexed and Searched by OracleAS Portal* (continued)

Spreadsheet Formats	
Format	**Version**
Lotus 1-2-3 Charts (123)	2, 3, 4, 5
Microsoft Excel for Windows (XLS)	2.2 through 2003
Microsoft Excel for Windows XML format	2003 (No formatting extracted)
Microsoft Excel for Macintosh (XLS)	98
Microsoft Excel Charts (XLS)	2, 3, 4, 5, 6, 7
Microsoft Works Spreadsheet (S30,S40)	1, 2, 3, 4
OpenOffice (SXC)	1, 1.1
StarOffice (SXC)	6, 7
Applix Presents (AG)	4.0, 4.2, 4.3, 4.4
Presentation Formats	
Format	**Version**
Corel Presentations (SHW)	6, 7, 8, 10, 2000, 2002, 11
Lotus Freelance Graphics (PRE)	2, 96, 97, 98, Millennium Edition R9, 9.8
Microsoft PowerPoint for Windows (PPT)	95 through 2003
Microsoft PowerPoint for Macintosh (PPT)	98
Microsoft Project (MPP)	98, 2000, 2002 (XP)
Microsoft Visio (VSD)	6
Microsoft Visio XML format	2003 (No formatting extracted)
OpenOffice (SXI, SXP)	1, 1.1
StarOffice (SXI, SXP)	6, 7 (No formatting extracted)
Display Formats	
Format	**Version**
Adobe Portable Document Format (PDF)	1.1 (Acrobat 2.0) to 1.5 (Acrobat 6.0)

TABLE 5-1 *File Formats That Can Be Indexed and Searched by OracleAS Portal* (continued)

For this example, create a text file on your local machine called sports.txt. In that file, type **football hockey basketball baseball**. Then save the file. Go back to your browser and add an item by clicking the Add Item icon in the bar above the empty region. Select the radio button next to Item Types and select File in the drop-down box. Click Next. Click the Browse button to the right of the File Name text box and select the sports.txt file you just created. Give it a display name of **Sports** and in the description field, type **soccer lacrosse**. Leave the rest of the fields the way they are and click Finish. The sports.txt file will be uploaded to your portal, and you will be taken back to the Edit Page window in your browser (Figure 5-3).

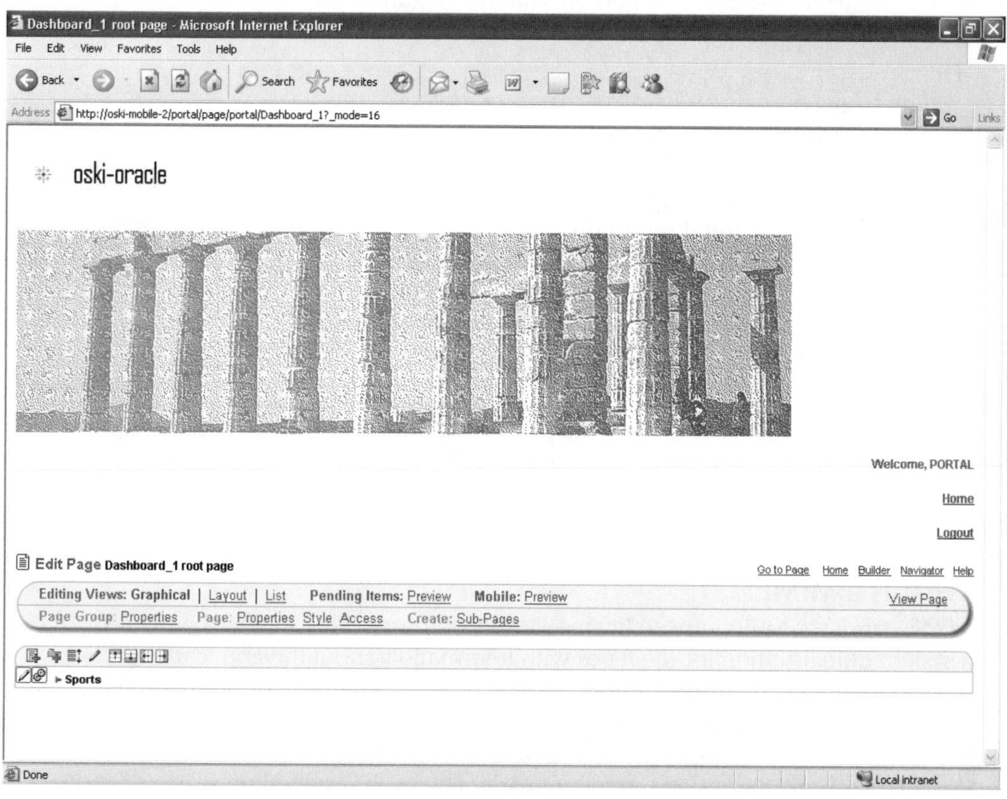

FIGURE 5-3 *The Edit Page screen displaying the newly added content*

On the top right of the page, there is a link called View Page. Click that link to show how the page will be displayed. Clicking the Sports link will display the contents of the file in the browser. If the link pointed to a file with an extension that was associated with a MIME (see the sidebar "What Is a MIME?") plug-in for your browser (say, a .doc file which is associated with Microsoft Word), the appropriate program would have executed and displayed in your browser.

Searching OracleAS Portal Content

Click the back button in your browser to return to the Edit Page screen. Create a new region and click the Add Portlet icon on that region. In the Search text box, type **search** to find the search portlets in the repository. Single-click Basic Search to move that portlet to the Selected Portlets window (Figure 5-4). Click OK.

TIP

You may be wondering where the search portlets came from. As part of the OracleAS Portal installation, a set of seeded portlets is installed. There are seeded portlets for things like searching the content in your portal repository, displaying login screens, doing basic portal administration, etc. These seeded portlets are part of every OracleAS Portal installation and are available to all developers and page designers.

Click the View Page link to view the page. Note the Search portlet on the top of the page. Type any of the keywords in the file we just uploaded in the search text

What Is a MIME?

MIME stands for Multipurpose Internet Mail Extensions. This standard provides a system of registration for file types with information about the applications needed to process them. This information is used by your browser to execute the appropriate program on your computer to display the content. For example, files with a .pdf extension are automatically displayed with Adobe Acrobat Reader (assuming that Adobe Acrobat Reader has been installed on your system, of course).

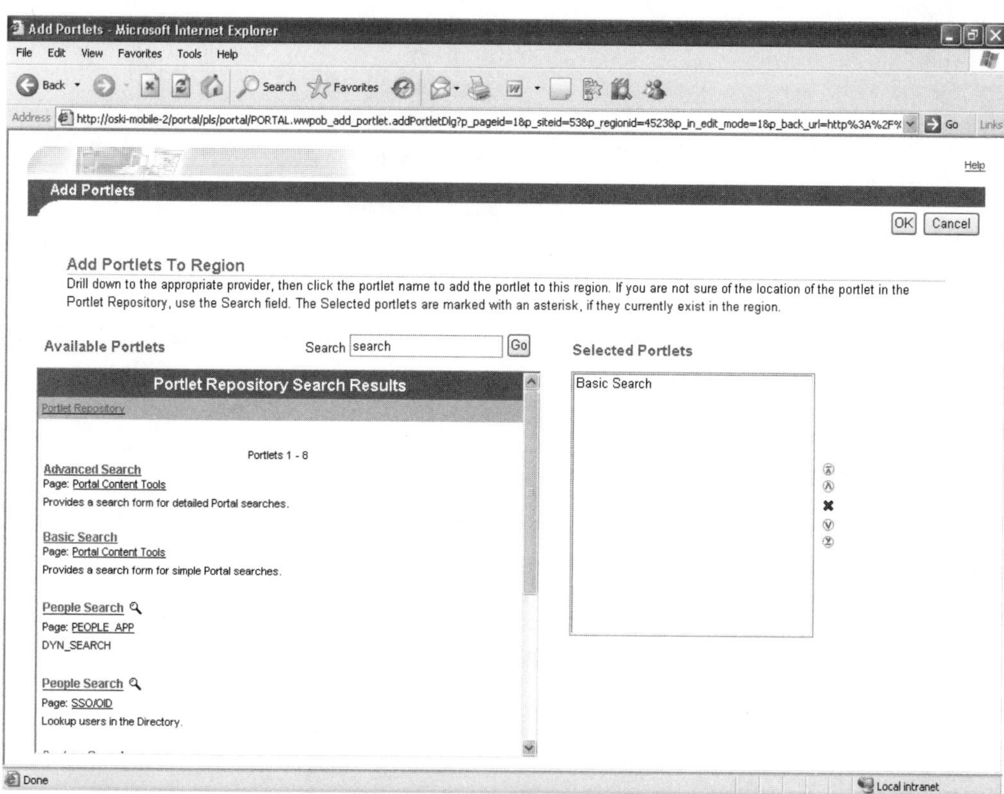

FIGURE 5-4 *The Selected Portlets window*

box. Remember, the following things are searchable: the title, the description, and the content, so any of the four sports in the sports.txt file (football, hockey, basketball, baseball) should be searchable along with the description (soccer, lacrosse) and the title (sports.txt). Type any combination of those keywords into the search dialog and click Search (Figure 5-5).

How come no results were returned? The answer lies in the fact that the indexes that maintain information about the content in our portal are not built dynamically. That is, they are not updated automatically when new content is added. The indexes must be rebuilt manually whenever new content is added. Luckily, this is an easy procedure and can be automated. The procedure to run is the SYNC procedure in

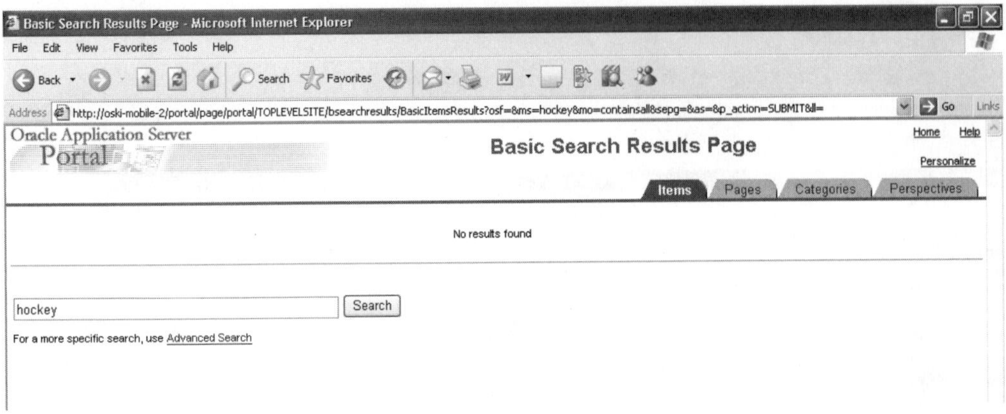

FIGURE 5-5 *The Search Results window*

the WWV_CONTEXT package owned by the PORTAL user in the infrastructure database. You can run it from a SQL*Plus session:

```
SQL*Plus: Release 10.1.0.4.2 - Production on Mon Sep 11 10:25:24 2006

Copyright (c) 1982, 2005, Oracle.  All rights reserved.

Connected to:
Oracle Database 10g Enterprise Edition Release 10.1.0.4.2 - Production
With the Partitioning, OLAP and Data Mining options

SQL> exec wwv_context.sync;

PL/SQL procedure successfully completed.
```

You can also run it from within OracleAS Portal by performing the following steps:

1. Go back to the Navigator by clicking the Navigator link on the top right of the screen.
2. Click the Database Objects tab.
3. In the Find text box on the top right of the screen, type **wwv_context**.
4. Click the Show Properties link.

5. Scroll down until you see the procedures and packages in the wwv_context package (Figure 5-6).
6. Click the small icon next to the SYNC procedure.

After the procedure successfully executes (signified by a check mark displayed on the screen when run from the OracleAS Portal Navigator), return to the Navigator by clicking the Navigator link on the top right of the screen. Click the Page Groups tab, then the View Root Page link next to the Dashboard_1 page group. In the search text box on the top of the screen, enter one of the search items again. The Search page will now correctly display the results of the search (Figure 5-7).

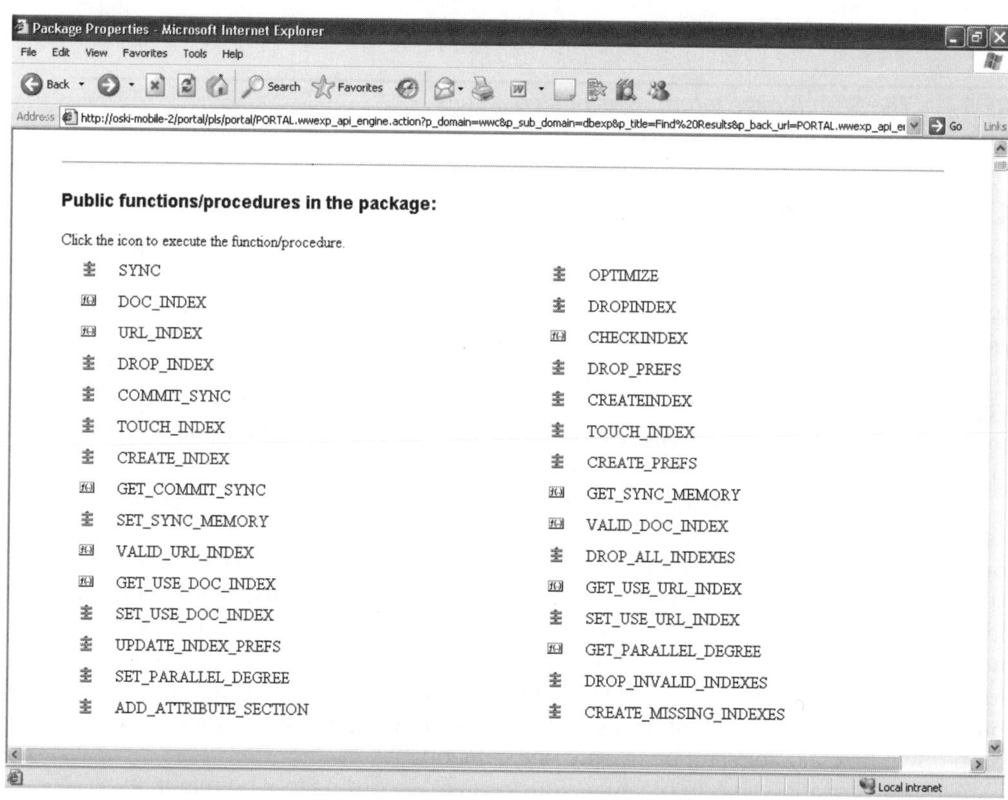

FIGURE 5-6 *The list of procedures and functions in the wwv_context package*

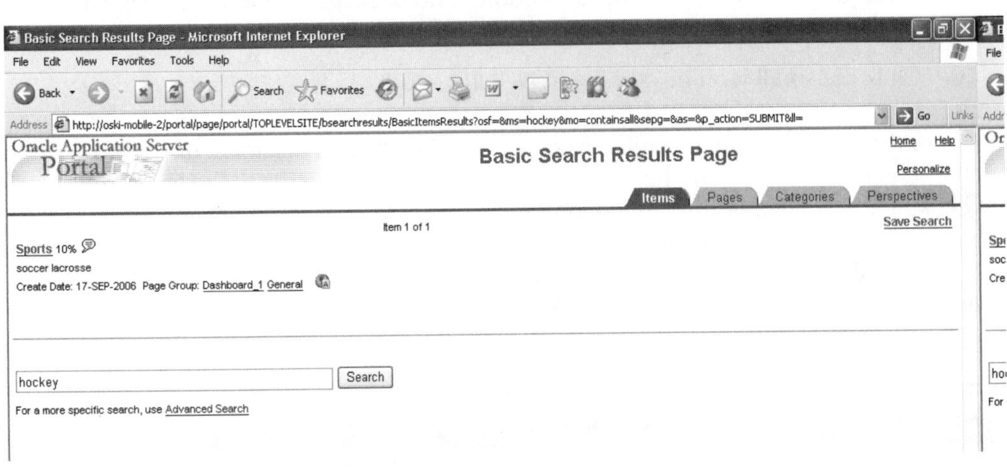

FIGURE 5-7 *The Search page returning expected results*

Categories and Perspectives

Categories and perspectives are ways of organizing the content that is in your portal repository. In general, categories are used to group items by their content, that is, what purpose they serve for your company or organization. Perspectives are used to organize the content according to who might be interested in seeing it. Right now, these concepts may be hard to visualize, but when we look at the advanced search capabilities of OracleAS Portal in the next section, having the ability to group information using these concepts will be invaluable, particularly when your portal site grows to the point where it contains a large amount of content.

By default, only one category is created: general. Categories and perspectives can be created at either the page group level or the shared objects level. A category or perspective created at the page group level will only be available to the root and subpages of that page group; a category or perspective created at the shared objects level will be available across all pages, subpages, and page groups. A category does not have many attributes (the only attribute gives content administrators the ability to associate an image with it), so the creation of a category is a relatively simple process. When adding content, you can specify your new category in the Category drop-down box. An item can be in only one category.

Perspectives allow you to organize your content according to who might be interested in seeing it. The process of creating a perspective and the attributes that can be defined for a perspective is virtually identical to those of a category. The main difference is that an item can belong to multiple perspectives, whereas an item can belong to only one category. Also, no perspectives are created by default.

Advanced Search

Go to the Edit Page screen for your page and click the Add Portlets icon for a region that has been defined as a portlet region. In the Add Portlets To Region page, type **search** in the Search text box and click Go. This will list the eight seeded portlets that Oracle provides you to add searching capabilities to your portal. Earlier, we added the Basic Search portlet to our page. This time, add the Advanced Search portlet by single-clicking it. Click OK to return to the Edit Page screen (Figure 5-8).

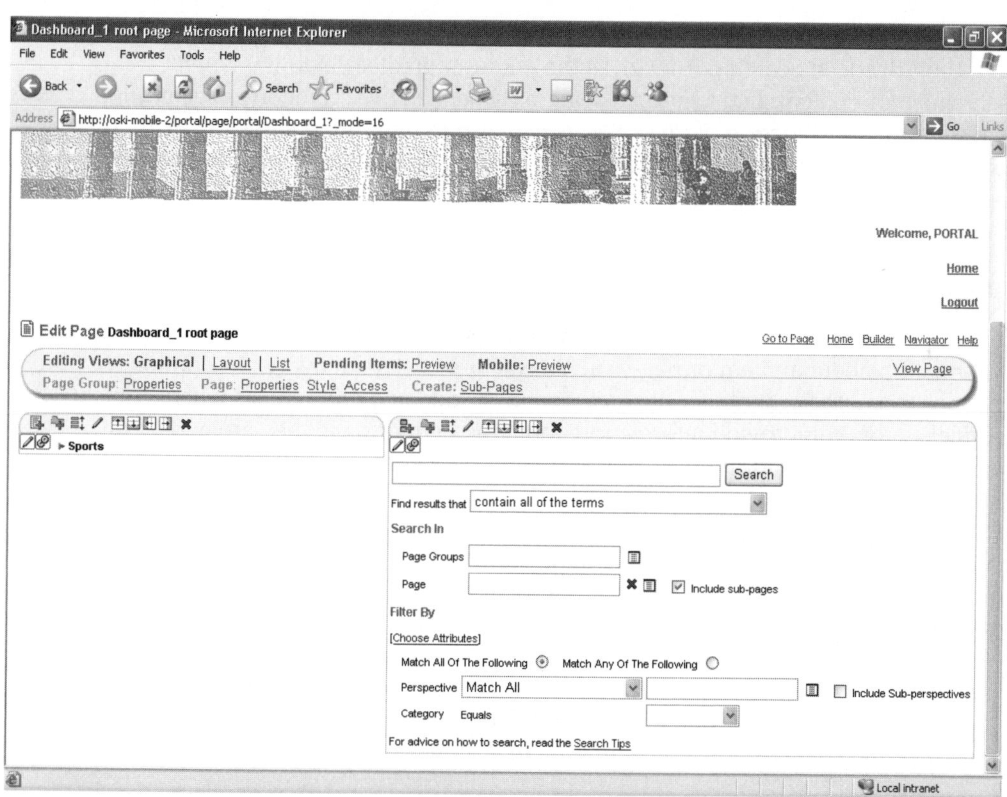

FIGURE 5-8 *The Edit Page screen with an Advanced Search portlet placed on it*

Why Would I Want to Use the Basic Search Portlet?

Since the Advanced Search portlet has so many more features than the Basic Search portlet, you may be wondering why the Basic Search portlet would ever be used. In reality, the Basic Search portlet is used more often than the Advanced Search portlet. Why? Most end users won't understand many of the options available in the Advanced Search portlet. Before reading this book, would you have known what a "page group" or a "perspective" was? Unless you had experience with content management systems, the answer is probably no. The ability for end users to use the Advanced Search portlet effectively comes down to training.

The Advanced Search portlet gives the end user greater flexibility when searching for content. End users can searc h by perspective, category, page group, page, or any combination of these. Users can also search for all items in a particular category or perspective by leaving the search text box blank and selecting the appropriate category or perspective.

Page Group Attributes

Content attributes are associated with item types and page types, and they store information about an item or page, such as the associated category, description, or perspective(s). These attributes are included in the add and edit screens where content administrators can provide information about the item or page they are adding or editing. Content administrators can create their own item types and page types and specify exactly what information they want users to supply by choosing which attributes to include. In addition, page group administrators can create their own attributes for containing extra information. You can add attributes at either the Page Group level or the Shared Objects level. To add an attribute at the Page Group level, click the page group link on the Navigator, click the Attributes link, and then click Create New . . . Attribute on the top left of the page. To add an attribute at the Shared Objects level, click the Shared Objects link on the Navigator, click the Attributes link, then click Create New . . . Attribute on the top left of the page. Table 5-2 lists the built-in item attributes that are provided with OracleAS Portal.

Attribute	Description
Author	The name of the author of the item.
Category	The name of the category to which the item or page belongs.
Description	A short text description of the item or page.
Display Name	The display name of the item or page.
Display Option	Information about how the item or portlet should be displayed: Item Displayed Directly In Page Area Link That Displays Item In Full Browser Window Link That Displays Item In New Browser Window
Enable Item Check-Out	Information about whether or not the item can be checked out and checked in. This provides document control, allowing groups of users to edit items and not overwrite each other's work. Users cannot edit items that are checked out by another user.
Expiration Period	Information about how long an item should be displayed on a page.
Image	The image associated with the item or page.
Image Alignment	Information about where the item image should appear in the page.
Keywords	Keywords that describe the content or purpose of the item or page. When a user performs a search, the user's search criteria are compared to the keywords to find a match.
Perspectives	The names of the perspectives associated with the item or page.
Publish Date	The date (in the format, DD-MON-YYYY HH12:MI PM) when the item should start being displayed to users.
Rollover Image	The second image associated with the item or page. This image is displayed whenever a user moves the mouse cursor over the original image on a navigation bar or tab.

TABLE 5-2 *A List of Built-in Page Attributes*

Getting Content Approved

One of the powerful features of OracleAS Portal is the ability to create approvals for your content. Approvals allow content administrators to define a user or group of users who must approve the content before it becomes available on your portal site. Oracle provides built-in portlets that give approvers the ability to see what items are waiting for their approval. Likewise, there are portlets that content administrators (submitters) can use to see the status of items awaiting approval. Before approvals can be used, however, they must be enabled. Approvals are enabled or disabled at the Page Group level. Once they are enabled, the pages that make up that page group can have the approval process enabled or disabled for each of them.

To enable approvals, go to the OracleAS Portal Navigator, click the Page Groups tab and click the Properties link next to one of your page groups. About three-quarters of the way down on the Configure tab is a section called "Approvals and Notifications." By default, Approvals and Notifications are disabled. Click the Edit link and select the check box next to Enable Approvals and Notifications. After you click OK on that page, you are returned to the properties page for the page group. Notice, however, that there's a new tab along the right side of the screen: "Approval" (Figure 5-9).

TIP

The second check box on the Edit Approvals and Notifications page, "Allow Page to Override the Page Group Approval Process," is what gives content administrators the ability to define different approval processes for different pages. If that box is left unchecked (as it is by default), all pages associated with that page group will use the approval process defined at the page group level to approve content. As such, if that box is left unchecked, there is no need to place an Approval tab on any of the pages' properties. If that box is checked, however, an Approval tab will appear on the properties page for all of the pages of that page group. For the simple exercises in this chapter, there's no need to check that box. Just remember where it is if the time comes for you to define different approval processes for different pages within a page group.

It is on this page that the approval process is defined. The Approval Routing List at the top is where you define the users and/or groups who will need to approve an item before it appears on an OracleAS Portal page. Every time you add a user or a

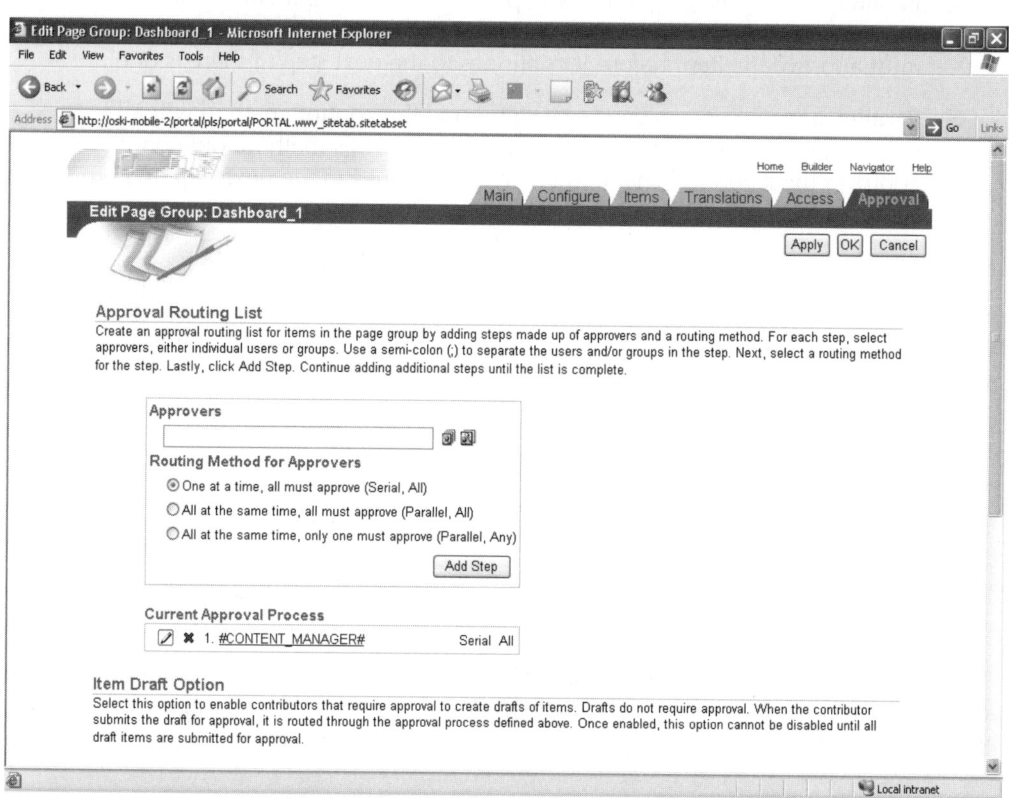

FIGURE 5-9 *Page Group Properties with the Approval tab displayed*

group of users in this box, it is considered a step in the approval process. There are three Routing Methods that can be assigned to each step:

- **Serial, all** Users assigned to a step using this routing method will see the approval notification one at a time. For example, if Nancy, Bob, and Jane are part of the VP group and one of the steps uses this routing method, Nancy will see the approval notification first. Bob and Jane won't see it until Nancy approves the item. In this method, all approvers must approve the item before it continues to the next step (if there is one).

- **Parallel, all** Users assigned to a step using this routing method will all see the approval notification at the same time. In this method, all approvers must approve the item before it continues to the next step (if there is one).
- **Parallel, any** Users assigned to a step using this routing method will all see the approval notification at the same time. In this method, only one approver must approve the item before it continues to the next step (if there is one).

The current list of approvers appears right below that box. By default, an approval process is automatically created. In Figure 5-9, you'll see it contains a special group called #CONTENT_MANAGER#. There are three special groups you can use:

- **#PAGE_GROUP_MANAGER#** Any user or group with the page group privilege Manage All, or the global privilege Manage All on the object type All Page Groups
- **#PAGE_MANAGER#** Any user or group with the page privilege Manage
- **#CONTENT_MANAGER#** Any user or group with the page privilege Manage or Manage Content. Privileges are discussed in detail in Chapter 10.

To the right of the Approvers text box are two small icons. The first icon allows you to browse and select individual OracleAS Portal users to add to the approval step. The second icon allows you to browse and select groups.

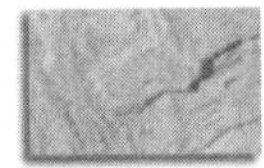

TIP
Users and groups are discussed in Chapter 10, but for now know that there's a many-to-many relationship between users and groups. One user can belong to many groups, and one group can contain many users. For instance, you may have a VP group that contains users Nancy, Bob, and Jane. Nancy may also belong to the IT group, and Bob may also belong to the Accounting group. If you assign the VP group to one of the approval steps, Nancy, Bob, and Jane will be involved in approving the content (depending on what routing method is used).

Below the Approvers box is the Current Approval Process box. To remove a step, click the small red X to the left of the step. The pencil icon to the left of the X allows you to edit the step. The only editing you can do to a step is to redefine the routing process. Click the X now to remove the #CONTENT_MANAGER# step. Click the Browse Groups icon to the right of the Approvers text box. You will see a pop-up window similar to Figure 5-10.

If you are working on a new OracleAS Portal installation, the pop-up window on your screen should look very similar to Figure 5-10. If you have added additional groups, they will show up in the pop-up window. By default, OracleAS Portal comes

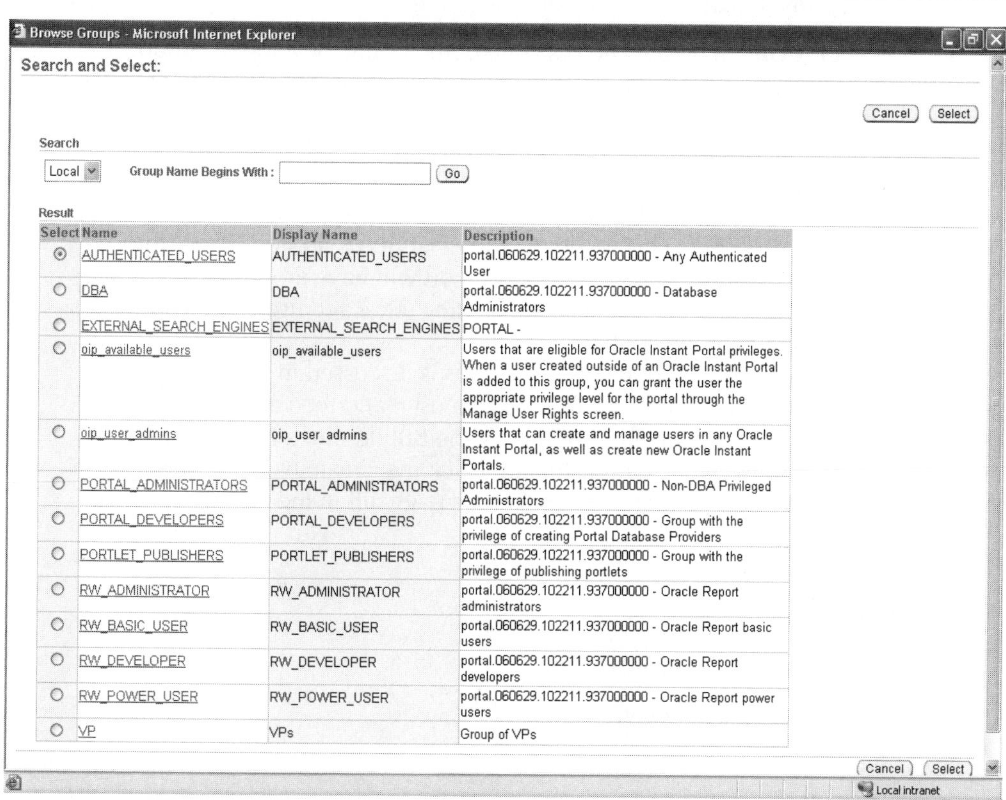

FIGURE 5-10 *The list of OracleAS Portal groups*

with some standard groups (these will be discussed in greater detail in Chapter 10). The following is a list of the groups you should concern yourself with for now:

- **AUTHENTICATED_USERS** Any user who logs on becomes a member of this group.
- **DBA** Any user assigned to this group has privileges to alter objects in the infrastructure database.
- **PORTAL_ADMINISTRATORS** Users in this group can do things like create or modify users or groups and change portal settings.
- **PORTAL_DEVELOPERS** Users in this group can create new portlets but do not have any authority to create or modify pages.
- **PORTLET_PUBLISHERS** The opposite of the portal_developers group: users in this group have page privileges, but no privileges to design or modify portlets.

Out of the box, none of these groups are good candidates for the approval process. You certainly could use them—you may have a system-type document that needs approval from all DBAs or a company logo that needs approval from the PORTLET_PUBLISHERS group—but more likely, you will have groups based on the structure of your organization (VP, Legal, Accounting, etc,) and users in those groups will be called upon to approve content.

In Chapter 10, the creation of users and groups is discussed in detail, but for now, follow these steps to create a group, create a user, and then assign that user to a group. In the OracleAS Portal Navigator, click the Builder link on the top right of the screen, and then select the Administer tab. Click the Create New Groups link on the bottom right of the page. In the Create Groups page, fill in the following fields:

- **Name** VP
- **Display Name** VPs
- **Description** Group of VPs
- **Make this group privileged** Checked
- **Owners** Portal
- **Members** Portal
- **Roles Assignment** Select All

Your screen should look like Figure 5-11. Click Submit, and then click Done.

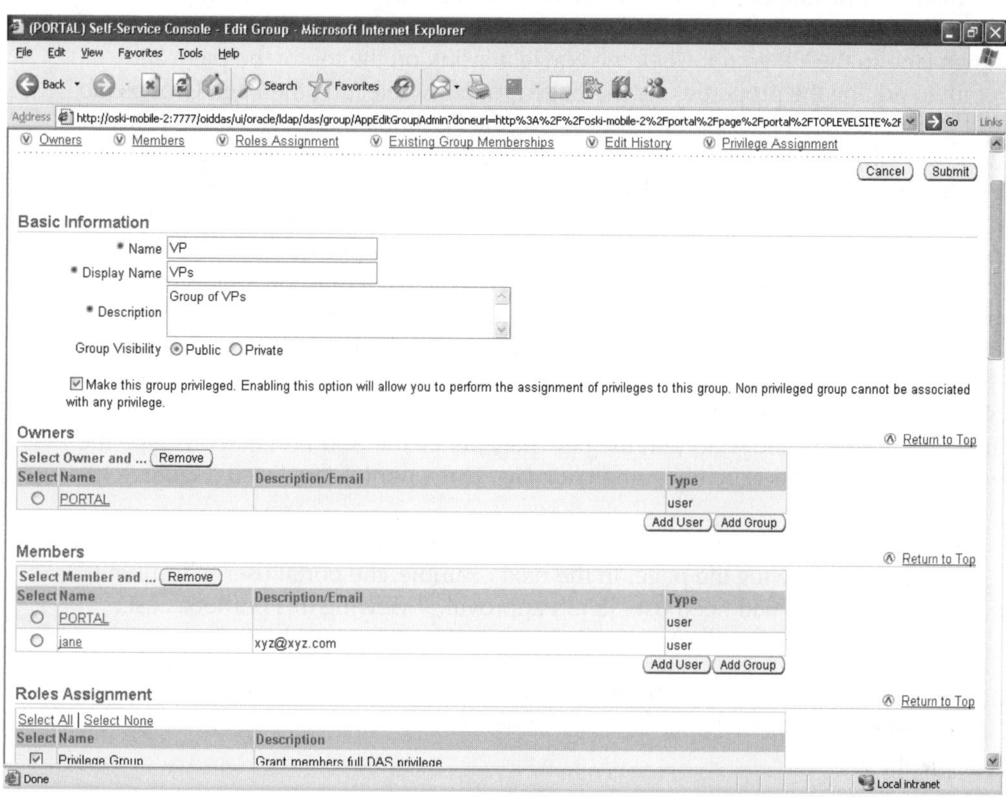

FIGURE 5-11 *The Create Group page*

Click the Create New Users link in the top right of the Administer tab. Only enter the following fields:

- **Last Name** Smith
- **User ID** jane
- **Password** jane01
- **Confirm Password** jane01
- **Email Address** xyz@xyz.com

Click Submit and then Done. We've now created an OracleAS Portal group named "VP" and an OracleAS Portal user named "jane." Later we'll come back and assign jane to the VP group. Click the Navigator link on the top of the page and return to editing the properties for the page group, by selecting the Page Groups tab and then selecting the Properties link next to the Dashboard_1 page group. Click the Approval tab and then click the Browse Groups icon next to the Approvers text box. Select the radio button next to VP and click Select. Select "All at the same time, all must approve (Parallel, All)" for the Routing Method and click Add Step. Further down on the page, click the check box next to "Require Approval for All Users"; then click OK. Now, any content that is added to the page must be approved by everyone in the VP group before it is displayed. Click OK to return to the OracleAS Portal Navigator. Next, let's create a page that has the Approver portlets on them.

Click the Dashboard_1 page group link, then click the Pages link. Click Create New Page on the top left of the screen. Give the page a name of **Approver_Page** and click Finish. In the region on the new page, click the Add Portlet icon. Type the word **approval** in the search box and click Go. Three portlets are listed (Figure 5-12):

- **My Approval Status** This portlet will list items that have been submitted by the user viewing the page. In the next example, the portal user will submit an item that will need user jane's approval. If viewing this portlet as user portal, the item will show up. When user jane views it, she won't.
- **Pending Approvals Monitor** This portlet will list all items that are awaiting approval. It is designed for page owners to see items in the list awaiting approval.
- **My Notifications** This portlet will list items the viewer of the page is responsible for. This is the opposite of the My Approval Status portlet. Using the routing list we created above, user jane will see an entry here, but user portal won't.

Select all three portlets and place them on the page; click OK to return to the Edit Page screen. After doing that, click the Page: Access link along the top of the page. In the Grantee text box in the middle of the page, enter **jane** and make sure View is selected in the drop-down box to the right. Click Add to give the jane user view privileges on that page.

We now want to make Approver_Page the default page for user jane when she logs in, along with making jane a member of the VP group. Click the Builder link on the top right of the page. Type **jane** in the Portal User Profile portlet on the right-

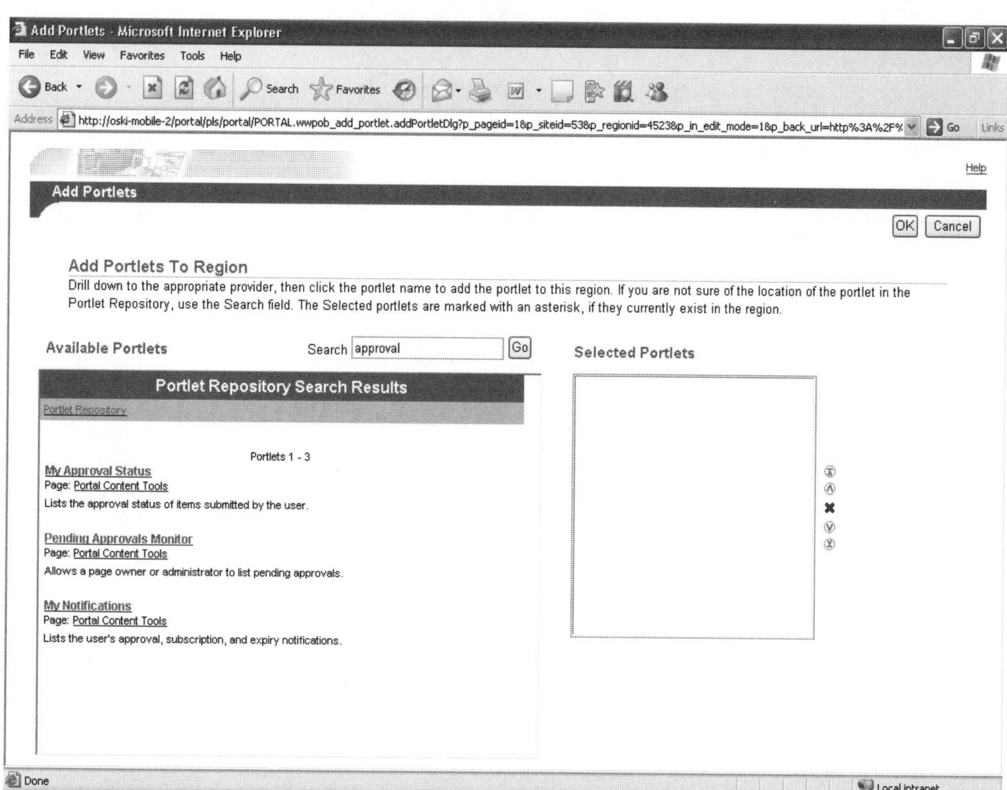

FIGURE 5-12 *The three approval portlets in the seeded repository*

hand side of the page and click Edit. In the Edit Portal User Profile screen, click the small icon next to the Default Group text box. Click the radio button next to VP and click Select. Scroll down on the Edit Portal User Profile screen and click the small icon next to the Default Home Page text box. Click the small plus sign next to the Dashboard_1 page group and click the Return Object link next to approver_page. Check the box right below that titled "Clear the Cache in Web Cache for User" (Figure 5-13). Click OK. User jane now has a default group of VP and has a default page (what she sees when she logs in) of the approver_page. Next, we'll add an item to the Dashboard_1 root page, and then log in as user jane to see the approvals waiting for her.

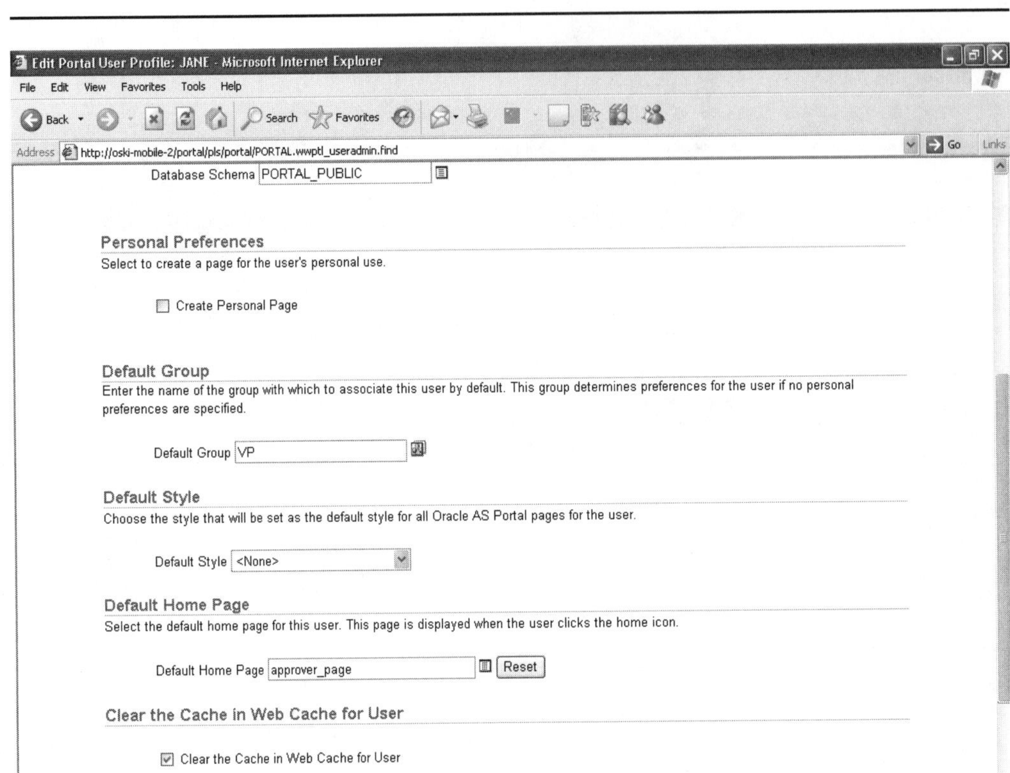

FIGURE 5-13 *The Edit User page*

Return to your page by clicking the Navigator link, the Page Groups tab, and finally, the Edit Root Page link next to the Dashboard_1 page group. If you don't have an item region on your page, create one now. In the item region, click the Add Item icon. Select Item Types and make sure "File" is in the drop-down box. Click Next. Click the Browse button next to the File Name text box and select a file off of your hard disk (it doesn't matter what it is; if you have a small text file that would be perfect for this example). Give the item a display name and click Finish.

When you return to the Edit Page In Graphical Mode screen, the content added now has "Pending" next to it (Figure 5-14). Since you are the creator of the page, you can see the item in edit mode. If you click the View Page link on the top right of the page, the page is displayed without the content, since it has not been approved yet. Terminate your browser by clicking the X in the very top right of your browser window (see the sidebar "Why It's Important to Close Your Browser").

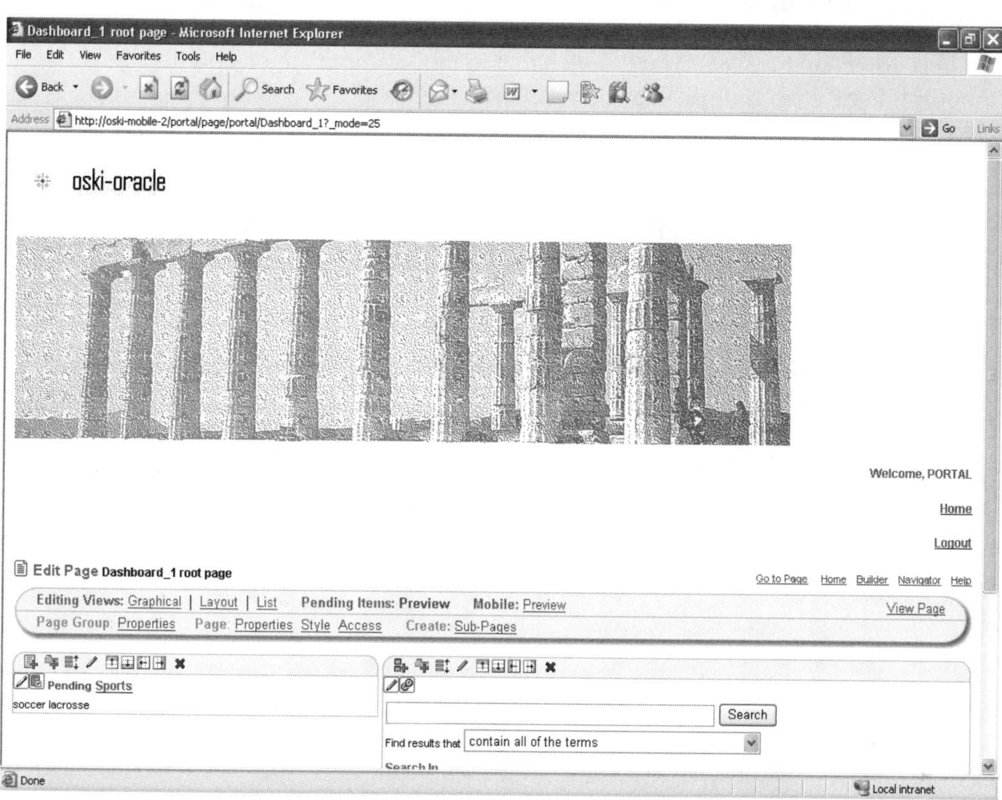

FIGURE 5-14 *The Dashboard_1 root page with a pending item on it*

Why It's Important to Close Your Browser

Was it necessary to close the browser? Couldn't we just log out of OracleAS Portal and log in again as the jane user? Yes, we could have done that, but OracleAS Portal keeps track of authentication information by way of cookies and strange things can happen when logging on and off as different users to test development work. It's always safe to close the browser and start up again when performing tests like this. One technique I would definitely not recommend is to have multiple instances of Internet Explorer running simultaneously—this is almost always a recipe for disaster. I usually use IE for one user and Firefox for the other. That way, you don't have to close the browser all the time.

Start up your browser again and this time, log in to your portal site as jane/jane01. You will be taken to the approvals page with the three approvals portlets we created earlier (Figure 5-15). You'll notice that in the My Notifications portlet, the "Approval Item" item is displayed. User jane can then select that item by clicking it, taking her to the Approval Notification Details Page. Here, she can enter comments in the Approver Comments field toward the bottom of the page and either accept or reject the content (Figure 5-16). For this example, enter the text **This is not complete – more work needed** in the Approver comments field and hit the Reject button.

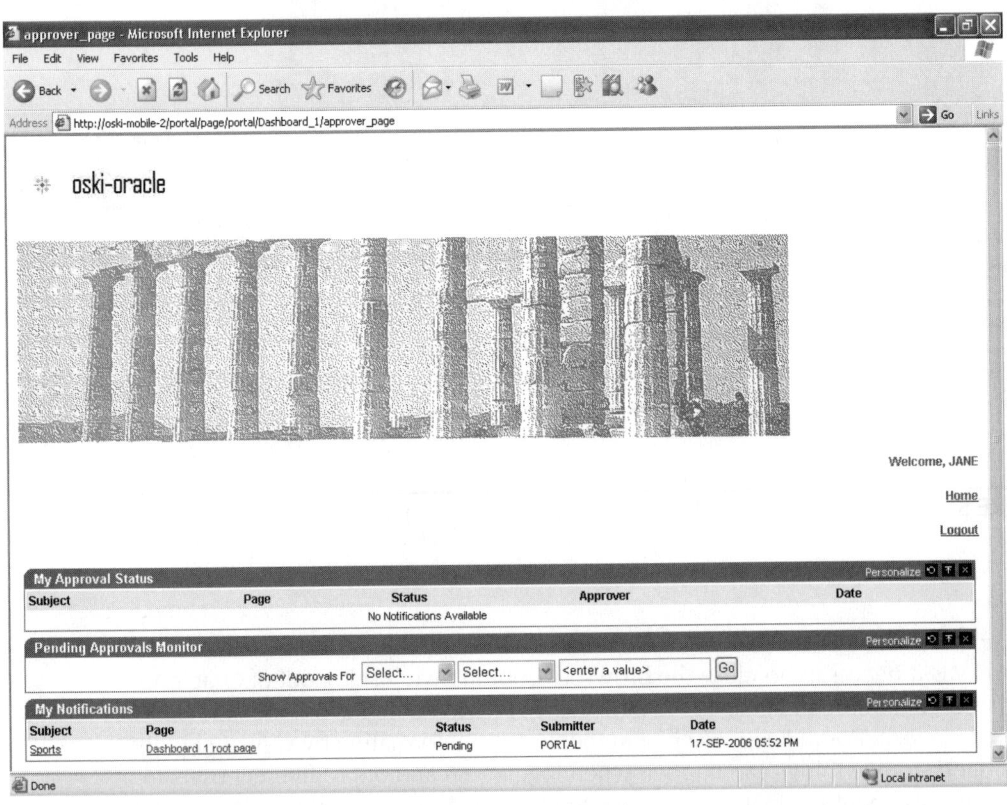

FIGURE 5-15 *The jane user's default page*

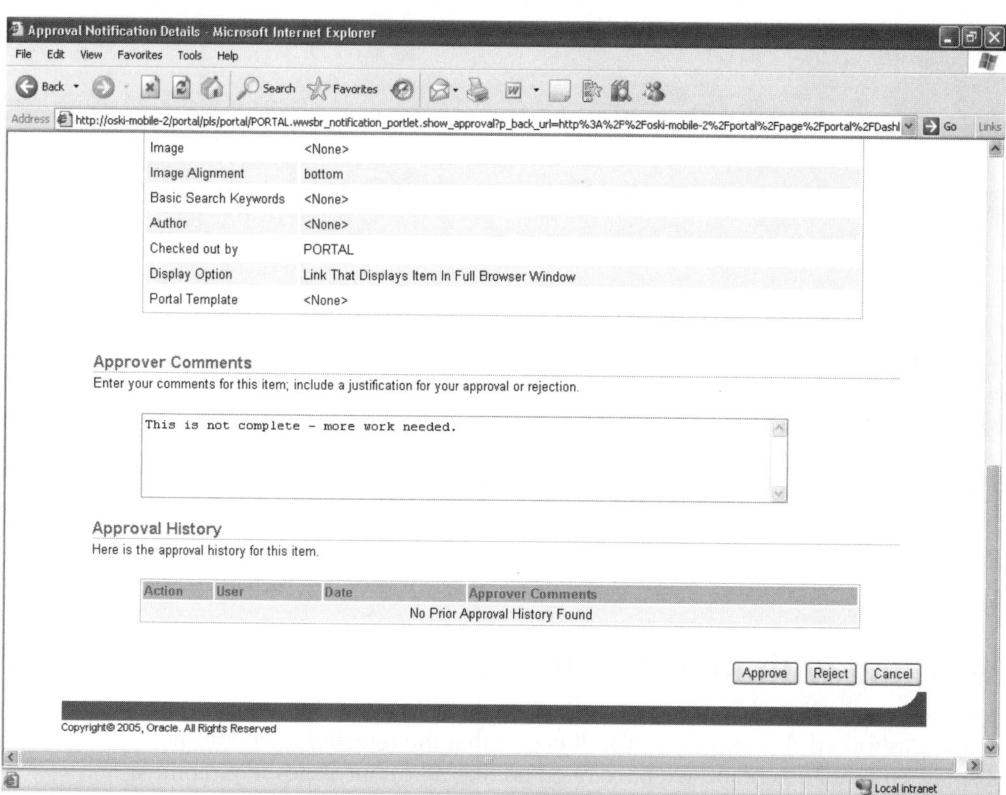

FIGURE 5-16 *The Approval Notification Details page*

Log out and log back in as the portal user. The approvals page is not the default page for the portal user, so you'll have to navigate to it by selecting the Navigator link on the top right of the page, clicking the Page Groups tab, clicking the Dashboard_1 page group link, clicking the Pages link, and finally clicking the Approver_Page link to display the page. You'll notice that the approver portlets automatically update to reflect the user viewing them. As the portal user, you will see entries in the three portlets based on the portal user. In the My Approval Status portlet, click the Rejected link under the Status column. Here you can view the comments that go along with the rejection of the item (Figure 5-17).

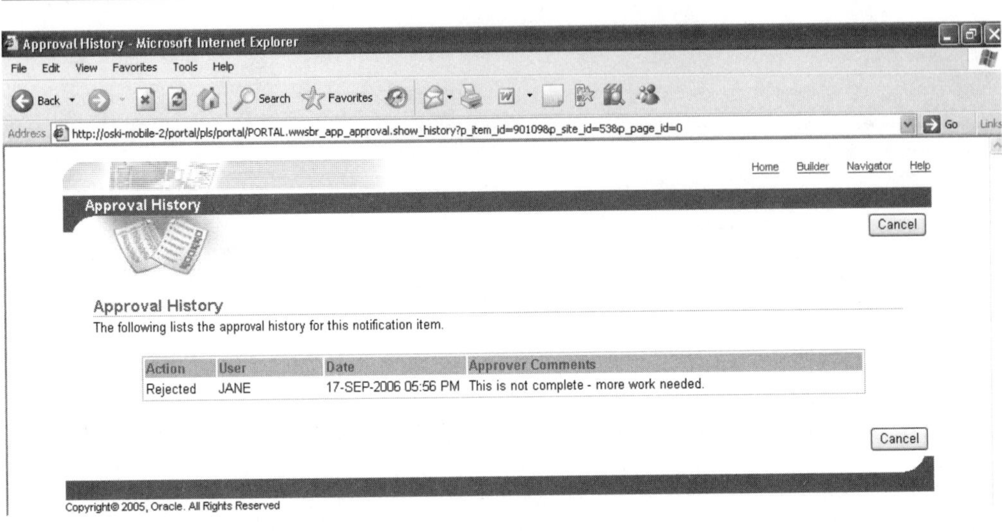

FIGURE 5-17 *The listing of items and their status*

Working with Rejected Items

If an item gets rejected, it needs to be fixed and resubmitted. Return to the root page of the Dashboard_1 page group. You'll notice that the rejected item does not display. Up until this point, we have been editing all of our pages in Graphical mode. To work with items, there is another mode that gives us access to some features specific to items: List mode. Click the List link next to Editing Views: on the top left of the page. This editing view (Figure 5-18) displays a list of items on the page along with links, buttons, and drop-down boxes that correspond to actions that can be performed on items. List mode is great for dealing with items but does not have any features for dealing with portlets (you'll notice that List mode does not even display *any* type of portlet information). The check boxes to the left of each item, along with the Select All and Select None links right above them, give content administrators the ability to perform bulk actions on large pieces of content, greatly saving time spent on administrative duties. You could, for example, click the Select All link, select Expire from the drop-down box, and click Go to manually expire all content on a page in one action.

You might think the Edit link to the left of an item will give content administrators the ability to edit the item. This is not the case, however. The Edit link allows content

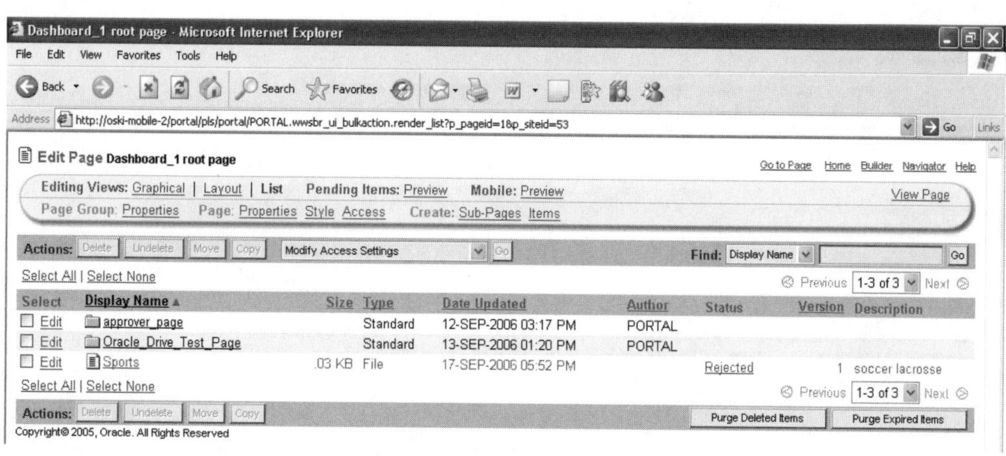

FIGURE 5-18 *Editing the Dashboard_1 root page in list mode*

administrators to edit the attributes of the item that are stored within the OracleAS Portal repository. Clicking that link will display the Edit Item screen that was displayed when you first added the item to the item region of the Dashboard_1 root page. You might think that clicking the link under the Display Name column would allow you to edit the item, but this is also incorrect. Clicking that link only serves to display the item. To actually edit the item, you must use the appropriate tool (Microsoft Word for a .doc file, Notepad for a .txt. file, etc.) to perform your edits and then add the item back into the OracleAS Portal repository.

Item Versioning

Before editing the file and adding a new version of the file back into the repository, click the Page: Properties link on the top left of the page and then click the Items tab. In the Item Versioning section at the top of the page, you'll notice three choices: None, Simple, and Audit (Figure 5-19). "Simple" prompts the user as to how they want to update an item: the user can either overwrite the existing item or create a new version. "Audit" always creates a new version of the item when it is updated. By choosing Simple or Audit, you can set up an item versioning system for items within your repository. For most sites, item versioning is implemented as a means of recovering items that have accidentally been overwritten or to retrieve older items that are to be used as templates for newer items.

Edit Page: Dashboard_1 root page - Microsoft Internet Explorer

File Edit View Favorites Tools Help

Address http://oski-mobile-2/portal/pls/portal/PORTAL.wwpob_page_edit.pageEdit

Home Builder Navigator Help

Main | Template | Style | Access | Items | Optional | Parameters | Events

Edit Page: Dashboard_1 root page

Apply | OK | Cancel

Item Versioning

Select the level of item versioning to use for the page: None always overwrites the previous version of the item, Simple offers the user a choice of overwriting the previous version or archiving it in the database, Audit always archives the previous version.

Item Versioning ○ None ⦿ Simple ○ Audit

Portal Template Assignment

Choose a portal template to render items in this page. Item types that use portal templates include text, PL/SQL, URL, HTML and text files.

No portal templates are available for use in this page group.

Default WebDAV Types

Choose the item types you want to use for files added to this page using WebDAV. For example, you can choose to have all zip files added as Zip File items rather than Simple File items so that they can be unzipped within the page.

Default Regular Files: File
Default Zip Files: Zip File
Default Image Files: File

Default Region

Select a default portlet region and a default item region for the page.

Default Region Type: Default Item Region

Local intranet

FIGURE 5-19 *The Item Versioning section of the Items tab*

NOTE

The use of item versioning is not mandatory, but it is one of those things that uses minimal system resources and takes such a small amount of time to set up that it's usually in your best interest as a content administrator to take the time to configure this feature.

Set Item Versioning to Simple for the page. Edit the item with the appropriate tool and save it. Now, click the Edit link next to the item on the list mode page of the Dashboard_1 root page. The Edit File page now has an Item Version Control section at the top of the page (Figure 5-20). The content administrator responsible for this item now has the following options:

- **Add Item As New Version, but not as Current Version** This option is good for saving "draft" versions of items in the repository.
- **Add Item As New and Current Version** This option is for adding a newly modified version of an item.
- **Overwrite Current Version** Replaces the current version of the item. Use care when using this option—the existing version of the item is gone forever if this option is used.

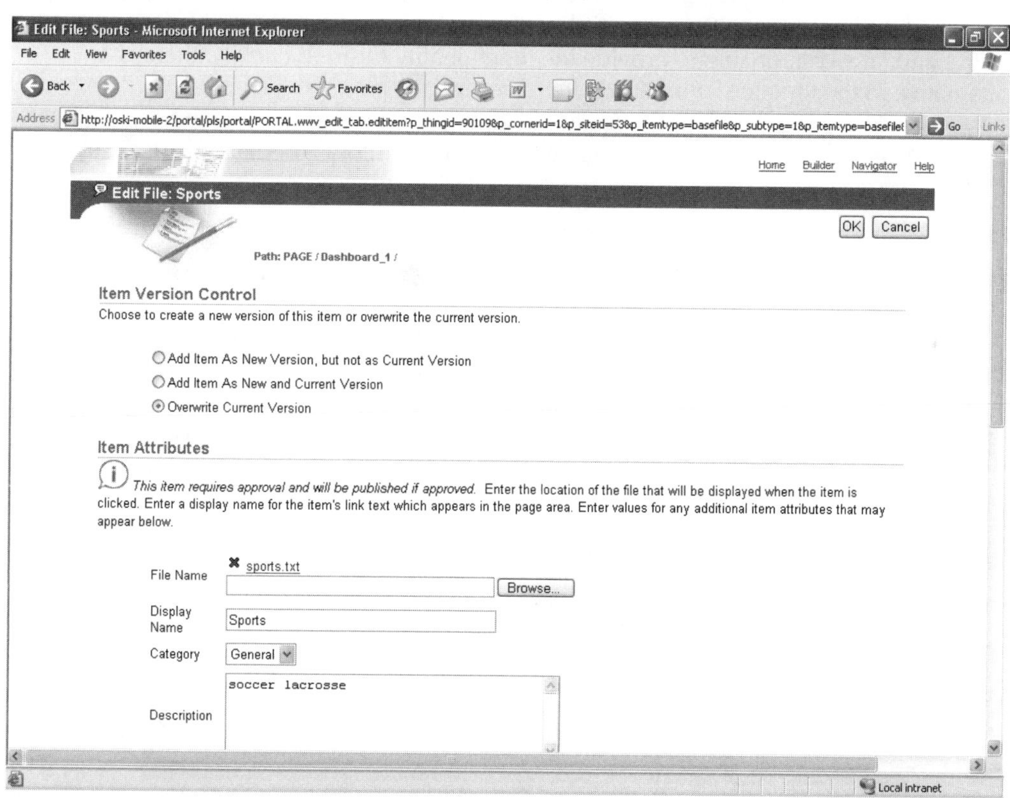

FIGURE 5-20 *The Add Item page with an Item Version Control section displayed*

Select Add Item As New And Current Version, specify a new file in the File Name field, and click OK. You are returned to the Edit page in List mode. Note that the status of the item has changed from Rejected to Pending and a new column, Version is displayed showing the value of 2. Clicking the version number takes you to a screen that allows you to recover previous versions of the item if you wish (Figure 5-21).

Using Oracle Drive

In the section "Items" earlier in this chapter, the process of adding items was demonstrated. The process of using the OracleAS Portal wizards is fine if you need to add a few items, but what if you need to add hundreds (or thousands) of items to your content repository? Also, consider this business requirement: you want a daily-generated report (or reports) added to your OracleAS Portal repository automatically. In both of these scenarios, the wizards described earlier will be, at best, cumbersome to use and, at worst, unable to provide the functionality desired. Luckily, there is an alternative to the OracleAS Portal Add Item wizards.

Oracle Drive is a stand-alone product that maps a drive from a machine running Microsoft Windows to the OracleAS Portal repository. For example, let's say

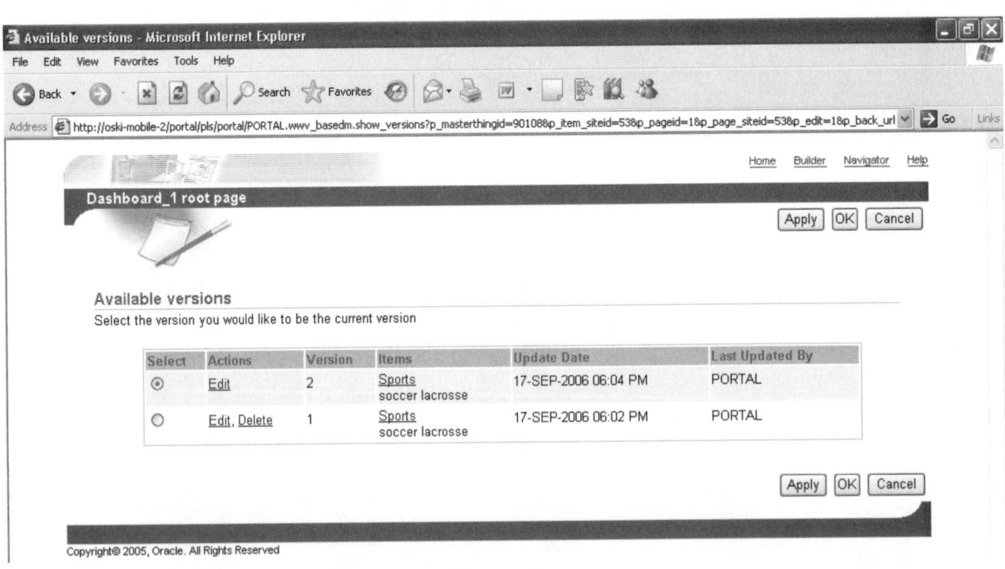

FIGURE 5-21 *The See Item Version History page*

you have a server running a version of Microsoft Windows in your organization that generates daily reports every night. You could place Oracle Drive on that server and map one of its drives (say P: for "Portal") to the OracleAS Portal repository. Page groups that you have created in OracleAS Portal show up as directories when Oracle Drive maps the drive. Subpages of the page groups show up as subdirectories in the mapped drive in Windows Explorer. You could then write a small batch file to execute and copy the file(s) from the directory that holds the daily reports on your server to the appropriate page (directory) on the P: drive. Once the file is copied over, it is available on the OracleAS Portal page immediately. For a brief refresher on the OracleAS Portal page, see the sidebar "OracleAS Portal Page."

The other scenario involves moving large pieces of content to your repository. Once Oracle Drive has mapped a drive letter to your repository, that drive can be used in any program or batch file as if it were a locally connected drive. Most likely, you will use Windows Explorer to move files around. As shown in Figure 5-22, the mapped drive reflects all of the pages you have created within OracleAS Portal. You can then use the cut/copy/paste features of Windows Explorer to move large pieces of content to you portal.

When you copy files into your repository, you'll notice that they don't copy as quickly as copying files around on your local drives. The slight lag is due to three factors: 1) the time it takes to copy your file across the network to the server, 2) the time it takes Oracle to convert the file into a BLOB (binary large object) and store it in the infrastructure database, and 3) the time it takes the OracleAS Portal engine to update the repository to reflect the fact that there's a new piece of content in it.

Oracle Drive is not part of the Oracle Application Server. It is only available as a separate download from Oracle's Technology Network site. Point your browser to: http://www.oracle.com/technology/software/products/cs/index.html. On that page,

OracleAS Portal Page

Two things to note: A page, as you may remember, is made up of different regions—it's entirely possible to have more than one region on a page. If the file is copied to a page (directory), how does the OracleAS Portal Page Engine know which region on the page to place the item? As you will see, for a page with more that one content region, one of the regions is defined as the default region for the page. You will see how to change that if needed. Also, if approvals have been set up for the page (as discussed in the preceding section) the content is *not* immediately available—the necessary users will need to approve it before it shows up on the page.

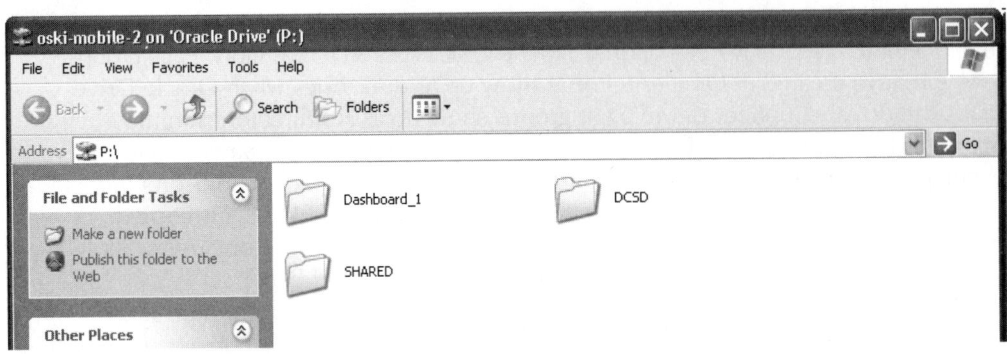

FIGURE 5-22 *Windows Explorer showing the mapped drive (P:) to the OracleAS Portal repository*

there is a link for Oracle Drive. As of the time of this writing (May 2007), the latest version is 10.2.0.0.5. Download and install Oracle Drive on your PC.

The first task after running Oracle Drive is to create a new service. Click the Service button and select New from the drop-down box. Give the service a meaningful name and select a user that has Manage Content privileges in your portal.

CAUTION
By default, OracleAS Portal is created with a default user named portal that has all privileges. This user is equivalent to the sys user in the database. As such, it should be used with extreme caution, as it is possible to do anything in OracleAS Portal when logged in as that user.

Enter the server name that your portal is running on and click the Advanced button on the bottom right of the window. If the mid-tier of your application server is using a port other than the standard HTTP port (80), enter it here. In the Server Directory: field, enter the standard portal directory, which is **dav_portal\portal**. Click OK to close the Service Properties window, select what drive letter you would like to use locally, and click Connect to map a network drive to your OracleAS Portal repository. When Oracle Drive attempts to make the connection, it will prompt you for the OracleAS Portal user's password. After entering that, a new window will pop up on your desktop, showing the contents of the OracleAS Portal repository page structure (Figure 5-23).

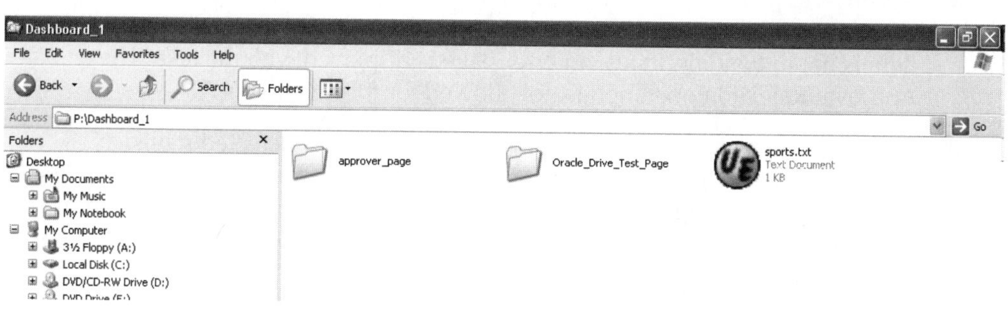

FIGURE 5-23 *The mapped drive to the OracleAS Portal repository*

You can tell if Oracle Drive is running by the existence of a small icon that looks like a globe with two small computer terminals in front of it. Along with the ability to drag and drop and cut and paste to this directory, you also have new options when you right-click any folder or item while Oracle Drive is running. When right-clicking a folder in your OracleAS Portal repository, you have three new options:

- **Set Properties** Selecting this opens a Web browser and displays the Page Properties for the page.
- **Change Access Control** Selecting this opens a Web browser and displays the Access tab in the Page Properties for the page.
- **View Page** Selecting this opens a Web browser and displays the OracleAS portal page.

When right-clicking an item in your OracleAS Portal repository, you have five new options:

- **Set Properties** Selecting this opens a Web browser and displays the Item Properties.
- **Preview Content** Selecting this opens a Web browser and displays the content (provided that a MIME type has been defined for the extension of the content—Microsoft Word for .doc files, for example).
- **View Versions** Selecting this opens a Web browser and displays the version history of the item.

- **Approve/Reject** If the item is in Pending status, a new Web browser page is opened and the screen to accept or reject the item is displayed. If the item is not in Pending status, an error page is displayed with the text "The Approval/Rejection operation is not allowed for this document."
- **Submit for Approval** If the item does not exist or is in Rejected status, a new Web browser page is opened and the Add Item screen is displayed. If the item is in Pending or Active status, then an error page is displayed with the text "Sorry, the Submit for Approval operation is not allowed for this document."

Since folders in drives that are mapped to the OracleAS Portal repository correspond to pages and files correspond to items, if you create a new folder in Windows Explorer, does it create a new page in the repository? The answer is yes. In Windows Explorer, right-click anywhere on a blank page of the window that has the mapped drive displayed. Select New from the drop-down menu and then select Folder. Name your new folder **Oracle_Drive_Test_Page**. Return to the OracleAS Portal Navigator in your Web browser and click the Page Groups tab if it's not already selected. Click the Dashboard_1 page group, and then click the Pages link. You should see a new page there called Oracle_Drive_Test_Page (Figure 5-24).

As mentioned earlier, a page can have multiple item regions on it. If you were to use Windows Explorer to copy content to a page (folder) that had multiple item regions on it, how would Oracle know which region to place the item? The answer to this lies in the fact that a single region is always designated as the default item

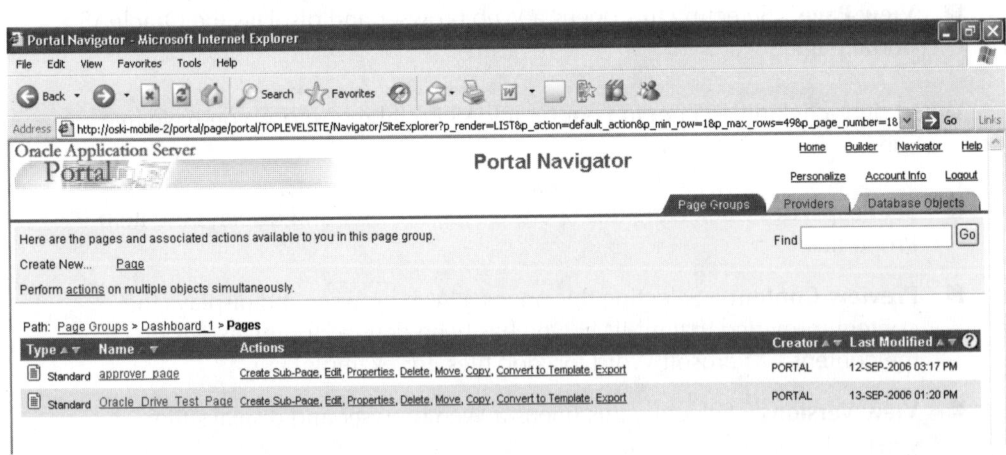

FIGURE 5-24 *The New Oracle_Drive_Test_Page page displayed in the OracleAS Portal Navigator*

region for the page. Any content copied to a page using a tool like Oracle Drive will use that region for the item's placement.

To see how this works, edit the newly created Oracle_Drive_Test_Page. By default, a single region is defined for the page. Create a new region to the right of the existing region. Click the pencil icons for both regions and define them as Items regions. Click the Page Properties link on the top left of the page and click the Items tab. On the bottom of the page, there is a section titled Default Region (Figure 5-25). Here, content administrators can select the region they wish to define as the default region on the page. To test this, select the new region as the default region, click OK, then use Windows Explorer to copy a file (or set of files) to the Oracle_Drive_Test_Page folder. Refresh the page displayed in your browser.

Why isn't the content there? Under normal circumstances it would be, but since we defined an approval chain for the page group, all pages that are part of that page group have the approval chain assigned to them. Click the List link in the top left of

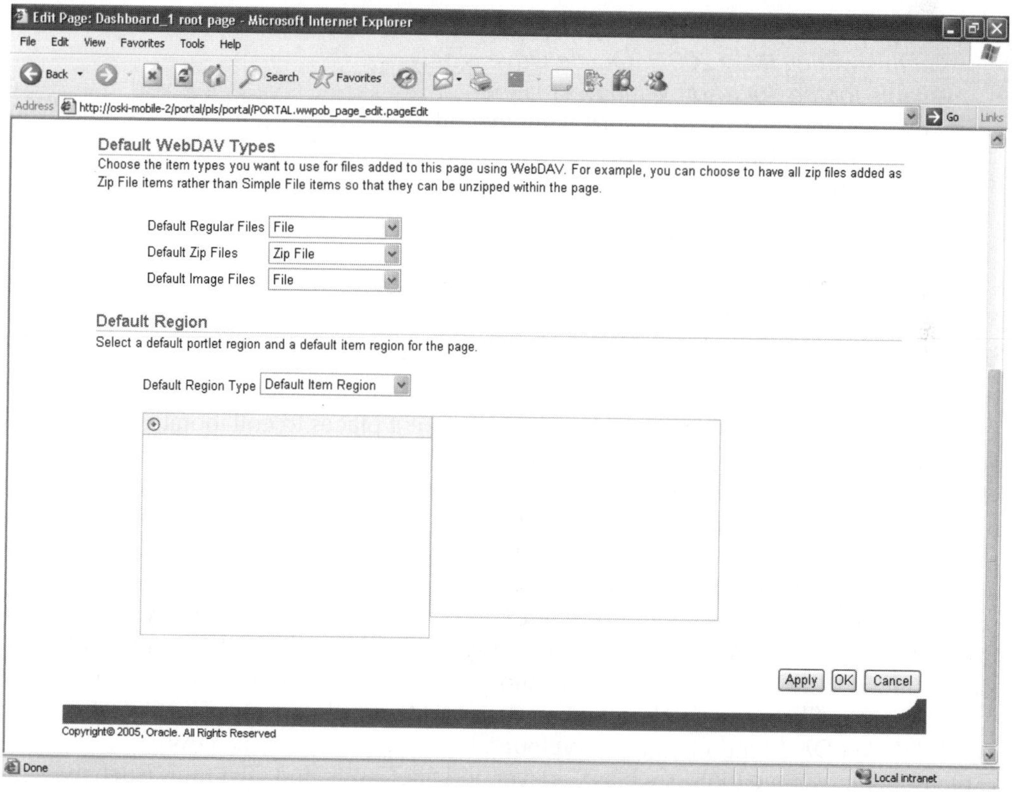

FIGURE 5-25 *The Default Region section of the Items tab*

the screen to edit the page in list mode. You will see the item (or items) with a status of Pending. Click the Pending link and approve it. Click the View Page link in the top right of the page and you will see the content displayed.

Automating Content Addition

Since the OracleAS Portal repository is mapped to a drive, the Microsoft Windows operating system sees the repository as just another drive on the system. Accordingly, it is possible to develop a simple batch file to copy reports (or other files) to the OracleAS Portal repository. Consider a server that generates reports on a nightly basis and stores them in the D:\Daily_reports directory. A simple batch file like the following listing can be scheduled with the built-in Task Scheduler tool to automatically add all PDF documents to the repository mapped to the P: drive:

```
D:
cd \Daily_reports
move /Y *.pdf p:\Oracle_Drive_Test_Page
```

TIP

As of this writing (May 2007), Oracle Drive is only available for the Microsoft Windows platform. It is possible, however, to use a third-party tool (like Hummingbird's Connectivity) to map Unix/Linux drives to your Windows server. Files on that drive can then be moved/copied to a repository-mapped drive, allowing you to automate content addition from a Unix/Linux server to your OracleAS Portal repository.

WebDAV

WebDAV (the term stands for Web-Based Distributed Authoring and Versioning) is a standard developed to allow users located in different places to collaboratively author Web documents. Oracle Drive uses WebDAV standards to communicate with the OracleAS Portal repository, but it is certainly not the only tool you can use. By using WebDAV, Oracle Drive is often referred to as a WebDAV client. Any tool, regardless of platform, that supports WebDAV can be used to communicate and add, modify, or delete OracleAS Portal content. This makes developing with a third-party tool like Dreamweaver (discussed in Chapter 4) incredibly easy to use with OracleAS Portal. With WebDAV integration, anything generated in a third-party tool can be added to the OracleAS Portal repository without the need to leave the tool to manually move files around. Almost all modern HTML development tools support WebDAV. WebDAV support can also be found in Java clients (such as DAV Explorer), open-source tools (such as Cadaver and SiteCopy), and GUI tools (such as Apple's Goliath).

The Content Management APIs

Up until this point, this chapter has concerned itself with the graphical content management tools available to content administrators working with OracleAS Portal. Sometimes, however, the need arises to programmatically modify content within your repository. Oracle provides a set of Application Programming Interfaces (APIs) that allow you to use PL/SQL to make changes to content in your repository. Developers can use the following five main packages to manipulate OracleAS Portal content:

- **WWSBR_API** This package contains APIs for manipulating content in the portal schema of the OracleAS Metadata repository. With this package, you can do things like add, move, modify, or delete items, and create, modify, or delete page groups, perspectives, categories, etc.
- **WWSRC_API** This package contains APIs for performing searches on content in the portal schema of the OracleAS Metadata repository.
- **WWSEC_API** This package contains APIs for controlling access to content in the portal schema of the OracleAS Metadata repository.
- **WWCTX_API** This package contains APIs for managing a session context for a specific user.
- **WWPRO_API_INVALIDATION** This package contains APIs for invalidation. For more information on Oracle APIs, see the sidebar "Content Management APIs."

Content Management APIs

OracleAS Portal has been around for quite some time and has gone through some significant changes. In some of the major releases, terminology of various OracleAS Portal elements has been changed. This fact can make it very confusing for Oracle developers using the Content Management APIs. Many of the tables, procedures, and functions have names that use "old" naming conventions. Even worse, you will occasionally have to write code that mixes new and old terminology. For instance, "page groups" were referred to as "content areas" in older versions of OracleAS Portal. Many times, you will need to reference a page group in your code by its internal ID, which is usually defined as caid (Content Area ID). The other terminology changes you should be aware of include: "pages" (which used to be referred to as "folders") and "navigation pages" (which used to be referred to as "navigation bars"). This takes a while to get used to, but it'll become second nature after you've written code for a while.

By default, only the portal user has access to the content management APIs. Even though the examples in this book use the portal schema for simplicity's sake, it is always a bad idea to do any development work within OracleAS Portal as the portal user. To grant access to the content management APIs to another OracleAS Portal user, you must run a script in the database as the portal user.

NOTE
The portal user in the database is different from the portal user in OracleAS Portal. The password for the database portal user is randomly generated upon installation of the Oracle Application Server and is stored in the Oracle Internet Directory (OID). If you have access to OID, run it and navigate to Entry Management, cn=OracleContext, cn=Products, cn=IAS, cn=Infrastructure Databases, OrclReferenceName=orcl, OrclResourceName=portal. In the bottom right of the program is an attribute called orclpasswordattribute. Use that value to log in to the infrastructure database.

After using a tool like SQL*Plus to log in to the database as the portal user, you must run a script that is located on the server running OracleAS Portal. This script is called provsyns.sql and is located in the ORACLE_HOME/portal/admin/plsql/wwc directory, where ORACLE_HOME is the base directory when the Oracle Application Server mid-tier was installed. Run this script as

```
@provsyns.sql <schema>
```

where <schema> is the name of the schema you wish to grant access to.

Setting the Context

Just because you can log in to the database with SQL*Plus as the portal user, that doesn't mean you have access to the content management APIs yet. One more step needs to be performed before you can run the procedures and functions that make up the APIs and get meaningful results. This step is called "Setting the Session Context." From Oracle's documentation:

> All of the content management APIs and the secure views assume that the context has been set for the functions to execute as a specific portal user. If you call an API from within a browser session

(for example, a database provider or PL/SQL item), the context is set automatically to the user who is currently logged in to the portal. If you call an API from a Web provider or an external application (for example, SQL*Plus or Portal Services), you must set the context to a specific user by using the wwctx_api.set_context API.

Luckily, this code is relatively simple. Earlier in this chapter, we created a user name "jane" with a password of "jane01." To set our context to be the jane user, the beginning of our code might look something like this:

```
declare
p_user_name varchar2(60) := 'JANE';
p_password varchar2(60) := 'jane01';
      p_company varchar2(60) := null;
begin
      wwctx_api.set_context(p_user_name,p_password,p_company);
end;
/
```

It is necessary to set the context before you execute any code that queries any of the content management APIs, so the preceding code fragment will need to be included in any of your PL/SQL procedures or functions. To execute the set_context procedure outside of a PL/SQL block in a SQL*Plus session, use the exec command:

```
exec wwctx_api.set_context('JANE','jane01',null);
```

If we had assigned a company to the jane user when creating her, we would have to replace the "null" at the end of the preceding command with the name of the company. If you don't set the context before executing statements against the Content Management API tables, you'll see error messages similar to this listing:

```
SQL> select id, name from wwsbr_all_folders where caid=53;
select id, name from wwsbr_all_folders where caid=53
                                                     *
ERROR at line 1:
ORA-14551: cannot perform a DML operation inside a query
ORA-06510: PL/SQL: unhandled user-defined exception
ORA-06512: at "PORTAL.WWCTX_SSO", line 1637
ORA-06502: PL/SQL: numeric or value error
```

In virtually every function or procedure that content administrators and developers can use to manipulate content, you need to know the page group ID you're dealing with, the page ID within the page group, and the region ID of the page. Optionally, if you wish to work with a specific item, you will need to know the item's ID also. The following list of queries shows how to determine the internal values of page groups, pages, regions, and items.

Determining Page Group IDs

The first thing we need to determine is the internal ID of the page group we are working with. The following query will determine that for us:

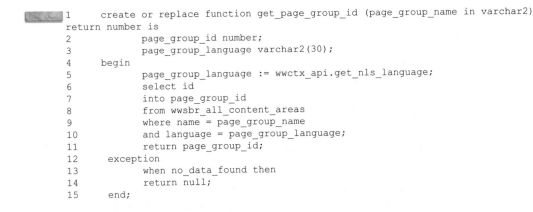

```
select id
from wwsbr_all_content_areas
where name = <Page group Name>;
```

The <Page Group Name> in this example is the internal name of the page group, not the display name (the one that shows up in the OracleAS Portal Navigator). We have been working with a page group called 'Dashboard_1' in all of the examples in the book so far. To determine the ID for the Dashboard_1 page group, we could execute a query like this in a tool like SQL*Plus:

```
SQL> select id
  2  from wwsbr_all_content_areas
  3  where name = 'Dashboard_1';

        ID
----------
        53
```

Instead of having to use the code in the preceding listing over and over again, you could put it into a function, where you could pass in the name of the page group and have the function return the Page Group ID (line numbers have been added for reference):

```
create or replace function get_page_group_id (page_group_name in varchar2) return number is
        page_group_id number;
        page_group_language varchar2(30);
begin
        page_group_language := wwctx_api.get_nls_language;
        select id
        into page_group_id
        from wwsbr_all_content_areas
        where name = page_group_name
        and language = page_group_language;
        return page_group_id;
 exception
        when no_data_found then
        return null;
 end;
```

A few things are worth noting about the preceding listing:

- Line 1 declares the function, specifying what parameter will be passed to it (page_group_name) and what type of value the function will return (a number).
- Lines 2 and 3 declare local variables that will be used inside the function.
- Line 5 determines the language of the page by calling the get_nls_language function in the wwctx_api package and assigns that value to the local variable named page_group_language.
- Lines 6–10 define the select statement. The main thing to note here is the "into" statement on line 7: The variable page_group_id will hold the value returned by the query.
- Line 11 returns the page_group_id value.
- Lines 12–14 return a null value if no page group with the name passed to the function is found.

With this function in place, you could assign the value of the page group ID to a variable in your PL/SQL code like this:

```
page_group_id := get_page_group_id('Dashboard_1');
```

Determining Page IDs

Now that we have the page group ID, we need to determine the ID of the page within the page group we wish to work with. The following query will do that for us (again, line numbers have been added for reference):

```
1       select id
2       from wwsbr_all_folders
3       where name = <Page Name>
4       and caid = 53
```

Line 4 is the key of this listing. The value (53) is from the query in the previous section that was used to determine the page group ID. The column name (caid) is a leftover from earlier versions of OracleAS Portal when page groups were called content areas. If we wanted to see all of the pages associated with the 'Dashboard_1' page group, we could use the function we created in the previous section to make this query a little more dynamic:

```
SQL> select id, name
  2  from wwsbr_all_folders
```

```
  3  where caid = get_page_group_id('Dashboard_1');

        ID NAME
---------- ----------------------------------------
     86105 Oracle_Drive_Test_Page
     84141 approver_page
         1 Dashboard_1
     70117 SAMPLE_BANNER1
```

Note that the root page of the page group has the same name as the page group. As in the preceding section, we can create a function to return the page ID:

```
create or replace function get_page_id (page_group_name in varchar2, page_name in
varchar2) return number is
      page_id number;
      page_group_language varchar2(30);
begin
      page_group_language := wwctx_api.get_nls_language;
      select id
      into page_id
      from wwsbr_all_folders
      where caid = get_page_group_id(page_group_name)
      and name = page_name;
      return page_id;
exception
      when no_data_found then
        return null;
end;
```

With this function in place, you could assign the value of the page ID to a variable in your PL/SQL code like this:

```
page_id := get_page_id('Dashboard_1', 'Oracle_Drive_Test_Page');
```

To test this function, you could write and execute an anonymous block of PL/SQL code like this:

```
SQL> set serveroutput on
SQL> declare page_id number;
  2  begin
  3     page_id := get_page_id('Dashboard_1', 'Oracle_Drive_Test_Page');
  4     dbms_output.put_line(page_id);
  5  end;
  6  /
86105

PL/SQL procedure successfully completed.
```

Note that the output (86105) matches the listing of pages shown earlier in the 'Dashboard_1' page group query.

If you only know the name of the page group and the page and want to find the page group ID and page ID with one query, you could execute a query like this:

```
select f.caid "Page Group ID",
f.id "Page ID"
from wwsbr_all_content_areas c,
wwsbr_all_folders f
where f.name = <Page Name>
and c.id = f.caid
and c.name = <Page Group Name>
```

The output of that query would look something link this:

```
SQL> select f.caid "Page Group ID",
  2  f.id "Page ID"
  3  from wwsbr_all_content_areas c,
  4  wwsbr_all_folders f
  5  where f.name = 'Dashboard_1'
  6  and c.id = f.caid
  7  and c.name = 'Dashboard_1';

Page Group ID    Page ID
------------- ----------
           53          1
```

Determining Region IDs

Now that we know how to determine the page group ID and the page ID, we need to determine the region ID for the page. The following query will list the regions on the root page of the Dashboard_1 page region:

```
select distinct r.id "Region ID",
r.type "Type"
from wwsbr_all_content_areas c,
wwsbr_all_folders f,
wwsbr_all_folder_regions r
where f.name = '<Page Name>'
and c.name = '<Page Group Name>'
and c.id = f.caid
and f.id = r.folder_id
and f.caid = r.folder_caid
and r.allow_content = 1;
```

The output from this query would look like this:

```
SQL> select distinct r.id "Region ID",
r.type "Type"
from wwsbr_all_content_areas c,
wwsbr_all_folders f,
wwsbr_all_folder_regions r
where f.name = 'Dashboard_1'
and c.name = 'Dashboard_1'
and c.id = f.caid
and f.id = r.folder_id
and f.caid = r.folder_caid
and r.allow_content = 1;

 Region ID Type
---------- --------------------------
      2532 ITEM
```

Again, you can create a function to return a region ID by passing the function the page group name, the page, and the region sequence (the first region you created on the page would be 1, the second would be 2, etc.):

```
create or replace function get_region_id (page_group_name in varchar2, page_name in
varchar2, region_seq in number) return number is
      region_id number;
begin
      select id
      into region_id
      from wwsbr_all_folder_regions
      where folder_caid = get_page_group_id(page_group_name)
      and folder_id = get_page_id(page_group_name, page_name)
      and seq = region_seq;
      return region_id;
exception
      when no_data_found then
        return null;
end;
```

To test this function, you could write and execute an anonymous block of PL/SQL code like this:

```
SQL> set serveroutput on
SQL> declare region_id number;
begin
    region_id := get_region_id('Dashboard_1', 'Dashboard_1', 1);
    dbms_output.put_line(region_id);
end;
/
2532

PL/SQL procedure successfully completed.
```

Note how the value (2532) matches the query shown earlier in the Dashboard_1 page region listing.

Determining Item IDs

Now that we know how to determine the page group ID, the page ID, and the region ID, we can finally get down to the item IDs:

```
SQL> select i.id ItemID, i.display_name title
  2  from wwsbr_all_items I
  3  where i.caid = get_page_group_id('Dashboard_1')
  4  and i.folder_id = get_page_id('Dashboard_1', 'Dashboard_1')
  5  and i.folder_region_id = get_region_id('Dashboard_1', 'Dashboard_1',
1)
  6  and i.active = 1
  7  /

   ITEMID  TITLE
----------------------------------------------------------------------------
    88101  AFC Predictions
```

Line 3 determines the page group ID, line 4 determines the page ID, and line 5 determines the region ID.

Using the Content Management APIs

Now that we know how to identify all of the pieces of our OracleAS Portal pages (page groups, pages, regions, and items), it's time to start using the Content Management API functions to programmatically make changes to our repository. One of many things you can do using the Content Management APIs is change the properties of an item. Suppose, for example, I wanted to programmatically change the name of the item on my Dashboard_1 root page from AFC Predictions to AFC Predictions 2006. The APIs include a package called wwsbr_api, which has a procedure in it called set_attribute. Developers can use this procedure to change the item name:

```
SQL> declare item_id number;
begin
 select i.id
 into item_id
 from wwsbr_all_items I
 where i.caid = get_page_group_id('Dashboard_1')
 and i.folder_id = get_page_id('Dashboard_1', 'Dashboard_1')
 and i.folder_region_id = get_region_id('Dashboard_1', 'Dashboard_1', 1)
 and i.active = 1
 and i.display_name = 'AFC Predictions';
 wwsbr_api.set_attribute(
  p_site_id => get_page_group_id('Dashboard_1'),
```

```
    p_thing_id => item_id,
    p_attribute_site_id => wwsbr_api.SHARED_OBJECTS,
    p_attribute_id => wwsbr_api.ATTRIBUTE_TITLE,
    p_attribute_value => 'AFC Predictions 2006');
   -- Process cache invalidation messages.
   wwpro_api_invalidation.execute_cache_invalidation;
  end;
  /

PL/SQL procedure successfully completed.
```

Refreshing the page will show the content with a new title (Figure 5-26).

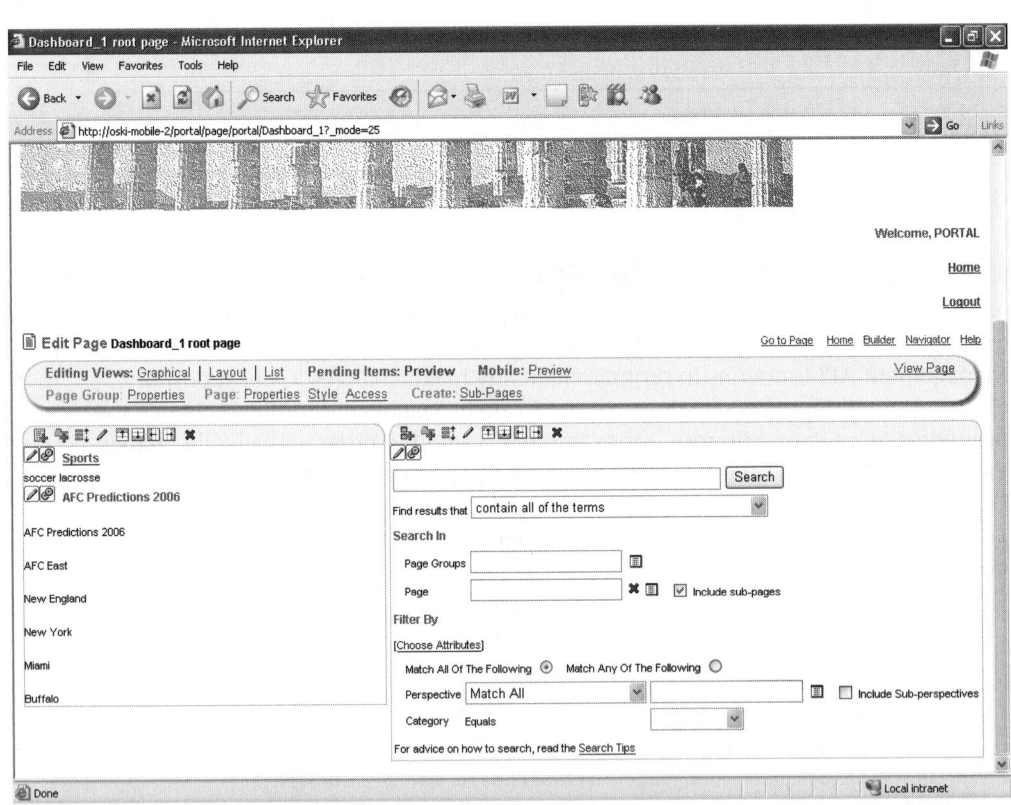

FIGURE 5-26 *The page showing the renamed item*

The following table lists the attributes that can be altered programmatically for base items:

Attribute	Constant	Value (p_attribute_value)
Author	wwsbr_api.ATTRIBUTE_ AUTHOR	Any varchar2(50) value
Category	wwsbr_api.ATTRIBUTE_ CATEGORY	<pagegroupid>_<categoryid>
Character Set	wwsbr_api.ATTRIBUTE_ CHARSET	wwsbr_api.VALUE_BIG5 wwsbr_api.VALUE_EUC_JP wwsbr_api.VALUE_GBK wwsbr_api.VALUE_ISO_8859 wwsbr_api.VALUE_SHIFT_JIS wwsbr_api.VALUE_US_ASCII wwsbr_api.VALUE_UTF8 wwsbr_api.VALUE_WINDOWS_1252
Description	wwsbr_api.ATTRIBUTE_ DESCRIPTION	Any varchar2(2000) value
Display Name	wwsbr_api.ATTRIBUTE_ TITLE	Any varchar2(256) value
Display Option	wwsbr_api.ATTRIBUTE_ DISPLAYOPTION	wwsbr_api.IN_PLACE to display the item directly in place wwsbr_api.FULL_SCREEN to display the item in the full browser window wwsbr_api.NEW_WINDOW to display the item in a new browser window
Enable Item Check-out	wwsbr_api.ATTRIBUTE_ ITEMCHECKOUT	wwsbr_api.ENABLE_ITEM_FOR_ CHECK_OUT wwsbr_api.DISABLE_ITEM_FOR_ CHECK_OUT
Expiration Period	wwsbr_api.ATTRIBUTE_ EXPIRATIONPER	wwsbr_api.PERMANENT to un-expire the item Any numeric value to set the expire mode to NUMBER. Any date value greater than the publish date to set the expire date to the value passed and the expire mode to DATE
File	wwsbr_api.ATTRIBUTE_ FILE	The path and filename of the file that you want to upload
Image	wwsbr_api.ATTRIBUTE_ IMAGE	The path and filename of the image that you want to upload
ImageMap	wwsbr_api.ATTRIBUTE_ IMAGEMAP	Any varchar2(4000) value

Attribute	Constant	Value (p_attribute_value)
Image Alignment	wwsbr_api.ATTRIBUTE_ IMAGEALIGN	wwsbr_api.ALIGN_TEXT_TOP wwsbr_api.ALIGN_ABSOLUTE_ BOTTOM wwsbr_api.ALIGN_ABSOLUTE_ MIDDLE wwsbr_api.ALIGN_BOTTOM wwsbr_api.ALIGN_RIGHT wwsbr_api.ALIGN_TOP wwsbr_api.ALIGN_LEFT wwsbr_api.ALIGN_MIDDLE wwsbr_api.ALIGN_BASELINE wwsbr_api.ALIGN_IMAGE_ ABOVE_LINK
Item Link	wwsbr_api.ATTRIBUTE_ ITEM_LINK	<pagegroupid>_<itemid>
Item Template	wwsbr_api.ATTRIBUTE_ ITEM_ TEMPLATE	<pagegroupid>_<itemtemplateid>
Keywords	wwsbr_api.ATTRIBUTE_ KEYWORDS	Any varchar2(2000) value
Mime Type	wwsbr_api.ATTRIBUTE_ MIME_ TYPE	Any of the MIME type constants in the WWSBR_API package. For example: wwsbr_api.VALUE_TEXT_ HTML wwsbr_api.VALUE_TEXT_PLAIN wwsbr_api.VALUE_IMAGE_GIF For a list of the available MIME type constants, refer to the OracleAS Portal PL/SQL API Reference on Portal Center: http://portalcenter.oracle.com. In the Portal Focus Areas section, click Portlet Development, then in the APIs and References section, click PL/SQL API Reference.
Name	wwsbr_api.ATTRIBUTE_ NAME	Any varchar2 (256) value. Specify a name that is unique within the page and all its tabs and subpages.
Page Link	wwsbr_api.ATTRIBUTE_ PAGE_LINK	<pagegroupid>_<pageid>
Perspectives	wwsbr_api.ATTRIBUTE_ PERSPECTIVES	<pagegroupid>_<perspectiveid>Separate multiple perspectives with commas. Non-existing perspective IDs are identified by the API. Only those perspectives that are available to the page group are added to the item.
PL/SQL	wwsbr_api.ATTRIBUTE_ PLSQL	Any varchar2(2000) value
Publish Date	wwsbr_api.ATTRIBUTE_ PUBLISHDATE	Any date value. This is a required attribute.
Rollover Image	wwsbr_api.ATTRIBUTE_ ROLLOVERIMAGE	The path and filename of the image file that you want to upload

Attribute	Constant	Value (p_attribute_value)
Smart Link	wwsbr_api.ATTRIBUTE_ SMARTLINK	wwsbr_api.VALUE_ACCOUNT_INFO wwsbr_api.VALUE_ADVANCED_ SEARCH wwsbr_api.VALUE_BUILDER wwsbr_api.VALUE_COMMUNITY wwsbr_api.VALUE_CONTACT wwsbr_api.VALUE_EDIT_PAGE wwsbr_api.VALUE_FAVOURITES wwsbr_api.VALUE_HELP wwsbr_api.VALUE_PORTAL_HOME wwsbr_api.VALUE_CUST_MOBILE_ HOME_PAGE wwsbr_api.VALUE_NAVIGATOR wwsbr_api.VALUE_PAGE_GROUP_ HOME wwsbr_api.VALUE_PERSONAL_PAGE wwsbr_api.VALUE_CUSTOMIZE_ PAGE wwsbr_api.VALUE_PORTLET_ REPOS_REF_STATUS wwsbr_api.VALUE_PORTLET_ REPOS wwsbr_api.VALUE_PROPERTY_ SHEET wwsbr_api.VALUE_REF_PORTLET_ REPOS wwsbr_api.VALUE_REFRESH_ PAGE wwsbr_api.VALUE_SUBSCRIBE
Smart Text	wwsbr_api.ATTRIBUTE_ SMARTTEXT	wwsbr_api.VALUE_SMART_TEXT_ CURRENT_DATE wwsbr_api.VALUE_SMART_TEXT_ CURRENT_PAGE wwsbr_api.VALUE_SMART_TEXT_ CURRENT_USER
Text	wwsbr_api.ATTRIBUTE_ TEXT	Any varchar2(4000) value
URL	wwsbr_api.ATTRIBUTE_ URL	Any URL value up to varchar2(2000)
Version Number	wwsbr_api.ATTRIBUTE_ VERSION_NUMBER	Any positive number. The number does not have to be an integer. Specify a version number that is unique; that is, it should not be the same as any existing version of the item. If you supply a value that is the same as an existing version number for the item, then it will be set to one more than the highest version number for the item.

Using the fields in this table, you could write a PL/SQL procedure to expire all items in a particular region tomorrow at midnight:

```
declare item_id     number;
       tomorrows_date    date;
       cursor loop_thru_items is
             select i.id
             from wwsbr_all_items i
             where i.caid = get_page_group_id('Dashboard_1')
             and i.folder_id = get_page_id('Dashboard_1', 'Dashboard_1')
             and i.folder_region_id = get_region_id('Dashboard_1', 'Dashboard_1', 1)
             and i.active = 1;
begin
       select to_date(sysdate+1) into tomorrows_date from dual;
```

```
12          open loop_thru_items;
13          loop
14                fetch loop_thru_items into item_id;
15                exit when loop_thru_items%notfound;
16                wwsbr_api.set_attribute(
17                       p_site_id => get_page_group_id('Dashboard_1'),
18                       p_thing_id => item_id,
19                       p_attribute_site_id => wwsbr_api.SHARED_OBJECTS,
20                       p_attribute_id => wwsbr_api.ATTRIBUTE_EXPIRATIONPER,
21                       p_attribute_value => tomorrows_date);
22                wwpro_api_invalidation.execute_cache_invalidation;
23          end loop;
24    end;
```

Note the following about this listing:

- Lines 3–9 define a cursor that is used to find all of the items in a specific region.
- Line 11 gets tomorrow's date (sysdate + 1) and assigns it to a variable called tomorrows_date.
- Line 12 opens the cursor defined in lines 3–9.
- Line 13 begins to loop through all of the items in the region.
- Line 14 fetches the item ID into a variable called item_id.
- Line 15 sets the exit condition for the loop.
- Lines 16–21 call the set_attribute procedure for each item in the region and set the ATTRIBUTE_EXPIRATIONPER attribute to the value in the tomorrows_date variable.
- Line 22 is a call to a procedure called execute_cache_invalidation. Many of the APIs automatically generate cache invalidation messages for the pages that are affected by the changes. Therefore, you should always call wwpro_api_invalidation.execute_cache_invalidation at the end of your routine to process these messages. If you do not call this procedure, your changes may not be visible until the affected pages are invalidated through other means. There is no need to call execute_cache_invalidation more than once. For example, if you are adding or updating multiple items in a loop, call execute_cache_invalidation when the loop is complete.

After you execute this procedure, you can check the item by clicking on the small pencil icon next to the item when editing the page in Graphical mode. If you scroll down to the Expiration Period field, you will see a value similar to what is in Figure 5-27.

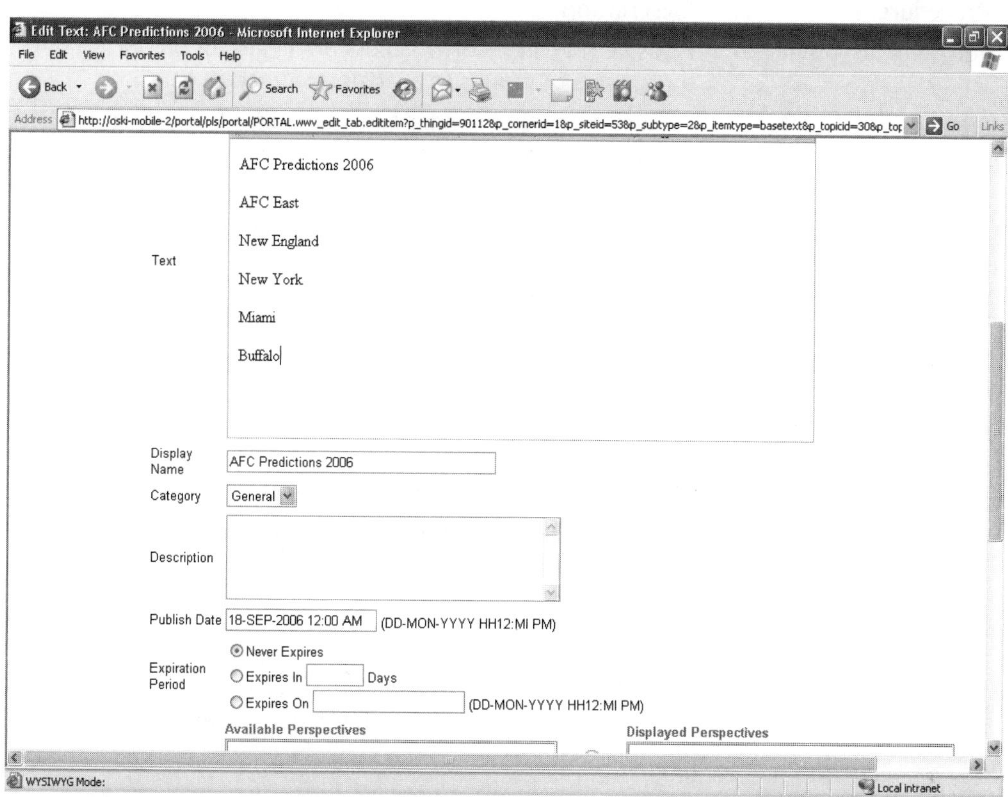

FIGURE 5-27 *The Item Attributes page showing the new expiration date*

The wwsbr_api Package

The wwsbr_api package has many useful procedures and functions for manipulating content programmatically. The following table lists the procedures and functions in this package and a brief description of each:

Procedure	Description
add_category	Creates a new category in a page group.
add_content_area	Creates a new page group.
add_folder	Creates a new page in a page group.
add_item	Creates a new item on a specified page in a page group.

Procedure	Description
add_item_ils_privileges	Adds item-level security access privileges for one or more users or groups to a single specified item.
add_item_post_upload	Creates a new item on a page and links it to existing document(s) in the document table.
add_perspective	Creates a new perspective in a page group.
approve	Approves an item that has been submitted for approval.
check_in_item	Checks in an item, provided it is checked out.
check_out_item	Checks out an item, provided the item is enabled for check-out.
clear_cmef_context	Clears the Content Management Event Framework (CMEF) context.
copy_folder	Copies a page within the same page group.
copy_item	Copies an item to a page either within the same page group or across page groups.
delete_folder	Deletes a page.
delete_ils_privilege	Deletes the item-level security access privileges for a user or group on a single specified item.
delete_item	Deletes an item present in a particular page and page group.
enable_ils_for_item	Enables item-level security for a specified item.
inherit_folder_ privileges	Causes an item that is enabled for item-level security to inherit its privileges from the page on which it resides.
modify_folder	Modifies a page's properties.
modify_item	Modifies an item in a particular page and page group.
modify_item_post_ upload	Modifies an item and links it to existing document(s) in the document table.
move_category	Moves a category within a page group.
move_folder	Moves a page to be another page's subpage within the same page group.
move_item	Moves an item either within the same page group or across page groups.
move_perspective	The procedure to move a perspective within a page group.

Procedure	Description
reject	Rejects an item that has been submitted for approval.
set_attribute	Modifies attribute values for a particular version of an item.
undelete_item	Undeletes an item (and its subitems).
upload_blob	Uploads document content to the document table.

NOTE

For more information on these functions and procedures and the parameter types involved in calling them, see the Oracle online PL/SQL reference for OracleAS Portal at: http://www.oracle.com/technology/products/ias/portal/html/plsqldoc/pldoc1014/index.html.

Additional Useful Packages

As mentioned earlier, there are four other packages of interest to the content administrator/developer:

- The wwsrc_api package
- The wwsec_api package
- The wwctx_api package
- The wwpro_api_invalidation package

Tables 5-3, 5-4, 5-5, and 5-6 list the functions and procedures in these packages.

Procedure	Description
category_search	Searches for categories and returns the category results rows in the form of an array of wwsbr_all_categories records.
get_all_items_xml	Returns an XML document describing the given item result set from the search result array of items.
get_all_pages_xml	Returns an XML document describing the given page result set from the search result array of pages.

TABLE 5-3 *Procedures and Functions in the wwwsrc_api Package*

Procedure	Description
get_item_xml	Returns an XML document describing the given item from the search result record for this resource.
get_page_xml	Returns an XML document describing the given page from the search result record for this resource.
item_search	Searches for items and returns the item results rows in the form of an array of wwsbr_all_items records.
page_search	Searches for pages and returns the page results rows in the form of an array of wwsbr_all_folders records.
perspective_search	Searches for perspectives and returns the perspective results rows in the form of an array of wwsbr_all_perspectives records.
specify_attributes	Builds up the search attribute criteria for the search APIs (item_search(), page_search(), etc.) by storing the attributes in an array based on wwsrc_runtime_attr_varray() objects.

TABLE 5-3 *Procedures and Functions in the wwwsrc_api Package* (continued)

Procedure	Description
accessible_objects	Gets a list of objects accessible to a user, checking for a specific privilege.
accessible_objects	Gets a list of objects accessible to a user, checking for a number of privileges.
activate_portal_user	Activates an existing but inactive OracleAS Portal 10*g* user.
add_group_to_list	Adds a group as a member to another group.
add_portal_user	Adds a Portal profile entry to the OracleAS Portal 10*g* repository.
add_user_to_list	Adds a user to a group.
clear_package_cache	Clears the package-level cache.
copy_privileges	Copies all privileges from a source object to a destination object.

TABLE 5-4 *Procedures and Functions in the wwsec_api Package*

Procedure	Description
create_list	Creates a group in OID and returns the corresponding group profile ID for the portal.
db_user	Returns the database schema name to which the user is associated, given the name of an OracleAS Portal 10*g* user.
deactivate_portal_user	Deactivates an OracleAS Portal 10*g* user.
delete_group_from_list	Deletes a group from the list of members of another group.
delete_list	Deletes a group from OID and any associated references to the group.
delete_portal_user	Deletes an OracleAS Portal 10*g* user profile entry from the portal schema, given a user name.
delete_user_from_list	Deletes a user from the membership list of a group.
get_authorization_function	Gets the name of the function used for function-based authorization.
get_defaultgroup	Returns the default group for a specified user.
get_granted_group_privilege	Gets the highest privilege that a group has on a given object.
get_granted_user_priv_code	Gets the granted privilege code that a user has on a given object.
get_granted_user_privilege	Gets the highest privilege that the user has on the specified object.
get_list_members	Deprecated as of Oracle9iAS Portal 9.0.2, since the groups are maintained in OID, which does not support an API to read the membership information if the number of members becomes very large. Gets a list of the members of a group of type 'LIST' when given a group ID.
get_manager	Returns the user name of a specified user's manager.
get_member_record	Deprecated as of Oracle9iAS Portal 9.0.2, since the membership information is maintained in OID and there is no member ID attribute, which is required as an input parameter for this function. Gets a member's record from the wwsec_member$ table.
get_privilege_level	Checks the highest privilege that a user has on a given object.
get_public_objects	Gets a list of objects granted to PUBLIC array.

TABLE 5-4 *Procedures and Functions in the wwsec_api Package* (continued)

Procedure	Description
grantee_list	Returns a list of grantees for a named object and specified owner.
group_id	Gets the group ID for a specified group name.
group_info	Returns group information, given a group ID.
group_name	Returns the group name when given a group ID.
has_privilege	Checks whether a user has a certain privilege.
has_privilege	Checks whether a user has one of a list of privileges.
has_privilege	Checks whether a specified user has a specified privilege.
id	Returns a person ID, given a user name or Globally Unique Identifier (GUID).
id_sso	Returns a person ID, given a user name or GUID and also validates that a user exists in the OID Server and OracleAS Portal 10*g*.
is_group_owner	Deprecated as of Oracle9iAS Portal 9.0.2, since the membership information is maintained in OID and there is no member ID attribute, which is required as an input parameter for this function. Checks whether a member is a group's owner.
is_privilege_at_least	Checks whether a specified user, or group to which a user belongs, has a privilege on a specified object that is at least as high as the privilege specified.
is_privileged_by_auth_function	Checks the authorization by calling the authorization function.
is_user_in_direct_group	Checks whether a user was individually granted membership in a specific group.
is_user_in_group	Checks whether a user belongs to a specific group.
list_id	Gets the group ID of a list within a site.
lists	Deprecated as of Oracle9iAS Portal 9.0.2, since the groups are stored in OID and are not scoped by site ID. Gets a list of list type groups.
modify_portal_user	Updates personal and business-related information about an OracleAS Portal 10*g* user.
person_info	Returns user information, given a person's ID.

TABLE 5-4 *Procedures and Functions in the wwsec_api Package* (continued)

Procedure	Description
person_info	Returns user information, given a user name.
privilege_list	Returns a list of privileges for a specified object_type_name.
publish_group	Deprecated as of Oracle9iAS Portal 9.0.2, as groups are stored in OID, which does not support this property. Sets the group to be publishable or nonpublishable.
remove_group_acl	Removes a group's privileges.
remove_user_acl	Removes a specified privilege from a user.
set_authorization_function	Sets the name of a function to be used for function-based authorization.
set_defaultgroup	Sets the default group for a specified user.
set_group_acl	Creates an entry in the Access Control List that grants a privilege on a specified object to a specified group.
set_user_acl	Gives a user a specified privilege in the OracleAS Portal 10*g*.
update_group_acl	Changes a group's privilege in the Access Control List.
update_group_owner	Modifies group ownership for a group that is a member of another group.
update_list	Updates general information for a specified group.
update_user_acl	Changes a user's privilege in the Access Control List.
update_user_owner	Modifies group ownership for a user.
user_in_groups	Deprecated as of Oracle9iAS Portal 9.0.2, since groups are now stored in OID and do not necessarily have a local shadow entry with an ID. Returns a list of group IDs when given a user name.
user_name	Returns a user name, given a person's ID.
users_in_group	Deprecated as of Oracle9iAS Portal 9.0.2, since the group memberships are being maintained in OID and implementation of this API becomes prohibitive. OID does not provide a direct API to return the members of a group, so recursive calls would have to be made to the directory to get the users who are indirect members. This function is not being used anywhere in the Portal code. Gets the list of all the users in a specific group.

TABLE 5-4 *Procedures and Functions in the wwsec_api Package* (continued)

Procedure	Description
clear_context	Clears the session context.
get_authentication_level	Gets the authentication level of the user.
get_base_url	Returns the base URL, also known as the URL prefix.
get_bidi_imagename	Returns the image name appropriate for the selected language.
get_company_name	Returns the company name associated with an Oracle Portal user.
get_dad_name	Gets the value of the DAD_NAME CGI variable.
get_db_user	Gets the name of the database schema corresponding to the current user of the system (as determined by the session context).
get_direct_doc_path	Returns the path to a file stored in the Oracle Portal repository.
get_doc_access_path	Gets the value of the DOC_ACCESS_PATH CGI variable.
get_flex_proc_path	Generates a fully qualified URL for flexible parameter passing from a relative URL.
get_gateway_iversion	Returns the internal version number of the gateway used to access the repository.
get_host	Gets the hostname and port of the server.
get_host_lowercase	Gets the hostname and port of the server in lowercase.
get_http_accept	Gets the value of the HTTP_ACCEPT CGI variable.
get_http_accept_charset	Gets the value of the HTTP_ACCEPT_CHARSET CGI variable.
get_http_accept_encoding	Gets the value of the HTTP_ACCEPT_ENCODING CGI variable.
get_http_accept_language	Gets the value of the HTTP_ACCEPT_LANGUAGE CGI variable.
get_http_language	Returns the HTTP language used by the current Oracle Portal user.
get_http_oracle_ecid	Gets the value of the HTTP_ORACLE_ECID CGI variable.
get_http_referer	Returns the HTTP Referer header value.
get_http_user_agent	Gets the value of the HTTP_USER_AGENT CGI variable.
get_http_x_oracle_assert_user	Gets the value of the HTTP_X_ORACLE_ASSERT_USER CGI variable.

TABLE 5-5 *Procedures and Functions in the wwctx_api Package*

Procedure	Description
get_image_path	Returns the path to the location of the product images.
get_ip_address	Gets the IP address of the client from the session context.
get_last_updated	Gets the time the session was last updated.
get_login_time	Returns the time that the current user logged in to Oracle Portal.
get_nls_language	Returns the NLS language used by the current Oracle Portal user.
get_nls_territory	Gets the NLS territory used by the current user of the system (as determined by the session context).
get_oracle_cache_version	Gets the value of the HTTP_ORACLE_CACHE_VERSION CGI variable.
get_osso_user_guid	Gets the value of the OSSO_USER_GUID CGI variable.
get_path_alias	Gets the value of the PATH_ALIAS CGI variable.
get_path_info	Gets the value of the PATH_INFO CGI variable.
get_proc_path	Generates a fully qualified URL from a relative URL.
get_product_schema	Returns the name of the schema in which Oracle Portal is installed.
get_product_version	Returns the version string for the installation of Oracle Portal.
get_proxy_port	Retrieves the port number of the proxy server.
get_proxy_server	Returns the name of the proxy server.
get_public_schema	Returns the name of the public schema.
get_public_user	Returns the name of the public user.
get_query_string	Gets the value of the QUERY_STRING CGI variable.
get_remote_addr	Gets the value of the REMOTE_ADDR CGI variable.
get_request_charset	Gets the value of the REQUEST_CHARSET CGI variable.
get_schema_user	Gets the name of the schema user as returned by SELECT USER FROM DUAL.
get_script_name	Gets the value of the SCRIPT_NAME CGI variable.
get_script_prefix	Gets the value of the SCRIPT_PREFIX CGI variable.
get_server_name	Gets the value of the SERVER_NAME CGI variable.
get_server_port	Gets the value of the SERVER_PORT CGI variable.

TABLE 5-5 *Procedures and Functions in the wwctx_api Package* (continued)

Procedure	Description
get_server_protocol	Gets the Web server's protocol—http or https.
get_servlet_path	Generates a fully qualified URL to the Parallel Page Engine.
get_session_expire_time	Gets the time when the session will expire.
get_session_start_time	Gets the time when the session started.
get_sessionid	Gets current session ID for the session context.
get_sso_proc_path	Generates a fully qualified URL for the Login Server from a relative URL.
get_sso_product_version	Gets the SSO product version.
get_sso_query_path	Gets the URL prefix to use for HTTP queries to the login server.
get_sso_schema	Returns the Single Sign-On schema name.
get_subscriber_id	Determines the subscriber ID of an Oracle Portal user.
get_sysdate	Gets the system date as returned by SELECT SYSDATE FROM DUAL.
get_system_var_names	Gets the set of external system variable names.
get_system_var_value	Gets the value of an external system variable given its name.
get_translation_language	Gets the translation language used by the current user of the system.
get_user	Returns the user name of the current Oracle Portal user.
get_user_id	Returns the user ID of the user currently logged in.
get_x_oracle_cache_auth	Gets the value of the HTTP_X_ORACLE_CACHE_AUTH CGI variable.
get_x_oracle_cache_device	Gets the value of the HTTP_X_ORACLE_CACHE_DEVICE CGI variable.
get_x_oracle_cache_encrypt	Gets the value of the HTTP_X_ORACLE_CACHE_ENCRYPT CGI variable.
get_x_oracle_cache_lang	Gets the value of the HTTP_X_ORACLE_CACHE_LANG CGI variable.
get_x_oracle_cache_subid	Gets the value of the HTTP_X_ORACLE_CACHE_SUBID CGI variable.
get_x_oracle_cache_user	Gets the value of the HTTP_X_ORACLE_CACHE_USER CGI variable.
has_idle_timeout_exceeded	Checks if idle timeout has occurred.

TABLE 5-5 *Procedures and Functions in the wwctx_api Package* (continued)

Procedure	Description
is_context_set	Checks whether a session context is set.
is_in_login_server	Checks if the current request is executing in the SSO server.
is_logged_on	Returns a boolean indicator showing if the user is logged on.
is_proxy_required	Checks if a proxy is required to contact the specified URL.
is_session_authenticated	Checks if the session ID represents an authenticated session.
logged_on	Indicates whether the user is logged in, and returns a number instead of a Boolean value so that the value returned can be used as a condition for creating a view.
set_context	Sets the session context for a lightweight user.
set_nls_language	Sets the NLS language and territory of the current SQL*Plus-created portal session.
validate_system_var_name	Validates the given system variable name.

TABLE 5-5 *Procedures and Functions in the wwctx_api Package* (continued)

Procedure	Description
execute_cache_invalidation	The procedure is designed to perform invalidations from SQLPLUS.
invalidate_by_instance	Invalidates the OracleAS Web Cache, given a portlet instance ID.
invalidate_by_portlet	Invalidates the OracleAS Web Cache, given a portlet ID.
invalidate_by_provider	Invalidates the OracleAS Web Cache, given a provider ID.
invalidate_by_user_portlet	Invalidates the OracleAS Web Cache, given a user provider ID and portlet ID.
invalidate_by_user_provider	Invalidates the OracleAS Web Cache, given a user and provider ID.
invalidate_cache	Invalidates the OracleAS Web Cache, given a set of parameters that together define a URL.

TABLE 5-6 *Procedures and Functions in the wwpro_api_invalidation Package*

Exercises

- Exercise 1: Design a page that uses tabs to segregate content by major departments within an organization. Use Oracle Drive to copy content there.
- Exercise 2: Write a PL/SQL program to add all files from a specific directory into your OracleAS Portal repository. Wrap this program into a procedure that can be called using the exec command in SQL*Plus in which you pass the directory name as a parameter.
- Exercise 3: Write a PL/SQL program to create a new OracleAS Portal user. Wrap that program into a procedure that can be called using the exec command in SQL*Plus in which you pass the username and password as parameters.

Summary

Content management is the process of adding, deleting, modifying, and performing various other activities on things that you want available in your portal, but that do not necessarily fit into a traditional programming paradigm like a form, chart, or report. These things might consist of Microsoft Word documents, Adobe PDF files, images, movies, sound files—the list goes on and on. Virtually anything that can be converted into a file that can be stored on a computer can be used as content.

Every portal system on the market today has a series of methods for dealing with content. Only OracleAS Portal, however, provides such a rich set of both declarative (Web-based) and programmatic tools giving content administrators incredible flexibility when managing their content. The PL/SQL packages allow developers to write reusable, secure code that can perform complex manipulation of content easily. These features make OracleAS Portal the premier content management portal product on the market today.

CHAPTER 6

OmniPortlet and Web Clipping

Back in Chapter 1, we discussed the wizards that OracleAS Portal comes with for developing portlets. The wizards are fast, easy, and secure and allow developers to generate forms, reports, charts, and the like very quickly. Beginning OracleAS Portal developers and administrators can be productive in a very short period of time once they've been trained on the basics of wizard-based portlet development (referenced in Chapter 1), content management (Chapter 5), and page design (Chapters 3 and 4). The real beauty of using the wizards isn't in the portlets themselves but in the unbelievable amount of complex code the wizards generate to handle things like session/state management of objects, maintaining visual consistency (templates, colors, fonts, etc.), and enforcing the complex security rules that can be built into OracleAS Portal pages and portlets. Any developer who has attempted to create even the most simple of Web pages that references a database securely can attest to the complexity of these tasks.

Since the wizards handle all of this "plumbing" for you, why go anywhere else? The answer lies in the fact that with any wizard-based tool, there are some serious limitations and most developers run up against these pretty quickly. As mentioned in Chapter 1, Oracle, while still supporting the OracleAS Portal development wizards, is clearly moving away from that development paradigm. As evidence of this, consider where the documentation for the wizards is in the Oracle Application Server Portal Developer's Guide: in the appendix, almost as an afterthought. The majority of the Developer's Guide is devoted to things like Java development (discussed in this book in Chapters 7 and 8) and advanced tools like OmniPortlet and Web Clipping. White papers from Oracle that discuss future enhancements and direction of OracleAS Portal almost never reference any enhancements planned for the development wizards. Most of the enhancements talk about things like adding OracleAS Portal–specific features to the Application Development Framework (ADF). To learn more about the ADF, see the sidebar "Application Development Framework (ADF)."

Using the built-in OracleAS Portal development wizards (fast, but limited) and developing portlets with Oracle JDeveloper and ADF (difficult, but flexible) are not the only two choices available to portlet developers. There are two technologies available in OracleAS Portal 10.1.4 that bridge the gap between the simplicity of the development wizards and the functionality of Java development. These two technologies are called OmniPortlet and Web Clipping.

What Is OmniPortlet?

OmniPortlet is a special type of portlet that attempts to provide the best of both worlds: declarative use (for ease) with a large number of source and display options (for power). Creating an OmniPortlet is different from the process of creating a portlet using the programmatic wizards referenced in Chapter 1. To use the OracleAS Portal wizards to create a portlet, perform the following steps:

1. Create a Database Provider in the OracleAS Portal Navigator if one doesn't exist already.
2. Select that Database Provider, and then select the object you wish to create (form, report, calendar, etc.).
3. Follow the wizards to generate the portal component.
4. Expose the component as a portlet.
5. Edit the page and place the portlet in a region on the page.

To create an OmniPortlet, perform the following steps:

1. On your page, add the seeded OmniPortlet portlet.
2. Define your OmniPortlet.

As you can see, there is no need to use database providers at all when using OmniPortlets. The OmniPortlet is part of the page, as opposed to the wizard-generated portlet being part of a database provider.

NOTE
You can think of a provider as a container of portlets. A provider can be used to set privileges and attributes of all portlets associated with that provider. Providers are discussed in greater detail in Chapters 7 and 8.

Application Development Framework (ADF)

ADF (Application Development Framework) is included with Oracle JDeveloper. The ADF is an end-to-end application framework that builds on J2EE standards and open-source technologies to simplify and accelerate implementing service-oriented applications. Oracle ADF can greatly simplify the development of applications that search, display, create, modify, and validate data from Oracle databases that use Web, wireless, desktop, or Web service interfaces. The combination of Oracle JDeveloper and ADF gives developers an environment that covers the full development lifecycle from design to deployment, with drag-and-drop data binding and visual UI design. Oracle JDeveloper and ADF are discussed in Chapter 7.

The OmniPortlet Wizard

The best way to learn about OmniPortlets is to build one. After this section, we'll go back and look at each of the major choices presented to you when defining your OmniPortlet individually. Edit the Dashboard_1 root page and click the Add Portlet icon in one of your portlet regions. Click the Portlet Builders folder on the left-hand side of the page, and then click the OmniPortlet link to move it to the Selected Portlets window. Click OK to return to the page. As you can see from Figure 6-1, the OmniPortlet is on the page, but has not been defined yet. Click the Define link in the OmniPortlet to be taken to the OmniPortlet Wizard.

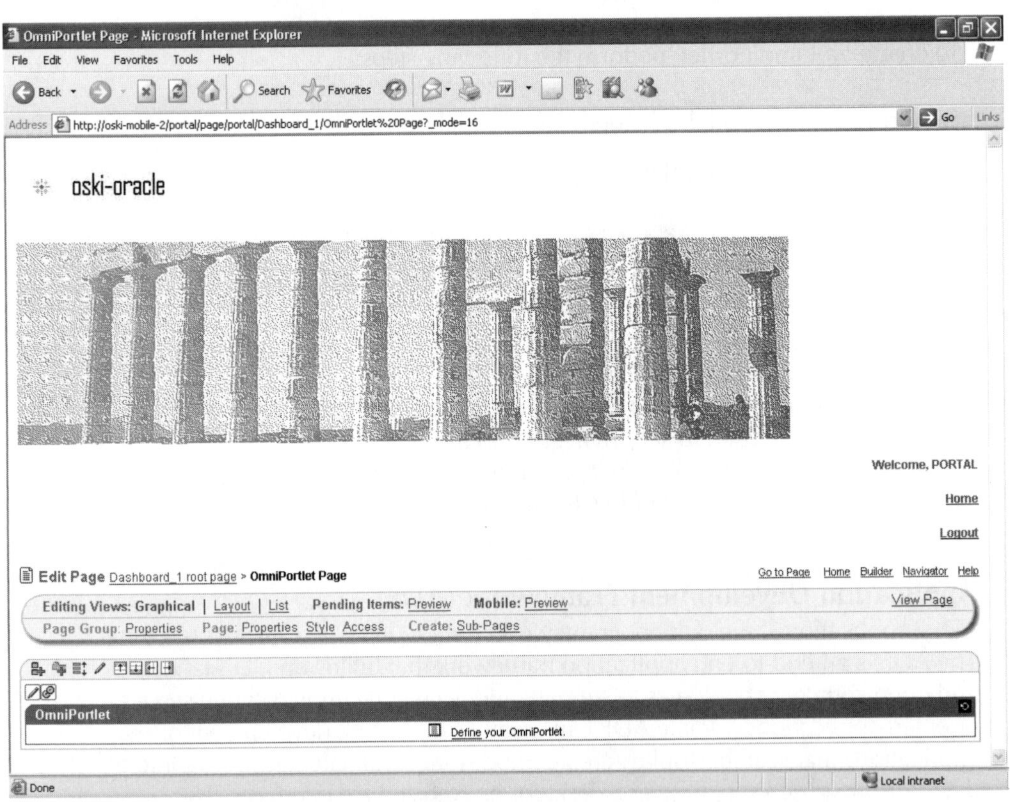

FIGURE 6-1 *The OmniPortlet before definition*

The first page of the OmniPortlet Wizard gives developers five choices from which they can get data:

- **Spreadsheet** Many organizations keep data in spreadsheets. Saving data in these spreadsheets using a standard format allows the data to be moved between applications easily. A common format used today is CSV (character-separated values), which is nothing more that a text file representing the data in the spreadsheet with a specified character used to separate fields.
- **SQL** If you want to query data from a data source, use this option. In most organizations, the data source will be an Oracle database, but unlike when using the OracleAS Portal development wizards, you are not limited to Oracle databases. Any data source that has a Type 4 JDBC driver can be used. Later in this chapter, we'll discuss the JDBC drivers you can download from Oracle. This makes OmniPortlet extremely valuable for creating portlets that pull data from numerous data sources throughout your organization.
- **XML** OmniPortlet can also be configured to read data that is in XML format.
- **Web Service** A *Web service* is a set of messaging protocols, programming standards, and network facilities that expose business functions to authorized users over the Web. OmniPortlet can treat a Web service as if it is a data source and query information from it.
- **Web Page** This option allows developers to use existing Web content as a source of data.

There are five steps in the OmniPortlet Wizard: Type, Source, Filter, View, and Layout. The Filter and View pages are all pretty much the same regardless of what you select on the Type screen. The second and fifth pages of the wizard (Source and Layout), differ greatly depending on what is selected for Type (affecting the Source page) and View (affecting the Layout page). Since SQL is the most common choice, select that for this example and click the Next button in the top right of the screen. You will see a screen similar to Figure 6-2.

In the middle of the page is the Connection section. This is where you define your data source for the OmniPortlet. Click Edit Connection to see the Edit Connection page (Figure 6-3).

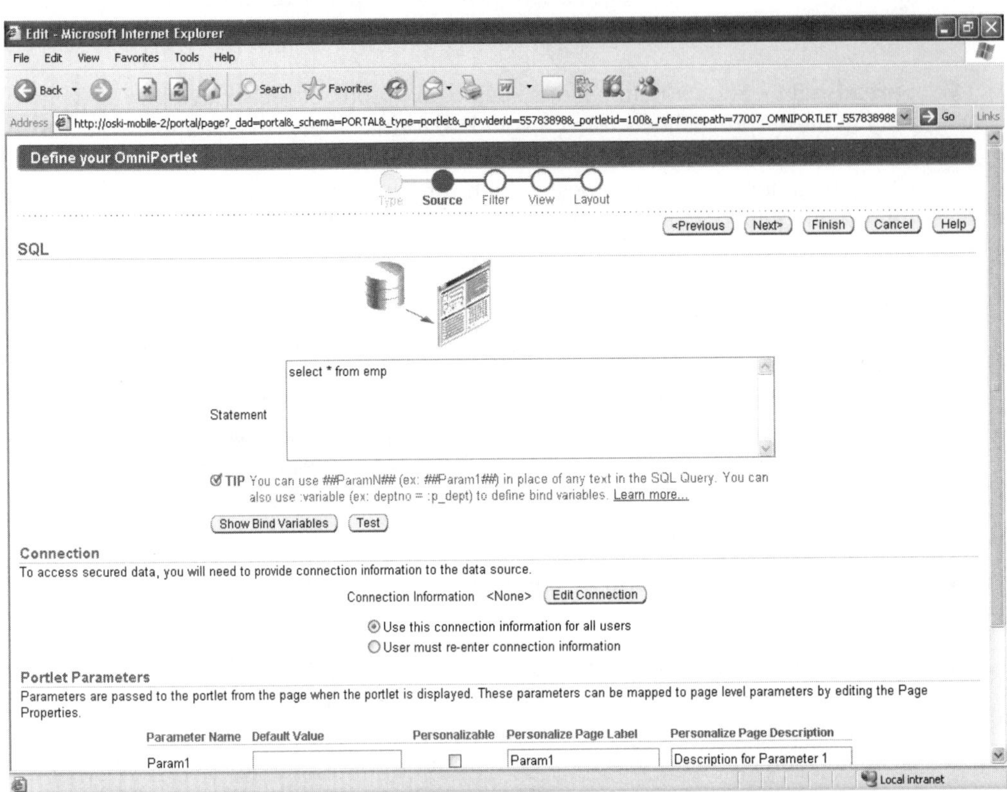

FIGURE 6-2 *The Source page of the OmniPortlet Wizard after "SQL" was selected*

Data Sources

On this screen, developers define where the data is coming from. By default, a connection is already defined to your infrastructure database. Click the flashlight icon to the right of the Connect Name box. You will see a pop-up box with the name of your infrastructure instance (by default, it's ORCL, unless your application server administrator chose a different name for the infrastructure database during installation). Under normal circumstances, you would never store data in your infrastructure database, but for the examples in this book, we will use a schema called portal_demo inside of the infrastructure database, so select ORCL (or whatever the name of your infrastructure database is) from the pop-up window, enter **portal_demo** as the username and the password for the portal_demo schema.

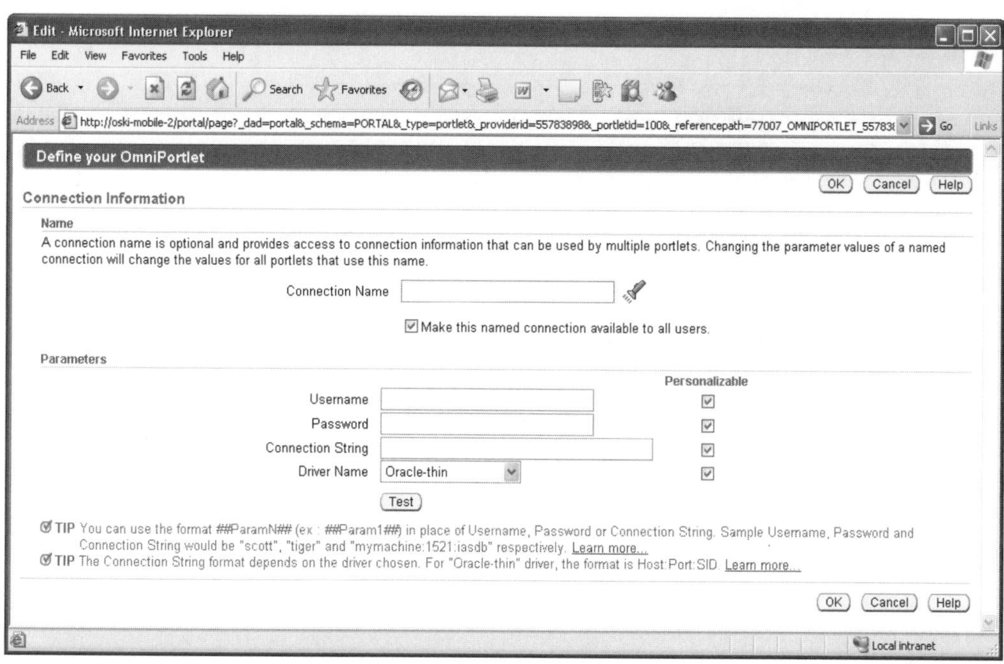

FIGURE 6-3 *The Connection Information screen for the OmniPortlet*

Click the Test button in the middle of the screen. You should see a pop-up window that says "Connection Successful."

Click OK to return to the OmniPortlet Wizard. By default, the SQL query "Select * from emp" is in the Statement box. Click the Test button below that to test the query. You should see a box with results from the emp table in it. Click Close to close the pop-up window. At the bottom of the page is the Portlet Parameters section. In Chapter 4, we discussed Page Parameters and how they can be used to pass information between pages. We'll re-visit this part of OmniPortlet development in the section "Page Parameters" later in this chapter. Click Next.

Defining Filters and Views

The next page of the wizard, the Filter page (Figure 6-4), is where developers can limit and order the rows that are returned by the query defined on the previous page of the wizard. The top section, Conditions, can be used to limit data by certain criteria. Selecting the drop-down box under Column will list all of the columns

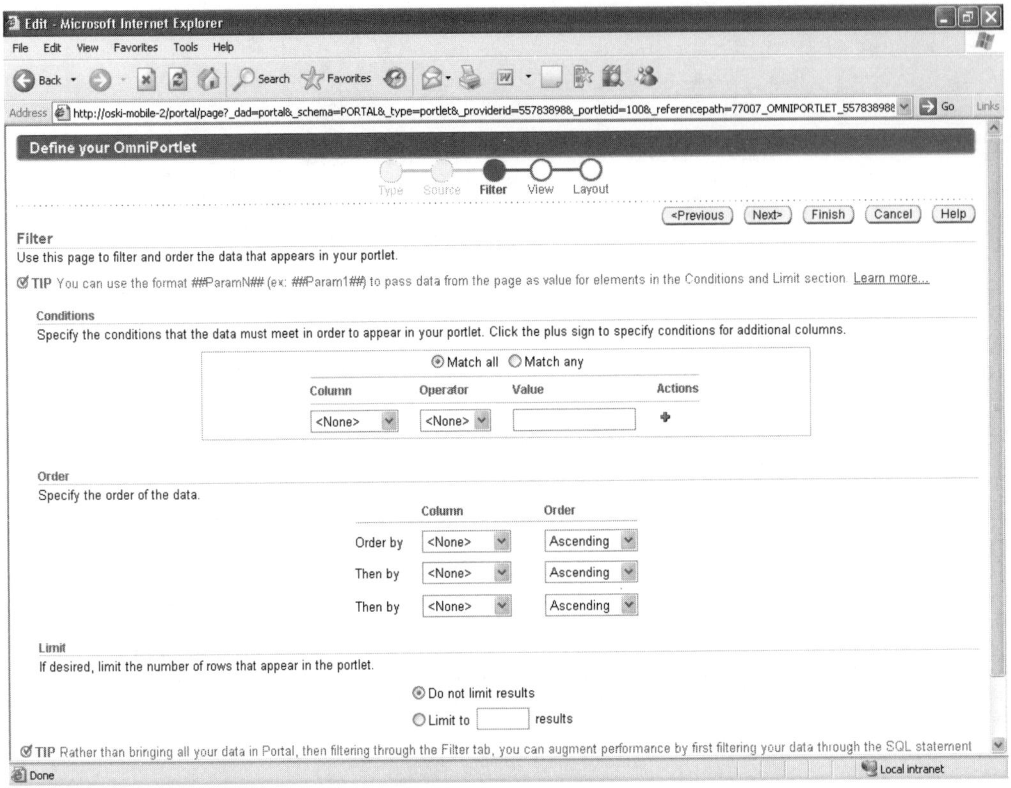

FIGURE 6-4 *The Filter page of the OmniPortlet Wizard*

returned by the previous step. The operator drop-down lists all of the operators you can apply, and the third column, Value, is where a developer specifies the value for the condition. Clicking the plus sign on the left adds the specified condition to the condition list and allows developers to add a second condition (if desired).

The middle section, Order, gives developers the ability to sort the way information is returned. There are only three fields you can sort by, and there is no way to add more fields to sort by. The last section, Limit, allows developers to specify how many rows are returned. Be careful when using this option however: no Next or Previous buttons or links are provided, so if you limit the rows returned to something small, those are the only records displayed. This may have practical applications but can be confusing for end users not trained on this functionality.

NOTE
*It's always more efficient to limit data returned in the query than it is to specify a limiting condition here. For example, if you only wanted to return those employees in department 10, you could create a condition on the Filter page, but it would be more efficient to write a SQL statement like this on the Source page: select * from emp where deptno = 10;*

The View page is the next page of the wizard. On this wizard page, developers define things like the title and header and footer text displayed, the layout style, and the caching rules for the portlet. The most important section on this page is the Layout section. In this section, developers have six basic choices of how they would like their portlet to present data to end users:

- **Tabular** The most "traditional" of the six choices, tabular displays data in a table format with columns and rows.
- **Chart** In this format, you must return at least three columns, one of which must be a numeric field: one column representing the x-axis of your graph, one representing the y-axis, and the numeric field representing the data.
- **News** This format returns data that usually consists of a "title" and a "body," in the same way a story in a newspaper would consist of a headline and the body of a story.
- **Bullet** This format returns values in either a bulleted or numbered list.
- **Form** This format allows page designers to create a portlet where they have control over the headings for each field displayed.
- **HTML** This format gives page designers the greatest control over the look of the portlet by requiring the coding of HTML. This layout also requires the use of HTML substitution tags for the fields to be displayed on the OmniPortlet similar to the substitution tags for HTML Content Layouts and HTML Page Skins discussed in Chapter 4.

Each of these layouts is discussed later in this chapter.

The final section on this page is called Caching. Caching plays a large role in OracleAS Portal. The construction of complex pages with many portlets and content regions can take a long time. Caching helps by saving previously generated portlets and pages so that when a second (or a third, fourth, fifth, etc.) request for a page is submitted, the OracleAS Portal engine can use the saved version instead of generating the page from scratch over and over again. By default, the caching status for an OmniPortlet is set to 60 minutes. This means that after the initial portlet is called by an end user, it is "saved" and the cached version is shown to everyone else requesting that portlet for the next 60 minutes. If you have a portlet that requires up-to-the-minute (or up-to-the-second) information (like a stock-quote portlet, for example), you will need to adjust the caching settings accordingly.

Layout

The final page of the OmniPortlet Wizard will differ greatly depending on which layout is selected in the previous step. A tabular layout, for example, produces two sections on the Layout page: Tabular Style and Column Layout. The Tabular Style section has two choices: Plain and Alternating (displays every other row in an alternating color to make it easier to read) and the Column Layout (gives developers the ability to change the column header, the order of columns displayed, alignment, actions) and a URL to redirect the user to if the column is clicked). A Chart layout style produces a completely different Layout page with three sections: Chart Style, Column Layout, and Chart Drilldown. Each one of the layouts will be discussed later in this chapter.

OmniPortlet Type: CSV

There are three ways to use a spreadsheet file in your OmniPortlet:

- You can upload it to the server running your OracleAS Portal instance.
- You can make it available in a directory on a server that has an HTTP server running that can access that directory.
- You can upload the spreadsheet as a piece of content and reference it there.

The second option is pretty rare; in most cases, developers will use either the first option or the third option. To use the first option, you need to upload the CSV file to the server running your OracleAS Portal instance, but in which directory? If you look at the CSV URL text box in Figure 6-5, you'll see a default value of "/htdocs/omniPortlet/sampleData/employees.csv".

The root directory that the OmniPortlet engine searches from starts in the ORACLE_MID_TIER_HOME/j2ee/OC4J_Portal/applications/portalTools/OmniPortlet directory. As an example, on the server used for the examples in this book, the OracleAS Mid-Tier is installed in C:\ORACLE\MT_HOME, so the OmniPortlet engine is looking for the employees.csv file in the present example in the C:\ORACLE\MT_HOME\ j2ee\OC4J_Portal\applications\portalTools\OmniPortlet\htdocs\omniPortlet\sampleData directory.

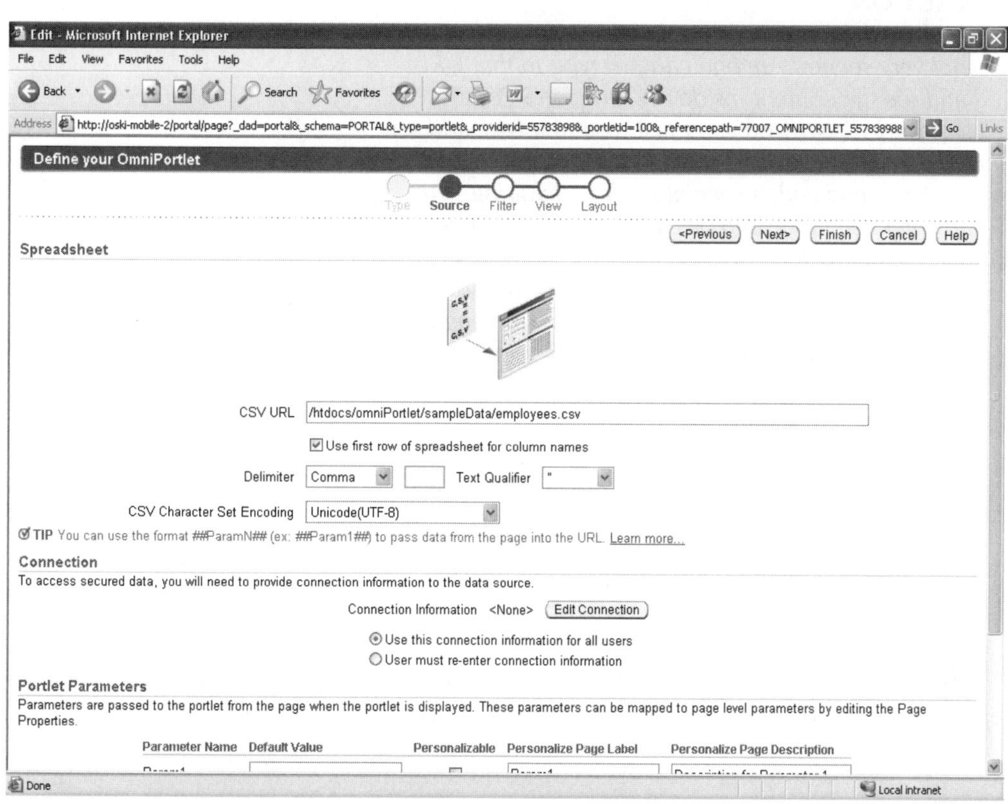

FIGURE 6-5 *The OmniPortlet Source page for a CSV type*

NOTE
For the examples in this chapter, I'm using a .csv file called Auto Records.csv. You can download this file from my Web site, http://www.oski-oracle.info/.

You can also use the third option to add a CSV file as a content item into the OracleAS Portal repository and then use a link to that in the CSV URL field. To do this, create a new content item region on the Dashboard_1 root page and click the Add Item icon in that region. Add a .csv file you want to use. When the Edit page for the Dashboard_1 root page displays after adding the item, right-click the link representing the .csv file and select Copy Shortcut. Return to the OmniPortlet CSV Wizard and paste the copied shortcut into the CSV URL field.

CAUTION

At this point you might be thinking, "Wow, that's not very secure! Anyone can just type in that URL and see the content inside my OracleAS Portal repository." No, you can't just type in a URL and see content. To demonstrate this, click Next. You will be presented with a special screen, requiring you to enter username and password information before the content will be displayed (this screen does not appear for .csv files stored in the operating system [method #1]). You can also test this by opening up a new browser. To see this, start another Internet Explorer window by selecting the Internet Explorer from your Start menu — don't open up a new browser window by selecting File | New | Window in Internet Explorer (if you do, authentication cookies are shared between the windows). In that new Internet Explorer window, paste in the URL. You'll be prompted to log in before the OracleAS Portal engine will display the content (Figure 6-6).

The check box next to "Use first row of spreadsheet for column names" does exactly what it sounds like—in succeeding wizard steps, the values specified in the

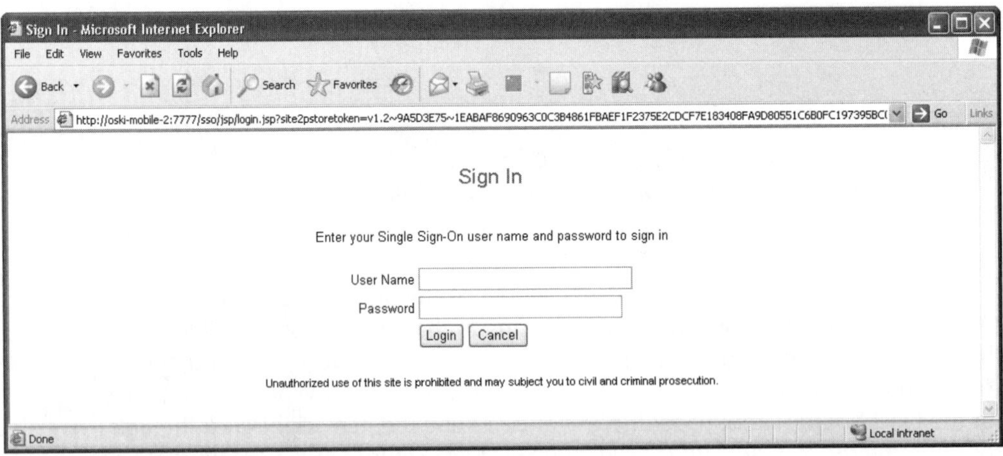

FIGURE 6-6 *The login window after attempting to view content before authentication*

first row of your spreadsheet will be used to identify columns if this box is checked. Most .csv files use a comma as their field delimiter. If you have used something else, you can change it here. The connection information will specify the credentials needed to access this file securely. The bottom section, Portlet Parameters, will be discussed in the section "Page Parameters" later in this chapter. Clicking the Next button on the top right of the screen brings us to the Filter page discussed earlier. Select any filters and ordering you wish to apply to the OmniPortlet and click Next.

The View page, as mentioned before, has six layout styles that can be applied to your OmniPortlet. This example will go over all six of them, but that won't be repeated for the other types of portlets.

OmniPortlet Views: Tabular

The tabular view is the most common and has the fewest number of options. The Layout screen that corresponds to the Tabular view (Figure 6-7), only gives the

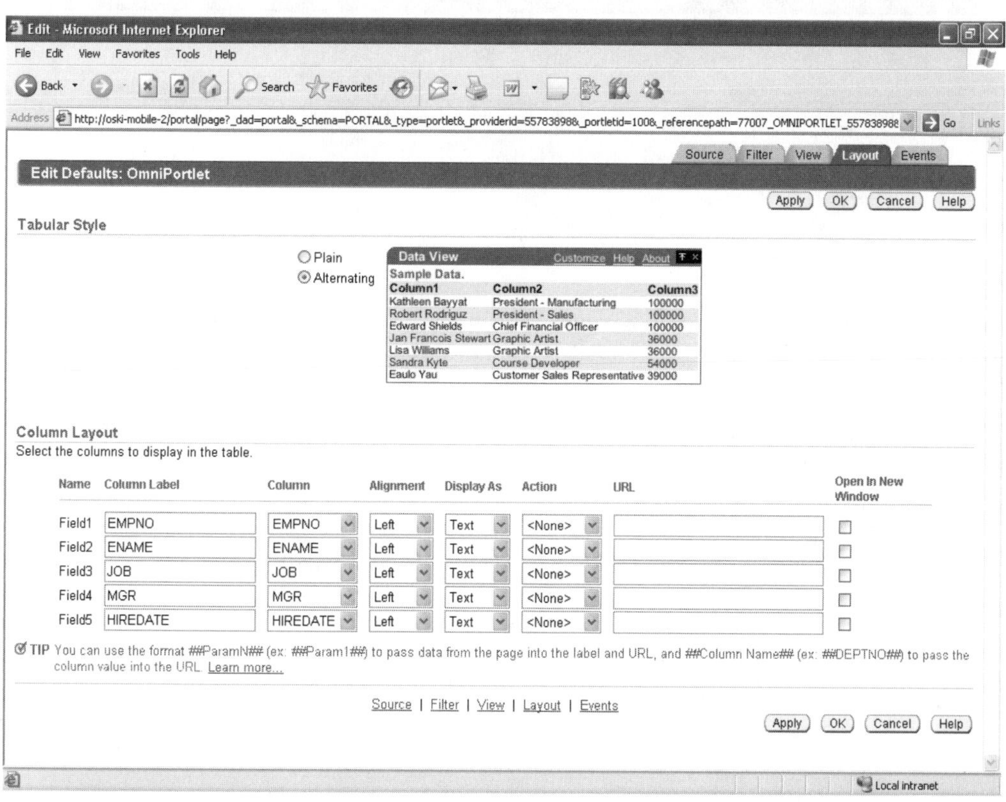

FIGURE 6-7 *The Layout screen corresponding to the Tabular view*

developer the option of choosing "Alternating" (which alternates colors between each row of returned data to make it more easily visible) and altering the column layout. In the Column Layout section, developers can change the column title, the order of displayed columns, how they are aligned and displayed, what action is taken if they are clicked, and a URL that can redirect the end user if they click on the data. If you chose the check box next to "Use first row of spreadsheet for column names" on the Source page of the wizard, the Column Labels column will be populated with those values. Experiment with the Column Label, Column, and Alignment fields and click Finish to generate your OmniPortlet (Figure 6-8).

To edit your OmniPortlet, click the pencil icon in the top left of the OmniPortlet. You are returned to the OmniPortlet Wizard in Edit mode. The steps in the OmniPortlet Wizard are replaced by tabs in the top right of the screen.

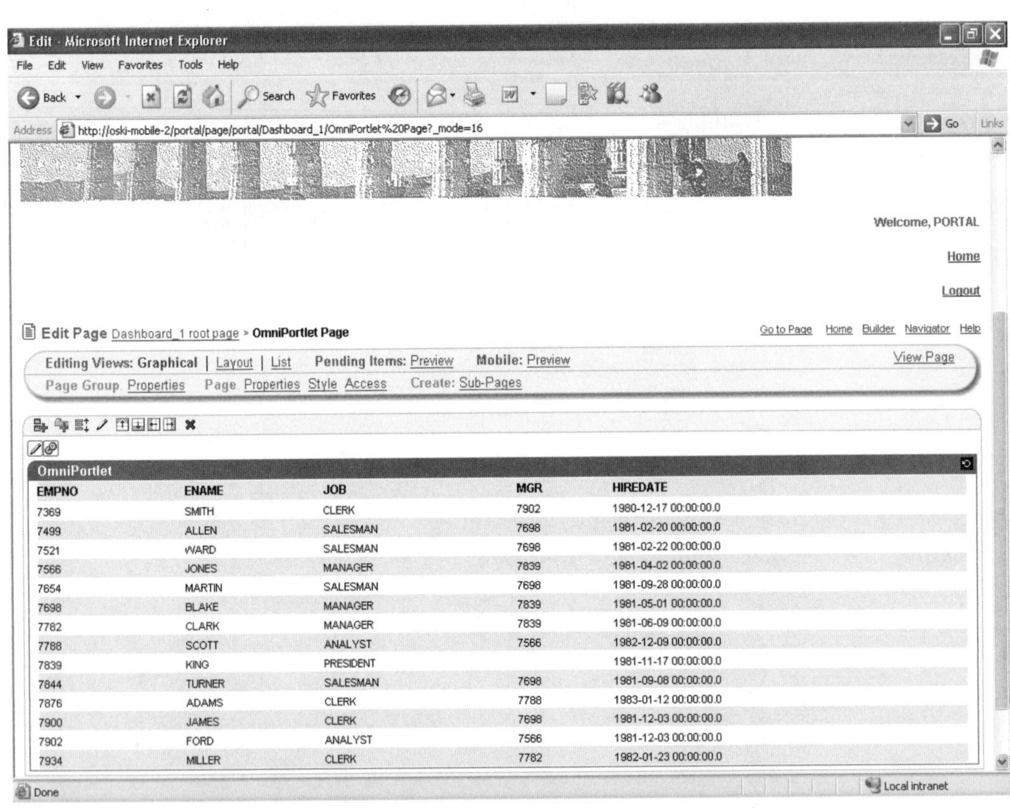

FIGURE 6-8 *The Dashboard_1 root page with the OmniPortlet displayed*

OmniPortlet Views: Charts

Click the View tab and change the layout style of your OmniPortlet to "Chart." Click the Layout tab. This tab (Figure 6-9) gives you the opportunity to define three basic types of charts: Bar, Pie, and Line. Selecting the radio button in the Chart Style section will display an example of what the chart might look like in the Data View graphic next to the radio buttons. Below the Data View graphic is a set of parameters developers can use to change things like the size (Height and Width) of the graph, if a legend is displayed in the graph, and whether 3-D effects are applied to the graph.

Below that is the Column Layout section. Here you specify what will be used for the x-axis (the Group), the y-axis (the Category), and the data to be plotted (the

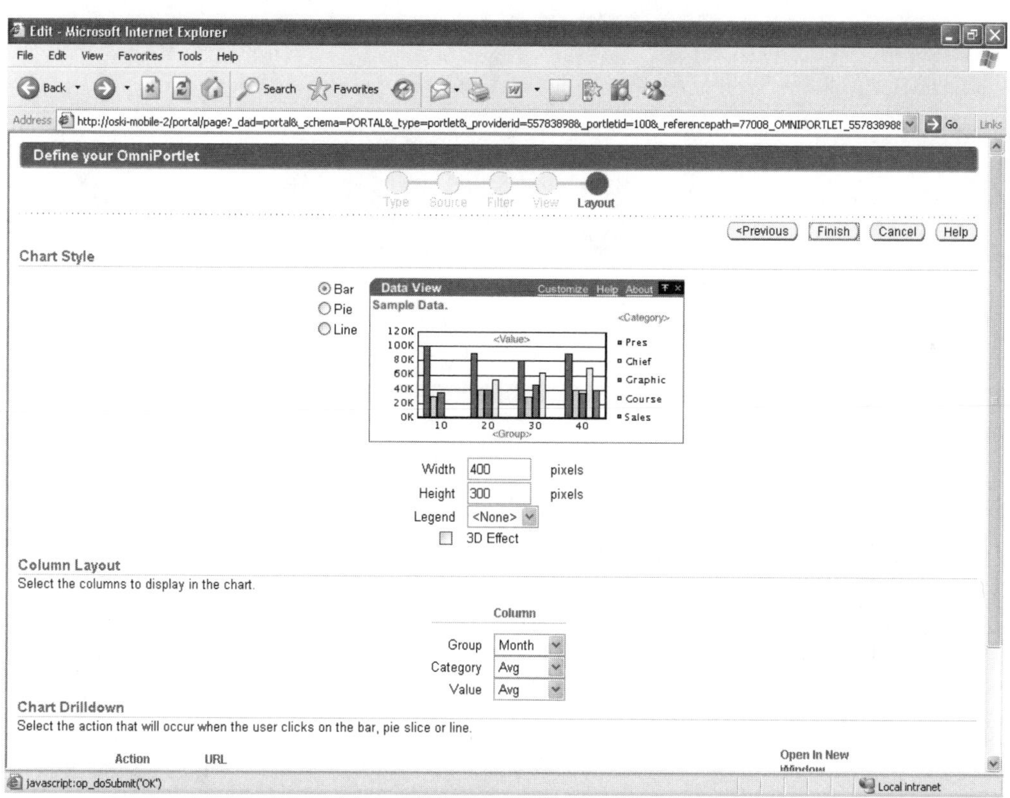

FIGURE 6-9 *The Layout screen corresponding to the Chart view*

Value). For my "auto records" spreadsheet, I used the Month as the group, and my average fuel mileage (the Avg field) as both the Category and the data (Figure 6-10).

OmniPortlet Views: News

Click the View tab, change the layout style of your OmniPortlet to News, and click the Layout tab (Figure 6-11). There are two sections: News Style and Column Layout. In the News Style section, developers have three choices: Plain, Logo, or Scrolling. Plain is self-explanatory; Logo prompts for an image to be displayed next to each news item, and Scrolling prompts for the size of the OmniPortlet window and allows end users to scroll as data expands out of the window.

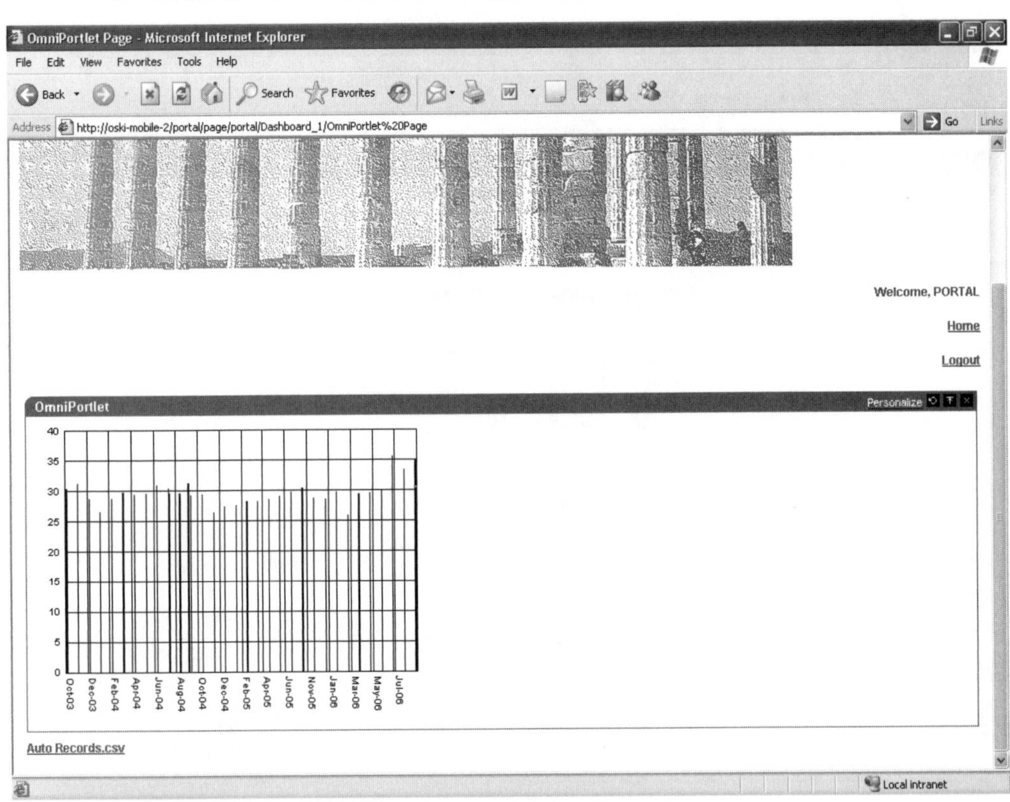

FIGURE 6-10 *The OmniPortlet with a graph displayed*

NOTE

If you remember back in Chapter 4, we discussed the concept of HTML Content Layouts. In the section by that name, we walked through an example of creating a scrollable region. You can use the "scrollable" option here to create a single portlet that scrolls, or you can create a "Plain" or "Logo" OmniPortlet and then apply that OmniPortlet to a region that has a scrollable HTML Content Layout assigned to it.

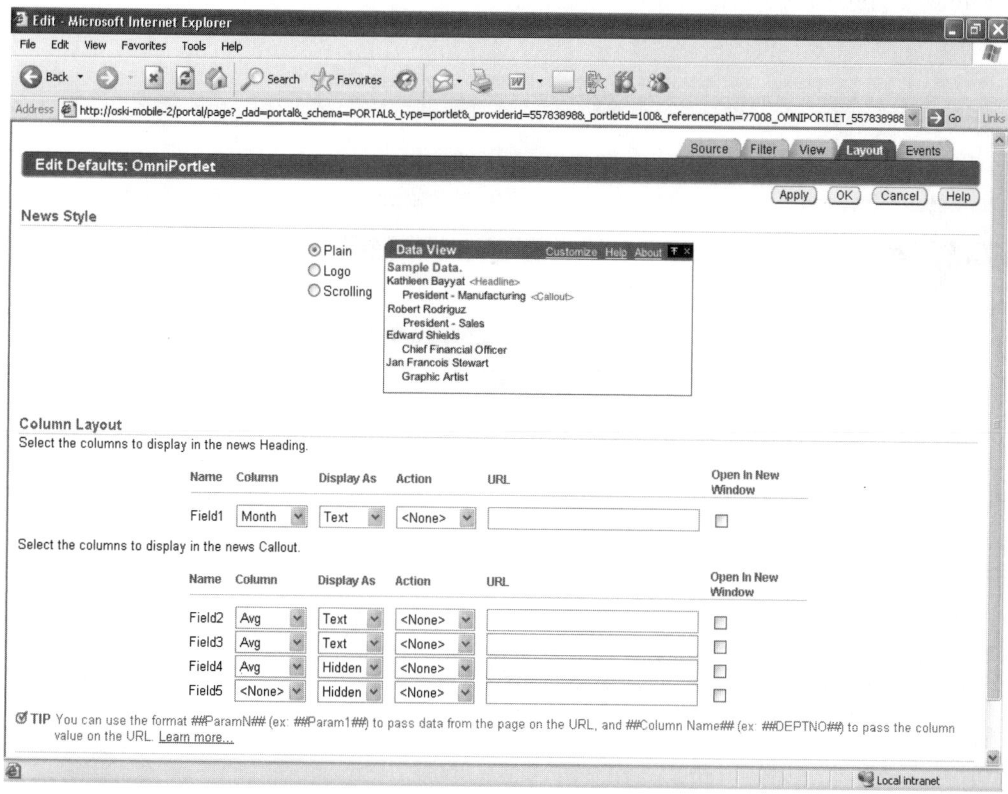

FIGURE 6-11 *The Layout screen corresponding to the News view*

In the Column Layout section, you specify what field will be used as the "Header" and what fields will be used as the "Callout." Furthermore, you can re-order the callout fields, change how they are displayed, specify actions and URLs if the user clicks them, and determine whether or not they should display in a new window when clicked. Experiment with the different settings and click OK to see your work.

OmniPortlet Views: Bullet

The Bullet view is pretty straightforward. The Layout screen (Figure 6-12) gives developers the option of nine different types of bullets: discs, circles, squares, numbers, lowercase letters, uppercase letters, lowercase roman numerals, uppercase Roman numerals or none. The Column Layout section allows developers to specify what data will be displayed and how it will be displayed.

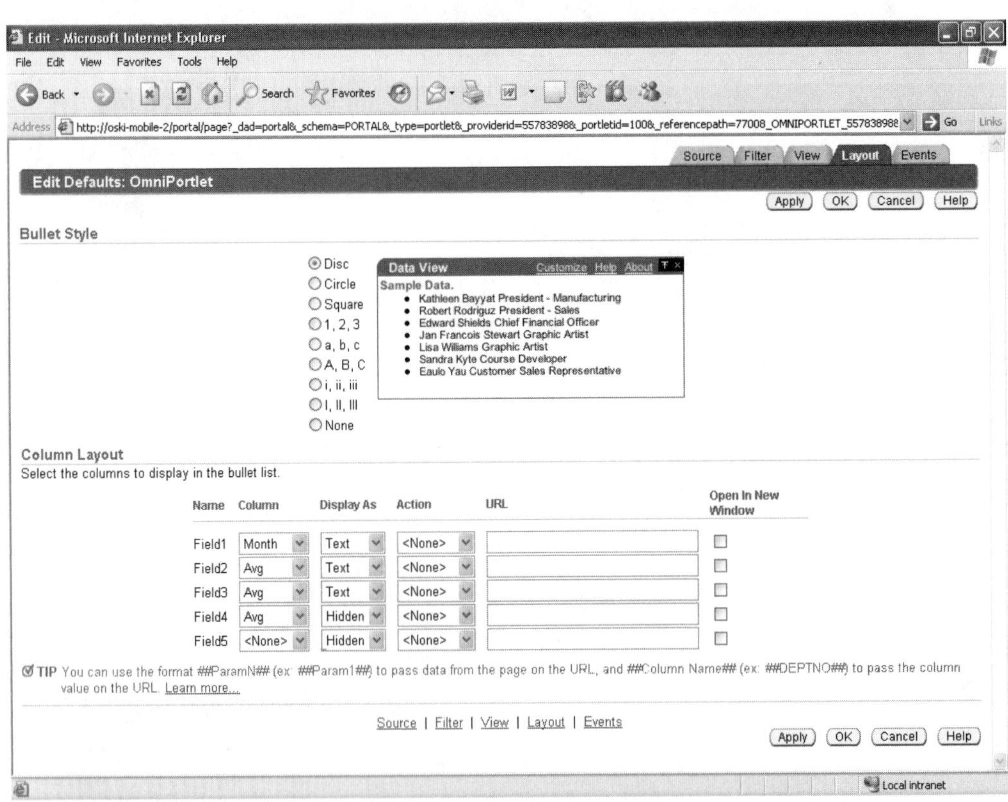

FIGURE 6-12 *The Layout screen corresponding to the Bullet view*

OmniPortlet Views: Form

The Form view is also simple. Instead of displaying information in a traditional tabular format (with a single set of column names displayed along the top), the form view displays column information for every record returned. The only options on the Layout screen (Figure 6-13) are the choice of horizontal or vertical form styles and the usual column layout options.

OmniPortlet Views: HTML

The HTML view offers interesting possibilities for OmniPortlet developers/designers. After you select HTML in the View page of the OmniPortlet Wizard, the Layout tab displays three free-form text boxes in which developers can write their own HTML

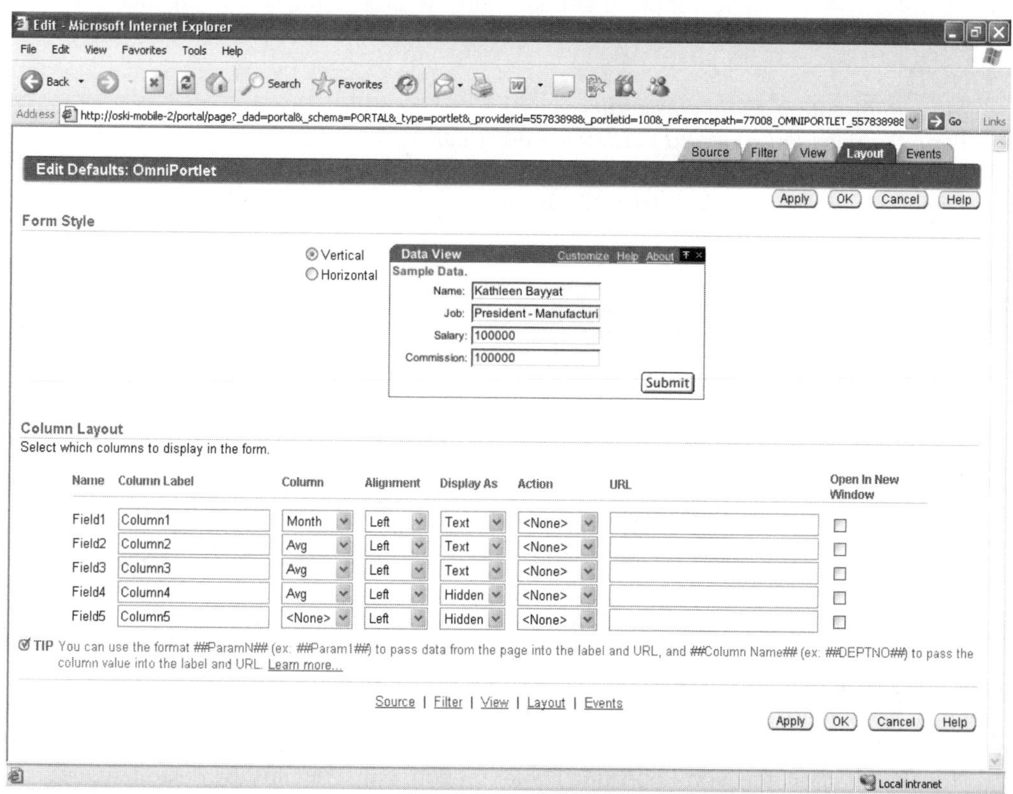

FIGURE 6-13 *The Layout screen corresponding to the Form view*

code. OracleAS Portal tries to help you out by populating the three sections with default HTML code. For the example spreadsheet we've been using in this chapter, the code populated in the Non-Repeating Heading section looks like this (line numbers have been added for reference):

```
1       <TABLE BORDER='0' WIDTH="100%">
2       <TR CLASS='PortletSubHeaderColor'>
3       <TH CLASS='PortletHeading1'>Month</TH>
4       <TH CLASS='PortletHeading1'>Mileage</TH>
5       <TH CLASS='PortletHeading1'>Gal</TH>
6       <TH CLASS='PortletHeading1'>Avg</TH>
7       </TR>
```

Line 1 constructs an HTML table with no border. Line 2 defines a table row (TR) and an element identifier for the table. In this case, the CLASS attribute assigns the class PortletSubHeaderColor to the row. The CLASS attribute has several roles in HTML: as a style sheet selector or for general-purpose processing by user agents.

NOTE
More information about classes like PortletSubHeaderColor and PortletHeading1 can be found in Section E.2.4 of the Oracle Application Server Portal User's Guide (10.1.4), Oracle Part # B13809-04.

Lines 3–6 define the headings used, based on the first row of the .csv file. Line 7 signals the end of the table row, </TR>.

The repeating section contains code that will loop, depending on how many rows are retrieved:

```
1       <TR CLASS='PortletText1'>
2       <TD>##Month##</TD>
3       <TD>##Mileage##</TD>
4       <TD>##Gal##</TD>
5       <TD>##Avg##</TD>
6       </TR>
```

Line 1 creates a new HTML table row for each row queried from the data source and uses a different class called PortletText1 to set the visual attributes for the data. The data from the data source is referenced by ##data##. Replace the "data" part with the names of your fields. Be sensitive to the fact that they must match exactly.

The final section, the Non-Repeating Footer section, only contains, by default, a single line to end the table definition. HTML will ignore anything it doesn't understand, so feel free to experiment with different HTML tags.

OmniPortlet Type: SQL

If you want your OmniPortlet to display information queries from a relational database, this is the type to choose. By default, OmniPortlet is set up to query information from Oracle databases (naturally), but you are not limited to that. Oracle provides DataDirect JDBC (Java Database Connectivity) drivers for the following relational databases:

- IBM DB2 UDB
- Informix Dynamic Server
- Microsoft SQL Server
- Sybase Adaptive Server

TIP

You can download and install these drivers from the Oracle Technology Network site. See Section I.2.4 of the Oracle Application Server Portal Configuration Guide, Oracle Part # B19305-03, for more details.

Earlier in this chapter (Figure 6-2), we looked at the Source page of the OmniPortlet Wizard when the SQL type was selected. That page is divided into three sections: SQL, Connection, and Portlet Parameters. In the SQL section, the query that drives the OmniPortlet is defined. Developers have the option of using bind variables in this query.

Bind variables can be useful for increasing the efficiency of parsing and caching of the SQL statement on the server side. Bind variables are used to replace a single value in SQL or PL/SQL, such as a character string, number, or date. Specifically, bind references may be used to replace expressions in SELECT, WHERE, GROUP BY, ORDER BY, HAVING, CONNECT BY, and START WITH clauses of queries. Bind references may not be referenced in FROM clauses or in place of reserved words or clauses. You create a bind reference by typing a colon (:) followed immediately by the column or parameter name.

To see how bind variables work, enter the following query in the Statement box:

```
select * from portal_demo.emp
where deptno = :p_dept_no
```

The colon (:) before the p_dept_no variable defines the variable as a bind variable that will need to be resolved before the query is run. Click the Show Bind Variables button in the middle of the page to see a listing of the bind variables.

You could enter a value here (say 10 or 20) and click Test to see the results, but what would be the point of that? If you wanted to see the employees in department 20, you could just write that into the SQL statement, or use the Filter tab to limit the rows returned. Why go through all of this extra work to define a bind variable? The real power of bind variables comes into play in connection with parameters.

TIP
I've hinted at it numerous times in this chapter and in Chapter 4, but parameters are discussed in the section "Page Parameters" later in this chapter.

The Connection section (also referenced earlier—see Figure 6-3) is where the source of your data is defined. This is a great leap forward from the OracleAS Portal wizards mentioned in Chapter 1. Oracle strongly recommends that you not keep any of your organization's data (referred to in Oracle's documentation as consumer data) in the infrastructure database. If you use the OracleAS Portal development wizards, the only way to access data not in the infrastructure database is to first create a link from the infrastructure database to your data source, and then to reference that database link in the SQL that populates the forms, report, etc. Maintaining this can become a chore for DBAs and OracleAS Portal administrators. Using the connection manager in OmniPortlet, you specify the connection information in the wizard, and a JDBC driver is used to connect to the consumer database without having to administer database links.

OmniPortlet Type: XML

XML (Extensible Markup Language) was developed by the World Wide Web Consortium, the governing body for Web standards. It allows designers to create their own customized tags, enabling the definition, transmission, validation, and interpretation of data between applications and organizations. Since creators or XML data can define their own tags and structure, there has to be some way to tell the recipient how the data is organized. The XML features of OmniPortlet give developers three ways of doing this:

- The data is in <ROWSET>/<ROW> format. If the data is provided in this format, no further transformations need to be applied. OmniPortlet can take data in a file with this format and display it immediately. The default file Oracle gives you to test (departments.xml) is an example of XML data in <ROWSET>/<ROW> format. If you look at the URL in Figure 6-14, you'll notice that it looks similar to the CSV URL in Figure 6-5. OracleAS Portal uses the same directory location to start searching for the specified file.

- The data comes with an XSL filter. An XSL (Extensible Stylesheet Language) file is a file that defines the presentation of an XML document and is used to translate XML documents into other formats (like the <ROWSET>/<ROW> format).
- You want to use an XML schema to describe the data. An XML *schema* is a description of a type of XML document, typically expressed in terms of constraints on the structure and content of documents of that type. An XML schema provides a view of the document type at a high level of abstraction.

NOTE
If you are transforming your data, the end result needs to be in ROWSET/ROW format for OmniPortlet to display it.

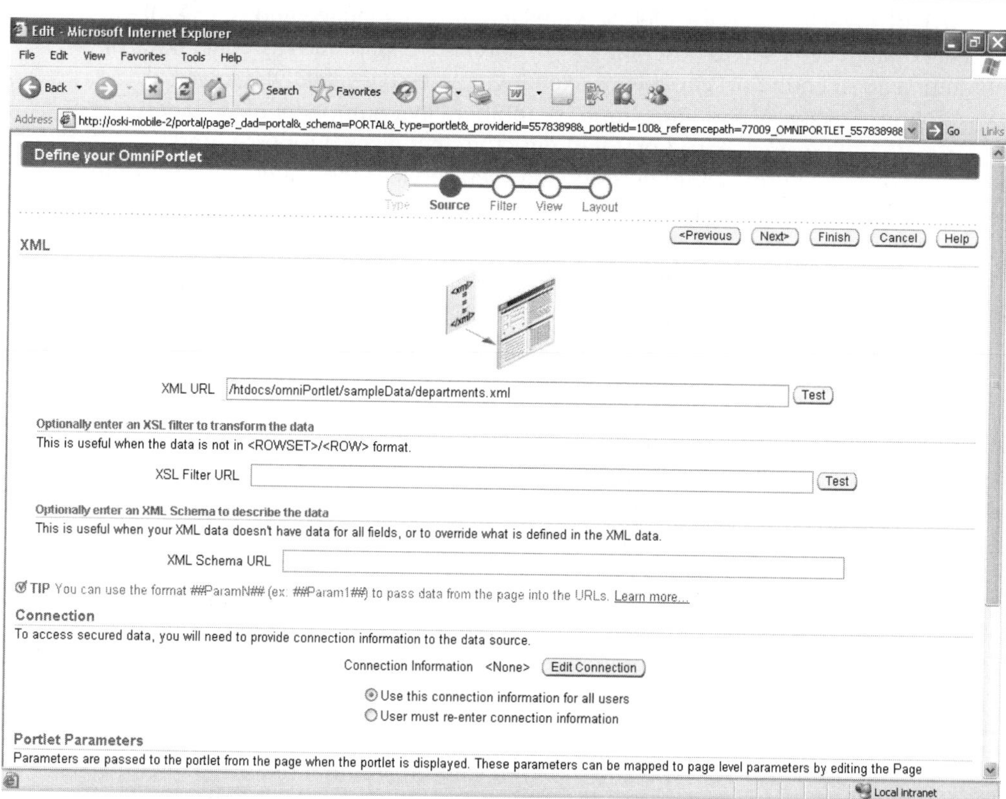

FIGURE 6-14 *The Source page for an XML OmniPortlet*

OmniPortlet Type: Web Service

The simple definition of a Web service is a collection of protocols and standards used for exchanging data between applications and systems. Having said that, there are entire books devoted to those protocols and standards, so don't be misled by that simple definition. Web services are complex and usually require a great amount of effort to design and implement. If you have designed your own Web services or want to get access to existing external Web services, you can use this type of OmniPortlet to retrieve information. This type of OmniPortlet is not designed for developers to create Web services—it is designed to "consume" them.

NOTE
When you use a Web service to get information, it is often referred to as consuming a Web service.

The Source page for a Web service (Figure 6-15) prompts for something called a WSDL URL. WSDL stands for Web Service Definition Language and is an XML-formatted language used to describe a Web Service's capabilities as collections of communication endpoints capable of exchanging messages. UDDI, Universal Description, Discovery and Integration, is another key component of Web Services. UDDI is an online, XML-based protocol directory that gives businesses and organizations a uniform way to describe the Web services they offer, discover other companies' Web services offerings, and gather the methods required to conduct business with other companies. UDDI uses WSDL as its language.

For the example in this chapter, you can use a Web service provided by Oracle. In the WSDL URL, enter:

```
http://webservices.oracle.com/WeatherWS/WeatherWS?WSDL
```

The Web service is designed to take in a single parameter (a ZIP code) and return a weather forecast for that ZIP code. Click Show Methods to see the method associated with this Web service. As you can see, there is only one: giveMeSomeWeatherInfo. Click Show Parameters. One parameter is displayed: param0. This parameter takes the ZIP code and displays the weather forecast for that ZIP code. Enter your ZIP code in that field and click Finish. The portlet is displayed, but some of the fields need tweaking. Click the small pencil icon in the top left of the portlet and select the Layout tab. Give columns meaningful names in the Column Label column and change the img column to display as an Image.

OmniPortlet Type: Web Page

The OmniPortlet Web Page type and the Web Clipping section of this chapter go hand-in-hand. Web Clipping is a technology unique to OracleAS Portal that allows

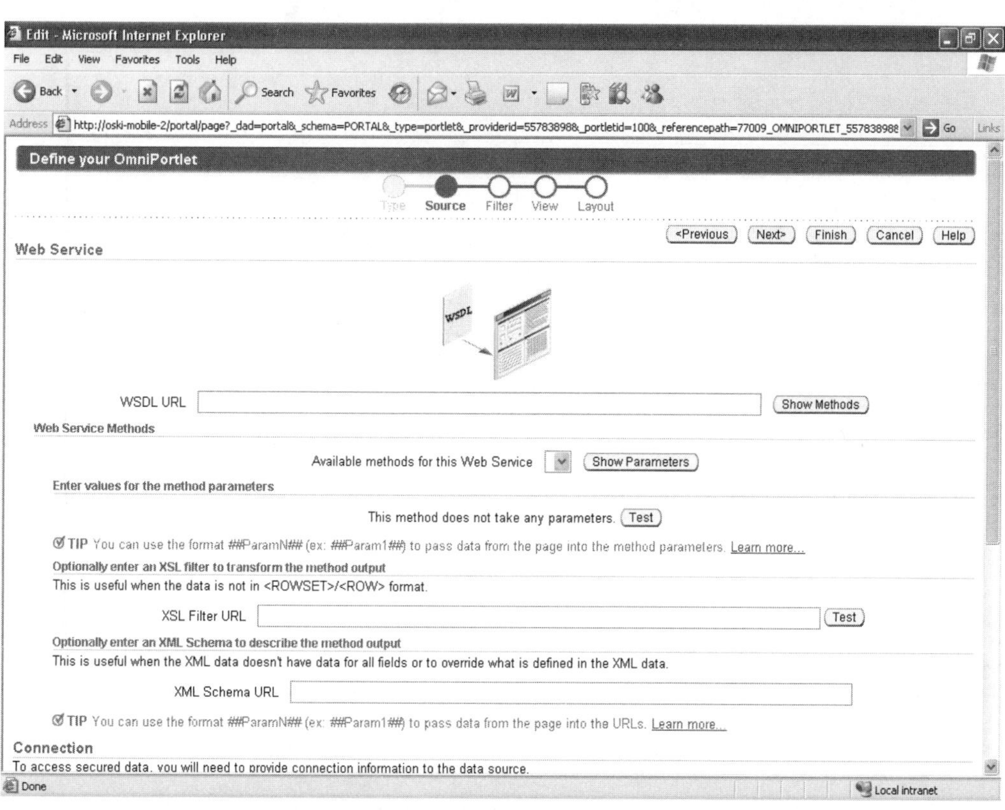

FIGURE 6-15 *The Source page for a Web service*

page designers to "grab" an existing Web page (or, more impressively, a part of an existing Web page) and place that grabbed piece on their OracleAS Portal page. The grabbed page is dynamic, so if the source page changes, the OracleAS Portal page changes automatically. This feature gives page designers an incredible amount of functionality without requiring any programmatic knowledge whatsoever.

To use this feature, you will need access to either the Internet or some internal Web site. The Source page for the Web Page type has the usual Portlet Parameters section at the bottom, but it only has one option on the top of the page: the Select Web Page button (Figure 6-16). When you click this button, a prompt for the Web page to be grabbed is displayed. This prompt then leads you into the Web Clipping studio, where developers can select a Web page, or part of a Web page to include

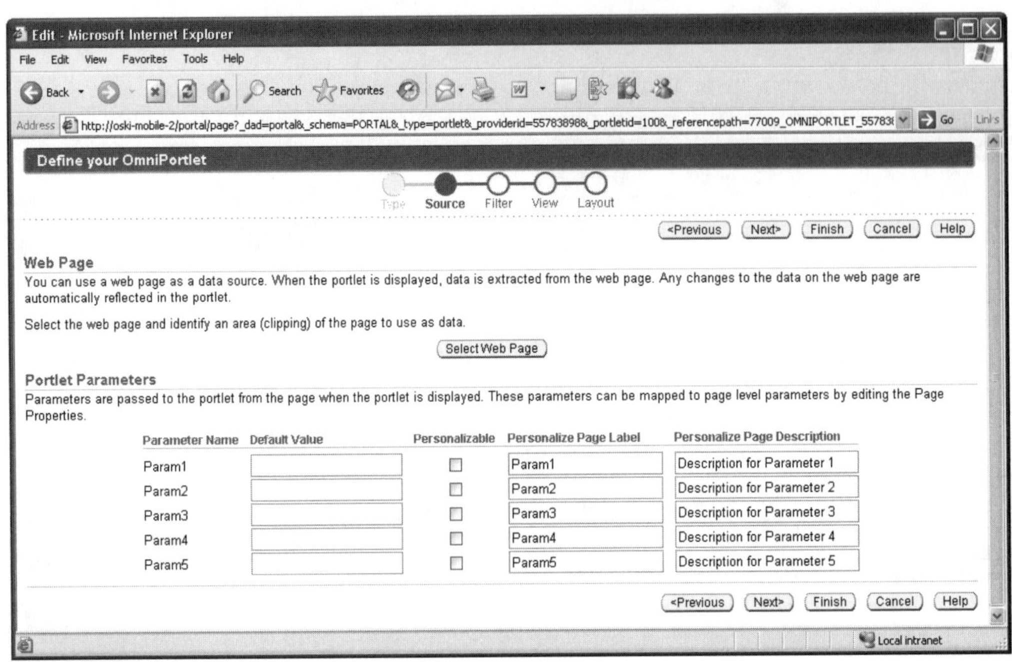

FIGURE 6-16 *The Source page for a Web Page OmniPortlet*

in their OmniPortlet. For more information about Web Clipping and the Web Clipping Studio, see the section "Web Clipping" later in this chapter.

Page Parameters

The ability to use parameters is especially valuable when discussing OmniPortlets. OmniPortlets, unlike portlets created with the OracleAS Portal development wizards, are fully "parameter-aware" and can be used to create a dynamic environment. In the following example, we're going to create two pages: one with an OmniPortlet that passes a parameter and another with an OmniPortlet that accepts a parameter.

Page groups can be set up to accept or deny parameters. By default, page groups are set to accept parameters, but it's always a good idea to check. If the page group does not accept parameters, you won't see an error message—the portlet on that page simply will display with incorrect information. To check the status of parameters in your page group, return to the OracleAS Portal Navigator and click the Properties link next to the Dashboard_1 page group. Select the Configure tab and scroll down to the Parameters and Events section. If parameters are enabled, it will say, "Page/portlet parameters and events are enabled." If, for whatever reason, you don't want parameter and event capabilities, click Edit and de-select the Enable Parameters And Events check box on the following screen.

In every Oracle Application Server installation that includes the infrastructure database and OracleAS Portal, a demonstration schema called PORTAL_DEMO is created. In this schema, there is a table called EMP with the following structure:

```
SQL*Plus: Release 10.1.0.4.2 - Production on Tue Sep 26 08:21:43 2006
Copyright (c) 1982, 2005, Oracle.  All rights reserved.
Connected to:
Oracle Database 10g Enterprise Edition Release 10.1.0.4.2 - Production
With the Partitioning, OLAP and Data Mining options
SQL> show user
USER is "PORTAL_DEMO"
SQL> desc emp
 Name                                      Null?    Type
 ----------------------------------------- -------- --------------------
 EMPNO                                     NOT NULL NUMBER(4)
 ENAME                                              VARCHAR2(10)
 JOB                                                VARCHAR2(9)
 MGR                                                NUMBER(4)
 HIREDATE                                           DATE
 SAL                                                NUMBER(7,2)
 COMM                                               NUMBER(7,2)
 DEPTNO                                             NUMBER(2)
```

The first OmniPortlet that we're going to create will list the employees and their departments. We will make the department column a link and pass the department number to our second OmniPortlet, which will display a graph showing the number of employees in each department. On the Dashboard_1 root page, place an OmniPortlet in one of the portlet regions. Define the OmniPortlet and select the following options:

1. Type screen: Select SQL.
2. Source screen:
    a. Enter **select ename, hiredate, deptno from portal_demo.emp** in the Statement field.
    b. Enter connection information for the portal_demo user in the infrastructure database.

3. Filter screen: Take all defaults.
4. View screen:
   a. Change Title to **Employees**.
   b. Select Tabular for Layout Style.
5. Layout screen:

For Field1:

- Column Label: **Emp Name**
- Column: **ENAME**

For Field2:

- Column Label: **Hire Date**
- Column: **HIREDATE**

For Field3:

- Column Label: **Dept**
- Column: **DEPTNO**
- Action: **Hyperlink**
- URL: Leave blank for now—we'll come back to this.

Now, let's create a new page that will hold an OmniPortlet that will accept a parameter and display the number of employees in a department in a graph. Create a new subpage in the Dashboard_1 page group (call it Employee_Graph_Page), and place an OmniPortlet in the default region on that new page. Define the OmniPortlet with the following fields:

1. Type screen: Select SQL.
2. Source screen:
   a. Enter **select count(*) from portal_demo.emp where deptno = ##Param1##** in the Statement field.
   b. Enter connection information for the portal_demo user in the infrastructure database.

c. Enter **10** in the Default Value field for Param1 in the Portlet Parameters section.

3. Filter screen: Take all defaults.

4. View screen:

   a. Change Title to **Employee Count**.

   b. Select Chart for Layout Style.

5. Layout screen: In the Column Layout section, change Group, Category, and Value to **Count_**.

Initially, the graph will display with a value of 3 (the number of employees in department 10, since we entered 10 for the value of Param1 in the default value field on the Source screen).

Now that we have a portlet that can accept a parameter, we need to define how to map a page parameter to the portlet parameter. On the Employee_Graph_Page, click the Page: Properties link on the top left of the page. Click the Parameters tab (Figure 6-17). Create a new page parameter called **dept_no** and click Add. In the Page Parameter Properties section, give the dept_no parameter a default value of 10. In the Portlet Parameter Values section, click the OmniPortlet link to expand the portlet parameters that you can pass to this portlet. The five parameters here correspond to the five parameters listed in the Source page when defining the OmniPortlet (Figures 6-2, 6-5, 6-14, 6-15, and 6-16). To define the dept_no page parameter to the Param1 OmniPortlet parameter, select the drop-down box next to Param1 and choose Page Parameter. When the next drop-down box appears to the right, select dept_no.

After you click OK, the page is re-displayed with the graph showing a value of 3, which, again, corresponds to the number of employees in department 10. The next thing we're going to do is re-visit the OmniPortlet on the root page of the Dashboard_1 page group, but before we do that, click the View Page link in the top right of the page and copy the URL that is displaying the current page. It should look something like this:

```
http://oski-mobile-2/portal/page/portal/Dashboard_1/Employee_Graph_Page
```

where oski-mobile-2 will be replaced with the name of your server. To copy this, highlight the URL in your browser and type CTRL-C.

Return to editing the Dashboard_1 root page and click the small pencil icon in the upper left of your OmniPortlet. Click the Layout tab and in the URL field next to the DEPTNO column, type CTRL-V to paste in the URL you just copied. By doing this,

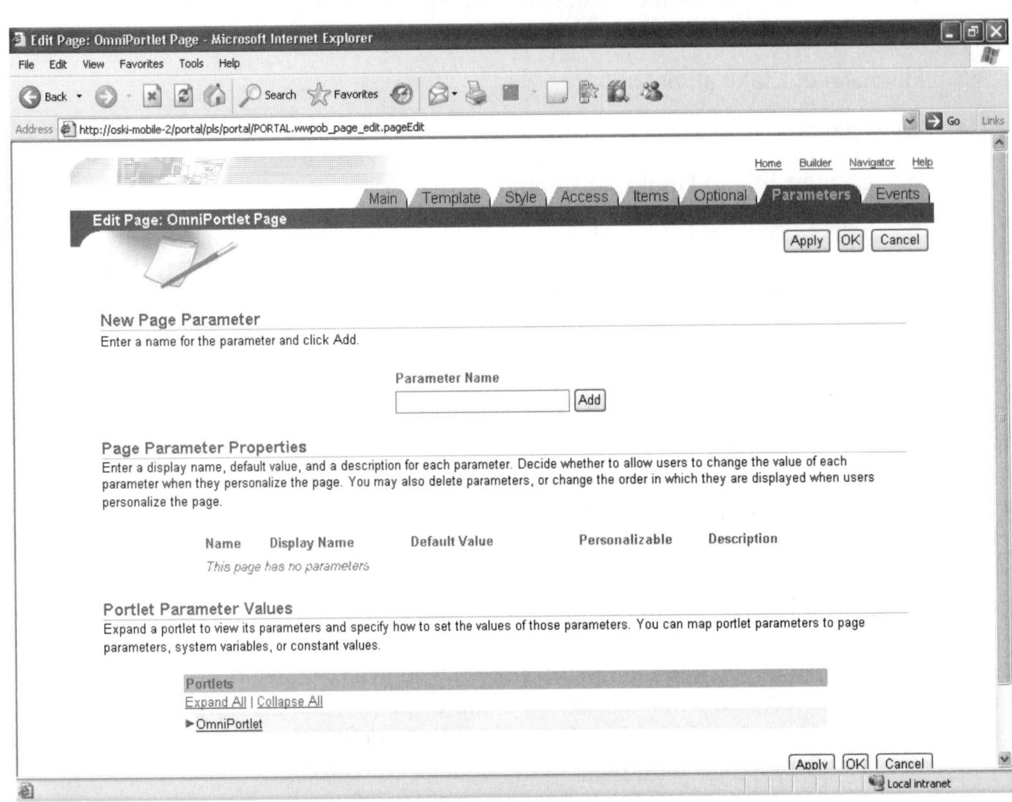

FIGURE 6-17 *The Parameters tab of the Page Properties*

you are instructing OmniPortlet to follow the link to the Employee_Graph_Page and display that page with the graph. If you just left it like that, however, the graph would always display the default value for the graph (3 employees corresponding to department 10). We need a way to pass the value the user is clicking to the Employee_Graph_Page. Edit the URL so it looks like this:

```
http://oski-mobile-
2/portal/page/portal/Dashboard_1/Employee_Graph_Page?dept_no=##DEPTNO##
```

where, again, oski-mobile-2 is replaced by your server name. At the end of the line, we've added the following text:

```
?dept_no=##DEPTNO##
```

The first part of the URL (everything before the '?') is the OracleAS Portal URL path to the page. You can see that it references the OracleAS Portal Page Engine (http://oski-mobile-2/portal/page/portal), then the Page Group (/Dashboard_1), and then the subpage (/Employee_Graph_Page). Everything specified after the question mark consists of page parameters. In this case, we are going to pass a single value to a page parameter that we have already defined (dept_no), and the value passed will correspond to the column in the OmniPortlet that we have selected in the SQL statement on the Source page when defining the portlet. In order to reference those columns, developers need to use the special notation of two pound signs before and after the column name (##DEPTNO##). Once that field is defined, click OK to return to the Edit page of the Dashboard_1 root page (Figure 6-18). Click any of the links and you will be taken to the Employee_Graph_Page with the correct value displayed for the department selected.

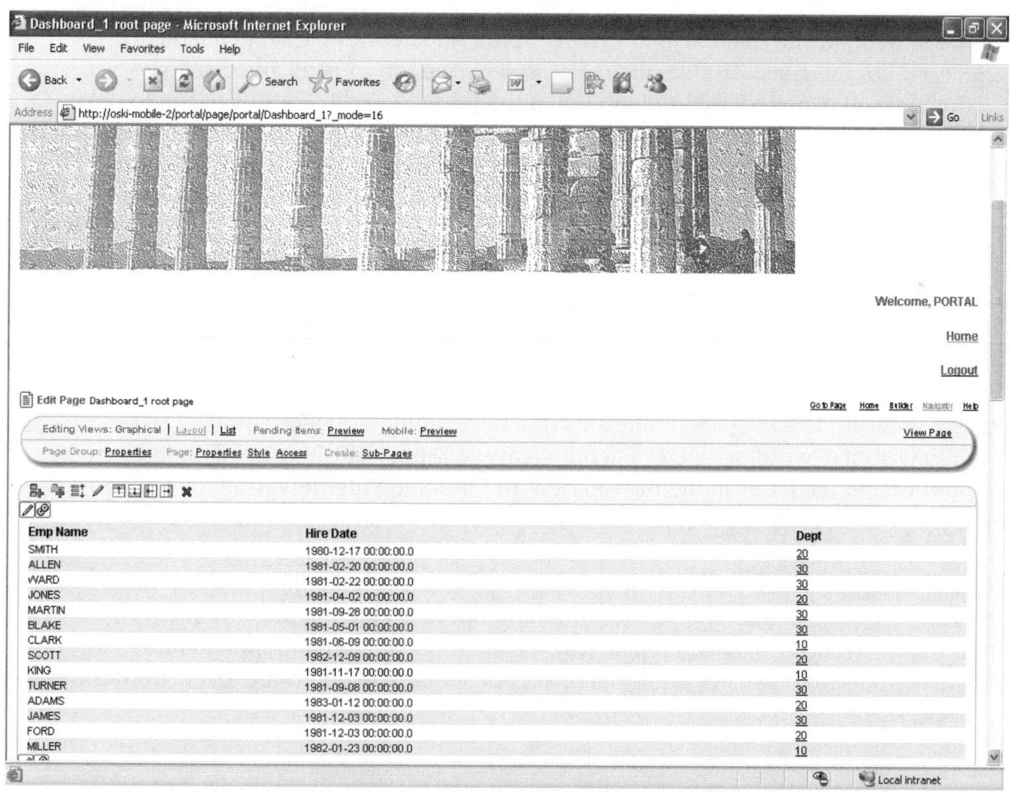

FIGURE 6-18 *The OmniPortlet with the Dept column turned into links*

For the exercises at the end of this chapter, we will explore using parameters in different types of OmniPortlets.

Web Clipping

Web Clipping is an exciting technology that allows OracleAS Portal Page Designers to construct OracleAS Portal Web pages from existing Web pages (whether internal or external) with no programming knowledge whatsoever. OracleAS Portal allows page designers to grab a page or part of a page and place that grabbed section on to their OracleAS Portal pages. Furthermore, page designers can pass login parameters to the page to be grabbed to display privileged information.

Using Web Clipping

To see how this works, edit the Dashboard_1 root page and click the Add Portlet icon in a portlet region on that page. Click the Portlet Builders link and select the Web Clipping Portlet. Click OK to return to editing the page. Since no Web clipping has been defined yet, the text "No Web clipping selected. Click 'Edit Default' to select one for all users, or 'Personalize' to select one for yourself." is displayed. Click the small pencil icon in the top left of the portlet to edit. For this example, let's create a Web Clipping portlet that queries information from the Oracle news page. In the URL field, enter **http://www.oracle.com/corporate/pressroom/index.html**. After specifying a Web page to "clip," you are taken to the Web Clipping Studio (Figure 6-19).

The page you selected to clip is displayed with a header along the top of the screen with four icons: Cancel, Section, Select, and Help. The two icons we're most interested in are the Section and Select icons. If you choose Select here, the entire page will be selected and returned to the Web Clipping portlet. If you choose Section, the Web Clipping Studio engine will try to divide the page selected into logical sections. Clicking Section results in a page similar to Figure 6-20.

You'll notice two differences: each logical section has a Choose link in its top left corner and the icons along the top right of the screen are now: Cancel, Section Smaller, Section Larger, Unsection, and Help. While the Web Clipping Studio uses some sophisticated code to break the page into logical sections, it may not section a complex page the way you want it to. By selecting Section Smaller, you can force the Web Clipping Studio engine to further attempt to divide the page in question into smaller sections. You can repeatedly click the Section Smaller link to further divide the page into smaller and smaller sections until you get to the level you wish to display.

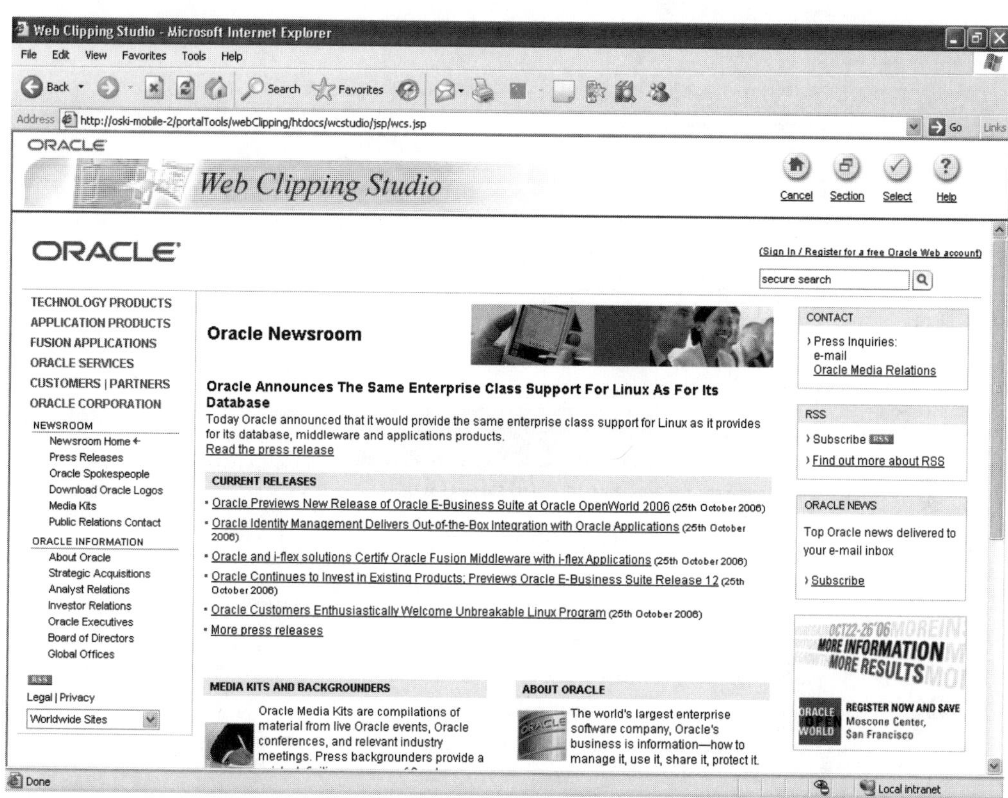

FIGURE 6-19 *The Web Clipping Studio*

NOTE

In theory, you can keep dividing the page down to the point where every single item on the page is its own section. It's not terribly practical to do that, however. For most of the pages I've used the Web Clipping Studio on, I've not had to section a page more than once or twice.

In this example, we want to get the News section in the middle of the page. If we click the Choose link right above the Oracle Newsroom heading, we'll get the

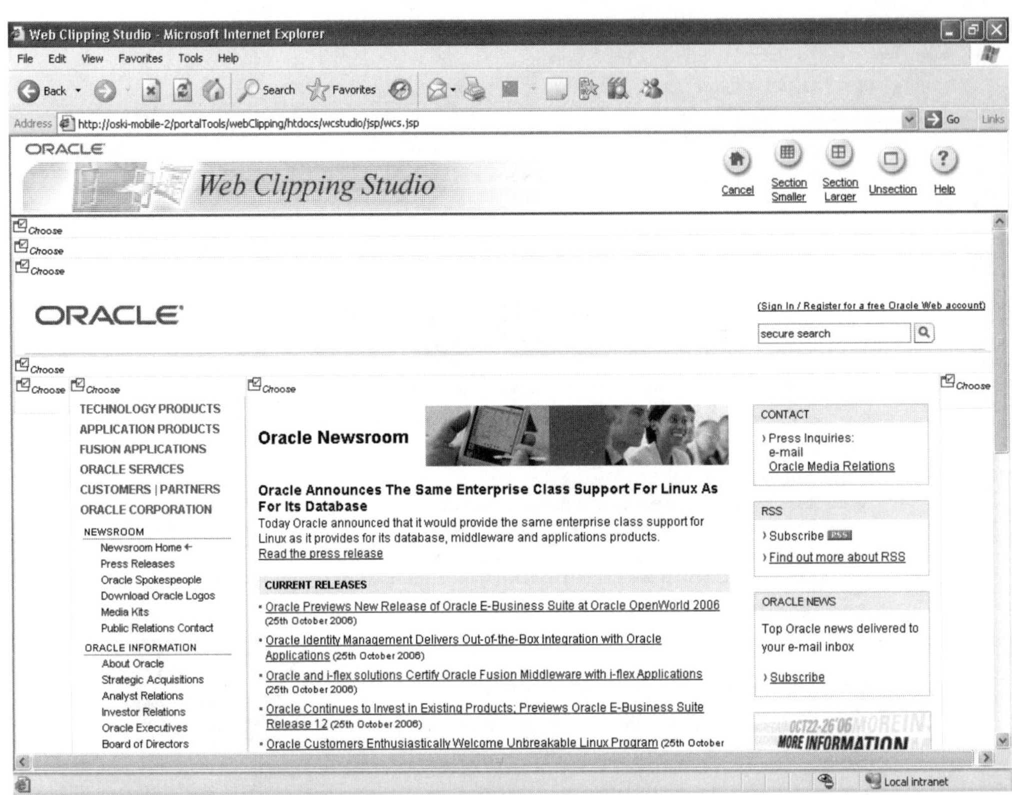

FIGURE 6-20 *A Web page after the Web Clipping Studio has sectioned it*

entire middle section, including the Media Kits and Backgrounders section and the About Oracle section, among others. Click the Section Smaller link in the top right of the page – you'll notice that the Web Clipping Studio engine divides the pages into smaller chunks (Figure 6-21). Click the Choose link to the top left of the section right above the first news story (in this example, it's the Choose link right above the news story that starts "Oracle Previews New Release of Oracle E-Business . . ."). The Web Clipping Studio page then re-displays with only the section you've selected. If that looks OK, click the Select button on the top right of the screen. The Web Clipping Portlet properties page is displayed (Figure 6-22).

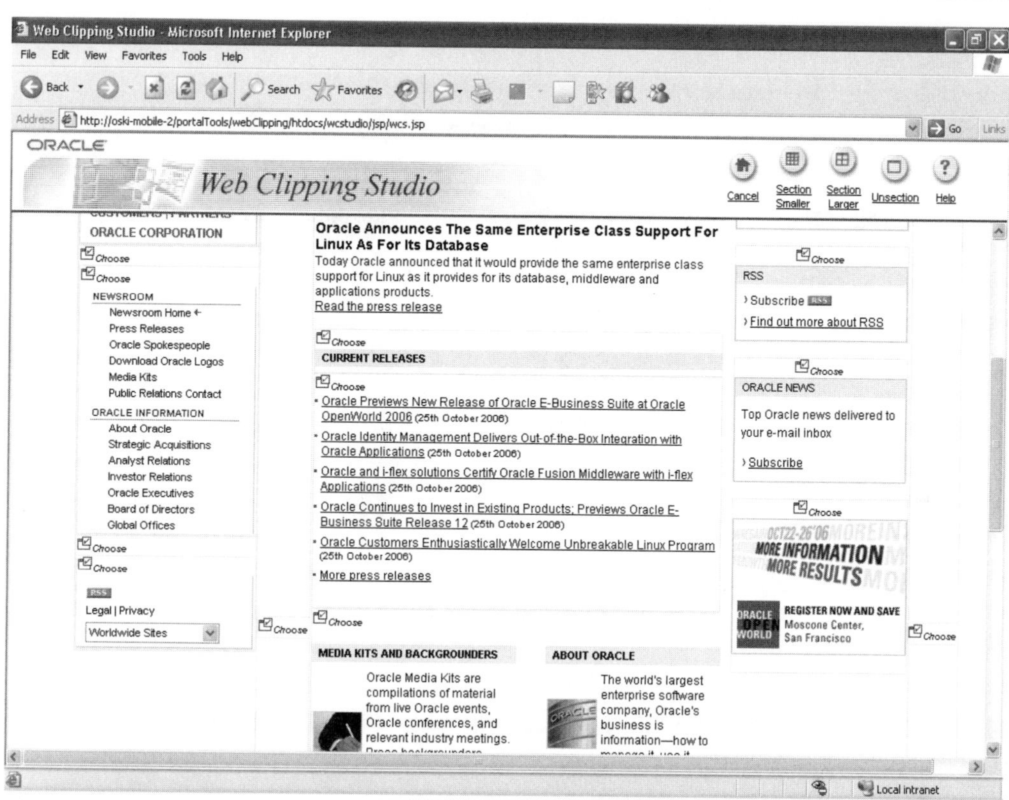

FIGURE 6-21 *The Oracle Web Page divided into smaller chunks*

Enter a title for the Web Clipping portlet and click OK. You will see a dynamic display of the data queried from the data source on your Web page (Figure 6-23).

One of the really amazing features of the Web Clipping Studio is its ability to remember login information when you define your Web Clipping portlet. For example, let's say that I have a Gmail account and I want to access my messages through an OracleAS Portal page. On one of the pages of the Dashboard_1 page group (it doesn't matter which one), place a new Web Clipping portlet in one of the portlet regions. Enter **http://www.gmail.com** in the URL Location field (if you have an account with another Web-based mail provider and would like to use that as you

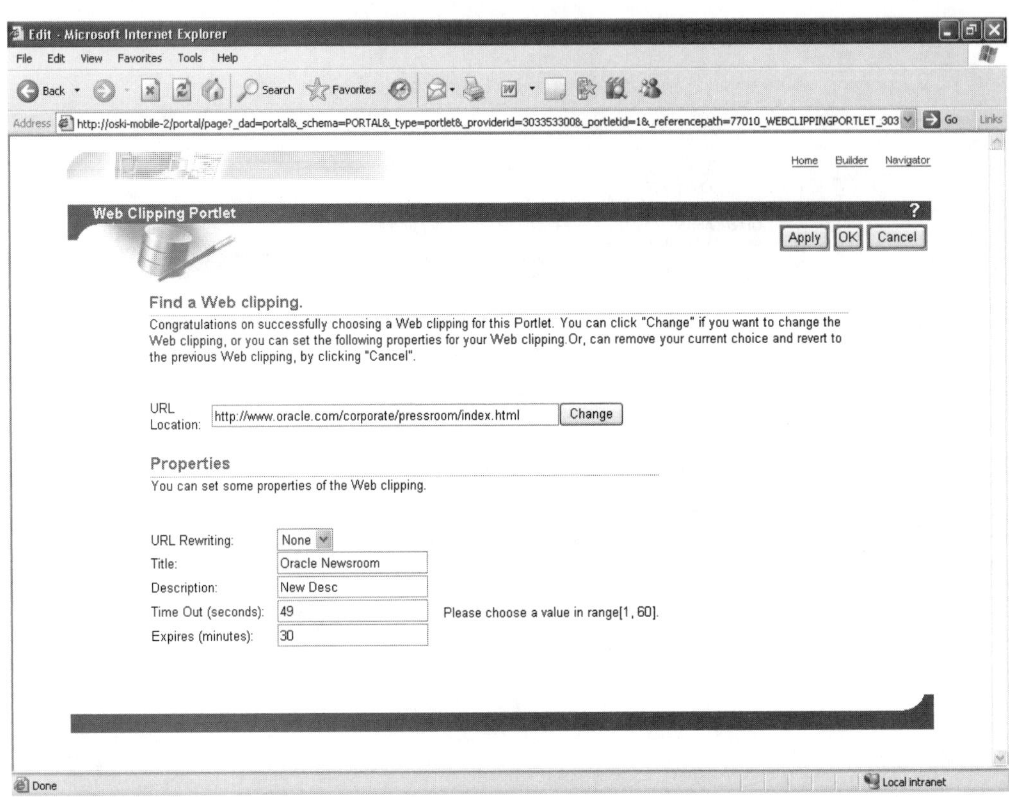

FIGURE 6-22 *The Web Clipping Portlet Properties page*

go through this example, feel free to do so). Click Start. Before using the Section link in the top right of the Web Clipping Studio screen, log in to your e-mail account. Then, click the Section link in the top right of the screen and select the Choose link above the region that displays your current e-mails. You may have to use the Section Smaller link to get to the exact part of the page you want. You should see a screen similar to Figure 6-24.

If the preview screen looks okay, click the Select link. Click OK in the Web Clipping Portlet attributes page and you are returned to the Web page with the portlet displayed. The Web Clipping portlet remembers the login you specified when creating the portlet, so you can place this portlet on other pages, give view

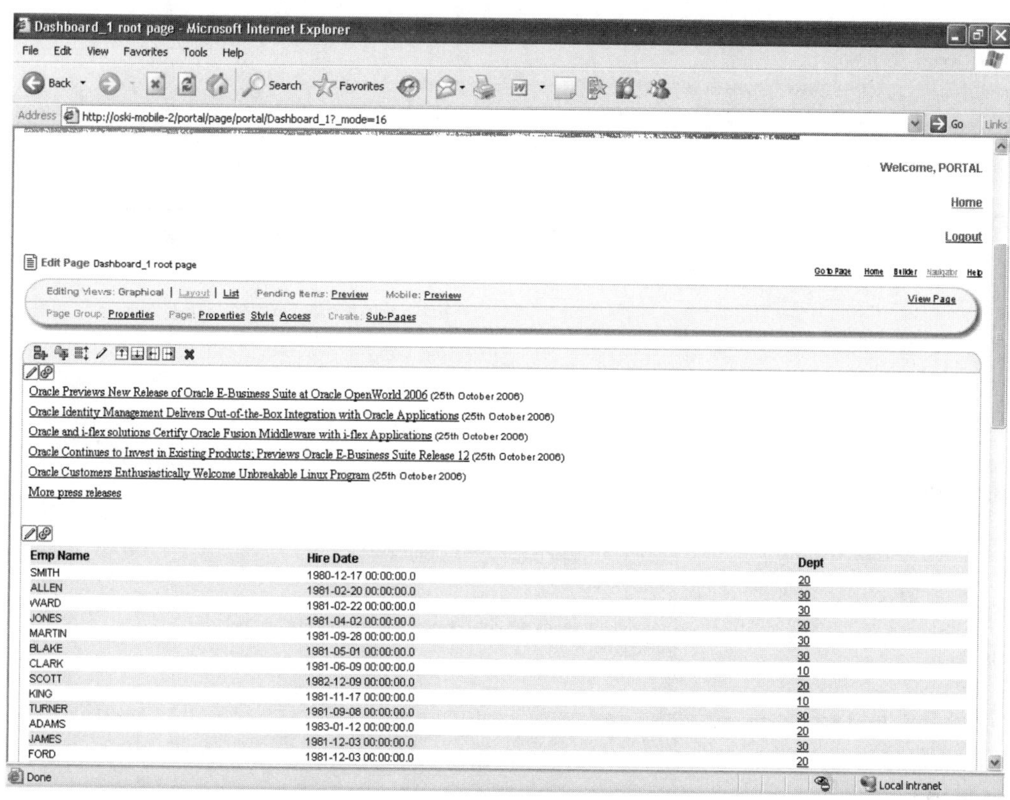

FIGURE 6-23 *The Web page with data queried from Oracle's news site*

privileges on those pages, and log in to your portal as a different user to see the information (Figure 6-25).

CAUTION

Be careful when using this technique. If any other user has access to this OracleAS Portal page, that user will see your e-mail information without having to know your username and password. This holds true for any sensitive information you use the Web Clipping Studio for.

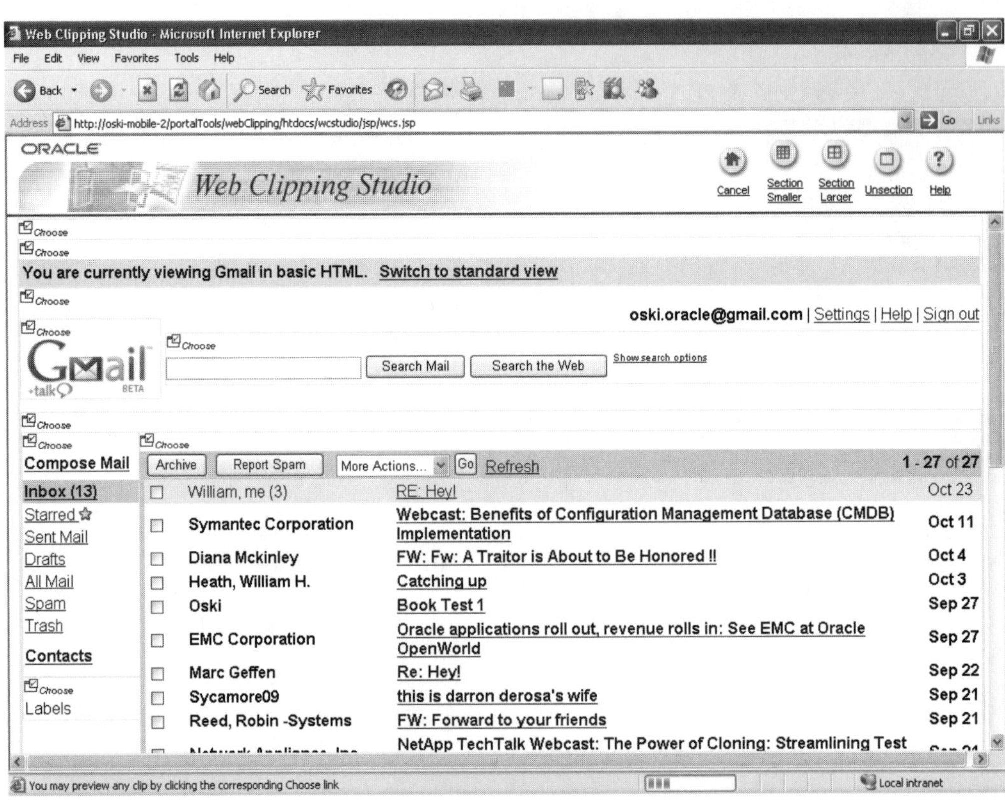

FIGURE 6-24 *The e-mail information for my account on Gmail*

Exercises

- Exercise 1: Design an OmniPortlet that queries data from a table in the PORTAL_DEMO schema in the infrastructure database. Design a second OmniPortlet on the same page that accepts a parameter. Return to the first OmniPortlet and make the source URL of one of the fields to be the same page. Display the page and notice how OracleAS Portlet repaints the page when different values are selected in the first OmniPortlet.

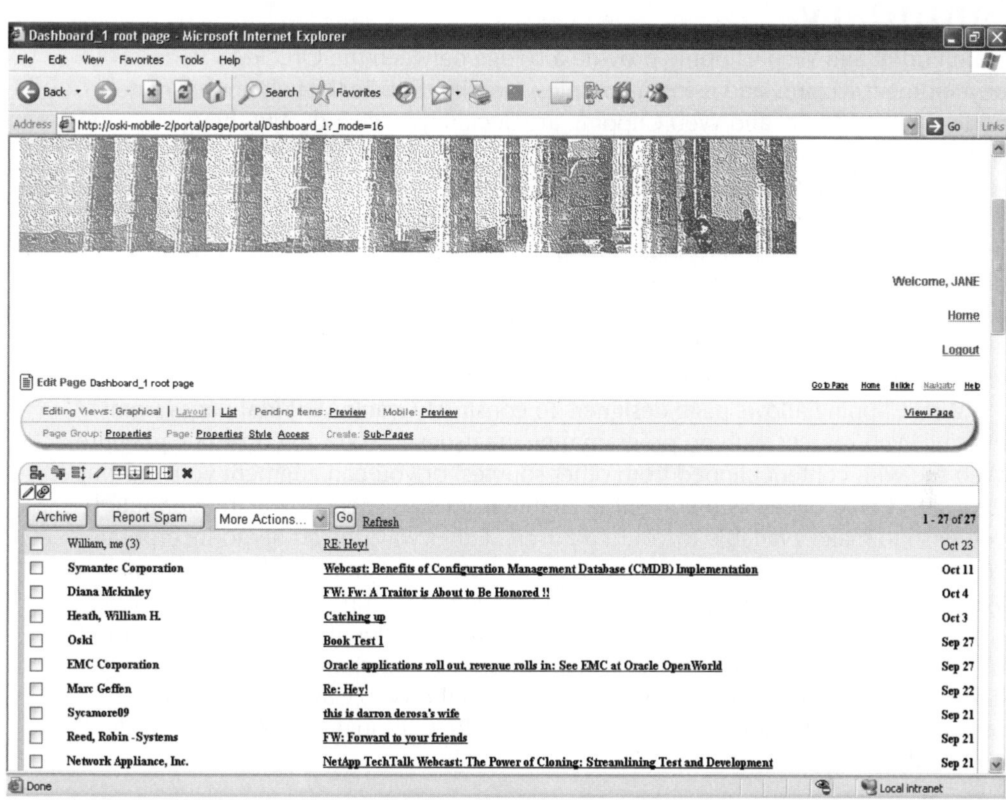

FIGURE 6-25 *The Web Clipping page viewed by a different user (Jane)*

- Exercise 2: Design an OmniPortlet with Graph as the layout and a Pie Chart as the Chart Style. Use the Chart Drill Down section to display another page with the value clicked on the pie chart passed to the other page as a parameter.
- Exercise 3: Use Web Clipping Portlets to gather news articles about a specific topic and create an OracleAS Portal page to aggregate those news stories.

Summary

OmniPortlet and Web Clipping provide a bridge between the OracleAS Portal development wizards and using a complex tool like Oracle JDeveloper to create portlets. OmniPortlet and Web Clipping are declarative wizards, but they overcome some of the limitations associated with the other OracleAS Portal declarative wizards discussed in Chapter 1.

OmniPortlet can query data from numerous data sources and display that information in a variety of formats. None of these sources or formats requires any programming knowledge beyond the basic understanding of the structure of the data sources and the way information is to be displayed to end users. OmniPortlets also can accept and pass parameters easily so that end users can have a dynamic experience when using your portal.

Web Clipping allows page designers to construct OracleAS Portal pages from existing Web sources with no programming whatsoever. You can construct an entire Web site with content clipped from other sources, or you can augment your existing OracleAS Portal pages with content available from sites specializing in information you wish to make available to your end users. Either way, the ability to incorporate content from virtually any site on the Web with no programming whatsoever makes Web Clipping an incredibly powerful tool for OracleAS Portal page designers.

If you need greater functionality than the OracleAS Portal wizards can provide but are not ready to undertake the task of becoming proficient in Java and Oracle JDeveloper, the combination of OmniPortlet and the Web Clipping Studio can provide you with the tools needed to create production-quality Web sites quickly and easily.

PART III

Development

CHAPTER 7

Writing Portlets with Java

The OracleAS Portal Development wizards referenced in Chapter 1 and the OmniPortlet and Web Clipping wizards discussed in Chapter 6 are examples of what Oracle refers to in its documentation as declarative portlet development. In this development model, developers declare *what* they want (as opposed to *how* to get what they want) and various wizards generate the actual code that runs behind the scenes. While it is possible to modify the code after it is generated, this is not the intent of the declarative development wizards—the generated code is very difficult to maintain and enhance. The preferred way to enhance your portlet using the declarative development method would be to run the wizards again to make modifications and to generate a new version of the portlet.

While this is certainly a valid way to develop portlets, most developers run into the limitations of the wizards fairly quickly. Because of their nature, the wizards need to make basic assumptions about how a portlet looks and behaves—not every possible option can be exposed through a wizard. The only way to get full control of your portlets is to develop them in either of the two native languages OracleAS Portal supports: PL/SQL or Java. This chapter focuses on Java and how to use Java-based development tools to build and deploy Java-based OracleAS Portal portlets.

Writing a chapter on using Java to develop portlets is not easy, not because of the techniques used, but rather because of the fundamental assumptions that have to be made when discussing those techniques. In their seminal book, *Oracle JDeveloper 10g Handbook*, (Oracle Press, 2003), authors Avrom Roy-Faderman, Peter Koletzke, and Paul Dorsey start the introduction by saying, "This is not the only book you will need to learn how to create Java-based web applications."

Yikes! And that's from a 750+ page book!

This is not intended to be a criticism in any way. Both the Java language and the Oracle JDeveloper development environment are so rich and complex that no one volume could possibly cover all salient points of interest. In fact, if you are interested in serious Java development using Oracle JDeveloper, consider the *Oracle JDeveloper 10g Handbook* along with *Oracle JDeveloper 10g for Forms and PL/SQL Developers* by Peter Koletzke and Duncan Mills (Oracle Press, 2006) to be required reading.

It is in this spirit that I am undertaking this chapter. This chapter is not designed to teach Java, Oracle JDeveloper, or the Application Development Framework (ADF). While the basics of each of these will be covered, it is my sincere hope that you will continue expanding your Java/JDeveloper/ADF knowledge by taking advantage of the reference materials alluded to in this chapter. In an attempt to make things easier, I have divided this chapter into ten basic steps you will need to perform to successfully develop and deploy Java-based portlets to your portal. Some of these steps, thankfully, only need to be performed once.

NOTE

This chapter is not intended to teach the Java language or how to make the most of the Oracle JDeveloper development environment. This chapter will only discuss those features of Java and Oracle JDeveloper that are relevant to portlet development. To learn more about Java, consider Java SE6, The Complete Reference by Herbert Schildt (McGraw-Hill, 2007). To learn more about Oracle JDeveloper, consider the two JDeveloper books named in the text. To learn more about ADF, consider the ADF Developer's Guide (search Oracle's technology network [http://www.oracle.com/technology/index.html] for part number B28967-01), the ADF Guide for Forms/4GL Developers (Oracle part number B25947-01), and the ADF Recommended Reading page at http://www.oracle.com/technology/products/jdev/tips/muench/requiredreading/index.html.

Step 1: Download the Portal Add-in for Oracle JDeveloper

There are many Java development environments available today, and any of these environments can be used to create Java-based portlets to be deployed to the Oracle Application Server. Oracle provides, however, an add-in for its Oracle JDeveloper product that makes developing and deploying portlets much easier. An *add-in* is a small piece of code added to the Oracle JDeveloper environment to enhance its functionality. The portal add-in consists of a wizard that will generate much of the underlying code for you. There are two significant differences to the code generated by the OracleAS Portal declarative development wizards discussed in Chapters 1 and 7, however:

- The code generated by the Oracle JDeveloper Portal Wizard consists *only* of the basic framework of the portlet—to make the portlet useful, you will have to add the necessary business logic.
- Since the code generated by the Oracle JDeveloper Portal Wizard consists only of the basic framework of the portlet, the wizard was designed to generate code to be modified and enhanced using the Oracle JDeveloper development tool.

As of this writing (May 2007), the portlet add-in is only needed for Oracle JDeveloper 10.1.2. The latest version of Oracle JDeveloper (10.1.3.2.0) has portlet development functionality built in. In some of Oracle's marketing materials, Oracle JDeveloper 10.1.3.2.0 is referred to as WebCenter. If you are using WebCenter, you can skip the "Step 2: Install the Portal Add-In for JDeveloper" and the "Step 5: Check the Installation of the Portal Add-In in JDeveloper" sections later in this chapter.

In early 2006, Oracle started giving away Oracle JDeveloper for free. If you haven't downloaded it yet, go to the Oracle downloads page (http://www.oracle.com/technology/software) and follow the instructions to download Oracle JDeveloper.

Oracle maintains a page on its technology site devoted to OracleAS Portal development. Point your browser to: http://portalcenter.oracle.com/. On this page you will find numerous resources for planning, administering, and developing for your portal. In the bottom right of the page is a link called Portal Developer Kit. Clicking that link takes you to the Portal Development Kit downloads page (http://www.oracle.com/technology/products/ias/portal/pdk.html). On this page you can download the Portal Development Kit (PDK), as we will do in a later step, and get various pieces of documentation and white papers. In the middle of the page is a section titled Portal Extension for JDeveloper. Click the Portal Extension for Oracle JDeveloper link and save the Zip file. After saving the Zip file, use a file compression tool to unzip the portal-addin-install.jar file.

TIP
You should make extensive use of both the http://www.oracle.com/technology/products/ias/portal/ and http://www.oracle.com/technology/products/ias/portal/pdk.html pages. Developers will find numerous while papers and code examples here dealing with advanced portlet development topics. Much of the information found here is not available anywhere else.

Step 2: Install the Portal Add-in for JDeveloper

The installation of the portal add-in is relatively simple. Shut down Oracle JDeveloper if it is running and issue the following command from a command prompt:

```
java -jar portal-addin-install.jar <JDeveloper home>
```

For example, if Oracle JDeveloper was installed in the c:\oracle\jdev1012 directory, your command would look like this:

```
java -jar portal-addin-install.jar c:\oracle\jdev1012
```

You should see output similar to the following:

```
Installing "/opt/jdev/10g/jdev/lib/ext/portal-addin.jar"
Installing "/opt/jdev/10g/jdev/lib/ext/wsrp-container.jar"
Installing "/opt/jdev/10g/jdev/lib/ext/oracle-portlet-tags.jar"
Installing "/opt/jdev/10g/jdev/lib/ext/ptlshare.jar"
Installing "/opt/jdev/10g/jdev/lib/ext/pdkjava.jar"
Installing "/opt/jdev/10g/jdev/lib/ext/jazn.jar"
Installing "/opt/jdev/10g/jdev/lib/ext/jazncore.jar"
Installing "/opt/jdev/10g/jdev/lib/patches/jaxb-api.jar"
Installing "/opt/jdev/10g/jdev/lib/patches/jaxb-libs.jar"
Installing "/opt/jdev/10g/jdev/lib/patches/jaxb-impl.jar"
Installing "/opt/jdev/10g/jdev/lib/patches/namespace.jar"
Installing "/opt/jdev/10g/jdev/lib/patches/relaxngDatatype.jar"
Installing "/opt/jdev/10g/jdev/lib/patches/xsdlib.jar"
Install successful. You may now start JDeveloper.
```

Step 3: Download the OracleAS PDK

The OracleAS PDK contains a set of portlet-building APIs that you can use to create programmatic portlets. If you are considering using Oracle JDeveloper to build and create portlets, you should install the development kit as part of your application server install. If this is not available to you, you can use the APIs locally by downloading the PDK from the URL listed in the preceding section and by installing it into a local OC4J instance that you can use to run and test your applications. For more information on this, see http://www.oracle.com/technology/products/ias/portal/html/installing.pdkjava.v2.html.

The only thing you are actually installing is the sample applications that come along with the PDK, but you certainly don't have to do that. You can get good use out of the PDK without installing any of the applications—the code examples that are part of the download can be invaluable in your Java-development efforts.

What Is OC4J?

Following the PDK installation instructions can be confusing for developers beginning to use Java to create portlets. OC4J (the name stands for Oracle Containers for Java) is Oracle's method of providing a Java environment to the Oracle Application Server. A container has attributes that can be set to tell all applications deployed to that container how to behave. Some of the things you can set include: directories where applications are deployed, if the OC4J container is clustered, the ports various Java processes like EJBs use, data sources for applications deployed to that container, security for applications through JAZN (Oracle's JAAS [Java Authentication and Authorization Service] implementation) settings, JMS (Java Message Service) settings, etc. Sometimes, however, developers want to work in an environment that does not include a full-blown application server. For those cases, Oracle provides a simple OC4J container that developers can install locally on their machines to develop and test against. You can download this local OC4J container by browsing to http://www.oracle.com/technology/products/ias/portal/pdk.html and then clicking the Download The Pre-Seeded OC4J link.

You can omit this step if you use the Oracle JDeveloper Portlet Creation Wizard to build the portlet. If the PDK libraries are installed on the Oracle Application Server, simply deploy the portlet. If the libraries haven't been installed, you can always package them with the portlet (in the same EAR file).

Step 4: Understand Portlet View Modes

A portlet has various view modes. These view modes define the user's interaction with the portlet and how the portlet behaves under certain conditions. The following information defines the various portlet view modes:

- **Shared Screen mode** A portlet uses Shared Screen mode to appear on a page with other portlets. This is the mode most people think about when they envision a portlet. Portlets are rendered inside HTML table cells when in Shared Screen mode. This means a portlet can display any content that can be rendered within a table cell, including, among other technologies, HTML, plug-ins, and Java applets. The actual size of the table cell is variable, depending on user settings, the browser width, and the amount and style of content in the portlet. When developing portlets, remember that your portlet will share a page with others and you cannot completely control its dimensions and placement.

- **Edit mode** A portlet uses Edit mode to allow users to customize the behavior of the portlet. Edit mode provides a list of settings that the user can change. These customizable settings may include the title, type of content, formatting, amount of information, defaults for form elements, and anything that affects the appearance or content of the portlet.
- **Edit Defaults mode** A portlet uses the Edit Defaults mode to allow page designers to customize the default behavior of a particular portlet instance. Edit Defaults mode provides a list of settings that the page designer can change. These customizable settings may include the title, type of content, formatting, amount of information, defaults for form elements, and anything that affects the appearance or content of the portlet. These default customization settings can change the appearance and content of that individual portlet for all users. Because Edit Defaults mode defines the system-level defaults for what a portlet displays and how it displays it, this mode should not be used as an administrative tool or for managing other portlets. Page designers access Edit Defaults mode from the Customize page when they choose Customize For Others. The link is labeled Edit Defaults on the banner of the wire frame diagram of that portlet. When you click Edit Defaults, a new page appears in the same browser window. The portlet typically creates a Web page representing a dialog box to customize the portlet instance settings. Once the settings are applied, you are automatically returned to the original page. Portal users typically access a portlet's Edit mode by clicking Customize on the portlet banner. When you click Customize, a new page appears in the same browser window. The portlet typically creates a Web page representing a dialog box to choose the portlet's settings. Once you apply the settings, you automatically return to the original page.
- **Preview mode** A portlet uses Preview mode to show the user what the portlet looks like before adding it to a page. Preview mode visually represents what the portlet can do. Portal users typically access a portlet's Preview mode by clicking its Preview icon from the Add Portlet page. A window then displays the preview of the chosen portlet. The user then has the option to add that portlet to the page. Portal administrators may access Preview mode from the Portlet Repository. Note that the portal does not draw the portal banner when rendering the portlet in this mode.

- **Full Screen mode** Portlets use Full Screen mode to show more details than possible when sharing a page with other portlets. Full Screen mode lets a portlet have the entire window to itself. For example, if a portlet displays expense information, it could show a summary of the top ten spenders in Shared Screen mode and the spending totals for everyone in Full Screen mode. Portlets can also provide a shortcut to Web applications. If a portlet provided an interface to submitting receipts for expenses in Shared Screen mode, it could link to the entire expense application from Full Screen mode. Portal users access a portlet's Full Screen mode by clicking the title of the portlet.
- **Help mode** A portlet uses Help mode to display information about the functionality of the portlet and how to use it. The user should be able to find useful information about the portlet, its content, and its capabilities with this mode. Portal users access a portlet's Help mode by clicking Help in the portlet banner.
- **About mode** Users should be able to see what version of the portlet is currently running, its publication and copyright information, and how to contact the author. Portlets that require registration may link to Web-based applications or contact information from this mode, as well. Portal users access a portlet's About mode by clicking About on the portlet banner. A new page appears in the same browser window. The portlet can either generate the content for this new page or take the user to an existing page or application.
- **Link mode** A portlet uses Link mode to render a link to itself that displays on a mobile page. When the user clicks the link, the portlet is called in Show mode but with a different content type.

When the Oracle JDeveloper Portal Wizard runs, it will ask you to provide code for each of these modes, if applicable, for your portlet.

Step 5: Check the Installation of the Portal Add-in in JDeveloper

You can test the installation by performing the following steps:

1. Start Oracle JDeveloper 10*g* (10.1.2).

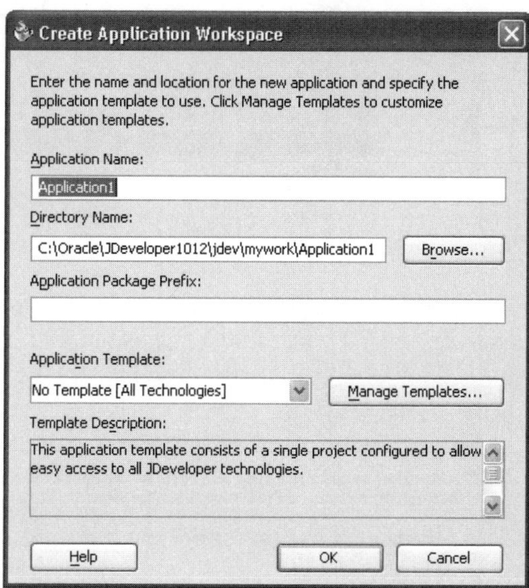

FIGURE 7-1 *The Create Application Workspace dialog in Oracle JDeveloper*

2. Create a new Application Workspace by right-clicking Applications in the Application – Navigator window on the left of the screen. Give the Application Workspace a meaningful name (Figure 7-1) and click OK.
3. Right-click your project under Applications in the Applications Navigator and select New.
4. In the New Object Gallery, expand the Web Tier node on the left-hand side.
5. Select the Portlets node.
6. Ensure two items are visible and selectable: Java Portlet and Oracle PDK Java Portlet (Figure 7-2).

Step 6: Decide Which Type of Portlet to Build

One of the fundamental choices you will face when building Java-based OracleAS Portal portlets is whether to use the Oracle PDK (Portal Development Kit) or to build

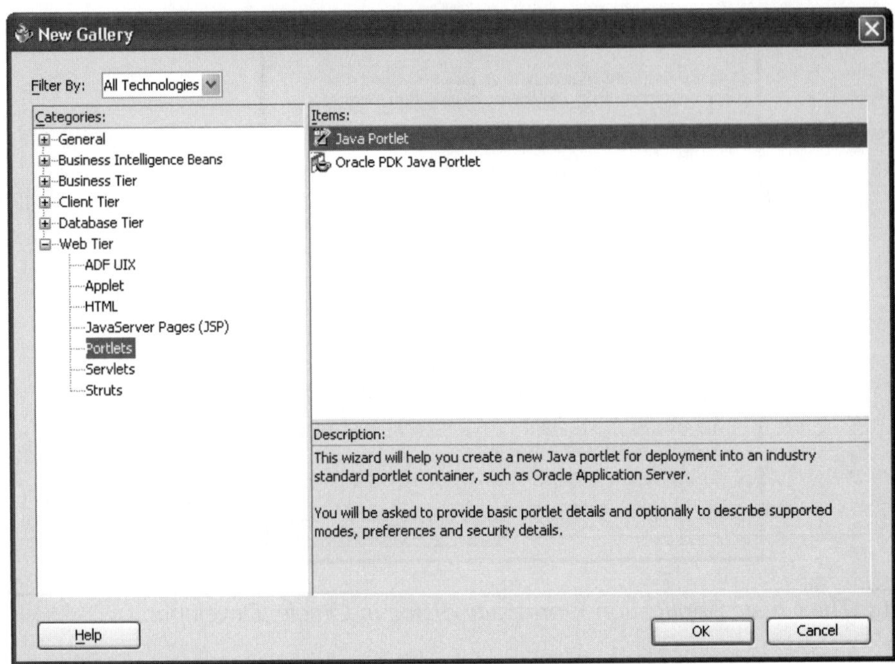

FIGURE 7-2 *The Java Portlet and Oracle PDK Java Portlet selections in the New Gallery window*

your portlet to an open standard. There are pros and cons to each of these approaches:

Method	Pros	Cons
Oracle PDK	Oracle PDK optimized for rapid development; mature API; large knowledge base of PDK-based solutions available.	Can only be deployed to an Oracle-based application server.
Open Standard	Can be deployed to any JSR 168–compliant application server; JSR 168 portlets deployed to Oracle's portlet container are automatically exposed through WSRP and can be consumed by any third-party WSRP-compliant portal.	Requires a greater knowledge of Java-based APIs; doesn't support inter-portlet communication, doesn't support the export/import of portlet customizations.

Open Standard: JSR 168

As mentioned earlier, OracleAS Portal is not the only portal product on the market. IBM, BEA, Microsoft, and JBoss (now part of Red Hat), to name a few, all make competing portal products. The Java community, in response to the request from developers desiring interoperability of portlets between different platforms, came up with a standard for portlets and portal development. This standard allows developers to code their portlets in such a way that they can be deployed to any application server–based portal environment that conforms to this standard.

Requests for new Java APIs are submitted to the Java Community Process and are called Java Specification Requests (JSRs). The JSR for portlet development is called JSR 168. JSR 168's stated purpose is as follows: "To enable interoperability between Portlets and Portal, this specification will define a set of APIs for Portal computing addressing the areas of aggregation, personalization, presentation, and security." JSR 168 defines container services, which provide the following:

- A portlet API for coding portlet functionality
- The URL-rewriting mechanism for creating user interaction within a portlet container
- The security and personalization of portlets

To see more detail about this specification, go to http://jcp.org/en/jsr/detail?id=168.

The Oracle PDK

The OracleAS Portal Developer Kit (PDK) provides developers with the necessary libraries to create portlets that take full advantage of all OracleAS Portal features. Since the PDK is designed by Oracle for OracleAS Portal, it is far more comprehensive than the JSR 168 standard. Portlets written with PDK features have full access to all of OracleAS Portal's advanced features, including integration with external applications, seamless integration with Oracle's LDAP implementation (Oracle Internet Directory), and access to classes and methods specifically written for developers interested in Oracle-based solutions. Oracle's development framework, known as Application Development Framework (ADF), is being updated to include more OracleAS Portal–specific functionality. With a rich development environment and a framework specifically designed for developer productivity, the combination of Oracle JDeveloper, the Application Development Framework, and the Portal Development Kit provides developers with all of the necessary tools to create complex portal-based applications quickly, securely, and easily.

Step 7: Use the Wizard to Build the Portlet

As mentioned in the preceding step, you can build two types of portlets with the Portal Add-in Wizard for Oracle JDeveloper: a portlet based on the Oracle PDK or a portlet based on the JSR 168 standard. The following two sections deal with each of these methods.

Building an Oracle PDK-Based Portlet

By choosing this option, developers can quickly build a portlet that has access to all features included in the Oracle Portal Development Kit. The drawback to building a PDK-based portlet is the fact that it cannot be deployed to anything other than Oracle Application Server (for more pros and cons, see the table earlier in this chapter). If you do not need to deploy your portlets to multiple application server environments, a portlet of this type is easier to build and contains more functionality than JSR 168–based portlets. To start building your PDK-based portlet, follow the steps in the section "Step 5: Check the Installation of the Portal Add-in in JDeveloper" in this chapter and select Oracle PDK Java Portlet in Figure 7-2. Selecting OK brings you to the Welcome screen for the Java Portlet Wizard. Click the Skip This Page Next Time box to suppress the Welcome screen. Click Next.

On the Step 1 of 7: Portlet Description page of the Oracle PDK Portlet Wizard (Figure 7-3), you are asked for basic information about your portlet. Everything entered here will be used by OracleAS Portal to display information about your portlet. For instance, the Portal Name field is what OracleAS Portal uses internally to store information about your portlet. It cannot contain any spaces or special characters. The next field, Display Name, is what the OracleAS Portal Navigator will use to display your portlet. This name will also be used when selecting portlets to be placed on a page (something we will do later in this chapter). The Description field is a simple text field used to help developers organize their portlets. The timeout information allows developers to specify how long the OracleAS Portal engine should try to render (display) the portlet before giving up and what message should be displayed if the engine is unable to render the portlet in the given time frame.

For this example, give the portlet the following values:

- **Portlet Name** BasicEmpPortlet
- **Display Name** Basic Employee Portlet
- **Description** My first Java-based portlet
- **Timeout (seconds)** 40
- **Timeout Message** Unable to render portlet

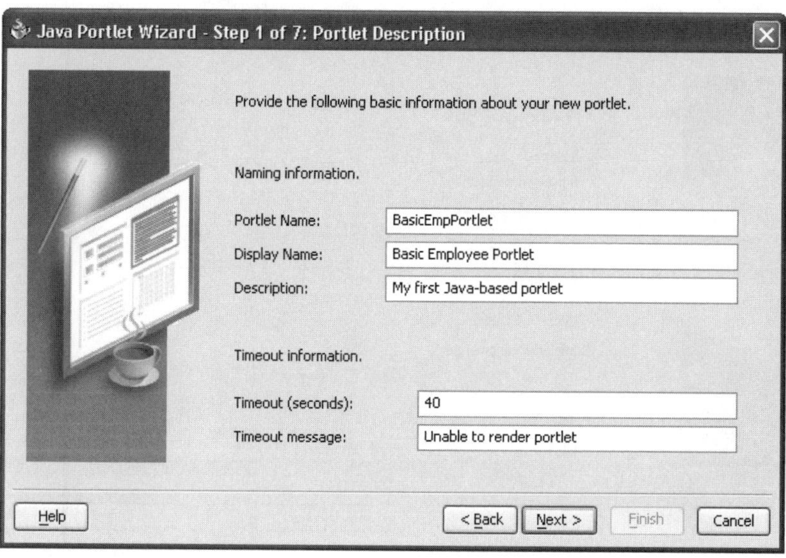

FIGURE 7-3 *Step 1 of the PDK Portlet Wizard*

Click Next. On the Step 2 of 7: Show Modes page of the wizard (Figure 7-4), developers are asked about the details of the different view modes discussed in the section "Step 4: Understand Portlet View Modes" of this chapter. Not all of the modes listed in that section are available in this wizard, as some of the modes are specific to JSR 168 portlets.

The Show Page check box corresponds to Shared Screen Mode for the portlet. This is where the portlet is displayed as part of an OracleAS Portal page and is where your end users will spend most of their time interacting with your portlet. The Implementation Style drop-down box gives developers four basic ways of displaying the information on a page: JSP (JavaServer Page), HTTP Servlet, HTML File, or as a Java class. JSPs give developers a great deal of functionality while keeping complexity relatively low (particularly when combined with Oracle JDeveloper's graphical editing tools), so unless there is a specific reason not to use JSPs, this is the selection you will use most of the time. By default, the filename associated with this page is populated as <PortletName>ShowPage.<implementation style>. You can change this if you'd like, but keeping track of oddly named files can become a chore, so in most cases, it's best to take the default.

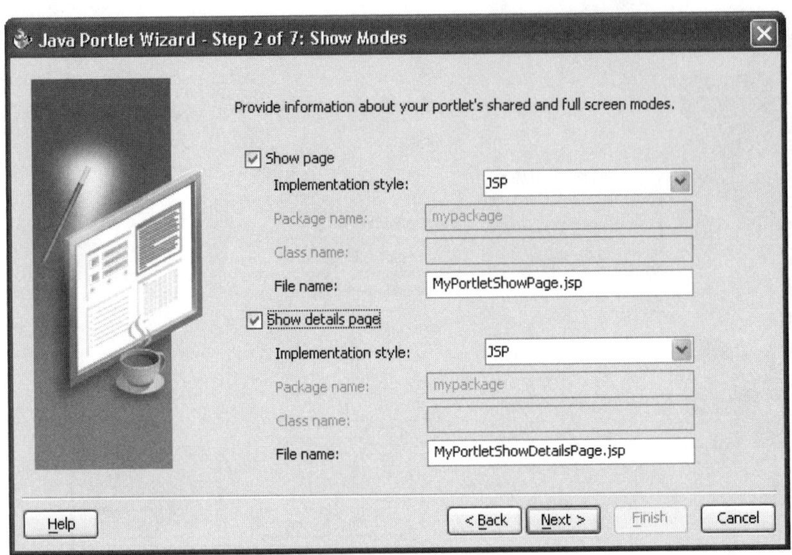

FIGURE 7-4 *Step 2 of the PDK Portlet Wizard*

The Show Details Page section at the bottom of this page of the wizard corresponds to the Full Screen Mode section described in the section "Step 4: Understand Portlet View Modes" of this chapter. If this section is selected, a file will be generated that, when selected, shows the portlet in an entire browser window. This is a very rare use of OracleAS Portal portlets, but for this example, select the Show Details Page check box, leave the defaults for that section and click Next.

On the Step 3 of 7: Customize Modes page of the wizard (Figure 7-5), there are two sections, Edit Page and Edit Defaults Page, which correspond, respectively, to the Edit Mode and Edit Defaults Mode descriptions in the section "Step 4: Understand Portlet View Modes" of this chapter. For this example, make sure both are selected and have JSP as their Implementation style. Leave the default File Name and click Next.

On the Step 4 of 7: Additional Modes page of the wizard (Figure 7-6), there are two sections: Help Page and About Page which correspond, respectively, to the Help Mode and About Mode descriptions in the section "Step 4: Understand Portlet View Modes" of this chapter. For this example, make sure both are selected and have JSP as their Implementation style. Leave the default File Name. Click Next.

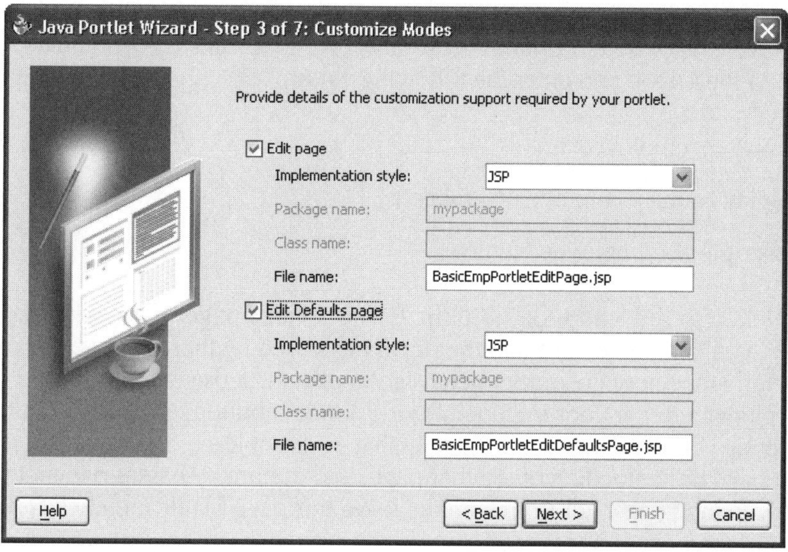

FIGURE 7-5 *Step 3 of the PDK Portlet Wizard*

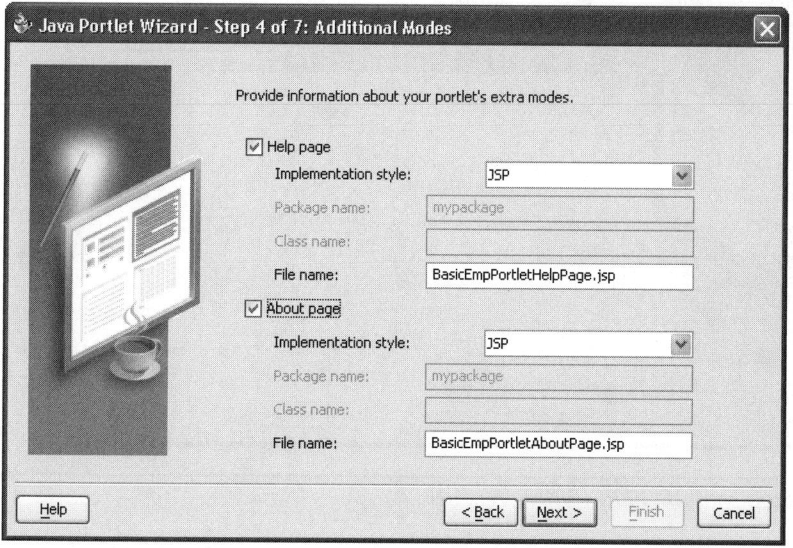

FIGURE 7-6 *Step 4 of the PDK Portlet Wizard*

On the Step 5 of 7: Public Portlet Parameters page of the wizard (Figure 7-7), you can add parameters that can be used to influence how the portlet is displayed. Parameters were discussed in Chapter 6. For this example, click the Add button on the bottom of the screen and enter the following values:

- **Name** p_employee_no
- **Display Name** Employee Number
- **Description** Employee Number

Click Next. On the Step 6 of 7: Public Portlet Events page of the wizard (Figure 7-8), you can add events and the parameters used by those events that can be used to influence how the portlet behaves. An event is a user action defined by a portlet developer. User actions include clicking a link, a button, or another control on a Web page. A page designer can specify that an event forces the reloading of the current page or the loading of another page, and optionally passes parameters to the newly loaded page. For this example, leave this page blank and click Next.

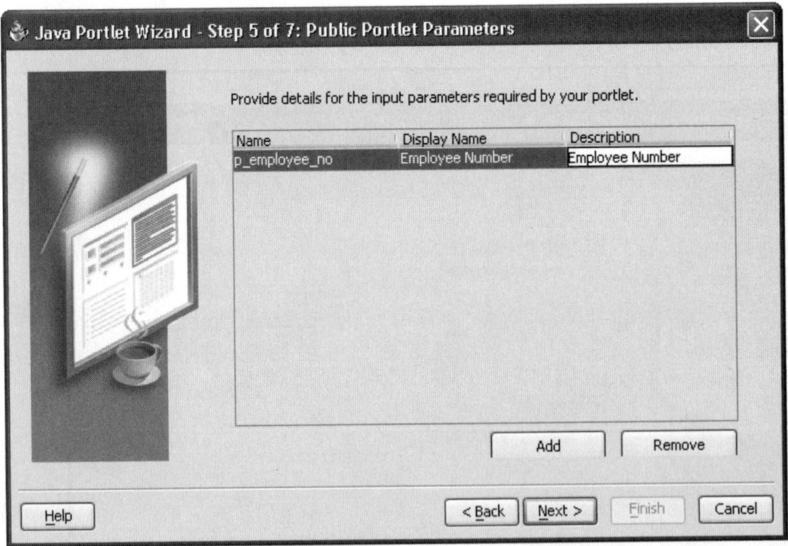

FIGURE 7-7 *Step 5 of the PDK Portlet Wizard*

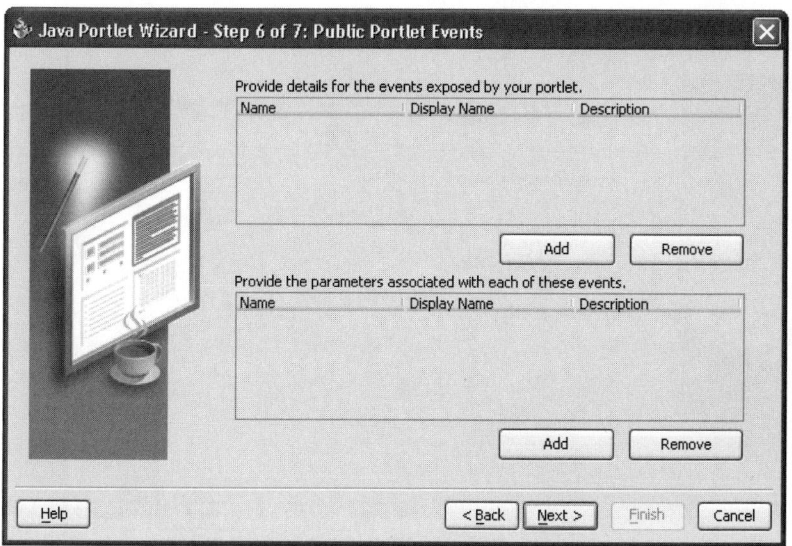

FIGURE 7-8 *Step 6 of the PDK Portlet Wizard*

The final step, Step 7 of 7: Provider Description (Figure 7-9), allows you to define the name of the provider and files associated with the deployment of your portlet. For more about providers, see the sidebar "Providers."

Providers

Providers can be thought of as "parents" to portlets. A portlet cannot exist without being associated with a provider (technically, OmniPortlets, discussed in Chapter 6, do not belong to a developer-created provider, but that's a special case). Things like security can be defined at the provider level, and these attributes will cascade down to all members (portlets) of the provider.

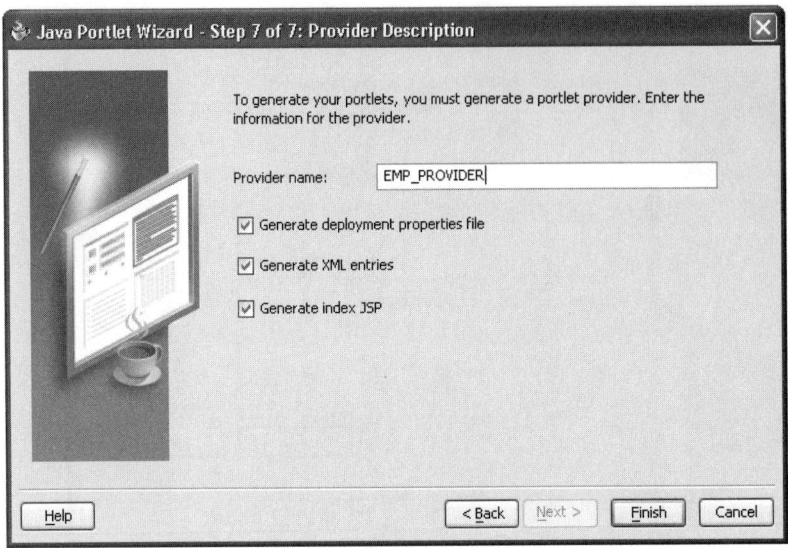

FIGURE 7-9 *Step 7 of the PDK Portlet Wizard*

If you use the declarative portlet wizards discussed in Chapter 1 to create your portlets, you must first create a Database Provider. A Database Provider uses PL/SQL as its engine and stores portlets in the infrastructure database. If you choose to create portlets using Oracle JDeveloper, you must create a Web Provider. A Web Provider is called, using HTTP requests, by OracleAS Portal and returns portlet content in HTML or XML. Web Providers are appropriate for Web-accessible information sources.

NOTE

As part of the code-generation process, a provider definition file will be generated automatically for you. This definition file, provider.xml, can then be used to register the portlet provider into the OracleAS Portal repository. Later on in this chapter, in the section titled "Step 10: Deploy and Register the Portlet," we will do just that.

On this page of the wizard, there is an entry for the provider name and three check boxes:

- **Generate deployment properties file** Checking this box will automatically generate the properties file for your application. There is almost no reason not to have this box checked. Even if you determine that this file is not needed, you can always leave this box checked, generate the file, and then remove it from your project at a later time.
- **Generate XML entries** Checking this box will generate the XML file for your provider. Again, it's very rare that you would not want to generate this file.
- **Generate index JSP** This will generate a simple file named index.jsp you can use to test your portlet. It does not get deployed (moved) to your Application Server and generates a very small .jsp file, so there's no real need to de-select this.

Give your provider a name of **EMP_PROVIDER** and leave all three check boxes checked. When you click OK, the files for your portlet are generated and you are returned to an Oracle JDeveloper screen similar to Figure 7-10.

In the Application Navigator on the left-hand side of the screen, you'll notice that the following files have been generated for you:

- **EmpPortletAboutPage.jsp** This file is the About page for your portlet. It is generated only if you selected the About Page check box on Step 4 of the Portal Wizard.
- **EmpPortletEditDefaultsPage.jsp** This file is the Edit Defaults page for your portlet. It is generated only if you selected the Edit Defaults Page check box on Step 3 of the Portal Wizard.
- **EmpPortletEditPage.jsp** This file is the Edit page for your portlet. It is generated only if you selected the Edit Page check box on Step 3 of the Portal Wizard.
- **EmpPortletHelpPage.jsp** This file is the Help page for your portlet. It is generated only if you selected the Help Page check box on Step 4 of the Portal Wizard.

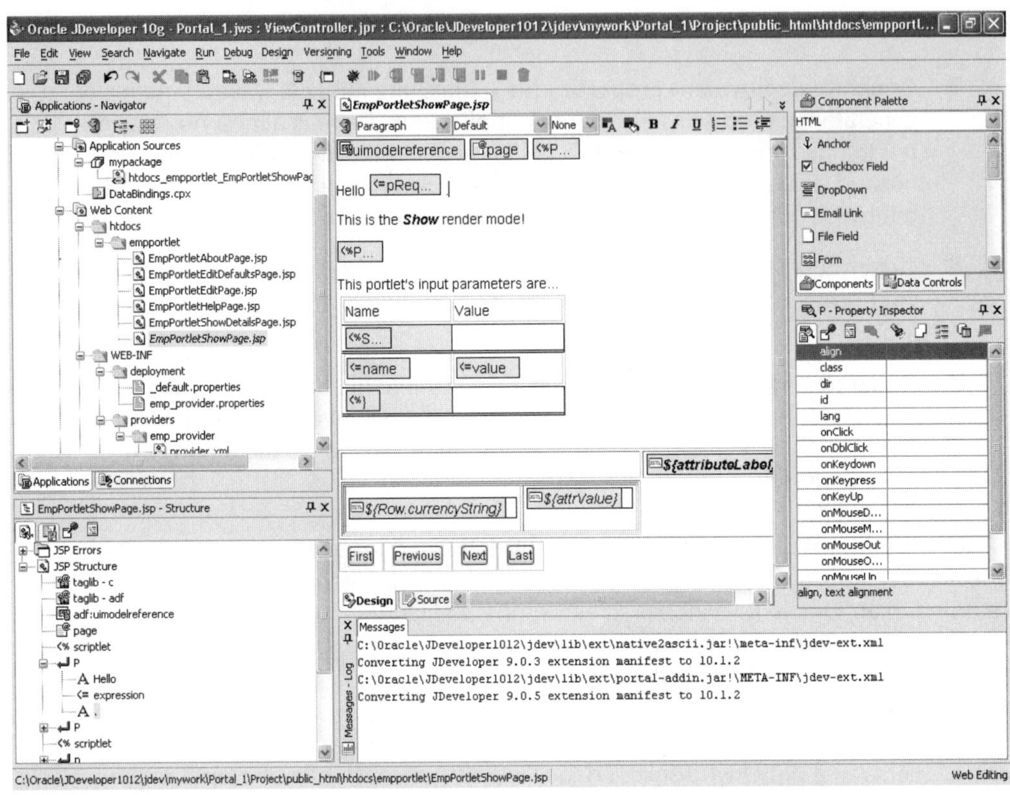

FIGURE 7-10 *Oracle JDeveloper with the PDK wizard-generated files displayed*

- **EmpPortletShowDetailsPage.jsp** This file is the Show Details page for your portlet. It is generated only if you selected the Show Details Page check box on Step 2 of the Portal Wizard.
- **EmpPortletShowPage.jsp** This file is the Show page for your portlet. It is generated only if you selected the Show Page check box on Step 2 of the Portal Wizard.
- **_default.properties** When portlets are associated to a provider, they normally have their own properties file, which defines the service class and loader classes for the portlet along with the specification of the provider.xml

file, which lists additional attributes for the portlet, along with renderer class and parameter information. In this example, the file right below this one (emp_provider.properties) serves that purpose. If there are multiple portlet providers deployed in the same Web application, this file points to the default portlet provider in the Web application.

- **emp_provider.properties** As mentioned in the preceding item, this file defines characteristics for the application.
- **provider.xml** This file defines a Web provider, its portlets and the location of the content to be displayed in the portlets. This file describes the behavior of the provider and its portlets.
- **web.xml** The web.xml file is what's known as a deployment descriptor. A *deployment descriptor* file describes how components of an application are deployed and assembled into a specific environment. In this case, the components are the files in this section that make up the portlet and the environment is the OracleAS Portal environment running on the Oracle Application Server. The Oracle Application Server uses the web.xml file to understand the components used by the application, as well as the environment variables and security requirements for the application.
- **index.jsp** This file is used to test the provider.

You can double-click any of the files in the Application Navigator and that file will be displayed in the middle part of the Oracle JDeveloper screen. JSPs are displayed with two tabs along the bottom of the main window: Design and Source. This is one of the most powerful features of Oracle JDeveloper. By selecting the Design tab, you can use graphical elements to construct your page. Along the top of the window, there are drop-down boxes for sectioning, font selection, and font size, along with graphical elements for setting the background and foreground colors, and standard text buttons for bolding, underlining, making bulleted and numbered lists, etc. With a graphical element fully integrated with the Oracle JDeveloper environment, developers can save time coding necessary details.

Another important feature is the Property Inspector located on the middle right of the page. The Property Inspector allows developers to quickly assign attributes to graphical elements so that they can create complex JSPs quickly. To see how this works, single-click any element that has properties associated with it. In the example in Figure 7-11, I've single-clicked the page directive on the top right of the page. Note how the Property Inspector changes to show the properties of the page directive. At the bottom of the Property Inspector is a small text box that changes to display a description of the property, depending on which property is selected.

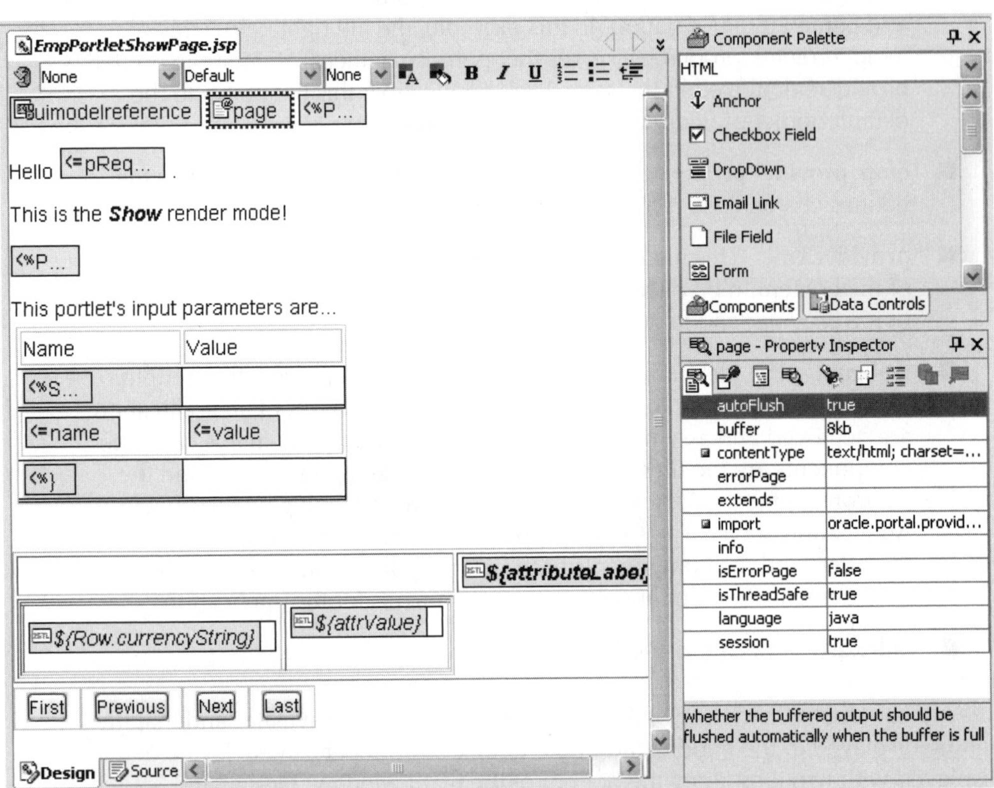

FIGURE 7-11 *The Property Inspector showing values for the page directive*

The Source tab, at the bottom of the main window in the middle of the Oracle JDeveloper screen, shows the code that goes along with the JSP. Both the Design and Source tabs are dynamic; that is, when a change is made on one tab, it is automatically reflected in the other. As a simple example, click the Source tab and find the following lines:

```
<P>Hello <%= pReq.getUser().getName() %>.</P>
<P>This is the <cTypeface:Bold><cTypeface:Italic>Show</i></b> render mode!</P>
```

Add this line in between those two lines:

```
<P>Your Portal Server Name is <%= pReq.getServerName() %>.</P>
```

Now click the Design tab again. You'll see that a new line has been added to the design page (Figure 7-12). If you are more of a visual developer, you can create the same effect graphically by doing the following:

1. With the Design tab selected, type the text **Your Portal Server Name is** in any space in the Design window.
2. In the Component Palette in the top right of the screen, select JSP from the drop-down box.
3. Click and drag the Expression tag next to the text you entered in Step 1.
4. When the Create JSP Expression dialog window pops up, enter **pReq.getServerName()**.
5. Click the Source tab to see the new code.

In the top left of the Oracle JDeveloper window is an icon that looks like a bunch of floppy disks stacked on one another. This is the Save All icon, which will save all files in your project if they haven't been saved already or if they've been modified. Click that icon now. You now have a fully functioning portlet that can be deployed to an Oracle Application Server. As it is, this portlet is not particularly useful. Later in this chapter, in the section "Revisiting the Add Business Logic Step," we'll revisit this portlet and add business logic to it.

Building a JSR 168 Portlet

The wizards for building a JSR 168 portlet are different than the OracleAS PDK Portlet wizards, but the concept is the same: answer questions about how you would like your portlet to look and behave, generate the basic infrastructure code, and then go back and add business logic in Oracle JDeveloper. To build a JSR 168 portlet, follow these steps:

1. Right-click Applications in the Applications Navigator, select New from the drop-down menu, select General in the Categories pane, and select Application Workspace in the Items pane.
2. Click OK and give your application workspace a meaningful name (in this example, I chose JSR168_Portlet_1).
3. Right-click Project underneath your new application workspace in the Application Navigator and select New.

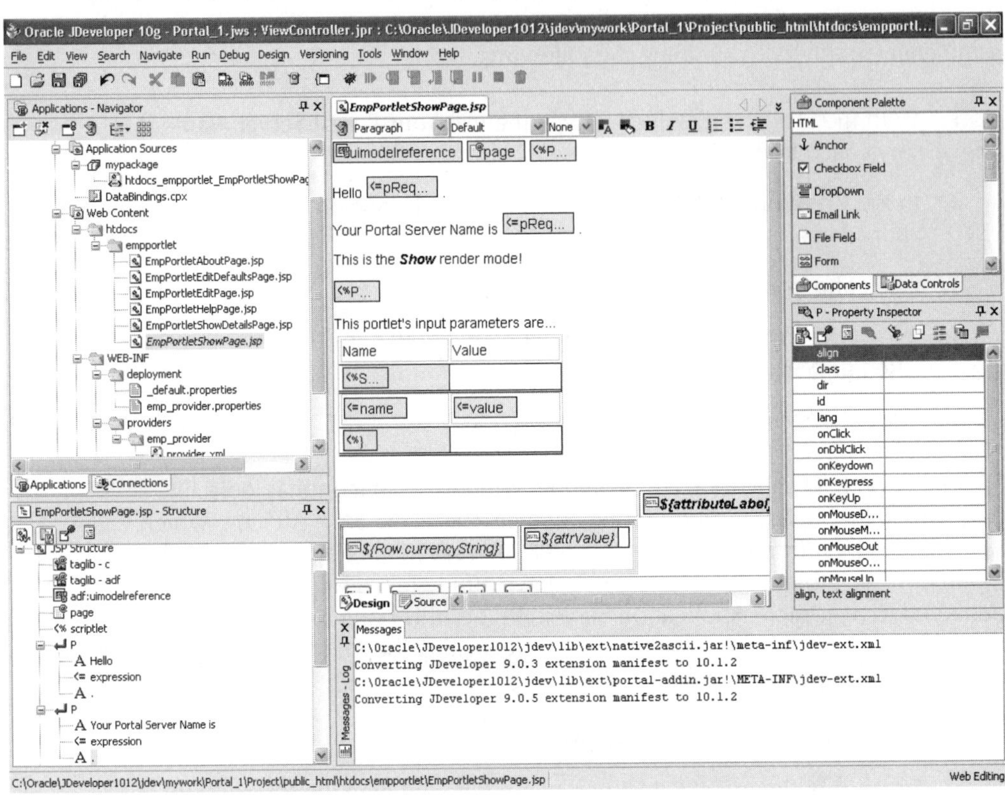

FIGURE 7-12 *The Design page of the JSP showing the new field*

4. In the New Gallery window, click the small plus sign next to Web Tier in the Categories pane and select Java Portlet in the Items pane.

You are now in the Java Portlet Wizard for Oracle JDeveloper. Select the Skip This Page Next Time check box if the Welcome page displays. Click Next. You'll notice, right from the start, that the wizard prompts for different information. In Step 1 of 7: General Portlet Properties (Figure 7-13), you are prompted for the following information:

- **Class** Wikipedia provides this definition of a class: "In object-oriented programming, classes are used to group related variables and functions.

A class describes a collection of encapsulated instance variables and methods (functions), possibly with implementation of those types together with a constructor function that can be used to create objects of the class." While the discussion of object-oriented concepts is beyond the scope of this book, know that a class is the fundamental building block of all Java code.

- **Package** A package is defined as a mechanism for organizing Java classes into namespaces. A namespace is just what it sounds like: a space that has a name, where the Java classes live.
- **Default Language** If you wish to deploy your application using a different language, you can select a value from the drop-down box.
- **Customizable** If this check box is selected, code will be selected for the Edit mode of the portlet.

For this example, give the class a name of **JSR168_Portlet_1**, leave the package name as mypackage, leave the Default Language as English, and make sure the Customizable check box is checked. Click Next.

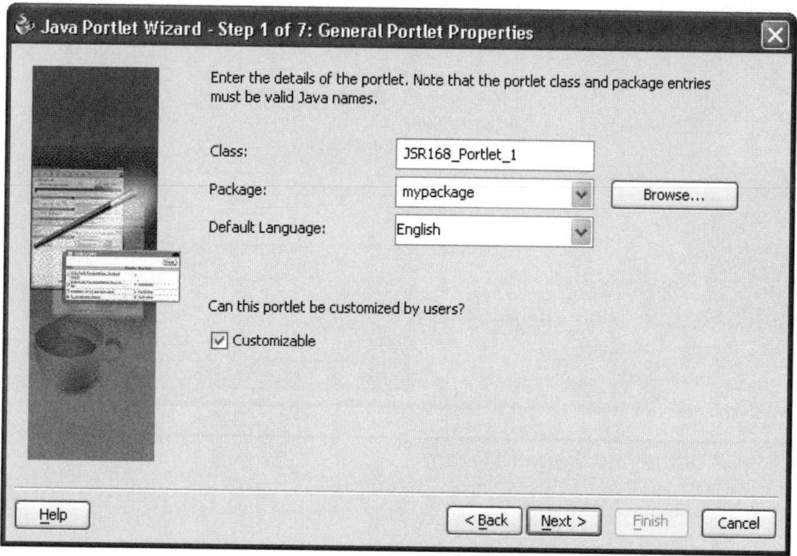

FIGURE 7-13 *Step 1 of the Java Portlet Wizard*

On the Step 2 of 7: Name and Attributes page of the wizard (Figure 7-14), the Display Name, Portlet Title, and Short Title fields each have short descriptions below them. The description field is for organizational purposes only. The Keywords field provides additional information about a page or item so that users can easily locate the page or item during a search. For this example, leave all the fields with the default values and click Next.

On the Step 3 of 7: Content Types and Portlet Modes page of the wizard (Figure 7-15), there are only two modes listed (as opposed to the six possible modes for Oracle PDK portlets in the previous section): view and edit. Edit will only appear if the Customizable check box is selected in the first page of the wizard. You might think that clicking the Add button at the bottom of the dialog box would allow you to add modes, but that is not the purpose of the Add button. That button can be used to add content types, each of which has its own modes.

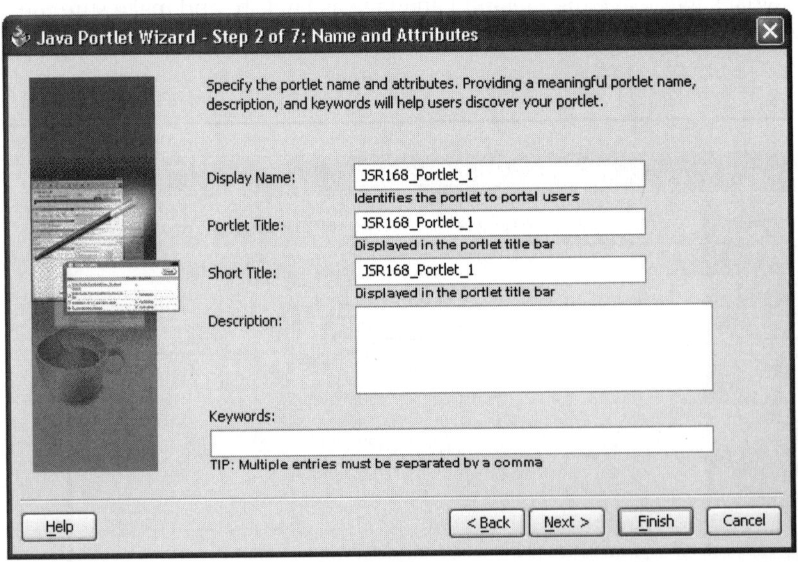

FIGURE 7-14 *Step 2 of the Java Portlet Wizard*

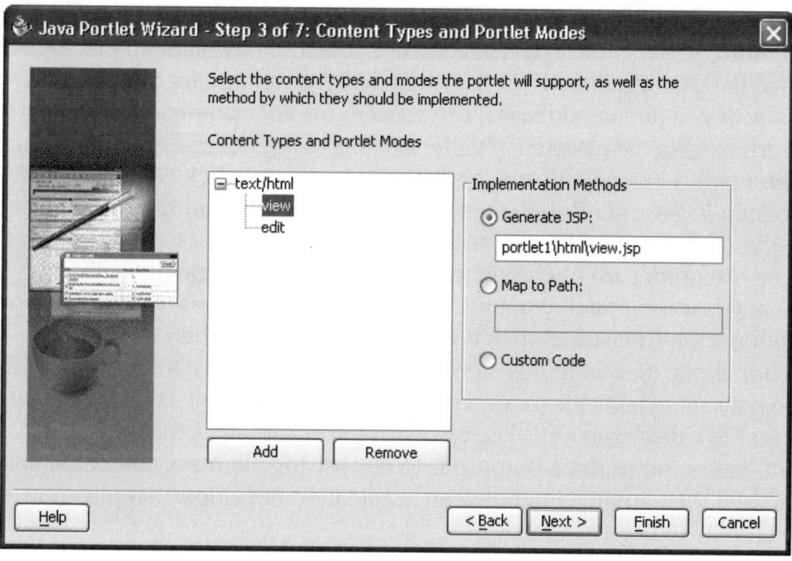

FIGURE 7-15 *Step 3 of the Java Portlet Wizard*

NOTE
If you click Add, you will note that there are five additional types you can add to your JSR 168–based portlet: text/xml (for displaying XML data), text/plain (for displaying plain text), text/vnd.oracle.mobilexml (for displaying XML data on mobile devices), application/xhtml+xml (for invoking an XHTML viewer through a browser), and application/xml (for invoking an XML program through a browser). Each of these additional content types has only one mode associated with it: view.

For this example, click the View and Edit tree nodes and make sure the Generate JSP: radio button is selected when each of the tree nodes is selected. Click Next.

On the Step 4: Customization Preferences screen (Figure 7-16), a single preference, Portlet Title, is defined by default. You can add additional preferences by clicking Add. By default, if you leave Portlet Title as an available preference, the code to have the user modify the portlet title will be generated for you automatically. If you define additional preferences for your portlet, you will have to write the code to take the preference value and make the necessary modifications to your portlet. For this example, leave the default values and click Next.

On the Step 5: Security Roles screen (Figure 7-17), you can specify security roles for the portlet. In a traditional deployment of a JSR 168–based portlet, the files that make up the portlet are packaged (put together) into a single file with a .war extension called, appropriately enough, a WAR file (WAR stands for Web Archive). A WAR file has a specific structure that must be adhered to (when we look at deploying our application in a later step, we'll see that Oracle JDeveloper handles most of the packaging tasks for us automatically). One of the files that makes up a WAR file is a file called web.xml. The web.xml file is known as the Web application deployment descriptor; its main purpose is to convey the elements and configuration information of a Web application between application developers, application

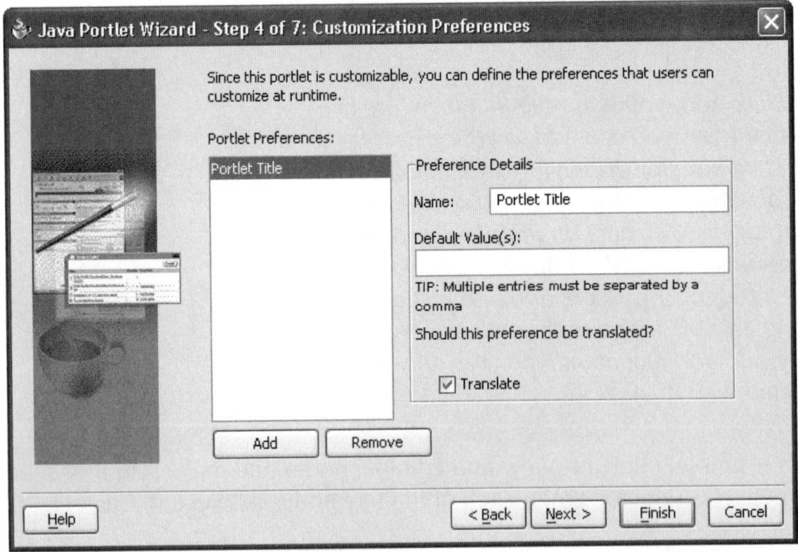

FIGURE 7-16 *Step 4 of the Java Portlet Wizard*

assemblers, and deployers. In certain cases, declarative security (a security rule such as one defined for an OracleAS Portal page or portlet) is not sufficient. In these (rare) cases, an application can be coded so that it takes advantage of what is referenced in the Java world as programmatic security. Programmatic security allows developers to take advantage of methods in the HttpServletRequest interface to impose another level of security in their applications. For this example, do not create any security roles but just click Next.

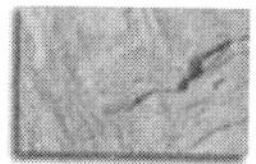

NOTE
To get more information about programmatic security, see the Java Servlet 2.4 Specification, Chapter 13 at http://jcp.org/aboutJava/communityprocess/final/jsr154/index.html.

On the Step 6 of 7: Caching screen (Figure 7-18), you can improve the performance of your portlets by keeping them in memory for a specific period of time.

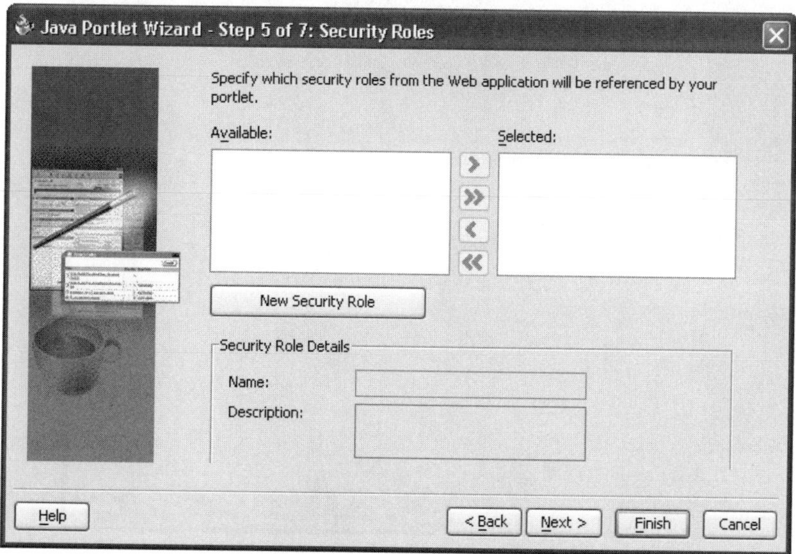

FIGURE 7-17 *Step 5 of the Java Portlet Wizard*

Technically, cached content isn't necessarily stored in memory; depending on the implementation, it can be stored on a hard disk. The point here is that you don't have to regenerate the HTML snippet for the OracleAS Portal portlet if you cache it.

This feature is useful for portlets that do not need up-to-the-second information. A cached portlet is saved in memory the first time it is generated by the OracleAS Portal Page engine. All requests for that portlet after the first time are generated from the saved version in memory up until the expiration time threshold is reached, after which, the portlet is generated from scratch again. For this example, leave Do Not Cache By Default selected and click Next.

On the final step, Step 7 of 7: Initialization Parameters (Figure 7-19), you have the option of defining parameters that can be used to influence the behavior of the portlet. This page differs from the Customization Parameters screen in that initialization parameters can be used to change things like the data returned in the portlet, whereas customizations are used to change (usually) how the portlet is displayed to the end user. For this example, click New and add a parameter with the name **p_emp_no**, a value of **Employee_num**, and a description of **Employee Number**. Click Finish.

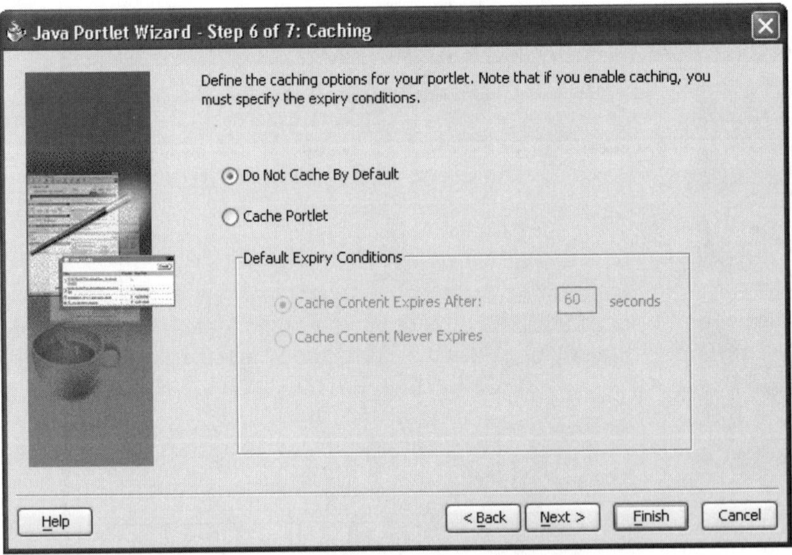

FIGURE 7-18 *Step 6 of the Java Portlet Wizard*

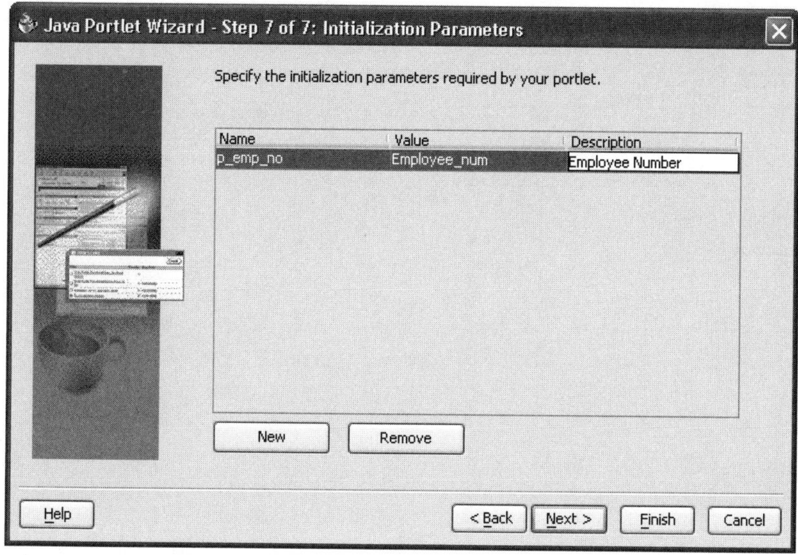

FIGURE 7-19 *Step 7 of the Java Portlet Wizard*

When complete, you'll notice that a number of files have been generated for your project (Figure 7-20), as explained in the following sections.

<Application Workspace>.java

If you generated the Oracle PDK project in the preceding section of this chapter, you'll remember that no .java files were generated at all. This is because, as part of the Oracle Application Server, Oracle has created methods and classes that could be used within .jsp pages to provide portal-specific functionality. The first couple of lines in the EmpPortalShowPage.jsp file (from the preceding section) look like this:

```
<%@page contentType="text/html; charset=windows-1252"
        import="oracle.portal.provider.v2.render.PortletRenderRequest"
        import="oracle.portal.provider.v2.http.HttpCommonConstants"
        import="oracle.portal.provider.v2.ParameterDefinition"
%>
```

For JSR 168–based portlets, however, you can't use Oracle-specific classes and methods, as the whole point of JSR 168–based portlets is the ability to deploy them

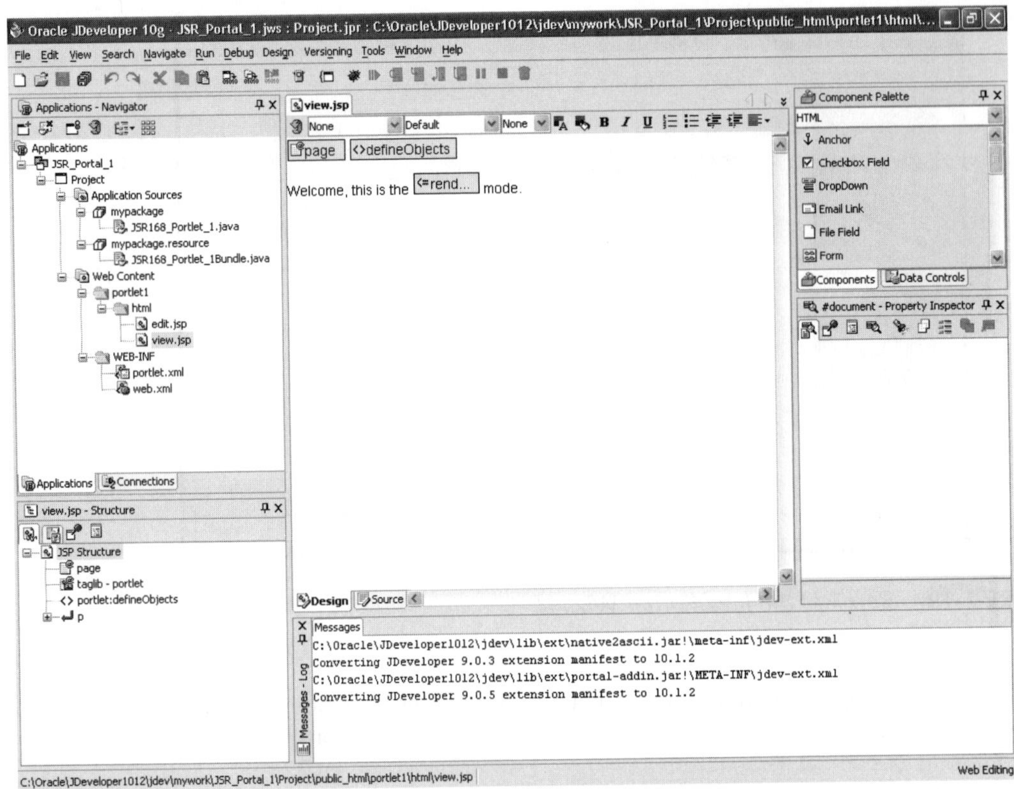

FIGURE 7-20 *Oracle JDeveloper with the Java wizard–generated files displayed*

on any JSR 168–compliant Web server. As such, much of the "plumbing" code for the portlet is found in this Java file (JSR168_Portlet_1.java in this example). The first couple of lines in your generated file should look something like this:

```
package mypackage;

import java.io.IOException;
import java.util.StringTokenizer;
import javax.portlet.*;
import mypackage.resource.JSR168_Portlet_1Bundle;
```

It is the "import javax.portlet.*;" line that imports the JSR 168–specific functionality for the portlet.

<Application workspace>Bundle.java

This .java file (in our example, JSR168_Portlet_1Bundle.java) is known as a *resource bundle* file. Resource bundle files contain locale-specific objects. Developers can use this mechanism to write code that is independent of the user's locale. This way, a program can be easily translated into different languages, handle multiple languages at once, and have new locales added easily at a later date.

edit.jsp

This file corresponds to the portlet in Edit mode, discussed in the section "Step 4: Understand Portlet View Modes" of this chapter. This page will contain anything specified on the Step 4: Customization Preferences page of the Oracle Java Wizard in Oracle JDeveloper. Again, remember that the default, Portlet Title, will have code to modify the title of the portlet generated automatically, but any other parameters you add will require code to make them functional.

view.jsp

This file corresponds to Shared Screen mode, discussed in the section "Step 4: Understand Portlet View Modes" of this chapter, which is where your end users will spend most of their time interacting with your portlet.

portlet.xml

This is a file unique to the JSR 168 specification. portlet.xml contains initialization parameters for the portlet. This file is similar in nature to the provider.xml file for PDK-Java portlets. This file describes the portlets in a given portlet application.

web.xml

The web.xml file is what's known as a deployment descriptor. A *deployment descriptor* describes how components of an application are deployed and assembled into a specific environment. In this case, the components are the files in this section that make up the portlet and the environment is the OracleAS Portal environment running on the Oracle Application Server. The Oracle Application Server uses the web.xml file to understand the components used by the application, environment variables, and security requirements for the application.

In the top left of the Oracle JDeveloper window is an icon that looks like a bunch of floppy disks stacked on one another. This is the Save All icon, which will save all files in your project if they haven't been saved already or if they've been modified. Click that icon now. You now have a fully functioning JSR 168–based portlet that can be deployed to any application server that supports the JSR 168 standard.

Step 8: Add Business Logic

After using the wizard to construct that basic framework of your portal application, you can begin to add business logic to it. As a developer, this is where you will spend most of your time. So as not to bog down the flow of the steps, adding business logic will be covered in the section later in this chapter entitled "Revisiting the Add Business Logic Step."

Step 9: Establish a Connection to an Application Server

Oracle JDeveloper gives developers the ability to deploy directly to an application server without having to build and transport the various files needed for a typical deployment. To establish a connection to the application server, follow these steps:

1. Under Connections, right-click and select New Application Server Connection. Click the Connections tab in the middle left of the screen to display the Connections Navigator. Right-click Application Server and select New Application Server Connection from the drop-down box.
2. Enter a meaningful connection name (I chose Local_AppServer for the examples in this section) and choose Oracle Application Server 10*g* as the connection type. Click Next.

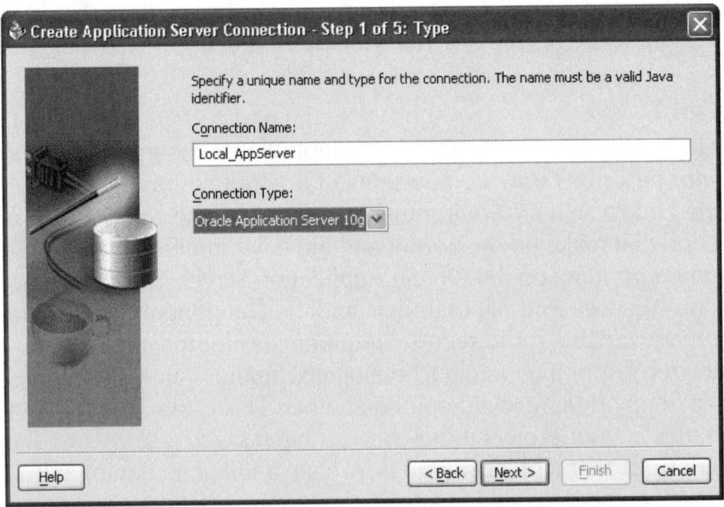

3. Enter the admin user's username (probably ias_admin, unless you or your application server administrator has created another user for administration

duties) and password. Select Deploy Password to not be prompted again for the password. Click Next.

4. Enter the following information:

- **Enterprise Manager OC4J Host Name** Usually, this will be the name of the host where the middle-tier is installed.
- **Enterprise Manager OC4J HTTP Port** This is the port of the mid-tier installation. By default, Oracle tries to use port 1810 and then tries succeeding higher numbers if that port is used. If your infrastructure and mid-tier are installed on the same server, then the infrastructure will default to 1810 and the mid-tier will default to 1811.
- **Remote Server's Oracle Home Directory** This is the home directory where the Oracle mid-tier is installed. Be careful to specify the directory exactly, as it must reflect the operating system the Oracle Application Server mid-tier is running on. For example, if the mid-tier is running on a Microsoft Windows server, the directory might look like this: C:\oracle\mid-tier-home. If the mid-tier is running on a Linux or Unix server, the directory name might look something like this: /u01/oracle/mid-tier. For more information on directory names, see the sidebar called "Naming Conventions for Directories."
- **OC4J Instance Name (optional)** An OC4J container is used to hold deployed applications. These containers have attributes that can be set to influence how the applications deployed to that container look and behave. Every Oracle Application Server mid-tier has an OC4J container called home. If you don't specify an OC4J container, your application will be deployed there. If you have a specific OC4J container you wish to deploy to, specify it here. Click Next.

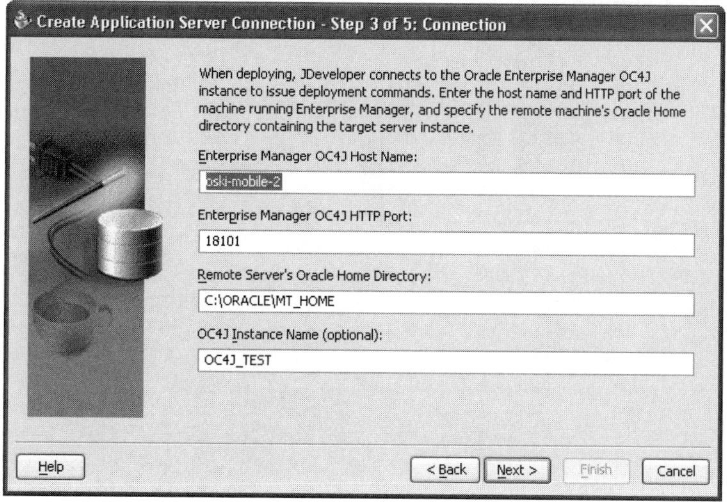

- **RMI Server URL** RMI (the term stands for Remote Method Invocation) is an API that allows objects to be instantiated and used in a distributed application. Enterprise JavaBeans (EJBs) commonly use RMI. The RMI port number may be found in ${OC4J_HOME}/j2ee/home/config/rmi.xml and usually defaults to 23791. To specify this value, use this format: ormi://<server>:<port>. My mid-tier is installed on a server called oski-mobile-2, so my specification looks like this: ormi://oski-mobile-2:23791.
- **RMI Username/Password** Enter a username, such as admin, having RMI login privileges on the OC4J instance within the Oracle Application Server. Since our application does not use EJBs or RMI, don't worry about these for now. Click Next.

5. Test the connection by clicking the Test Connection button on the top of the page.

Naming Conventions for Directories

Under normal circumstances, Microsoft Windows is not case-sensitive regarding directory names. For example, the following is my root directory on my laptop:

```
c:\>dir
 Volume in drive C is System
 Volume Serial Number is 2091-4B19

 Directory of c:\

06/29/2006  12:24 AM                 0 AUTOEXEC.BAT
09/12/2006  01:25 PM    <DIR>          Cakewalk Projects
06/29/2006  12:24 AM                 0 CONFIG.SYS
06/29/2006  12:32 AM    <DIR>          Documents and Settings
10/18/2006  02:52 PM    <DIR>          Downloads
06/29/2006  09:14 AM    <DIR>          Drivers
09/13/2006  10:52 PM    <DIR>          extract
07/13/2006  01:20 PM    <DIR>          JB2Driver
09/16/2006  04:28 PM    <DIR>          Loops
10/19/2006  12:21 PM    <DIR>          MP3s
09/07/2006  09:57 AM    <DIR>          ORACLE
10/19/2006  01:46 PM    <DIR>          Program Files
06/29/2006  12:42 AM    <DIR>          swsetup
10/12/2006  09:56 AM    <DIR>          TEMP
06/29/2006  12:43 AM    <DIR>          W309BF33
10/24/2006  09:31 AM    <DIR>          WINDOWS
08/15/2006  12:24 PM    <DIR>          wmpub
               7 File(s)         26,830 bytes
              16 Dir(s)  26,639,306,752 bytes free
```

If I want to see the contents of my MP3s directory, case-sensitivity doesn't matter. I can see it this way:

```
c:\>dir mp3s
 Volume in drive C is System
 Volume Serial Number is 2091-4B19

 Directory of c:\mp3s

10/19/2006  12:21 PM    <DIR>          .
10/19/2006  12:21 PM    <DIR>          ..
10/14/2006  11:03 PM    <DIR>          Brown James - Star Time 1991
10/14/2006  11:14 PM    <DIR>          CCR
10/03/2006  05:13 PM        97,934,976 dylan - Live 1975.mp3
10/03/2006  06:16 PM        60,237,696 dylan - Modern Times.mp3
10/05/2006  03:16 PM    <DIR>          Hendrix Jimi
10/12/2006  01:13 PM    <DIR>          Petty Tom
02/05/2006  09:02 PM        40,127,893 REM - Document.WMA
02/05/2006  06:50 PM        44,735,389 Rolling Stones - Exile on
Main St..WMA
              10 File(s)  3,133,725,362 bytes
               7 Dir(s)  26,639,306,752 bytes free
```

Or this way:

```
c:\>dir MP3s
 Volume in drive C is System
 Volume Serial Number is 2091-4B19

 Directory of c:\MP3s

10/19/2006  12:21 PM    <DIR>          .
10/19/2006  12:21 PM    <DIR>          ..
10/14/2006  11:03 PM    <DIR>          Brown James - Star Time 1991
10/14/2006  11:14 PM    <DIR>          CCR
10/03/2006  05:13 PM        97,934,976 dylan - Live 1975.mp3
10/03/2006  06:16 PM        60,237,696 dylan - Modern Times.mp3
10/05/2006  03:16 PM    <DIR>          Hendrix Jimi
10/12/2006  01:13 PM    <DIR>          Petty Tom
02/05/2006  09:02 PM        40,127,893 REM - Document.WMA
02/05/2006  06:50 PM        44,735,389 Rolling Stones - Exile on
Main St..WMA
              10 File(s)  3,133,725,362 bytes
               7 Dir(s)  26,639,306,752 bytes free

c:\>
```

But when specifying the Remote Server's Oracle Home directory, you must specify exactly the way the dir command displays the directory on the server. My middle-tier is installed in

```
C:\ORACLE\MT_HOME>
```

So I have to specify this directory all in CAPS at this prompt.

Step 10: Deploy and Register the Portlet

Deployment is a fancy word for packaging and moving your code from your development environment to your server. Since Java and J2EE applications can become rather complex, the deployment of applications has become its own subject. Thankfully, Oracle JDeveloper greatly simplifies the deployment of applications by checking the files in your application for syntactical correctness and by assuring the necessary files are deployed to the correct locations on your server. For this example, we'll take the application created in the section "Building an Oracle PDK-Based Portlet" of this chapter, deploy it, register the provider with the OracleAS Portal repository, and display it on a page. Perform the following steps to ensure a successful deployment of your application:

1. In your project, right-click web.xml and select Create War Deployment Profile. Click OK.
2. In the save deployment profile screen, change the name to something meaningful. Click Next.
3. In the WAR Deployment Profile Properties dialog (Figure 7-21):
   - Click General on the left-hand pane and change the war and ear filenames to something meaningful.
   - Change the Enterprise Application Name to something meaningful.
   - Make sure the Specify J2EE Web Content Root radio button is selected and give the Context Root a meaningful name. Remember this name; we're

going to need it in an upcoming step. For this example, I am calling my J2EE Web Context Root EmpPortlet.

- Select File Groups | WEB-INF/lib | Contributors on the left-hand side. In the Libraries Selected For Deployment section, select Portlet Development. Click OK.

4. Deploy to the Oracle Application Server by right-clicking the deployment profile.

5. Choose Deploy To and select the previously created app server connection (Local_AppServer for this example).

6. Wait for the Deployment Finished message in the log page and verify that there were no error messages.

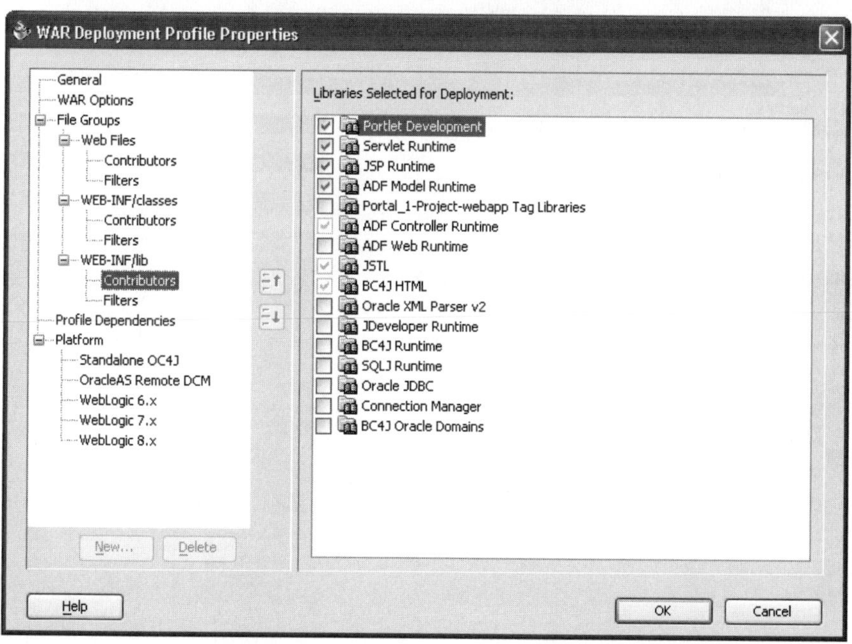

FIGURE 7-21 *The WAR Deployment Profile Properties dialog*

We're almost there. The application has been deployed to the application server, but the OracleAS Portal repository doesn't "know" about it yet. We have to manually register a new provider and tell the repository where to find the new application. This is the step when you tell OracleAS Portal where to look for the remotely running portlet provider. Log in to OracleAS Portal as a user with administration privileges and select the Administer tab. Click the Portlets subtab and click the Register A Provider link in the middle of the page. Give your provider a Name, Display Name, Timeout specification, and Timeout Message and click Next.

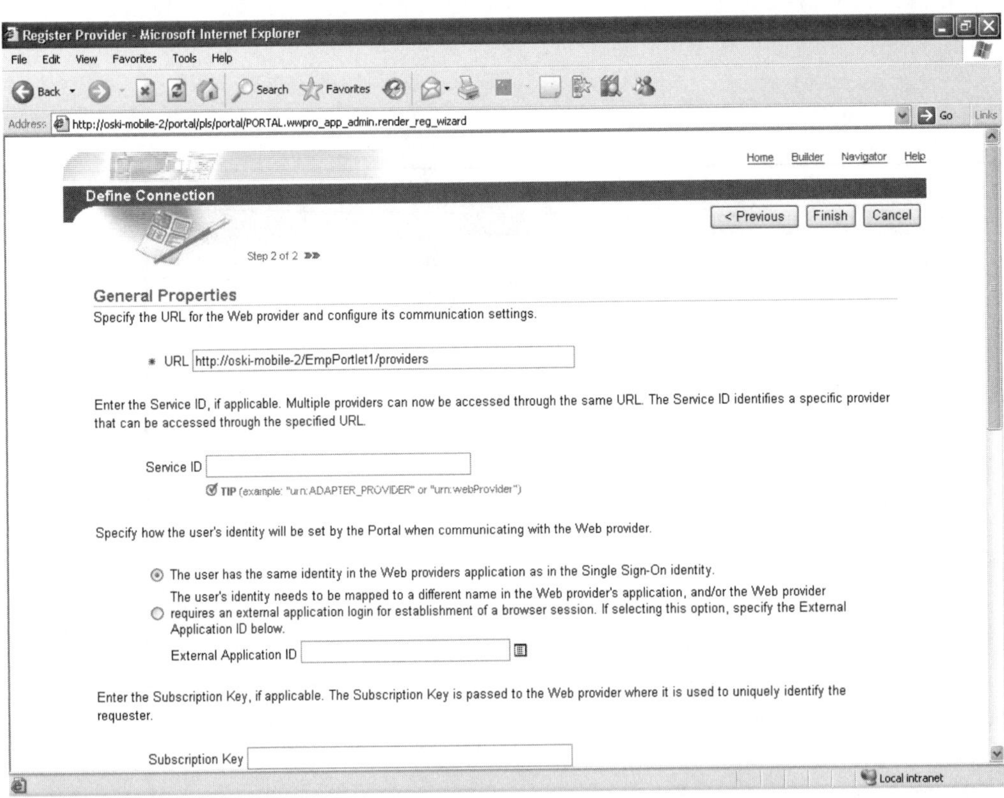

FIGURE 7-22 *Connection information for the new provider*

Remember how I mentioned earlier that you will need to remember the value of the J2EE Context Root you specified in Oracle JDeveloper right before you deployed the application? Here is where we need it. The URL for the General Properties of this portlet has the following format:

```
http://<server name>/<J2EE Context Root>/providers
```

The server I have been using for the examples in this chapter is called oski-mobile-2, and the example context root I used earlier was EmpPortlet. Based on this, my URL looks like this:

```
http://oski-mobile-2/EmpPortlet/providers
```

Leave all other fields on that page as their defaults and click OK (Figure 7-22). If everything was specified correctly, you will see a page similar to Figure 7-23.

Now that the provider is registered, click OK to return to the Portal Builder page. It's now time to place the portlet in the provider we just registered on a page. Click the Navigator link on the top right of the page, and then select the Page Groups tab.

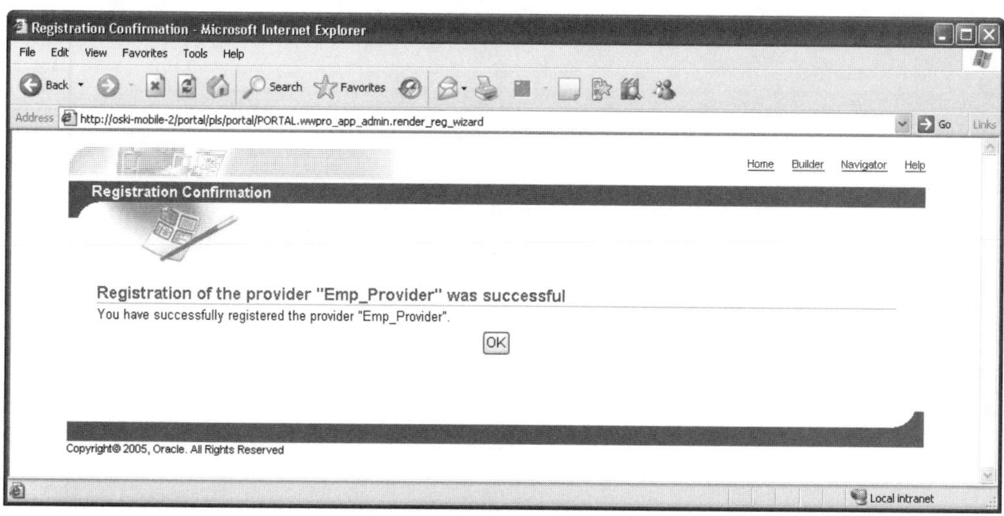

FIGURE 7-23 *Successfully registering the new provider*

Edit a page and click the Add Portlet icon in one of your portlet regions on that page. Click the Portlet Staging Area link; you should now see the new provider name you just registered in the previous step (Figure 7-24). Clicking that provider name will display the portlet you deployed from Oracle JDeveloper. Click that portlet to move it on to the page. Click OK to be returned to the Edit view of the page. Your Oracle JDeveloper portlet should display (Figure 7-25).

The portlet displays with the line "p_employee_no – No values have been submitted yet." Let's change the page to display something there. First, we have to define a page parameter. Click the Page: Properties link in the top left of the page and click the Parameters tab. On the Parameters tab, enter a name of **p_employee_no** in the Parameter Name field in the middle of the page and click Add. In the Portlet Parameter values section at the bottom of the page, click Employee Portlet. Next to Employee Num, select Page Parameter, and then select p_employee_no in the next drop-down box (Figure 7-26). Click OK to accept these parameters.

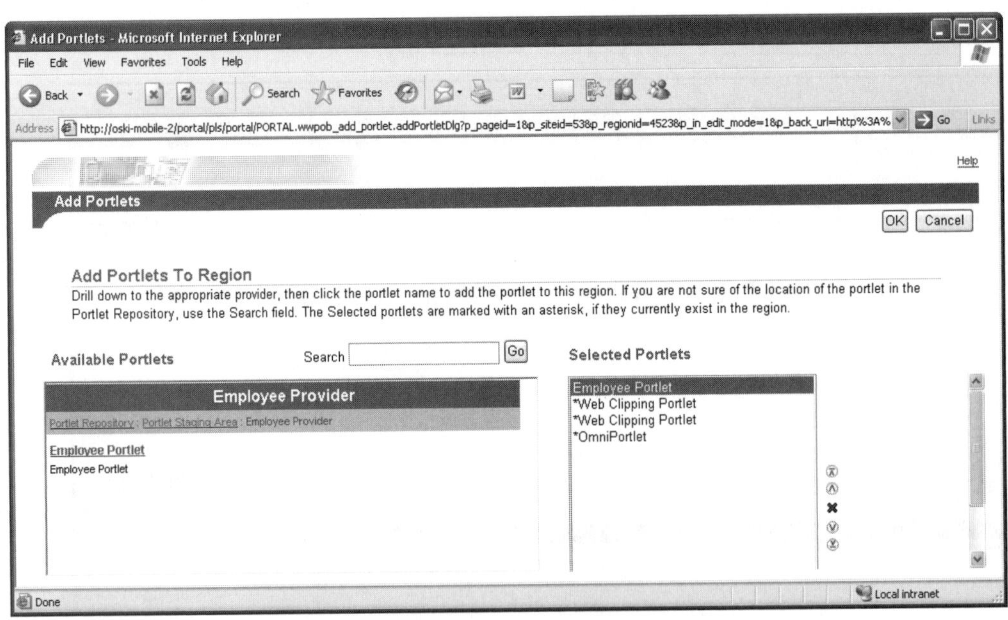

FIGURE 7-24 *Adding the new portlet to a page*

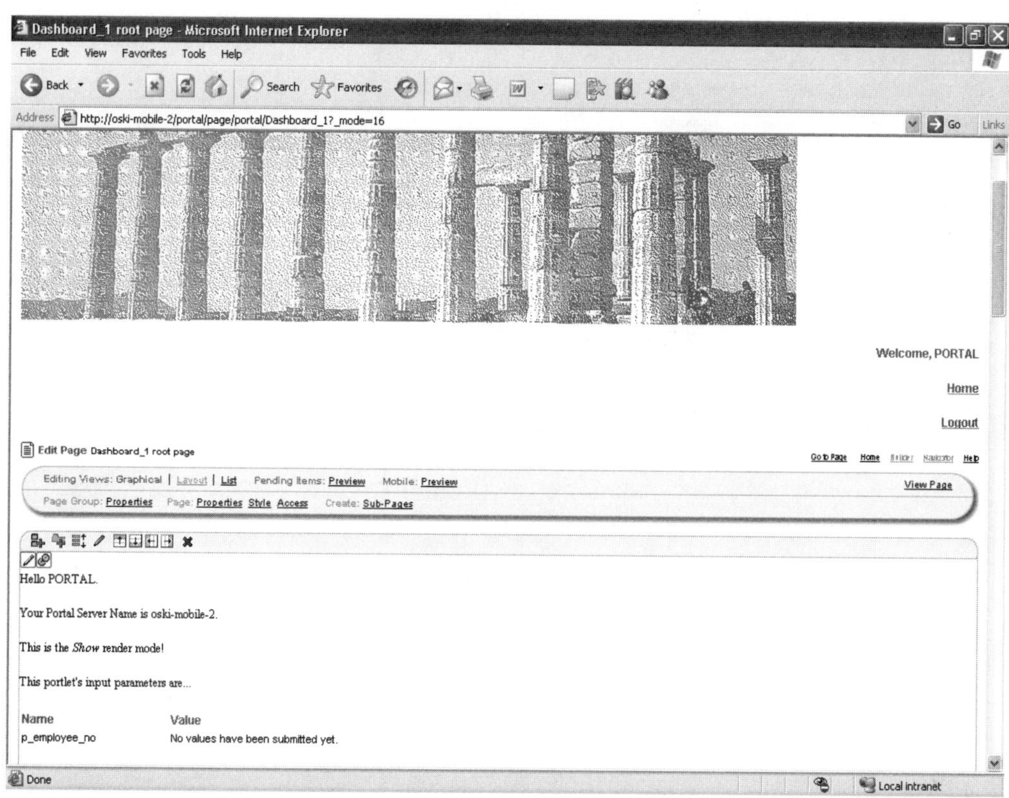

FIGURE 7-25 *The OracleAS Portal page with the JDeveloper portlet displayed*

You are then returned to the edit page. Change the URL in your browser by adding **&p_employee_no=10** to the end of the URL. It should now look something like this:

```
http://oski-mobile-2/portal/page/portal/Dashboard_1?_mode=16&p_employee_no=10
```

The ampersand (&) is used to separate parameters passed to Web applications. In this case, we changed the URL to include a new parameter named p_employee_no,

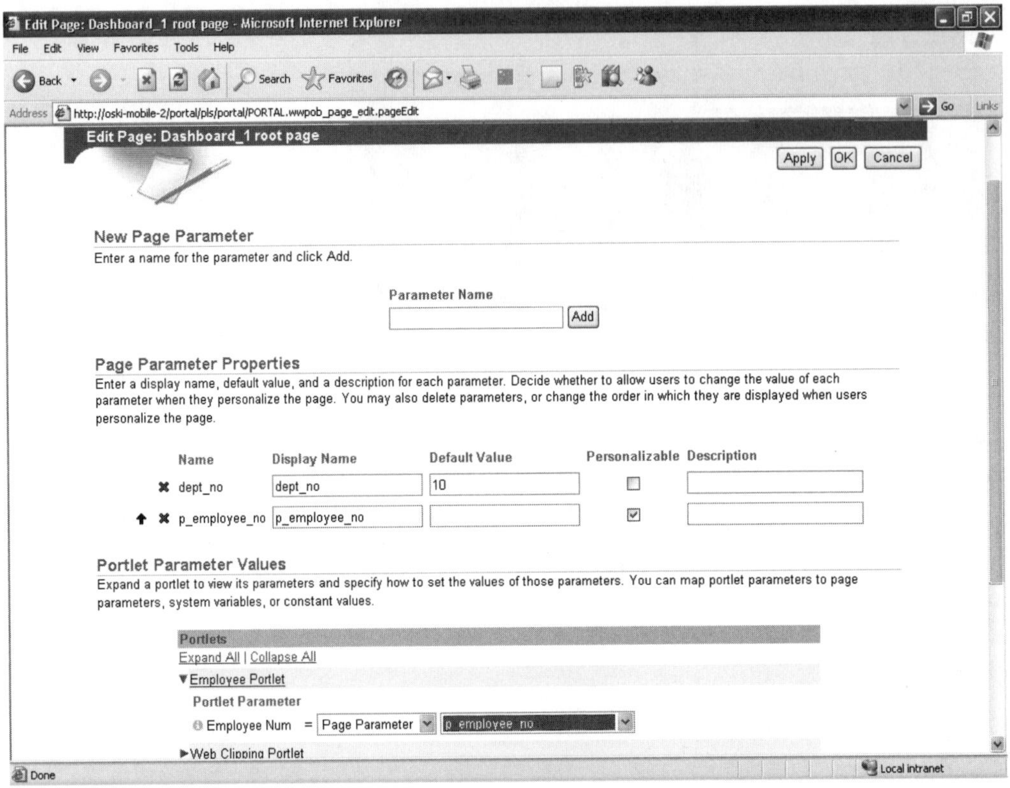

FIGURE 7-26 *Adding a new page parameter*

and we assigned that parameter a value of 10. The Parameter tab that is part of the properties page for this OracleAS Portal page allowed us to map a page parameter to a parameter in one of the portlets on the page. Once that was done, the portlet displays with the correct value (Figure 7-27).

Revisiting the Add Business Logic Step

The portlets we've created in the preceding step work, but they are not terribly functional. Let's add some logic to query information from the database and display it back to the user. For this example, we'll make extensive use of the graphical functionality of Oracle JDeveloper to simplify our development.

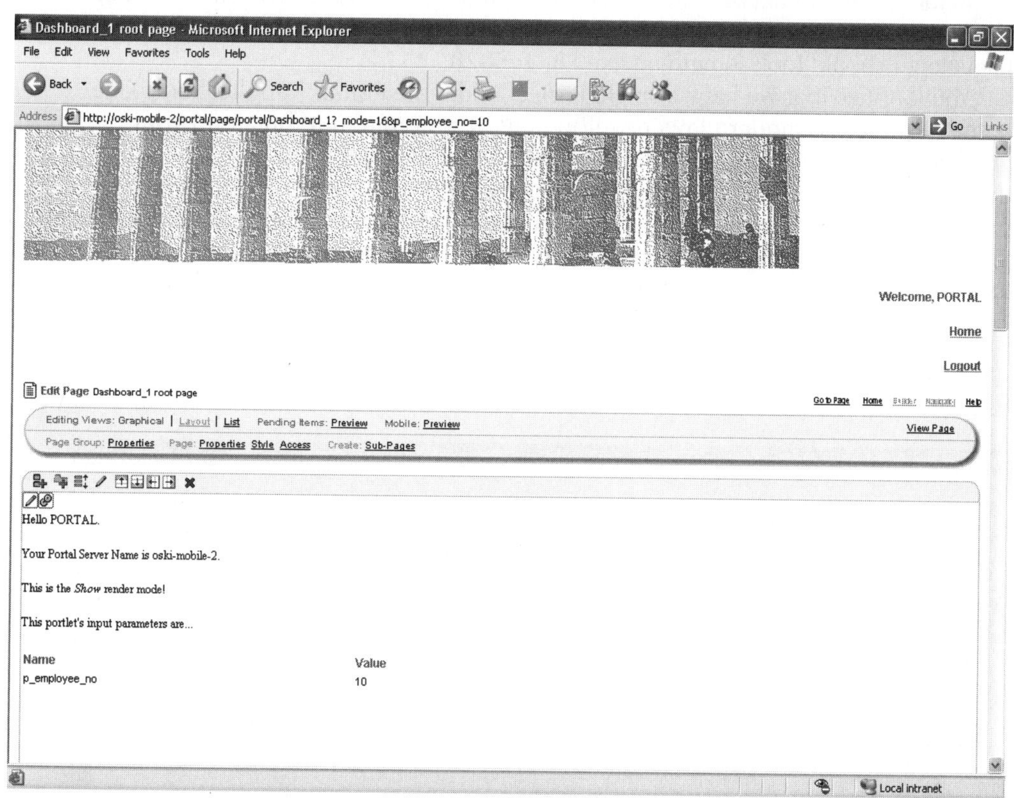

FIGURE 7-27 *Displaying the JDeveloper portlet with a parameter value passed to it*

The Application Developer Framework (ADF)

The Application Developer Framework (ADF) is defined by Oracle like this: "Oracle ADF is a comprehensive productivity layer for J2EE developers. It simplifies building applications as a set of business services with Web, Wireless, and Rich Client interfaces. ADF accelerates development with ready-to-use J2EE Design Pattern implementations and metadata-driven components that you'd otherwise have to code, test, and debug by hand." ADF is used within Oracle JDeveloper to greatly reduce the amount of time developers spend writing database-centric applications.

Return to the portlet built in the section "Building an Oracle PDK-Based Portlet." If you followed the instructions in that section, the Applications Navigator in Oracle JDeveloper should look something like Figure 7-28.

You'll notice that we have a single Project under the Portal_1 application space named Project. In modern Java development, it is common to break up your applications into multiple sections. The most common paradigm used today is a development method called model-view-controller (MVC). Under this method, the code to model the database (model) is separated from the code used to display graphical elements to the user (view), which in turn is separated from the business logic (controller). In Oracle JDeveloper, these sections are usually divided into two projects: one called Model and one called ViewController.

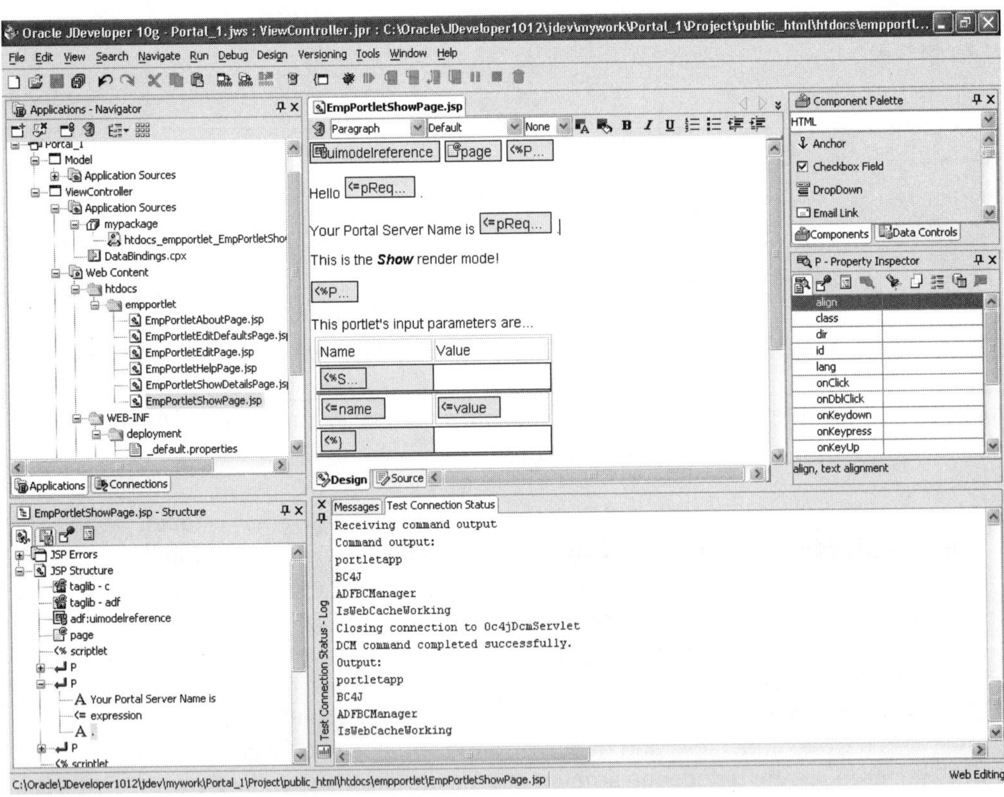

FIGURE 7-28 *Oracle JDeveloper with the PDK portlet loaded*

NOTE
Like everything else related to Java development in general and Oracle JDeveloper development specifically, it doesn't have to be done this way; this is just the most common way of developing complex Web-based applications.

The "Project" project that was generated for us by the Portal Add-in Wizard in Oracle JDeveloper effectively generated the ViewController part of our application. To make things easier, single-click the Project node in the Applications Navigator, and then select File | Rename from the Oracle JDeveloper menu. Rename the Project.jpr file to ViewController.jpr. Click Save. The Applications Navigator will redisplay with ViewController as a node.

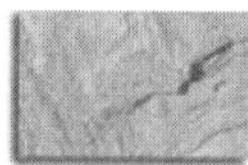

CAUTION
Be careful when doing this. Even though we changed the filename to display ViewController in the Application Navigator, the directory structure of all of the files still points to the Project directory. This is not an issue if you use Oracle JDeveloper to deploy applications as we did in the section "Step 10: Deploy and Register the Portlet" of this chapter, but if, for whatever reason, you need to manually deploy an application, changing this can cause headaches.

We now need a new project that will be used to model the database. Right-click the Portal_1 node and select New Project from the drop-down box. In the New Gallery window, select General | Projects in the Categories pane and select Empty Project in the Items pane. Click OK. Give the project a name of **Model**. With Model selected in the Applications Navigator, right-click and select New. In the Categories pane, select Business Tier | Business Components and in the Items pane, select Business Components Diagram (Figure 7-29). Click OK. Give the business components diagram a name of **EmployeeBCD** and click OK. You are then taken to the Business Components Diagram (BCD) editor. Oracle JDeveloper provides drag-and-drop functionality so that developers can graphically place the components they need from the database on to the BCD. Before we can use this functionality, however, we must establish a connection to the database.

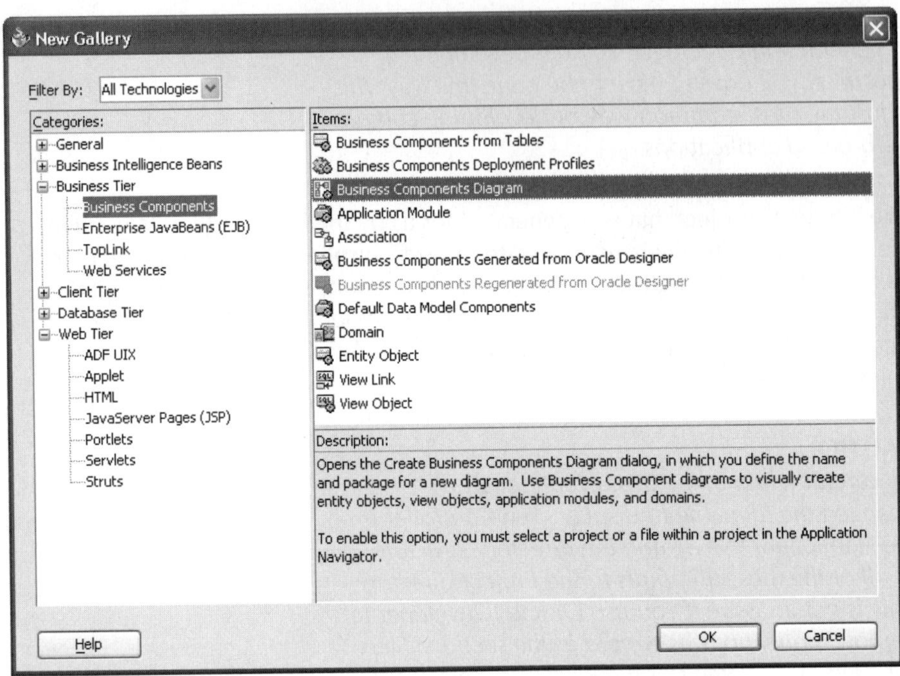

FIGURE 7-29 *Selecting a business components diagram for the JDeveloper project*

Click the Connections tab in the middle left of the screen. Right-click the database node and select New Database Connection. Give the connection a meaningful name and make sure Oracle (JDBC) is selected as the Connection Type. Click Next. Enter a username and password (and optionally a role). For this example, I am going to use the portal_demo schema in the infrastructure database. Click Next. In the Step 3 of 4: Connection page of the wizard, enter the hostname of the application server, the listener port number, and the instance name of the infrastructure database. Click Next. In the final screen, click the Test Connection button. Click Finish.

In the Connections Navigator, click the small plus sign next to the database connection you just created. Click the plus sign next to the PORTAL_DEMO schema, and then click the plus sign next to the Tables node. Click and drag the EMP table on to the EmployeeBCD (Figure 7-30). Make sure Business Component Entity Objects is selected and click OK. By doing this, you have created what is called an *entity object*. From Oracle's documentation: "Entity objects are business components that encapsulate the business model, including data, rules, and persistence behavior, for items that are used in your application. For example, entity objects can represent: elements of the logical structure of the business, such as

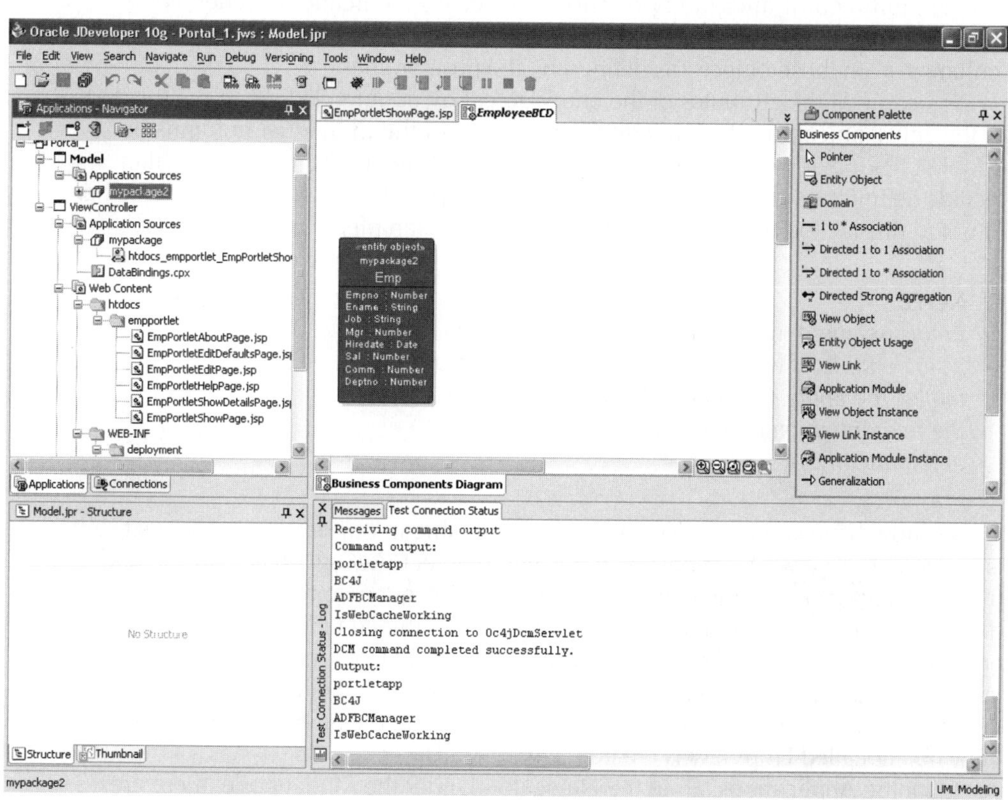

FIGURE 7-30 *The EmployeeBCD business components diagram with the EMP entity object dragged onto it*

product lines, departments, sales, and regions; business documents, such as invoices, change orders, and service requests; physical items, such as warehouses, employees, and equipment. Entity objects map to single objects in the datasource. In the vast majority of cases, these are tables, views, synonyms, or snapshots in a database. Advanced programmers can base entity objects on objects from other datasources, such as spreadsheets, XML files, or flat text files. When entity objects are based on database objects, columns in the database object map to single entity object attribute in the entity object. The definitions of these attributes (reflected in the entity object's XML file) reflect the properties of these columns, including data types, column constraints, and precision and scale specifications. When entity objects are based on objects from other datasources, entity object attributes map to 'columns' from those objects, as defined by the programmer."

You can edit the attributes of the entity object by double-clicking in the header of the entity object, or you can edit the attributes of the individual columns by double-clicking any of the column names. Some of the attributes you can alter include defining validation rules, the methods generated for the entity object, whether or not to display tooltips for the fields, etc. For this example, leave all defaults.

NOTE
In this example, we're only going to query data from a single table. If we were to query data from multiple tables, the Entity Object editor would maintain the referential integrity defined in the database automatically.

We now have an entity object that models a table in our database. The next step is to generate a view object based on this entity object. A *view object* gathers and filters the data stored in the entity object, uses a SQL query to form a collection of data, and can comprise multiple entity objects (e.g., joined tables). Right-click the entity object and select Generate | Default Data Model Components. If the Welcome page appears, click Skip This Page Next Time and click Next. Accept the default values for this view object by clicking Finish on the Step 1 of 2 page. A new view object called EmpView is created (Figure 7-31).

Click the Applications tab in the Navigator. Under the Model node, there are now four files: AppModule, Emp, EmployeeBCD, and EmpView. Click and drag the EmpView view on to the EmployeeBCD. The Emp entity object is inside the EmpView view object (Figure 7-32). This signifies the fact that the EmpView view object is using the Emp entity object as its source. You can edit the attributes of the view object by double-clicking it. Here, you can change the query that is used to pull data from the data source, change tuning attributes, add your own custom properties, etc.

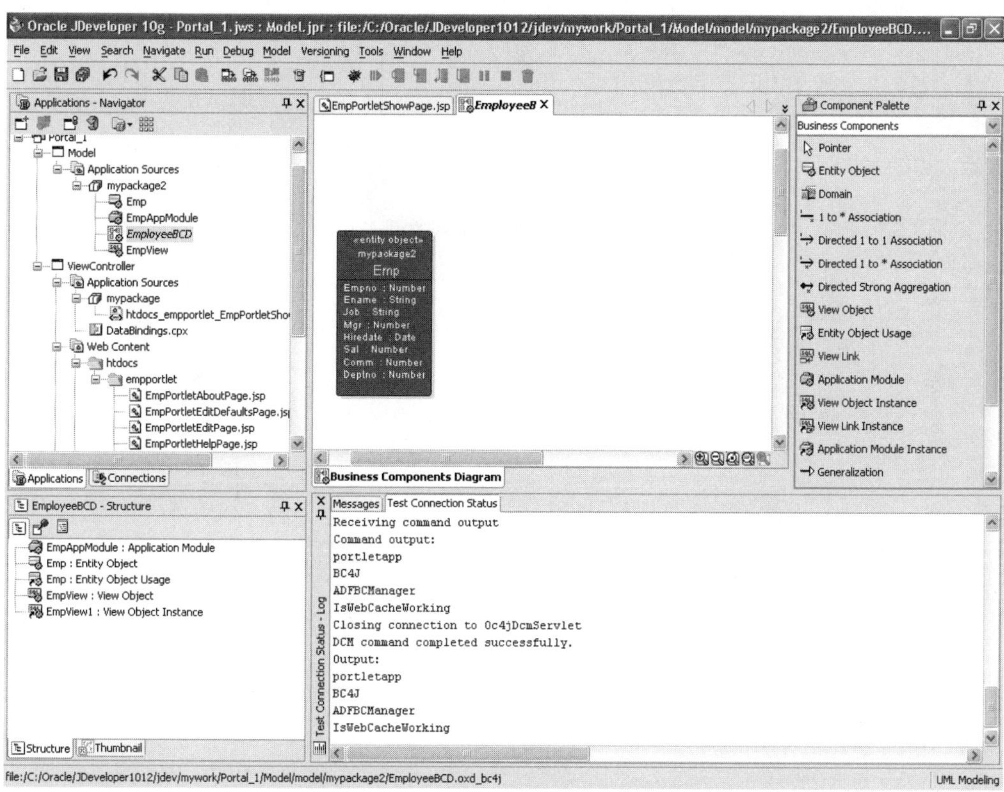

FIGURE 7-31 *The EmpView object created in the Application Navigator*

TIP

Without getting into the gory details of why entity objects and view objects are essential to streamlined Java/Oracle application development, you should understand that the concept of persistence—the ability of data to outlive the process that created it—is extremely important when it comes to Java-based applications accessing relational databases. The Oracle Application Development Framework is doing a tremendous amount of work behind the scenes to make this happen with minimal impact to your development efforts. For more information about ADF and persistence, see the reference materials listed earlier in this chapter.

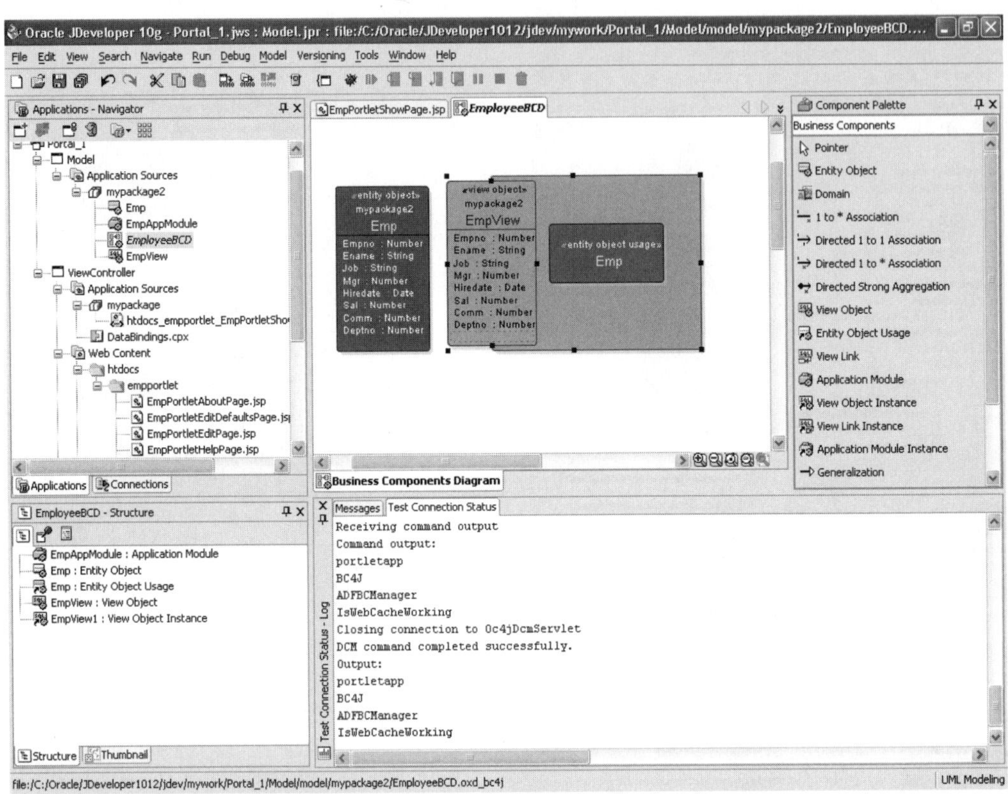

FIGURE 7-32 *The EmployeeBCD business components diagram with the EmpView view object*

Next, we need something called an application module. An *application module* is a service object that coordinates view objects for a specific task (such as a form to display the employee data). On the top right side of the Oracle JDeveloper screen, there is a window called the Component Palette. Make sure Business Components is selected in the drop-down box and drag and drop Application Module on to a blank spot of the EmployeeBCD screen. Give it a meaningful name (in this example, I called it EmpAppModule) and then drag the EmpView view object into the application module (Figure 7-33). Just like the entity object and the view object, you can edit the application module's attributes by double-clicking it.

Normally, this is where you would begin creating the .jsp page to hold your view objects, but the Portal Add-in Wizard for Oracle JDeveloper has done that for us already. Double-click the EmpPortletShowPage.jsp file in the ViewController node of the Application Navigator. If the Design tab is not selected, select it now. In

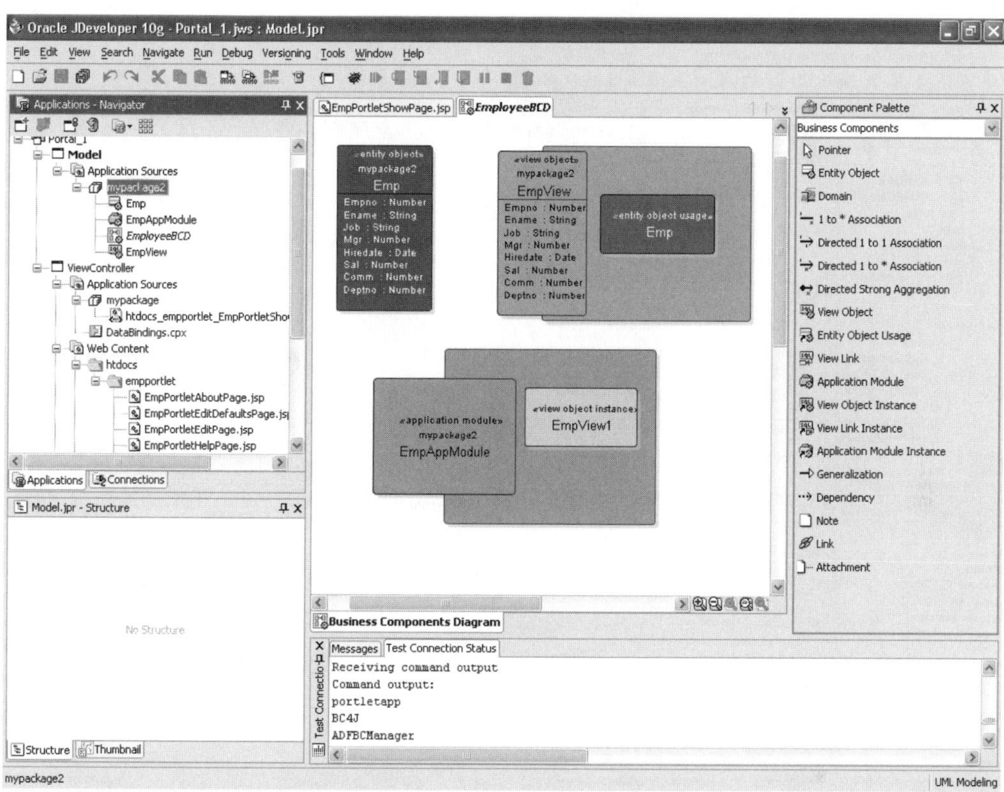

FIGURE 7-33 *The EmpAppModule with the EmpView view object dropped into it*

the top right of the Oracle JDeveloper window is a selection titled Data Control Palette. In that window, there should be a node called EmpAppModuleDataControl (the name is based on what I called the application module in the preceding paragraph). Click the small plus sign to the left of that to expand the objects associated with that data control. Single-click the EmpView1 node. Notice how the Drag And Drop As drop-down box at the bottom of the Data Control Palette gets populated. Leave Read-Only Table selected and drag and drop the EmpView1 View object onto a blank spot of the EmpPortletShowPage.jsp page (Figure 7-34).

Finally, we can add a button that will allow us to scroll through our records. In the Data Control Palette in the top right of the Oracle JDeveloper window, click the small plus sign next to the EmpView1 view object. If you scroll to the bottom of that list, you'll see a folder with another small plus sign next to it called Operations. Click that small plus sign to see a list of buttons you can use.

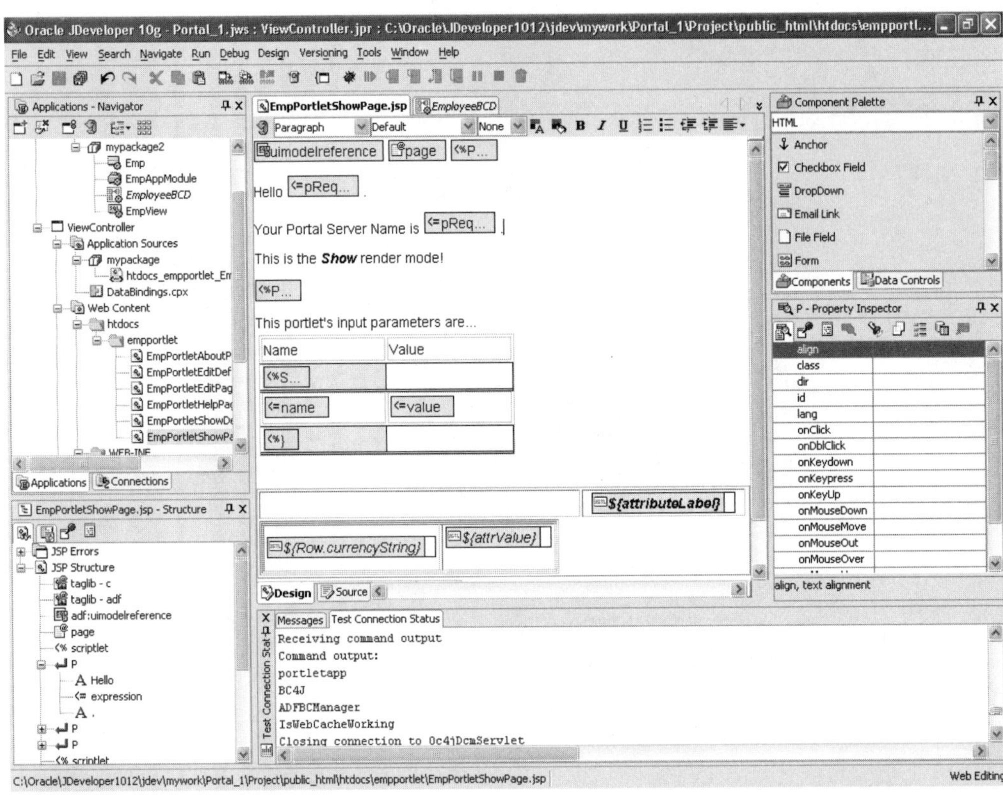

FIGURE 7-34 *The EmpPortletShowPage.jsp page with the EmpView1 view object placed on it*

NOTE

This can be confusing because there's another Operations folder right below that. The second Operations folder only has Commit and Rollback as button options, while the top Operations folder has things like Create, Find, Execute, etc. The top Operations folder (the one with Create, Find, Execute, etc.) is a subset of the EmpView1 view object, while the second Operations folder (the one with only Commit and Rollback) is a subset of the application module.

By default, the portlet will return the first ten rows from the portal_demo.emp table. There are 14 rows in that table. Click and drag the Next button to right below the table that has the records (Figure 7-35).

Deploy your application by right-clicking the EmpPortlet.deploy file and deploying to the application server. Go into OracleAS Portal and re-display the page you placed the portlet on. You should see a page similar to Figure 7-36.

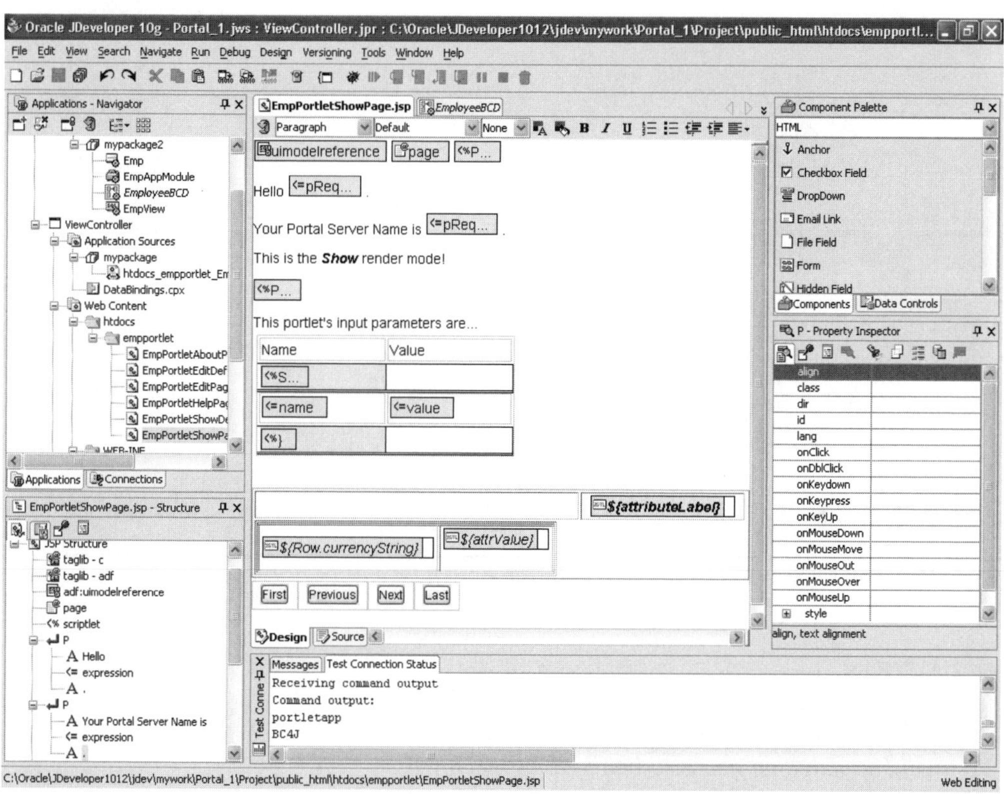

FIGURE 7-35 *Adding the Next button to the EmpPortletShowPage.jsp page*

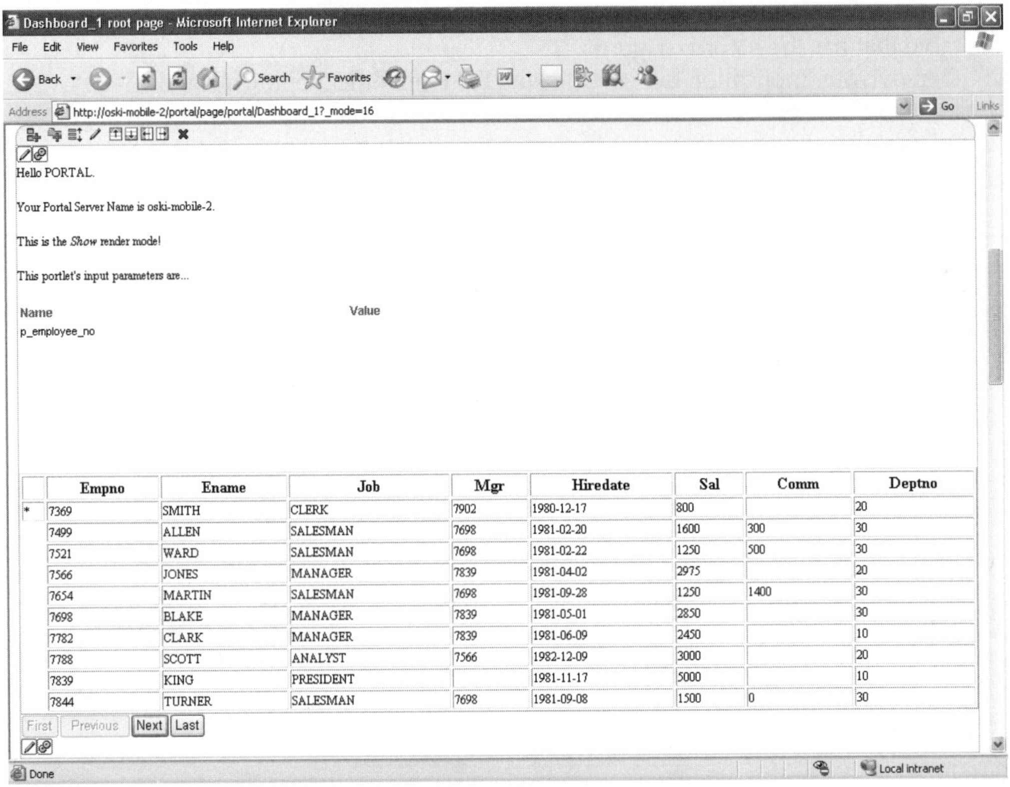

Dashboard_1 root page - Microsoft Internet Explorer

File Edit View Favorites Tools Help

Address http://oski-mobile-2/portal/page/portal/Dashboard_1?_mode=16

Hello PORTAL.

Your Portal Server Name is oski-mobile-2.

This is the *Show* render mode!

This portlet's input parameters are...

Name	Value
p_employee_no	

	Empno	Ename	Job	Mgr	Hiredate	Sal	Comm	Deptno
*	7369	SMITH	CLERK	7902	1980-12-17	800		20
	7499	ALLEN	SALESMAN	7698	1981-02-20	1600	300	30
	7521	WARD	SALESMAN	7698	1981-02-22	1250	500	30
	7566	JONES	MANAGER	7839	1981-04-02	2975		20
	7654	MARTIN	SALESMAN	7698	1981-09-28	1250	1400	30
	7698	BLAKE	MANAGER	7839	1981-05-01	2850		30
	7782	CLARK	MANAGER	7839	1981-06-09	2450		10
	7788	SCOTT	ANALYST	7566	1982-12-09	3000		20
	7839	KING	PRESIDENT		1981-11-17	5000		10
	7844	TURNER	SALESMAN	7698	1981-09-08	1500	0	30

First Previous Next Last

Done Local intranet

FIGURE 7-36 *The OracleAS Portal page with the new JDeveloper portlet placed on it*

CAUTION

*Before you right-click the EmpPortlet.deploy file and attempt to deploy your portlet again, there is a small anomaly that needs to be fixed, especially if you plan on viewing the page using Internet Explorer 6 or 7. Since we have added ADF components, we need entries in the web.xml file to "bind" the ADF components to the various files that use those components. There are filter mappings created in the web.xml file for *.jsp files, but for some reason, Internet Explorer 6 or 7 doesn't seem to pick them up. We can fix this by adding a mapping that tells* *the application server to bind all files to the ADF components. Edit the web.xml file by double-clicking it. There is a section of filter mappings that starts like this:*

```
<filter-mapping>
  <filter-name>ADFBindingFilter</filter-name>
  <url-pattern>*.jsp</url-pattern>
</filter-mapping>
<filter-mapping>
  <filter-name>ADFBindingFilter</filter-name>
  <url-pattern>*.jspx</url-pattern>
</filter-mapping>
<filter-mapping>
```

Right before that, add these lines:

```
<filter-mapping>
  <filter-name>ADFBindingFilter</filter-name>
  <url-pattern>/*</url-pattern>
</filter-mapping>
```

Exercise

Create a Java-based portlet that displays information queried from a database table as a graph. Hint: look at the values presented in the Drag And Drop As drop-down box that's part of the Data Control Palette.

Summary

The declarative development wizards referenced in Chapter 1 are great for developing and deploying simple, database-centric portlets, but the complex business rules in place at most organizations today usually force developers to abandon declarative development pretty quickly. To unleash the full power of OracleAS Portal, developers need to embrace advanced technologies like Java and Oracle JDeveloper.

Oracle is fully aware of the complexity of Web-based application development and the pressures put upon developers. To address this, Oracle provides their Java-based development tool, Oracle JDeveloper, to developers free of charge. While Oracle JDeveloper 10.1.2 does not provide native support for OracleAS Portal development out of the box, a simple add-in can be used to give developers using Oracle JDeveloper an environment that makes portlet development fast and easy. Combined with the Application Development Framework and the Portal Development Kit, Oracle JDeveloper is the premier development environment for sophisticated, production-quality portlets.

In January 2007, Oracle released WebCenter, an upgrade to Oracle JDeveloper. WebCenter has full OracleAS Portlet development capabilities built into it. Steps 1–5 in this chapter do not have to be performed for WebCenter—all other content in this chapter is applicable for using WebCenter to develop and deploy OracleAS and JSR 168-based portlets.

CHAPTER 8

Advanced Development Topics

ou're probably familiar with the phrase "hitting a moving target." The implication, many times, is that whatever you're trying to accomplish is made that much harder because the real world keeps intruding. Modern Web development provides a double-whammy: not only is the target moving, but the tools that developers use to hit the moving target are themselves changing and evolving. Imagine using a bow and arrow to hit a target that keeps moving and every time you shoot an arrow, somebody comes along and gives you a new bow to use—this is what most Web developers face today.

OracleAS Portal is not a closed system. The developers and architects who created OracleAS Portal were smart enough to design it in such a way that it can integrate with new technologies relatively easily. By doing this, they have ensured that organizations who invest their resources in OracleAS Portal development do not have to worry about obsolescence. OracleAS Portal fully embraces Java and Java-based standards that allow developers to integrate these new technologies into their portal development efforts easily. One of the most popular new technologies is called Service-Oriented Architecture (SOA). This chapter discusses how SOA and OracleAS Portal complement each other.

This chapter does not provide a detailed explanation of the technologies that compose SOA—there are entire books devoted to each of these subjects. Rather, this chapter focuses on how Oracle has provided ways for OracleAS Portal to take advantage of these technologies to make your end-user experience more fulfilling.

Service-Oriented Architecture

It's almost impossible to pick up a computer magazine or development book that doesn't have some reference to service-oriented architecture. SOA means a lot of different things to different people (type define:SOA on Google), but for our purposes, we are concerned with Oracle's vision of SOA and, more specifically, Oracle's vision of how OracleAS Portal makes SOA accessible for developers and end users.

Portals were born from the simple desire to provide a one-stop destination for information in an enterprise. That information could come from production databases, data warehouses, legacy applications, business intelligence tools, ERP systems—the list goes on and on. In addition to this, portals provide end users with functionality unique to the portal experience: the ability to customize the data and the way the data is displayed. Traditional reporting tools limit data presentation, but with a portal, an end user can customize virtually all aspects of the data and the way the data is presented (within reasonable limits, of course).

Another benefit of portals is the ability to present a visually consistent interface to end users. This may sound trivial, but its importance should not be underestimated—many otherwise great applications have fallen into disuse because of a poor user interface. Not only do portals provide a visually consistent environment for elements defined within the portal itself (portlets and content), but they can provide a visually consistent interface to external applications. By using these technologies, developers and page designers using OracleAS Portal can integrate external, Web-based applications into OracleAS Portal. This technique provides three benefits:

- **Visual consistency between applications** OracleAS Portal handles all of the page design and display functions.
- **A single point of security** OracleAS Portal's Single-Sign On (SSO) technology allows administrators to grant access to external applications through OracleAS Portal, so end users do not have to log in multiple times to access multiple applications.
- **SOA-like benefits** One of the core benefits of investing in SOA technologies is the ability for end users to remain productive even if a server (or set of servers) goes down for any reason. OracleAS Portal's integration feature allows end users to continue interacting with Portal to do their job even if one of the external applications goes down.

NOTE
It's important to note that the last of these three points uses the term "SOA-like." Developing portlets and placing them on pages as discussed throughout this book is not a "true" SOA environment. OracleAS Portal does, however, provide many of the benefits of an SOA environment without any specialized coding.

From a developer's point of view, portlets provide additional benefits. All portal systems come with predefined (seeded) portlets that can be used right out of the box. Many times, much of the functionality required can be satisfied using these seeded portlets. Another benefit includes the reduction in development time. Many portal products contain code-generating wizards that can be used to construct a significant part of the portlet (if not all of it). Also, since most portals are integrated with their respective application servers, deploying portlets is usually a trivial task. This fact makes prototyping easy and shortens the feedback loop between developers and end users, leading to applications better tailored toward end users' needs.

As portals began to grow in popularity, a disturbing trend began to emerge, however: that of the specialized portal. Many organizations, in their haste to implement this new technology, did not coordinate goals among levels and departments within their organization. The result was a hodgepodge of specialized portals within the organization, resulting in portal infrastructures that had high costs of ownership, redundant services, little or no reuse, and a myopic, departmental focus. In short, these departmental, specialized portals became exactly the opposite of what the original idea of portals promised.

Goals of an SOA Application

Ask a CIO or CTO what the goals of an SOA application are and you'll probably get many answers. All SOA projects, however, share several fundamental goals:

- Better visibility (auditing, reporting) for predicting change
- Ability to easily change the process
- Incremental rollout of new and updated applications
- Improved productivity
- Compression of total processing time (real time)
- Greater connectivity to systems, services, and people
- Improved ability to predict and respond to change
- Enhanced organizational productivity
- A simplified information technology environment
- Leverage of existing investments
- Immediate value to users
- Cure for information overload through a single, highly intuitive, and interactive user experience
- Significant business and IT benefits, such as making aggregated information available to users who require specific data to do their jobs
- Personalization of information for increased productivity and better decision making
- Leverage of existing assets/investments in guided business processes
- Improved communication and collaborations

- Improved customer service and supplier relations
- A single secure point to aggregate and deliver services
- The #1 expected benefit: Seamless plug and play of different technology providers and/or custom legacy code

OracleAS Portal: The Face of SOA

Oracle, in its marketing materials, refers to OracleAS Portal as "the face of SOA." What, exactly, is meant by that? By embracing some of the advanced topics discussed in this chapter, Oracle has shifted OracleAS Portal's focus from creating portals that were "information-centric" to ones that are "application-centric." To state it more simply, Oracle now markets OracleAS Portal less as a development tool to create applications that access data and display it to end users (information-centric) and more of a tool that can be used to integrate various applications in an environment that provides security, visual consistency, scalability, and reliability (application-centric). Obviously, information and the access to information are what development tools and applications are all about, so information is still very much at the heart of all things Portal, but as organizations shift from dedicated applications to those that can be served up as services, OracleAS Portal provides an excellent "face" on which to build your Web-centric services.

What does OracleAS Portal provide for those organizations wishing to implement an SOA environment?

- **A unified technology stack with complete application-level services** OracleAS Portal provides a sophisticated page engine, security model, caching (both through OracleAS Portal and the Web Cache components of the Oracle Application Server), page design tools, and the ability to integrate with external applications.
- **Common portal services for single sign-on, personalization, search, management, and more** OracleAS Portal is a mature portal environment that provides all of the advanced features that end users, administrators, and developers expect from a modern portal environment.
- **Support for interoperability standards** The WSRP standard and the JSR-168 specification are supported.
- **WSRP** Web Services for Remote Portlets (WSRP) is a standard for Web Portals to access and display portlets that are hosted on a remote server. WSRP is a communication protocol between portal servers and portlet containers. Combined with Java Portlet Services (a specification that defines a set of APIs to enable interoperability between portlets and portals,

addressing the areas of aggregation, personalization, presentation, and security), these standards enable developers to integrate their applications from any internal or external source as portlets with WSRP portals. Building portal pages becomes as simple as selecting portlets from the OracleAS Portal repository.

- **JSR-168** JSR-168 is a Java Community Process (JCP) Java Specification Request (JSR). This specification defines how portlets are created for any Java Web Portal. Developers can use a tool like Oracle JDeveloper to create a JSR-168-based portlet, and then deploy that portlet to any JSR-168-compliant Application Server.
- **Portal services preconfigured for common use cases** These include decision dashboards, business processes, collaboration, publishing, application integration, and more.

Portals will lead the charge by virtue of their ability to offer the preceding features, not to mention these further advantages:

- **Improved ability to predict and respond to change** You can bring key services from Oracle SOA Suite to provide better visibility into your business. Portals also offer integrated and automated processes that can be monitored and optimized as conditions change, along with a service-oriented environment that allows you to quickly implement and deploy new capabilities to eliminate inefficiencies and improve productivity.
- **Increased productivity** By gaining easy access to a variety of useful business content such as industry news, research reports, financial information, and other information, employees can be more productive. Content is accessible from users' desktops via the portal, and individual users or business units can customize an onscreen dashboard to get the exact information they need in support of their job roles.
- **Improved communications and collaboration** The numerous communication channels available with a portal, including a calendaring system, dynamic banners, and scrolling headlines, enable better communications and more collaboration among employees, customers, and business partners.
- **Tailored information and services** Managers can tailor information and services to the needs of particular user communities.
- **Improved customer service and supplier relations** Customer service representatives can handle all customer communications, regardless of where the communications are generated. Organizations can better

coordinate with suppliers and other business partners, who can use portals to access current accounts and invoices, view product delivery information, order parts, or schedule deliveries.

- **Better decision-making** By accessing up-to-date information that's critical to the business, such as demand forecasts and market trends, managers are able to make more informed decisions quickly. Managers can also view executive dashboards with up-to-date business intelligence from across the organization.
- **Leverage of existing investments** These composite applications present information following the step-by-step logic of the process, which reduces confusion and mitigates the chance of the process breaking. All of this is integrated along with services, such as content management or identity management, of the underlying portal platform.
- **Access to relevant performance metrics** You can collaborate and take actions via interaction with business processes.
- **A standards-based framework** This provides for integrating heterogeneous applications and technology environments.

In short: SOA provides flexibility in the back end: component management, security, and business rules, as well as policies, events, alerts, and monitoring administration. OracleAS Portal gives you the assembly and presentation technologies to implement SOA-based solutions.

OracleAS Portal and SOA: The Challenges

Even with this new focus, there are still challenges to overcome, dealing mainly with flexibility and speed:

- The use of portlets and the portlet model can be constraining—there is still a need for greater flexibility.
- Web Services can be implemented a multitude of different ways, and the portlet style of Web Services is not always the most efficient or appropriate.
- Portlet standards are limited in scope and adoption—while standards like Web Services for Remote Portlets (WSRP) and JSR-168 provide a foundation for portlet integration and interoperability, there are still significant gaps in these standards.
- Portals offer limited integration capabilities but must provide performance gains.

- Integration is primarily visual. Today, most portals provide a way of integrating external applications visually by incorporating them as portlets. There is a demand in many organizations for portlets and portals to interact directly with these external applications.
- Communication is largely point-to-point (application to portal) and synchronous. Greater interaction with external applications (including advanced features like asynchronous transactional capabilities) is needed for modern Web-based application development.
- Complex business processes require extensive custom programming. Not only is that code hard to develop, implement, and maintain, but many organizations duplicate development efforts by having similar logic in disparate applications.

SOA and What It Addresses

Service-oriented architecture addresses the need for both flexibility and speed. SOA provides standards-based, course-grained services. When designing the processes that will deliver the applications services, the designer needs to consider the appropriate granularity of the process. Fine-grained services are business functions that require a lot of communication, and each service is designed to do a small part of the work. Consumers of fine-grained services are required to make many service calls to accomplish the desired business function. Course-grained services are business functions that require very little communication, each service being designed to do a relatively large amount of work. Consumers of course-grained services are required to make minimal service calls to accomplish the desired functionality.

SOA also provides loosely coupled composite applications. "Loosely coupled" describes a resilient relationship between two or more computer systems that are exchanging data. Loosely coupled systems are considered useful when either the source or the destination computer system is subject to frequent changes. A composite application is an application built by combining multiple services. A composite application consists of functionality drawn from several different sources within a service-oriented architecture. The components may be individual Web services, selected functions from within other applications, or entire systems whose outputs have been packaged as Web services (often legacy systems).

At the very core of SOA is a concept that is similar to OracleAS Portal: components and services must be separated and independent of the applications that consume them. In addition to this, all SOA systems, like OracleAS Portal, must be easily modified and adaptable to changing business conditions and opportunities. Without these fundamental attributes, SOA systems would be too complex to be of any significant use.

SOA offers a comprehensive life cycle for management of information and applications:

- **An integrated service environment (ISE) to develop services** An ISE provides the following:
- **Service abstraction** Also referred to as service interface–level abstraction, this is a principle that encourages developers to establish services as "black boxes," intentionally hiding their underlying details from potential consumers. By limiting what is made public about a service to what is documented in the service contract, a high degree of separation can be achieved between what becomes private (hidden) and public (consumable). This is desirable because it supports the loosely coupled relationship.
- **Business process modeling** Business process modeling is the activity of representing both the current and future processes of an enterprise, so that the current process may be analyzed and improved. BPM is typically performed by business analysts and managers who are seeking to improve process efficiency and quality. The process improvements identified by BPM may or may not require IT involvement, although that is a common driver for the need to model a business process.
- **A development environment** For Oracle-based SOA environments, Oracle JDeveloper provides numerous tools that allow developers to implement and integrate SOA technologies (using a product like the Oracle SOA Suite) quickly and easily.
- **A productivity layer/framework** Oracle has been working diligently to add functionality to the Application Developer Framework (ADF). The ADF is a mature framework that allows developers to create sophisticated applications easily.

NOTE
In the Oracle Application Development Framework Developer's Guide for Forms/4GL Developers 10g Release 3 (10.1.3.0) (available at http://download-west.oracle.com/docs/html/B25947_01/toc.htm), Chapter 33, "Working with Web Services," contains an excellent section titled "Publishing Application Modules as Web Services."

- **Rapid application maintenance** Oracle JDeveloper provides the most comprehensive development environment for developing and deploying applications and application services for SOA environments.
- **A multiprotocol enterprise service bus (ESB) to integrate applications** An enterprise service bus (ESB) refers to a software architecture construct, implemented by technologies found in a category of middleware infrastructure products usually based on standards, that provides foundational services for more complex architectures via an event-driven and standards-based messaging engine (the bus). An ESB generally provides an abstraction layer on top of an implementation of an enterprise messaging system, which allows integration architects to exploit the value of messaging without writing code. Contrary to the more classical enterprise application integration (EAI) approach of a monolithic stack in a hub-and-spoke architecture, the foundation of an enterprise service bus is built of base functions broken up into their constituent parts, with distributed deployment where needed, working in harmony as necessary. ESB does not implement a service-oriented architecture (SOA) but provides the features with which one may be implemented. Contrary to common belief, ESB is not necessarily Web-services based. ESB should be standards-based and flexible, supporting many transport mediums. Based on EAI rather than SOA patterns, it tries to remove the coupling between the service called and the transport medium.
- **A services registry for discovering and managing the lifecycle of services** All SOA software products rely on an underlying UDDI Registry as a core repository and system of record for service data. UDDI is an acronym for Universal Description, Discovery, and Integration, a platform-independent, XML-based registry for businesses worldwide to list themselves on the Internet. UDDI is an open industry initiative enabling businesses to publish service listings and discover each other and define how the services or software applications interact over the Internet. A UDDI business registration consists of three components: 1) White Pages—address, contact, and known identifiers, 2) Yellow Pages—industrial categorizations based on standard taxonomies, and 3) Green Pages—technical information about services exposed by the business. UDDI is one of the core Web Services standards. It is designed to be interrogated by SOAP messages and to provide access to Web Services Description Language documents describing the protocol bindings and message formats required to interact with the Web services listed in its directory.

- **A BPEL-based orchestration engine to tie services into business processes** Business Process Execution Language is a business process modeling language that is executable. It is serialized in XML and aims to enable programming by large groups of people (or smaller groups over longer time periods). "Programming in the large" generally refers to the high-level state transition interactions of a process—BPEL refers to this concept as an Abstract Process. A BPEL Abstract Process represents a set of publicly observable behaviors in a standardized fashion. An Abstract Process includes information such as when to wait for messages, when to send messages, when to compensate for failed transactions, etc. Programming in the small, in contrast, deals with short-lived programmatic behavior, often executed as a single transaction and involving access to local logic and resources such as files, databases, etc. BPEL's development came out of the notion that programming in the large and programming in the small required different types of languages.
- **A business rules engine to enable business policies to be captured and automated** A business rules engine is a software system that helps manage and automate business rules. The rules a business follows may come from legal regulation, company policy, or other sources. The rules engine software, among other functions, may help to register, classify, and manage all these rules; verify consistency of formal rules, infer some rules based on other rules, and relate some of these rules to information technology applications that are affected or need to enforce one or more of the rules. Rules can also be used to detect interesting business situations automatically. For any IT application, the business rules change more frequently than the rest of the application code. Rules engines or inference engines are the pluggable software components that separate the business rules from the application code. This allows the business users to modify the rules frequently without the need of IT intervention and hence allows the applications to be more adaptable with the dynamic rules. In previous-generation applications, data was meant to be dynamic and was supposed to be operated upon by the logic and rules to get the desired results. Data dynamics are no longer the only need of the hour, but the focus has been shifted to the dynamic rules.
- **Web Services management and security solutions** These are to enforce authentication and authorization policies on services and to monitor services and processes for compliance to SLAs.

> **Service Level Agreements**
> A service level agreement (SLA) is a formal negotiated agreement between two parties. It is a contract that exists between customers and their service provider, or between service providers. It transcripts the common understanding about services, priorities, responsibilities, guarantees, etc. It then specifies the levels of availability, serviceability, performance, operation, or other attributes of the service such as billing. An SLA is more business oriented and easier to understand. Its technical specifications are commonly described through either an SLS (service level specification) or an SLO (service level objective). An SLS is a technical interpretation of an SLA. It is therefore intended as an operational guideline for the implementation of the service. An SLO is a subset of an SLS, which contains some service parameters for the goals to be achieved by the SLS.

- **Business Activity Monitoring (BAM) solutions** These provide real-time visibility into business entities and their interactions, and enable services to be optimized.

OracleAS Portal and SOA share many common characteristics:

- Clear separation of services from consuming applications
- Capability to accommodate heterogeneous IT environments
- Centrality of Web Services standards

The Back End: SOA

On the back end, or the technologies that are not exposed to the end user, SOA works in conjunction with OracleAS Portal by providing the "plumbing" behind the scenes:

- OracleAS Portal defines and implements how services are enabled, secured, orchestrated, managed, optimized, etc.
- OracleAS Portal provides a complete, layered architecture.

- OracleAS Portal provides process and message orientation (as opposed to functional/object orientation).

The Front End: OracleAS Portal

On the front end, or the technologies that are exposed to the end user, OracleAS Portal provides these benefits:

- OracleAS Portal consumes and assembles services for use by end users.
- OracleAS Portal provides a message/notification process.
- Process-driven composite applications are easily exposed via OracleAS Portal.
- OracleAS Portal brings the power of SOA to line-of-business users.

Key Components: Portal/SOA Solutions

Numerous OracleAS Portal technologies make the implementation of SOA-based application easier:

- Single interface, multiple uses
- Portals bring reusability and loose coupling principles of SOA to the UI level
- Complementary services
- An easy-to-use, yet fairly robust, environment for deploying service-oriented applications
- End-user customization and profile-based personalization
- Interportlet communication and workflow for basic composite application assembly
- Presentation-layer integration
- OmniPortlet (see Chapter 6)
- Web Clipping (see Chapter 6)
- Browse/Section/Clip a Web Page
- Publish as a Portlet

- A wizard-driven tool to capture and "portletize" content from existing Web sites
- Fuzzy Logic for improved fault tolerance
- Access to secure Web content using authentication/HTTPS
- Capability to manage and publish content (see Chapter 5)
- Self-service content management and publishing
- Windows desktop integration: Oracle Drive and WebDav
- Extensibility via APIs and Content Management Event Framework (CMEF)
- Portal standards

Oracle JDeveloper (see Chapter 7) provides a way for developers to create portlets that take advantage of SOA capabilities easily. Some of Oracle JDeveloper's SOA/Portal features include

- The ability to generate J2EE code automatically (JPDK or JSR168)
- Built-in support for SAP, PeopleSoft, and JD Edwards
- Extensibility to other systems through reusable patterns
- Use of interportlet communication to assemble composite applications with parameters and events
- The ability to generate JSR-168 portlets
- The ability to deploy to Oracle's Java Portlet Container
- The ability to automatically expose generated portlets to remote portals through WSRP
- The Oracle JDeveloper Java Portlet Wizard: build, deploy, and run a portlet on a portal page in three minutes
- Compatibility with WSRP 1.0 and 2.0
- Management of producers through EM

The Oracle SOA Suite in conjunction with Oracle's Business Intelligence Suite provides these SOA features:

- Below-the-glass integration: BI, BPEL, BAM
- Oracle's Business Intelligence tools, Oracle Reports, and Oracle Discoverer, which provide sophisticated reporting environments for organizations desiring both canned and ad hoc reporting capabilities for their end users. Both Oracle Reports and Oracle Discoverer can be integrated easily into OracleAS Portal (see Chapter 11). With OracleAS Discoverer, developers can
- Create context-driven dashboards using the Worksheet Portlet and parameters
- Drill down into Discoverer Viewer
- Analyze both relational and OLAP data
- Take advantage of intuitive, in-place analysis capabilities
- Personalize their dashboards with parameters

In January 2007, Oracle released a new product called Oracle WebCenter Suite. WebCenter Suite provides a wide range of new capabilities and Web 2.0 services targeted at the J2EE developer seeking to develop dynamic and context-rich user experiences. Using WebCenter capabilities, developers can build and deploy JavaServer Faces (JSF) applications that consume portlets or build and deploy portlets that can be consumed by Oracle Portal. Key developer-oriented features of Oracle WebCenter Suite include

- A framework that augments JSF by providing components for binding portlets and content and for customizing the application at run time
- Components that are directly integrated into the design-time experience and implemented as an extension to Oracle JDeveloper
- A complete set of embeddable Web 2.0 content, search, collaboration, and communication services
- Support of key portlet and content integration standards, including JSR-168, JSR-170, and WSRP 2.0

Oracle's SOA Suite provides architects with all of the tools they need to implement SOA/OracleAS Portal applications:

- A comprehensive native BPEL implementation
- An easy-to-use modeling tool
- Rich management and monitoring
- A declarative mechanism to achieve service integration below the UI
- Human touch points exposed through the Portal
- Dashboard views for real-time and historical process monitoring
- Real-time activity monitoring
- Capability to monitor business processes in real time
- Capability to provide heterogeneous information access
- Capability to correlate KPIs to business processes
- Capability to change processes to adapt to business environment changes
- Root-cause analysis
- Business process monitoring
- Event-based alerting

Where Do I Start?

It is essential to understand that SOA impacts every aspect of business and IT within your organization. Without an organization-wide commitment to bringing these technologies to implementation, it is bound to fail. Having said that, it is recommended to implement a phased approach:

- **Identify your key business areas first.** Be careful; there may not be agreement on this topic. Don't let a disagreement at this phase derail the entire project.
- **Identify key business objectives and define success.** Defining success can often be the most challenging phase of the project. Be careful not to set goals too high or too low.

- **Look to improve business processes in key areas.** "Process" is the key word here. Often, the simple act of defining and measuring a key process within an organization improves it organically.
- **Implement an incremental and measured approach.** "Measured" is the key word in this point. Without a concrete measuring system, your SOA efforts may never be implemented.
- **Define and prioritize your problem domain.** The process of identifying and defining potential bottlenecks in your organization is often the key element in the success or failure of an SOA project.
- **Consider ramp-up time during implementation.** Since SOA affects all aspects of an organization, the shift needed to reap the benefits often takes time.
- **Understand technology and multiple back-end systems.** SOA will integrate data and processes from multiple, disparate systems. Understanding these systems and how they integrate is essential to SOA success.
- **Adhere to standards.** This usually requires some extra effort from both management and developers, but it is well worth it in the long run.
- **Understand existing business processes and services, or create new business processes and services.** If business processes are not fully defined (or not defined at all), now is the time to do it.
- **Consider extending beyond the organization's boundaries.** Consider including customers, partners, suppliers, content, and services.

So how should one build a portal solution that takes advantage of the benefits of Portal and SOA? Oracle's Middleware products and technology, including Oracle Application Server and Oracle SOA Suite, are designed and architected for this very purpose. In Oracle's view of an SOA platform (and this is a key fact to note) OracleAS Portal is an integral component. How services provide interaction with a user is done via OracleAS Portal.

Summary

A portal can be used for information sharing, collaboration, and operations and is designed to be the single source of interaction with corporate information and the focal point for conducting day-to-day business. Service-oriented architecture (SOA) offers greater business agility and reduced IT costs when compared to the Web and client/server architecture. OracleAS Portal, coupled with supporting Oracle Middleware components, can be used to deliver SOA-based solutions that join up business processes. Specifically, you can build a portal interface and portlets that surface business processes orchestrated through Oracle BPEL Process Manager within the context of a single business identity into an Oracle Portal page. This is achieved by an out-of-the-box BPEL worklist portlet that exposes BPEL processes and sample BPEL portlets that allow you to develop custom UIs to support business processes. A portal can be a logical and appropriate first step toward SOA implementation because

- OracleAS Portal lends itself to SOA approaches by its fundamental nature.
- OracleAS Portal delivers immediate value to users.
- OracleAS Portal can be used to create compelling interfaces using Oracle Portals as touch points to your business processes.

Portals are the face of SOA and provide the following benefits and tools upon which to build your application-centric services:

- Provides a unified delivery vehicle for all end-user services
- Is customizable
- Is available anywhere
- Connects people, information, and processes
- Delivers a seamless user experience
- Hides complexity
- Provides context
- Empowers knowledge workers with information and productivity tools

Oracle Resources

The following are two excellent Oracle resources:

- "Oracle Application Server Portal 10*g* Release 2 (10.1.4) – Customized Portlets with BPEL" (Oracle Technical Note, http://www.oracle.com/technology/products/ias/portal/pdf/portal_10gr2_bpel_customized_portlets.pdf)
- "Oracle SOA Suite and Enterprise Portals – Enhance Employee Productivity with Process-Centric Portals" (Oracle White Paper, http://www.oracle.com/technology/products/ias/portal/pdf/oracle_soa_suite_portals.pdf)

PART IV

Administration

CHAPTER 9

Site Administration and Performance Tuning

ut of the box, OracleAS Portal does not require any administration. If you wanted to, you could run OracleAS Portal with all of its default settings and have a perfectly usable portal environment for your developers and end users. But that's like saying you could install an Oracle database, not perform any administration on it, and start using it. Technically, it is possible to do this, but it wouldn't be very smart.

There are certain OracleAS Portal settings you will want to alter to tailor your portal to specific needs. OracleAS Portal provides numerous settings that allow administrators to change things like the main page users see when they type in the portal's URL in their browser, the amount of content users can upload to the portal repository, if users can create their own personalized pages, etc. There is also the concept of performance tuning, which will inevitably rear its ugly head as your portal grows and greater numbers of end users access it. Also, you will be presented with errors in your portal every now and then. It is important that you know where to look when you begin to resolve these errors.

Along with these responsibilities, an OracleAS Portal administrator is sometimes also tasked with the creation and administration of new users and groups. User/group administration and OracleAS Portal security features are discussed in Chapter 10. This chapter will discuss the basic OracleAS Portal administration and performance monitoring duties every OracleAS Portal administrator should be familiar with.

In order to follow along with the examples in this chapter, you will need to log in to your portal as a user with administration privileges. You can tell if the user you have logged in as has administration privileges by the existence of the Administer tab on the Portal Builder screen after you have logged in. If that tab is not there, have your OracleAS Portal administrator grant you administration privileges. There are numerous ways to do this; for more information see Chapter 10.

What Is Administration?

OracleAS Portal administration is the process by which tasks are performed that affect the OracleAS Portal environment. Usually, there is a member of the organization that is dedicated to this task. Sometimes, that person is also tasked with setting up users and maintaining security, but sometimes, especially when the portal is big and has a large number of users, there is a separate person dedicated to this task.

As we have seen is previous chapters, most things you can do in OracleAS Portal (create pages, add content, etc.) are performed within OracleAS Portal itself via a Web browser. Administration of OracleAS Portal is no different. Most administration duties can be performed while logged in to OracleAS Portal as a user with administration privileges. Log in to your OracleAS Portal now and click on the Administer tab on the top right of the screen (Figure 9-1).

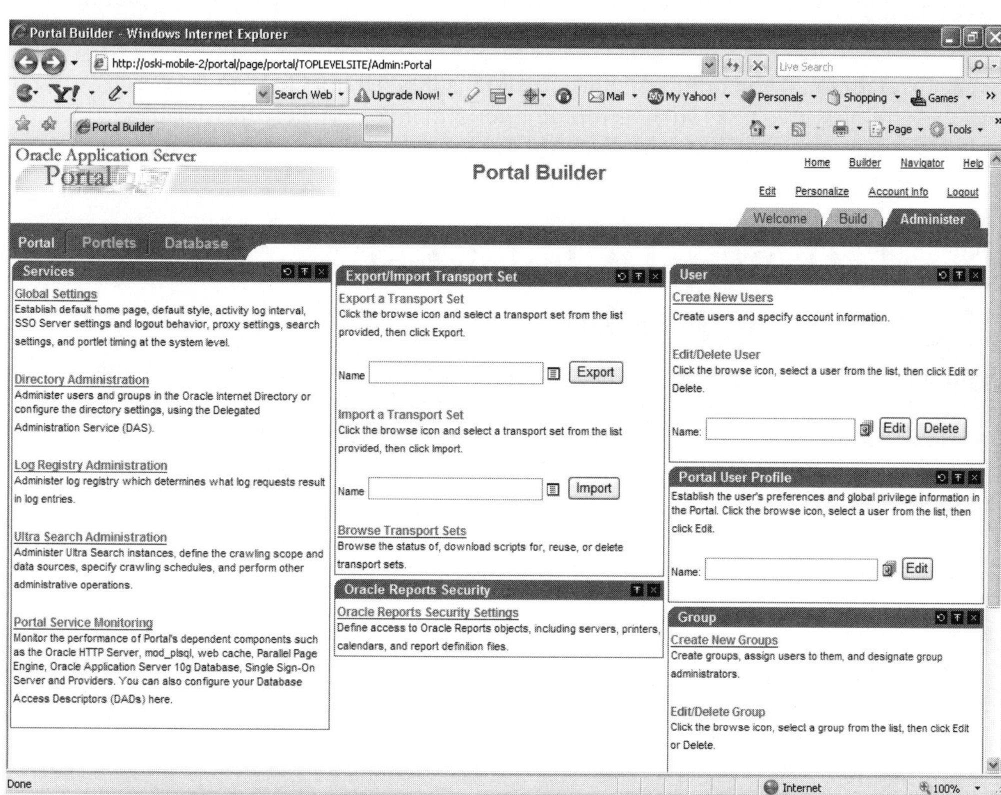

FIGURE 9-1 *The Administration tab of the OracleAS Portal Builder with the Portal subtab displayed*

There are three subtabs in the top left of the screen:

- **Portal** The portlets on this subtab allow administrators to alter settings that affect the entire portal. From here you can alter what page is displayed when users first connect to your portal, change log file settings, import or export parts of your portal, and administer users and groups. The four portlets on the right side of the Portal subpage (User, Portal User Profile, Group and Portal Group Profile) will be discussed in Chapter 10.
- **Portlets** The portlets on this subtab allow administrators to view and refresh the portlet repository and register or modify providers and provider groups. Back in Chapter 7, in the section "Step 10: Deploy and Register the

Portlet," we registered a provider after creating and deploying one as part of the portlets developed with Oracle JDeveloper in that chapter.

- **Database** The portlets on this tab allow administrators to perform basic administrative tasks such as monitor performance and view the database configuration on the infrastructure instance that is part of the Oracle Application Server installation.

OracleAS Portal Administration: The Services Portlet

In the top left of the Portal subtab, there is a portlet titled Services. The links in this portlet allow administrators to change some of the basics settings of how OracleAS Portal behaves. The first link, Global Settings, takes you to a page (Figure 9-2) that allows administrators to change basic settings for your portal. Along the top, there are seven tabs:

- Main
- Configuration
- SSO/OID
- Cache
- Mobile
- Proxy
- Search

Main

This tab has the following sections:

- **Default Home Page** This is page users see when they enter the URL of your portal site. By default the Portal Builder page is the first page users see. When you are ready to turn your portal site over to end users, you will want to change the default page.
- **Default Style** Styles, discussed in Chapter 3, define visual attributes of your pages and the things placed on them, such as portlets, items, and tabs. Any style you create as part of the Shared Objects section under Page Groups in the Portal Navigator will show up in this list.

- **Personal Pages** Selecting this option will automatically create a personal page when new users are created on the system. A personal page is a page that an end user, with no development privileges, can use to create a personalized page with content or portlets that have been made public. See the section "Personal Pages" later in this chapter for more information.
- **Portal File Quota** This section allows administrators to set a limit on the amount of content stored in the portal and the maximum file size of a piece of content that can be added to a page.
- **Self-Registration Options** This section allows administrators to set up a mechanism where users can self-register themselves. Similar to the method described in the section "Getting Content Approved" in Chapter 5, an Approval Routing List can be set up that requires approval from a user or set of users before a self-registering end user gets access to the portal site. See the section "Self-Registration" later in this chapter for more information.
- **E-Mail (SMTP) Host** Self-registered users can be notified when they have been approved. If you wish to notify users via e-mail and have access to an SMTP server, you can enter that information here.
- **Error Page** OracleAS Portal provides a standard error page to display to users when an unanticipated event happens. If you wish to create your own error message page, you can do so within OracleAS Portal and reference it here.
- **Version Information** Although there is nothing you can set here, this section is very important. If, for whatever reason, you need to deal with Oracle Support regarding an OracleAS Portal issue, one of the first questions they will ask you is what version you are running. Here is where you find that exact information.

Configuration

This tab has the following sections:

- **Default JPDK Instance** This defines the location of the SOAP router information for the default Java Portal Development Kit instance for your portal. There is almost no reason to ever change this setting.
- **Provider Offline Message** If, for whatever reason, a provider should go offline, you can specify what message is to be displayed to the end user here. Providers are also called producers under the WSRP standard.
- **URL Connection Timeout** This field defines how long the OracleAS Portal Engine should continue to attempt to contact a site before giving up. This

field does not apply to providers; edit the provider itself to specify the provider timeout.

- **Activity Log Interval** This field specifies how long OracleAS Portal will maintain log information in its tables. OracleAS Portal uses two tables to store log entries and switches between them according to the value specified here.
- **Temporary Directory** Certain operations within OracleAS Portal require temporary files to be created. You can specify which directory on your server these files are to be placed here.
- **Cookie Domain** The cookie domain specifies the scope of the OracleAS Portal session cookie. The default, if no value is specified, is the hostname of the listener that generated the cookie response.

SSO/OID

This tab has the following sections:

- **SSO Server Settings** This section specifies how OracleAS Portal identifies itself to the server running Oracle's Web-security product, Oracle Internet Directory. Unless you are changing the architecture of how your Application server is installed, you should never have to change these values.
- **Oracle Internet Directory Settings** When using the portlets on the Portal subtab of the Administration tab to create new users and groups, entries are created in Oracle Internet Directory for those new users and groups. Oracle Internet Directory is an implementation of an industry standard called LDAP (Lightweight Directory Access Protocol). LDAP uses a tree structure to store information about users. This section allows you to change the default settings for how the trees are constructed when creating new users and groups.
- **Cache for OID Parameters** There are pages created automatically for creating and modifying users and groups. If you need to change those for whatever reason, the cache that stores information about those pages needs to be refreshed. You can do this by selecting the Refresh Cache For OID Parameters check box and clicking OK.
- **Directory Synchronization** When a user or group is modified, the OracleAS Portal engine needs to be notified. This section specifies if the OracleAS Portal engine is notified automatically and the interval of when the messages are sent. There is almost never any reason to turn this off.

Cache

The OracleAS Web Cache is a piece of the Oracle Application Server. The OracleAS Web Cache is designed to reduce response time by caching frequently requested pages. The OracleAS Web Cache has sophisticated logic built into it that allows the caching engine to cache parts of Web pages. This allows the caching engine to cache certain parts of pages and dynamically build other parts of pages, resulting in faster response times. This tab contains two sections:

- **Web Cache Invalidation Settings** This specifies where invalidation settings are sent to. Unless you are changing the architecture of your Oracle Application Server installation, you will never have to touch this setting.
- **Clear Web Cache** If, for whatever reason, you wish to clear the Web cache, you can do so in this section. You can also clear all Web cache entries for a specific user. This option is generally only used in diagnostic and testing scenarios.

Mobile

This tab contains options for users who wish to access your portal using a mobile device.

Proxy

A proxy server is used to connect outside of a firewall. A firewall is a hardware or software solution that has filters that can deny unauthorized or potentially dangerous material from entering the system. If your organization makes use of these, you can specify a proxy server on this tab.

Search

This tab contains the following sections:

- Search Results Page
- Advanced Search Link
- Search Properties
- Internet Search Engine
- Oracle Text Properties
- Oracle Text Based URL
- Enterprise Search Engine Settings

Search Results Pages

By default, two results pages come installed as part of your OracleAS Portal installation: the Basic Search Results page and the Search Results page. If you want to replace these pages with your own, create the results pages and specify them here. When end users use the Basic Search or Advanced Search portlets, the results will be displayed in the page you specify here.

Advanced Search Link

An Advanced Search link is displayed on all Basic Search portlets as follows: "For a more specific search, use 'Advanced Search.'" When end users click the Advanced Search link on the Basic Search portlet, they are redirected to the Advanced Search Page automatically. If you want end users to be redirected to a different search page, or to a URL (like http://www.google.com/), specify that value here.

Search Properties

This specifies the number of results returned per page for a search.

Internet Search Engine

An Internet search engine link can be displayed on all Advanced Search portlets. You can specify a special link for searching the Internet by entering values here.

Oracle Text Properties

Back in Chapter 5 we discussed content and content management features. Content (like text files or Microsoft Word documents) is converted into things the database can understand (in technical terms, a Binary Large Object, or BLOB) and is stored in the database. Oracle Text adds powerful text search and intelligence text management to the Oracle database, in this case the infrastructure database of Oracle Application Server. OracleAS Portal uses the Oracle Text functionality to extend its search capabilities. There are two check boxes in this section:

- **Enable Oracle Text Searching** Thisenables Oracle Text. All text-type attributes are included in the search, and in addition the following content is indexed:
- **Files** files in binary format can be indexed provided the file format is filterable by Oracle Text.
- **Web pages that URLs (in URL attributes) point to** The content must be plain text or HTML.

- **Enable Themes and Gists** Select this check box to display additional information for items (documents/files) when they are returned in search results:
- **View major themes in a chart** A theme shows the nouns and verbs that occur most frequently.
- **View a short summary about the content (gist)** Gists are derived from how frequently those nouns and verbs appear.

Oracle Text Base URL

Oracle Text needs a base URL to resolve relative URLs into fully qualified absolute URLs when building the Oracle Text index. If no value is specified, the relative URLs are not indexed and, therefore, any URL content that the relative URL points to cannot be searched.

Enterprise Search Engine Settings

Use these options to control whether portal content can be indexed by Enterprise Search Engines (ESEs). In the future, other enterprise search engines, such as Oracle Secure Enterprise Search, will be able to search secure portal content. When this technology becomes available, more documentation will be published on Oracle's Technology Network site, http://www.oracle.com/technolgy/products/ias/portal/documentation.html.

The next link in the Services portlet on the Portal subtab of the Administration page is titled Directory Administration. Clicking that link takes you to a page that looks a little different than the OracleAS Portal pages we've been working with in this book (Figure 9-2).

The Oracle Identity Management Self-Service Console page is outside of OracleAS Portal. You'll notice that the URL for the page usually takes you to a different server (if the infrastructure and mid-tier installation of your Oracle Application Server are on different machines) or to a different port on the same server (if the infrastructure and mid-tier installations are on the same server). We are now in the infrastructure part of the Oracle Application Server where all security information is stored. Depending on your privileges, you may see up to four tabs along the top right of the screen:

- **Home** This is a Welcome page that describes the types of things you can do in the Self-Service console.
- **My Profile** To see information about yourself, click this tab. In Chapter 10 we will explore the creation and modification of users, groups, and user and group attributes.

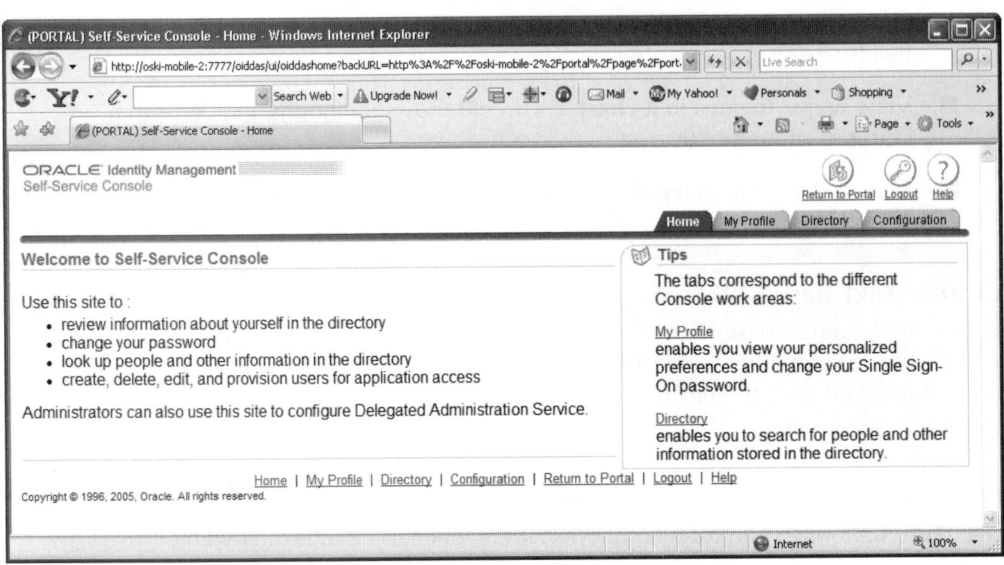

FIGURE 9-2 *The Self-Service Console*

- **Directory** This tab allows you to edit information about any user or group in the system. You can also create users and groups by selecting the appropriate subtab and clicking Create.
- **Configuration** This tab allows administrators to change the basic settings of the tree that Oracle Internet Directory uses to store user and group information. In most cases, you will never have to alter these values.

Click the Return to Portal link on the top right of the page to exit the Self-Service Console.

NOTE
Technically, the URL discussed in the first paragraph of this section may also use the same port as the portal, as it is possible in some scenarios to set up your DAS in the mid-tier Oracle home.

The next link, Log Registry Information (Figure 9-3), allows administrators to define how much information is written to the OracleAS Portal log files. By default, a Log Registry Record with every option (Domain, Sub-Domain, Name, etc.) is enabled for all entries. If, for whatever reason, you don't want that much information written to the log file, you can click the small pencil icon under the Edit heading and change the values to limit what is written to the log files. Be careful when using this option, however, as limiting options can make it harder to track down errors.

CAUTION
With the introduction of OracleAS Web Cache into the OracleAS Portal architecture, some actions logged in OracleAS Portal Activity Log tables have become inaccurate. These actions include View, Execute (for Reports, Charts, and Hierarchies), and Show. The Activity Log tables and views still remain in the OracleAS Metadata Repository, as all other logged actions remain accurate. There are a number of database views you can use to view information in these log tables—see section 7.4 of the Portal Configuration guide (http://download-east.oracle.com/docs/cd/B14099_19/portal.1014/b19305/cg_monit.htm#sthref1274).

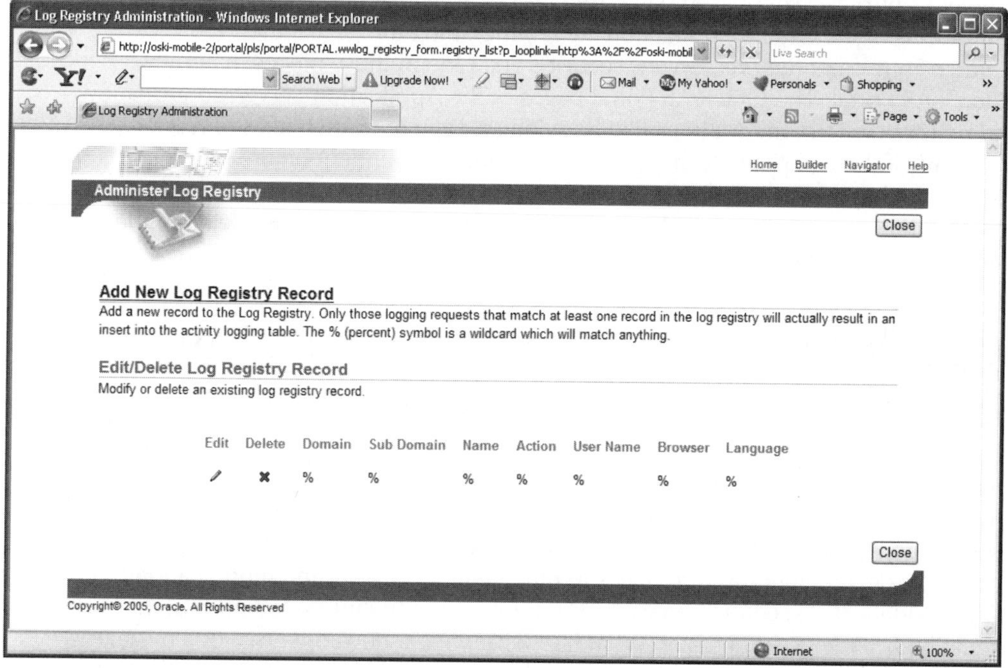

FIGURE 9-3 *The Log Registry Information page*

The next link in the Services portlet on the Portal subtab of the Administration page is titled Ultra Search Administration. Oracle Ultra Search is an Oracle product that is built on Oracle Database and Oracle Text technologies to provide uniform search-and-locate capabilities over multiple repositories, which can include Oracle databases, other ODBC-compliant databases, IMAP mail servers, etc. Oracle Ultra Search uses a "crawler" to collect documents. You can schedule crawlers to find documents in external or internal Web sites and store that information in their own repositories. This link will take you outside the Portal Administration pages and into the UltraSearch Administration pages.

NOTE
A full discussion of Oracle Ultra Search is beyond the scope of this book. For more information, see the Oracle Ultra Search Administrator's Guide, Oracle part number B14041-01.

The next link in the Services portlet is titled Portal Service Monitoring. Clicking this link directs you to a special part of the Oracle Application server called the Oracle Enterprise Manager Application Server Control (Figure 9-4). The Application Server Control is a set of Web pages that allows administrators to monitor and alter all aspects of the Oracle Application Server, including things like the Web Cache, Oracle Forms and Reports servers, security, etc. One of those pieces, naturally, is OracleAS Portal. The OracleAS Portal pages of the Application Server Control allow administrators to monitor things like how long a page or portlet takes to render (display), if the components that OracleAS Portal is dependent on are running or not, and what the settings for the OracleAS Portal cache are, among others. We'll look at the Oracle Enterprise Manager Application Server Control in detail in the section "Performance Tuning" later in this chapter.

OracleAS Portal Administration: The Export/Import Transport Set Portlet

Because OracleAS Portal gives instant feedback (as soon as you make a change to a page, any user who references that page sees the new result immediately), it's tempting to have just one OracleAS Portal environment: end users can log in and see the pages they're interested in, and developers can log in and use the page design or development wizard pages to make enhancements and modifications. For small portals, this scenario can work, but for medium to large-sized portals, this situation is a recipe for disaster. What happens when a developer makes a mistake on a page? All end users immediately see that mistake. Also, there is no testing mechanism in place in this scenario. Developers can inadvertently expose incorrect

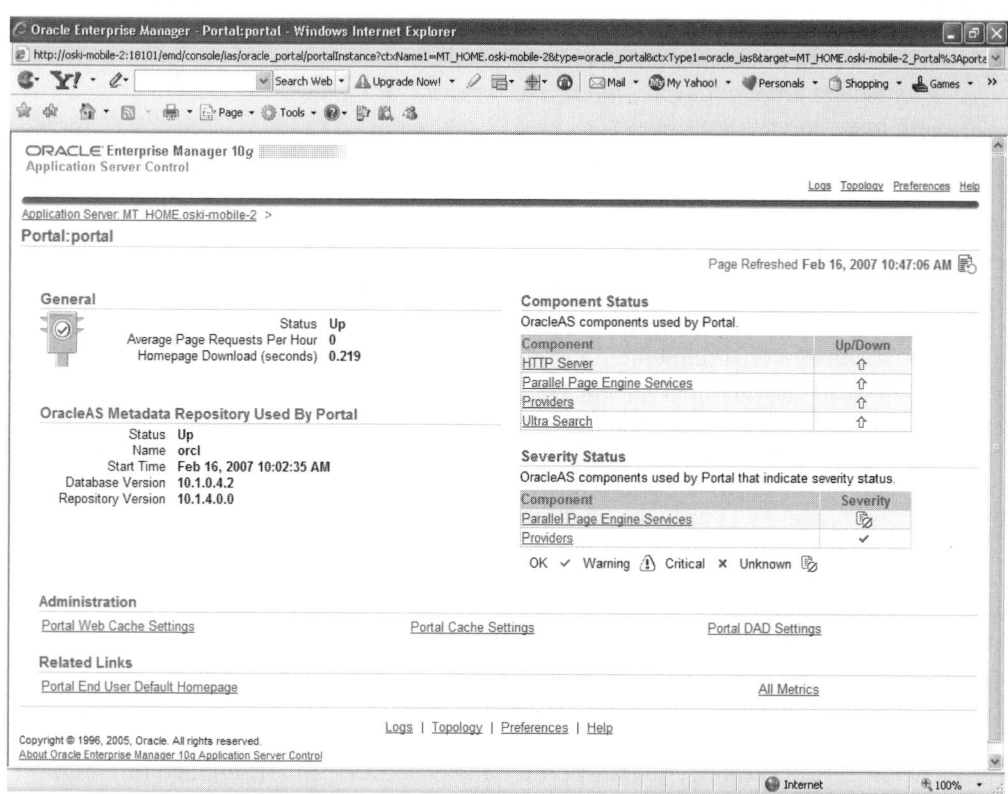

FIGURE 9-4 *The Oracle Enterprise Manager Application Server Control Portal Target page*

or inappropriate information to end users with no one to check or validate their work before it is deployed. The answer to this problem is to have multiple OracleAS Portal environments: one for production and another for development.

This is how Portal was designed from the start; i.e., everything in a single environment. This is why content approvals exist and how Oracle Technology Network (http://www.oracle.com/technology/index.html) and Oracle's main page (http://www.oracle.com/) work. Most users, however, would rather have multiple environments and move content between them. The key for a single environment is in adhering to development processes for pages (keeping them hidden until approved). Content addition, however, can easily be controlled by content approval processes (see Chapter 5).

NOTE
For large portals, it is conceivable to have even more OracleAS Portal environments: one for production, one for testing, one for development, and one for system integration.

If you've set up your environment with multiple OracleAS Portal environments, there has to be a way of moving code from one environment to another. But for most of the tasks we've performed in this book (page design, content management, etc.) we haven't written any code! We've used wizards or graphical editors to construct what we wanted—how do we get the code behind all of that stuff and move it to a different environment? Transport Sets are the answer.

If you've worked with older versions of Oracle Portal (e.g., 3.0.9.*x*), you will love Transport Sets. They maintain all of the dependencies of your OracleAS Portal objects automatically, so you don't have to worry about missing anything. If you've never worked with older versions of OracleAS Portal, count your blessings. The Export/Import process was arduous on those older systems and prone to errors, some serious enough to invalidate your entire portal!

A transport set is a collection of OracleAS Portal objects for an import or an export. It is made up of three pieces: the transport set, the extracted data, and a migration script. The transport set contains metadata (data about data) for the OracleAS Portal objects. The extracted data includes everything you specify when creating the transport set: pages, content, portlets, etc. The script is what you use to export and import the data.

In the process of creating the transport set, the process is "smart" enough to maintain all of the dependencies for all of the OracleAS Portal objects selected to be exported. What do I mean by dependencies? Consider this example: Let's say I want to move the Dashboard_1 page group from my development environment to my production environment. What dependencies are there in the Dashboard_1 page group? There's quite a list:

- The Root page of the page group
- Subpages of the page group
- Portal templates defined in the page group
- HTML templates defined in the page group
- Categories defined in the page group
- Navigation pages defined in the page group
- Perspectives defined in the page group

- Styles defined in the page group
- Attributes defined in the page group
- Page types defined in the page group
- Item types defined in the page group

Imagine if you had to export each one of those pieces individually? But wait—there's more:

- Portlets on the pages and subpages
- Provider definitions for the portlets on the pages and subpages
- Any object referenced from the Shared Objects section of the page group
- Content on the pages and subpages

Yikes! Without some method of maintaining dependencies, moving complex OracleAS Portal objects (like an entire page group) would be extremely difficult. Luckily, OracleAS Portal handles those complex dependencies for us.

Before we can use the export/import feature of OracleAS Portal, however, we first need to create a transport set. In OracleAS Portal, navigate to the Page Groups tab of the Portal Navigator. On the Page Groups tab (Figure 9-5), there is an Export link next to each page group (some seeded page groups like Portal Design-Time Pages can't be exported). Click the Export link next to the Dashboard_1 page group.

NOTE

You certainly don't have to export an entire page group. If you navigate to any of the subelements of the page group (subpages, templates, categories, etc.), you'll notice Export links next to any of those objects. Clicking those Export links will determine the dependencies for that object and only export what needs to be exported for a successful import to another system.

The Export Objects page displays (Figure 9-6). On this page, you can specify a name for your transport set or add the Dashboard_1 information to an existing transport set. You also have the option of exporting the security of all of the objects in the Dashboard_1 Page Group by selecting the Export Access Control Lists check box.

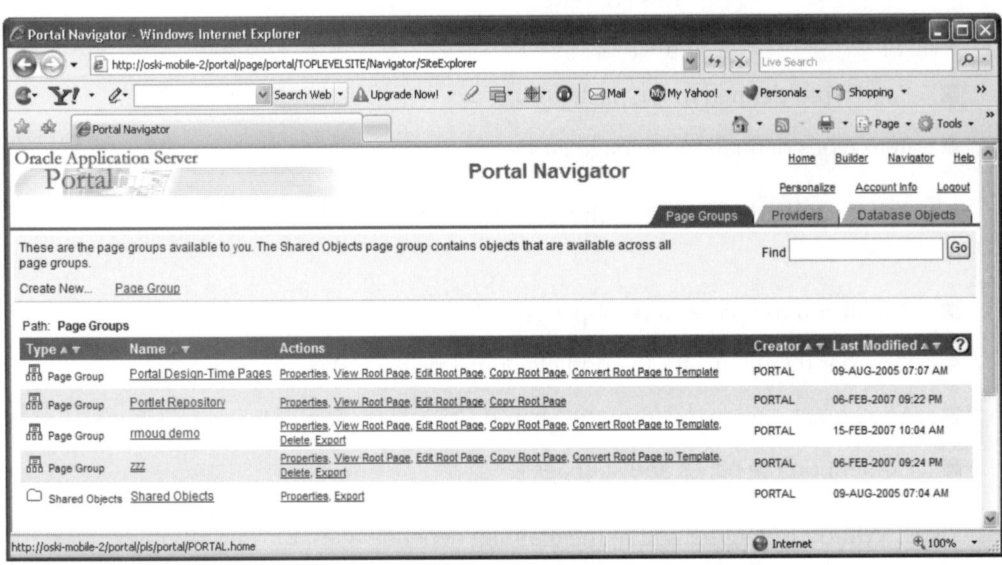

FIGURE 9-5 *The Page Groups tab in the OracleAS Portal Navigator*

Clicking Next takes you to the Transport Set Objects page (Figure 9-7). This page has three sections:

- **Explicitly Selected Objects** This section lists the OracleAS Portal objects selected by you for export. You can de-select objects here if you don't want to export them.
- **Referenced Objects** This section lists the objects that are directly or indirectly referenced by the explicitly selected objects in the preceding item. If you click the Replace On Import check box, the referenced object(s) will replace any existing objects with the same name when they are imported.
- **External Objects** These objects are the external dependencies of the exported objects. These objects are required to exist on the destination portal. If you wish to migrate shared objects and you have the appropriate privileges, add the external dependency to the transport set to make it an explicitly exported object. To be on the safe side, you can add all of these by selecting the top check box (which then highlights all of the check boxes) and click

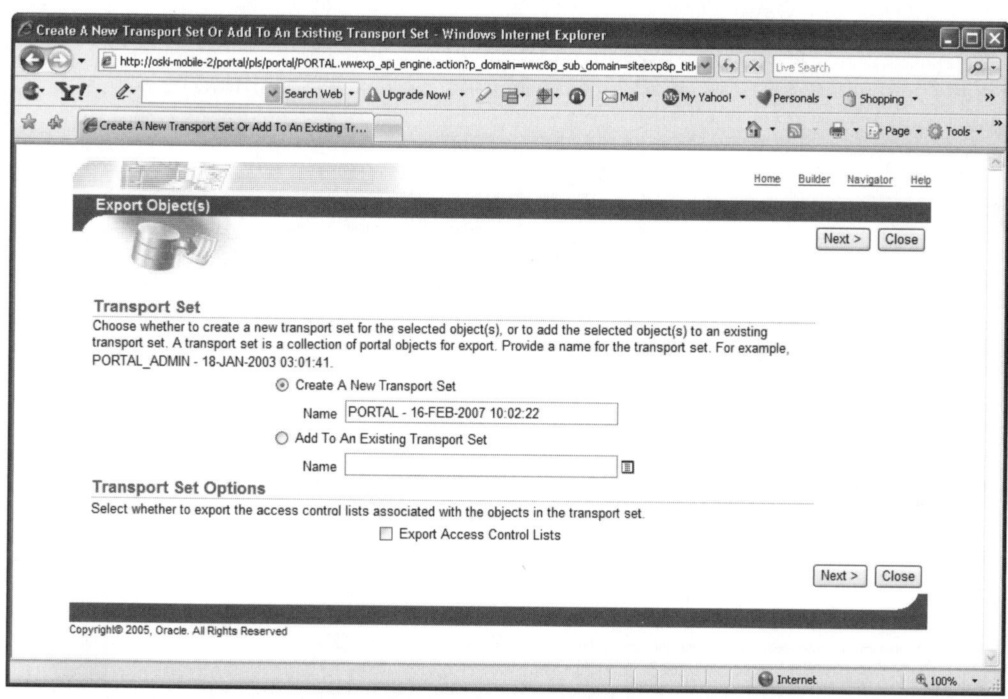

FIGURE 9-6 *The Export Objects page*

the Add To Transport Set button in the header of that section. When you do that, you are taken to another page, which asks for the import behavior (Replace on Import or leave existing object if a matching name is found).

It's entirely possible that these objects have their own dependencies (and those objects, in turn, have even more dependencies). Make sure you export everything you think you will need for your production portal.

It's also important not to export too much, however. For example, your developers may be working on a subpage of a page group that isn't ready for production yet. In that case, it's probably not a good idea to export the page group (or you can de-select the pages that are not ready for production)—you'll get all of the pieces of the page group, including the not-ready-for-production subpage(s).

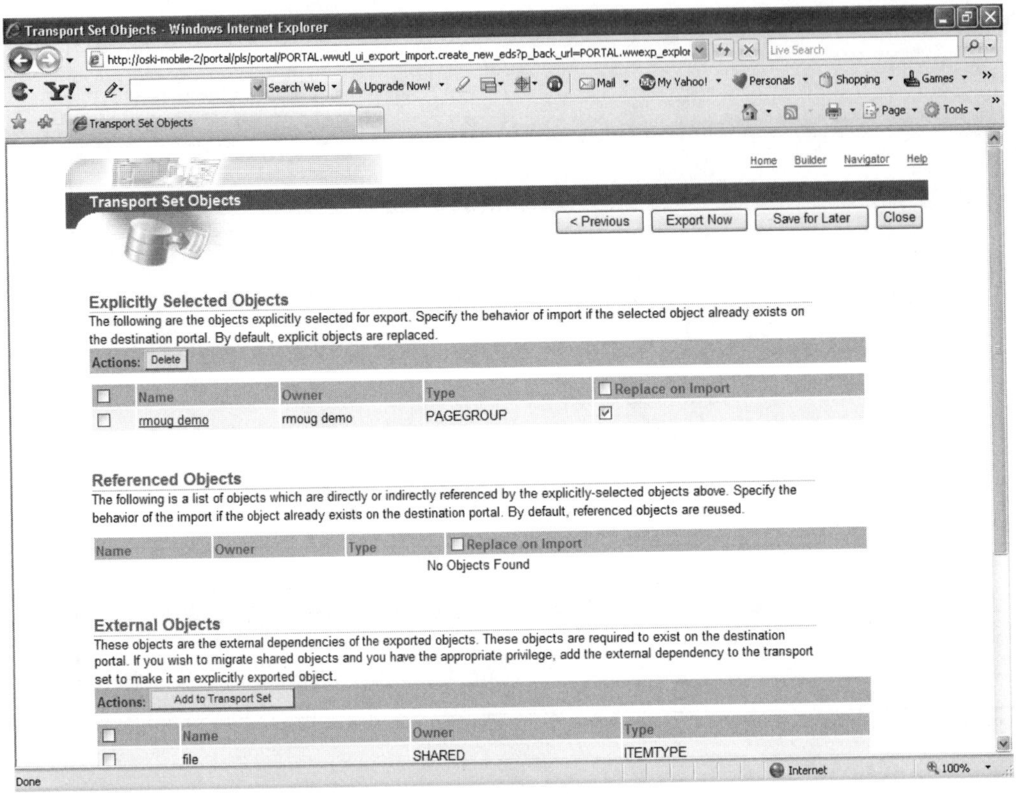

FIGURE 9-7 *The Transport Set Objects page*

When you are comfortable having selected the OracleAS Portal components you wish to export, click Export Now. The Download Scripts And View Log page is displayed (Figure 9-8).

If you're waiting for an "Export Complete" message to be displayed, you'll be waiting a long time. The only way to see if the export is complete is to click the View Log Of Actions link and look for lines like this at the bottom:

```
Completed On: 02-NOV-06 12:46:53
Detailed log information can be viewed here.
```

This can be very confusing for beginning OracleAS Portal administrators. The Export Now button makes it seem as if you've exported the OracleAS Portal data, doesn't it? That is not, however, what has just happened. All you have done is create the transport set, which marks the objects to be exported by copying the data to

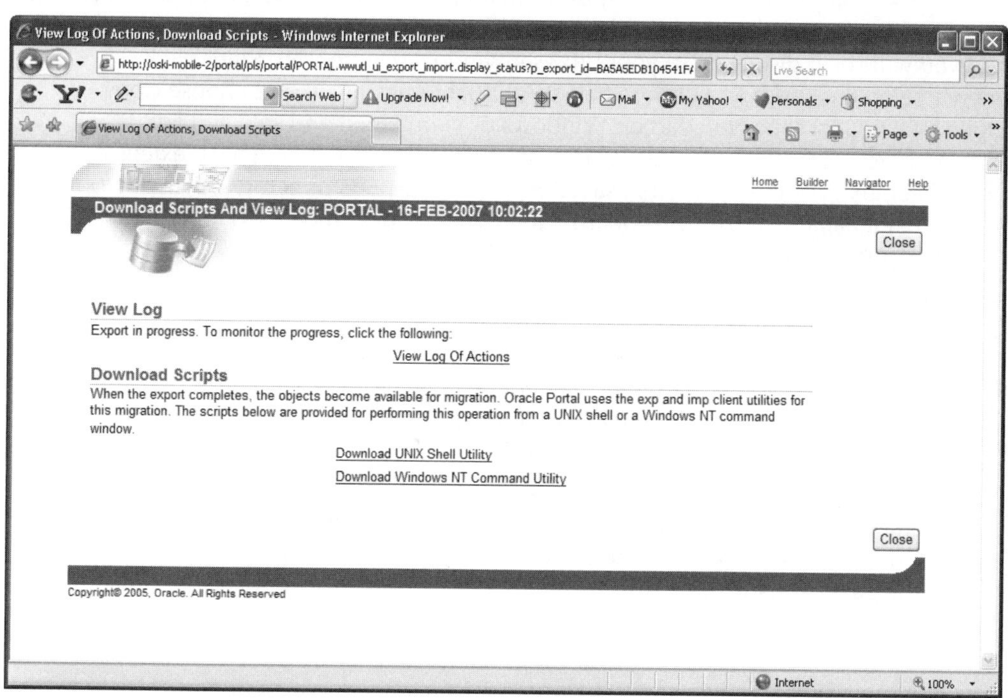

FIGURE 9-8 *The Download Scripts And View Log page*

transport-set tables in the infrastructure database. We now need to run a script to actually export the marked data from these transport-set tables into an export file for transfer to the destination portal.

Click OK to return to the Download Scripts and View Log page. There are two links on the bottom of the page: Download Unix Shell Utility and Download Windows NT Command Utility. The scripts displayed by each of these links are used for both exporting and importing the data. If you are exporting from a Unix server and importing to a Unix server, you only need the Unix script. Likewise, if you're going from Windows to Windows, you only need the Windows script. If you're moving between Unix and Windows, however, you'll need both scripts.

NOTE

You don't have to download these scripts right away; you can come back to this page later and download them at a later time.

For this example, I'm going to export from a Windows machine and import to a Windows machine, so I'll only need the Windows script. Click the script you need and you will see it displayed in your browser window (Figure 9-9). Right-click anywhere on this script and choose Select All. Right-click again and choose Copy. Open a text editor (like Notepad on Windows or vi on Unix) and selected Edit | Paste from the menu. Save the file with a .bat extension (save it with a .sh extension for Unix/Linux). For this example, I saved it in the c:\exports directory on my laptop and gave it a name of move_dashboard_1.bat. This script will be used for both importing and exporting.

TIP
The preceding paragraph was performed with Microsoft Internet Explorer. Other browsers may not behave the same way. You can always right-click the file link and select Save As to save the export/import file.

I can now use that script to export the data. The script needs parameters passed to it in order to work properly. If you try to run it without those parameters, it will display the parameters it expects:

```
C:\exports>move_dashboard_1.bat

  Usage:

  move_dashboard_1.bat  [-mode export_or_import][-s portal_schema]
      [-p portal_password][-c connect_string]
      [-pu portal_username][-pp portal_userpassword]
      [-company company_name][-d dump_file_name(s)]
      [-automatic_merge]

  -mode mode              Mode for invoking the Export Import Command
                          Line Utility
                          EXPORT mode :
                              Exports content to dump files using Oracle
                              exp utility
                          IMPORT mode :
                              Imports content from dump files using Oracle
                              imp utility

  -s portal_schema        Oracle database account for portal
                          (Mandatory) Default : portal

  -p portal_password      Oracle database password for portal
                          (Mandatory) Default : portal_schema

  -pu portal_username     Lightweight username for logging into
                          portal. Default : portal_schema
```

```
                          Applicable only in IMPORT mode

   -pp portal_userpassword Lightweight user password for logging
                          into portal Default : portal_username
                          Applicable only in IMPORT mode

   -company company_name   Company name (Eg : ORACLE)
                          If company name has space character(s),
                          enclose it in double quotes.
                          (Eg : "ORACLE FINANCE")
                          NONE for no company.
                          Default : NONE
                          Applicable only in IMPORT mode

   -c connect_string       TNS Connection Information to remote
                          database (Mandatory)

   -d dump_file_name(s)    Names(s) of files for Oracle exp or imp
                          utilities to write to or read from. If
                          multiple filename(s) are used,
                          they need to be separated by commas.
                          E.g.: FILE1.DMP,FILE2.DMP
                          Default : Script file name followed by
                          dmp extension
                          i.e. move_dashboard_1.dmp

   -automatic_merge        Automatically merge contents of dump
                          file on import
                          Applicable only in IMPORT mode

move_dashboard_1.bat [-mode export_or_import][-s portal_schema]
   [-p portal_password][-c connect_string]
   [-pu portal_username][-pp portal_userpassword]
   [-company company_name][-d dump_file_name(s)]
   [-automatic_merge]

Example to run the script in EXPORT mode
move_dashboard_1.bat  -mode export -s myportal -p myportal123
    -c mydb -d myexport.dmp

Example to run the script in IMPORT mode
move_dashboard_1.bat  -mode import -s myportal -p myportal123
    -pu expimp_usr -pp expimp_usr123 -company ORACLE
    -c mydb -d myexport.dmp

C:\exports>
```

Here's another confusing part for beginning OracleAS Portal administrators: the password, which is specified by the –p switch in the script, is *not* the password of the portal user in OracleAS Portal. It is the password of the portal user in the

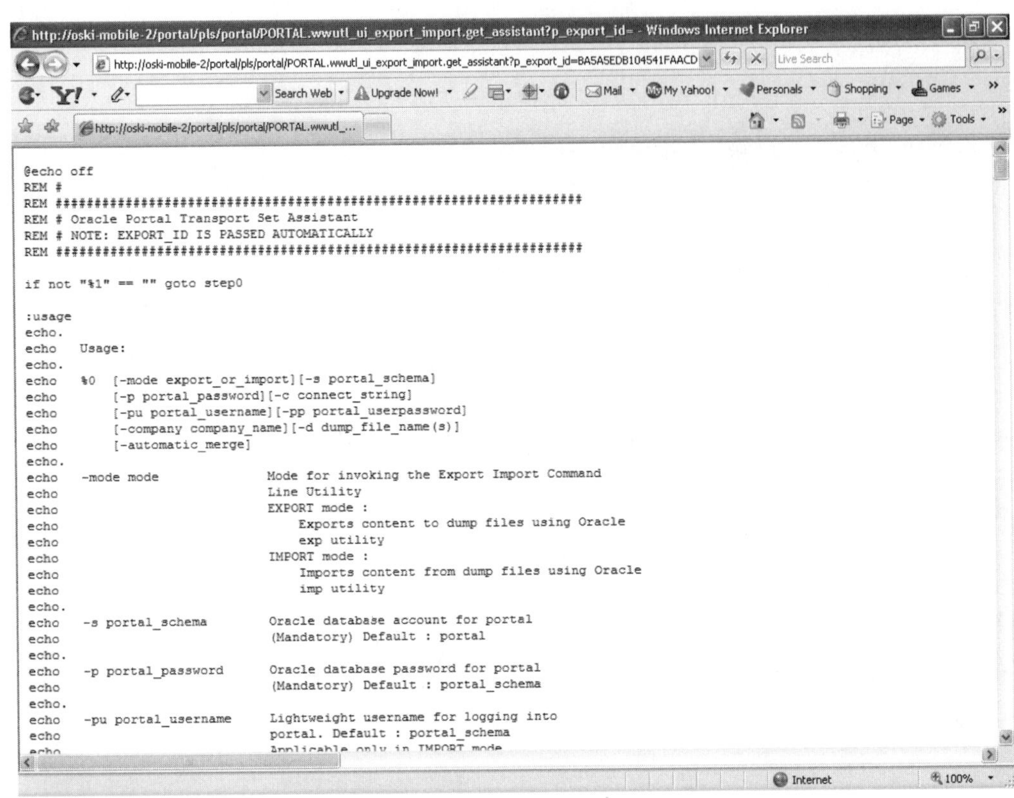

http://oski-mobile-2/portal/pls/portal/PORTAL.wwutl_ui_export_import.get_assistant?p_export_id= - Windows Internet Explorer
http://oski-mobile-2/portal/pls/portal/PORTAL.wwutl_ui_export_import.get_assistant?p_export_id=BA5A5EDB104541FAACD
@echo off
REM #
REM ##
REM # Oracle Portal Transport Set Assistant
REM # NOTE: EXPORT_ID IS PASSED AUTOMATICALLY
REM ##
if not "%1" == "" goto step0
:usage
echo.
echo Usage:
echo.
echo %0 [-mode export_or_import][-s portal_schema]
echo [-p portal_password][-c connect_string]
echo [-pu portal_username][-pp portal_userpassword]
echo [-company company_name][-d dump_file_name(s)]
echo [-automatic_merge]
echo.
echo -mode mode Mode for invoking the Export Import Command
echo Line Utility
echo EXPORT mode :
echo Exports content to dump files using Oracle
echo exp utility
echo IMPORT mode :
echo Imports content from dump files using Oracle
echo imp utility
echo.
echo -s portal_schema Oracle database account for portal
echo (Mandatory) Default : portal
echo.
echo -p portal_password Oracle database password for portal
echo (Mandatory) Default : portal_schema
echo.
echo -pu portal_username Lightweight username for logging into
echo portal. Default : portal_schema

FIGURE 9-9 *The Export/Import script associated with the Transport Set*

infrastructure database you are exporting from (commonly referred to as the portal schema password). Oracle generates a random password for this schema when the Oracle Application Server infrastructure instance is created. If it's random, how do you determine what it is?

To determine the (database) portal password, you'll have to use a tool called Oracle Directory Manager. This tool, installed on the server, is a graphical interface to Oracle Internet Directory, which is Oracle's implementation of the LDAP standard used for security. You can run this tool from the server via a Remote Desktop connection on Microsoft Windows or an X Window server on Unix/Linux. After running the program, you are presented with the logon screen (Figure 9-10).

The login requires specifying a username in LDAP format. By default, the username for Oracle Directory Manager to view all of the attributes we're interested in is orcladmin. To specify it in LDAP format, you must type in **cn=orcladmin**. Here,

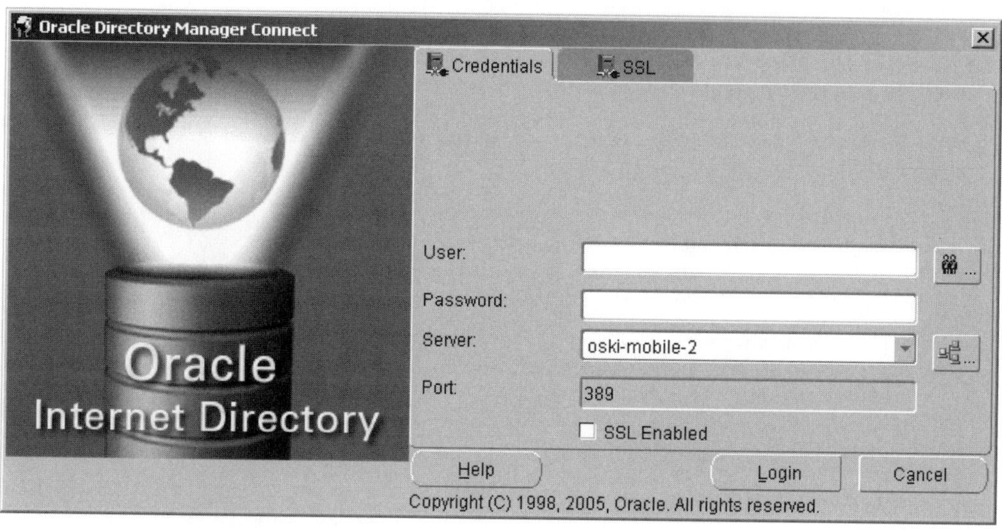

FIGURE 9-10 *The Oracle Directory Manager Login screen*

"cn" stands for common name; it used by LDAP products to identify users. The password will be the same as the instance password the person who installed Oracle Application Server chose during installation (this is also the default password for the portal user in OracleAS Portal—which is *not* the same thing as the randomly generated database portal password). After a successful login, you are presented with the main Oracle Directory Manager screen (Figure 9-11). On the left-hand side of this window, click the small plus sign next to Entry Management to expand it. Then click the following plus signs next to: cn=OracleContext, cn=Products, cn=IAS, cn=IAS Infrastructure Databases, and orclReferenceName=orcl.local; then click OrclResourceName=PORTAL. On the right-hand pane, there will be an entry called orclpasswordattribute:. This is the database portal password.

If your Oracle Application Server installation is on Unix or Linux, you can also use the following script to determine the portal schema password (make sure to type the line toward the end of the listing that starts with "$ORACLE_HOME/bin/ldapsearch" as one long line—don't hit ENTER to separate it on separate lines):

```
#!/bin/ksh
echo "\n================================="
echo "\n Get Schema Password From OID"
echo "\n================================="
echo "\nEnter the password of the cn=orcladmin user (usually the
ias installation password): \c"
stty -echo
```

```
read OIDPW
stty echo
#
if [[ -z $OIDPW ]]; then
   echo "OID Admin password required!"
else
   echo "\nEnter the name of the Host on which OID is installed : \c"
   read OIDHOST

   if [[ -z $OIDHOST ]]; then
      echo "No OID host specified!"
   else
      echo "\nEnter the OID Listen Port (default 3060): \c"
      read OIDPORT
      if [[ -z $OIDPORT ]]; then
         echo " - No OID Port specified, using default"
         OIDPORT=3060
      fi

      echo "\nEnter the desired Oracle schema name (default orasso): \c"
      read DBUSERNAME

      if [[ -z $DBUSERNAME ]]; then
         echo " - No schema value entered, using default"
         DBUSERNAME=orasso
      fi
      #
      echo "\nLooking up the ${DBUSERNAME} schema password
from $OIDHOST:$OIDPORT"
      echo "\n>\>\>\>\>\>\>\>\>\>\>\>\>\>\>\>\>\>\>\>\>"
      $ORACLE_HOME/bin/ldapsearch -h $OIDHOST -p $OIDPORT -D "cn=orcladmin"
-w "
$OIDPW" -b "cn=IAS Infrastructure Databases,cn=IAS,cn=Products,cn=OracleCon
text"
"orclResourceName=$DBUSERNAME" orclpasswordattribute
      echo "\n<<<<<<<<<<<<<<<<<<<<<<<<<<<<<<<<<<"
   fi
fi
```

Based on the "Example to run the script in EXPORT mode" section in the earlier listing, the following parameters need to be specified:

- **–mode** Import or export
- **–s** The name of the schema in my infrastructure database that hold my portal information. Defaults to portal.
- **–p** The portal database schema password
- **–c** The name of the infrastructure database in my tnsnames.ora file
- **–d** The name of the export file

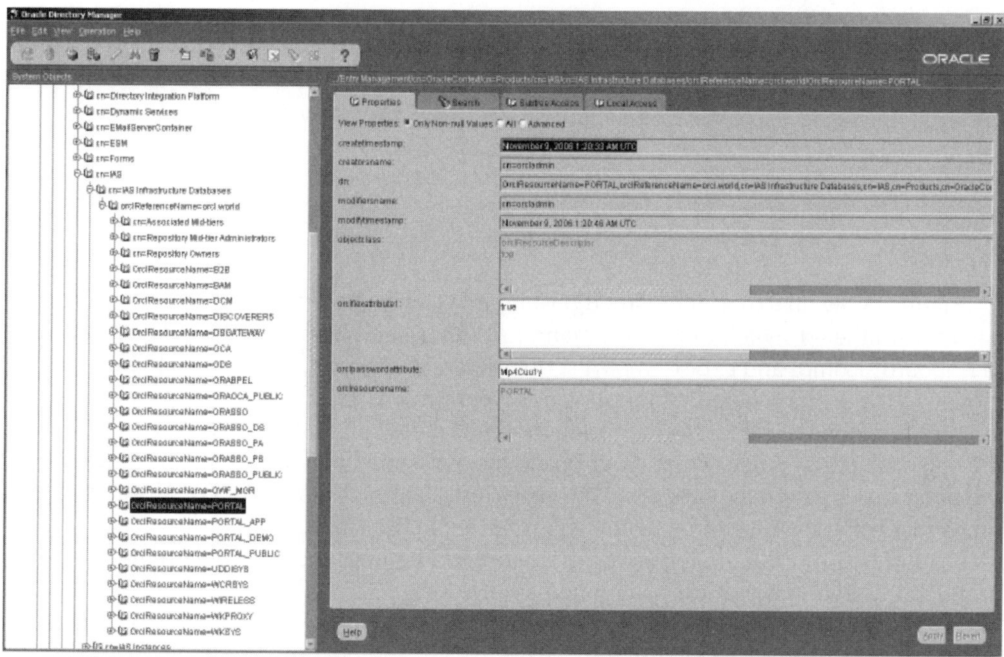

FIGURE 9-11 *The Main Oracle Directory Manager screen*

Based on the password I retrieved from Oracle Directory Manager in Figure 9-11, the export command on my computer looks like this:

```
C:\exports>move_dashboard_1.bat -mode export -s portal -p Dzyz79Z8 -c orcl  -d
dashboard_1.dmp
Verifying the environment variables...
Verifying the Oracle Client version...
export Mode Selected
Verifying the portal schema passed...
Verifying the availability of transport set...
Verifying the status of transport set...
Calling Oracle exp or imp utility based on the mode of operation....

Export: Release 10.1.0.4.2 - Production on Thu Nov 2 13:43:08 2006

Copyright (c) 1982, 2005, Oracle.  All rights reserved.

Connected to: Oracle Database 10g Enterprise Edition
Release 10.1.0.4.2 - Production
With the Partitioning, OLAP and Data Mining options
```

If everything was entered correctly, it will end like this:

```
. . exporting table       WWUTL_RW_TX_SYS_COMPDEF$          0 rows exported
. . exporting table       WWUTL_SRC_TX_DEPENDENCY$          0 rows exported
. . exporting table   WWUTL_PRO_TX_PROVIDER_PREFS$          9 rows exported
Export terminated successfully without warnings.

PL/SQL procedure successfully completed.

This part of the export/ import operation is now complete.
C:\exports>
```

There is now an export file named dashboard_1.dmp (based on what was passed with the –d switch to the command just described). Both the export file (dashboard_1.dmp) and export/import script (move_dashboard_1.bat) need to be moved to the server where the import is to be performed. Assuming you've done that, it's now time to import to the production instance. You will need to determine the database portal password on your production instance, which is different, since the password is generated randomly for every installation of OracleAS Portal. After doing that using the Oracle Directory Manager techniques described earlier, the move_dashboard_1.bat file to run again to import. The import command on the production server requires the following parameters:

- **–mode** Import or export
- **–s** The database portal user
- **–p** The password for the database portal user
- **–pu** The portal user who's going to own the objects to be imported
- **–pp** The password for the portal user who's going to own the objects to be imported
- **–company** The company of the portal user who's going to own the objects to be imported (this is optional)
- **–c** The name of the infrastructure database in my tnsnames.ora file
- **–d** The name of the export file

The –pu switch signifies the OracleAS Portal user to own the objects, and the –pu switch is for that user's password. Based on the settings of my production database, the import command on my production server looks like this:

```
move_dashboard_1.bat -mode import -s portal -p Q90vVtG2 -pu portal
-pp portal_prod -company TUSC -c PROD -d dashboard_1.dmp
```

We've imported the data to our production instance, so we're done, right? Not quite. The data is in the transport-set tables, but the OracleAS Portal Repository doesn't "know" about it yet. On your production instance, navigate to the Administer tab in OracleAS Portal and click the small icon next to the text box under the Import A Transport Set heading in the middle of the page. You will see a transport set with the same name as the one you exported from your development instance (Figure 9-12). Importing that transport set will populate the OracleAS Portal Repository with all of the necessary metadata (data about the OracleAS Portal objects). After that completes, the Dashboard_1 Page Group (with all of its components) will display in the Page Groups tab of the Portal Navigator on your production system. It is important to review the online log view for any errors during both import and export. The logs are detailed and are very useful for problem diagnosis.

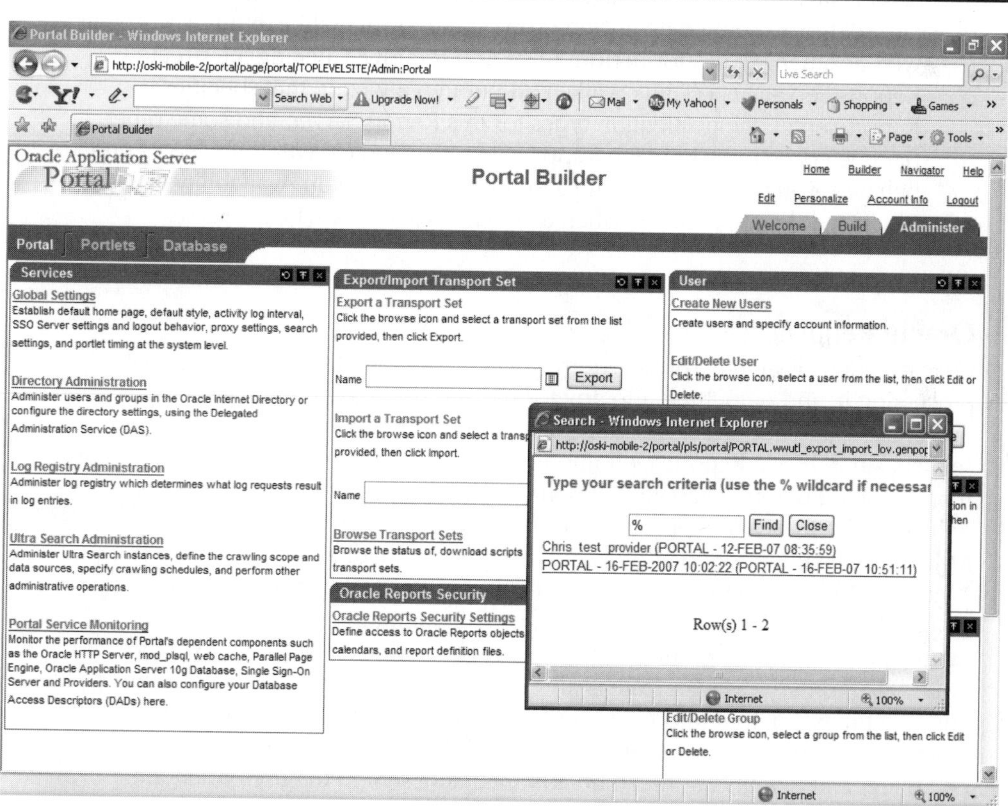

FIGURE 9-12 *Importing a Transport Set*

OracleAS Portal Administration: The Oracle Reports Security Portlets

In Chapter 11, techniques for integrating things like Oracle Forms, Oracle Reports, and Oracle Discoverer workbooks and worksheets are discussed. When taking an Oracle Report and integrating it with OracleAS Portal, there are additional portlets available to further define security settings for the Oracle Report in question. Clicking the Oracle Reports Security Settings link on the Administration tab displays a page with four portlets (Figure 9-13):

- **Reports Server Access** As part of the Oracle Application Server, there is a component installed called the Reports Server. This component is used to serve Oracle Reports to end users via their Web browsers. The Reports Servers take care of converting the report from Oracle Reports' native format (an .rdf file) to something a Web browser can display (like .html or a .pdf) as well as other settings for performance and security. Clicking the Create Reports Server Access link walks you through a wizard that specifies a Report Server, the destination types for this Report Server, and some other parameters defining how the Reports Server's interface with OracleAS Portal behaves. You can also associate a Reports Server with an Availability Calendar (discussed shortly) to define when that Reports Server will be available.

Oracle Reports

Oracle Reports is an enterprise reporting tool for taking data from any format, processing it, and outputting it to any format and destination. Oracle Portal is one of the many out-of-the-box destinations supported by the OracleAS Reports service. An RDF is a Reports Definition File that contains a binary representation of the metadata that defines the structure of the report (this is only one way to save a report definition—the other two are as a JSP file or an XML file). The Reports Server processes a report by loading the definition (JSP, XML, or RDF file), querying the defined data source, and formatting the data output as directed by the report definition. The output format may be any of many different types, including HTML, PDF, PostScript, XML, plain text, and more. The primary use case here is an Oracle Report being scheduled to run and dumping its output into a Portal page automatically once the report is finished. The Portal user does not have to wait for the Oracle Report to complete, and a notification can be automatically sent to the user when the report completes (which could take hours). The user can then visit the Portal page chosen for the report output to browse the result at his or her leisure.

- **Reports Definition File Access** Oracle Reports' native format is what is known as a Reports Definition File (.rdf). In this wizard, administrators can define access to an .rdf file on the server's file system. The Report Name is used to identify the Oracle Reports Report Definition File within OracleAS Portal. The Oracle Reports File Name specifies the name of the Oracle Reports Report Definition File. The Reports Printers listed are those that you have already added to OracleAS Portal (discussed shortly). If you want to include more parameters, click More Parameters and more rows will be added. You can also associate a Reports Definition File with an Availability Calendar (discussed shortly) to define when that Reports Definition File (or Reports JSP or XML file) will be available.

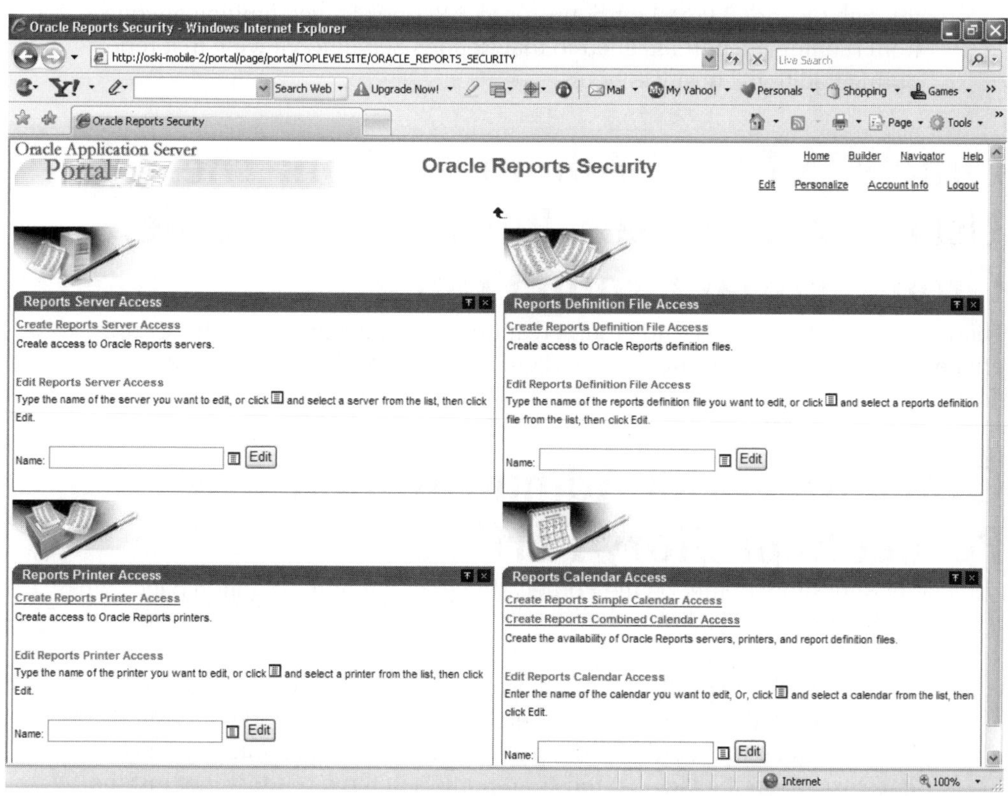

FIGURE 9-13 *The Oracle Reports Security portlets*

- **Reports Printer Access** The Create Reports Printer Access link will bring you to a wizard used for defining printers attached to your system that can be used by Oracle Reports displayed through OracleAS Portal. The Operating System Printer Name is used to identify the printer to the Reports Server. You can also associate a Reports Printer with an Availability Calendar (discussed next) to define when that Reports Printer will be available.
- **Reports Calendar Access** A Reports Calendar can be used to define times of the day when the other reports access parameters are valid. For instance, you could create a Reports Calendar called "Business Hours" that runs from 8 A.M. until 5 P.M., and assign a Reports Definition File Access entry to it. By doing so, you would arrange that OracleAS Portal users could only access that report during traditional business hours. That calendar could also be assigned to a printer, limiting anyone from printing any reports accessed through OracleAS Portal off-hours, or to a Reports Server, limiting anyone from running a report assigned to that Reports Server to viewing that report during traditional business hours.

OracleAS Portal Administration: The User Portlets: User, Portal User Profile, Group, Portal Group Profile

These portlets deal with user and group creation and modification and the security privileges associated with those users and groups. Users and groups are discussed in detail in Chapter 10.

OracleAS Portal Administration: The Portlet Repository Portlets

The Portlet Repository portlet on the Portlets subtab of the Administration page (Figure 9-14) contains three links:

- **Display Portlet Repository** Clicking this link displays a page that lists all of the portlets that have been registered in the OracleAS Portal repository. It looks similar to the Add Portlet page when designing an OracleAS Portal Page except for the fact that it lists all portlets in the repository, not just the ones page designers have access to.

- **Refresh Portlet Repository** If numerous developers are creating and modifying portlets and administrators are creating and using transport sets, it's possible that developers will get inconsistent results when working with portlets. If you want to reset everyone to get a consistent view of the registered portlets in the OracleAS Portal Repository, click this link. Depending on the size of your repository, you will be presented with a success screen after a minute or so.
  When you register a provider (or producer) with OracleAS Portal, a call is made to the remote provider (producer) for information about how many and what types of portlets are present in the provider (producer) definition.

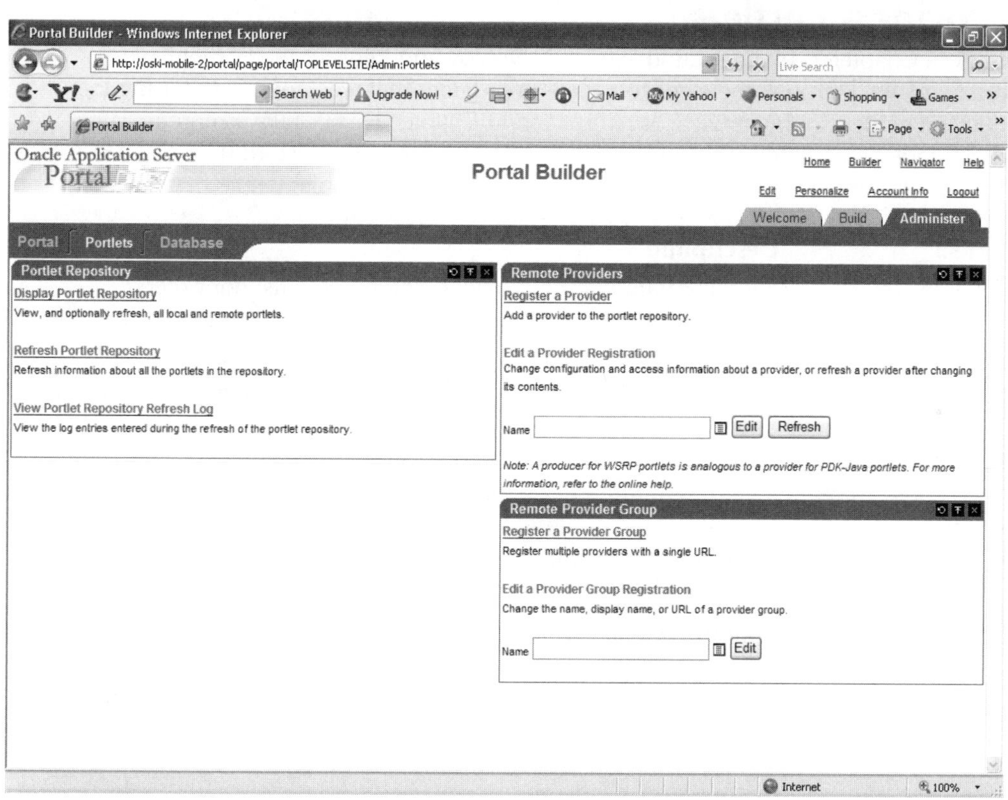

FIGURE 9-14 *The Portlets subtab of the OracleAS Portal Administration page*

The information that is collected is what is displayed in the OracleAS Portlet Repository. It is effectively a cache of remote provider (producer) definitions. When you choose to refresh the repository, it is as if you decided to register all the providers (producers) again all at the same time. All of the information cached in the repository is refreshed by contacting all the remote providers (producers).

- **View Portlet Repository Refresh Log** If, for whatever reason, there are errors when the Oracle AS Portlet Repository is refreshed, click this link to see a detailed list of messages written to the refresh log file.

OracleAS Portal Administration: The Remote Providers Portlets

Back in Chapter 7, in the section "Step 10: Deploy and Register the Portlet," we briefly walked through the steps to register a provider that was not created using the declarative development wizards referenced in Chapter 1. Let's take a more in-depth look at the fields in this wizard. On the first page of the wizard (Figure 9-15), you are prompted for the following fields, as shown in this table:

Field	Description
Name	Enter the name of the provider. The name must not exceed 200 characters or include spaces or special characters.
Display Name	Enter a name to display for the provider when it is referenced. The name must not exceed 200 characters. This display name appears in the Portlet Repository and in the Add Portlets screen with the provider's portlets listed beneath it.
Timeout	Enter the number of seconds Oracle Portal should try to connect to the provider before displaying the Timeout Message. The default value is 10 seconds.
Timeout Message	Enter the message to display when Oracle Portal cannot establish contact with the provider within the number of seconds specified in the Timeout field. The message displays within the body of the portlet. The message may not contain either mobile (mobileXML) or desktop (HTML) markup.

Field	Description
Implementation Style	Choose Database if the provider is written as a PL/SQL package. Oracle Portal communicates with the database provider by making local procedure calls. Choose Web if the provider is written as a Web application. Oracle Portal communicates with Oracle Web providers using SOAP over the HTTP protocol. These providers are generally written as Java code using the Oracle PDK-Java APIs. Choose WSRP if the provider is implemented as a WSRP producer. Oracle Portal communicates with WSRP producers using the WSRP V1 protocol.

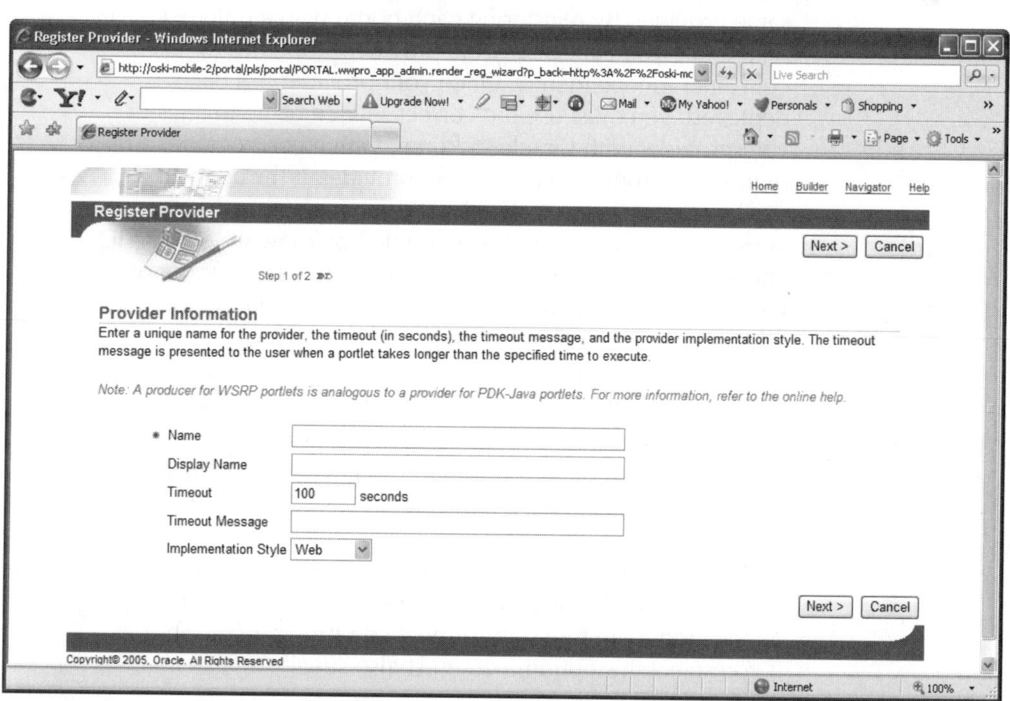

FIGURE 9-15 *The first page of the Register a New Provider Wizard*

The second page of the wizard asks for the following fields:

Field	**Description**
URL	Enter the base URL of the provider.
Service ID	Enter the service ID of the provider. The service ID identifies a specific provider at the URL specified. PDK-Java enables you to deploy multiple providers under a single adapter servlet. The providers are identified by a service name or service identifier. For example, you can register the PDK-Java samples provider using the URL http://mycompany.com/jpdk/providers and a service ID of urn:sample. Alternatively, you can use a URL of the form http://mycompany.com/jpdk/providers/sample, where the provider name (sample) is appended to the URL of the PDK-Java samples provider. In this case, you should leave the Service Id field blank. You can specify the service ID separately in cases where multiple portals are sharing the same provider. By registering each portal with a different service ID, you can specify the provider properties for each consumer independently. Once your provider has been deployed, you must use the correct service name to register your provider with OracleAS Portal, which ensures that requests are routed to the correct provider. If the adapter servlet receives a request without a service name, the request goes to the default provider. If you do not know the service ID, check the provider test page or contact the administrator of the provider. If you are using the Federated Portal Adapter, the URL points to the adapter, not the provider. Thus, you must enter a value for this field. In this case, the service ID would be the "urn:" followed by the name of the database provider.
User Identity	Select whether: The user has the same user name and password in the Web provider's application as in the Single Sign-On identity. The user's user name and password need to be mapped to a different user name and password in the Web provider's application, and/or the Web provider requires an external application login for establishment of a browser session. If you select this option, you must also specify an External Application ID.
External Application ID	If you chose to specify a separate user name and password for the Web provider's application, enter the external application's ID.

Field	Description
Subscription Key	Enter the key that is passed to the provider. This key uniquely identifies this Oracle Portal node as the requester.
Shared Key	Enter the encryption key that is shared with the provider. This key is used to encrypt and decrypt data communicated to the provider.
Web provider in same cookie domain as the portal	Select if the cookies created by the provider are in the same domain as the portal. If they are, the cookies are visible to the portal and are passed through to the browser. This facilitates better integration between the provider and Oracle Portal. It is also valid to set this if you are using the Federated Portal Adapter. The cookie domain is specified by the provider when it creates its cookies. If you select this option, any cookies created by this provider are forwarded to the user's browser and managed by the browser instead of Oracle Portal. Once managed by the browser, those cookies are sent to any other Web server that is accessed within the same browser session or that falls within the relaxed scope specified when the cookie was created. This can result in cookie collisions and strange errors/loss of sessions in totally unrelated Web applications. To minimize the possibility of cookie collisions, you should ensure that (1) any custom cookies created by the Web provider have names that are unique to that Web provider and (2) all portal instances accessed using the Federated Portal Adapter are configured with different DAD names. PDK-Java release 1 (JServ) Web providers requiring this setting are installed in uniquely named JServ servlet zones. PDK-Java release 2 (OC4J) Web providers should not use this setting if they use servlet sessions. This is because the name of cookie used to identify the session is always JSESSIONID. This name is specified as part of the Servlet 2.3 Specification. Relaxing the scope of a JSESSIONID cookie almost certainly causes session-related problems in other, totally unrelated, Web applications.
Public	Select if the provider does not require any user- or session-specific information.

Field	Description
User	Select if the provider requires user specific information. If you select this option, you can also choose a Login Frequency and select whether the provider also requires session specific information.
Login Frequency	Choose how often to call the provider's initSession method: Always if you want to call the provider's initSession method every time each user requests one of the provider's portlets. In practice the only time you should ever set the value to Always is when performing error diagnosis. Setting the value to Always can create some significant performance overhead, and this is one of the first settings to check if you have a performance problem. This option was introduced to work around some issues with early versions of OracleAS Portal and is only kept for backward compatibility. Once Per User Session if you want to call the provider's initSession method only the first time each user requests one of the provider's portlets. Never if you do not want to call the provider's initSession method when users request one of the provider's portlets.
Require portal user–specific session information	Select if the provider requires session-specific information, such as session ID and login time.
Middle Tier	Choose the proxy server to use for the connection to the provider from the middle tier for rendering portlets.
Portal Repository	Choose the proxy server to use for the connection to the provider from the portal database for getting information about the provider and its portlets.

OracleAS Portal Administration: The Remote Provider Group Portlets

Registering a provider group allows you to register multiple providers with a single URL. Managing providers as a group is a convenience to simplify manageability of large numbers of providers. All providers that belong to a particular provider group are listed in the Navigator. Click the link to the provider group to view all of its providers, and then click the Register link next to each provider you want to register with the portal.

OracleAS Portal Administration: The Database Subtab

On this subtab you can perform basic database administration tasks on the infrastructure database: create or edit schemas (including changing passwords, default/temporary tablespaces, profiles, selecting that schema for Portal users, and altering grants and roles), create or edit roles, and view numerous canned reports about your infrastructure database.

Personal Pages

Earlier in this chapter we mentioned the concept of personal pages. A personal page is a way of granting limited page-creation capabilities to end users. End users wouldn't normally have privileges to create their own pages, but with the popularity of personalizable Web pages like My Yahoo (http://my.yahoo.com/), personal pages was added as a feature to OracleAS Portal. With a personal page, a user can change the page to suit his or her interests.

In the section "OracleAS Portal Administration: The Services Portlet" earlier in this chapter, we noted the existence of a check box titled Create Personal Pages For New Users. After this box was checked, I created a new user named Oski2. If I then return to the OracleAS Portal Navigator, choose the Page Groups tab, and then select Shared Objects, I will see a link titled Personal Pages. Clicking this link will list the letters of the alphabet—there is a new entry under "O" for the Oski2 user I just created (Figure 9-16).

The personal page (Figure 9-17) contains five sections: a Favorites portlet, an External Applications portlet, and the two portlets related to approvals discussed in the section "Getting Content Approved" of Chapter 5, along with, on the right side of the page, a content portlet with a description of what end users can do with their personal page with a set of links to the OracleAS Portal help system. Clicking the Edit link in the top right of the page allows end users to edit their personal pages. For more information on editing OracleAS Portal Pages, see Chapters 3 and 4.

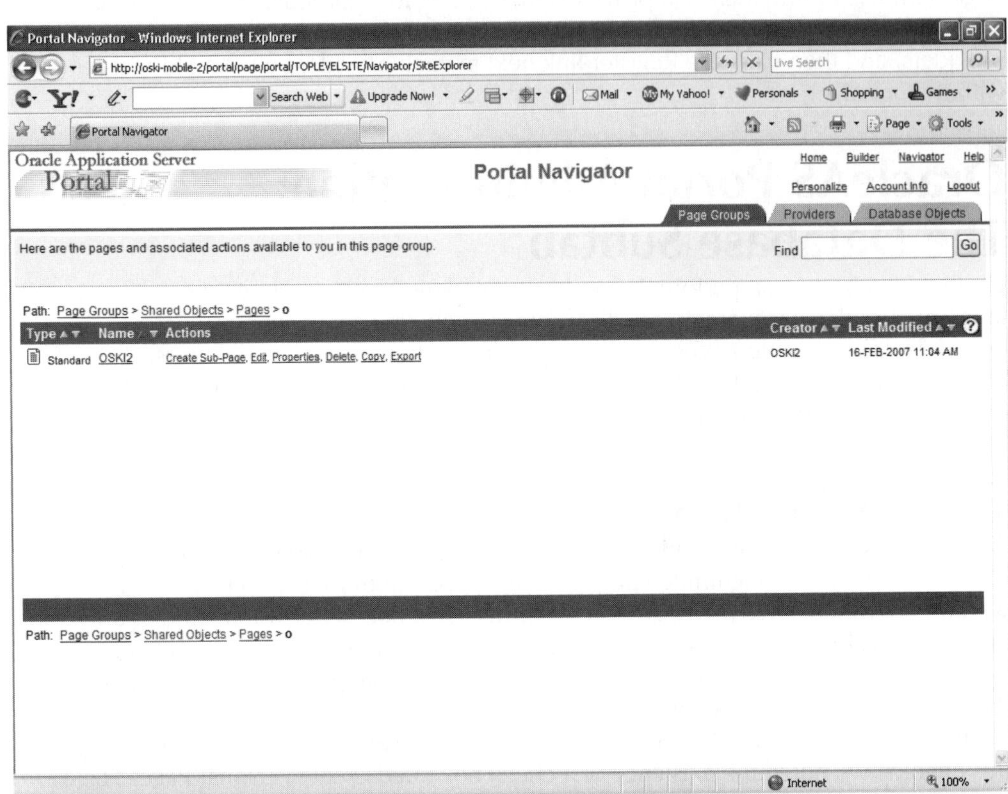

FIGURE 9-16 *A list of personal pages*

The PUBLIC User

We haven't discussed privileges much (users and security are discussed in detail in Chapter 10), but for now know that there is a special user in OracleAS Portal called PUBLIC. The PUBLIC user is, in fact, a pseudo-user. What does that mean? It means that you can't actually log in or do anything as the PUBLIC user, but you can use it when assigning privileges. Any page or portlet that grants a privilege or set of privileges to the PUBLIC pseudo-user has, in effect, granted that privilege or set of privileges to everyone on the system. Only portlets and content granted to either the user constructing their personal page or to the PUBLIC user will be available when a user builds their personal page. In Chapter 10 we will also discuss how to make the personal page the default page for the user.

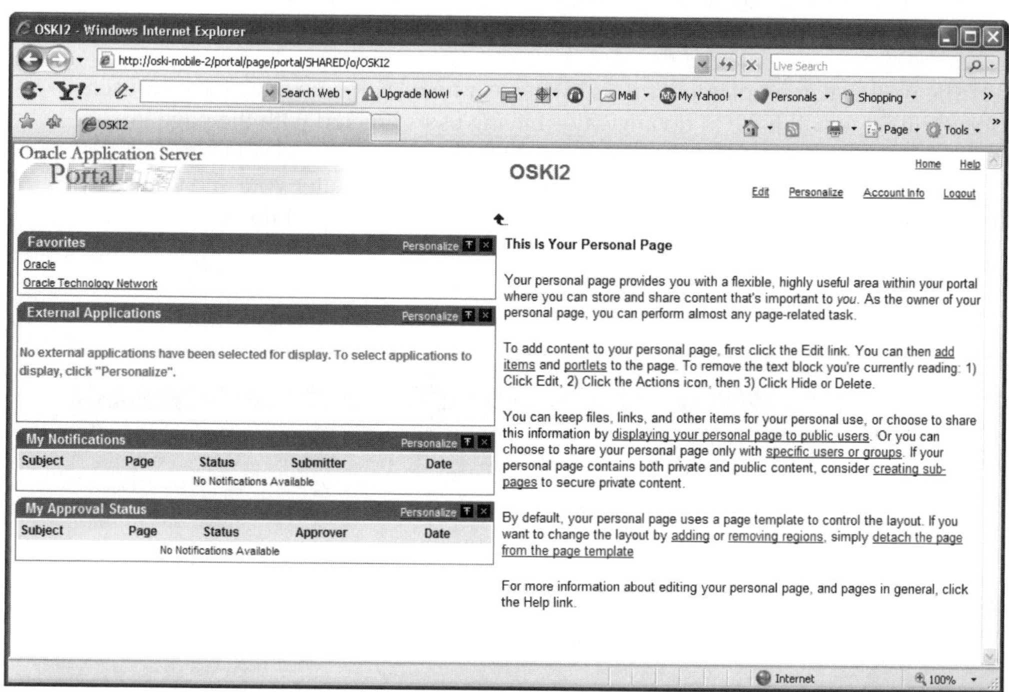

FIGURE 9-17 *The Personal page for the Oski2 user*

Self-Registration

Many Web sites allow end users, upon visiting them for the first time, to register with the site. Oftentimes, registering with the site gives end users access to advanced features of the site, such as personalization features. If your OracleAS Portal is going to be exposed to numerous (potential) users, the process of adding new users can become burdensome and time-consuming for OracleAS Portal administrators. If your portal is designed to provide public information that end users can tailor to their needs, then the self-registration feature of OracleAS Portal can save you a lot of administration work.

Earlier in this chapter, in the section "OracleAS Portal Administration: The Services Portlet," we saw an option that allows users to self-register themselves. In this section, we'll see how to implement that functionality. After selecting the Self-Registration option on the Services portlet on the Portal subtab of the Administration page, end users can add themselves to your portal site if they haven't already been created as OracleAS Portal users. The default main page (Figure 9-18), however, does not provide this functionality. You might think that a new user simply has to enter a new username and password to be prompted to create an account, but this is not the case.

The only way to implement this is to create a new Welcome page for your users (something you will have to do anyway—having users greeted with the page in Figure 9-18 is not something you would want for your production site), add a login portlet, customize the options for the login portlet and then alter your site to display the new Welcome page when users type in the URL for your portal site.

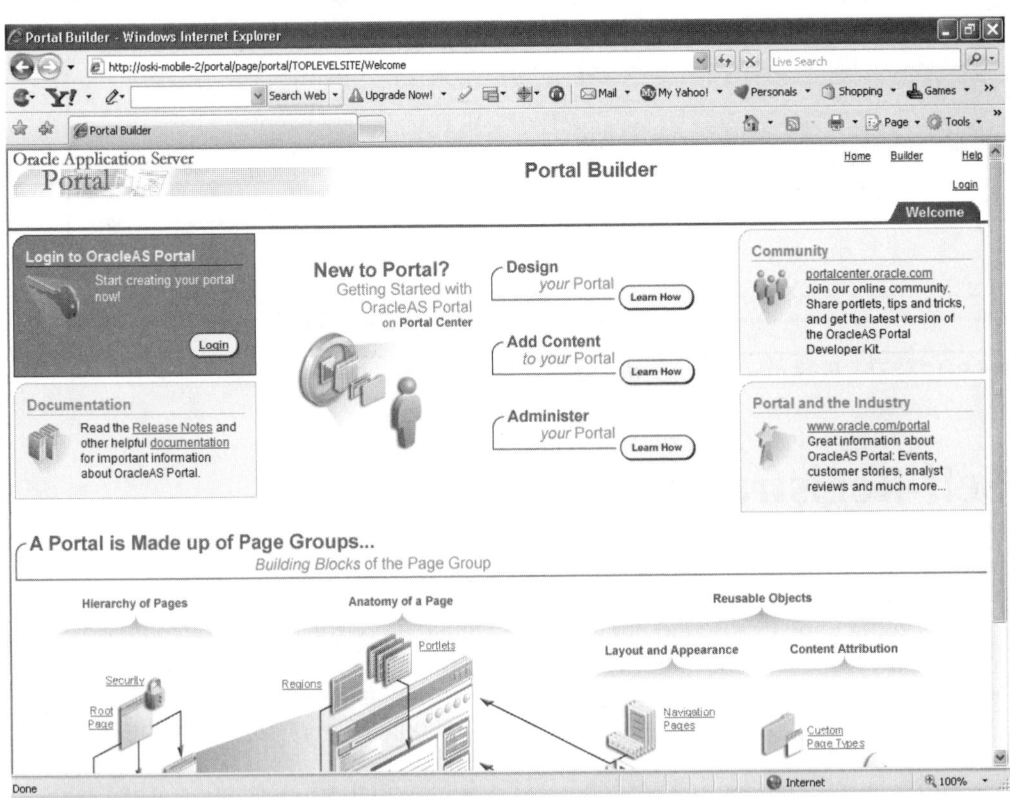

FIGURE 9-18 *The default Main page for OracleAS Portal*

Self-Registration Step 1: Create the Welcome Page

The Welcome page for your site can be anywhere in the Page Group hierarchy. The key security attribute to assign to this page is to make it PUBLIC, since no one will have logged in yet when they view it. In the OracleAS Portal Navigator, create a new Page Group called **Welcome**. By default, a root page is created automatically when a new Page Group is created. Click the Edit Root Page link in the middle of the OracleAS Portal Navigator page.

By default, a banner is created along the top of the screen and a single, undefined region is created below it. Click the red X in the banner region to delete it. In the region that is left over, click the Add Portlet icon and search for **login**. Select the Login portlet to place it on the page. Click OK to return to editing the page. Your Welcome page should look something like Figure 9-19.

Since we are already logged in, only the Logout link is displayed. When we access this page before logging in, we will see the Login portlet. After we log in, the Login portlet (which will now only consist of the Logout link) is all that will be displayed for users who do not have a default page to "land" to. For now, add a region below the one with the Login portlet. Click the Add Item icon in that region, select Built-In Navigation Types, and select Portal Smart Link in the drop-down box. Click Next. On the second page of the wizard, select Builder next to Portal Smart Link, enter **Builder** in the Display Name field, and click Finish. Add another item to that region by selecting the same thing on the first page of the Add Item Wizard, selecting Navigator in the Portal Smart Link field on the second page, entering **Navigator** in the Display Name field, and clicking OK. Your page should look like Figure 9-20.

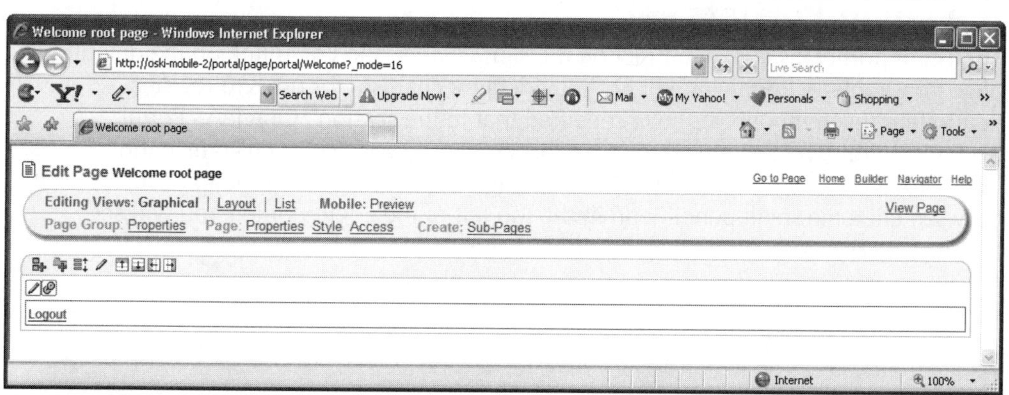

FIGURE 9-19 *The New Welcome page with the Login portlet placed on it*

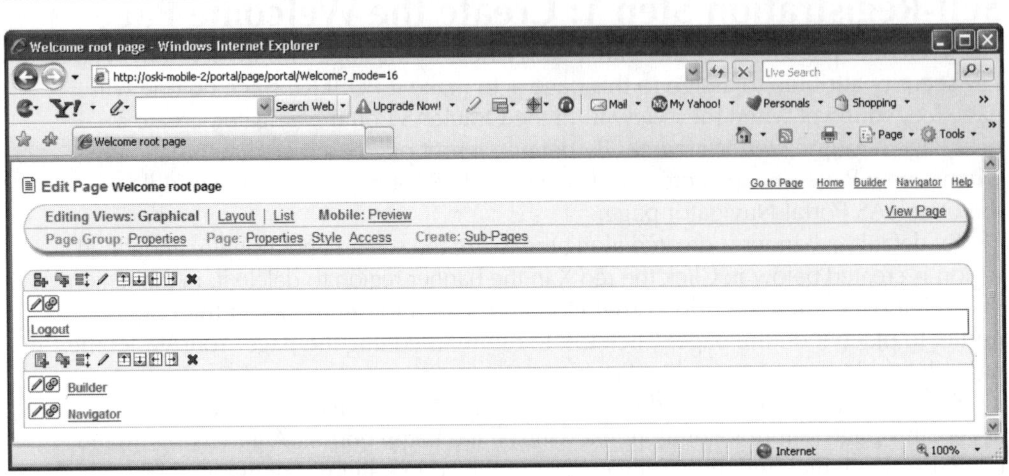

FIGURE 9-20 *The Welcome page with the additional links placed on it*

Next, we need to make this page available to users who have not logged in yet. Click the Properties link next to "Page:" on the top left of the page (be careful not to click the Properties link next to the "Page Group:" heading). Click the Access tab, and then click the check box next to Display Page To Public Users. Click OK to save your settings.

Self-Registration Step 2: Customize the Login Portlet

The Login portlet, as it is, will function the same way as the Login link on the default page for OracleAS Portal—it will not provide a mechanism for users to register themselves (even though we have specified that in the section "OracleAS Portal Administration: The Services Portlet" of this chapter). We need to customize the portlet to allow that functionality. With the page displayed in Edit mode in your browser, click the small pencil icon in the top left of the Login portlet. You will see the Customize screen for the Login portlet (Figure 9-21).

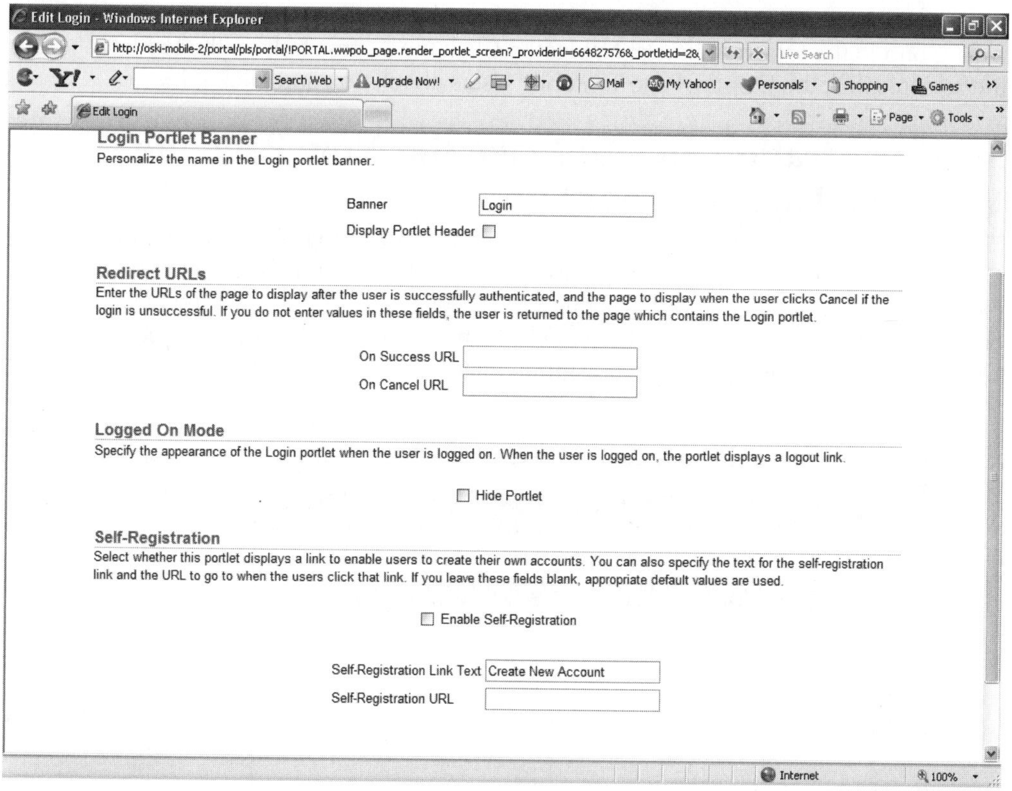
Edit Login - Windows Internet Explorer
http://oski-mobile-2/portal/pls/portal/!PORTAL.wwpob_page.render_portlet_screen?_providerid=664827576&_portletid=2&
Edit Login
Login Portlet Banner
Personalize the name in the Login portlet banner.
Banner
Login
Display Portlet Header
Redirect URLs
Enter the URLs of the page to display after the user is successfully authenticated, and the page to display when the user clicks Cancel if the login is unsuccessful. If you do not enter values in these fields, the user is returned to the page which contains the Login portlet.
On Success URL
On Cancel URL
Logged On Mode
Specify the appearance of the Login portlet when the user is logged on. When the user is logged on, the portlet displays a logout link.
Hide Portlet
Self-Registration
Select whether this portlet displays a link to enable users to create their own accounts. You can also specify the text for the self-registration link and the URL to go to when the users click that link. If you leave these fields blank, appropriate default values are used.
Enable Self-Registration
Self-Registration Link Text
Create New Account
Self-Registration URL
Internet
100%

FIGURE 9-21 *The Customize screen for the Login portlet*

The last section on that page, Self-Registration, is what needs to be customized. Clicking the Enable Self-Registration check box will add self-registration functionality to this portlet. If you want to change the name of the link that will be displayed in this portlet, you can alter the Self-Registration Link Text field. If you have a page designed for users to register themselves, you can add that in the Self-Registration URL field; otherwise, new users will be directed to Oracle's default self-registration page. For this example, leave the default values for the two text boxes and click OK.

Since this will be the page that portal users will see before they log in, we need to make it a public page. Edit the page by clicking the Edit Root Page next to the page group in the OracleAS Portal Navigator. Click the Access link on the top left of the screen. Click the Display Page To Public Users check box and click OK.

Self-Registration Step 3: Make the New Page the Welcome Page for Your Site

The final step involves making this new page the Welcome page for your site. In OracleAS Portal Builder, select the Administer tab. Select the Portal subtab and click the Global Settings link. The first section of the Global Settings page is titled Default Home Page. Click the small icon to the right of the text box and select the Return Object link next to the Welcome page group (Figure 9-22). Click OK.

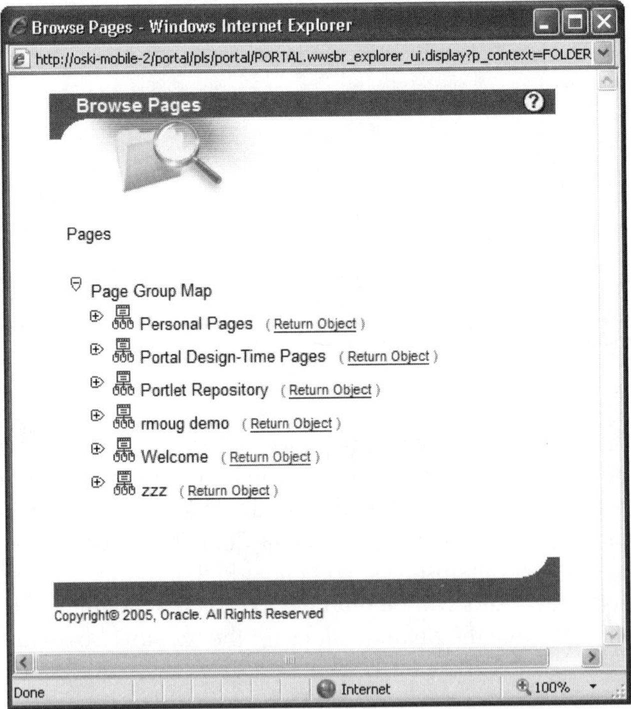

FIGURE 9-22 *The Selection window for the Default Home Page dialog*

CAUTION
I can't stress enough the importance of being careful when changing the Default Home Page for your site. There are two things you should check and double-check before changing the Default Home Page: 1) Make sure you have a login portlet on the page you plan on making the Default Home Page! If you don't, then you're stuck: the page everyone sees (including your developers and administrators) when they type in the URL in their browsers has no way to log in! There are ways around this, but they are really a pain. 2) Make sure the page you plan on making your Default Home Page has "Display Page To Public Users" selected in its Page Properties.

Open a new browser (don't open a new tab in Firefox or select File | New | Window in Internet Explorer, as cookies are shared between these browser sessions). Enter the URL of your site. You should see a page similar to Figure 9-23. Notice that there is a Create New Account link at the bottom of the screen. Clicking that link takes you the Self-Registration page (Figure 9-24). From here you can create a new OracleAS Portal user. Users, groups, and privileges are discussed in detail in Chapter 10.

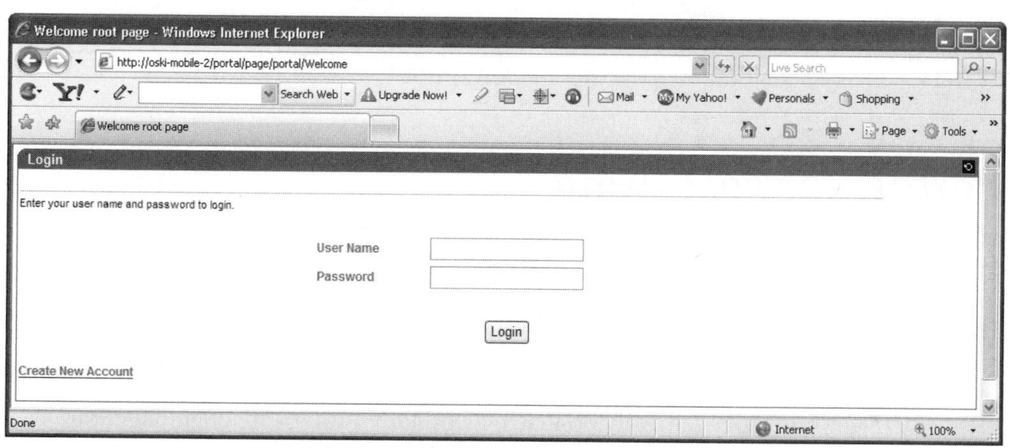

FIGURE 9-23 *The New Welcome screen*

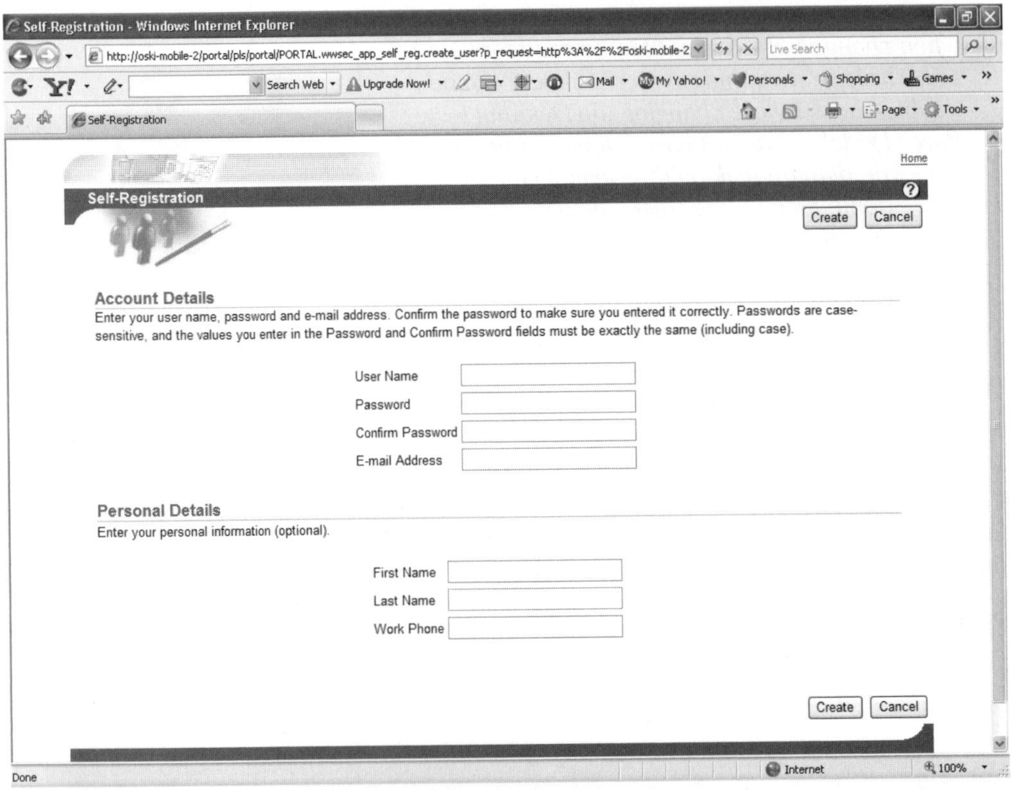

FIGURE 9-24 *The Self-Registration page of OracleAS Portal*

Performance Tuning

As systems become more and more complex, tuning those systems becomes exponentially more difficult. If your Java/Web-based/Oracle-driven application is performing poorly, where do you start looking? The database? The operating system? The network? The end user's browser settings? The JVM settings on your server? The other applications running on the client's machine? This list goes on and on.

Fortunately, Oracle provides a tool that, while not giving you the exact answer (does any diagnostic tool ever really do that?), gives administrators enough direction so that increasing the performance of their OracleAS Portal applications is made much easier. This tool is called the Oracle Enterprise Manager Application Server Control.

NOTE
An entire book could be written on tuning OracleAS Portal. In fact, one already has: The Oracle Application Server 10g Administration Handbook by John Garmany and Don Burleson (Oracle Press, 2004). This book contains large sections of performance-related topics throughout its text. It is an excellent guide for administering all Oracle Application Server components.

The Application Server Control (ASC) is a special version of Oracle Enterprise Manager that is designed to monitor and report on all of the processes that are running in conjunction with the Oracle Application Server. If you have experience with Oracle Enterprise Manager (OEM), know that the ASC is a different flavor of OEM—it is not used for administering databases. As such, the screens look completely different from the traditional OEM product. When Oracle Application Server is installed, the installer prompts you for the name of your middle-tier instance and a password. This password becomes the password for three things: getting access to the ASC, the portal password to log in to OracleAS Portal, and the orcladmin password to log in to Oracle Directory Manager. ASC is implemented as a combination of a stand-alone OC4J instance and a specialized OEM Agent program. These are started and stopped independently of the Oracle Application Server

The ASC attempts to use port 1156 on your server by default. If that port is being used, it attempts 1810, then one number higher until it finds a free port. If your infrastructure and middle tiers are installed on the same machine, the ASC for the infrastructure is probably using 18100 and the ASC for the middle tier is probably using 18101. The OracleAS Portal components are on the middle tier, so point your browser to that server with the appropriate port number. The user name to log in to the ASC is ias_admin, and the password is the one specified during installation. After logging in, you will be asked which instance of the Oracle Application Server you wish to view. Select the middle tier. You will then see a page similar to Figure 9-25.

NOTE
You will see the instance selection screen only if your OracleAS Portal metadata is in the same database instance as your Identity Management metadata. If you chose to install your OracleAS Portal metadata into a separate database instance from your Identity Management metadata, you will be taken directly to the main page (unless you have multiple mid-tiers associated with the one Product Metadata repository).

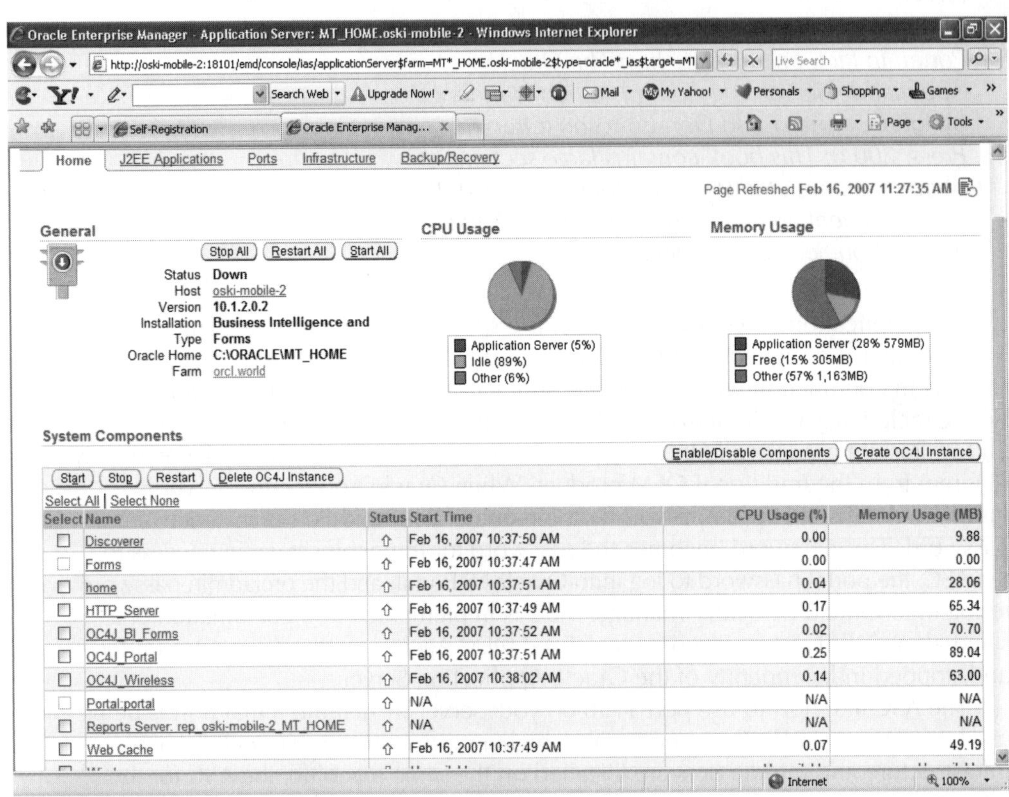

FIGURE 9-25 *The Oracle Enterprise Manager Application Server Control Main page for the middle tier*

There is a lot of information presented here. On the Home tab (which is selected by default), there is a General section at the top and a System Components section in the middle. The two System Components that will be of interest to us are the OC4J_Portal and Portal:Portal components.

Since Web servers (like the Apache Web server included with Oracle Application Server) and the Java language/J2EE specifications are maintained by separate entities (The Apache Foundation and Sun Microsystems, respectfully), coordinating changes in these products and having them work together is a continuing challenge. Vendors that sell a J2EE-compliant Web server have their own methods of providing a Java environment. In Oracle's case, this method is called OC4J.

OC4J stands for Oracle Containers for J2EE, which provides a Java environment to the Apache Web server included with Oracle Application Server. An Oracle Application Server instance can have multiple OC4J containers running simultaneously. Each of these containers has numerous attributes that can be set differently, depending on the needs of the applications that are deployed to the container. For example, an application may have strict security requirements that can be implemented within a specific OC4J container.

The list of System Components in Figure 9-25 contains a combination of OC4J containers, components specific to the Oracle Application Server, and special components designed to provide information about specific pieces of the Oracle Application Server. Special components are for informational purposes only—you cannot alter any settings on the Oracle Application Server through these special components. Notice the grayed-out check box to the left of the Portal:Portal component—this is an indication that it cannot have any actions applied to it and is a special component.

NOTE

The check box is grayed out because Enterprise Manager Application Server Control cannot apply any opmn control actions to this process (start/stop/restart, enable/disable, delete). In Portal:portal's case, all these actions are performed against OC4J_Portal. All actions exposed by the ASC are implemented at the low level by either the opmn or dcm executable (depending upon whether they are control actions or configuration actions).

The OC4J_Portal component is an example of an OC4J container, and the Portal:Portal component is an example of a special component. Click the OC4J_Portal link in the System Components section. The Home screen (Figure 9-26) provides basic information related to things like CPU Usage, Memory Usage, and Active Sessions for the container. The most important piece of information on this page, however, is contained in the All Metrics link in the bottom left of the page. Clicking this link brings you to a page that can be used to monitor real-time statistics for your portal. As an example, click the small plus sign next to OC4J Servlet Metrics, and then click the Servlet – Requests Per Second link. You'll see a list of the different servlets in your portal.

NOTE

Portal:portal means this is a Portal instance and the Database Access Descriptor (DAD) name is portal. By default the DAD will always be portal. Earlier versions of Oracle Portal, however, allowed you to use other DAD names, so if you are working with an upgraded Portal instance where the DAD name was created as something else, you will see Portal:<DAD_name>.

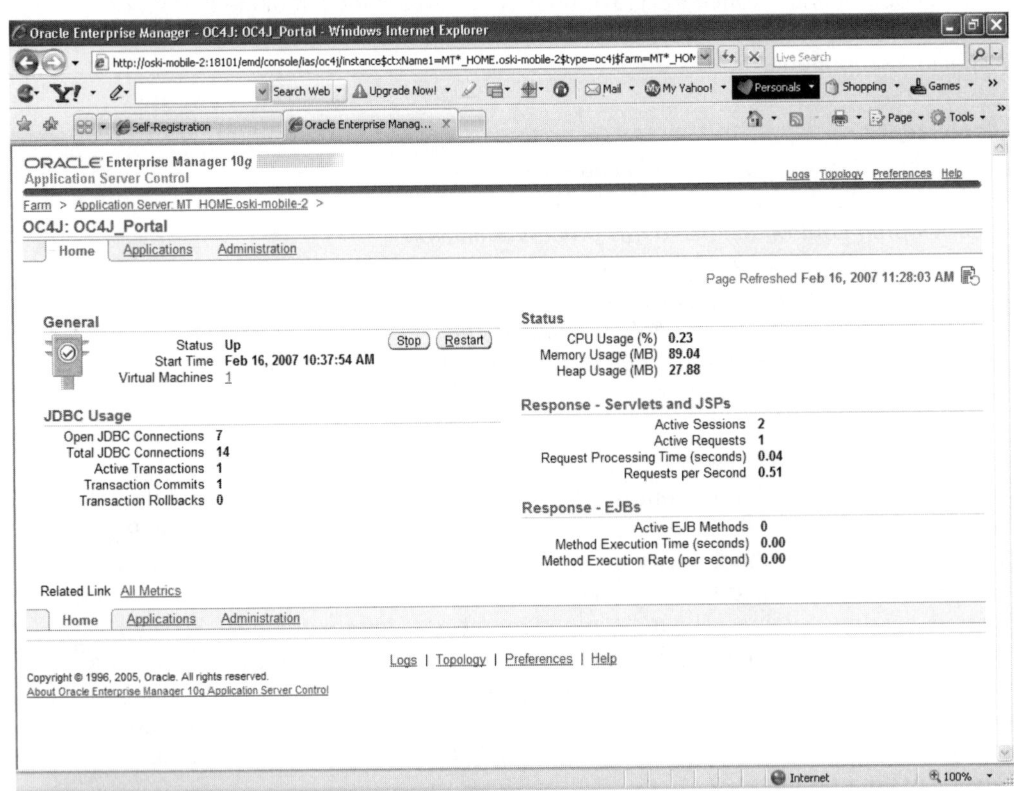

FIGURE 9-26 *The Home screen of the OC4J_Portal System Component*

In another browser, log in to OracleAS Portal, navigate to a page, and refresh it a couple of times. Now return to your browser with ASC running and click the sunglass icon next to one of the servlets. You should see activity for your servlet displayed on a graph (Figure 9-27). Information like this can be used to determine how many people are concurrently connecting to your portal, which pages and portlets are the most popular, etc. The All Metrics page provides a wealth of information regarding the state of your portal. To learn more, see the sidebar "The All Metrics Page."

The other system component of interest to us is the Portal:Portal system component. In the breadcrumb menu in the top left of the screen, click the Application Server link to return to the main ASC page. Click the Portal:Portal system component link. You will see a page similar to Figure 9-28.

The metrics pages we looked at for the OC4J_Portal instance are available for all OC4J instances. This page is unlike any of the OC4J pages in the sense that it has

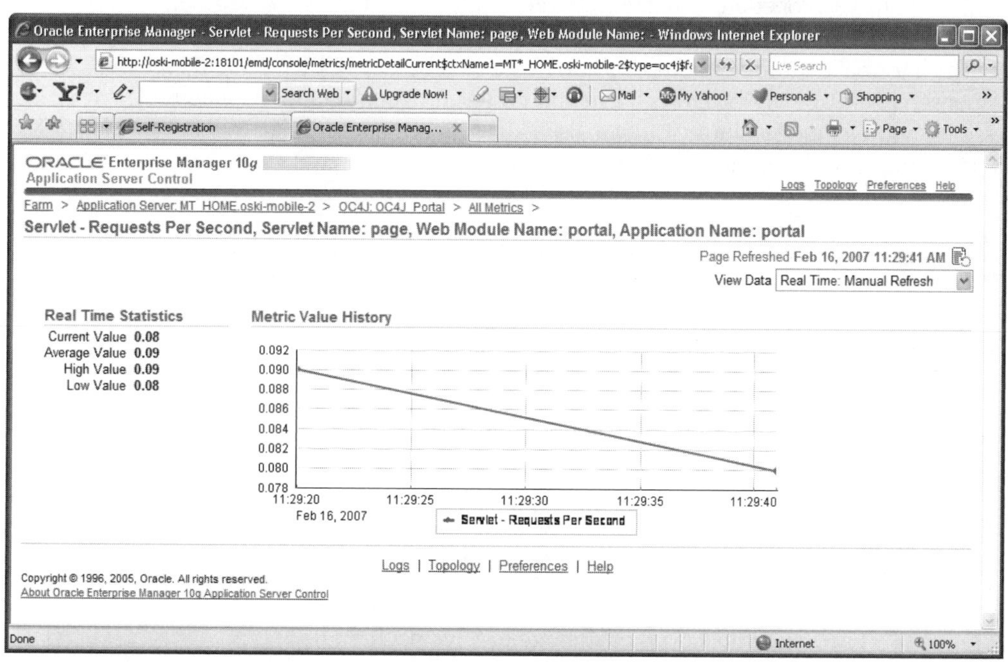

FIGURE 9-27 *Real-time metric information for Portal Components*

The All Metrics Page

It is important to note that the All Metrics page is useful only if your ASC has been running for a relatively significant period of time, as all metric information is held in memory and is lost each time ASC is restarted. This can be alleviated if you have a full OEM instance installed; you can configure the OEM Agent to upload all the same metrics into a central OEM repository where they are held for 30 days (and can then be archived). Oracle Application Server Portal performance reports can be generated using the Performance Reporting Scripts, which have been available since Oracle9*i*AS Portal Release 1 (3.0.9.8.3). These scripts allow an OracleAS Portal administrator to load Portal log files into a database table (using SQL*Loader) and run SQL*Plus reports on them. The scripts can be downloaded from http://portalcenter.oracle.com/ for Oracle Application Server Portal middle tier versions 3.0.9.8.3 and higher, and 9.0.2.3.0 and higher. In Oracle Application Server Portal 10*g*, the scripts and readme files are located in the Portal directory in the mid-tier Oracle_Home. The statistics collected indicate how long the overall request took, how much of that time was spent in the user's procedure, what user made the request, whether a database connection was obtained from the connection pool, what type of caching was used, etc. The information from these reports can be viewed by day or by hour and includes Response Time, Page Views, Errors, Page and Portlet Timeouts, Logins, Concurrent Sessions, and Unique Sessions. You can also extract information similar to the information that was available in the Oracle9*i*AS Portal Release 1 (3.0.*x*) monitoring portlets, such as

- What is the peak login time per day?
- How many logins per day does the portal receive?
- How long have portlets been taking to execute?
- What is the slowest portlet?
- How many total hits does the portal receive each day?
- Most/least popular portlets
- How often are users viewing a page or portlet?
- How many unique users have logged in each day?
- Which portlets were called?
- How many hits does each page receive each day?
- How many hits does each portlet receive each day?
- Request breakdown by IP address or host name

For more information on this rather large topic, see: http://www.oracle.com/technology/products/ias/portal/html/admin_monitor_10g_diagnostics_analytics.html.

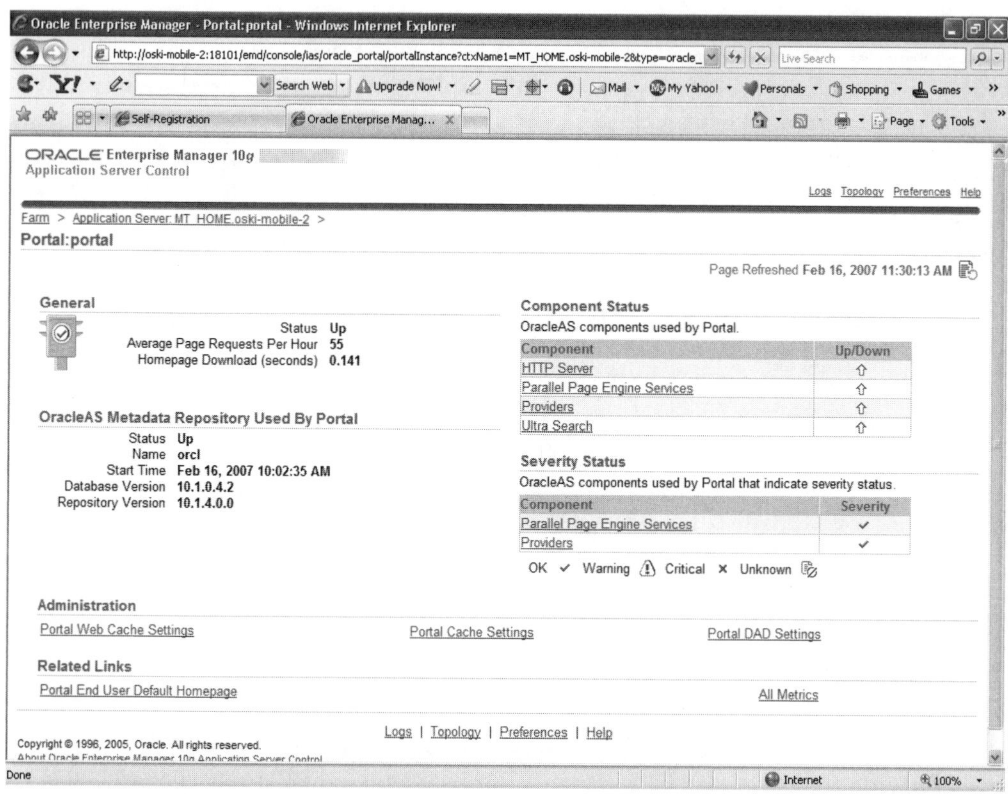

FIGURE 9-28 *Portal system component*

been specifically designed to display detailed OracleAS Portal information. On this page, general information such as status, page requests per hour, and component status are displayed. On the right-hand side of the page, click either of the Providers links (they both take you to the same page (Figure 9-29).

This page is great for getting specific information about OracleAS providers and portlets. In the top section of the page, there is a section titled Providers. This section provides performance information for all portlets, grouped into the three basic categories of portlets: database, Web, and WSRP. Below that, the section titled Performance breaks down performance information for each provider. You can then drill down into a provider to see performance information for the individual portlets deployed to that provider (Figure 9-30).

Back on the Portal:portal main page (Figure 9-28), there is another All Metrics link in the bottom right of the page. This is similar to the All Metrics link we saw on

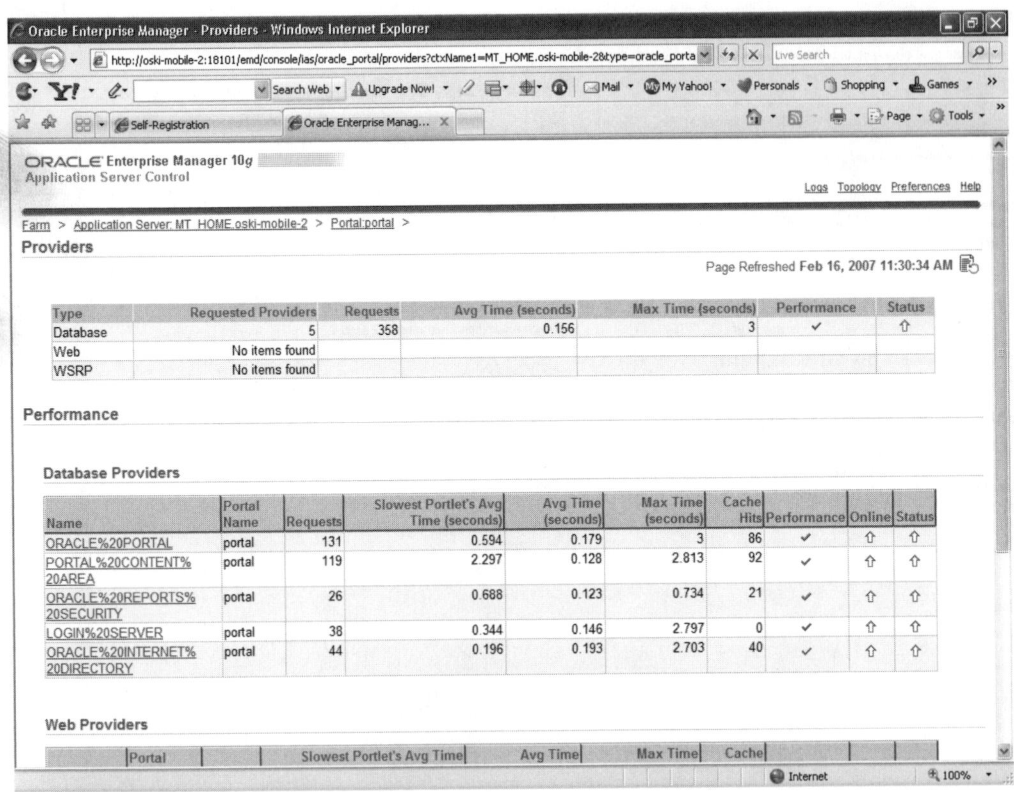

FIGURE 9-29 *The Providers Statistics page*

the OC4J_Portal page. The metrics provided here give even more OracleAS Portal-specific information that you can run in real time. None of these metrics will help bad Java code run any faster, but it can help you pinpoint where the bottlenecks are on your system.

Implementing SSL

SSL, or Secure Sockets Layer, is a protocol for transmitting secure information over the Internet. All communication between server and client is encrypted to prevent unauthorized access during transmission. In some situations, it may be beneficial (or a requirement) to implement SSL for your OracleAS Portal to prevent sensitive

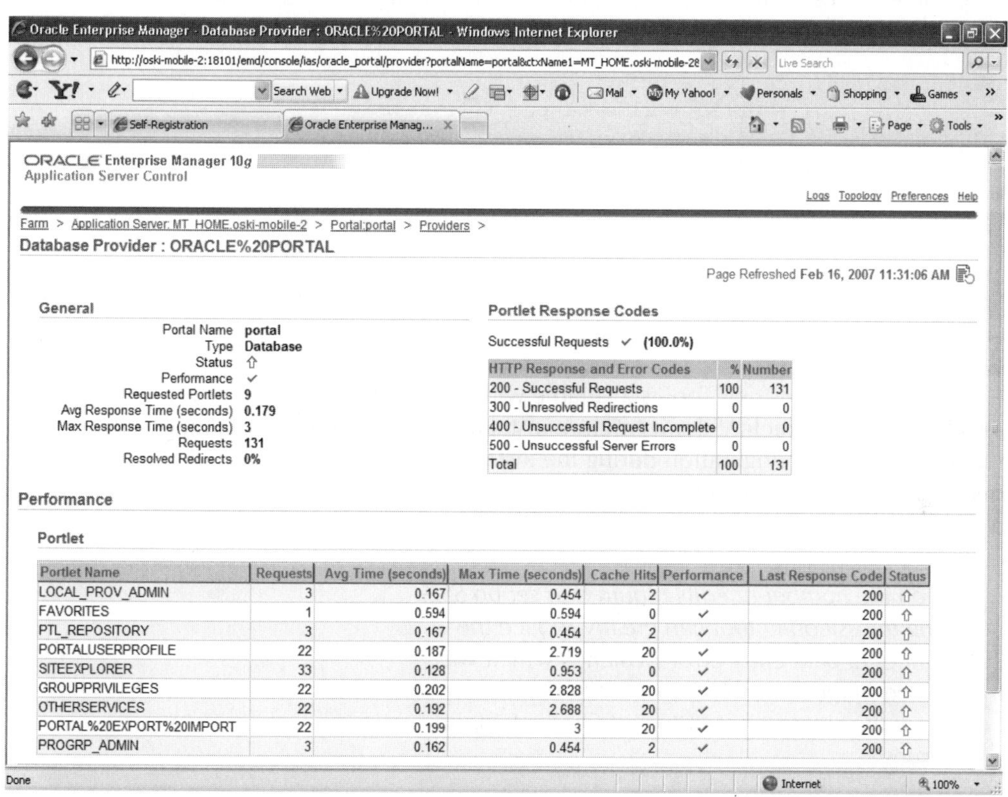

FIGURE 9-30 *The Portlet Statistics page*

information from falling into the wrong hands. This section provides an overview of the most common SSL configurations for OracleAS Portal and describes the procedures necessary to implement them.

OracleAS Portal uses a number of different components (such as the Parallel Page Engine, Oracle HTTP Server, and OracleAS Web Cache), each of which may act as a client or server in the HTTP communication. As a result, each component in the Oracle Application Server middle tier may be configured individually for the protocols of HTTPS rather than HTTP. The 10.1.2 release of the Oracle Application Server introduces the SSL Configuration Tool, which helps automate many of the manual steps currently required for configuring SSL. The SSL Configuration Tool executable is located in the ORACLE_HOME/bin directory of your middle-tier installation, and its usage syntax is as follows:

```
SSLConfigTool ( -config_w_prompt
                | -config_w_file <input_file_name>
                | -config_w_default
                | -rollback )
                [-dry_run]
                [-wc_for_infra]
                [-secure_admin]
                [-opwd <orcladmin_pwd>]
                [-ptl_dad <dad_name>]
                [-ptl_inv_pwd <ptl_inv_pwd>]
```

The SSL Configuration Tool is available with any Oracle Application Server installation type. OracleAS Infrastructure installations are the only installation type that supports SSL configuration during the installation. This option is available on one of the installation screens.

TIP
Given the number of edits required to set up SSL, using the sslconfig tool can greatly reduce the chances of data entry error (which is why it was created in the first place), as configuring SSL is one of the greatest generators of Oracle Support Requests.

If you install Oracle Application Server and choose to make some configuration changes before running the SSL Configuration Tool, you should run the tool and then refer to the SSL Configuration Tool log files to verify that your changes were not overwritten. The SSL Configuration Tool creates log files in the directory from which the tool is run. A new log file is created each time the tool is run. For these reasons, it is suggested that you create a separate directory from which you can run the SSL Configuration Tool. Table 9-1 describes the command-line options for the SSL Configuration Tool.

Before using these recommended methods to configure SSL, you must confirm that OracleAS Portal is working correctly in the (default) non-SSL configuration. To test this, you must ensure that the following portal tasks work without errors:

- The OracleAS Portal home page is accessible.
- Users can log in to OracleAS Portal.
- Edits to content are shown immediately.

Parameter	Description
–config_w_prompt	Runs in interactive mode.
–config_w_file <input_file_name>	Runs in silent mode using the values specified in the <input_file_name> file. This input file should be an XML file. See Oracle Application Server Administrator's Guide for more information.
–config_w_default	Runs in silent mode using the values specified in the portlist.ini and ias.properties files. These values would be correct at install time; these files are not updated with any subsequent configuration changes post install, however.
–rollback	Reverts to the previous state before the command was last run. SSO registration will be done using a virtual host and port.
–dry_run	Prints the steps without implementing them.
–wc_for_infra	Forces an OracleAS Web Cache to be used as a load balancer for an infrastructure environment.
–secure_admin	Secures the OracleAS Web Cache and Enterprise Manager administration ports (the ports used to display Application Server Control Console).
–opwd <orcladmin_pwd>	Sets the Oracle administrator password. This parameter is required.
–ptl_dad <dad–name>	Sets the OracleAS Portal DAD name. If no name is specified, the default portal will be used.
–ptl_inv_pwd <ptl_inv_pwd>	Sets the Portal invalidation password used to send invalidation to OracleAS Web Cache.

Table 9-1 *Command-Line Options for the SSL Configuration Tool*

If any connection should be secured with SSL, it is the connection between the browser and OracleAS Single Sign-On. The password should be protected by SSL in transit between the browser and OracleAS Single Sign-On. For at least a minimal level of security, you should configure your installation with this option. All of the subsequent SSL configurations assume that you have configured SSL for OracleAS Single Sign-On.

After you have successfully performed the checks just described, you can use either of the following two methods to configure SSL to OracleAS Single Sign-On:

- Configuring SSL to OracleAS Single Sign-On Using the SSL Configuration Tool
- Configuring SSL to OracleAS Single Sign-On Manually

Configuring SSL to OracleAS Single Sign-On Using the SSL Configuration Tool

To configure this option using the SSL configuration tool, follow these steps:

1. Enable SSL on the OracleAS Infrastructure that has Identity Management installed. Run the SSL configuration tool in the infrastructure Oracle home, as shown in the following example for Windows. In this example, config_w_default is used to run the tool in silent mode using the values specified in the portlist.ini and ias.properties files and opwd is the Oracle administrator password. If no password is specified, you will be prompted to enter the password. Enter **n** when prompted by the script to configure your site to accept browser requests using the SSL protocol.

```
SSLConfigTool.bat -config_w_default -opwd <orcladmin_pwd>
```

NOTE
In the previously described configuration of SSL, you must re-register the OracleAS Single Sign-On middle-tier partner application. Because the OracleAS Single Sign-On middle-tier partner application is still non-SSL, you must re-register it as non-SSL. Therefore, the re-registration of mod_osso needs to specify the non-SSL URL of the OracleAS Single Sign-On middle tier for the mod_osso_url parameter to ssoreg.

2. After enabling SSL on the OracleAS Infrastructure that has Identity Management installed, you must protect OracleAS Single Sign-On URLs. When the single sign-on server is enabled for SSL, you must specify that HTTP access be limited to those hosts that must access the server using this protocol. This is especially true in the case of those computers hosting the OracleAS installer and OracleAS Portal. In ORACLE_HOME/sso/conf/sso_apache.conf, locate and uncomment the three directives that follow; then provide a value for the Allow From parameter.

3. Invoke the first directive if you are installing a release 9.0.2 middle tier with a release 10.1.2 single sign-on server. This directive enables the installer to access the single sign-on server over HTTP. Replace <your_domain_name> with the fully qualified host name of the middle tier on which the installer is located; then uncomment the line. If you plan to install from more than one location, enter just a domain name.

```
<Location "/pls/orasso/*[Ss][Ss][Oo][Pp][Ii][Nn][Gg]">
Order deny,allow
Deny from all
#  Allow from <your_domain_name>
</Location>
```

4. OracleAS Portal must use HTTP to access the URL that provides a list of external applications. The directive that follows enables such access. Replace <your_domain_name> with the fully qualified Portal host name; then uncomment the directive. If you have more than one Portal database, enter just the domain name for these databases.

```
#<Location "/pls/orasso/*[Aa][Pp][Pp][Ss]_[Ll][Ii][Ss][Tt]">
#  Order deny,allow
#  Deny from all
#  Allow from <your_domain_name>
#</Location>
```

5. Versions of OracleAS Portal that predate release 9.0.2 use HTTP to verify whether a user exists in the single sign-on database. This last directive enables verification. Again, replace <your_domain_name> with the fully qualified Portal host name; then uncomment the directive. If you have more than one Portal database, enter just the domain name for these databases.

```
#<Location "/pls/orasso/[Oo][Rr][Aa][Ss][Ss][Oo].
wwsso_app_admin.validate_user*">
#  Order deny,allow
#  Deny from all
#  Allow from <your_domain_name>
#</Location>
```

6. After editing sso_apache.conf, update the repository for Distributed Cluster Management:

```
ORACLE_HOME/dcm/bin/dcmctl updateConfig -v -d
```

7. Run the SSL Configuration Tool in the middle-tier Oracle home or multiple middle-tier Oracle homes, as shown in the following example for Windows. Where config_w_prompt is passed to run the SSL Configuration Tool in

interactive mode, ptl_inv_pwd is the portal invalidation password and opwd is the Oracle administrator password. If no password is specified, you will be prompted to enter the password. Choose No when prompted to configure HTTPS.

```
SSLConfigTool.bat -config_w_prompt -ptl_inv_pwd <ptl_inv_pwd> -
opwd <orcladmin_pwd>
```

8. Set the OracleAS Single Sign-On query path URL. OracleAS Portal maintains the URL prefix of OracleAS Single Sign-On, which accesses certain information through HTTP calls from the database using the UTL_HTTP package. These calls must be done through HTTP rather than HTTPS. As a result, even if OracleAS Portal and OracleAS Single Sign-On are configured to use HTTPS, you must still have access to an HTTP port on OracleAS Single Sign-On to support these interfaces. The calls made across this interface are required to obtain the list of external applications to allow customization of the External Applications portlet and to perform the mapping of OracleAS Single Sign-On user names to external application user names. To set this URL prefix, and the OracleAS Single Sign-On Query Path URL, perform the following steps:

    a. Log in to OracleAS Portal as the portal administrator.

    b. Click the Administer tab.

    c. Click the Portal tab.

    d. Click Global Settings in the Services portlet.

    e. Click the SSO/OID tab.

    f. Edit the Query Path URL Prefix under the SSO Server Settings. Enter a URL for OracleAS Single Sign-On. On the server used for the examples in this book it would be: http://oski-mobile-2:7777/pls/orasso.

At this point, configuration is complete for SSL communication to OracleAS Single Sign-On.

Securing OracleAS Portal Pages

Once you secure the OracleAS Single Sign-On communication, the next option is to secure the communication to the "front door" of OracleAS Portal, which is OracleAS Web Cache. In this configuration, OracleAS Web Cache can forward the request to the Oracle HTTP Server, which is acting as the OracleAS Portal middle tier, using HTTP for better performance. Similarly, the Parallel Page Engine requests for portlet content that loop back to OracleAS Web Cache can request the content using HTTP.

After you have successfully performed the checks described in the previous section (the OracleAS Portal home page is accessible, users can log in to OracleAS Portal, and edits to content are shown immediately), you can use either of the following two methods to configure SSL to the OracleAS Portal Main page:

- Configuring SSL to OracleAS Web Cache Using the SSL Configuration Tool
- Configuring SSL to OracleAS Web Cache Manually

For space purposes, only Configuring SSL to OracleAS Web Cache Using the SSL Configuration Tool is discussed.

Configuring SSL to OracleAS Web Cache Using the SSL Configuration Tool

To configure SSL for OracleAS Web Cache, perform the following tasks:

1. Create a Wallet. See the section "Creating a Wallet" later in this chapter for details.
2. Run the SSL Configuration Tool in the middle-tier Oracle home to set up SSL for OracleAS Web Cache, as shown in the following example for Windows, where config_w_default is used to run the tool in silent mode using the values specified in the portlist.ini and ias.properties files and opwd is the Oracle administrator password. If no password is specified, you will be prompted to enter the password. Enter the following values when prompted by the script: **y** when prompted to configure your site to accept browser requests using the SSL protocol and **n** when asked if your Oracle HTTP Server accepts requests in SSL protocol.

   ```
   SSLConfigTool.bat -config_w_default -opwd <orcladmin_pwd>
   ```

3. Register Web providers or Provider groups. See the section "Registering Web Providers or Provider Groups Exposed over SSL" later in this chapter.
4. Add the Web provider server certificate to the trusted certificate file. See the section "Augmenting the Portal Tools Trusted Certificate File" later in this chapter for details.
5. Enable access for Oracle Ultra Search. See the section "Enabling Access for Oracle Ultra Search" later in this chapter.
6. Re-register OracleAS Portal as an Oracle Ultra Search content source. See the section "Re-Registering OracleAS Portal as an Oracle Ultra Search Content Source" later in this chapter.

Creating a Wallet The various components of OracleAS Portal use the Oracle Wallet Manager to store the certificates for the secure communication. The first step in this process is to obtain a certificate from a Certificate Authority (for example, OracleAS Certificate Authority, VeriSign, GTE CyberTrust, etc.). To obtain a digital certificate from the relevant signing authority, submit a Certificate Request (CR) uniquely identifying your server to the signing authority.

1. Open the Oracle Wallet Manager in the middle-tier MID_TIER_ORACLE_HOME. On Unix, enter **owm** from the command prompt. On Windows, invoke Oracle Wallet Manager from the Start menu.
2. Choose Wallet | New. On Unix, the wallet is stored in the following location by default: /etc/ORACLE/WALLETS/<Account Name creating the Wallet>. On Windows, the wallet is stored in the following location by default: \Documents And Settings\<Account Name creating the Wallet>\ORACLE\WALLETS.
3. Create a password for the wallet.
4. Click Yes to accept the option to create a CR.
5. Fill out the Certificate Request dialog with details that uniquely identify your server. The following table shows some sample values for the various fields in the Certificate Request dialog.

Field Name	**Sample Values**
Common Name	www.tusc.com
Organizational Unit	WebServices
Organization	TUSC
Locality/City	Lombard
State/Province (Do not use abbreviations; the value specified for state or province must be completely spelled out.)	Illinois

6. Click OK. A dialog will inform you that the certificate request was created successfully. The Certificate node in the Wallet Navigator will change to Requested.
7. Save the wallet in a convenient directory, for example,

```
MID_TIER_ORACLE_HOME\webcache\wallets\VeriSignWallet
```

8. Send the CR to the chosen Certificate Authority (CA). Certificates are issued by trusted third parties known as Certification Authorities (CA), for example, OracleAS Certificate Authority or VeriSign. For details on how to obtain a certificate, check the appropriate vendor's Web site.
   Depending on the CA, you may need to cut and paste the certificate request in their Web page or export the CR to a file for subsequent uploading to the site.
9. Select the Certificate node in the Wallet Navigator.
10. Highlight the Certificate text in the Certificate Request field. Make sure to include the BEGIN/END NEW CERTIFICATE REQUEST lines.
11. Copy and paste into the Certificate Request field on the CA's Web site.

To export the certificate request,

1. Choose Operations | Export Certificate Request.
2. Choose the Name and Location of the CR file. A Status Line Message will confirm the successful export of the CR.
3. Once exported, the CR can be uploaded to the CA's Web site.

Once the CA has processed the request, the User Certificate is forwarded to you either as text within an e-mail or as a simple file that is downloaded from a given Web page. If you are using a trial Root Certificate or have chosen a CA, which is not currently installed in the Oracle Wallet Manager, you must first import the CA's Trusted Certificate before importing your server-specific User Certificate. To import the trusted certificate,

1. Choose Operations | Import Trusted Certificate.
2. Depending on the CA, choose Paste The Certificate or Select A File That Contains The Certificate.
3. Select the appropriate certificate file or paste in the text from the e-mail. Oracle Wallet Manager expects base-64-encoded root certificates.
4. Click OK.

A status line message should appear indicating that the certificate was successfully imported. When you import the server-specific User Certificate, the certificate node in the tree structure should also display as Ready. If the certificate import fails, then it is possible that the Certificate is in a format that the Oracle Wallet Manager does not support. In this case, you need to convert it to a supported format before importing. The easiest way to do this is through the certificate Import and Export Wizards within a browser. The following steps are for the Internet Explorer browser:

1. In Internet Explorer, select Tools | Internet Options.
2. Click the Content tab.
3. Click Certificates.
4. Click the Trusted Root Certification Authorities tab.
5. Select Import and follow the wizard to import the certificate.
6. Highlight the newly imported certificate from the list.
7. Click Export and follow the wizard to the Export File Format page.
8. Choose Base-64 encoded X.509.
9. Click Next and give the certificate a filename.
10. Click Next.
11. Click Finish.
12. In Oracle Wallet Manager, choose Operations | Import Trusted Certificate.

Once the Trusted Root Certificate has been successfully imported into the Oracle Wallet Manager, you may then import the server-specific User Certificate. To import the server's user certificate,

1. Choose Operations | Import User Certificate.
2. Based on the CA, choose Paste The Certificate or Select A File That Contains The Certificate.
3. Select the appropriate certificate file or paste in the text from the e-mail.
4. Click OK.

A status line message should appear indicating that the User Certificate has been successfully imported. Having imported the certificate, it is important to save the wallet with the Autologin functionality enabled. This step is required because OracleAS Web Cache accesses the wallet as the process starts, and the wallet password is not held by OracleAS Web Cache. If this property is not set, OracleAS

Web Cache immediately shuts down if running in SSL mode. To set this property, perform the following steps:

1. Choose the Trusted Certificate you just imported from the list in the Oracle Wallet Manager.
2. Check Wallet | AutoLogin, if it is not already checked.
3. Choose Wallet | Save.

Registering Web Providers or Provider Groups Exposed Over SSL To register a Web provider that is exposed over SSL, you must have a copy of the root certificate of the certificate authority used by the Web provider. If the Web provider is using an unknown or uncommon certificate authority, you need to add the appropriate root certificate (using Base-64-encoded X.509 format) to the set of trusted certificates recognized by the Oracle Database hosting the OracleAS Metadata Repository containing the OracleAS Portal schema. To register Web providers or provider groups, perform the following steps:

1. Change directory to ORACLE_HOME/javavm/lib/security/ on the Oracle home containing the Oracle Database hosting the OracleAS Metadata Repository containing the OracleAS Portal schema.
2. Create a backup of the truststore file cacerts, for example, cacerts.bak.
3. Execute the following command to add the required certificate to the trust store:

```
$ORACLE_HOME/jdk/bin/keytool -import -alias <aliasName> -file
<root_certificate_file_name> -trustcacerts -v -keystore
$ORACLE_HOME/javavm/lib/security/cacerts
```

4. Provide the trust store password, and type **Yes** when prompted for confirmation.

If your portal schema is located in an OracleAS Metadata Repository database that was created using the OracleAS Metadata Repository Creation Assistant and if the release of that Oracle Database is earlier than 10*g* (10.1.0.*x*), these steps do not need to be performed.

Augmenting the Portal Tools Trusted Certificate File If you use the Web Page data source of OmniPortlet provider, you are doing a loopback to the Web Clipping provider and so need to add the Web provider server certificate to the trusted certificate file pointed to by the <trustedCertificateLocation> tag in OmniPortlet provider.xml file. The default certificate file is the ca-bundle.crt file, located in the MID_TIER_ORACLE_HOME/portal/conf directory.

To do this, perform the steps that follow, which are based on the Internet Explorer browser. The steps may differ slightly if you are using another browser for capturing and exporting the necessary certificate.

1. Capture the necessary certificate: Point your browser to the Web Clipping provider test page: http://<host>:<port>/portalTools/webClipping/providers/webClipping. You should see a Security Alert dialog box that shows "The security certificate was issued by a company you have not chosen to trust. View the certificate to determine whether you want to trust the certifying authority." or something similar. Click View Certificate, and then go through the following steps to export the certificate into a temporary file:
    a. Select the Details tab.
    b. Select Show: <All> in the drop-down list, and click Copy To File. Run the Export wizard to export the certificate in Base-64-encoded X.509 format into a temporary file MID_TIER_ORACLE_HOME/portal/conf/providertemp.cer.
2. Append the certificate in the temporary file to the certificate file used by OmniPortlet provider (default is MID_TIER_ORACLE_HOME/portal/conf/ca-bundle.crt).

Enabling Access for Oracle Ultra Search For Oracle Ultra Search to access secure Web sites, you need to import certificates into the crawler's trust store and the Oracle Application Server Containers for J2EE (OC4J) JVM's trust store. By default, the OC4J JVM recognizes certificates of well-known certificate authorities. However, if the secure portal instance uses a self-signed certificate or a certificate signed by an unknown certificate authority, then you must import the portal's certificate into the OC4J JVM's truststore. The OC4J JVM default truststore is located at ORACLE_HOME/jdk/jre/lib/security/cacerts. To add the required certificate to the trust store, perform the following steps:

1. Change directory to ORACLE_HOME/jdk/jre/lib/security/ on the middle tier.
2. Create a backup of the truststore file cacerts, for example, cacerts.bak.
3. Execute the following command to add the required certificate to the trust store:

```
$ORACLE_HOME/jdk/bin/keytool -import -alias <aliasName> -file
<root_certificate_file_name> -trustcacerts -v -keystore
$ORACLE_HOME/jdk/jre/lib/security/cacerts
```

4. Provide the trust store password, and type **Yes** when prompted for confirmation.

The preceding steps also need to be performed on the OracleAS Infrastructure containing the Oracle Ultra Search crawler.

Re-Registering OracleAS Portal as an Oracle Ultra Search Content Source If you use Oracle Ultra Search to crawl your portal and you reconfigure SSL throughout OracleAS Portal, you must re-register OracleAS Portal as a content source with Oracle Ultra Search. To do this, perform the following steps:

1. Access the Oracle Ultra Search administration tool:
    a. Click Ultra Search Administration in the Services portlet. The Services portlet is on the Portal subtab of the Administer tab on the Portal Builder page.
    b. Log in. If OracleAS Portal was configured using Oracle Enterprise Manager, the Oracle Ultra Search instance is not configured automatically and therefore the Ultra Search Administration link in OracleAS Portal will not work. To set this up, you must create an Oracle Ultra Search instance.
2. On the Instances tab, click Apply to set the instance. If you have more than one instance, make sure to select the instance you want to manage first.
3. On the Crawler tab, enter the Cache Directory Location and the Crawler Log File Directory. These directory locations are on the computer where Oracle Application Server middle tier is installed, for example, /tmp for the Cache Directory Location and /tmp for the Crawler Log File Directory.
4. On the Sources tab, click the Oracle Sources subtab, choose Oracle Portal (Crawlable) from the Create Source drop-down list, and click Go. Edit the OracleAS Portal data source and customize the types of documents the Oracle Ultra Search crawler should process. HTML and plain text are the default document types that the crawler will always process. You can add other document types, such as MS Word Doc, MS Excel Doc, and PDF.
5. Enter OracleAS Portal registration details:
    a. Enter the Portal Name.
    b. For URL base, enter the base URL for the portal. Use the format

    ```
    http://<host>:<port>/pls/<portal_DAD>/<portal_schema>
    ```

    c. Click Register Portal.
6. Select the page groups that you would like to create data sources for and then click Create Portal Data Sources. You can optionally edit each of the

portal data sources to add content types for processing. For example, you can add the MS Word Doc, MS Excel Doc, and PDF Doc types. A page group is available as a crawlable data source, when either the option Display Page To Public Users is set on its root page (Edit Page:Access tab) or the View privilege is granted to PUBLIC (Edit Page Group: Access tab).

7. Finally, on the Schedules tab, schedule the indexing of the portal data sources:
    a. Click Create New Schedule and enter a Name for the schedule.
    b. Click Proceed To Step 2 and specify synchronization schedule details.
    c. Click Proceed To Step 3, select Portal from the drop-down list and then click Get Sources.
    d. Move the sources over to the Assigned Sources box and click Finish.

Clicking the Status link for the source enables you to optionally run the synchronization immediately. Once you have registered OracleAS Portal as an Oracle Ultra Search content source, you can register the Ultra Search provider with OracleAS Portal.

1. In the Remote Providers portlet, click Register a Provider. By default, the Remote Providers portlet is on the Portlet subtab of the Administer tab on the Portal Builder page.
2. Fill in all the fields on the first step of the wizard.
    a. Your Timeout setting affects how long pages take to render if the portlet is not responding, so do not set it too high.
    b. Leave Implementation Style set to Web.
    c. Click Next to continue.
3. Enter the URL for the Ultra Search provider. By default this is

    ```
    http://<host>:<port>/provider/ultrasearch/servlet/soaprouter
    ```

4. Set the Service ID to be "ultrasearch."
5. Change the Login Frequency to Once Per User Session and then click Next.
6. Click the Browse Groups icon, select AUTHENTICATED_USERS, and grant Execute privileges.
7. Finally, click Finish.

Once the provider is registered with OracleAS Portal, you can add the Ultra Search portlet to portal pages. Check that an entry exists for Oracle Ultra Search in the OC4J_Portal configuration file data-sources.xml. For detailed instructions, see the Oracle Ultra Search Administrator's Guide, available from the Oracle Technology Network at http://www.oracle.com/technology/. If the entry is missing, the Ultra Search portlet cannot access the Oracle Ultra Search instance and you will see the following error when the portlet is placed on the page:

```
ORA-20000: Oracle Ultra Search error WKG-10602: Instance does
not exist ORA-06512: at "WKSYS.WK_ERR", line 179 ORA-06512: at line 1
```

When you create or register a new provider, a page is created in the Portlet Repository under Portlet Staging Area to display portlets for that provider. This page is not visible to all logged-in users. It is visible to only the user who published the provider, and the portal administrator. The publisher or portal administrator can change the provider page properties to grant privileges to appropriate users and groups, as required.

For more information about configuring SSL in OracleAS Portal, see the Oracle Application Server Portal Configuration Guide (Oracle Part Number B14037-03), Chapter 6.

Using the Log Loader

Inevitably, you will get an error message when working with OracleAS Portal. Was the message generated by portal itself, or the Java portlet that was in the process of being rendered? Maybe it was the database, or a network message. Without some sort of logging system, it would be almost impossible for OracleAS Portal administrators to find error messages quickly and fix them.

The Oracle Enterprise Manager Application Server Control has a link at the bottom of all of its pages, named Logs. Clicking this link takes you to the View Logs page of the ASC (Figure 9-31).

TIP

The Logs link also appears at the top right. This link is context sensitive, so if you click the Logs link from the Portal:portal page, you will automatically end up at the logs page with the Portal:portal component already selected.

As you can see, there are a lot of log files that Oracle Application Server uses to keep track of diagnostic information. If you know you're looking for log information related to OracleAS Portal, you could move the OC4J_Portal and Portal:portal

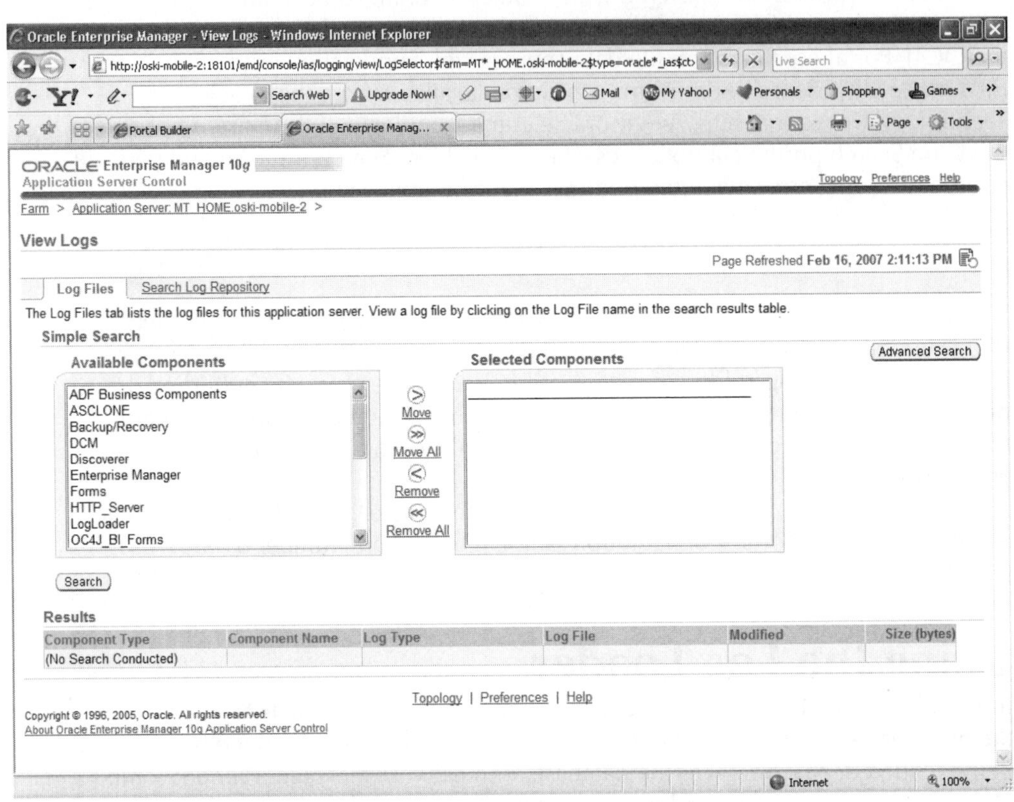

FIGURE 9-31 *The View Logs page of the Application Server Control*

components to the Selected Components box and click the Search button in the bottom left of the screen. This, however, only returns a list of all of the log files that the components have written to (Figure 9-32). There is no way to specify what you are looking for (like an error number) or when you would like the search results to reflect (you probably don't care if the OC4J_Portal component wrote to the application.log file six months ago).

The log file associated with the Portal:portal is the portal metadata repository (database) log file. By default, this log file is not created upon install, as often the database is physically located on a different server than the middle tier where the log loader and ASC are running. It is good practice to set up the portal repository log post-install and NFS-mount the file system it is located on in such a way that all

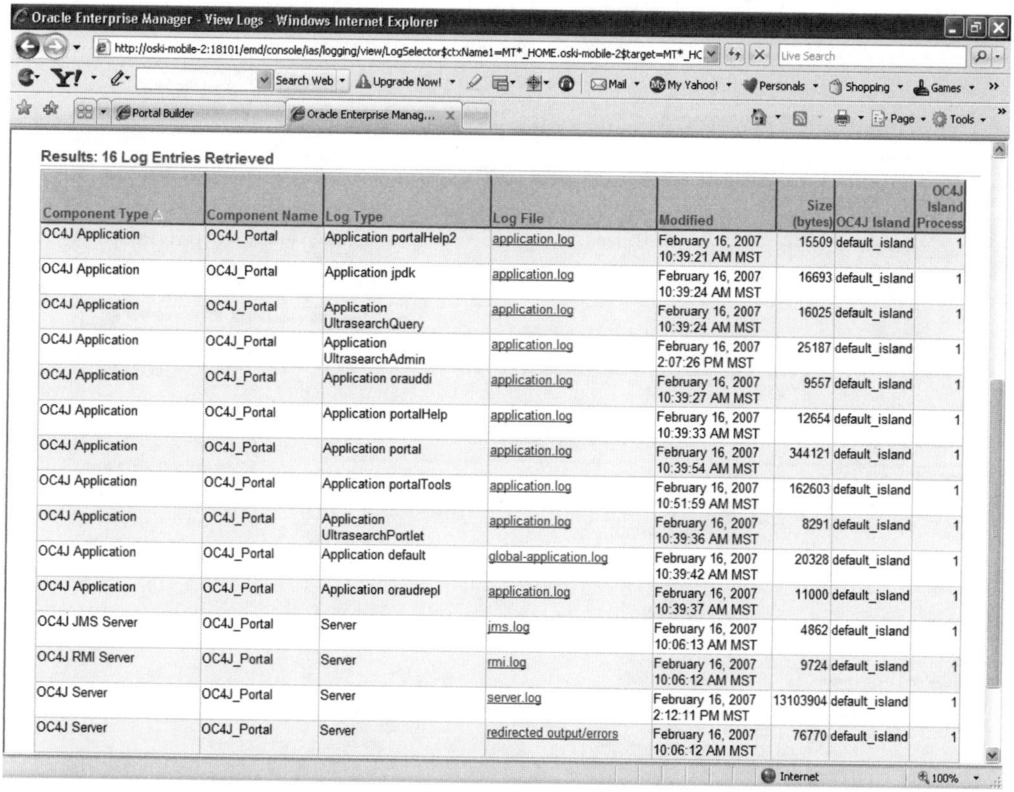

Oracle Enterprise Manager - View Logs - Windows Internet Explorer

Results: 16 Log Entries Retrieved

Component Type	Component Name	Log Type	Log File	Modified	Size (bytes)	OC4J Island	OC4J Island Process
OC4J Application	OC4J_Portal	Application portalHelp2	application.log	February 16, 2007 10:39:21 AM MST	15509	default_island	1
OC4J Application	OC4J_Portal	Application jpdk	application.log	February 16, 2007 10:39:24 AM MST	16693	default_island	1
OC4J Application	OC4J_Portal	Application UltrasearchQuery	application.log	February 16, 2007 10:39:24 AM MST	16025	default_island	1
OC4J Application	OC4J_Portal	Application UltrasearchAdmin	application.log	February 16, 2007 2:07:26 PM MST	25187	default_island	1
OC4J Application	OC4J_Portal	Application orauddi	application.log	February 16, 2007 10:39:27 AM MST	9557	default_island	1
OC4J Application	OC4J_Portal	Application portalHelp	application.log	February 16, 2007 10:39:33 AM MST	12654	default_island	1
OC4J Application	OC4J_Portal	Application portal	application.log	February 16, 2007 10:39:54 AM MST	344121	default_island	1
OC4J Application	OC4J_Portal	Application portalTools	application.log	February 16, 2007 10:51:59 AM MST	162603	default_island	1
OC4J Application	OC4J_Portal	Application UltrasearchPortlet	application.log	February 16, 2007 10:39:36 AM MST	8291	default_island	1
OC4J Application	OC4J_Portal	Application default	global-application.log	February 16, 2007 10:39:42 AM MST	20328	default_island	1
OC4J Application	OC4J_Portal	Application oraudrepl	application.log	February 16, 2007 10:39:37 AM MST	11000	default_island	1
OC4J JMS Server	OC4J_Portal	Server	jms.log	February 16, 2007 10:06:13 AM MST	4862	default_island	1
OC4J RMI Server	OC4J_Portal	Server	rmi.log	February 16, 2007 10:06:12 AM MST	9724	default_island	1
OC4J Server	OC4J_Portal	Server	server.log	February 16, 2007 2:12:11 PM MST	13103904	default_island	1
OC4J Server	OC4J_Portal	Server	redirected output/errors	February 16, 2007 10:06:12 AM MST	76770	default_island	1

FIGURE 9-32 *Results from a basic search of Application Server log files*

relevant log loader processes may access it. You will also need to register this new log file with your log loader for it to start loading logs. See section K.2.3.5, "OracleAS Metadata Repository," of the Portal Configuration Guide for more info (http://download-east.oracle.com/docs/cd/B14099_19/portal.1014/b19305/cg_app_k.htm#sthref2744).

Fortunately, the Oracle Application Server provides a tool that can be used to organize all of the application server's log files. This tool is called Log Loader, but because of its use of system resources, it is not activated by default. Click the Search Log Repository tab on the top left of the screen. A search page with many more options is displayed (Figure 9-33).

Before you can use this page, however, the Log Loader must be running. Click the Log Loader button in the top right of the page. When the Log Loader page

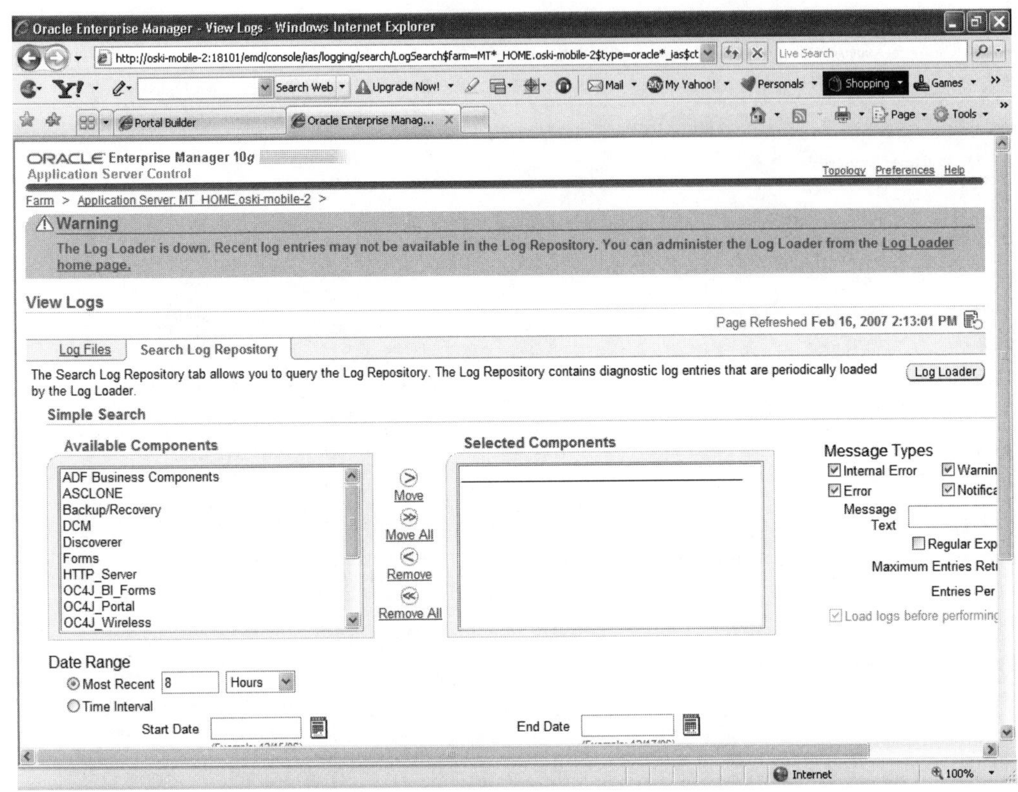

FIGURE 9-33 *The Search Log Repository page*

appears, click Start and then click Start And Load Existing Logs. After a minute or so (depending on the size of your application server log files), you will see a confirmation page. Click OK to return to the Log Loader page. Click the View Logs link in the top left to return to the View Logs page. The log loader takes all registered log files and collates them into a large XML repository where searches may be made across components easily.

Now, we have the ability to specify what we're looking for and when the message was generated. Click the Move All link in the middle of the page to select all log files. Under message types, de-select all of the check boxes and enter **ora-** in the Message Text field. Change the Date Range field to only search for the previous 4 hours and click Search. You will see a result similar to Figure 9-34.

You can get more information about any of the messages by clicking the check box next to them and clicking the View Details button at the top of listing.

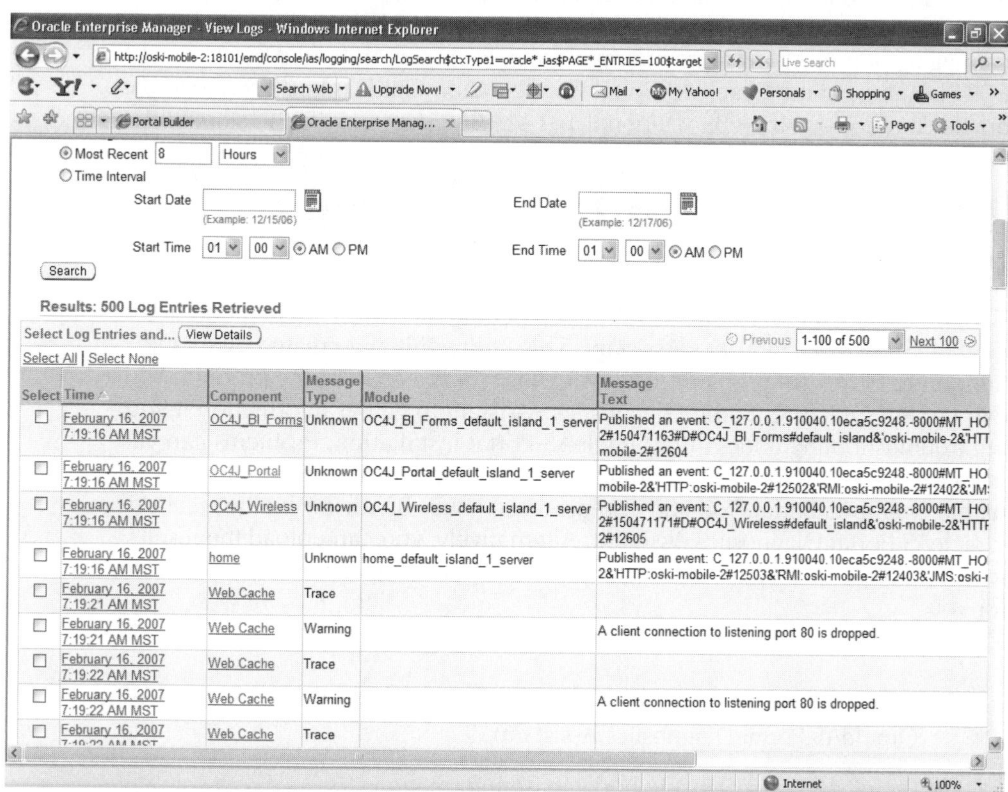

FIGURE 9-34 *Results using the Log Loader*

One of the most important benefits of using the log loader repository is that it allows you to use the ECID feature for tracking and diagnosing issues. OracleAS Portal makes use of an ECID (Execution Context Identifier), which is a unique number assigned to a request and attached to the information recorded for that request. As a request is passed from one component to another, the ECID can be incremented to form a sequence. This means that an individual request can be tracked through any number of components by following this ECID sequence.

An ECID is generated by the first Oracle Application Server component to receive a request without an ECID. ECID generation is available in OracleAS Web Cache, Oracle HTTP Server, remote Oracle Providers runnin1g in OC4J, and the Parallel Page Engine (PPE). An ECID is generated only if it does not already exist. In this release, logging of OracleAS Portal invalidations in the OracleAS Web Cache now includes the ECID of the original request. This can be used to relate invalidations to original edits or personalizations. Oracle Containers for J2EE (OC4J) can include the ECID with each log entry it writes, which can be useful for debugging purposes. For more information on ECID see Appendix K.2.1, "Enabling ECID Logging" of the OracleAS Portal Configuration Guide (http://download-east.oracle.com/docs/cd/B14099_19/portal.1014/b19305/cg_app_k.htm#sthref2691).

The OracleAS Portal Diagnostics Assistant

The discussion of diagnostics would not be complete without a mention of the OracleAS Portal Diagnostics Assistant. This utility, initially created by Oracle Support to help with problem diagnosis, now ships as part of the product. You can use the OracleAS Portal Diagnostics Assistant to gather information if you are troubleshooting issues after OracleAS Portal installation. Problems can vary from accessing the OracleAS Portal to users getting errors at different levels within OracleAS Portal. You can also diagnose issues by reviewing the results from OracleAS Portal Diagnostics Assistant. Alternatively, you can upload the results to Oracle Support Services so that they can assist in troubleshooting the problem for you.

The generated report includes the following sections:

- Errors and violations summary (available only if violations are detected by OracleAS Portal Diagnostics Assistant)
- OracleAS Portal Repository database information
- OracleAS Single Sign-On database information
- Oracle Internet Directory diagnostics report
- Oracle Text diagnostics report
- Apache error log file analysis

In addition, all OracleAS Portal–related configuration files and log files are collected and zipped for your convenience. To generate diagnostics information using OracleAS Portal Diagnostics Assistant, perform the following steps:

1. Check the Support and Metalink section on OTN at http://www.oracle.com/technology/ for the latest update/patch information for OracleAS Portal Diagnostics Assistant. Download the latest OracleAS Portal Diagnostics Assistant script. Support/Upgrade is located in the Product Information section.

2. Ensure that the ORACLE_HOME environment variable is set to the correct OracleAS Portal middle-tier Oracle home directory. If you try to run OracleAS Portal Diagnostics Assistant from a database Oracle home directory, it fails and no diagnostics information is collected.

3. Navigate to the location where you downloaded and unzipped OracleAS Portal Diagnostics Assistant.

4. Run OracleAS Portal Diagnostics Assistant on Unix. Parameters for the Portal Diagnostic Assistant are listed in Table 9-2.

```
pda.csh
-schema <portal schema name>
-password <portal schema password>
-connect <Portal connect string>
-ssoSchema <SSO schema name>
-ssoPassword <SSO schema password>
-ssoConnect <SSO connect string>
[-apacheLogDir <directory name>]
[-apacheLogName <file name>]
[-logFileLimit <number of rows>]
[-show]
[-showall]
```

Run the script without any parameters to get Help information.

The following is an example of running OracleAS Portal Diagnostics Assistant on a Unix platform:

```
# Set the environment
#
setenv ORACLE_HOME /oracle/productsAS
#
# Run PDA
#
pda.csh \
-schema portal  \
-password <portal_password>  \
-connect abc.oracle.com:1521:orcl1 \
-ssoSchema orasso \
-ssoPassword <orasso_password> \
-ssoConnect defg.oracle.com:1521:orcl2
-show
```

Parameter	Description
–schema	Name of the OracleAS Portal schema. This parameter is mandatory. Default = Portal.
–password	Password for the OracleAS Portal schema. This parameter is mandatory. Default = portal_schema.
–connect	Connect string for the OracleAS Portal schema. Use the format <host>:<port>:<sid>. This parameter is mandatory.
–ssoSchema	Name of the OracleAS Single Sign-On schema. This parameter is mandatory.
–ssoPassword	Password for the OracleAS Single Sign-On schema. This parameter is mandatory.
–ssoConnect	Connect string for the OracleAS Single Sign-On schema. Use the format <host>:<port>:<sid>. This parameter is mandatory.
–apacheLogDir	Directory for Oracle HTTP Server error log file. This parameter is optional. Default = ORACLE_HOME/Apache/Apache/logs.
–apacheLogName	Error log filename. This parameter is optional. Default = error_log.
–logFileLimit	The number of rows in the error log file. This parameter is optional. Default = 10000.
–show	Generates diagnostics information with only the necessary set of queries. This is the default mode for generating diagnostics information when no other parameters are selected.
–showall	Generates diagnostics information with all the queries. This mode has an additional query that retrieves all the portal objects and their privileges from the relevant security table. Because of this, generating diagnostics information in the –showall mode takes a very long time.

Table 9-2 *Parameters for the Portal Diagnostic Assistant*

To run OracleAS Portal Diagnostics Assistant on Windows, follow these steps:

1. Start up a command prompt, and run the following command:

```
pda.cmd
-schema <portal schema name>
-password <portal schema password>
-connect <Portal connect string>
-ssoSchema <SSO schema name>
-ssoPassword <SSO schema password>
-ssoConnect <SSO connect string>
[-apacheLogDir <directory name>]
[-apacheLogName <file name>]
[-logFileLimit <number of rows>]
[-show]
[-showall]
```

2. Open the latest HTML report (pda.htm) in a browser window and use the information to help diagnose any OracleAS Portal issues.

Exercise

Modify your Welcome page so that it has the professional look of a production Web site. You can find other sites on the Internet using OracleAS Portal to get ideas for your Welcome page by searching for "pls/portal" on Google.

Summary

As we have seen in this chapter, administration of OracleAS Portal can include anything from changing the page users see when they first access our portal to setting up the secure sockets layer to secure our portal. The administration of OracleAS Portal is made easier through the various Web pages included as seeded pages within OracleAS Portal and the performance tuning pages included as part of the Oracle Enterprise Manager Application Server Control. By using these pages effectively, OracleAS Portal Administrators can minimize the time and resources needed to keep their OracleAS Portal site running smoothly.

CHAPTER 10

OracleAS Portal Users and Security

he World Wide Web, as it exists today, was never originally intended for transactional interaction with end users. For this reason, applications that run in a Web browser and that require a security model usually involve incredible amounts of complex code that maintains a user's identity throughout the session. Developers have been assisted in developing these security models through the use of frameworks in the last couple of years, but it is still an arduous task made even more complex through the need for comprehensive testing before moving a Web-enabled application to production status. All of the features and functionality of OracleAS Portal that we've discussed so far in this book would be of limited value if the security mechanism used to authenticate users was difficult to administer. Thankfully, OracleAS Portal has a fully integrated system for creating and maintaining users and security so that the gory details of creating secure OracleAS Portal portlets and pages are hidden from administrators. In this chapter, we will discuss how to create and administer users, the concept of groups, which allow privileges to be assigned to users en masse, and how the OracleAS Portal engine evaluates privileges when an end user requests an OracleAS Portal page.

How OracleAS Portal Handles Security

When data is stored in an Oracle database and a database administrator wants to give access to a user, the database administrator usually creates a new user in the database and then grants privileges to that user so that the user can see the information. The privilege can be either a system privilege or an object privilege. A *system* privilege allows the user to do something to the database such as create a table or modify an index. An *object* privilege allows the user to do something to a specific object in the database such as query the data from the EMPLOYEE table owned by the HR user, as an example. Much like database users, users of OracleAS Portal are afforded similar properties, but instead of system privileges like "create table" or "modify index," the system privileges are related to OracleAS Portal tasks like creating page groups or modifying a provider. Furthermore, Oracle Portal separates privileges into different scopes, Instance and Global. While a given privilege may be granted to the user, the scope defines to which objects that privilege may be applied. Instance level allows the action against a named object, while Global allows the privilege to be assigned to any object of the named type.

The Administer tab is available to any OracleAS Portal user who logs in with administration privileges. Clicking this tab in the Portal Builder will display the OracleAS Portal Administration page (Figure 10-1). On the right side of the page are four portlets that will be used to add and modify users and groups.

The top portlet, User, creates new OracleAS Portal users or modifies existing ones. Clicking the Create New Users link takes you to a Delegated Administration Service (DAS) unit, which is a targeted subcomponent of the overall Oracle Identity

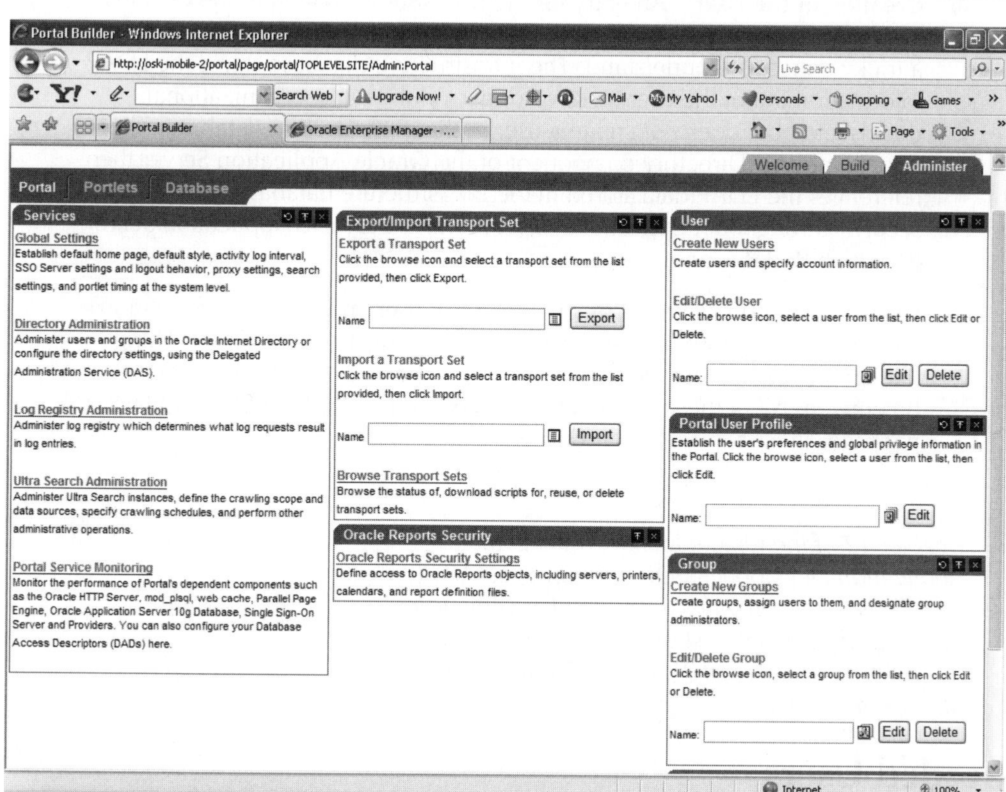

FIGURE 10-1 *The OracleAS Portal Administration page*

Management Self-Service Console. On this page, administrators can enter the details of the new OracleAS Portal user they would like to create. There are a couple of important things to note on this page:

- **The URL** If you are working on a system that has both the infrastructure and mid-tier installed on the same machine, you'll notice that the URL is referencing a new port number. If you are working on a system where the infrastructure and mid-tier are installed on different machines, you'll note that the URL now references the server where the infrastructure is installed. The creation of new users is handled by Web pages in the infrastructure instance, and you are taken there to create and modify users. When you are finished creating or modifying a user, you are returned to your OracleAS Portal administration page.

- **Creation of the User** An entry for the new user is created in the Oracle Internet Directory, not as a user in the infrastructure database. This can be a tricky concept to understand. The infrastructure database stores the LDAP information about the user (password, personal details, organizational details, etc.) but does *not* create a user in the infrastructure database. The Oracle Internet Directory component of the Oracle Application Server then references the LDAP data stored in the infrastructure database to enforce security throughout applications deployed to the Oracle Application Server (of which Portal is one).
- **User Information** When creating an LDAP user, much more information can be entered about the user than when creating a database user. Things like employee number, work numbers, office, and even a home address can be entered. All of these fields can be referenced by both PL/SQL and Java packages in an application as desired.

TIP
Chapter 12 of the Oracle Identity Management Application Developer's Guide, "DBMS_LDAP PL/SQL Reference," provides a wealth of information. See http://download-west.oracle.com/docs/cd/B14099_19/idmanage.1012/b14087/dbmsldap_ref.htm#OIMAD009.

Seeded Users

By default, a number of OracleAS Portal users are created automatically when OracleAS Portal is installed. These users have different capabilities and are used to set up your portal. The following users and their capabilities are installed by default:

- **PORTAL** This is the superuser for the portal. In a standard installation, the user name is PORTAL. This user account has the highest privileges because it is granted all the global privileges available in the portal. The initial password for PORTAL is the password that is supplied when naming the middle-tier instance during the Oracle Application Server installation. This user is also an Oracle Instant Portal administrator for every Oracle Instant Portal, regardless of who created them.
- **ORCLADMIN** Similar to PORTAL, this account is granted the highest privileges in OracleAS Portal. For DBAs reading this, this account is similar to the SYS account that is created automatically when creating a database instance. This account is created for the Oracle Application Server administrators and uses the password that is supplied when naming the

middle-tier instance during the Oracle Application Server installation. This user is also an Oracle Instant Portal administrator for every Oracle Instant Portal, regardless of who created them.

- **PORTAL_ADMIN** Is a privileged OracleAS Portal user account with administrative privileges excluding those that would give the user the ability to obtain higher privileges or perform any database operations. This user cannot edit any group or manage privileges on any schema or shared object. This account is typically intended for an administrator who manages pages and provisions user accounts. The initial password for PORTAL_ADMIN is the password that is supplied during the Oracle Application Server installation.
- **PUBLIC** This account identifies unauthenticated access to the OracleAS Portal. Once a user logs in, the user name changes from PUBLIC to the user name by which the user is authenticated. When granting portal privileges on individual objects that do not have an explicit check box for granting the object to Public, this user can be identified as the grantee of the privilege to grant access to it for unauthenticated users.

NOTE
There is a default group included with OracleAS Portal called Authenticated Users. This group refers to any user who has logged in (authenticated) to OracleAS Portal. Any security privilege granted to an authenticated user will apply to any user who has logged in. Any privilege granted to the PUBLIC user, in contrast, applies to anyone accessing the OracleAS Portal resource, whether they are logged in or not.

Default Schemas

One of the concepts that many OracleAS Portal administrators struggle with is the difference between users in OracleAS Portal and users in the infrastructure database. OracleAS Portal users are called "lightweight" users, and their information is stored in a part of the Oracle Application Server called Oracle Internet Directory (OID). OID uses a standard called LDAP (Lightweight Directory Access Protocol) to store information about users. One of the interesting things about the LDAP standard is that it does not mandate how the information about your users should be stored. Oracle, being Oracle, decided to use a database to store that information. The information stored about OID users is not stored in a traditional relational-database way. For example, when a lightweight user is created, there is *no* corresponding database user created. There is simply an entry created in a database table (or set of tables) that holds the lightweight user's information (this information is encrypted in the database). The OID component of the Oracle Application Server is then used to access the information in those tables, and OracleAS Portal then takes the response from OID to determine whether to give or deny access to an OracleAS Portal component.

When you work with OracleAS Portal creating portlets and pages, the objects you create need to be stored someplace. Oracle uses the infrastructure database installed with the Oracle Application Server to store those objects. For this reason, there are schemas created in the infrastructure database to hold the various OracleAS Portal objects:

- **PORTAL** This schema contains the OracleAS Portal database objects and code. To execute Web-requested procedures, Portal Services uses N-Tier authentication to connect to the schema to which the lightweight user accounts are assigned (by default, PORTAL_PUBLIC). The default name for this schema in a standard OracleAS Portal installation is PORTAL. This can be a confusing concept for new users of OracleAS Portal—there is an LDAP user named PORTAL and a database user named PORTAL. They are completely different types of users: the LDAP user is for Web applications (like OracleAS Portal) and the other is a database user. They also have different passwords—the LDAP PORTAL user uses the password specified when the middle-tier is installed, and the database PORTAL user has its password generated randomly during installation.
- **PORTAL_PUBLIC** This is the schema that all lightweight users are mapped to by default. All procedures publicly accessible through the Web have the execute privilege granted to PUBLIC, which makes them accessible through this schema. In a standard OracleAS Portal installation, this schema is named PORTAL_PUBLIC.
- **PORTAL_DEMO** This schema is used to hold some demonstration code. The installation of this schema is optional.
- **PORTAL_APP** This schema is used for external JSP application authentication.

Creating Users

To create a new OracleAS Portal user, follow the process mentioned earlier in this chapter—log in to your portal as a user with administration privileges (like portal or orcladmin), click the Administer tab on the top right of the page, and then click the Create New Users link in the top right. You will see a page similar to the one shown Figure 10-2.

NOTE
Usernames in OracleAS Portal are not case-sensitive; however, they are stored in the LDAP directory in the case in which they were entered. Hence, if you access the LDAP directory directly, you must be aware of the case that was used to create the user in the first place.

The Oracle Identity Management Self-Service Console is the page where new OracleAS Portal users are created. There is a lot of information that can be added for a user (much more that creating a database user), but only a few of the fields are mandatory. The links along the top of the screen (Additional Personal Details,

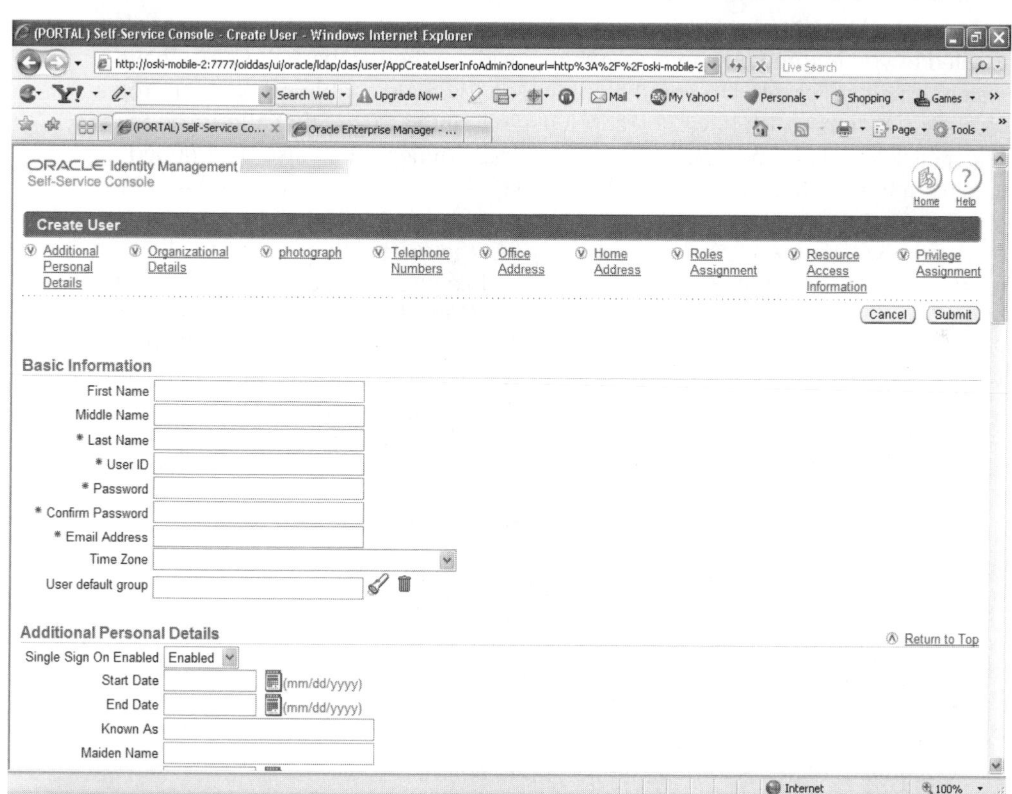

FIGURE 10-2 *The Oracle Identity Management Self-Service Console*

Organizational Details, etc.) can be used to jump to those sections of this page. At the very bottom of the page are three sections dealing with privileges: Roles Assignment, Resource Access Information, and Privilege Assignment. These sections will be discussed shortly.

The fields marked with an asterisk are the only mandatory fields that need to be entered when creating a new user. User ID and Password are the fields your user will use to log in to your portal. All of the other fields on this page (Organization Details, Telephone Numbers, etc.) are stored in the infrastructure database and can be referenced programmatically in your portal if so desired. The attributes that can be used to search for a user are definable within the full Oracle Identity Management Self-Service Console. These attributes are used for the search lists of values (LOVs). The bottom three sections on the page deal with user privileges.

User Privileges

If you've worked with databases, you know that, as a user, you need certain privileges granted to you before you can do anything inside of the database. You may have system privileges granted to you that allow you to create a table or index or drop a sequence. You may also have object privileges granted to you that allow you to select or delete data from a specific table. These privileges can also be grouped together into roles that can then be granted to database users to make the assignment of privileges easier in large systems.

Similarly, OracleAS Portal has a privilege-based system that is used to allow or restrict users to OracleAS Portal–based objects like pages and portlets. At the bottom of the Oracle Identity Management Self-Service Console page is a section called Privilege Assignment (Figure 10-3). In this section, administrators can explicitly assign system privileges to the users they create. If the new user is not granted any of these privileges, the Administer tab will not display for this user when that user logs in. Just like a database user, an OracleAS Portal user can be granted these privileges implicitly via a role (discussed shortly).

NOTE

While it is possible to directly assign privileges to a user, it is recommended that any OracleAS Portal security policy be based around a role-based access control (RBAC) philosophy: privilege assignment is never granted explicitly to an individual user but rather is provisioned through the appropriate role assignment. OracleAS Portal allows you to enforce an RBAC model by unchecking the Enable Privilege Assignment In DAS option on the SSO/OID tab of the global settings page.

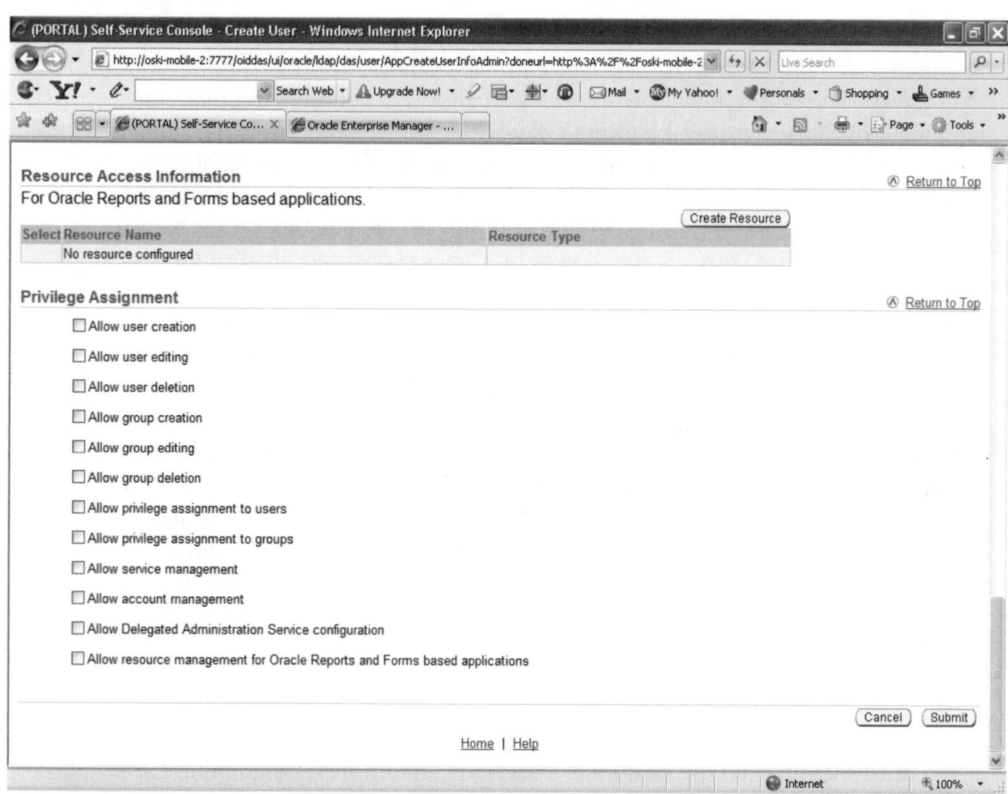

FIGURE 10-3 *The Privilege Assignment section*

Right above the Privilege Assignment section of the Create User page is a section titled Resource Access Information. This section is commonly used to link database credentials (a username/password combination) with OracleAS Portal users for Oracle Reports and Oracle Forms.

Resource access descriptors (RADs) are not limited to the use of Oracle Forms and Oracle Reports, however. They can be used to define credentials for any external application that does not have a standard Web interface. For more information about Oracle Forms and Reports, see the sidebar "Other Oracle Reports and Forms-Based Applications."

Other Oracle Reports and Forms-Based Applications

If you are not familiar with Oracle's other development products, understand that Oracle Forms is a development tool that allows developers to create applications that are driven by Oracle databases quickly and easily. Oracle Reports allows developers to create complex reports from Oracle databases quickly and easily. Two of the components of the Oracle Application Server are called Forms Server and Reports Server, and they do exactly what their names suggest; namely, the Forms Server serves up Oracle Forms applications to users in their Web browsers, and the Reports Server does the same for Oracle Reports. In order for Oracle Forms and Oracle Reports to populate their respective forms and reports with data, however, they need to communicate (log in) to an Oracle database. If you have an Oracle Form or Oracle Report that is used by two or three users, giving them the username and password for the database is probably not a big deal, but what if you have an Oracle Form or Report that is used by 500 or 5,000 users? Giving out the username and password is not such a good idea. In those circumstances, you can use the Resource Access Information section to associate an Oracle Single Sign-On (SSO) account with a corresponding database credential to give those users access to the data on the Oracle Form or Oracle Report without making them explicitly log in to the database.

The third section from the bottom is a section called Roles Assignment. Here, you can assign a role to an OracleAS Portal user. Any privileges granted to the role are automatically granted to that user when they become a member of that group. You can create your own roles, but by default, several roles are created when OracleAS Portal is installed:

- **Privilege Group** This group's description says "Grant members full DAS privileges." DAS (the name stands for Delegated Administration Services) is a component of Oracle Internet Directory, which is the LDAP component of the Oracle Application Server. It allows users and application administrators to perform trusted proxy-based administration of directory information. You can assign administrative responsibilities according to business requirements and control security policies for different components of the enterprise.
- **Oracle Collaboration Suite Users** This group is for users for whom the Oracle Collaboration Suite home page is the default page. Oracle

Collaboration Suite is an Oracle Application Server–based product from Oracle that makes use of OracleAS Portal for many of its features.

- **DBA** This group is for users who need administration privileges in the infrastructure database for OracleAS Portal. When a user's role is granted in the OracleAS Portal Navigator, a tab called Database Objects will appear giving that user the ability to create or drop schemas as well as full privileges on any of the objects in those schemas. It is important to note that this applies to the Oracle Application Server infrastructure database only, not to any of the consumer databases that your organization will use to drive your OracleAS Portal applications.
- **PORTAL_ADMINISTRATORS** Members of this group are granted privileges to perform administration tasks in Portal such as the tasks discussed in this chapter (create/modify OracleAS Portal users and groups) and those mentioned in Chapter 9.
- **PORTLET_PUBLISHERS and PORTAL_DEVELOPERS** Traditionally, although not always, there is a division of labor when it comes to creating Web-based applications, resulting in two distinct skill sets: Web designers, who are focused on a Web site's design (and less concerned with the programmatic functionality of the site), and Web developers, who focus on the functionality and are less focused on the site's design. In that spirit, there are two roles created to reflect this. PORTLET_PUBLISHERS have privileges to design pages and place portlets on pages, but do not have privileges to create portlets. Likewise, PORTAL_DEVELOPERS have the ability to create portlets, but no privileges to create pages or place their portlets on pages. You are certainly not limited to these roles, as you can create roles that model the division of responsibilities within your organization, but they provide a good starting point for setting up your OracleAS Portal responsibilities.
- **UDDI Unlimited Quota Users Group, UDDI Publishers Group, UDDI Replicators Group, UDDI Administrators Group** UDDI (the term stands for Universal description, discovery, and integration) is used when developing and deploying Web services. UDDI is an online directory that gives businesses and organizations a uniform way to describe their services, discover other companies' services, and understand the methods required to conduct business with a specific company. It serves as a specification for maintaining standardized directories of information about Web services, recording their capabilities, location, and requirements in a universally recognized format. It is seen (with SOAP and WSDL) as one of the three foundation standards of Web services.

The Portal User Profile

When you clicked the Create New Users link in Figure 10-1, you were taken to the Oracle Identity Management Self-Service Console, which allowed you to enter basic information about the new OracleAS Portal user. There's another link on the OracleAS Portal Administer tab that allows you to enter more information about the new OracleAS Portal user. After creating the new user as described in the preceding section, enter that user's name in the Portal User Profile portlet on the Administer tab of OracleAS Portal and click Edit to be taken to the Edit Portal User Profile page (see Figure 10-4). This page is divided into two tabs: Preferences and Privileges.

Preferences Tab

On the Preferences tab, there are six sections:

- **Portal Privileges** If you want to quickly disable a user, you can do so here. That user's objects (Pages, Portlets, etc.) remain in the repository, but that user can no longer log in if the check box is unchecked.
- **Database Schema** As mentioned earlier, all of the objects generated or created within OracleAS Portal need to be stored someplace. The schema defined here serves as the default schema to store these objects. Normally, when a new provider is created a schema is specified to store all of that provider's objects. Whatever is specified here will show up as the default schema when the provider is defined.
- **Personal Page** Create a personal page for the user.
- **Default Group** A user can be the member of numerous groups. One of those groups can be specified as the default group. This is important when defining a default page for the user (see the Default Home Page bullet point that follows).
- **Default Style** Styles are used to control the overall look of an OracleAS Portal page. A user can have a default style applied to all of his or her pages here.
- **Default Home Page** Here, you can define a home page for a specific user. There are three levels OracleAS Portal checks when determining what page to display to the end user after that user logs in:
- Is there a default home page defined for this user? If so, that page is displayed.
- Is there a default home page defined for the default group for the user? If so, that page is displayed.

- If there is no page defined for the user or the default group, then the default page for the site is displayed.
- **Clear the Cache in Web Cache for User** When changes are made to a user's profile, they don't always show up immediately because of OracleAS Portal's caching capabilities. You can make the change occur immediately by clicking the Clear the Cache in Web Cache for User check box and by clicking either Apply or OK. Note that entries in the cache are keyed against the individual username (if user-level caching is enabled). Clearing the cache will remove the user-specific entries from the cache but has no effect on system-level cached objects accessed by the user.

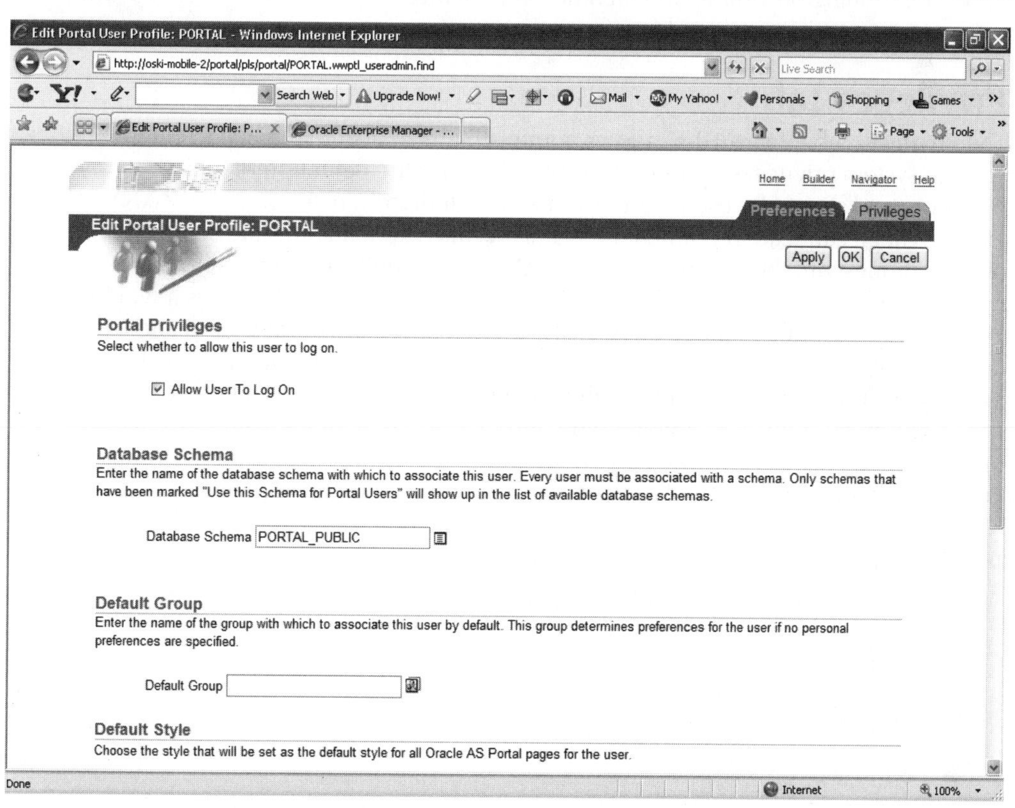

FIGURE 10-4 *The Preferences tab of the Edit Portal User Profile screen*

NOTE
This is another frustrating point for new OracleAS Portal users. A cache is a piece of memory (usually) that holds recent requests. When a user makes another request, the cache is checked to see if the information is already there. If it is, the cache can serve up that information to the end user very quickly, saving processing and response time. In Oracle Application Server 10g, there are sophisticated caching programs both in the Application Server itself (a component called the Web Cache) and in the portal component. Additionally, all major browsers have their own cache running on your local machine—any of these can (temporarily) report "old" information.

Privileges Tab

The Privileges tab (Figure 10-5) allows administrators to assign OracleAS Portal–specific system privileges to users. This tab allows for the definition of global privileges and should be used with extreme care. Indiscriminate use of any "ANY_xxx" privilege can lead to unintended results. While explicit grants are scoped to the object on question, the assignment of an "ANY_xxx" privilege gives just that: the right to apply the granted action on *any* object of that type in the Portal as a whole. For example, granting Manage on ANY_PAGE to a user allows that user to access (and modify) any page in the system, regardless of the user's individual rights on the page. These privileges effectively grant superuser privileges (at least at the level specified) on all objects of a given type and determine what the user can do regarding page design. The page is divided into three main sections: Page Group Privileges, Portal DB Provider Privileges, and Administration Privileges.

Page Group Privileges

This section is divided into the following privileges:

- All Page Groups
- All Pages
- All Styles
- All Providers
- All Portlets

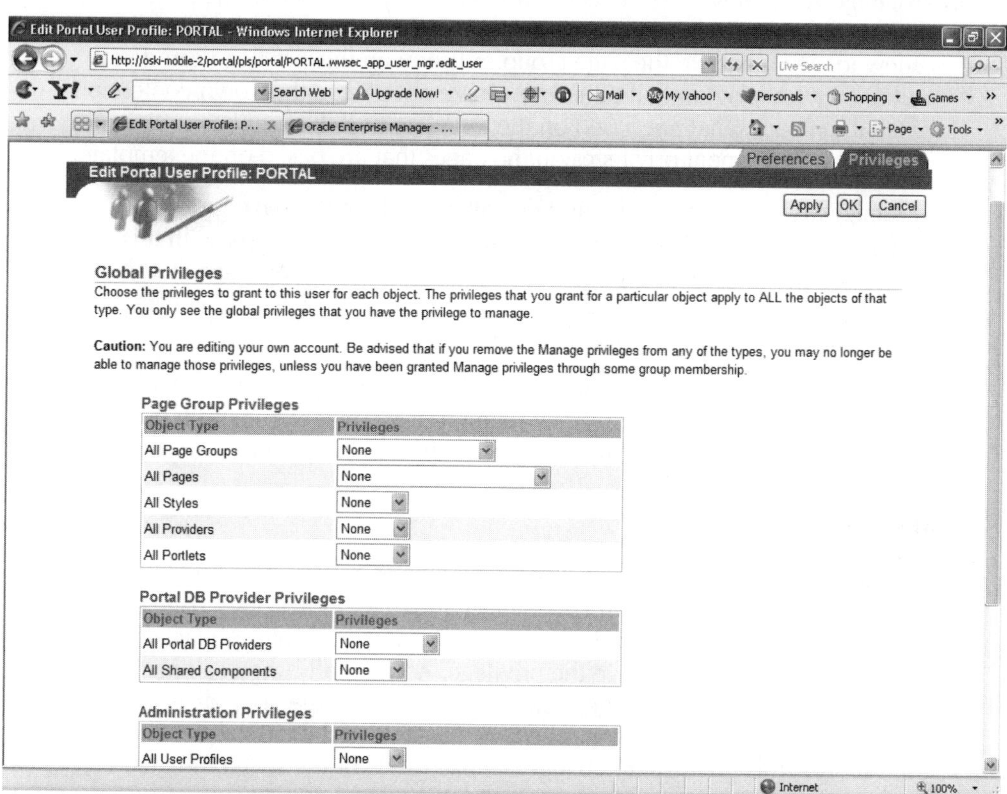

FIGURE 10-5 *The Privileges tab of the Edit Portal User Profile screen*

All Page Groups

- **Manage All** Perform any task within the page group. The Manage All privilege includes all other page group privileges: Manage Classifications, Manage Templates, Manage Styles, and View. A user with this privilege is called the page group administrator.
- **Manage Classifications** Create, edit, and delete any category, perspective, attribute, custom item type, and custom page type in the page group. A user with this privilege must also have the page group privilege View to view pages in this page group. Users with this privilege cannot delete item or page types they have created if the portal contains items or pages based on the type. Such users must first obtain privileges on the items and pages.

- **Manage Templates** Create, edit, and delete any template in the page group. A user with this privilege must also have the page group privilege View to view pages in the page group. A user with this privilege can delete a tab on a template only if other users have not placed their own content on the tab on pages that are based on the template or if the user has sufficient content management privileges on the pages that are based on the template.
- **Manage Styles** Create, edit, and delete any style in the page group, and change the style applied to any page in the page group. A user with this privilege can also view any page in the page group. The Manage Styles privilege does not provide grantees with any personalization privileges on the page groups on which it is granted.
- **View** View the content of any page in the page group, but cannot add, remove, show, or hide any content within those pages. A user with this privilege can also preview any externally published portlet in the page group.

All Pages

- **Manage** A user with the page privilege Manage can perform any operation on the page or tab. The Manage privilege includes all the other page or tab privileges. Such users can add regions to a page and create subpages under the page on which they have the privilege. Additionally, they can perform all of the actions listed for the Manage Content privilege, as well as control page or tab access and the page style or the style of the tab's regions. For a user with this privilege to change the page style or the style of the tab's regions, the page group option Allow Privileged Users To Manage Style must be selected at the page group level. Selecting this option enables the user to apply a different style when editing the page or the tab's regions. If this option is not selected at the page group level, only users with the page group privilege Manage All or Manage Styles can apply a different style to the page or the tab's regions. There is a second page group option for controlling page styles called Allow Privileged Users To Personalize Page Style. When this option is selected, users with at least the page privilege Personalize (Style) can apply a different style when personalizing the page. If a page is based on a template, users with the Manage privilege may not be able to control page or tab access and style. There are two template-level options, Enable Pages To Have Different Access and Enable Pages To Use Different Style, that control whether page designers can specify different access and style settings. These template-level options must be selected; otherwise, page or tab access and style settings cannot be changed on pages that use the template, even though users have the Manage privilege.

- **Manage Content** Users with the page or tab privilege Manage Content can add, edit, hide, show, share, and delete any item, subitem, portlet, or tab on the page or tab's defined regions. Such users can also personalize pages according to the personalize page privileges and can view the page.
- **Manage Items With Approval** A user with the page or tab privilege Manage Items With Approval can add or edit items on the page or tab, but the changes are published only after the defined approval process is complete. This page privilege is available only when approvals are enabled on the page's page group. If approvals are enabled, but an approval process is not defined, users with this privilege can add, edit, or copy items on the page or tab without approval. In other words, when approvals are enabled but an approval process is not defined, the page privilege Manage Items With Approval becomes equivalent to the page privilege Manage Content with regard to items. This privilege is not available for mobile pages. Users with the page or global privilege Manage Items With Approval can also personalize the pages on which they have the privilege and can view the page.
- **Manage Style** A user with the page or tab privilege Manage Style can change the style of the page and regions on the page or regions on the tab. The Manage Style privilege includes all of the page personalization privileges and the View privilege on the pages on which it is granted. For a user with the Manage Style privilege to change the style of a page or a region on a tab, the page group option Allow Privileged Users To Personalize Page Style must be selected for the page's page group. This option is available on the Main tab of page group properties. If a page is based on a template, users with the Manage Style privilege may not be able to control the style of the page. The template-level option Enable Pages To Use Different Style must be selected on the template to enable users with the Manage Style privilege to change the style of a page that is based on the template. This privilege is not available for mobile pages.
- **Personalize Portlets (Full)** A user with the page or tab privilege Personalize Portlets (Full) can alter his own view of the page by changing the style of the page; adding portlets to the page; and deleting, moving, hiding, or showing any portlet on the page. For a user with this privilege to change the style of a page or of a region on the tab, the page group option Allow Privileged Users To Personalize Page Style must be selected for the page or tab's page group. Such users can also view any page on which they have the privilege. Changes made under Personalize privileges are visible only to the user who made them. For example, if a user with the Personalize Portlets (Full) privilege deletes a portlet from a page or tab, other users will still see that

portlet. Similarly, if a user with the Personalize Portlets (Full) privilege adds a portlet to a page or a tab, only that user will see the portlet.

- **Personalize Portlets (Add-Only)** A user with the page or tab privilege Personalize Portlets (Add-Only) can alter their view of the page by changing the style of the page; adding portlets to the page; and deleting, hiding, or showing the portlets that they add. Such users can also view any page on which they have the privilege. For a user with this privilege to change the style of a page or of a region on a tab, the page group option Allow Privileged Users To Personalize Page Style must be selected on the page or tab's page group. Changes made under the privilege Personalize Portlets (Add-Only) are visible only to the user who made them. For example, if a user with this privilege adds a portlet to a page, only that user will see the portlet.
- **Personalize Portlets (Hide-Show)** A user with the privilege Personalize Portlets (Hide-Show) can change the style on their view of the page or of regions on a tab, and hide, show, or rearrange (re-order) any portlet within the current region on their view of the page or regions. Such users can also view any page on which they have the privilege. For a user with this privilege to change a style, the page group option Allow Privileged Users To Personalize Page Style must be selected on the page or tab's page group. Changes made under the privilege Personalize Portlets (Hide-Show) are visible only to the user who made them. For example, if a user with this privilege hides a portlet on a page, that portlet is hidden only for that user; other users will still be able to see the portlet.
- **Personalize (Style)** A user with the page or tab privilege Personalize (Style) can apply a different style to their view of the page or of regions on a tab. Such users can also view any page on which they have the privilege. For a user with this privilege to change a style, the page group option Allow Privileged Users To Customize Page Style must be selected on the page or tab's page group. Changes made under the page privilege Personalize (Style) are visible only to the user who made them. For example, if a user with this privilege applies a different style to a page, other users will still see the page with the original style. If a page is based on a template, users with this privilege may not be able to control the style of the page or of the region on the tab. The template-level option Enable Pages To Use Different Style must be selected on the template to enable users with the Personalize (Style) privilege to change the style of a page that is based on the template. This privilege is not available for mobile pages.

- **View** A user with the page or tab privilege View can view the content of the page or tab but cannot add, remove, show, or hide any of that content.
- **Create** A user with the page or tab privilege Create can create a page.

All Styles

- **None** No global style privileges are granted.
- **Manage** A user with Manage privilege can create, edit, and delete any style in any page group.
- **View** A user with View privilege can view any style in any page group.
- **Publish** A user with Publish privilege can make any style in any page group public for other users to use.
- **Create** A user with Create privilege can create styles in any page group. Users or groups with this privilege can also edit and delete the styles they create.

All Providers

- **None** No global provider privileges are granted.
- **Manage** A user with Manage privilege can register, edit, deregister any provider, and display and refresh the Portlet Repository. Also allowed to grant edit abilities on any provider.
- **Edit** A user with Edit privilege can edit any registered provider.
- **Publish** A user with Publish privilege can register and deregister any provider.
- **Execute** A user with Execute privilege can view the contents of any provider.
- **Create** A user with Create privilege can register portlet providers. On the provider the user (or group) creates, the user gets a Manage privilege; therefore, the user can perform all operations (including edit and deregister) on the particular provider that the user has created.

All Portlets

- **None** No global portlet privileges are granted.
- **Manage** A user with Manage privilege can create, edit, or delete any portlet in any provider.
- **Edit** A user with Edit privilege can edit any portlet in any provider.
- **Execute** A user with Execute privilege can execute any portlet in any provider. Users or groups with these privileges can see all portlets even if the portlet security is enforced. The Show link appears in the Navigator for all portlets.
- **Access** A user with Access privilege can view any portlet in any provider.
- **Publish** A user with Publish privilege can publish any page, navigation page, or Portal DB Provider portlet to the portal, making it available for adding to pages.

Portal DB Provider Privileges

These privileges determine what the user can do regarding portlet creation.

All Portal DB Providers

- **None** No global application privileges are granted.
- **Manage** A user with Manage privilege can edit, delete, or export any Portal DB Provider, and create, edit, delete, or export any portlet in any Portal DB Provider. A user with this privilege can also grant access to any Portal DB Provider and any portlet in any Portal DB Provider.
- **Edit Contents** A user with Edit Contents privilege can edit or export any portlet in any Portal DB Provider.
- **View Source** A user with View Source privilege can view the package specification and body and run any portlet in any Portal DB Provider. This privilege is intended primarily for users or groups who may want to look at a portlet's source so they know how to call it.
- **Customize** A user with Customize privilege can run and customize any portlet in any Portal DB Provider.

- **Run** A user with Run privilege can run any portlet in any Portal DB Provider.
- **Create** A user with Create privilege can create Portal DB Providers. Users or groups with this privilege can edit, delete, and export the providers they create and create, edit, delete, and export any portlet in them.

All Shared Components

- **None** No global shared component privileges are granted.
- **Manage** A user with Manage privilege can create, view, copy, edit, delete, and export any shared component in any Portal DB Provider, view and copy any system shared component, and grant access to any non–system shared component.
- **Create** A user with Create privilege can create shared components in any Portal DB Provider, view and copy any system shared component, and view any shared component. Users and groups with this privilege can view, copy, edit, delete, and export the shared components they create.

Administration Privileges

Privileges here determine what the user can do regarding portal administration.

NOTE
Although the Administration Privileges section contains the five following sets of privileges, only the first (All User Profiles) is shown in Figure 10-5.

All User Profiles

- **None** No global user profile privileges are granted.
- **Manage** A user with Manage privilege can edit any user profile and grant this privilege to other users and groups.
- **Edit** A user with Edit privilege can edit any user profile.

All Group Privileges (profiles)

- **None** No global group profile privileges are granted.

- **Manage** A user with Manage privilege can edit any group profile and grant this privilege to other groups. The Privileges tab of the group profile allows the user to assign those privileges to the group. The Manage privilege provides the Edit privilege and the ability to grant it to others.
- **Edit** A user with Edit privilege can edit any portal group profile (setting the default home page and default mobile home page). The ability to change any group's description, memberships, and owners is controlled by the Oracle Internet Directory access control policies, which are administered through membership in the OracleDASEditGroup group.

All Schemas

- **None** No global schema privileges are granted.
- **Manage** A user with Manage privilege can create, edit, and drop any schema; grant access to any schema; create, edit, drop, and rename any database object in any schema; and query, update, delete, and insert data in any table or view in any schema. Users or groups with this privilege can compile any function, procedure, package, or view in any schema; execute any function, procedure, or package in any schema; and grant access to any database object in any schema.
- **Modify Data** A user with Modify Data privilege can create schemas; query, update, delete, and insert data in any table or view in any schema; and compile any function, procedure, package, or view in any schema. Users or groups with this privilege can execute any function, procedure, or package in any schema and edit, drop, and grant access to the schemas they create.
- **Insert Data** A user with Insert Data privilege can create schemas and can query and insert data in any table or view in any schema. Users or groups with this privilege can edit, drop, and grant access to the schemas they create.
- **View Data** A user with View Data privilege can create schemas, query data in any table, or view data in any schema. Users or groups with these privileges can edit, drop, and grant access to the schemas they create.
- **Create** A user with Create privilege can create schemas. Users with these privileges can also edit, drop, and grant access to the schemas they create.

If you want a user or group to access the Schemas portlet on the Administer Database tab of the Builder page, either make the user or group a member of the DBA group or explicitly grant the user or group View privileges on the Administer Database tab. If you do not grant these privileges, the user or group will still be able to use the Navigator to access schemas.

All Logs

- **None** No global log privileges are granted.
- **Manage** A user with Manage privilege can edit or purge any log and grant this privilege to others.
- **Edit** A user with Edit privilege can edit or purge any log.
- **View** A user with View privilege can view any log.

All Transport Sets

- **None** No global transport set privileges are granted.
- **Execute** A user with Execute privilege can export and import objects that are not shared.
- **Manage** A user with Manage privilege can edit or purge any import or export sets and grant this privilege to others.

Creating Groups

A group, as mentioned earlier, is a way to group users and privileges. A user can be made a member of a group and then inherit any privileges assigned to that group. To create a group, return to the Administer tab of the OracleAS Portal and click the Create New Groups link in the middle right of the page. The Create Group page of the Oracle Identity Management Self-Service Console is displayed (Figure 10-6).

Here, you can create new groups and assign roles to them. You can also add users and other groups to your new groups. When you're finished creating a group, click Submit to return to the Administer tab of OracleAS Portal. For more information on groups, see the sidebar "Public vs. Private Groups."

Public vs. Private Groups

In the middle of Figure 10-6 is a radio button titled Group Visibility with two choices: Public and Private. Most of the time, you will be creating Public groups, but Private Groups serve an important purpose also. Private Groups were intended for defining groups available to the individual (such as e-mail lists). Some OracleAS Portal Administrators, however, try to use this functionality to "hide" a group, rather than relying on group membership or ownership. In general, it is recommended that groups be defined as Public and secured using the appropriate owner/membership to limit the access. Using private groups in conjunction with Global group privileges can lead to unexpected results (example: a "hidden" group can be visible unexpectedly because a user has a global edit group privilege). Likewise, defining a group as a privileged group allows for the definition of a role (to appear in the create user/groups screens). Defining a privileged and/or Public role changes the definition of a group from a simple aggregation to a security role.

Just as with creating users, there's another link that allows you to add more information about your group. On the bottom right of the Administer tab, there's a portlet titled Portal Group Profile. Type in the name of the group you just created and click Edit in that portlet (Figure 10-7).

Like the Portal User Profile, the Portal Group Profile also has two tabs: Preferences and Privileges. The Preferences page allows administrators to specify the default style and home page for members of this group. If a user is a member of more than one group, these settings will only be applied if this group is defined as the user's default group.

The Privileges tab is identical to the Privileges tab for the user we saw earlier, in Figure 10-5. When there's a conflict between privileges granted to a user and privileges granted to a group of which the user is a member, the higher privilege will be enforced. For example, if a user has only been granted View privileges on All Page Groups but belongs to a group where Manage All has been granted on All Page Groups, the user will have Manage All privileges on All Page Groups.

Object Privileges

Up until this point, we've been discussing system privileges—OracleAS Portal privileges like creating or editing pages or modifying users. The other set of privileges incorporated in OracleAS Portal involves object privileges, the ability to view a

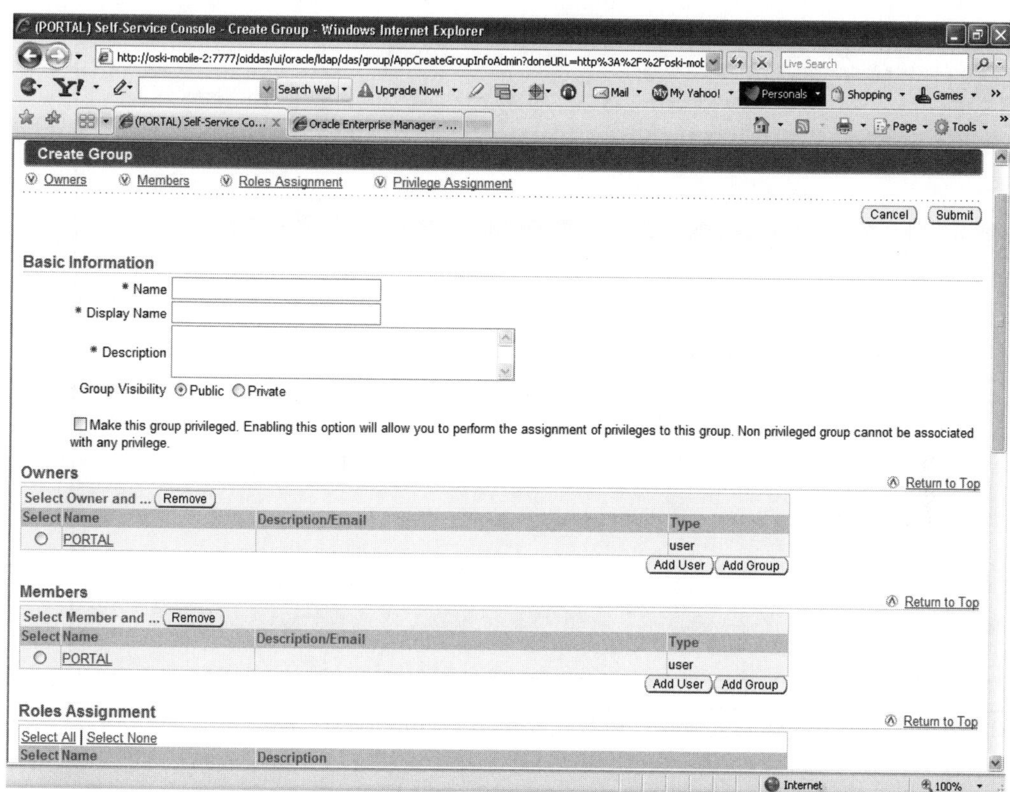

FIGURE 10-6 *The Create Group page of the Oracle Identity Management Self-Service Console*

portlet or modify an existing item. The key to understanding object privileges is understanding the concepts of hierarchies and inheritance.

OracleAS Portal portlets do not exist in isolation. Every portlet you develop must be associated with something called a provider. An OracleAS Portal Provider is the entity that serves up one or more portlets. As mentioned in Chapter 1, this is another example of Oracle's one-to-many relationship within OracleAS Portal. The one-to-many relationship is between providers (the one) and its portlets (the many). Why is this system in place? As your portal grows, it is likely that you will develop numerous providers, portlets, and pages, as well as manage many pieces of content. Providers provide administrators with a way of assigning attributes and privileges to a number of portlets at the same time, instead of having to assign these privileges to each portlet individually. Let's look at an example.

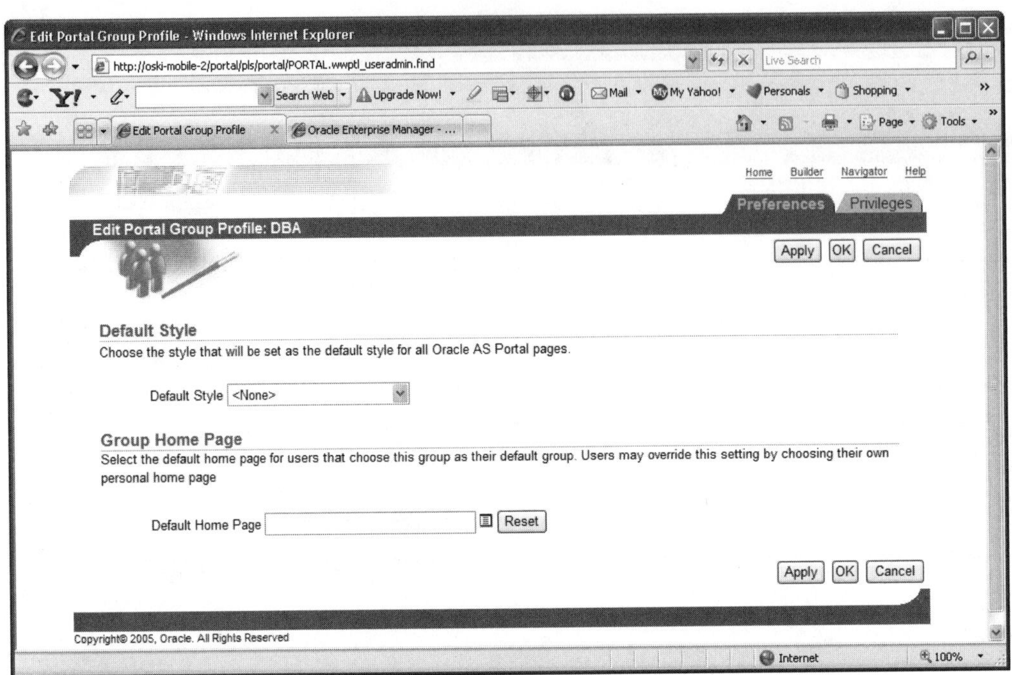

FIGURE 10-7 *The Preferences tab of the Edit Portal Group Profile page*

Let's say you have developed a number of Human Resources portlets and they have been placed on a number of different OracleAS Portal pages. Keeping track of who can see what could quickly turn into an administrative nightmare. OracleAS Portal, however, provides a mechanism where a security administrator could assign privileges at the Provider level—all of the portlets associated with this provider would automatically inherit the privileges set at the Provider level. This way, if a member of the Human Resources department joined or left the company, the privileges for all of the Human Resources portlets could be granted or revoked at one time. There is a similar one-to-many relationship between OracleAS Portal page groups and pages—privileges can be set at the page group level and will automatically cascade down to individual pages.

There are other variations on this theme—you could, for example, not set any privileges at either the provider or page group level and set privileges at the page and portlet levels, respectively. You could also set privileges at the top levels (Page Groups and Providers) and override them at the lower levels (Pages and Portlets) according to your needs. OracleAS Portal provides security administrators with a multitude of choices when designing the security for their portals.

Let's take a look at security for portlets.

Portlet Security

As mentioned earlier in this chapter, portlet security can be set at either the portlet or provider level. In Figure 10-8, the OracleAS Portal Navigator is displayed with the Providers tab highlighted.

Here, you can see the names of the providers that are currently installed on your system. By default, Oracle provides a couple of providers that serve either as internal providers (holding various seeded portlets like the Create New User portlet) or as examples. Next to each of the providers is a series of links, one of which is Grant Access. If you select the Grant Access link, you will see a screen similar to Figure 10-9.

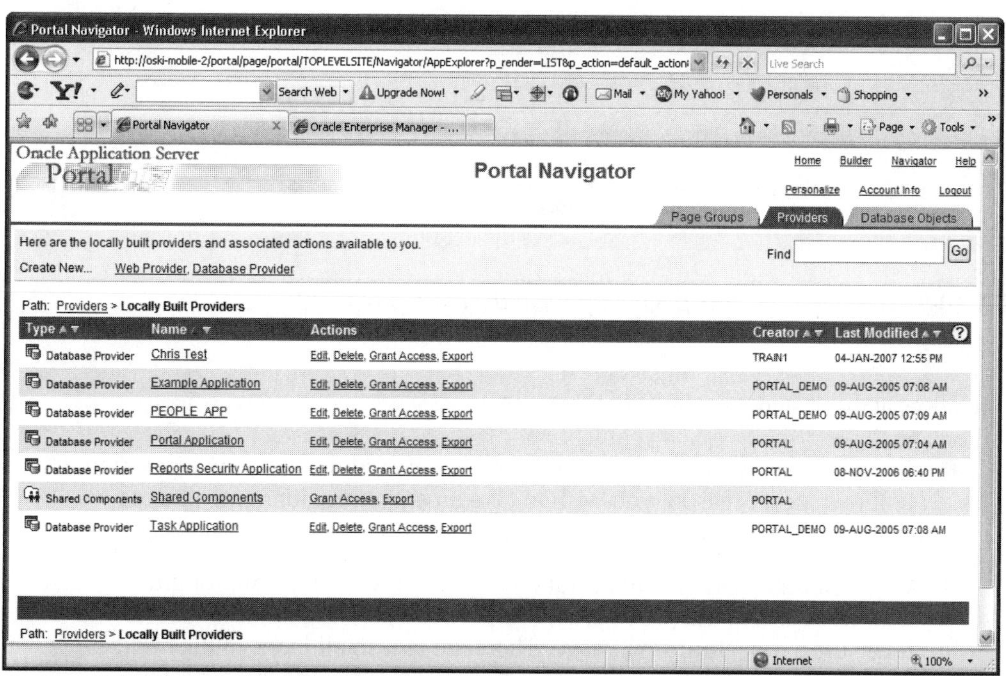

FIGURE 10-8 *The Providers tab of the OracleAS Portal Navigator*

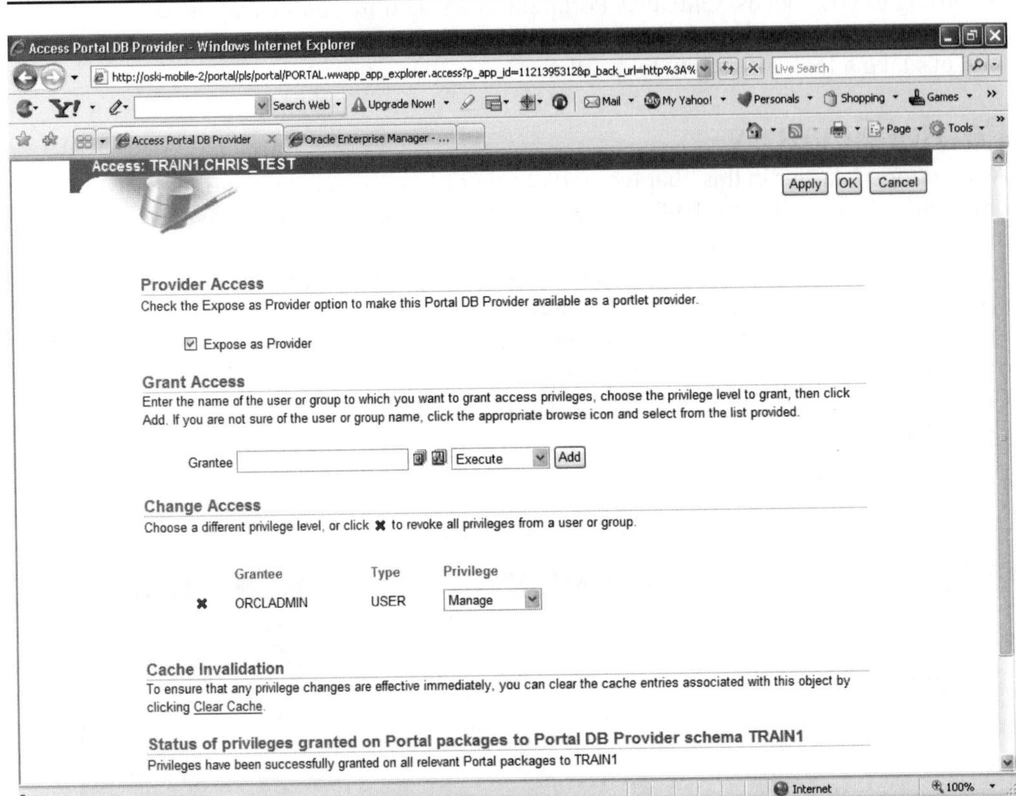

FIGURE 10-9 *The Grant Access page for a local database provider*

There are four major sections of this page:

- **Provider Access** By default, the Expose As Provider check box is selected. If, for whatever reason, you wish to take an entire provider and all of its portlets offline, you can de-select this check box.
- **Grant Access** Here, administrators can select what users and/or groups will get access to the provider and its portlets and which kind of access those users and groups will have. There are two small icons in the middle of the screen. The left icon pops up a window displaying the users on

your system for you to select. The right icon displays groups. If you grant a privilege to a group, any user who is a member of that group will inherit the privilege specified. The drop-down box to the right of the two small icons lists five privileges: Execute, Personalize, View Source, Edit, and Manage (for Remote Providers, this drop-down would contain Manage, Edit, Publish, and Execute). The table that follows lists portlet tasks and the privileges needed to perform those tasks for local database providers.

Action	Manage	Edit	View Source	Customize	Execute
Grant portlet privileges to other users	X				
Manage portlet locks	X	X			
Edit any portlet version	X	X			
Delete the portlet from the database	X	X			
Rename the portlet	X	X			
Export the portlet to another database	X	X			
Copy the portlet	X	X			
Generate the portlet PL/SQL package	X	X	X		
Monitor portlet usage	X	X	X		
View portlet's call interface, package spec, and body	X	X	X		
Customize the portlet	X	X	X	X	
Run the portlet	X	X	X	X	X
Add the portlet to the Favorites list	X	X	X	X	X

- **Change Access** This section allows you to change the privileges already granted to users or groups. Clicking the red X deletes the privilege entirely.
- **Cache Invalidation** As mentioned in various places in this book, OracleAS Portal specifically, and the Oracle Application Server in general, uses

sophisticated caching systems to improve performance. Sometimes, the caching system does not reflect changes you make immediately. To make any changes you made show up immediately, click the Clear Cache link in this section.

Now let's take a look at individual portlets. Click OK to return to the OracleAS Portal Navigator. This time, instead of clicking the Grant Access link next to one of the providers, click the provider itself. You are taken to the page of the provider that lists all of the portlets that are associated with that provider (Figure 10-10).

Next to each of the portlets, there is a Grant Access link. Clicking that link will take you to a page similar to Figure 10-11.

By default, there are three sections similar to the Grant Access page for providers (shown earlier in Figure 10-9):

- **Portal Access** This section is similar to the Provider Access section of Figure 10-9. By default, the portlet is available; if you want to take it offline for any reason, uncheck this box.

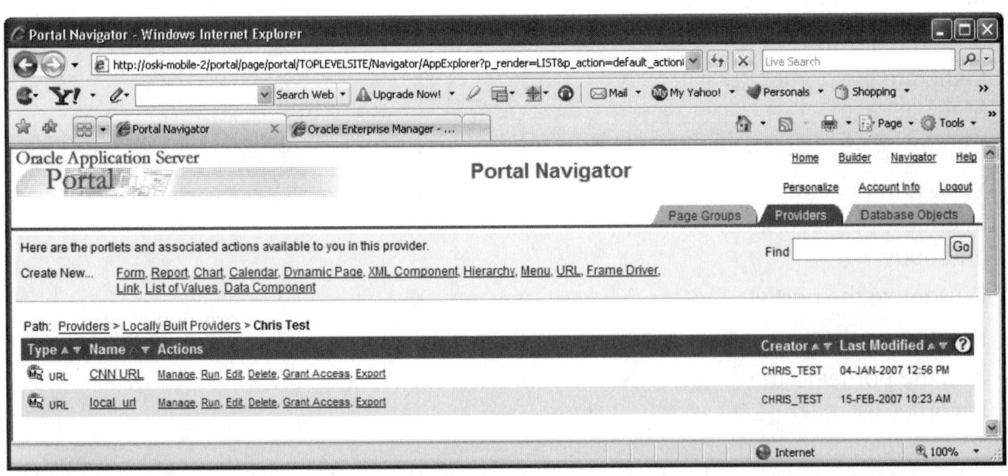

FIGURE 10-10 *The portlets page for a provider*

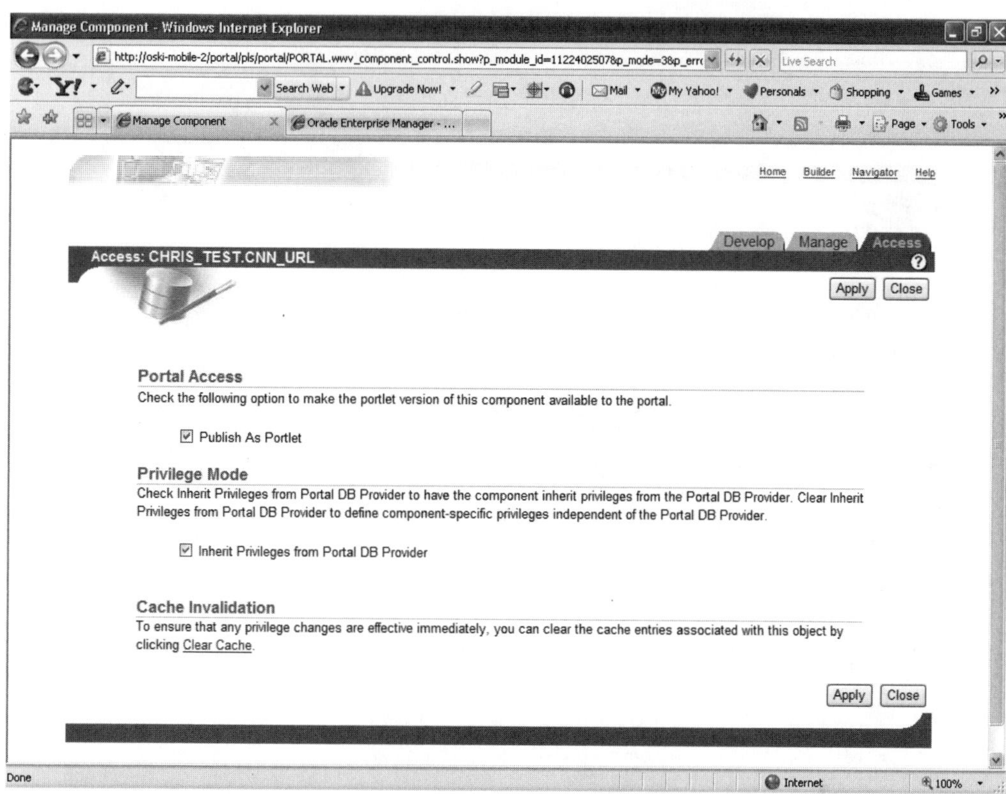

FIGURE 10-11 *The Grant Access page for an individual portlet*

- **Privilege Mode** By default, every portlet is set to inherit the privileges from the provider. If you don't want this option, de-select the check box and click the Apply button on the right side of the screen. The page will re-draw and look similar to Figure 10-12. As you can see, there are now Grant Access and Change Access sections that provide the same functionality as the provider Grant Access page in Figure 10-9.
- **Cache Invalidation** This section provides the same functionality as the Cache Invalidation section in Figure 10-9.

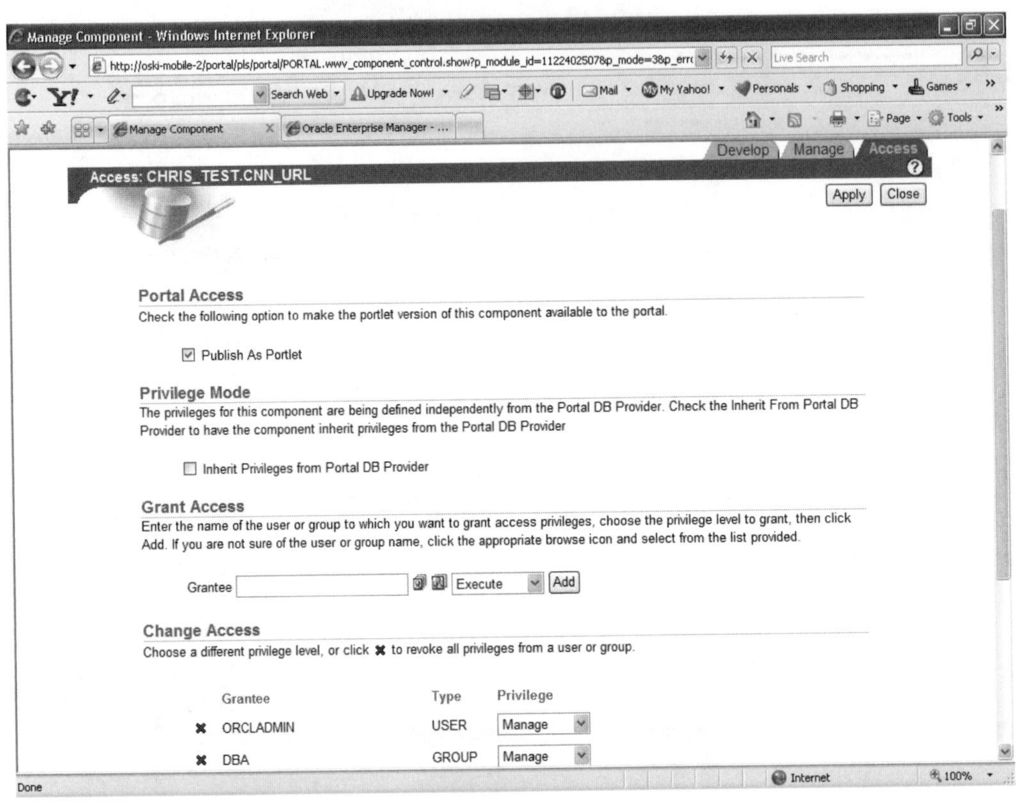

FIGURE 10-12 *The Grant Access page for a portlet without inheriting privileges from the provider*

Page Security

The concepts behind OracleAS Portal page security are very similar to those for portlet security described in the preceding section. Security can be set at the Page Group level and automatically cascade down to all subpages (and even to items on the page), or security managers can define security for each page individually if so desired. In the Page Groups tab of the OracleAS Portal Navigator, there is no Grant Access link like we saw for providers in the Providers tab. To see the security privileges for a page group, you must first click the Properties link next to the page group in question and then click the Access tab (Figure 10-13).

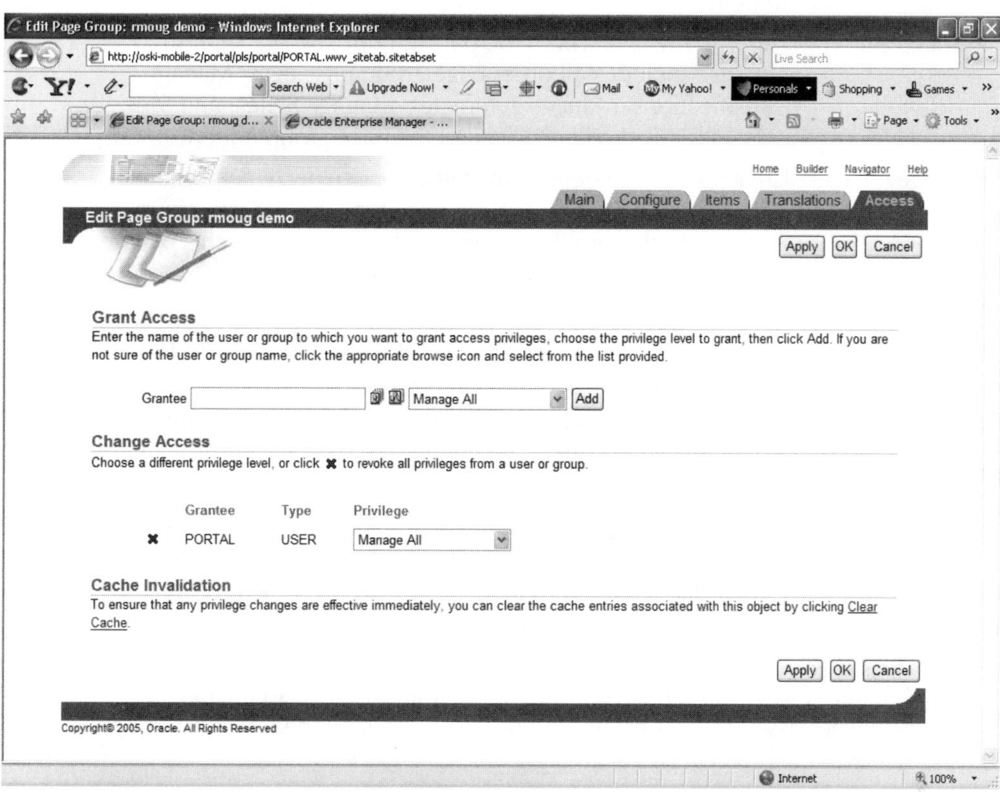

FIGURE 10-13 *The Access tab for an OracleAS Portal page group*

There are three main sections on this page:

- **Grant Access** In this section security administrators define users and groups who have access to this page group. The two small icons in the middle of this line allow administrators to select users or groups. There are five privileges that can be set at the Page Group and/or Page level: Manage All, Manage Classifications, Manage Templates, Manage Styles, and View. The actions that can be performed with each of these privileges are described in the following table.

Privilege	Actions
Manage All	Perform any task within the page group. The Manage All privilege includes all other page group privileges: Manage Classifications, Manage Templates, Manage Styles, and View. A user with this privilege is called the page group administrator.
Manage Classifications	Create, edit, and delete any category, perspective, attribute, custom item type, and custom page type in the page group. A user with this privilege cannot view the pages in this page group unless he or she also has the View privilege.
Manage Templates	Create, edit, and delete any page template in the page group. A user with this privilege cannot view the pages in this page group unless he or she also has the View privilege.
Manage Styles	Create, edit, and delete any style in the page group, and apply a different style to any page in the page group. A user with this privilege can also view any page in the page group.
View	View the content of any page in the page group, and preview any externally published portlet in the page group. A user with this privilege cannot add, remove, show, or hide any content within the pages in the page group.

- **Change Access** In this section security administrators can change the privileges assigned to users and groups. The red X on the left-hand side removes the privilege.
- **Cache Invalidation** This section serves the same purpose as the Cache Invalidation section shown in Figures 10-9 and 10-11.

The Root Page

Every page group has at least one OracleAS Portal page associated with it. This page is called the *root* page. There is a special access page for the root page, but it cannot be accessed from the OracleAS Portal Navigator. The only way to get to it is to click the Edit Root Page link in the navigator, click the Graphical mode in the top left of the screen (if not in Graphical mode already), and then click the Access link next to Page: in the top left of the screen (Figure 10-14).

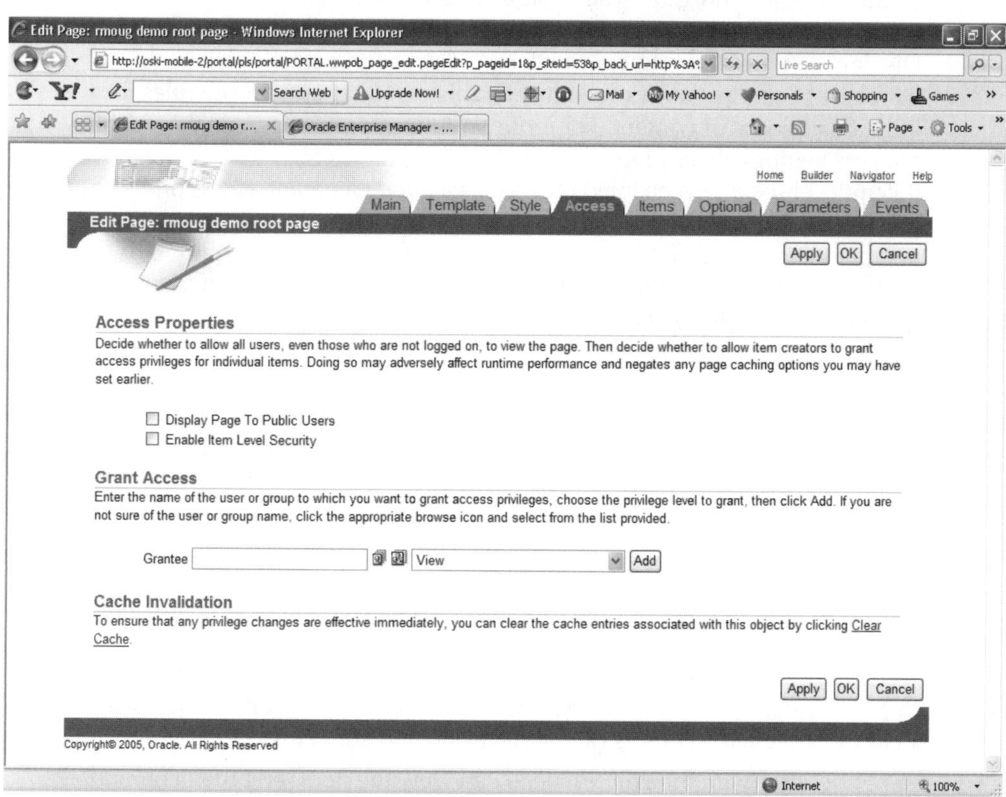

FIGURE 10-14 *The Access tab for a root page*

There are three sections on this page:

- **Access Properties** On the root page you can specify if this page is viewable by Public users, i.e., those who have not logged in (this is available on all pages if page privileges are not inherited from page group). It is common to define a page other than Oracle's default page for OracleAS Portal as your default page for your site. Since you want users to be able to see it (and presumably log in), you'll have to make it a Public page by selecting the Display Page To Public Users check box. The second check box, Enable Item Level Security, allows security administers to set up security rules for individual pieces of content. For more on Access properties, see the sidebar "Access Settings" later in the chapter.

If item-level security is enabled on your page, you can grant access privileges to individual items. Item-level security is a mechanism that allows controlled and granular access to specific items in a page. As a content contributor, when you add a new item to a page, you can decide if you want to make the item accessible to certain users or groups. Users or groups who are not on the item's access control list are not able to view or edit the item. You must be logged in as an authorized user with the Manage Item or higher privileges on the item. Only the item creator or owner can grant access privileges to a specific item. The following table lists the privileges associated with items.

Item Privileges	Description
Manage	A user with the Manage privilege can view the item, edit the item, delete the item, and grant privileges on the item. The Manage privilege does not allow a user to add subitems under the item. Only users with the Manage Items With Approval or higher privileges on the page can add subitems.
Edit	A user with the Edit privilege can view the item, edit the item, and delete the item.
View	A user with the View privilege can view the item only.

- **Grant Access** This section serves the same purpose as the Grant Access section shown earlier in Figure 10-13. There are some additional privileges at this level, however, and they are listed here.

Privilege	Description
Manage	A user with the Manage privilege can perform any operation on the page. With this privilege you can perform all of the actions listed for the Manage Content privilege (listed next), as well as control the access and style of the page. Notes: For a user with this privilege to change the style of a page, the Allow Privileged Users To Manage Style option must be selected at the page group level. This allows the user to apply a different style when editing the page. If this option is not selected at the page group level, only users with the Manage All or Manage Styles page group privileges can apply a different style for the page. There is a second option for controlling styles at the page group level called Allow Privileged Users To Customize Page Style. When this option is selected, users with at least the Customization (Style) privilege on a page (described later in this table) can apply a different style when customizing the page. If a page is based on a template, users with this privilege may not be able to control the access and style of the page. There are two options at the template level, Enable Pages To Have Different Access and Enable Pages To Use Different Style, which control whether page designers can specify different access and style settings for the page. These must be selected; otherwise, the page access and style settings cannot be changed by users with this privilege.
Manage Content	A user with the Manage Content privilege can add, edit, hide, show, share, and delete any item, portlet, or tab on the page.

Privilege	Description
Manage Items with Approval	A user with the Manage Items with Approval privilege can add or edit items on the page, but the changes are published only after the defined approval process is complete. Notes: Users with this privilege cannot add portlets to a page. This privilege is only available if approvals are enabled. If approvals are enabled but an approval process is not defined, users with this privilege can add, edit, or copy items on the page without approval. This privilege is not available for mobile pages.
Manage Style	A user with the Manage Style privilege can change the style and region properties of the page. Notes: If a page is based on a template, users with this privilege may not be able to control the style of the page. The template-level option, Enable Pages To Use Different Style, controls whether page designers can specify different style settings for the page. This option must be selected; otherwise, the page's style settings cannot be changed by users with this privilege. For a user with this privilege to change the style of a page, the Allow Privileged Users To Customize Page Style option must be selected at the page group level. When this option is selected, users with this privilege on a page can apply a different style for the page. This privilege is not available for mobile pages.

Privilege	Description
Customize Portlets (Full)	A user with the Full Customize Portlets privilege can change the style of the page; add portlets to the page; and delete, move, hide, or show any portlet on the page. Notes: These changes are visible only to the user who made them. For example, if a user with the Full Customize Portlets privilege deletes a portlet from a page, other users will still be able to see that portlet on the page. Likewise, if a user with the Full Customize Portlets privilege adds a portlet to a page, only that user will see the portlet; other users will not. For a user with this privilege to change the style of a page, the Allow Privileged Users To Customize Page Style option must be selected at the page group level. When this option is selected, users with this privilege on a page can apply a different style when customizing the page.
Customize Portlets (Add-Only)	A user with the Add Only Customize Portlets privilege can change the style of the page; add portlets to the page; and remove, hide, or show the portlets that are added. Notes: These changes are visible only to the user who made them. For example, if a user with the Add-Only Customize Portlets privilege adds a portlet to a page, only that user will see the portlet; other users will not. For a user with this privilege to change the style of a page, the Allow Privileged Users To Customize Page Style option must be selected at the page group level. When this option is selected, users with this privilege on a page can apply a different style when customizing the page.

Privilege	Description
Customize Portlets (Hide-Show)	A user with the Hide-Show Customize Portlets privilege can change the style of the page and hide, show, or rearrange any portlet on the page. Notes: These changes are visible only to the user who made them. For example, if a user with the Hide-Show Customize Portlets privilege hides a portlet to a page, that portlet is hidden only for that user; other users will still be able to see the portlet. For a user with this privilege to change the style of a page, the Allow Privileged Users To Customize Page Style option must be selected at the page group level. When this option is selected, users with this privilege on a page can apply a different style when customizing the page.
Customization (Style)	A user with the Style Customization privilege can apply a different style to the page. Notes: These changes are visible only to the user who made them. For example, if a user with the Style Customization privilege applies a different style to a page, other users will still see the page with the fonts and colors of the original style. For a user with this privilege to change the style of a page, the Allow Privileged Users To Customize Page Style option must be selected at the page group level. When this option is selected, users with this privilege on a page can apply a different style when customizing the page. If a page is based on a template, users with this privilege may not be able to control the style of the page. The template-level option, Enable Pages To Use Different Style, controls whether page designers can specify different style settings for the page. This option must be selected; otherwise, the page's style settings cannot be changed by users with this privilege. This privilege is not available for mobile pages.

Privilege	Description
View	A user with the View privilege can view the content of the page but cannot add, remove, show, or hide any of that content.

- **Cache Invalidation** This section serves the same purpose as the Cache Invalidation section shown earlier in Figure 10-13.

Access Settings

From Oracle's documentation: "By default, items inherit the access settings that apply to the page or tab that hosts the item. Only users or groups who are authorized to access a given page or tab can access its items. When you enable item-level security for a page or tab, items initially use the same security that is applied to the page or tab. It's up to item owners to grant access to a given item to specific users and/or groups. Manage and Manage Content page-level privileges override item-level security privileges. However, item-level security takes precedence over other page-level privileges, such as Manage Style. If a user has Manage Style privileges on a page where item-level security is enabled, and item-level access privileges have been defined for the items, the user can work with the items based on the item-level privileges. Users may be granted a higher level of access to an item than they have on the page or tab that hosts the item. For example, users may have View privileges on a page or tab, allowing them to look at the page or tab, but not to change it. If an item owner explicitly grants Manage or Edit privileges to users, the users are authorized to edit the item, even though they can do nothing else to other objects on the page or tab. You can enable item-level security only on Standard pages and custom pages that are based on the Standard page type. There is no relationship between item-level security and item versioning. Item-level security has to do with who can access an item, and item versioning has to do with how older versions of an item are handled as newer versions are uploaded. Changes to the access settings of a page template affect all pages that are based on the template. However, if the template allows for the use of access settings that are different from those specified in the template, changes to the page template's access settings do not affect the pages that are based on the template."

Subpages

The Access tab for subpages can be reached by clicking the Properties link in the OracleAS Portal Navigator next to the subpage in question and then clicking the Access tab (Figure 10-15).

Subpages can inherit privileges from the page group, the same way an individual portal can inherit its privileges from its provider, as we saw earlier in Figure 10-11. To override privileges for the page, select the Specify Access Settings radio button. Unlike in the case of the page in Figure 10-11, there's no need to click Apply—the page automatically re-paints itself with the access settings described in Figure 10-14.

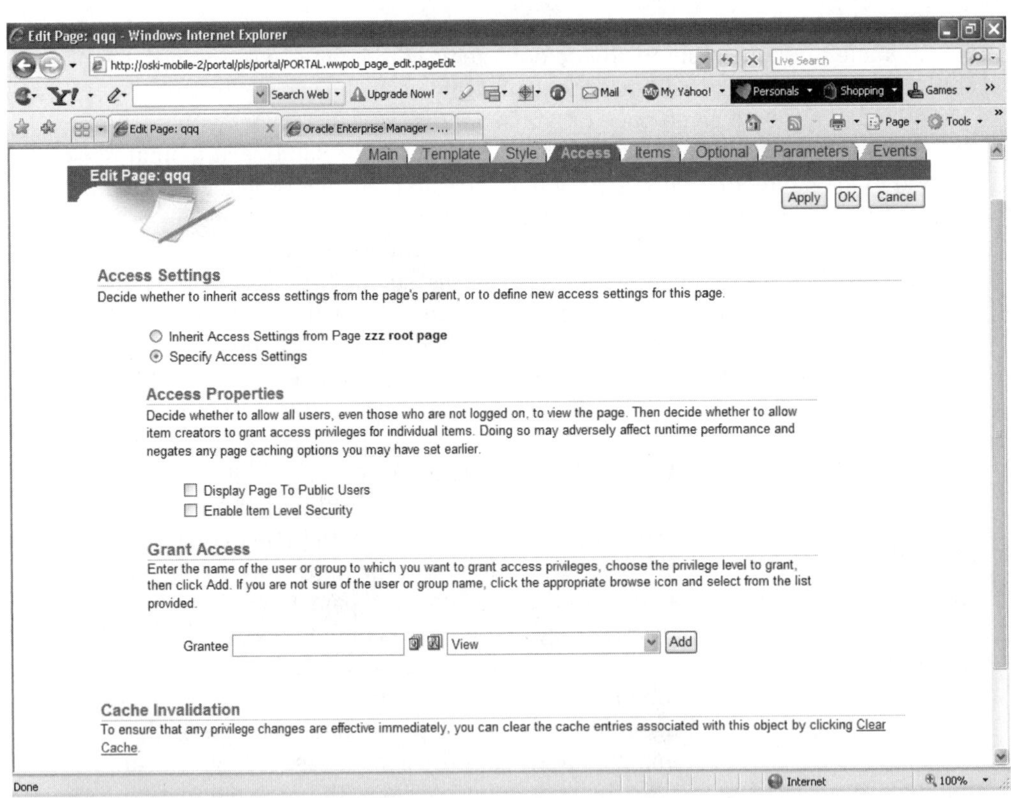

FIGURE 10-15 *The Access page for a subpage*

Portlet security overrides page security. What does this statement mean? Let's say there are two users, User A and User B, and two portlets, P1 and P2. The developer has granted the View privilege on P1 to P2 to both User A and User B. A page designer then creates a page, places P1 and P2 on the page, and grants view privileges on the page to Users A and B. Both users can see the page and see both portlets on the page. If the security manager then goes in and revokes the view privilege on P2 from User B, User B can still see the page, but only P1 will be displayed.

TIP
Just to make things tricky, User B could belong to a group that has view privileges on P2. In that case, User B would see P2 even though the View privilege was explicitly revoked from User B.

The security model in Oracle Portal 10*g* (10.1.4) extends beyond the simple permission model to include the access path used to enter the Portal. For example, although certain users may have permission to view a secured page within the Portal while they are at their place of work, the same cannot be said for when they are at a cyber café or working from home, accessing the corporate Web site over the Internet. The OracleAS Portal security model allows for the definition of a secured vs. unsecured access point. If the user enters the Portal via an unsecured network (such as the Internet), the security infrastructure will automatically disable components of the OracleAS Portal site. By default, this Authentication Modifier functionality allows for the following:

- Globally prevents any edits/customization of the Portal outside of the secured network
- Prevents viewing of specific pages outside of the secured network
- Prevents editing of a specific page outside of the secured network

NOTE
For more information, see the document "Expose Your Intranet Portal to the Outside World in a Secured Manner" at: http://www.oracle.com/technology/products/ias/portal/pdf/secured_inside_outside.pdf.

Exercise

Create users and groups with different privileges to understand how OracleAS Portal handles security. Eventually you will work with a user who sees something they shouldn't or can't see something they should. It is essential to understand OracleAS Portal's security mechanism to diagnose these types of issues quickly.

Summary

Web-based applications that rely on security mechanisms to restrict data and content from users are notoriously difficult to program and test. All of OracleAS Portal's features would be of limited value if security was arduous to set up and maintain. OracleAS Portal's security model allows security administrators to architect their portal in such a way that users, portlets, and pages can inherit privileges from groups, providers, and page groups, respectively. This model allows users to get access to the information they need quickly, with minimal administrative effort.

PART V

Miscellaneous

CHAPTER 11

Integrating Forms, Reports, and Discoverer into Portal

s dynamic and full-featured as OracleAS Portal is, it is certainly not the only development tool available from Oracle. In recent years, Oracle has made a concerted effort to web-enable their most popular development tools. As a result, the Oracle Forms, Oracle Reports, and Oracle Discoverer products do not support full web-based functionality. In fact, as of release 9*i* of Oracle Forms and Oracle Reports, deploying to a client (a PC in most cases) is no longer even supported—the Web is the only option to deploy your forms or reports.

Each of these tools has its own strengths and weaknesses; no one tool is perfect for every situation. These legacy tools provide Oracle developers with a robust feature set, seamless integration with Oracle databases, and a wealth of existing knowledge available via various Web resources (OTN, MetaLink, etc.). While OracleAS Portal is an exciting development environment, chances are your organization has existing Oracle Forms, Oracle Reports, and Oracle Discoverer Workbooks and Worksheets being used in production. For most organizations, it is not practical to discard all of their existing applications and begin coding OracleAS Portal Forms and Reports from scratch. Thankfully, Oracle provides a mechanism to ease your transition into OracleAS Portal development by facilitating the integration of existing Oracle Forms, Oracle Reports, and Oracle Discoverer Workbooks and Worksheets into OracleAS Portal. Developers can achieve the benefits inherent in OracleAS Portal, namely its robust security and its ease of visual consistency, while moving existing applications to the Web with relative ease.

It is also important to note that the forms and reports components of OracleAS Portal have a much smaller feature set and do not have all of the functionality of the Oracle Forms, Reports, and Discoverer products. Therefore, OracleAS Portal may not be the best choice as an exclusive tool to rewrite existing production applications in.

Is OracleAS Portal required to move existing Oracle Forms, Oracle Reports, and Oracle Discoverer Workbooks and Worksheets to the Web? No; it is entirely possible to move those components to the Web outside of OracleAS Portal. This chapter discusses the integration of existing Oracle Forms, Oracle Reports, and Oracle Discoverer Workbooks and Worksheets into web pages that are served up by the OracleAS Portal engine in Oracle Application Server 10*g* Release 2. We will discuss the various methods for incorporating these components into OracleAS Portal, the pieces that need to be in place before attempting to integrate these components (like creation and administration of Discoverer connections), and the various methods of security we can apply to these components.

This chapter discusses the following topics:

- Benefits of integration
- Native support

- Integration of Oracle Reports
- Integration of Oracle Forms
- Integration of Oracle Discoverer Workbooks and Worksheets

Benefits of Integration

The benefits of developing in OracleAS Portal are numerous: the elimination of fat-client-based applications and maintenance, the simple implementation of security, the implementation of a consistent visual interface via the use of user interface templates, and the declarative, wizard-based development approach, allowing a minimum of code to be written, just to name a few. There are, however, several considerations that must be taken into account before moving development to OracleAS Portal.

First, and foremost, a great deal of time and effort may have been spent using Oracle's other development tools (Forms, Reports, Discoverer) to build existing applications, and re-coding these applications may take resources that are impractical for many organizations to undertake. Second, Portal requires a new skill set and a new way of thinking; it may not be feasible to retrain all of your development staff. Finally, the forms and reports components in OracleAS Portal do not have the full feature set of the Oracle Forms and Oracle Reports products, which may further make it impractical to move production applications to OracleAS Portal. While these potential limitations may influence the types of applications to be developed in OracleAS Portal for your organization, it is important to note that Oracle has made a great effort to give developers and administrators the ability to incorporate existing applications into OracleAS Portal. This chapter is devoted to exploring these options.

Despite the preceding considerations, there are significant reasons for moving existing applications into OracleAS Portal. The most significant of these are security and the exploitation of Oracle Application Server 10*g*'s advanced security features, grouped together under the title Identity Management. It is not uncommon for developers and administrators to spend as much time and effort devising and implementing security rules for Web-based applications as they do coding and testing the application itself. OracleAS Portal provides an integrated security structure that allows administrators to quickly and easily maintain users within OracleAS Portal. OracleAS Portal pages can be designed to show or hide different portlets (in this case, the portlets would be your Oracle Forms, Reports, and Discoverer components), depending on the security privileges for your users defined in OracleAS Portal. Further security privileges can be granted to users allowing them to modify (or, in OracleAS Portal's terminology, "customize") individual portlets for their own purposes. The mechanism for these security features is handled automatically by the OracleAS

Portal engine and, in most cases, does not require any additional programming by the OracleAS Portal developer.

Another significant challenge for developers and administrators deploying Web-based applications involves the effort needed to maintain a consistent look and feel across the various pages that make up the Web-based application. There is nothing less professional than constructing a web site where end users are forced to visit pages that differ in font, colors, and basic page design. Because of the maturity of most web sites, we take this consistency for granted, but in most cases, a great deal of work needs to go into maintaining this consistency. OracleAS Portal provides numerous features like templates that allow developers and administrators to greatly reduce the amount of effort needed to deploy an application with consistent visual attributes.

Native Support

OracleAS Portal has native support for two of the three components mentioned in this chapter: Oracle Reports and OracleAS Discoverer Worksheets and Workbooks. Oracle Forms does not have native support in OracleAS Portal, but we can still integrate Oracle Forms by way of a URL.

NOTE
You won't see the term "native support" in any of the OracleAS Portal documentation. In this chapter, the term native support is used to describe those features of OracleAS Portal that have been designed specifically to work with the three Oracle development tools mentioned in this chapter: Oracle Forms, Oracle Reports, and Oracle Discoverer. There are OracleAS Portal-specific features explicitly designed for Oracle Reports and Oracle Discoverer, but none for Oracle Forms. Hence, OracleAS Portal is said to have native support for Oracle Reports and Oracle Discoverer, but no native support for Oracle Forms.

The Oracle Reports and Oracle Discoverer Worksheets become portlets, once we "tell" OracleAS Portal about them. These portlets can then be manipulated like any other portlet in the OracleAS Portal Portlet Repository and be placed on a page, be placed on a tabbed page, and/or have customization options defined for them that can be made available to power users. Since Oracle Reports and OracleAS Discoverer are supported natively in OracleAS Portal, there are certain OracleAS Portal–specific features associated with them that enhance the OracleAS Portal developer's ability to work with them. For example, developers have the ability to set up a calendar in OracleAS Portal that determines when a particular Oracle Report can be run via OracleAS Portal or when a particular printer can be accessed by that Oracle Report running via OracleAS Portal.

Just because OracleAS Portal has native support for Oracle Reports doesn't mean developers have to use those features. If we choose not to, however, we lose out on using any OracleAS Portal–specific functionality (like the calendars just mentioned). To integrate OracleAS Discoverer Worksheets and Workbooks, however, we will have to use OracleAS Portal–specific methods. We can also integrate Oracle Forms into OracleAS Portal, but since there is no native support, no OracleAS Portal–specific features are associated with the integration of Oracle Forms.

Component #1: Oracle Reports

During the installation of Oracle Application Server 10*g*, a component called a Reports Server was automatically created, if the Business Intelligence and Forms option was chosen. The Reports Server component of Oracle Application Server 10*g* allows administrators to take an existing Oracle Report (either an .rep or .rdf file) and view it over the Web via a web browser. To view the report in OracleAS Portal, at least one Reports Server must be up and running, as we will associate the Oracle Report with an Oracle Applications Server 10*g* Reports Server when we turn the Oracle Report into an OracleAS Portal portlet. As you will see, we are not limited to just one Reports Server. We can have numerous servers running to handle the load of reports being generated, or Reports Servers with specific functions, security, and priorities.

Upon installation of Oracle Application Server 10*g*, a Reports Server called rep_<hostname> was created. Most of the administrative duties of Oracle Application Server 10*g* can be handled graphically through the Enterprise Manager Application Server Control web site. To view the status of this Reports Server, enter the Enterprise Manager Application Server Control web site for your installation. Point your browser to

```
http://<hostname>:1810
```

where the hostname is the name of the machine where the middle tier (also referred to as the Application Server) is installed. For the examples in this chapter, a server named oski-2k3 is used, so the URL to reference this server would look like

```
http://oski-2k3:1810
```

The login user for the Enterprise Manager web site is ias_admin. The password is set during installation of the Oracle Application Server 10*g* mid-tier instance. If the infrastructure tier and middle tier are installed on the same machine, you will see a Farm page similar to Figure 11-1. If the infrastructure and the middle tier are on different servers, you will see a screen similar to the one in Figure 11-2.

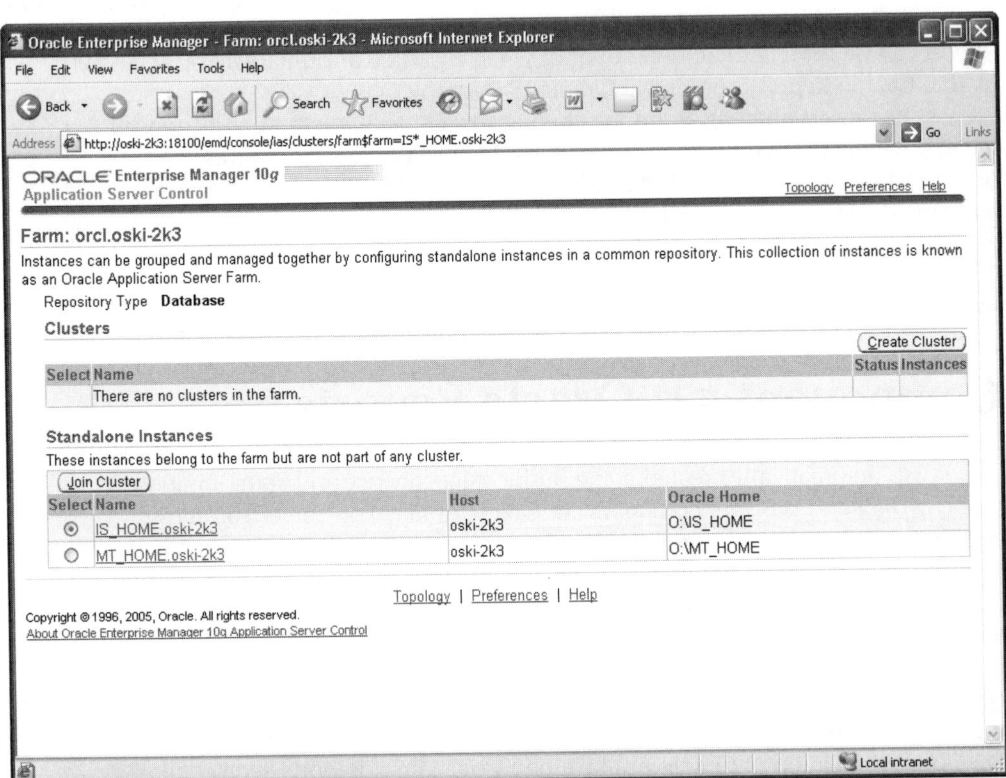

FIGURE 11-1 *The Enterprise Manager Application Control Farm page*

In this example, I have two instances of Oracle Application Server 10*g* installed on my server. One is called IS_HOME (for InfraStructure home) and one is called MT_HOME (for Application Server Mid-Tier home). The names of these Oracle Application Server 10*g* instances are arbitrary and are set during installation of Oracle Application Server 10*g*. The Forms, Reports, and Discoverer Servers are deployed in the middle tier, so click the Application Server link (MT_HOME.oski-2k3 in the preceding example). You will be taken to a screen similar to the one in Figure 11-2.

This screen lists all of the components that make up the middle tier (application server) for my installation. In the preceding example, there is a component called Reports:rep_oski-2k3. This is the Reports Server that was installed automatically

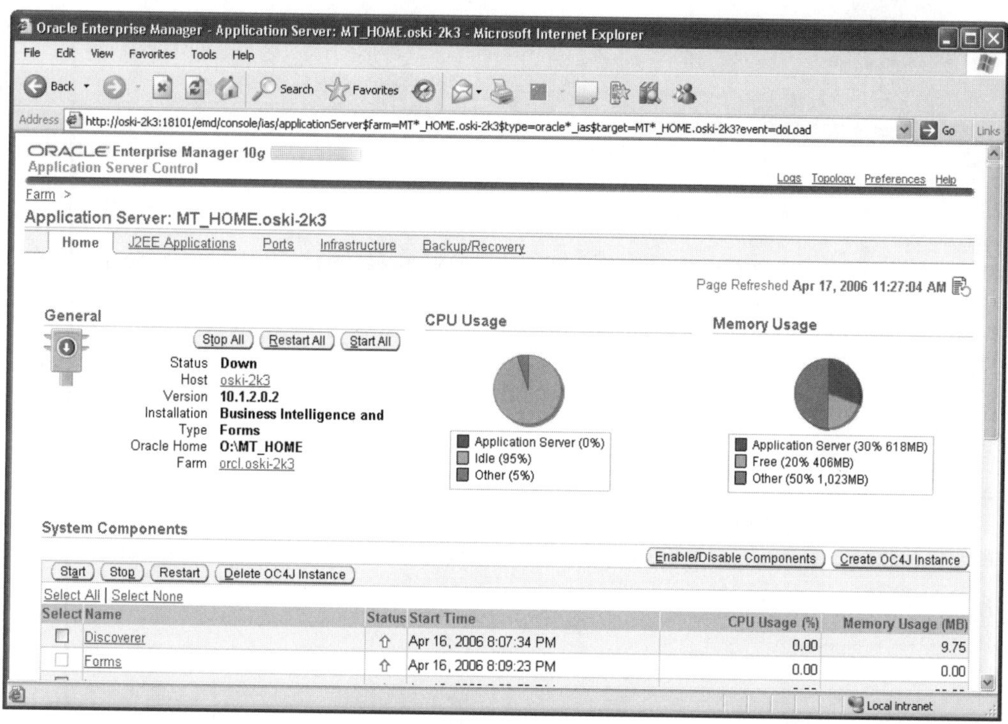

FIGURE 11-2 *The Enterprise Manager Web Page for the middle tier*

during the Oracle Application Server 10*g* installation on my server. If you want to test to see if the Reports Server is up, point your browser to

```
http://<Middle-tier server>:<port>/reports/rwservlet/showjobs?server=<server_name>
```

For the example server in this chapter, the URL would look like this:

```
http://oski-2k3/reports/rwservlet/showjobs?server=rep_oski-2k3_MT_HOME
```

The port number for the middle tier defaults to port 80, which is also the default HTTP port, so if your administrator has not changed the default settings, you do not have to specify the port. You should see a page similar to Figure 11-3.

To test that all of the pieces are in place to actually serve up Oracle Reports in your browser, point your browser to the Welcome page for the Application Server (Figure 11-4).

```
http://<Middle-tier server>:<port>
```

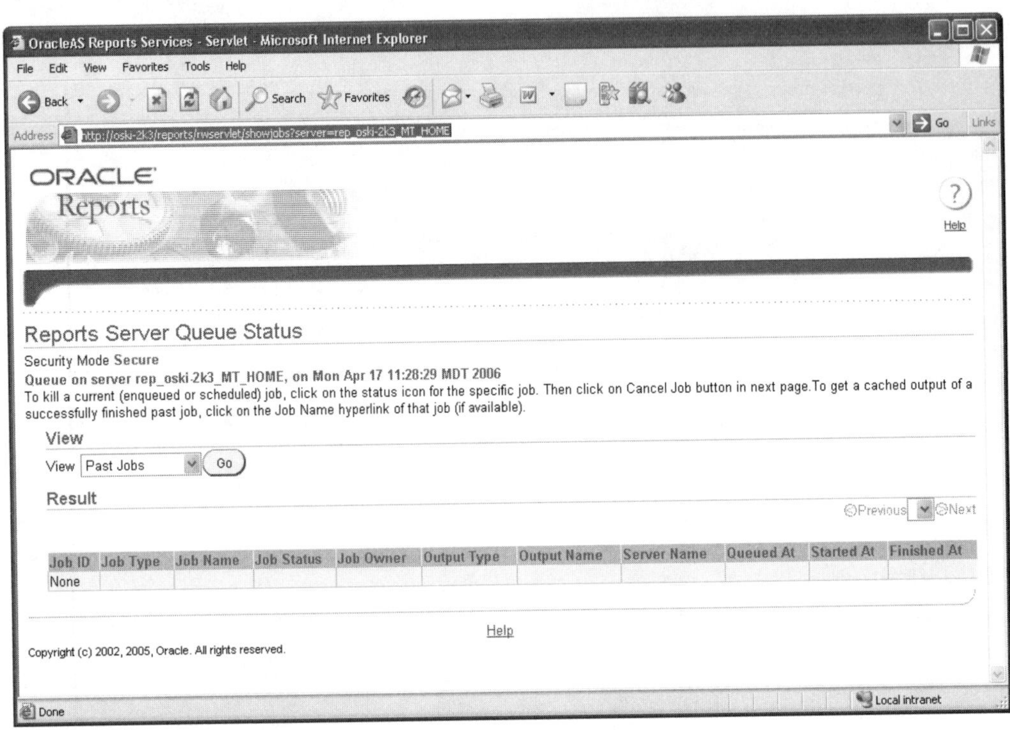

FIGURE 11-3 *The Showjobs page for the Reports Server*

For the example server in this chapter, the URL would look like this:

```
http://oski-2k3
```

Click the Demonstrations tab, then the Business Intelligence And Forms link, then the Reports Services link, and finally the Test A Paper Report On The Web link. You should see a screen similar to Figure 11-5.

Replace the Reports Server name with the name of the Reports Server you want to test. In my example, it's rep_oski-2k3. Replace the connect string with any valid connect string and change DesFormat to HTML 4.0. Leave the report name as test.rdf. Click Run Report. If you see a report in your web browser, the Reports Server is working.

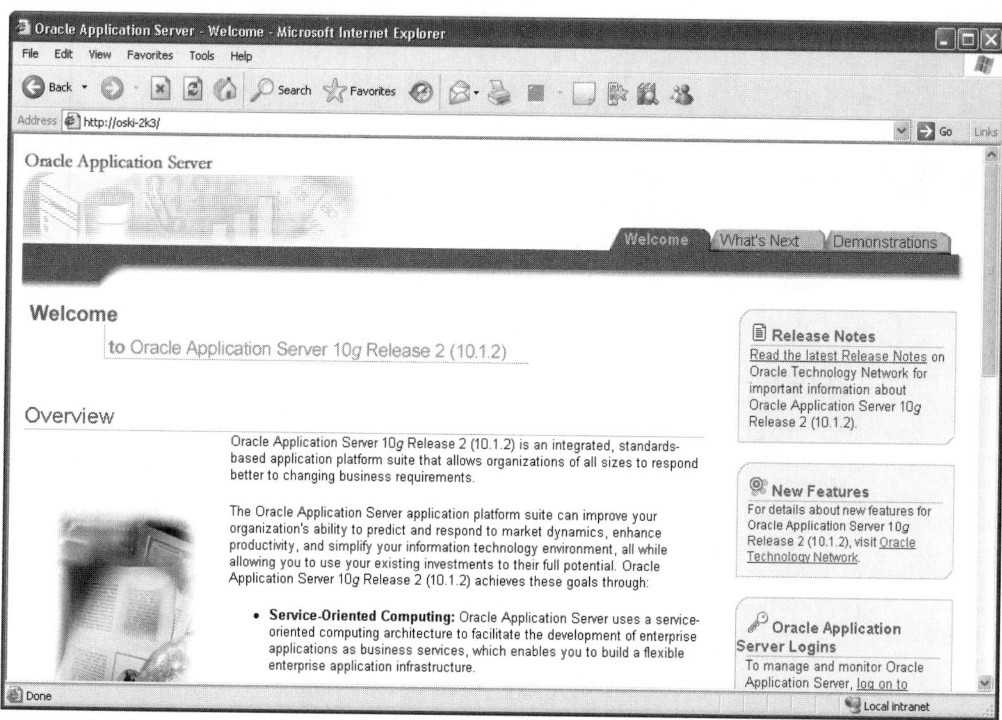

FIGURE 11-4 *The main page of the Application Server*

The reports component in OracleAS Portal is a very powerful way to develop web-based reports in a very short period of time. It does, however, have some serious limitations. Since the major components of Portal (Forms, Reports, Charts) are built using wizards, a significant amount of control is handled by the code generator. Any development environment that uses code generators as its primary way of developing application components will hide many of the component details away from the developer. In many cases, this is not a prohibitive factor for your development needs. In other cases, developers will need total control of their components and this development environment will fall short of their development needs. If, for whatever reason, this limitation prohibits the development of OracleAS Portal reports, developers can integrate existing reports developed in Oracle Reports into OracleAS Portal.

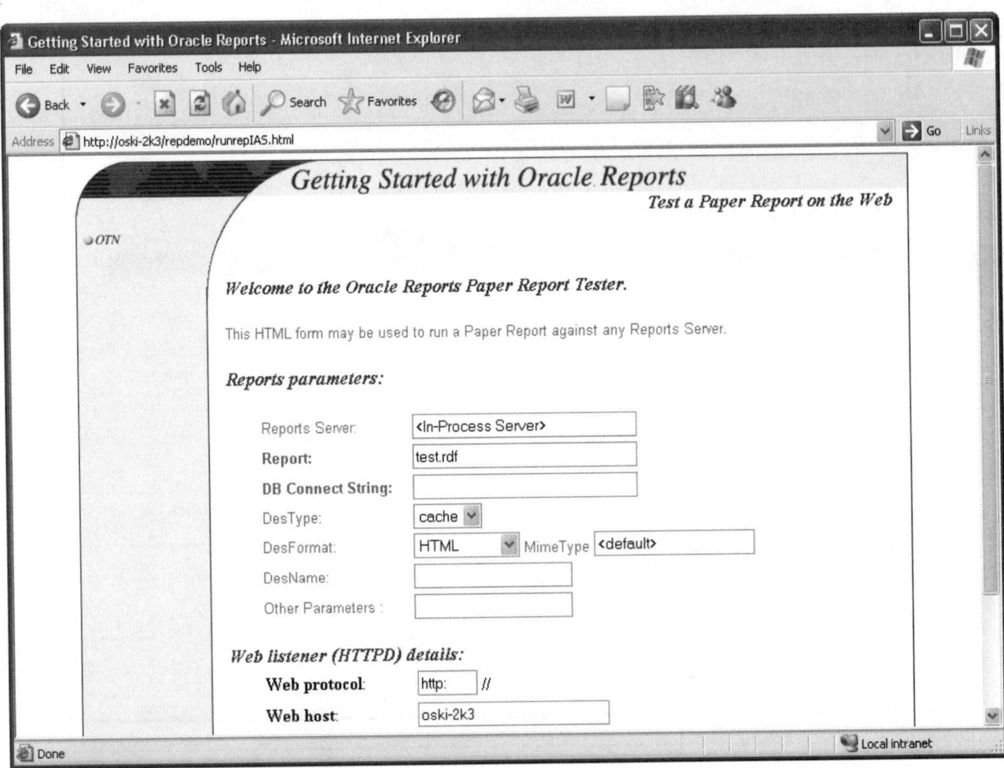

FIGURE 11-5 *Testing the Reports Server*

Reports Integration Method #1: Using the Portal URL Component

The simplest way to incorporate an Oracle Report into Portal is by way of a URL. This is not the native way of supporting Oracle Reports in OracleAS Portal, and while it is the quickest way to get an Oracle Report onto an OracleAS Portal page, it does not have the ability to use any of the Oracle Reports–specific functionality built into OracleAS Portal.

If you successfully ran the report from the Getting Started With Oracle Reports screen in Figure 11-5, you noticed that a new window popped up with a URL similar to

```
http://oski-
2k3/reports/rwservlet?destype=cache&desformat=HTMLCSS&%20server=rep_oski-
2k3_MT_HOME&report=test.rdf&userid=system/password@orcl
```

This URL can be used to create an OracleAS Portal component (a URL component) that can then be placed on an OracleAS Portal page. Assuming you've already created a Database Provider in OracleAS Portal, go into that provider and create a new URL component. Give it a name that is easily remembered. For this example (Figure 11-6), I used the name test_reports_url. When we get to the next step in this process, we'll use this URL component and place it on a page.

On the second step of the wizard, enter the URL just given (http://oski-2k3/reports/rwservlet?destype=cache&desformat=HTMLCSS& server=rep_oski-2k3_MT_HOME&report=test.rdf&userid=system/password@orcl), replacing the server name (oski-2k3) with your server name and the Reports Server (rep_oski-2k3_MT_HOME) with your Reports Server name. Click Finish and then Run As Portlet on the component summary page. You should see the report in your web browser. Click the Access tab on the component summary page and make sure Publish To Portal is checked.

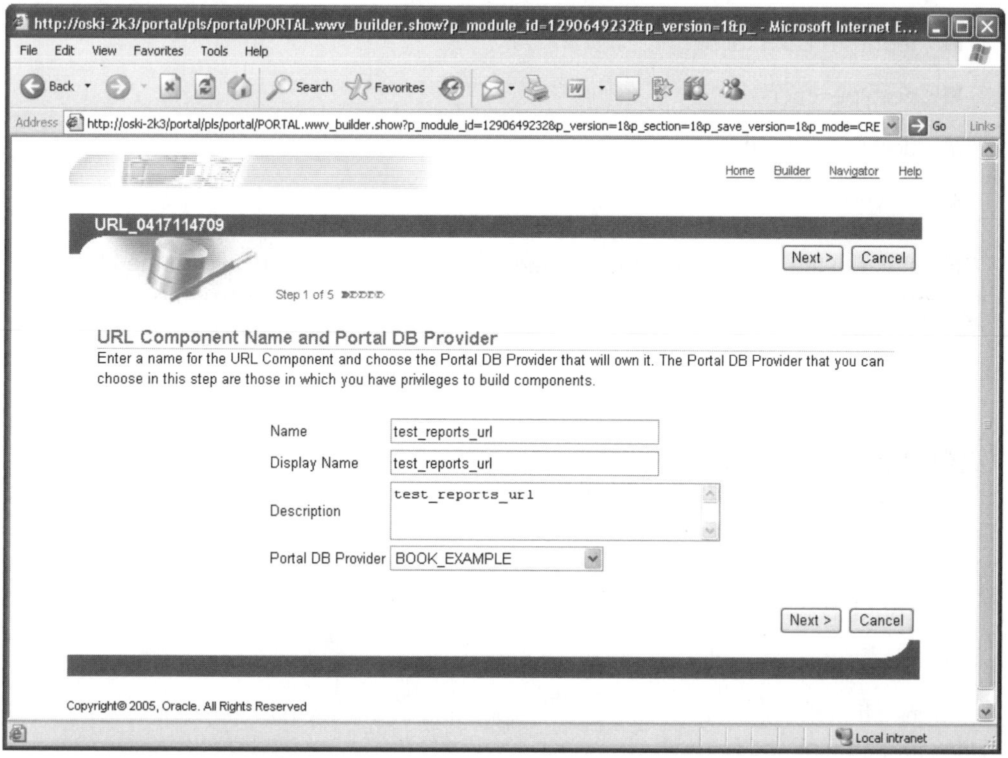

FIGURE 11-6 *Specifying the reports URL*

Securing the Reports URL

If you looked closely at the URL used to run the test report over the Web, you noticed that there was sensitive information in it; information we certainly don't want exposed in a URL for the entire world to see. How can we hide this information? The Reports Server can make use of something called a keymap file. This file hides the details of the report from the user's eyes by referencing a key in a file on the server. The keymap file for the Reports Server is called cgicmd.dat and is located in <Middle_Tier_Home>/reports/conf. Here's an example of some of the entries in that file:

```
orqa: report=breakb.rdf destype=cache desformat=html server=repserver
breakbparam: report=breakb.rdf destype=cache desformat=html server=repserver
userid=scott/tiger@mydb
```

The key name is to the left of the colon. The parameters associated with that key are to the right of the colon. The example contains two keys: orqa and breakparam. The orqa key uses the following parameters:

- report=breakb.rdf
- destype=cache
- desformat=html
- server=repserver

Note that in the keymap file, the parameters are separated by spaces (in the URL they were separated by ampersands). Our URL in this example looks like this:

```
http://oski-
2k3/reports/rwservlet?destype=cache&desformat=HTMLCSS&%20server=rep_oski-
2k3_MT_HOME&report=test.rdf&userid=system/password@orcl
```

We want to hide everything after the question mark, so we could create an entry in the cgicmd.dat file that looks like this:

```
test_report: destype=cache desformat=HTMLCSS server=rep_oski-mobile report=test.rdf
userid=system/password@orcl
```

We could then reference the keymap file with the following URL:

```
http://oski-2k3/reports/rwservlet?cmdkey=test_report
```

To see all of the parameters that can be specified in the keymap file, look at the syntax for rwclient and rwservlet in Appendix A of "Oracle Application Server Reports Services Publishing Reports to the Web 10*g* (9.0.4)," Oracle Part Number B10314-01. The most common parameters used are listed in Table 11-1.

Parameter	Description
ARRAYSIZE	Use ARRAYSIZE to specify the size (in kilobytes) for use with ORACLE array processing. Generally, the larger the array size, the faster the report will run.
AUTHID	Use AUTHID to specify the user name and, optionally, the password to be used to authenticate users to the restricted OracleAS Reports Server. User authentication ensures that the users making report requests have access privileges to run the requested report.
BUFFERS	Use BUFFERS to specify the size of the virtual memory cache in kilobytes. You should tune this setting to ensure that you have enough space to run your reports, but not so much that you are using too much of your system's resources.
DESFORMAT	Specifies the format for the job output. In bit-mapped environments, use DESFORMAT to specify the printer driver to be used when DESTYPE is FILE. In character-mode environments, use it to specify the characteristics of the printer named in DESNAME.
DESNAME	Use DESNAME to specify the name of the cache, file, printer, OracleAS Portal, or e-mail ID (or distribution list) to which the report output will be sent. To send the report output by e-mail, specify the e-mail ID as you do in your e-mail application (any SMTP-compliant application). You can specify multiple user names by separating them with commas, and without spaces.
DESTYPE	Use DESTYPE to specify the type of device that will receive the report output. If you have created your own pluggable destination via the Reports Destination API, this is how the destination you created gets called.
REPORT	Use MODULE or REPORT to specify the name of the report to run.
RUNDEBUG	Use RUNDEBUG to turn on error messages/warnings that would otherwise not be displayed. For example, with RUNDEBUG=YES, you might get the error message "Frame 1 overlaps but does not contain Frame 2." This situation may or may not be acceptable, depending on the job being run.
SCHEDULE	Use SCHEDULE to set the day, time, and frequency a report should be run. The default is to run the report once, now. Time values are expressed according to a 24-hour day (e.g., one P.M. is expressed as 13:00).

TABLE 11-1 *Common rwclient and rwservlet Parameters*

Parameter	Description
SERVER	Use SERVER to specify the name of the Reports Server you want to use to run this report.
SSOCONN	Use SSOCONN to specify one or more connect strings to use to connect to one or more data sources in a single sign-on environment.
TRACEOPTS	TRACEOPTS indicates the tracing information that you want logged in the trace file when you run the report.
USERID	Use USERID only if you're not using single sign-on. Use USERID to specify your Oracle user name and password, with an optional database name for accessing a remote database. If the password is omitted, then a database logon form opens automatically before the user is allowed to run the report.

TABLE 11-1 *Common rwclient and rwservlet Parameters* (continued)

If you want users to log on to the database, then omit the password portion of the USERID keyword from the report request. If you want users to log on every time they run report requests, then use the Reports key mapping file, cgicmd.dat, to specify the run-time command, and include the %D argument in the relevant key mapping entry. You can also use the SSOCONN parameter to reference a database resource for your OracleAS Portal user.

Things get a little confusing here: OracleAS Portal uses users created in Oracle's implementation of LDAP (Lightweight Directory Access Protocol) called Oracle Internet Directory. These LDAP users are not users in the database, even though the security information about these users is stored in the infrastructure database (confusing enough?). In order for these LDAP users who are not database users to have privileges to see (query) and potentially enter (insert), modify (update), and remove (delete) data in an Oracle database, a database resource must be set up for each of these LDAP users. The database resource is named, and then referenced with the SSOCONN parameter described in Table 11-1. LDAP users are commonly set up either in OracleAS Portal or by accessing the Oracle Internet Directory Delegated Authentication Server directly at: http://<infrastructure server>:<port>/oiddas.

This serves to hide the implementation details from the end user. The cgicmd.dat file is not read dynamically, however, so every change to it requires administrators to stop and start the OC4J_BI_FORMS component in the middle tier.

To put this component on a page, go back to the OracleAS Portal Navigator and click the Page Groups tab. If you don't have a page group defined, create one now. Edit the root page for your page group. You can edit the page in one of three ways: Graphical mode, Layout mode, or List mode. Select Layout Mode and then click Add Portlets in the main region of the page to see the Add Portlets page (Figure 11-7).

Click the name of your database provider. You should see Test_Report_URL (or whatever you named your URL) as one of the portlets that can be placed on this region. If it is not displayed, type **test_report_url** in the search field and click Go. Once it is displayed, single-click it to move it to the right-hand side (Selected Portlets) of the page. Your Portal page now has an Oracle Report integrated into it. Back on the Edit Page screen, click the Graphical link on the top left of the page. You should see the report (albeit clumsily placed) on the page.

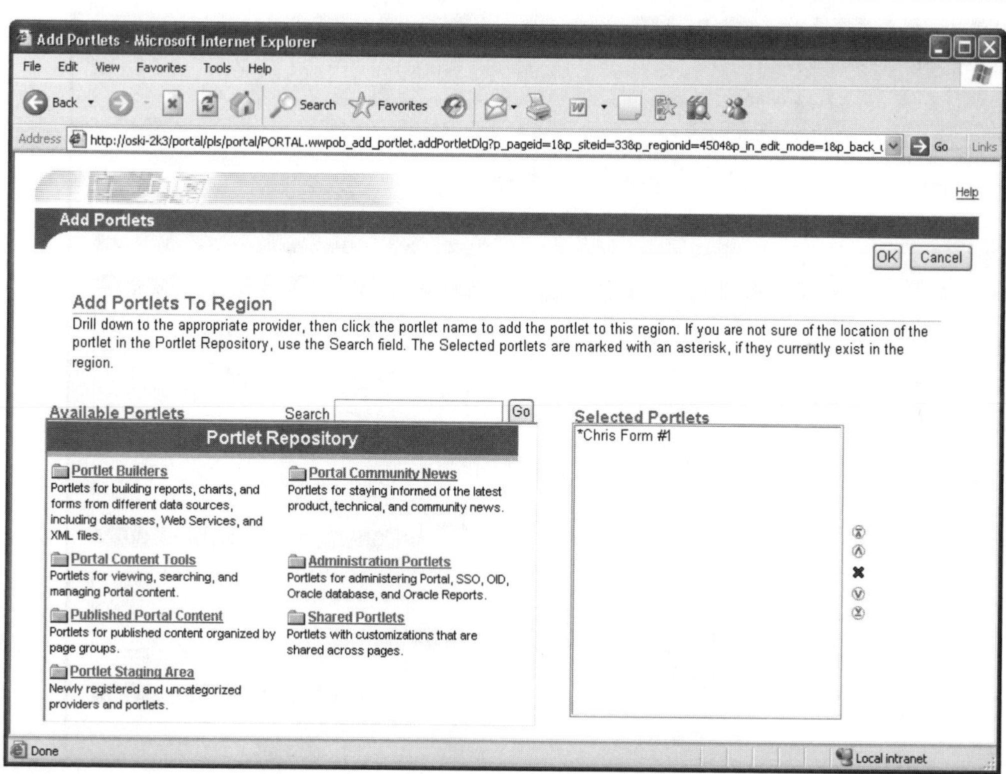

FIGURE 11-7 *Adding a portlet to a region*

Reports Integration Method #2: Using the Native Portal Method

Using the URL component is a quick way to get an Oracle Report on an OracleAS Portal page, but we can't use any of OracleAS Portal's native support for Oracle Reports to enhance our functionality with this method. If you're logged in to OracleAS Portal as a user with administration privileges, you'll see an Administer tab on the builder page (Figure 11-8).

If you click the Administer tab, and then on the Portal subtab on the top left of the screen, you will see a link on the bottom right that says Oracle Reports Security Settings. Clicking that link will take you to a page that looks like Figure 11-9.

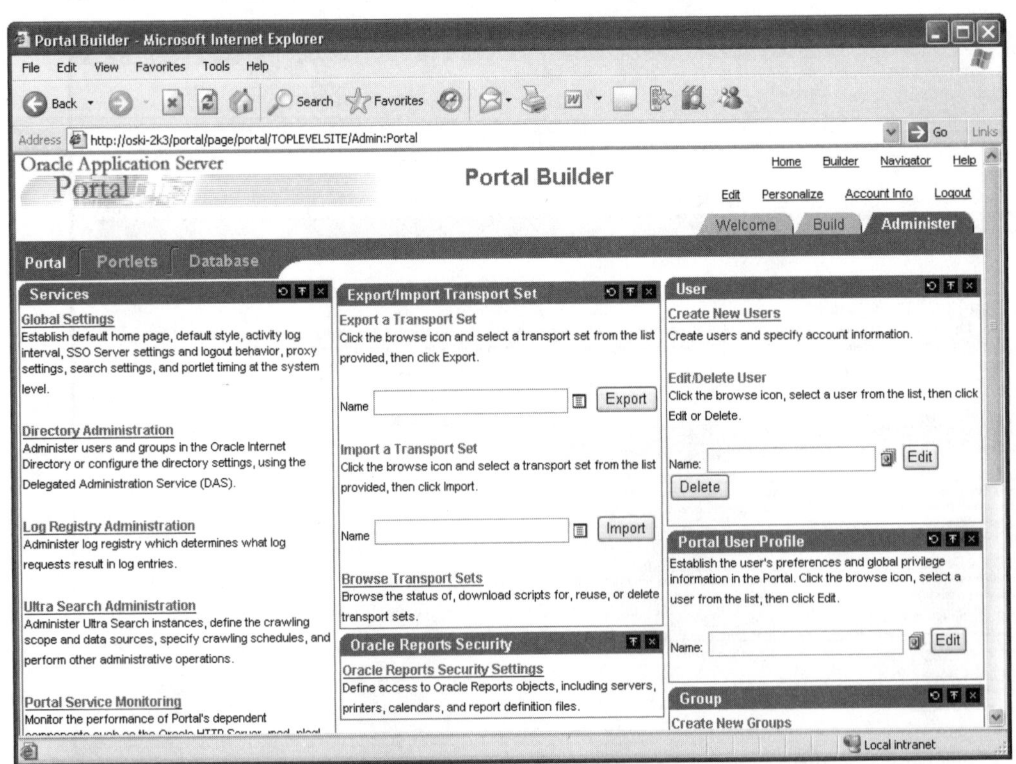

FIGURE 11-8 *The Portal subtab of the Administer tab*

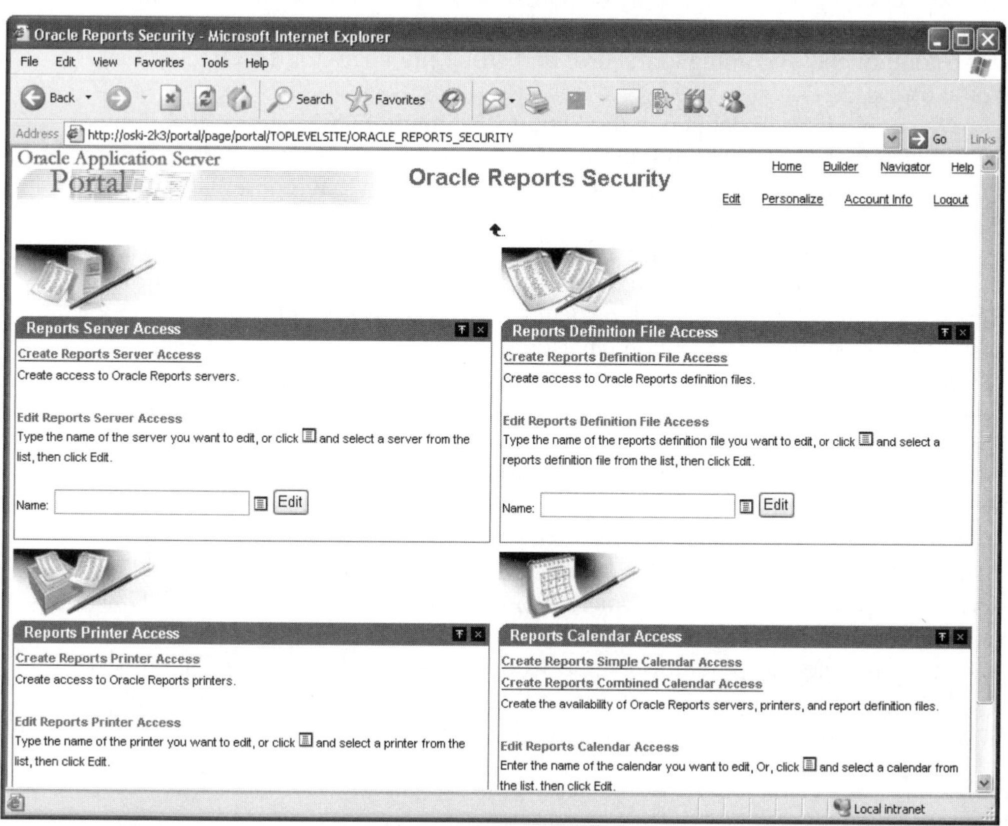

FIGURE 11-9 *The Oracle Reports Security page*

On this screen, we can define access to Reports Servers, access to .rdf files, access to printers, and access to report calendars. By using these features of OracleAS Portal, developers can use OracleAS Portal's security mechanisms and added functionality to restrict access to the various components of Oracle Reports. For example, an OracleAS Portal Calendar Access object can be created that limits access to nonbusiness hours, so that no report can be run during business hours, consuming precious system resources. That calendar object can then be associated to any combination of Reports Servers, .rdf files, and reports printers. If an attempt is made to access a Reports Server, .rdf file, or reports printer outside of the reports calendar access period (i.e., during working hours), the request fails and an error message is generated. Developers also have the ability to restrict access to any of these components according to the user and group privileges for the OracleAS Portal user.

When an .rdf file is defined in the Reports Definition File Access portlet, it must be associated with a Portal DB Provider. If that report has Publish To Portal checked in the Access tab of the component summary screen, then that report will show up as an available portlet to be placed on an OracleAS Portal page in the OracleAS Portal portlet repository. Depending on when the page is viewed, the report will then be displayed (if it falls within the calendar parameters associated with the Reports Server and .rdf file) or will display an error with absolutely no developer or system administration intervention whatsoever.

You can use keymap file entries when you define entries in the Reports Definition File Access portlet, but it's tricky to find and a little confusing to use. Click Create Reports Definition File Access. In Step 1 of the wizard, give the report a meaningful name. On the second step of the wizard, you'll start entering characteristics of the report: its name on disk, the Reports Server you want to use, etc. Here's the tricky part: when we get to the final step, we can specify a keymap entry to use; any parameters specified in that keymap entry will override anything you enter in these screens. To prove this, leave the Oracle Reports File Name field blank. Click Finish to generate the report definition file access for Portal.

Wait a minute—if we're finished, how do we specify what keymap file entry we want to use? If you click either the Run or Run As Portlet link on the component summary screen, you'll get the following error message:

```
REP-50004: No report specified on the command line
```

This makes sense, since we left the Oracle Reports File Name field blank. On the component summary screen, you'll see a link that says Personalize. Clicking this link will take you to the screen shown in Figure 11-10.

In the CGI/Servlet Command Key field enter **test_report** (or a suitable name for a key in your cgicmd.dat file) and click Save Parameters. Click the *x* in the top right to close the window and return to the Component Summary screen. Now click either Run or Run As Portlet and you should see your report. Once you have saved the parameter, the key specified in the CGI/Servlet field will always be used when this report is run in OracleAS Portal. The values have been taken from the cgicmd.dat file and have overridden the report's attributes that were specified in Step 2 of the wizard.

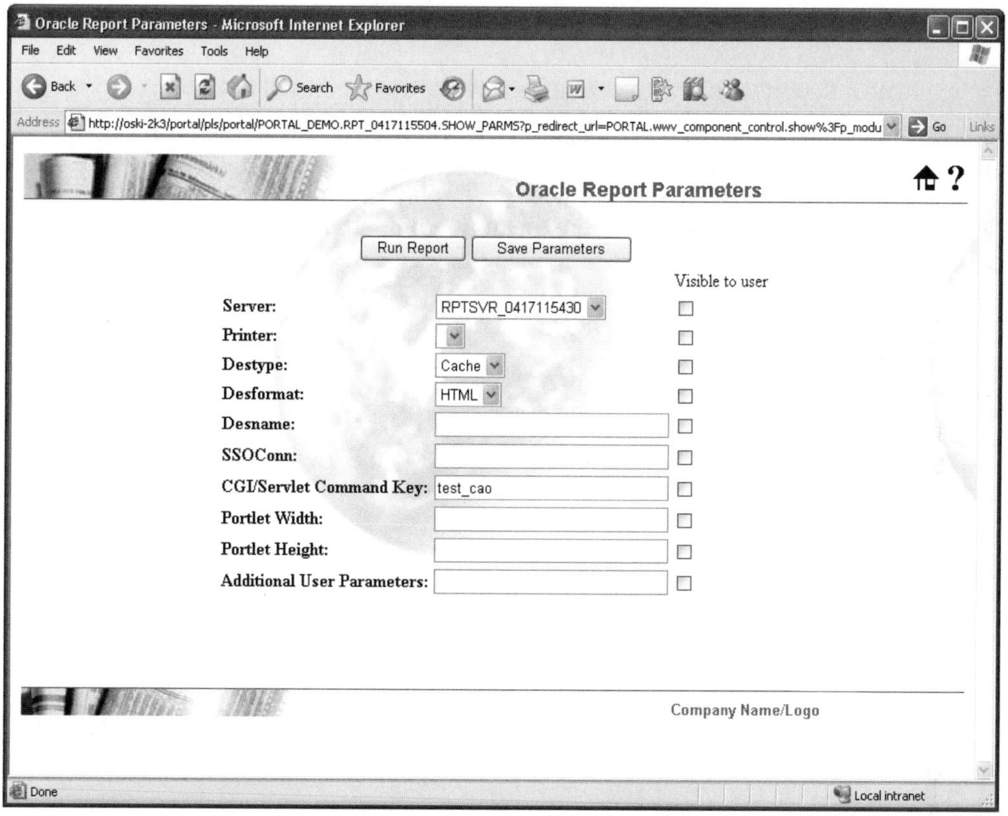

FIGURE 11-10 *The OracleAS Portal Report Parameters Page*

Reports Server Administration

As mentioned earlier, we are not limited to just one Reports Server. There is an executable called rwserver located in the <Middle_Tier_Home>/bin directory. This program can be used to stop, start, or create a Reports Server and, if running on the Windows platform, create a Reports Server as a Windows service. To start a Reports Server,

```
rwserver server=<Reports Server>
```

TIP
If the Reports Server you specify does not exist, a new one will be created.

To stop a Reports Server,

```
rwserver server=<Reports Server> shutdown=immediate
```

To create a Reports Server as a Windows service, use the install keyword:

```
rwserver server=<Reports Server> install autostart=yes
```

Oracle provides the rwservlet executable to display information about your Reports Server in your browser. Here are the most common parameters passed to rwservlet:

- **showjobs** Displays a Web view of Reports Server queue status.

  Example syntax:

  ```
  http://oski-2k3/reports/rwservlet/showjobs?server=rep_oski-2k3
  ```

- **showenv** Displays the rwservlet configuration file (rwservlet.properties).

  Example syntax:

  ```
  http://oski-2k3/reports/rwservlet/showenv
  ```

- **showmap** Displays rwservlet key mappings.

  Example syntax:

  ```
  http://oski-2k3/reports/rwservlet/showmap
  ```

- **showmyjobs** Displays the Reports Server queue status for a particular user.

  Example syntax:

  ```
  http://oski-2k3/reports/rwservlet/showmyjobs
  ```

Component #2: Oracle Forms

There is no native way to integrate Oracle Forms into OracleAS Portal, meaning that there are no OracleAS Portal–specific features for integrating and administering Oracle Forms within OracleAS Portal. In order to accomplish Forms–to–OracleAS Portal integration, we have to use a technique similar to method #1 for integrating Reports (i.e., using the URL component in Portal). First, we need to make sure the Forms Server is up and running. If you look back at Figure 11-2, you'll see a component called Forms. If the status arrow is a check mark, we're up and running.

NOTE

One thing to notice about the Forms component: the radio button next to the Forms component is grayed out. Normally, to stop, start, or restart a component, we select its radio button and then click Start, Stop, or Restart in the right middle of the page. Why can't we do that with the Forms component? The Forms component is dependent on the OC4J_BI_FORMS component. When it's up, the Forms component is up; when it's down, the Forms component is down. So the next question becomes, if they're dependent on each other, why are there two of them? There are many reasons, but the most important one is that there are performance metrics associated with the Forms Server that allow administrators to see how efficiently the Forms Server is working. These metrics are viewable by clicking the Forms link. There is also a screen after you click the Forms link to view and modify the Forms Server configuration files. By separating these two components, administrators can get detailed information about both the OC4J_BI_FORMS and FORMS components of the Oracle Application Server 10g middle tier.

To test your Forms Server, we're going to follow steps similar to when we tested the Reports Server. Point your browser to the Welcome page for the Application Server. If the infrastructure and the middle tier are on the same machine, the port number is probably 7778. If they are on separate machines, the port number is probably 7777:

```
http://<Middle-tier server>:<port>
```

You should see a page similar to the one shown earlier in Figure 11-4. Click the Demonstrations tab, then the Business Intelligence And Forms link, and then the Forms Services link next to the text that starts "Demonstrates a test form...." If this is the first time you're attempting to run an Oracle Form, you will be prompted to install a browser plug-in called JInitiator.

NOTE
Oracle JInitiator enables users to run Oracle Forms applications using Netscape Navigator or Internet Explorer. It provides the ability to specify the use of a specific Java Virtual Machine (JVM) on the client, rather than using the browser's default JVM. Oracle JInitiator runs as a plug-in for Netscape Navigator and as an ActiveX component for Internet Explorer. Oracle JInitiator does not replace or modify the default JVM provided by the browser. Rather, it provides an alternative JVM in the form of a plug-in. To get more information about JInitiator, refer to "Oracle Application Server Forms Services Deployment Guide 10g (9.0.4)," Oracle Part Number B10470-01, Appendix A.

After JInitiator installs, you should see a new browser window similar to Figure 11-11.

Securing the Form's URL

Unlike the URL we used to run our first report, the URL to run our form seems pretty innocuous:

```
http://oski-2k3/forms90/f90servlet
```

Not much sensitive information you can get from the address in Figure 11-11, is there? But how do we specify what form we want to run and what characteristics we want to specify? Here's where Oracle is throwing you a bit of a curve ball. The demo to run a test report does not use a keymap entry (we saw all of the report's details in the URL), but the demo to run a form does use a keymap entry, even though there doesn't appear to be one specified.

Oracle Forms, like Oracle Reports, uses a keymap file called the Forms Servlet Configuration File. It serves the exact same purpose as the Oracle Reports keymap file: namely, it hides sensitive details about the Oracle Form from the user's eyes in the URL of the browser. The Forms Servlet Configuration File is called formsweb.cfg and is located in <middle_tier_home>/forms90/server. The formats of the files are different, but the concept is the same: a key that will be referenced in the URL of the browser, followed by attributes that will determine what form is run and how the Forms Server is run in that particular Oracle Form. In Oracle's documentation, the keys in the formsweb.cfg file are called named configurations.

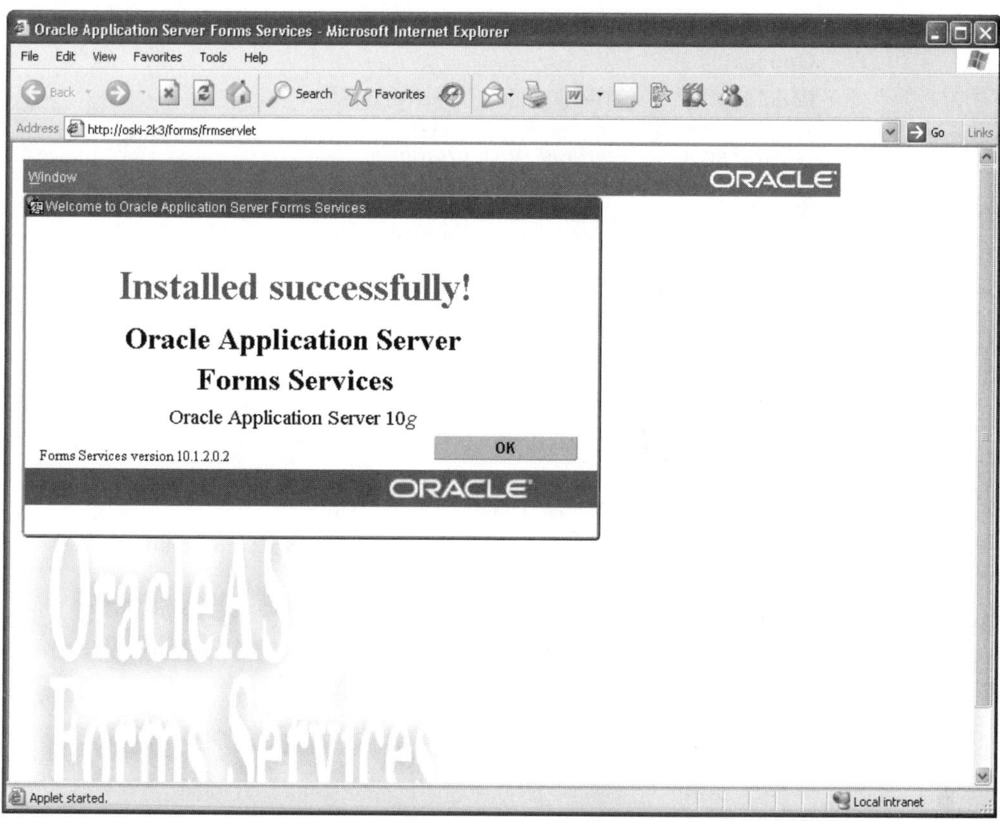

FIGURE 11-11 *The test page for the Oracle Forms Server*

In the cgicmd.dat file for the Reports Server, the entries have this format:

```
key: attribute1 attribute2 etc.
```

In the formsweb.cfg file for the Forms Server, the entries have this format:

```
[named configuration]
attribute1
attribute2
etc.
```

See Chapter 4 of the "Oracle Application Server Forms Services Deployment Guide 10*g* (9.0.4)" for a complete list of the parameters that can be specified. The most common parameters are specified in Table 11-2.

Parameter	Required / Optional	Parameter Value
baseHTML	Required	The default base HTML file.
baseHTMLJInitiator	Required	Physical path to HTML file that contains JInitiator tags.
connectionDis allowedURL	Required	This is the URL shown in the HTML page that is not allowed to start a new session.
IE	Recommended if there are users with Internet Explorer 5.0 or above browsers	Specifies how to execute the Forms applet under Microsoft Internet Explorer 5.0 or above. If the client is using an Internet Explorer 5.0 or above browser, either the native JVM or JInitiator can be used. A setting of "JInitiator" uses the basejini.htm file and JInitiator. A setting of "Native" uses the browser's native JVM.
log	Optional	Supports running and debugging a form from the Builder. Default value is Null.
form	Required	Specifies the name of the top-level Forms module (fmx file) to run.
userid	Optional	Login string. For example: scott/tiger@ORADB.
otherparams	Optional	This setting specifies command-line parameters to pass to the Forms run-time process in addition to form and userid. The default is otherparams=buffer_records=%buffer% debug_messages=%debug_messages% array=%array% obr=%obr% query_only=%query_only% quiet=%quiet% render=%render% record=%record% tracegroup=%tracegroup% log=%log% term=%term% Note that special syntax rules apply to this parameter when it is specified in a URL: a + may be used to separate multiple name=value pairs. See Section 3.3.4, "Specifying Special Characters in Values of Runform Parameters" in the "Oracle Application Server – Forms Services Deployment Guide" (http://download-west.oracle.com/docs/cd/B10464_01/web.904/b10470/basics.htm) for more information. For production environments, in order to provide better control over which runform parameters end users can specify in a URL, use the restrictedURLparams parameter.

TABLE 11-2 *The Most Common Parameters Specified*

Parameter	Required / Optional	Parameter Value
debug	Optional	Allows running in debug mode. Default value is No.
buffer	Optional	Supports running and debugging a form from the Builder. Subargument for otherparams. Default value is No.
log	Optional	Supports running and debugging a form from the Builder. Default value is Null.
pageTitle	Optional	HTML page title, attributes for the BODY tag, and HTML to add before and after the form.
serverURL	Required	/forms90/l90servlet (see Chapter 1, "Oracle Application Server-Forms Services Deployment Guide" (http://download-west.oracle.com/docs/cd/B10464_01/web.904/b10470/intro.htm)) for more information.
codebase	Required	Virtual directory you defined to point to the physical directory <ORACLE_HOME>/forms90/java, where, by default, the applet JAR files are downloaded from. The default value is /forms90/java.
imageBase	Optional	Indicates where icon files are stored. Choose between the following: "codeBase", which indicates that the icon search path is relative to the directory that contains the Java classes. Use this value if you store your icons in a JAR file (recommended). "documentBase", which is the default. In deployments that make use of the Forms Server CGI, you must specify the icon path in a custom application file.
logo	Optional	Specifies the .GIF file that should appear at the Forms menu bar. Set to NO for no logo. Leave empty to use the default Oracle logo.
width	Required	Specifies the width of the form applet, in pixels. Default is 650.
height	Required	Specifies the height of the form applet, in pixels. Default is 500.
separateFrame	Optional	Determines whether the applet appears within a separate window. Legal values: True or False.

TABLE 11-2 *The Most Common Parameters Specified* (continued)

Parameter	Required / Optional	Parameter Value
splashScreen	Optional	Specifies the .GIF file that should appear before the applet appears. Set to NO for no splash. Leave empty to use the default splash image. To set the parameter, include the filename (for example, myfile.gif) or the virtual path and filename (for example, images/myfile.gif).
background	Optional	Specifies the .GIF file that should appear in the background. Set to NO for no background. Leave empty to use the default background.
lookAndFeel	Optional	Determines the application's look and feel. Legal values: Oracle or Generic (Windows look and feel).
jinit_download_page	Required (Netscape only)	If you create your own version of the JInitiator download page, set this parameter to point to it. Default is /forms90/jinitiator/us/JInitiator/jinit.download.htm.
jinit_classid	Required (IE only)	Default is clsid:CAFECAFE-0013-0001-0009-ABCDEFABCDEF.
jinit_exename	Required	Default is jinit.exe#Version=1.3.1.9.
jinit_mimetype	Required (Netscape only)	Default is application/x-jinit-applet;version=1.3.1.9.
baseHTMLJInitiator	Required	Physical path to HTML file that contains JInitiator tags.
jpi_codebase	Required	Sun's Java Plug-in codebase setting.
jpi_classid	Required	Sun's Java Plug-in class ID.
jpi_download_page	Required	Sun's Java Plug-in download page.
em_mode	Required	1 is to enable. 0 is to disable. 1 indicates that all Enterprise Manager information is available, including metrics and servlet status. 0 indicates that only configuration information is available.
oid_formsid	Required	Configured during the OracleAS installation, so you do not need to change this.
ORACLE_HOME	Required	Configured during the OracleAS installation, so you do not need to change this.

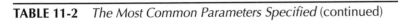

TABLE 11-2 *The Most Common Parameters Specified* (continued)

The URL for the Reports Server to read the cgicmd.dat file looks like this:

```
http://<server name>:<port>/reports/rwservlet?key
```

The URL for the Forms Server to read the formsweb.cfg file looks like this:

```
http://<server name>:<port>/servlet/f90servlet?config=named configuration
```

Wait a minute; the demo form that displayed in Figure 11-11 did not have a "config=" at the end of the URL. How did the Forms Server know what Oracle Form to display? At the beginning of the formsweb.cfg file, there is a "default configuration" section. Parameters specified in this section are used unless they are overridden by any named configurations referenced in the file. Since we didn't reference any, the default parameters were used. One of the default parameters is:

```
Form=test.fmx
```

We could have specified a named configuration like this:

```
[test_form]
form=test.fmx
```

and then specified the URL like this:

```
http://oski-2k3/servlet/f90servlet?config=test_form
```

Here's a strange quirk. Try this:

```
http://oski-2k3/servlet/f90servlet?config=bogusbogusbogus
```

Now, bogusbogusbogus does not exist in the formsweb.cfg file, yet the form gets displayed with no error message. Why? Remember that the named configurations override any parameters specified in the default configuration section. Since bogusbogusbogus isn't in the formsweb.cfg file, the values from the default configuration are used (including the one that says "form=test.fmx"). This is why it's a good idea to comment out the form= parameter in the default configuration section or redirect users and developers to a help page. As in the case of the cgicmd.dat file, if you make any changes to the formsweb.cfg file, you must bounce the OC4J_BI_FORMS component before any changes will take effect.

Integrating the Oracle Form into OracleAS Portal is as simple as creating a URL object and performing the steps we did in the section "Reports Integration Method #1: Using the Portal URL Component" earlier in this chapter. The URL

```
http://oski-2k3/servlet/f90servlet?config=<named configuration>
```

can be used to construct the OracleAS Portal component (a URL component) that can then be placed on an OracleAS Portal page. Assuming you've already created a Database Provider in OracleAS Portal, go into that provider and create a new URL component. Give it a name that is easily remembered. For this example (Figure 11-12), I used the name test_form_url. On the second step of the wizard, enter the URL just shown (http://oski-2k3/forms/frmservlet?config=<named configuration>). When we get to the next step in this process, we'll use this URL component and place it on a page.

Click Finish and then Run As Portlet on the component summary page. You should see the form in your web browser. Click the Access tab on the component summary page and make sure Publish To Portal is checked. You can now place this portlet on an OracleAS Portal page.

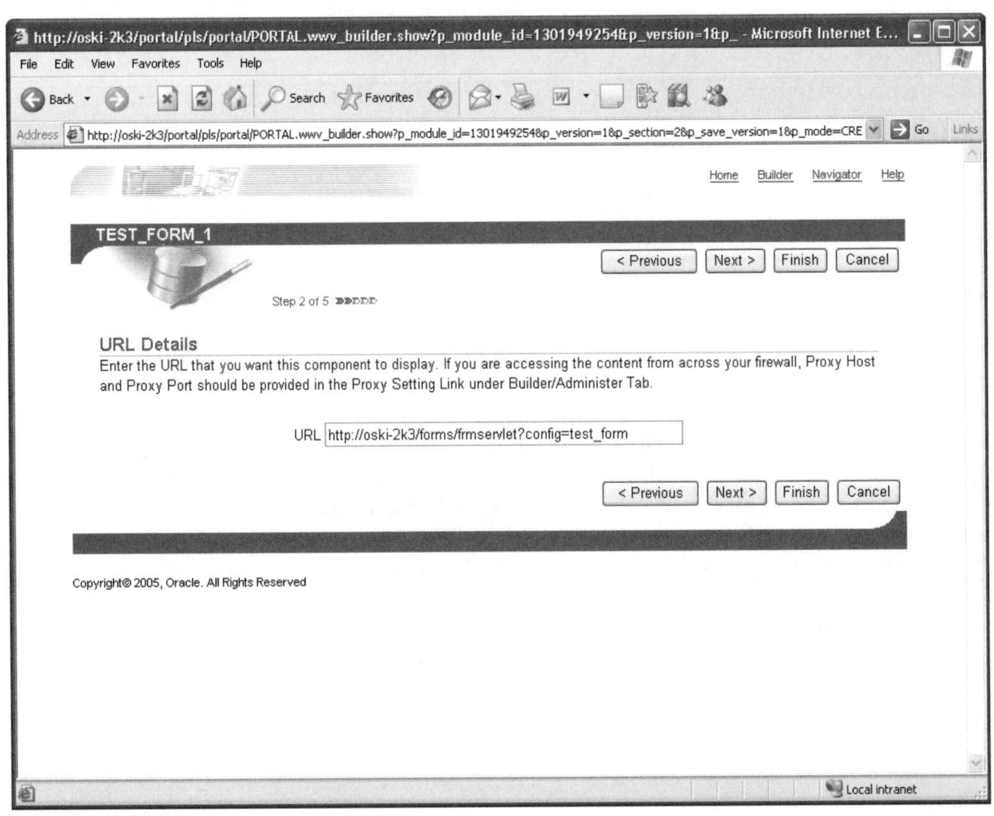

FIGURE 11-12 *Specifying the Oracle Forms URL for the OracleAS Portal component*

Component #3: Oracle Discoverer

Using either the URL or native methods to integrate Oracle Forms and Oracle Reports is a tricky, though relatively simple process. Incorporating OracleAS Discoverer Workbooks into Portal requires a significantly greater number of steps. To start with, there is native support for OracleAS Discoverer in Portal, but we have to "tell" OracleAS Portal about OracleAS Discoverer first. In Oracle's documentation, this is called "Registering the Discoverer Portlet Provider."

Registering the Discoverer Portlet Provider

The Discoverer Portlet Provider is a program that runs on the server and facilitates communication between the Discoverer Server and OracleAS Portal. Thankfully, the first part of this process has to be performed only once, because once the Discoverer Portlet Provider is registered with OracleAS Portal, it remains there. The other steps in the process, however, must be repeated for each Discoverer Worksheet we wish to incorporate into OracleAS Portal.

Before attempting to register the Discoverer Portlet Provider, we need to make sure all the pieces for OracleAS Portal and OracleAS Discoverer are in place and can "speak" to each other. Type the following in your browser:

```
http://<server>:<port>/discoverer/portletprovider
```

where <server> is the middle-tier server and <port> is the default port number of the middle-tier instance. In the examples in this chapter, I have been using a server named oski-2k3 with its middle tier installed on port 7778, so the URL on that server would look like this:

```
http://oski-2k3/discoverer/portletprovider
```

You should see a screen similar to the one shown in Figure 11-13.

TIP

If you don't see a screen like Figure 11-13, make sure the OracleAS Discoverer background process is running on your server. You can start all services by typing **opmnctl startall**. *If this does not fix your problem, check MetaLink docs 217185.1, 202268.1, and 236088.1 for suggestions on solutions.*

Next, we need to register the OracleAS Discoverer Portlet Provider in OracleAS Portal. Log in to OracleAS Portal as a user with Portal administration privileges. On

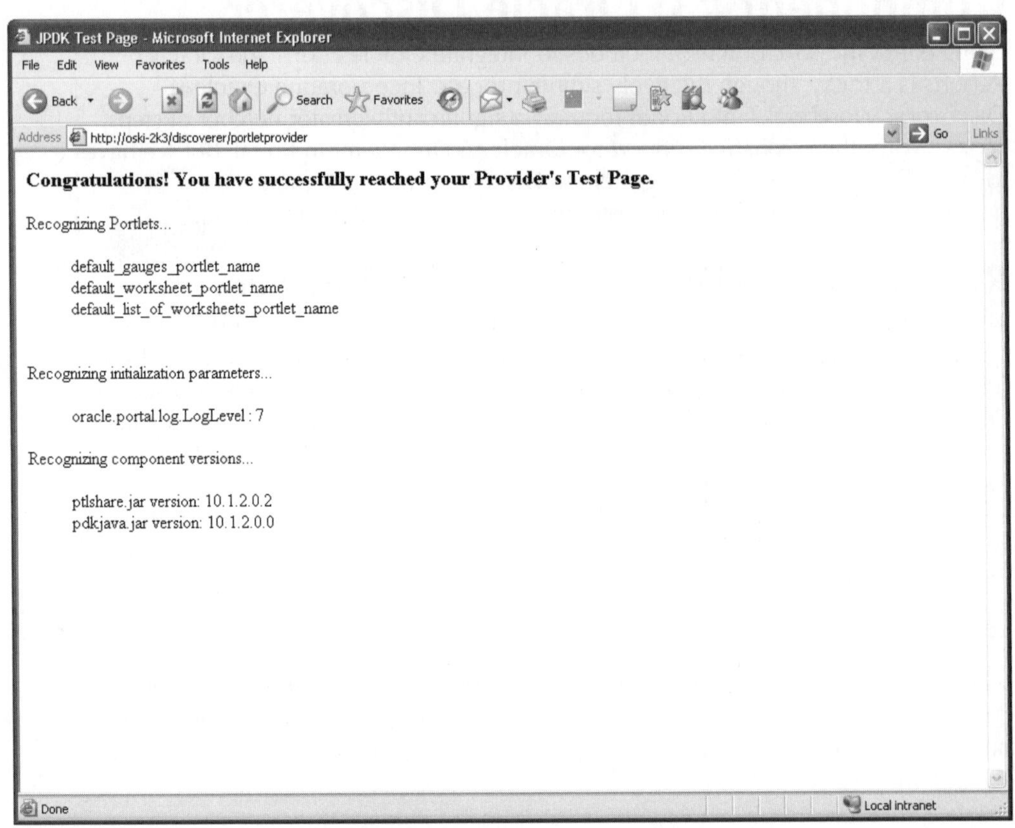

FIGURE 11-13 *Testing the Discoverer Portlet Provider*

the main OracleAS Portal page, click the Administer tab on the top right of the page, and select the Portlets subtab from the top left of the page. Click Register A Provider in the middle of the page (Figure 11-14).

The Name and Display Name fields in Step 1 of the Register a Portlet Provider Wizard can contain anything, but the Display Name is what will be displayed to developers when they attempt to add an OracleAS Discoverer Portlet to a page, so make it meaningful. Make sure Web is chosen for implementation style. Click Next to display the General Properties page.

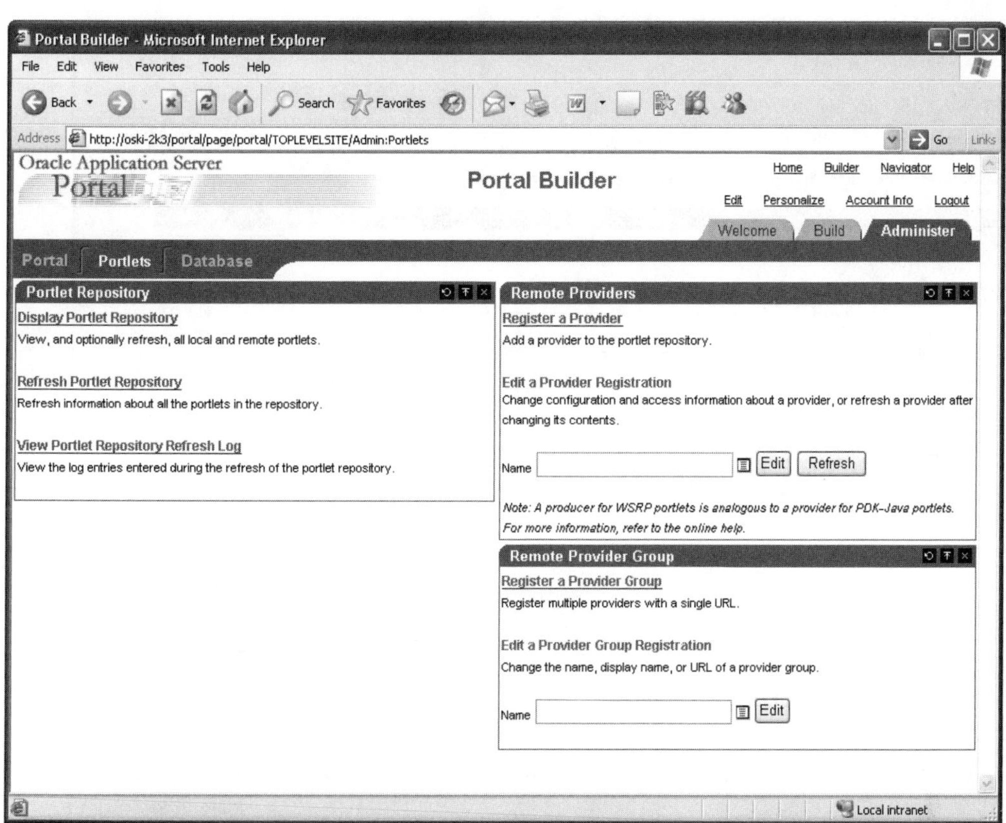

FIGURE 11-14 *The Portlets subtab of the Administer tab*

In the URL field, enter the URL we used to test the Discoverer Portlet Provider:

```
http://<server>:<port>/discoverer/portletprovider
```

Make sure the radio button starting with "The user has the same identity . . ." is selected (Figure 11-15).

Click Next. Unless you want to change the default grant access settings, you do not need to enter details in the control access page. Click Finish. The Discoverer Portlet Provider is now registered with Portal.

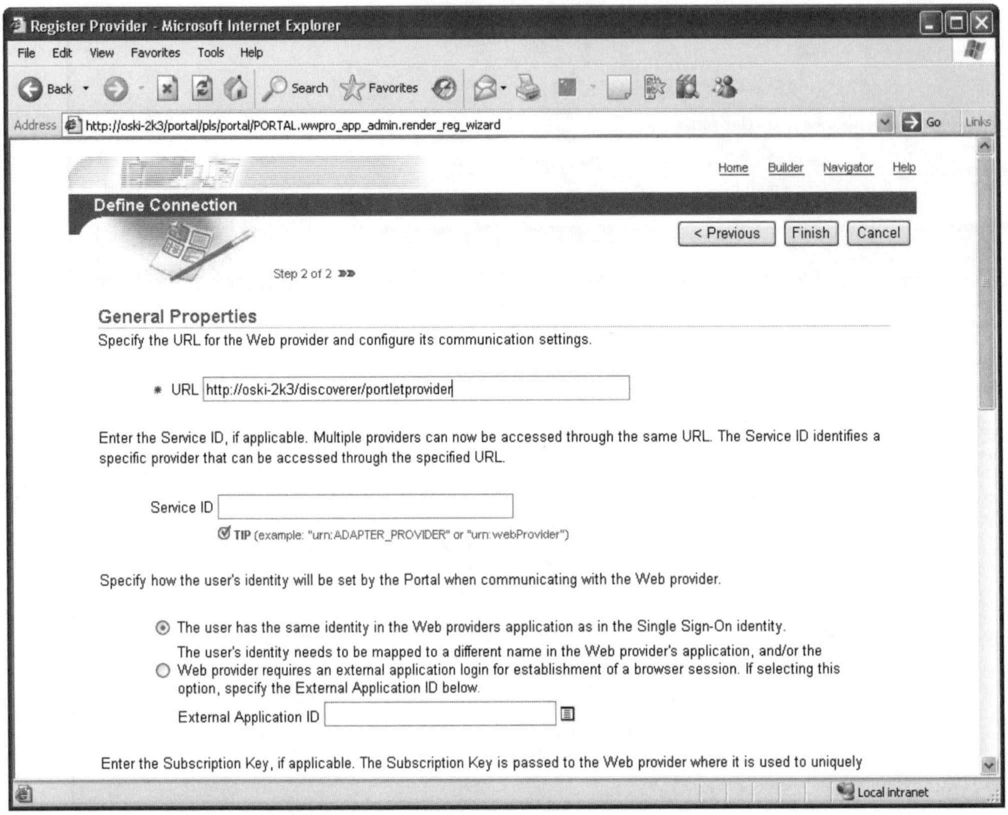

FIGURE 11-15 *Registering the OracleAS Discoverer portlet*

Creating a Discoverer Connection in Oracle Application Server 10*g*

Before we can add OracleAS Discoverer portlets to a page, we have to establish an OracleAS Discoverer connection for Oracle Application Server 10*g*. Back in Figure 11-2, the first system component listed for the middle tier was one called Discoverer. Clicking that link will take us to the screen where we can configure OracleAS Discoverer connections for Oracle Application Server 10*g*. Click the link that says Discoverer Public Connections. You will see a screen that looks like Figure 11-16.

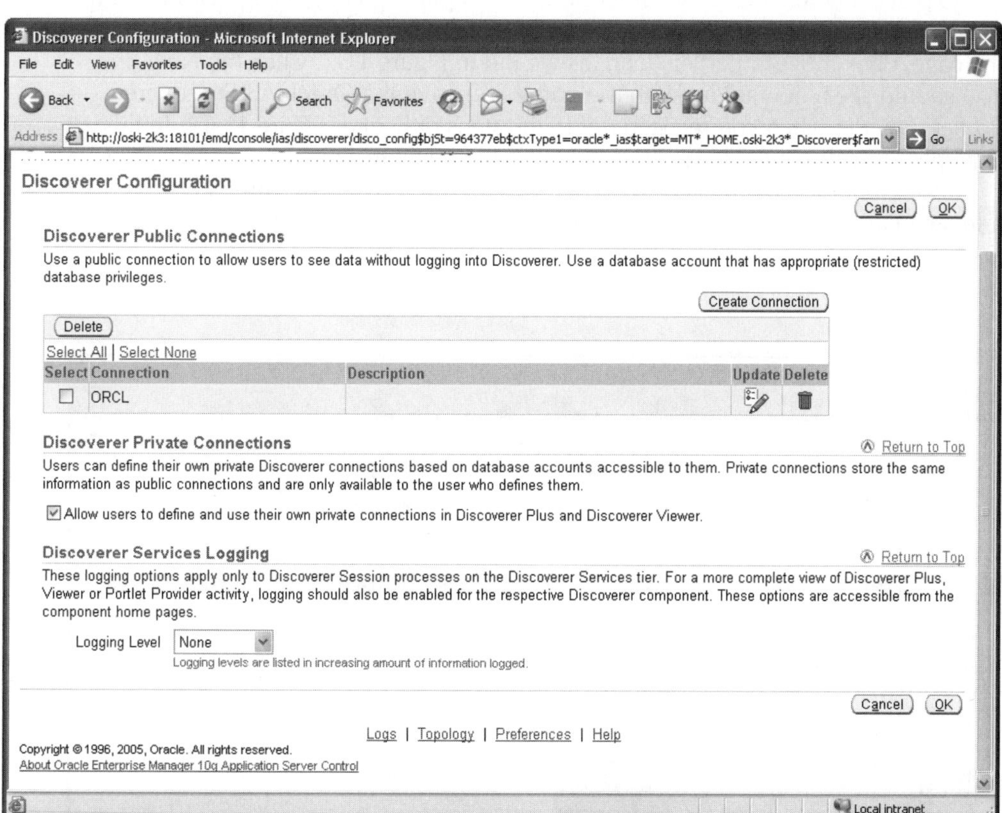

FIGURE 11-16 *Specifying an OracleAS Discoverer connection*

Click Create Connection and enter connection information for a user that has a Discoverer EUL (End-User Layer) built. The connect string entered here must match an entry in the tnsnames.ora file in the <Middle-Tier-Home>/network/admin directory on the server. When it comes time to configure an OracleAS Discoverer portlet after it has been placed onto an OracleAS Portal page, we will be asked to enter the name of the OracleAS Discoverer connection defined on this page. Different Workbooks and different OracleAS Portal pages can use the same OracleAS Discoverer connection.

To place an OracleAS Discoverer portlet on a page, go to the Page Groups tab and select a page group. Click the Layout link on the top of the page. In a region on the page, click the Add Portlets icon, as we did in Figure 11-7. Click the New link. You should see a new folder with the name you gave the OracleAS Discoverer Portlet Provider when you registered it in the steps right after Figure 11-13. In this example, it's called OracleAS Discoverer Provider (Figure 11-17).

If we click the OracleAS Discoverer Provider link, we have three choices: adding a Discoverer Gauges Portlet, a Discoverer Worksheet portlet, or a List of Database Workbooks portlet. Clicking the List Of Database Workbooks link will

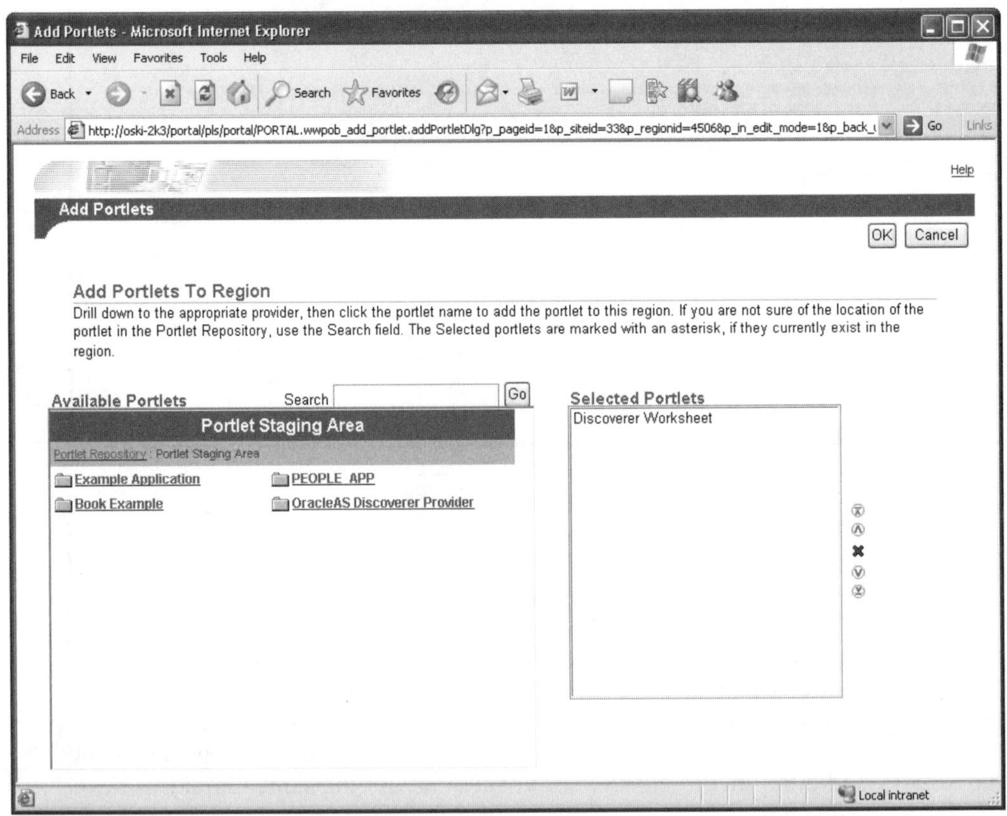

FIGURE 11-17 *The available portlets of the discoverer_provider*

place a portlet on the screen that allows end users to specify which OracleAS Discoverer Workbook they would like to view. If we click the Worksheet portlet, we will have to perform another step: configuring the portlet to specify which OracleAS Discoverer Worksheet we would like to view.

Click Worksheet, so that it appears on the right-hand side of the page under Selected Portlets. We will specify which Worksheet we want to display in the next step. Clicking OK on the top right part of the screen will take us back to the Page Layout screen. Click Graphical in the top left part of the screen to display the page graphically. You should see something like Figure 11-18.

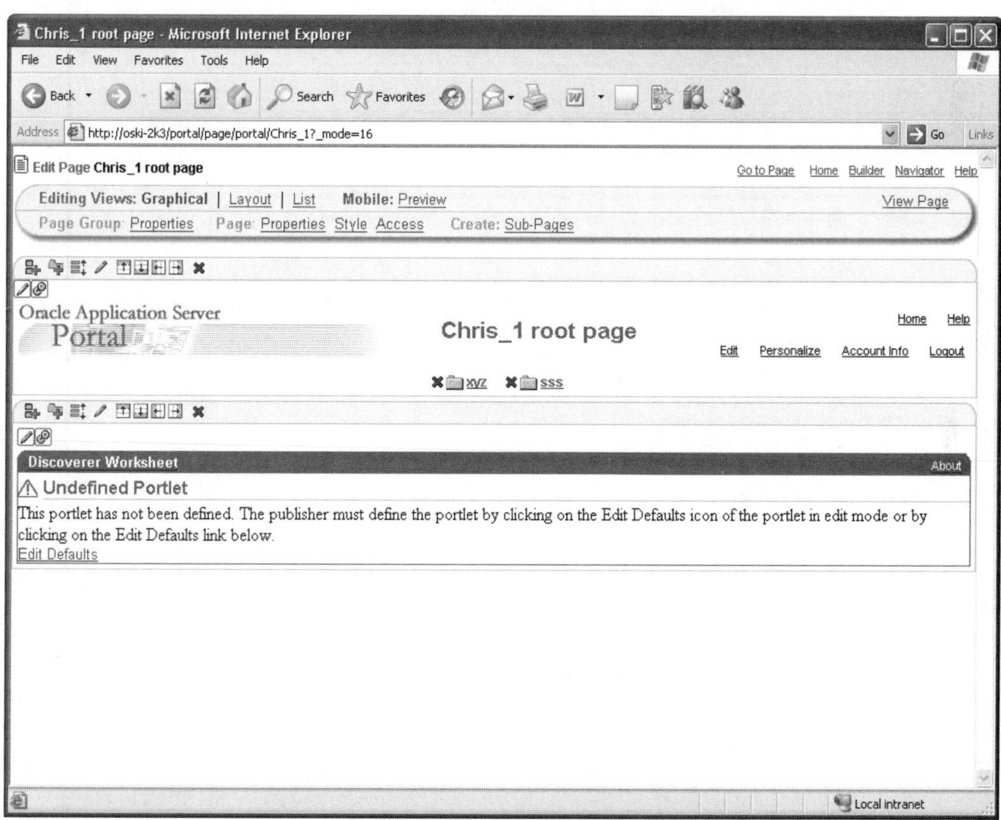

FIGURE 11-18 *Attempting to display the Oracle Discoverer Worksheet*

The error makes sense because we haven't defined which OracleAS Discoverer Worksheet we want to display yet. We can't do that by editing the page in Graphical mode; we can do it only by editing the page in Layout mode, so click the Layout link on the top-left side of the page. In the region where you added the Discoverer portlet, you should see a link that says Edit Defaults next to the Discoverer portlet. Clicking that link will take you to the Edit Worksheet Portlet Defaults Wizard. This wizard will step you through the definition of the Discoverer portlet.

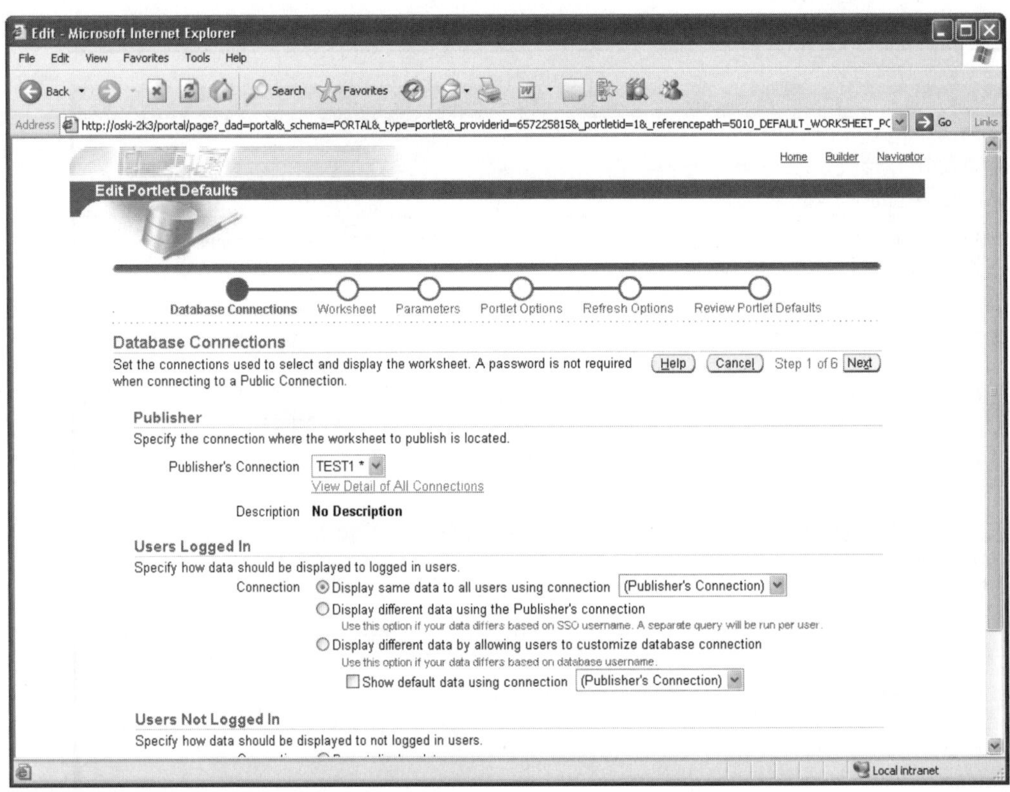

FIGURE 11-19 *The first page of the Edit Worksheet Portlet Defaults Wizard*

The Edit Worksheet Portlet Defaults Wizard

The first page of the Edit Worksheet Portlet Defaults Wizard asks us to enter the connection we created earlier in Figure 11-15. The wizard will then attempt to establish a connection to the instance that has a Discoverer End-User Layer (EUL) already built. On Step 1 of the wizard, the OracleAS Discoverer Workbooks available to us will be displayed. Leave the other selections with their default values for this example and click Next on the bottom right of the page (Figure 11-19).

On Step 2 of the wizard, we specify the Workbook and Worksheet to be displayed (Figure 11-20).

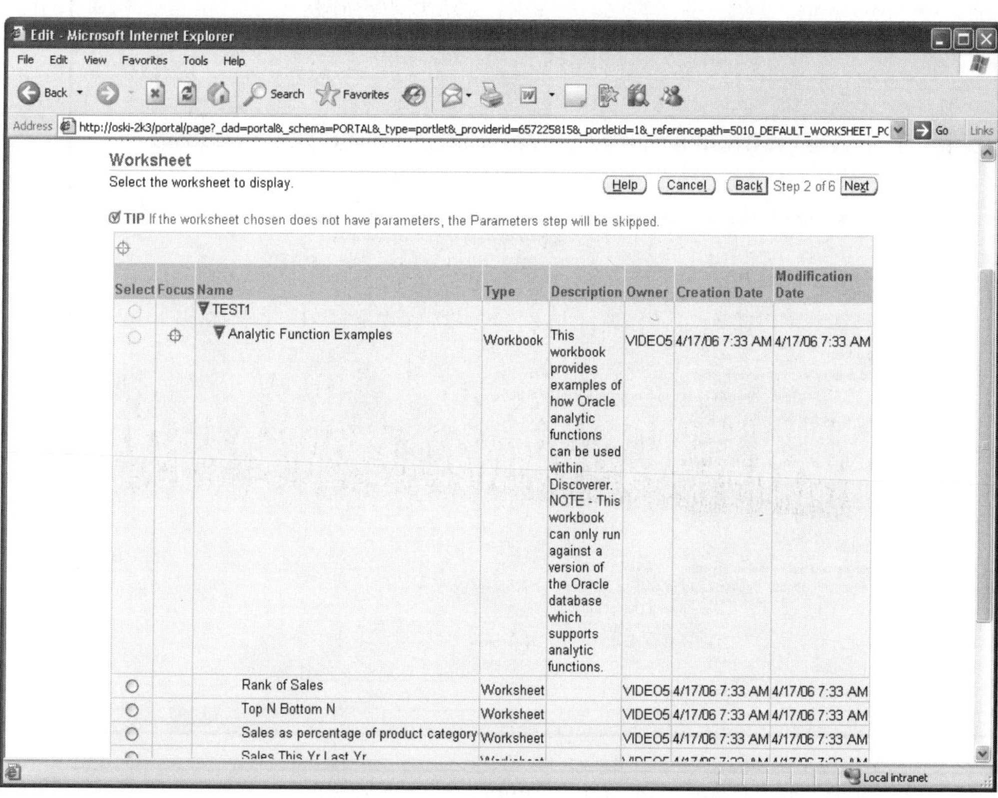

FIGURE 11-20 *The second page of the Edit Worksheet Portlet Defaults Wizard*

If there are any parameters associated with the Worksheet, we are taken to Step 3 of the Edit Worksheet Portlet Defaults Wizard, where we can specify parameter values. If there are no parameters associated with the Worksheet, we are taken directly to Step 4, the Portlet Settings page, where we can specify the title of the portlet (Figure 11-21).

The fifth step, the Refresh Options page (Figure 11-22), takes a little explaining. When the page is constructed and the OracleAS Discoverer portlet is rendered, it is cached so that subsequent calls to display the page occur quickly. This may be a

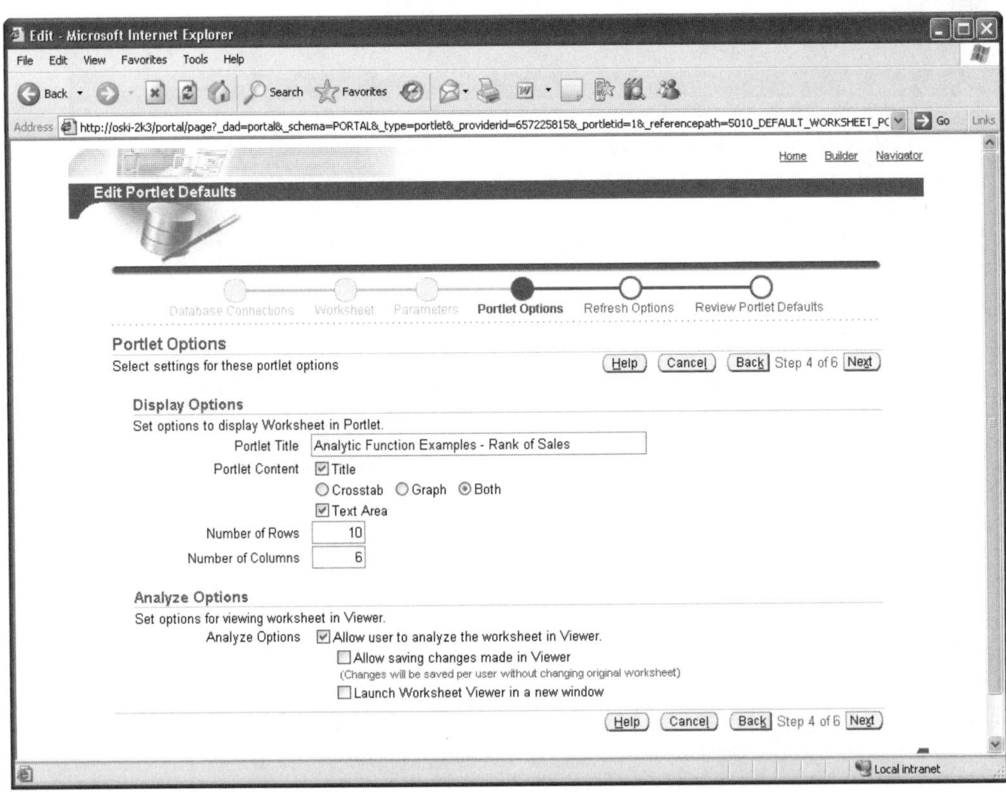

FIGURE 11-21 *Step 4 of the Edit Worksheet Portlet Defaults Wizard*

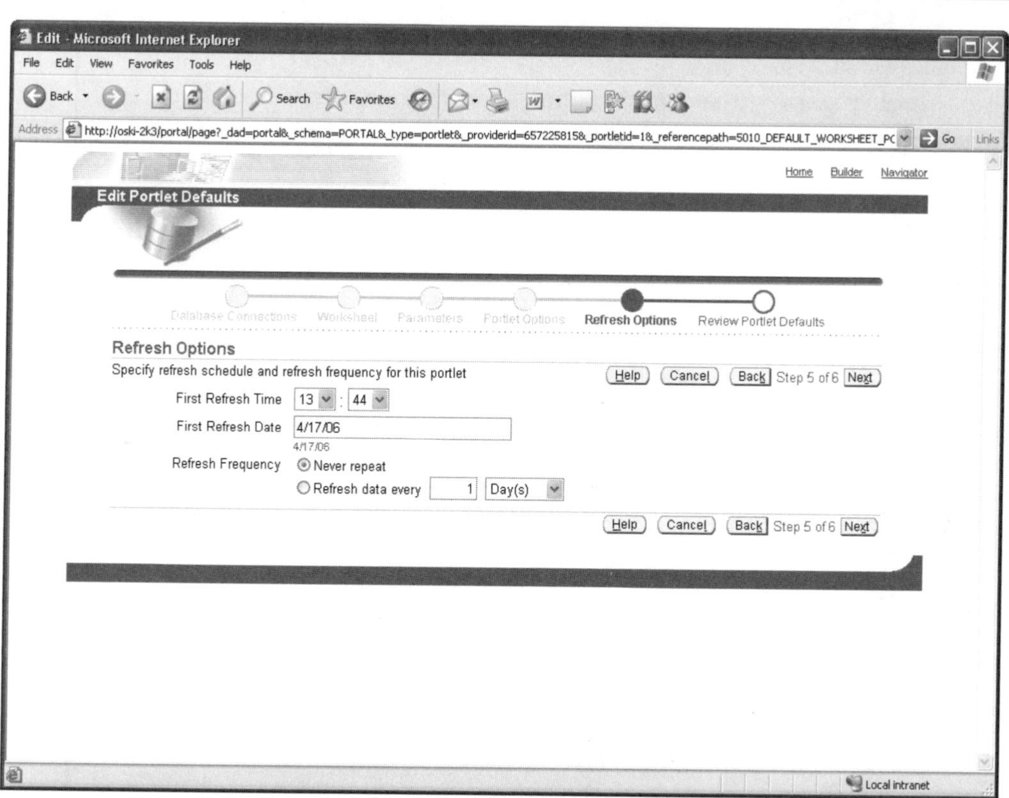

FIGURE 11-22 *The fifth page of the Edit Worksheet Portlet Defaults Wizard*

problem if the information on the OracleAS Discoverer portlet is dynamic and needs to be refreshed on a regular basis. You can specify a specific time or an interval to refresh the data in the OracleAS Discoverer portlet. The shortest refresh time that can be specified is one hour.

Finally, there is a review page to check all of your selections (Figure 11-23). After clicking Finish on the review screen, you can see the results of your work. You will automatically be taken back to the page layout screen. Click Graphical in the top right-hand part of the screen. You should now see the Discoverer report displayed similar to Figure 11-24.

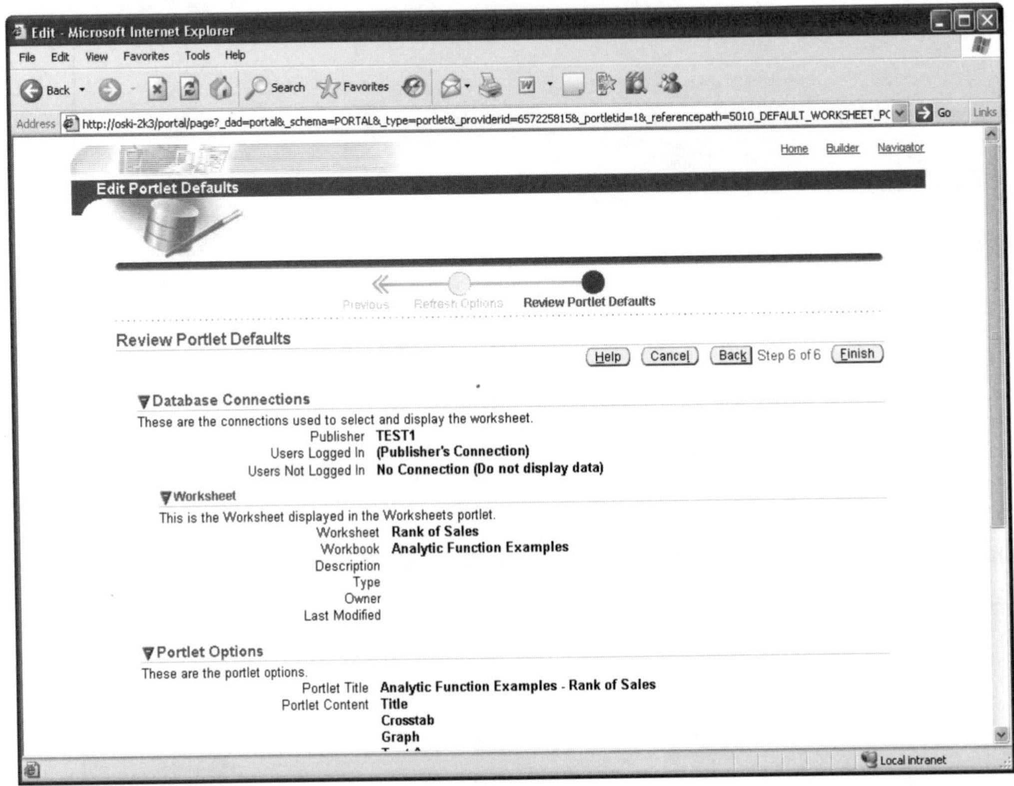

FIGURE 11-23 *The sixth and final page of the Edit Worksheet Portlet Defaults Wizard*

Click the View Page link in the top right of the screen to see how the page will look when deployed (Figure 11-25).

NOTE
Certain advanced OracleAS Discoverer features such as drill-downs are not available when you display your OracleAS Discoverer Worksheets in OracleAS Portal.

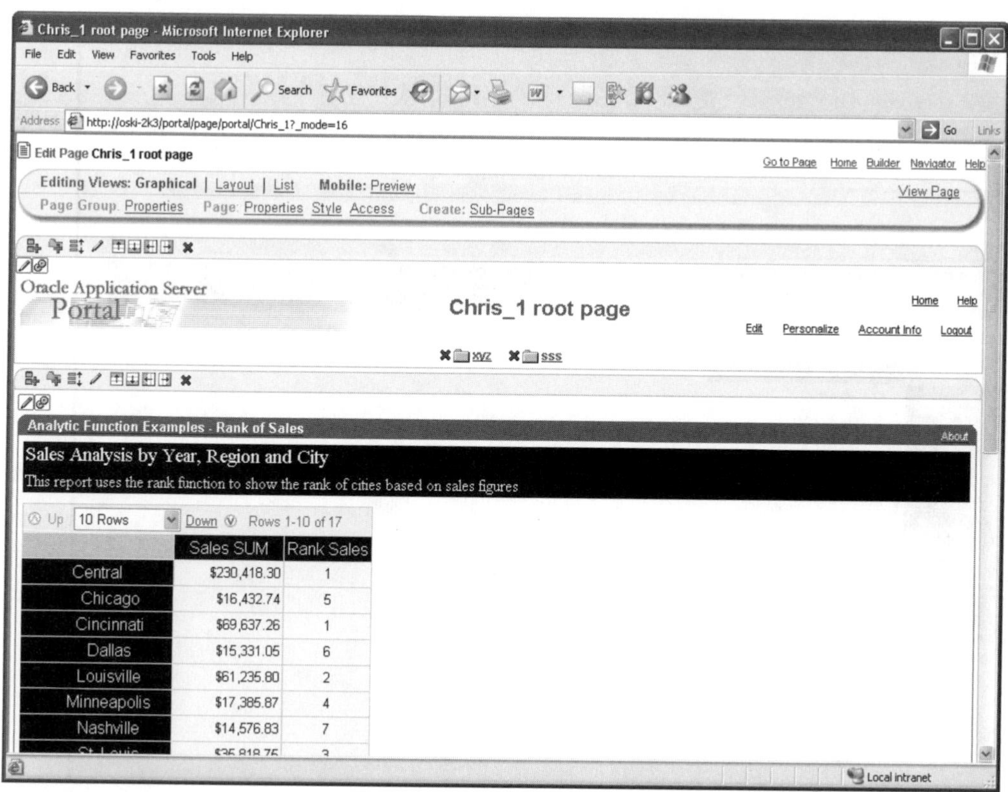

FIGURE 11-24 *The Discoverer Worksheet displayed in graphical mode*

Summary

The designers of OracleAS Portal have given developers and administrators enough flexibility to incorporate non-Portal items into OracleAS Portal sites relatively easily. There is native support for Oracle Reports and Oracle Discoverer Worksheets, and even without native support for Oracle Forms, there are still methods for incorporating these Oracle Forms into OracleAS Portal. Integrating these existing components gives developers and administrators the benefit of not having to duplicate any existing development work, while gaining all of the benefits that OracleAS Portal provides.

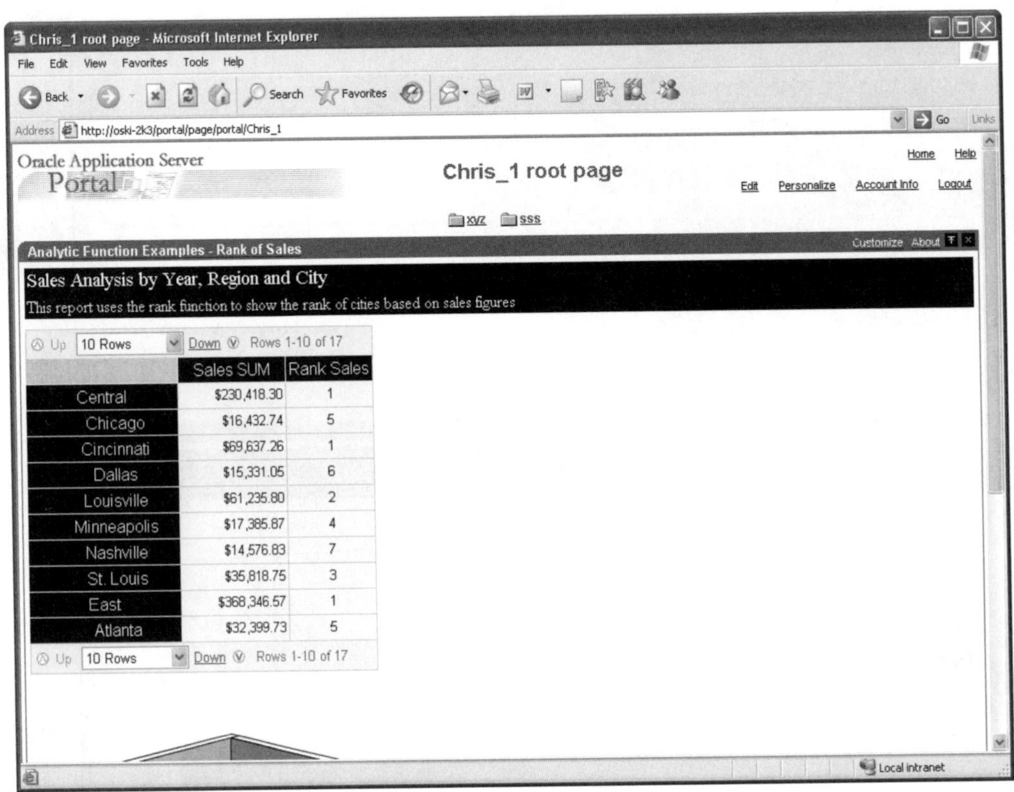

FIGURE 11-25 *The Discoverer Worksheet displayed as an OracleAS Portal portlet*

CHAPTER 12

Oracle Instant Portal

n Oracle's terms, a portal "enables you to interact with information from many different sources through a single interface. In OracleAS Portal terms, that interface is called a page. The portal itself is a collection of pages." Just about anyone who has surfed the Web is familiar with a portal; Yahoo.com, MSN.com, and even Amazon.com can be considered portals. Oracle's main product offering in the portal area is OracleAS Portal, which is part of the Oracle Application Server. OracleAS Portal used to be called WebDB, and the latest version of OracleAS Portal, as of May 2007, is 10.1.4.

OracleAS Portal is designed to provide end users and developers with a consistent environment in which to develop and view portal pages, content, and portlets. The OracleAS Portal development environment is itself a portal application, so new developers and users can see what it is like to interact with a set of portal pages immediately. While OracleAS Portal is relatively easy to learn and use (especially considering how complex development environments like Oracle JDeveloper or Microsoft Visual C# are), Oracle has been continually adding features and functionality to the OracleAS Portal product. As such, the latest incarnation of OracleAS Portal can present a relatively difficult task for new developers and users to master, particularly if the business needs are relatively simple.

What Is OracleAS Instant Portal?

According to Oracle's documentation, "Oracle Instant Portal provides instant out-of-the-box portals for secure publishing and content sharing, ideal for enterprises with a need for smaller-scale intranets or an internal communications hub. Unlike OracleAS Portal portals, Oracle instant portals are intended for user communities that have well-defined, somewhat limited needs for information sharing."

Why Does OracleAS Instant Portal Exist?

As Oracle has continued to add features to OracleAS Portal, its learning curve has increased dramatically. Many organizations have simple requirements, and the thought of devoting numerous resources to their portal development and maintenance is overwhelming. There is also the question of developing a simple portal to see if the technology is appropriate for a particular organization. OracleAS Instant Portal satisfies both of these requirements by limiting the number of options available to the portal developer (thus making portal creation and maintenance simpler), providing a simple and intuitive security model, and allowing the addition of content using a simple tool (Oracle Drive, discussed later). All of this allows Oracle Instant Portal developers to get their feet wet with OracleAS Portal quickly and easily.

Limitations

OracleAS Instant Portal is not intended to be a full-blown portal environment. As such, there are some serious limitations. First and foremost, OracleAS Instant Portal is designed as an environment to manage content. While it is possible to place portlets on your Instant Portal (and as you'll see, there are some default portlets available to you when you create your OracleAS Instant Portal), it was not intended for that functionality. OracleAS Instant Portal also has its own security model; if your business model requires you to create a complex security model, OracleAS Instant Portal may not be the right choice. Also, the options for visual templates are extremely limited—the freedom to create backgrounds, colors, fonts, and templates is not available in OracleAS Instant Portal.

NOTE
Originally, Oracle Instant Portal was created for small businesses to get them started with portals. Since many small businesses don't have dedicated portlet developers, Oracle didn't add portlet editing capabilities to Oracle Instant Portal.

Your First Instant Portal

To create your first Instant Portal, log in to OracleAS Portal and select the Build tab. At the bottom of the Build tab, you'll see a portlet entitled Oracle Instant Portal (Figure 12-1). From here, you can type a name in the Name field and create a new Instant Portal.

We'll talk about the XML file text box in a second. When you enter a name and click Create, you are presented with a screen similar to Figure 12-2. On this screen, you'll see the basics of what an OracleAS Instant Portal looks like. On the top middle of the screen is a small toggle button. On the page displayed in Figure 12-2, you are in View mode. You cannot make changes to your Instant Portal pages in this mode. Clicking this button will toggle the page into Edit mode, allowing you to make changes.

On the top left of the Oracle Instant Portal page, the name of your Instant Portal is displayed. You can change this name by clicking the text and replacing it while you're in Edit mode. The picture on the top right can be selected and replaced with a file from your local computer. That is the extent of changes you can make to the banner of your Instant Portal.

Below that is a series of tabs: Home, Company, Sales, etc. These tabs are created automatically if you do not specify an XML file when creating your Instant Portal. These tabs can be renamed or deleted; you can also add tabs to your OracleAS

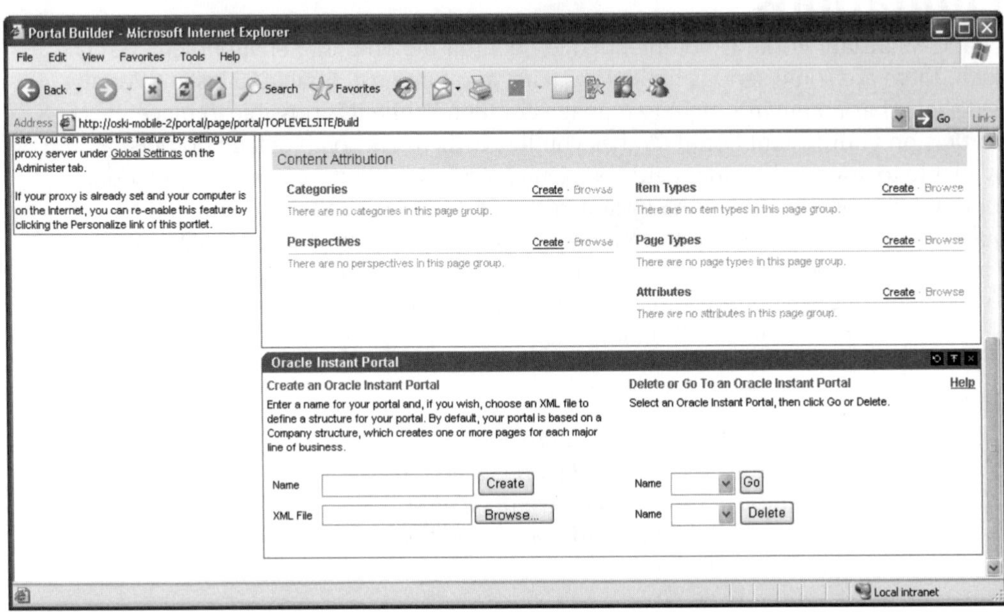

FIGURE 12-1 *The Create Instant Portal portlet on the OracleAS Portal Build tab*

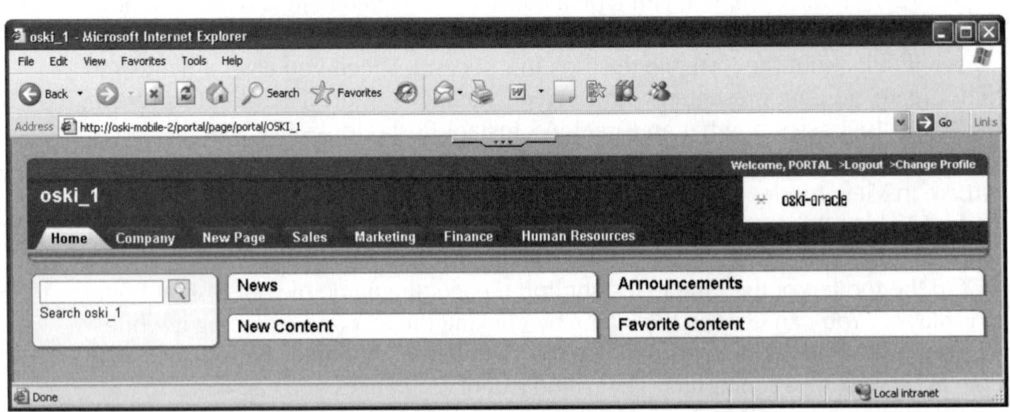

FIGURE 12-2 *Oracle Instant Portal in View mode*

Instant Portal. The XML file option in the OracleAS Instant Portal portlet on the Build screen allows developers to specify how they want their OracleAS Instant Portals to look when they are created. Oracle does not provide an example XML file for you to use; the only way to see what the format of the XML should look like is to query "Sample XML file" in the help system (Figure 12-3).

On the left-hand side of the Home tab is the Search portlet, which allows you to search your entire Instant Portal for relevant information. The other tabs also have a search portlet that allows you to search for information on just that page (and its subpages) or the entire OracleAS Instant Portal. When you create a new tab, this search portlet is created for you and placed on that tab automatically.

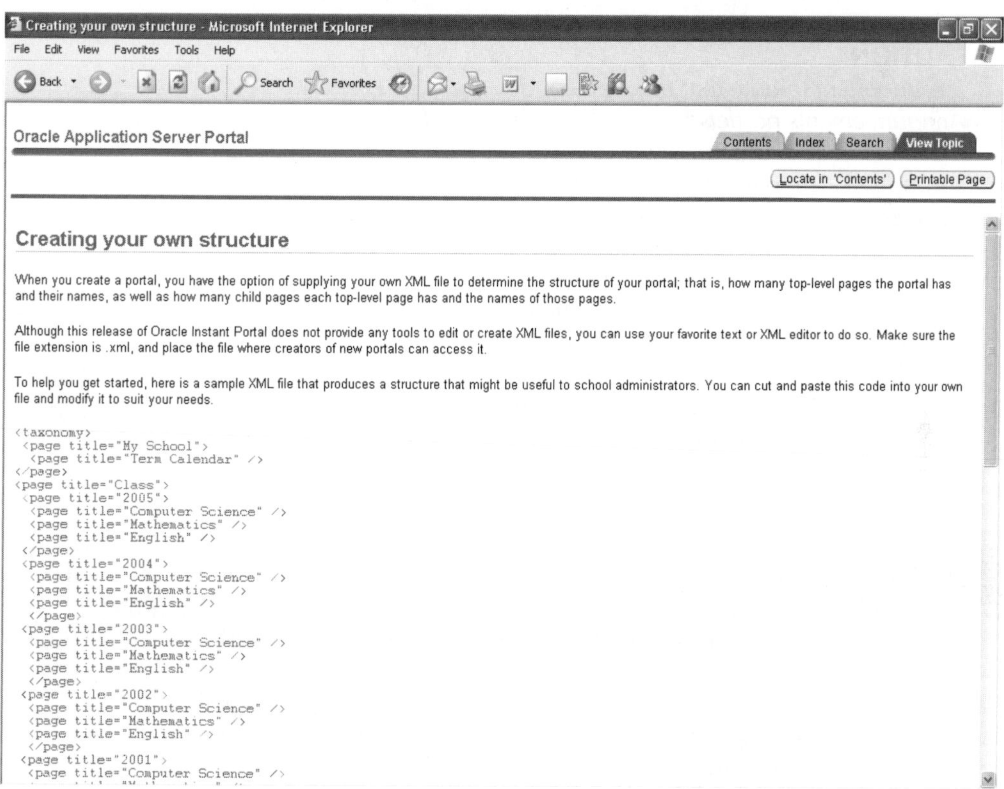

FIGURE 12-3 *The Sample XML file for Instant Portal*

Items (content) added to your Instant Portal are not immediately available to the search engine. By default, the indexing engine "wakes up" every 30 minutes and indexes any new content. You can also manually invoke the indexing engine. The following code can be run in the repository database as the portal user to update all necessary indexes:

```
exec wwv_context.sync();
```

The first tab (the Home tab in Figure 12-2) is unique in the sense that it can (and does) hold portlets. Any other tabs and subpages you create and modify cannot hold portlets. On the Home tab, there are four portlets. The News and Announcements portlets are tied to the first two subpages of the second (Company) tab. Any piece of content you place on those subpages will show up in those portlets.

CAUTION

It is important to note that the News and Announcements portlets on the Main tab are tied to the News and Announcement subpages on the second tab (Company) by their internal reference numbers. If, for whatever reason, you delete the second tab, any new tab that you create in the second position will not be tied to the News and Announcements portlets on the Home tab anymore. If you want to use the functionality of the portlets on the Home tab, never delete the second tab—always rename it. If that tab is deleted for whatever reason, you can get that functionality back, but it takes a little work: you'll need to re-create the tab, and then navigate to it. Look at the URL for the PageID. Add that PageID to the portlet customization on the home page.

The New Content portlet on the Home tab is exactly what it sounds like—any piece of content that is added to your OracleAS Instant Portal will be placed here. Favorite Content is a way of allowing end users to "tag" content. A small "home" icon is placed next to all content on OracleAS Instant Portal. When the user clicks that icon, the content is added to the Favorite portlet.

NOTE

If you wanted to, you could go into the Portal Navigator after the Instant Portal has been created and add portlets to this page, but Instant Portal was not intended for that purpose. You cannot see any other tabs or subpages of your OracleAS Instant Portal in the OracleAS Portal Navigator—all of the functionality of the additional tabs and subpages is handled programmatically, and no corresponding portal objects are created in the OracleAS Portal Navigator.

Click the toggle button in the top middle of the Instant Portal page to enter Edit mode (Figure 12-4). A series of editing buttons is displayed along the top, and a New Item button is displayed. The Home tab is a special tab, and the things you can add to it are limited. If you click the New Item button near the top left, you'll see that your only three choices are URL Item, Email Item, and Paste Item. On all other tabs, you have many more options.

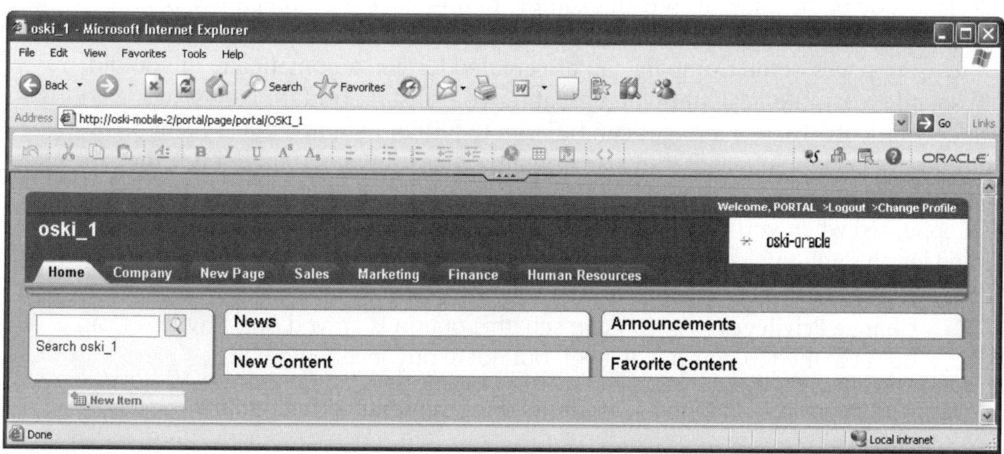

FIGURE 12-4 *The Oracle Instant Portal in Edit mode*

To see this, click one of the other tabs. You'll notice that you are not taken to the tab selected; rather, a set of icons appears above and to the right side of the tab you selected. From left to right, these icons represent:

- **Change Privileges** Clicking this icon brings up a menu where you can set privileges for the tab.
- **Add Top-Level Page** A top-level page is the equivalent of a tab. To add a new tab, select this option and a new tab will be created to the right of the existing tab.
- **Delete Top-Level Page** Deletes a tab.
- **Move Tab Left** Moves the selected tab one space to the left.
- **Move Tab Right** Moves the selected tab one space to the right.

The arrow in the circle to the right of the tab name navigates to that tab, so when you are in Edit mode, it takes two clicks to navigate to a tab. To change the name of the tab, simply click the name in Edit mode and type the new tab name.

Each tab has at least one page associated with it. You can also create subpages (for all tabs except the Home tab) whose titles are displayed hierarchically on the left-hand side of the page. To see an example of this, click the Company tab, and then click the small arrow in the circle to the right of the tab name (Figure 12-5).

Two subpages of the Company tab are created for you automatically (if you did not specify a sample XML file when creating your instant portal): News and Announcements. These subpages can be used to further organize the content of your instant portal. Subpages can also contain other subpages. Single-click the News subpage on the left side of the screen. A graphical menu, similar to the one that appeared when you clicked the tab name, appears directly above the subpage. Going left to right, the icons represent:

- **Change Privileges** As you can see, this option is grayed out. Privileges can be set at the tab (top-page) level, but not at any level below that.
- **Add Page** Clicking this icon drops down a menu with the following choices:
- **Add Page** Clicking this option creates a new subpage at the same level as the page selected.
- **Add Child Page** Clicking this option creates a new subpage that becomes a subpage of the page currently selected.

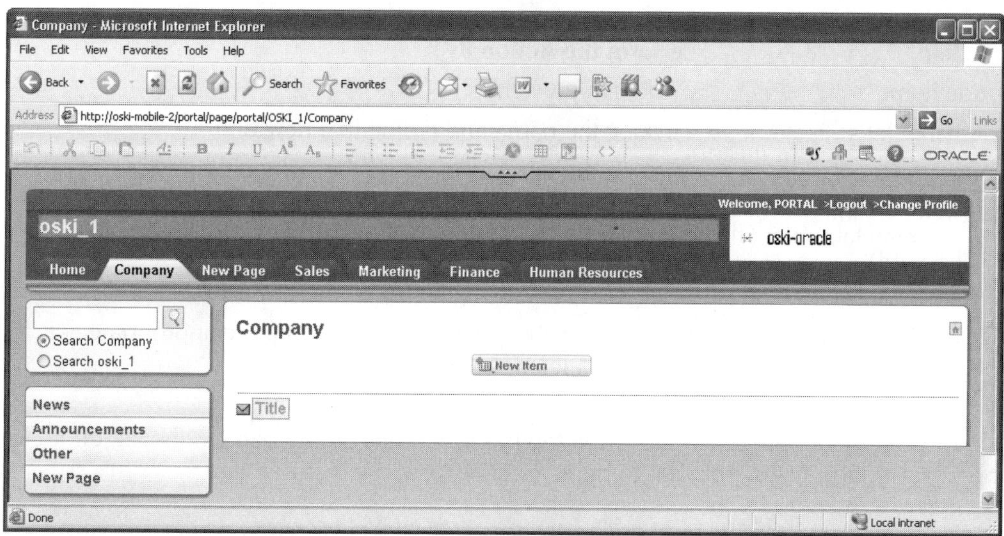

FIGURE 12-5 *The Company tab*

- **Cut Page** This option is very handy for moving a page to either a different subpage level or another tab. All of the content on the page is moved automatically.
- **Paste Page** Pastes a "cut" page to the current location as a page at the same level as the page currently selected.
- **Paste as Child Page** Pastes a "cut" page to the current location as a child page to the page currently selected.
- **Delete Page** Deletes a page.
- **Move Page Up** Moves the currently selected page one space up.
- **Move Page Down** Moves the currently selected page one space down.

The arrow in the small circle directly to the right of the selected page navigates to that page. Below the list of subpages is another button called Add Page. Clicking this button lists two choices: Add Page and Paste Page. They have the same functionality as the Add Page and Paste Page options just described. Using these options saves you one mouse click.

From here we can perform the following actions:

Action	Perform the Action By
Add items	Clicking New Item
Rename tabs	Clicking the name and typing in a new one
Move tabs	Clicking the tab and selecting the right/left arrows
Remove a tab	Clicking the tab and then selecting the trash can icon
Set security	Clicking the tab and then selecting the people icon
Add subpages	Selecting the Add Page icon on the lower left
Move/Delete subpages	Selecting a subpage and then selecting the appropriate move or delete icon

The Edit-mode format bar along the top has four icons on the right, to the left of the Oracle logo. Again, from left to right:

- **Select Style** This drop-down lists the color modes available for your Instant Portal. There are only ten choices, and new ones cannot be added. This is one of the limitations of Oracle Instant Portal designed to provide you with a simpler environment. Feel free to experiment with different styles; you can change back at any time. Just hover over a particular style to see it applied to a page—if you don't select it, it won't be applied.
- **Manage Users** This is the security button; it brings up the same dialog box as when you select the people icon when you click a tab in Edit mode. This dialog box allows you to set privileges for users of your Instant Portal (Figure 12-6). Here, you can define, at the Tab level, what privileges users have. Oracle Instant Portal has three basic privileges: View (the eyeball), Contribute (the pencil), and Manage (the wrench).
- **View** Allows users to see the content on a tab.
- **Contribute** Allows users to add, delete, or modify content on a page.
- **Manage** Allows users to view, add, delete, or modify content as well as carry out administrative tasks such as creating subpages and modifying privileges.

NOTE
It is important to note that this is the lowest level of granularity you can provide in Instant Portal. You cannot, for example, set rules for different pages and subpages under a tab—you can only set privileges at the tab level. Again, this limitation was designed to provide a simple Portal environment.

- **Go to Portal Builder** This icon takes you to the Navigator, which allows you to use that interface to make changes to your Instant Portal. Note that you can only make changes to the Home tab; all other tabs, pages, and subpages are Instant Portal objects and cannot be accessed from the Navigator.
- **Help** The final icon is the Instant Portal help system.

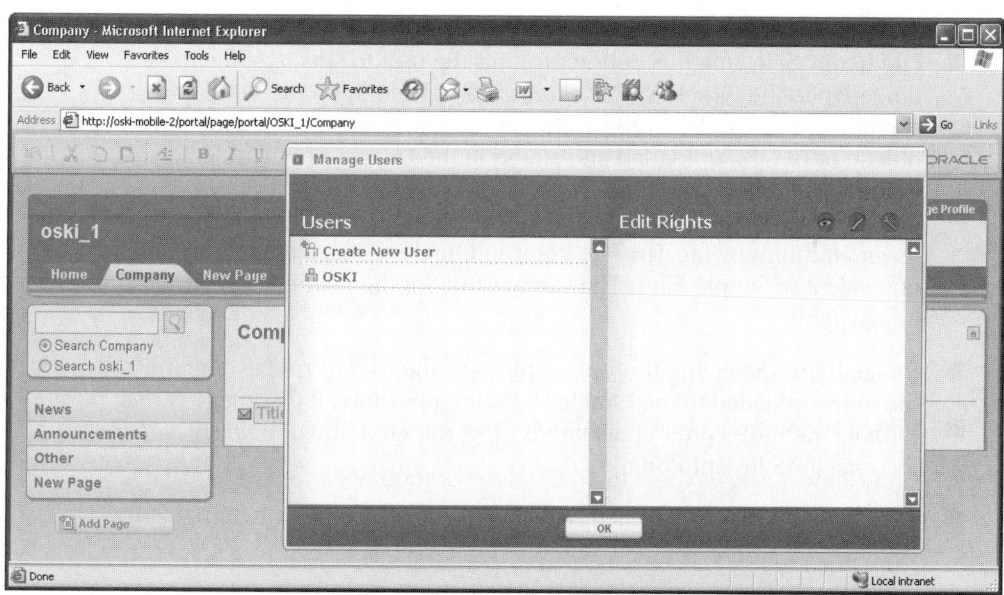

FIGURE 12-6 *The Manage Users dialog box for Oracle Instant Portal*

Adding Content Manually

On a tab other than the Home tab, click the New Item button on the middle of the page. The drop-down box contains seven choices:

- **Rich Text Item** Selecting this item opens a text editor where you can type in the content you wish to display. A Rich Text Item consists of three attributes: a Title, a Summary, and the text of the item. Different graphical modifiers (bold, italic, etc.) are available depending on which of the item's three attributes you are entering or modifying.
- **Expandable Rich Text Item** An Expandable rich text item is exactly the same as a Rich Text Item except for the existence of a small Expand button in the item (it's a small rectangle under the Summary of the item with an arrow pointing down). This Expand button allows end users to show (expand) the text of the item. This is particularly useful for large text items: instead of taking up the entire page, the title and summary of an item can be displayed. If end users wish to read the article, they can click the Expand button to view it.
- **File Item** Selecting this option prompts the user to specify a file to be uploaded to the OracleAS Portal repository. The file is converted into something that can be stored within an Oracle database (a binary large object, or BLOB), uploaded and stored in the Oracle Application Server infrastructure database.
  Back in Chapter 5, we discussed Files and Simple Files. Simple files have fewer attributes by far. The File Items in OracleAS Instant Portal are the equivalent of Simple Files. The same is true for the next item in this list: Image Items.
- **Image Item** Selecting this option prompts the user to specify a graphical file to be uploaded to the OracleAS Portal repository. If the image is in a format OracleAS Portal understands (.jpg, .tif, etc.), it will be displayed in the OracleAS Instant Portal.
- **URL Item** Selecting this item will place a small icon in the item that the user can click to be redirected to another web page.
- **Email Item** Selecting this item will prompt for a valid e-mail address. A small envelope icon is placed on the screen. When the user clicks that icon, the user's default e-mail client is invoked and the e-mail address specified is populated.

- **Paste Item** If an item has been cut from another page, it can be pasted here using this option.

Adding Content with Oracle Drive

Adding content to your OracleAS Instant Portal (or any portal for that matter) can be a tedious process, particularly if you have a significant amount of data to load. OracleAS Instant Portal, like OracleAS Portal, is WebDAV compliant, but setting up a WebDAV client can be a tricky and frustrating process. Oracle provides a simpler way, although they hide the download pretty well. On the http://www.oracle.com/technology/software/products/cs/index.html page for Collaboration Suite, you'll see a link for Oracle Drive. Oracle Drive facilitates the connection and mapping of a local drive to your Portal repository.

Figure 12-7 shows the connection screen for Oracle Drive. Once the connection is established, a drive is mapped locally on your computer, allowing you to drag and drop content from your PC to your repository. The tabs of your OracleAS Instant Portal show up as directories in your Oracle Drive-mapped network drive. All subpages show up as subfolders in the top-level folders.

NOTE

As of this writing (May 2007), the only operating system Oracle Drive is supported and available for is Microsoft Windows.

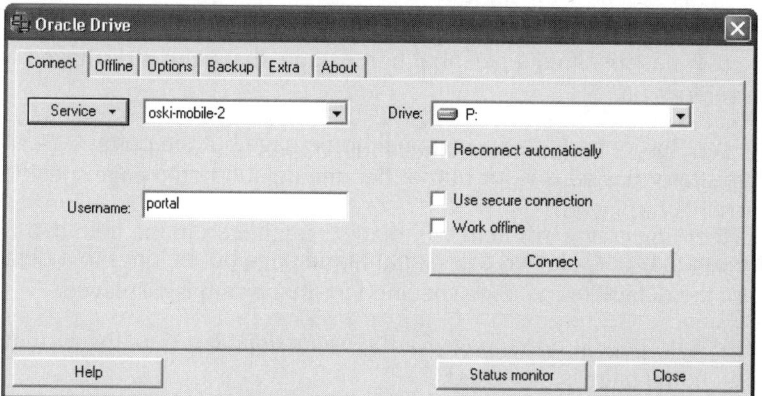

FIGURE 12-7 *The Oracle Drive Connection screen*

See the section "Using Oracle Drive" in Chapter 5 for more information on using Oracle Drive.

Defining a Landing Page

By default, the OracleAS Portal Builder page is defined as the page users are re-directed to after they log in to OracleAS Portal. This page is referred to as the *landing page*, because it is where users "land" after they log in. For developers or page designers, landing on the default builder page is perfectly acceptable. For end users, however, it is much more desirable to have them land on a page not related to portlet development or page design.

To change the landing page for a user, perform the following steps:

1. Log in to OracleAS Portal as a user with administration privileges.
2. Click the Builder link on the top-right of the screen if you are not already in the OracleAS Portal Builder.
3. Click the Administer tab on the right side of the screen.
4. In the Portal User Profile portlet on the right side of the screen, select the user whose landing page you'd like to change and then click Edit.
5. In the Default Home Page section of the Edit Portal User Profile page, select the page that will serve as that user's landing page.

The home page is the first page that is displayed to users after they log in to OracleAS Portal. Here's how the logic works:

- If the user has specified a personal home page, that page is displayed when the user logs on.
- If the user has not selected a personal home page but the portal administrator has set one for him or her, the default home page specified for that user is displayed.
- If the user has not selected a personal home page but belongs to a default group, the default home page specified for that group is displayed.
- If there is no default home page for the user's default group, the system default home page is displayed.

Summary

OracleAS Portal is a full-featured portal environment. For those developers and organizations unwilling or unable to dedicate the resources to learning, mastering, and maintaining the OracleAS Portal product or those organizations whose business requirements are simple and revolve around content and content management, Oracle Instant Portal provides a simple environment to create and deploy content-based portals quickly. While limitations exist in relation to the OracleAS Portal product, the ability to create and deploy content-based portals quickly and easily will appeal to many organizations.

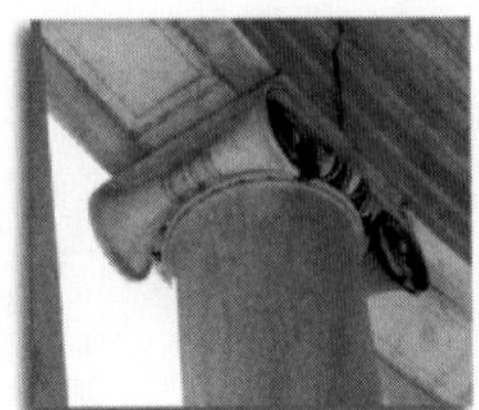

PART VI

Appendixes

APPENDIX A

Future Direction of OracleAS Portal

Virtually every Portal-related presentation done by an Oracle employee at the major Oracle conferences over the past year or so contains at least one slide that says "Portal is the Face of SOA."

Chapter 8 goes through the details of why service-oriented architecture and OracleAS Portal are such a good match. In a nutshell, Oracle is marketing OracleAS Portal as a tool to integrate various applications and data throughout your organization. SOA provides the "plumbing" underneath the user interface, and OracleAS Portal provides the UI.

The Statement of Direction link on the Oracle Portal Product Overview page (http://www.oracle.com/technology/products/ias/portal/product_overview_10g1014.html) doesn't mention SOA, but it is dated August 2005. Oracle's 10.1.4 New Features paper (http://www.oracle.com/technology/products/ias/portal/pdf/portal_1014_new_features.pdf) and Portal's Business Overview Whitepaper (http://www.oracle.com/technology/products/ias/portal/pdf/overview_10gr2_2_business.pdf) both discuss OracleAS Portal and SOA. The most comprehensive document outlining Oracle's commitment to OracleAS Portal as a key component of its SOA strategy, however, is available on the Portal Product Overview page (URL just given). While it is technically not a Statement of Direction, a lot can be discerned from a white paper titled "Oracle SOA Suite and Enterprise Portals – Enhance Employee Productivity with Process-Centric Portals." This paper can be downloaded at http://www.oracle.com/technology/products/ias/portal/pdf/oracle_soa_suite_portals.pdf.

APPENDIX B

OracleAS Portal Resources

here are surprisingly few really good Oracle Portal resources outside of Oracle's site (hence the motivation to write this book). The following is a list of sites I've used in my OracleAS Portal travels over the years.

- **Oracle Portal Center** You'll probably spend most of your time at Oracle's Portal Center site (http://www.oracle.com/technology/products/ias/portal/index.html). Just about anything directly related to OracleAS Portal can be found here.
- **Oracle Technology Network** On the main Oracle Technology Network (OTN) site (http://www.oracle.com/technology/index.html), don't be afraid to search for **Portal** in the Secure Search box. Some really cool Portal-related papers are not on the Portal Center site. For example, if you want to know how to integrate Application Express and Portal, search for **portal application express**. You'll be taken to http://www.oracle.com/technology/products/database/application_express/howtos/omniportlet_index.html, a page devoted to that subject.
- **The Oracle Forums** I'm surprised how few people use them. I've found countless answers to questions in the Oracle Forums, some directly from the developers who worked on the software. http://forums.oracle.com/ will get you to the main forums page; http://forums.oracle.com/forums/category.jspa?categoryID=13 will get you to the main page for the Application Server and all things Portal (make sure to scroll down to see all of the Portal categories). Be sure to use the search feature because it can definitely save you a lot of time, since postings don't always go in the category you would think they would.
- **http://tahiti.oracle.com/** Here is another site that doesn't get as much use as one would expect. The links here allow you to search through all of the documentation set for a specific Oracle product (like, say, the 10.1.2 version of the Application Server) in one location. This is great if you don't know where a particular subject is.
- **Oracle By Example** OBEs are tutorials on specific topics. The great thing is that each step of the process is spelled out so that you can learn a lot about OracleAS Portal indirectly by following the examples and by seeing how basic tasks are done. The main OBE page is http://www.oracle.com/technology/obe/start/index.html. The OBE page for Portal is http://www.oracle.com/technology/obe/obe_as_10g/portal/index.html.

In addition to these sites, Oracle University offers three OracleAS Portal courses:

- Build Corporate Portals (three days)
- Build Portlets with PL/SQL (two days)
- Build Portlets with Java (three days)

Oracle University's home page is http://education.oracle.com/.

APPENDIX C

Exercise Commentary

riginally, I was going to include an Exercise Commentary section in the book where I would walk through all of the exercises step-by-step. After writing up the first couple of exercise answers, I realized this was impractical for two reasons:

- **The amount of space it took up** Even a simple exercise took pages and pages of instructions to fully document. If I added screen shots, then it became ridiculously long.
- **It was BORING** I read back through the instructions—click this, highlight this, type that—and couldn't keep my eyes open. Only the heartiest of readers would be able to make it through. Plus, I was never able to figure out how much redundancy to leave out; for instance, by the fifth example, do I assume the reader knows what I mean when I say, "Go to the Portlets tab," or is it necessary to spell out each of the steps in case the reader skipped the first couple of exercises?

I finally arrived at an elegant solution: Flash-enabled movies that readers can view from my Web site. The Flash animations were made with a very cool tool called Wink (http://www.debugmode.com/wink/). Point your browser to http://www.oski-oracle.info/. On the home page, there are links for all of the exercises in this book, plus some things not in the book that I just thought were pretty cool. Feel free to distribute these little "movies"—just remember to credit the source (me).

As a side note, I'm a big believer in supporting shareware. I depend on commercial software in my day-to-day life, but I also depend on a plethora of shareware programs that I run every day. I'm one of the few people who have actually paid for my copy of WinZip, and I can't imagine doing my job without some of the tools on my laptop. Everyone eventually gets used to the "nag" screens in these programs, but just go ahead and send the check to those people writing the utilities you use every day. You'd be surprised how much of a difference you can make by doing the right thing. Plus it's good karma.

Other freeware/shareware tools I use on a regular basis include the following:

- **Audacity (http://audacity.sourceforge.net/)** This is an incredibly powerful audio-editing tool.
- **DB Power Amp (http://www.dbpoweramp.com/)** Converts your music files between just about any format you can imagine.
- **Winamp (http://www.winamp.com)** Windows Media Player? Yuck. Winamp is simple, sounds great, and gives me everything a music lover could want.

- **CCleaner (http://www.ccleaner.com)** "Crap" Cleaner for Windows. If I don't run it for a while, my system slows to a crawl.
- **Daemon Tools (http://www.daemon-tools.cc)** Allows you to mount .iso files as virtual drives on your system—very cool!
- **PuTTY (available from multiple sources)** This is a great SSH Telnet client.
- **Winmerge (http://www.winmerge.org)** This is a great tool for programmers who need to compare files.

And remember—pay for the software you use.

Index

References to figures are in italics.

A

B

C

D

E

F

G

H

I

J

P

T

U

V

W

X

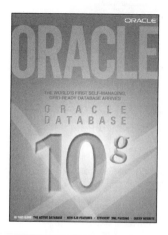

FREE SUBSCRIPTION

○ **Yes, please send me a FREE subscription to *Oracle Magazine*.** ○ **NO**

To receive a free subscription to *Oracle Magazine*, you must fill out the entire card, sign it, and date it (incomplete cards cannot be processed or acknowledged). You can also fax your application to +1.847.763.9638.
Or subscribe at our Web site at otn.oracle.com/oraclemagazine

○ From time to time, Oracle Publishing allows our partners exclusive access to our e-mail addresses for special promotions and announcements. To be included in this program, please check this circle.

○ Oracle Publishing allows sharing of our mailing list with selected third parties. If you prefer your mailing address not to be included in this program, please check here. If at any time you would like to be removed from this mailing list, please contact Customer Service at +1.847.647.9630 or send an e-mail to oracle@halldata.com.

signature (required) X date

name title

company e-mail address

street/p.o. box

city/state/zip or postal code telephone

country fax

YOU MUST ANSWER ALL TEN QUESTIONS BELOW.

① WHAT IS THE PRIMARY BUSINESS ACTIVITY OF YOUR FIRM AT THIS LOCATION? (check one only)
- □ 01 Aerospace and Defense Manufacturing
- □ 02 Application Service Provider
- □ 03 Automotive Manufacturing
- □ 04 Chemicals, Oil and Gas
- □ 05 Communications and Media
- □ 06 Construction/Engineering
- □ 07 Consumer Sector/Consumer Packaged Goods
- □ 08 Education
- □ 09 Financial Services/Insurance
- □ 10 Government (civil)
- □ 11 Government (military)
- □ 12 Healthcare
- □ 13 High Technology Manufacturing, OEM
- □ 14 Integrated Software Vendor
- □ 15 Life Sciences (Biotech, Pharmaceuticals)
- □ 16 Mining
- □ 17 Retail/Wholesale/Distribution
- □ 18 Systems Integrator, VAR/VAD
- □ 19 Telecommunications
- □ 20 Travel and Transportation
- □ 21 Utilities (electric, gas, sanitation, water)
- □ 98 Other Business and Services

② WHICH OF THE FOLLOWING BEST DESCRIBES YOUR PRIMARY JOB FUNCTION? (check one only)

Corporate Management/Staff
- □ 01 Executive Management (President, Chair, CEO, CFO, Owner, Partner, Principal)
- □ 02 Finance/Administrative Management (VP/Director/ Manager/Controller, Purchasing, Administration)
- □ 03 Sales/Marketing Management (VP/Director/Manager)
- □ 04 Computer Systems/Operations Management (CIO/VP/Director/ Manager MIS, Operations)

IS/IT Staff
- □ 05 Systems Development/ Programming Management
- □ 06 Systems Development/ Programming Staff
- □ 07 Consulting
- □ 08 DBA/Systems Administrator
- □ 09 Education/Training
- □ 10 Technical Support Director/Manager
- □ 11 Other Technical Management/Staff
- □ 98 Other

③ WHAT IS YOUR CURRENT PRIMARY OPERATING PLATFORM? (select all that apply)
- □ 01 Digital Equipment UNIX
- □ 02 Digital Equipment VAX VMS
- □ 03 HP UNIX
- □ 04 IBM AIX
- □ 05 IBM UNIX
- □ 06 Java
- □ 07 Linux
- □ 08 Macintosh
- □ 09 MS-DOS
- □ 10 MVS
- □ 11 NetWare
- □ 12 Network Computing
- □ 13 OpenVMS
- □ 14 SCO UNIX
- □ 15 Sequent DYNIX/ptx
- □ 16 Sun Solaris/SunOS
- □ 17 SVR4
- □ 18 UnixWare
- □ 19 Windows
- □ 20 Windows NT
- □ 21 Other UNIX
- □ 98 Other
- 99 □ None of the above

④ DO YOU EVALUATE, SPECIFY, RECOMMEND, OR AUTHORIZE THE PURCHASE OF ANY OF THE FOLLOWING? (check all that apply)
- □ 01 Hardware
- □ 02 Software
- □ 03 Application Development Tools
- □ 04 Database Products
- □ 05 Internet or Intranet Products
- 99 □ None of the above

⑤ IN YOUR JOB, DO YOU USE OR PLAN TO PURCHASE ANY OF THE FOLLOWING PRODUCTS? (check all that apply)

Software
- □ 01 Business Graphics
- □ 02 CAD/CAE/CAM
- □ 03 CASE
- □ 04 Communications
- □ 05 Database Management
- □ 06 File Management
- □ 07 Finance
- □ 08 Java
- □ 09 Materials Resource Planning
- □ 10 Multimedia Authoring
- □ 11 Networking
- □ 12 Office Automation
- □ 13 Order Entry/Inventory Control
- □ 14 Programming
- □ 15 Project Management
- □ 16 Scientific and Engineering
- □ 17 Spreadsheets
- □ 18 Systems Management
- □ 19 Workflow

Hardware
- □ 20 Macintosh
- □ 21 Mainframe
- □ 22 Massively Parallel Processing
- □ 23 Minicomputer
- □ 24 PC
- □ 25 Network Computer
- □ 26 Symmetric Multiprocessing
- □ 27 Workstation

Peripherals
- □ 28 Bridges/Routers/Hubs/Gateways
- □ 29 CD-ROM Drives
- □ 30 Disk Drives/Subsystems
- □ 31 Modems
- □ 32 Tape Drives/Subsystems
- □ 33 Video Boards/Multimedia

Services
- □ 34 Application Service Provider
- □ 35 Consulting
- □ 36 Education/Training
- □ 37 Maintenance
- □ 38 Online Database Services
- □ 39 Support
- □ 40 Technology-Based Training
- □ 98 Other
- 99 □ None of the above

⑥ WHAT ORACLE PRODUCTS ARE IN USE AT YOUR SITE? (check all that apply)

Oracle E-Business Suite
- □ 01 Oracle Marketing
- □ 02 Oracle Sales
- □ 03 Oracle Order Fulfillment
- □ 04 Oracle Supply Chain Management
- □ 05 Oracle Procurement
- □ 06 Oracle Manufacturing
- □ 07 Oracle Maintenance Management
- □ 08 Oracle Service
- □ 09 Oracle Contracts
- □ 10 Oracle Projects
- □ 11 Oracle Financials
- □ 12 Oracle Human Resources
- □ 13 Oracle Interaction Center
- □ 14 Oracle Communications/Utilities (modules)
- □ 15 Oracle Public Sector/University (modules)
- □ 16 Oracle Financial Services (modules)

Server/Software
- □ 17 Oracle9*i*
- □ 18 Oracle9*i* Lite
- □ 19 Oracle8*i*
- □ 20 Other Oracle database
- □ 21 Oracle9*i* Application Server
- □ 22 Oracle9*i* Application Server Wireless
- □ 23 Oracle Small Business Suite

Tools
- □ 24 Oracle Developer Suite
- □ 25 Oracle Discoverer
- □ 26 Oracle JDeveloper
- □ 27 Oracle Migration Workbench
- □ 28 Oracle9*i* AS Portal
- □ 29 Oracle Warehouse Builder

Oracle Services
- □ 30 Oracle Outsourcing
- □ 31 Oracle Consulting
- □ 32 Oracle Education
- □ 33 Oracle Support
- □ 98 Other
- 99 □ None of the above

⑦ WHAT OTHER DATABASE PRODUCTS ARE IN USE AT YOUR SITE? (check all that apply)
- □ 01 Access
- □ 02 Baan
- □ 03 dbase
- □ 04 Gupta
- □ 05 IBM DB2
- □ 06 Informix
- □ 07 Ingres
- □ 08 Microsoft Access
- □ 09 Microsoft SQL Server
- □ 10 PeopleSoft
- □ 11 Progress
- □ 12 SAP
- □ 13 Sybase
- □ 14 VSAM
- □ 98 Other
- 99 □ None of the above

⑧ WHAT OTHER APPLICATION SERVER PRODUCTS ARE IN USE AT YOUR SITE? (check all that apply)
- □ 01 BEA
- □ 02 IBM
- □ 03 Sybase
- □ 04 Sun
- □ 05 Other

⑨ DURING THE NEXT 12 MONTHS, HOW MUCH DO YOU ANTICIPATE YOUR ORGANIZATION WILL SPEND ON COMPUTER HARDWARE, SOFTWARE, PERIPHERALS, AND SERVICES FOR YOUR LOCATION? (check only one)
- □ 01 Less than $10,000
- □ 02 $10,000 to $49,999
- □ 03 $50,000 to $99,999
- □ 04 $100,000 to $499,999
- □ 05 $500,000 to $999,999
- □ 06 $1,000,000 and over

⑩ WHAT IS YOUR COMPANY'S YEARLY SALES REVENUE? (please choose one)
- □ 01 $500, 000, 000 and above
- □ 02 $100, 000, 000 to $500, 000, 000
- □ 03 $50, 000, 000 to $100, 000, 000
- □ 04 $5, 000, 000 to $50, 000, 000
- □ 05 $1, 000, 000 to $5, 000, 000

100103